THE OXFORD HANDBOOK OF

# LANGUAGE
# EVOLUTION

# OXFORD HANDBOOKS IN LINGUISTICS

## RECENTLY PUBLISHED

# THE OXFORD HANDBOOK OF

# LANGUAGE EVOLUTION

*Edited by*

## MAGGIE TALLERMAN

*and*

## KATHLEEN R. GIBSON

OXFORD
UNIVERSITY PRESS

**OXFORD**
UNIVERSITY PRESS

Great Clarendon Street, Oxford, OX2 6DP,
United Kingdom

Oxford University Press is a department of the University of Oxford.
It furthers the University's objective of excellence in research, scholarship,
and education by publishing worldwide. Oxford is a registered trade mark of
Oxford University Press in the UK and in certain other countries

First Edition published in 2012
First Edition published in paperback 2013

Impression: 1

Published in the United States of America by Oxford University Press
198 Madison Avenue, New York, NY 10016, United States of America

British Library Cataloguing in Publication Data
Data available

ISBN 978–0–19–954111–9 (hbk.)
978–0–19–967916–4 (pbk.)

Printed in Great Britain by
CPI Group (UK) Ltd, Croydon, CR0 4YY

# Contents

## PART I INSIGHTS FROM COMPARATIVE ANIMAL BEHAVIOUR

## PART III THE PREHISTORY OF LANGUAGE: WHEN AND WHY DID LANGUAGE EVOLVE?

## PART IV LAUNCHING LANGUAGE: THE DEVELOPMENT OF A LINGUISTIC SPECIES

## PART V LANGUAGE CHANGE, CREATION, AND TRANSMISSION IN MODERN HUMANS

# PREFACE AND ACKNOWLEDGEMENTS

This volume represents a snapshot of current knowledge and theories in the field of language evolution, and is written from the widely differing perspectives of the numerous academic disciplines that contribute to this fascinating and tantalizing field of study. The editors invited many dozens of the most eminent academics to contribute; a number, sadly, felt unable to take the time to write for a general audience, but 60 scientists at the top of their game did accept the invitation. To these colleagues, we extend a heartfelt thanks for all your efforts, including the time spent drafting and re-drafting chapters to our exacting standards. It is your life's work that has helped to make this volume a success, and we are grateful to you for sharing this research with the general reader.

What has resulted from these endeavours is a collection which, we hope, will be a standard work of reference for years to come. Language evolution is, however, a discipline that is moving extremely quickly. Even as we write, many new discoveries and developments are being reported and published. Of course, some of these apparent breakthroughs will prove ephemeral or illusory, but others will doubtless change the field. We have tried to avoid endorsing too soon any results which are not yet proven, but at the same time we have attempted to be—and to encourage our contributors to be—as up to date as possible.

The target audience for this volume comprises scholars and students of all the disciplines that contribute pieces of the language evolution puzzle: linguists, biologists, archaeologists, ethologists, neuroscientists, anthropologists, psychologists, geneticists, palaeontologists, and more. We have encouraged contributors to write with this general audience in mind as much as possible, and we hope that the results will be widely accessible to readers of all backgrounds.

We would like to extend a special massive thanks to Laura Bailey, a PhD student at Newcastle University, England, for her painstaking work in compiling and checking the list of references and finalizing the subject index. We probably drove her almost insane, but she completed her task on time and without complaint. We gratefully acknowledge the support of the Faculty of Humanities and Social Sciences at Newcastle, both in funding Laura's work and in allowing Maggie Tallerman leave from teaching for one semester in order to complete this volume. We also thank John Davey at Oxford University Press for his help and support over the long timespan of this project. Finally, we'd like to express our gratitude to our partners, S. J. and John, for their patience and forbearance in the face of our continuing need to work when we should have been taking holidays with them.

Maggie Tallerman, *Newcastle, England*
Kathleen R. Gibson, *Houston, Texas*
January 2011

# LIST OF FIGURES

# LIST OF TABLES

# LIST OF CONTRIBUTORS

**Stephen R. Anderson** is the Dorothy R. Diebold Professor of Linguistics, Psychology and Cognitive Science at Yale University. His interests in Linguistics cover all of the major subfields, although his work in recent years has focused on the theory of morphology. Among his publications, the 2004 book *Doctor Dolittle's delusion* (Yale University Press) discusses the gulf between human language and the communication systems of other species.

**Michael A. Arbib** was born in England, grew up in Australia, and is now University Professor, Fletcher Jones Professor of Computer Science, and Professor of Neuroscience (etc.), at the University of Southern California. His first book was *Brains, machines and mathematics*. His 39th book, co-edited with Derek Bickerton, is *The emergence of protolanguage: Holophrasis vs. compositionality* (Benjamins, 2010).

**Amy L. Bauernfeind** is a doctoral student in Hominid Paleobiology at the George Washington University, where she studies comparative primate neurobiology. Her research interests include variation in neural structure, neurodevelopment, and metabolism in the primate brain.

**Derek Bickerton** (PhD Cambridge) is Professor Emeritus of Linguistics at the University of Hawaii. He is best known for his work on creole languages, including the controversial Bioprogram Hypothesis, and on the evolution of language. His publications in the latter field include *Language and species* (University of Chicago Press, 1990), *Adam's tongue* (Hill & Wang, 2009), and *Biological foundations and origins of syntax* (MIT Press, 2009, edited with Eörs Szathmáry).

**Cedric Boeckx** is Research Professor at the Catalan Institute for Advanced Studies (ICREA), and a member of the Department of General Linguistics at the Universitat de Barcelona. His publications include *Islands and chains* (Benjamins, 2003), *Linguistic Minimalism* (OUP, 2006), *Bare syntax* (OUP, 2008), and *Language in cognition* (Wiley-Blackwell, 2009). He is founding co-editor of the Open Access journal *Biolinguistics*, and the founding editor of OUP's *Oxford Studies in Biolinguistics* monograph series.

**Rudolf Botha** is Emeritus Professor of General Linguistics at the University of Stellenbosch and Honorary Professor of Linguistics at Utrecht University. His research includes work on the evolution of language, morphological theory and word formation, and the conceptual foundations of linguistic theories. He is the author of twelve books, including *Unravelling the evolution of language* (Elsevier, 2003). He was the organizer of the Cradle of Language Conference held in 2006 in Stellenbosch, South Africa.

**Robbins Burling** has been concerned for a half-century with the linguistics and ethnology of north-eastern India and Bangladesh. He became interested in the evolution of the capacity for language when colleagues in archaeology asked 'When did language begin?' and he could only reply 'I dunno'. He is the author of *The talking ape: How language evolved* (OUP, 2005).

**Joan Bybee** was at the University at Buffalo from 1973–1989 and is now Distinguished Professor Emerita at the University of New Mexico. Her book *The evolution of grammar* (University of Chicago Press, 1994, with Perkins and Pagliuca) documents how unrelated languages create grammar using similar mechanisms. Works arguing that domain-general principles give rise to linguistic structure are *Phonology and language use* (CUP, 2001), *Frequency of use and the organization of language* (OUP, 2007), and *Language, usage and cognition* (CUP, 2010).

**Angelo Cangelosi** is Director of the Centre for Robotics and Neural Systems at the University of Plymouth. His PhD is from the University of Genoa, and he has been visiting scholar at the University of California, San Diego and the University of Southampton. He edited *Simulating the evolution of language* (Springer, 2002), and is currently co-editor-in-chief of the journal *Interaction Studies*. His primary work is on language learning and evolution in robots and embodied agents.

**Rebecca L. Cann** is a Professor of Genetics at the University of Hawaii, Manoa. Her interests include human evolutionary genetics and the molecular conservation genetics of endangered species. She is interested in the shared properties of modern endangered species and the early stages of human evolution. These include small population sizes, gender differences in behaviour, infectious disease risks, and geographical isolation.

**Andrew Carstairs-McCarthy** is a former Professor of Linguistics at the University of Canterbury, Christchurch, New Zealand. His main research interests have been morphology (*Allomorphy in inflexion*, Croom Helm, 1987) and the evolution of language (*The origins of complex language*, OUP, 1999). These two interests converge in his most recent book, *The evolution of morphology* (OUP, 2010).

**Nick Chater** is Professor of Behavioural Science at Warwick Business School. His research focuses on fundamental principles of cognition, and especially on reasoning, decision making, and language. His has co-edited or co-written six books, and has written over 200 papers. He is a Fellow of the Cognitive Science Society and Associate Editor of the journal *Psychological Science*.

**Dorothy L. Cheney** graduated from Wellesley College and received her PhD from the University of Cambridge, where her advisor was Robert A. Hinde. She was a post-doctoral fellow at Rockefeller University, working with Peter Marler. Together with Robert Seyfarth, she is the author of *How monkeys see the world* (University of Chicago Press, 1990) and *Baboon metaphysics* (Chicago, 2007). She is currently Professor of Biology at the University of Pennsylvania.

**Morten H. Christiansen** is Professor in the Department of Psychology and Co-Director of the Cognitive Science Program at Cornell University, as well as External Professor at the Santa Fe Institute. His research focuses on the interaction of biological and environmental constraints in the processing, acquisition, and evolution of language. He is the author of more than 125 scientific papers and has edited volumes on connectionist psycholinguistics, language evolution, and language universals.

**Frederick L. Coolidge** is a Professor in the Department of Psychology at the University of Colorado at Colorado Springs. He has a PhD in psychology and completed a postdoctoral fellowship in clinical neuropsychology. His research interests include behavioural genetics, cognitive archaeology, and psychological assessment. He has received three Fulbright Fellowships to India and has published five books. He has published articles in the *Journal of Human Evolution, Cambridge Archaeological Journal, PaleoAnthropology, Journal of Anthropological Research*, and elsewhere.

**Michael C. Corballis**, a New Zealander, completed his PhD from McGill University, and taught in the Department of Psychology there before being appointed to the University of Auckland in 1978, where he is currently Emeritus Professor of Psychology. He has published widely on various aspects of cognitive neuroscience, including laterality, imagery, and language. He is the author of *From hand to mouth* (Princeton University Press, 2002), and his new book *The recursive mind* (Princeton) will appear in 2012.

**Terrence W. Deacon** is Professor and Departmental Chair in Anthropology at the University of California, Berkeley. His research combines human evolutionary biology and neuroscience, with the aim of investigating the evolution of human cognition. It extends from laboratory-based cellular-molecular neurobiology to the study of semiotic processes underlying animal and human communication, especially language. Many of these interests are explored in his 1997 book, *The symbolic species: The coevolution of language and the brain* (W. W. Norton).

**Bart de Boer** did his PhD with Luc Steels at the Vrije Universiteit Brussel on the topic of self-organization in vowel systems. An adaptation of this thesis was published as *The origins of vowel systems* (OUP, 2001). He has also worked with Patricia Kuhl at the University of Washington on the evolutionary implications of infant-directed speech. Currently he works at the Universiteit van Amsterdam on the biological evolution of the vocal tract and on cultural evolution of speech.

**Francesco d'Errico** is a CNRS Director of Research attached to the University of Bordeaux, France. Focusing on the origin and evolution of symbolic behaviours and complex bone technologies, his research has questioned the dominant paradigm of a sudden European origin of modern cultures and identified the presence of older symbolic traditions in Africa, Europe, and the Near East. He has published several books and more than 200 papers, mostly in international journals.

**Frans B. M. de Waal** is a biologist with a PhD from the University of Utrecht, in the Netherlands. He is C. H. Candler Professor of Psychology at Emory University, and Director of the Living Links Center at the Yerkes National Primate Research Center, both in Atlanta, GA. He is the author of numerous books, including *The age of empathy* (Random House, 2009).

**Karl C. Diller** is researching the evolutionary genetics of language in the Cann laboratory (genetics) at the John A. Burns School of Medicine, University of Hawaii. His PhD in linguistics is from Harvard University. He was formerly Professor of Linguistics at the University of New Hampshire, where a special interest of his was the neurolinguistic foundations of second language acquisition.

**Merlin Donald** is Professor Emeritus, Queens University, Ontario; Honorary Professor, University of Aarhus, Denmark; and former Chair of Cognitive Science, Case Western Reserve University, Ohio. He is a Fellow of the Canadian Psychological Association and the Royal Society of Canada, and the author of *Origins of the modern mind: Three stages in the evolution of culture and cognition* (Harvard, 1991), and *A mind so rare: The evolution of human consciousness* (Norton, 2001).

**Robin I. M. Dunbar** is Professor of Evolutionary Anthropology at the University of Oxford, a Fellow of the British Academy, and co-director of the British Academy's Centenary Research Project. His principal research interests focus on the evolution of sociality in mammals, with particular reference to ungulates, primates, and humans.

**Dean Falk** is a palaeoanthropologist who specializes in brain evolution. She is a Senior Scholar at the School for Advanced Research in Santa Fe, New Mexico and at the Department of Anthropology, Florida State University. Her books include *Finding our tongues: Mothers, infants and the origins of language* (Basic Books, 2009), and *Bones to pick: How two controversial discoveries changed perceptions of human evolution* (University of California Press, 2011).

**W. Tecumseh Fitch** is Professor of Cognitive Biology at the University of Vienna. His main interests are in bio-acoustics and the evolution of cognition, particularly the evolution of human speech, language, and music, all studied from a broad comparative perspective. He is author of *The evolution of language* (CUP, 2010). He conducts experimental research on vocalization and cognition in humans and a variety of vertebrates, including chimpanzees, seals, deer, dogs, alligators, and parrots.

**Kathleen R. Gibson** is Professor Emerita of Neurobiology and Anatomy, University of Texas Medical School, Houston and Professor Emerita in the Department of Orthodontics, U.T. School of Dentistry. She has co-edited six books on the development and evolution of brains and cognition including *'Language' and intelligence in monkeys and apes* (CUP, 1990), *Tools, language and cognition in human evolution* (CUP, 1993), *Modelling the early human mind* (McDonald Institute for Archaeological Research, 1996), and *Evolutionary anatomy of the primate cerebral cortex* (CUP, 2001). She is currently co-editor with Jim Hurford of the Oxford Series, *Studies in the Evolution of Language.*

**Susan Goldin-Meadow** is the Beardsley Ruml Distinguished Service Professor at the University of Chicago, where she has taught for over 30 years. Her research interests focus on gesture—the home-made gestures children create when not exposed to language, and the gestures we all produce when we talk. She is the founding editor of the journal *Language Learning and Development*, and is the current president of the International Society for Gesture Studies.

**Katharine Graf Estes'** research investigates the processes underlying early language acquisition and the connection between early phonological and lexical representations. She received her PhD in developmental psychology from the University of Wisconsin-Madison in 2007. She is currently an Assistant Professor at the University of California, Davis. She has received funding from the National Institutes of Health and the National Science Foundation.

**Stevan Harnad,** External Member of the Hungarian Academy of Science, is author of or contributor to over 300 publications, including *Origins and evolution of language and speech, Lateralization in the nervous system, Peer commentary on peer review: A case study in scientific quality control, Categorical perception: The groundwork of cognition, The selection of behavior: The operant behaviorism of B. F. Skinner, Scholarly journals at the crossroads: A subversive proposal for electronic publishing,* and *Cognition distributed: How cognitive technology extends our minds.*

**Bernd Heine** is Emeritus Professor at the Institute of African Studies (Institut für Afrikanistik), University of Cologne. His 33 books include *Possession: Cognitive sources, forces, and grammaticalization* (CUP, 1997); *Auxiliaries: Cognitive forces and grammaticalization* (OUP, 1993); *Cognitive foundations of grammar* (OUP, 1997); with Derek Nurse, *African languages: An introduction* (CUP, 2000); *A linguistic geography of Africa* (CUP, 2008); with Tania Kuteva, *World lexicon of grammaticalization* (CUP, 2002); *Language contact and grammatical change* (CUP, 2005); *The* *changing languages of Europe* (OUP, 2006); and *The genesis of grammar* (OUP, 2007).

**William D. Hopkins** is Professor of Psychology and Neuroscience at Agnes Scott College. He also holds the appointment of Research Scientist within the Division of Developmental and Cognitive Neuroscience at the Yerkes National Primate Research Center of Emory University. His research focuses on the evolution of language and speech, and on the evolution of manual skills, such as grasping, bimanual coordination and tool use, as they relate to the emergence of population-level behavioural and brain asymmetries in non-human primates.

**Jim Hurford** is Emeritus Professor of Linguistics at the University of Edinburgh. He has an interest in reconciling traditions within and outwith linguistics which have tended to conflict. He works in a framework in which representation of grammars in individual minds interacts with properties of language used in communities, emphasizing the interaction of evolution, learning, and communication. He constructed early computer simulations of language evolution, and his books include *The origins of meaning* (OUP, 2007) and *The origins of grammar* (OUP, 2011).

**Vincent M. Janik** is a Reader in Biology in the School of Biology, University of St Andrews, UK. Previously, he was a postdoctoral research fellow at the Woods Hole Oceanographic Institution, USA and a Royal Society University Research Fellow at the University of St Andrews. His research concentrates on vocal communication in marine mammals and the evolution of complexity in animal communication and cognition.

**Simon Kirby** is Professor of Language Evolution at the University of Edinburgh and co-founder of the Language Evolution and Computation Research Unit. He has pioneered the application of computational and mathematical modelling techniques to traditional issues in language acquisition, change, and evolution. In particular, he has developed an experimental and computational approach to cultural evolution called Iterated Learning, which treats language as a complex adaptive system operating on multiple interacting timescales.

**Chris Knight** was for many years Professor of Anthropology at the University of East London. He is best known for his 1991 book, *Blood relations: Menstruation and the origins of culture.* He helped initiate the Evolution of Language (EVOLANG) series of international conferences and has published widely on the evolutionary emergence of language and symbolic culture.

**Tania Kuteva** is Professor of English Linguistics at the Heinrich-Heine-University of Düsseldorf, Germany. Apart from a number of articles in international journals, she has also published two books with Cambridge University Press and three with Oxford University Press, on grammaticalization, language contact, grammatical typology, and language evolution, four of which are co-authored with Bernd Heine. She is on the editorial board of the journal *Studies in Language*.

**David Lightfoot** writes on syntactic theory, language acquisition, and historical change. He argues that internal language change is contingent, taking place in bursts, and that this entails construing language acquisition as 'cue-based'. He has published eleven books, most recently *How new languages emerge* (CUP, 2006). He is a fellow of the American Association for the Advancement of Science and of the Linguistic Society of America. His main appointments have been at McGill, Utrecht, Maryland, and Georgetown. He served as Assistant Director of the National Science Foundation, returning to Georgetown to direct programmes in Communication, Culture & Technology and Interdisciplinary Cognitive Science.

**John L. Locke** is Professor of Linguistics, Lehman College, City University of New York. He completed his PhD at Ohio University and took postdoctoral training at Yale University and at Oxford. His most recent books are *Eavesdropping: An intimate history* (OUP, 2010) and *Duels and duets: Why men and women talk so differently* (CUP, 2011).

**Ann MacLarnon** is Director of the Centre for Research in Evolutionary Anthropology at Roehampton University. She has worked on a wide variety of areas in primatology and palaeoanthropology, with an emphasis on comparative approaches. Research topics include reproductive life histories and physiology, stress endocrinology and behaviour, and aspects of comparative morphology including the brain and spinal cord. Work on this last area led to the unexpected discovery that humans evolved increased breathing control for speech.

**Peter F. MacNeilage** has written over 120 papers and one monograph ( *The origin of speech*, OUP, 2008) on the nature and evolution of complex action systems. His conceptual contributions include the Frame/Content theory of the evolution of speech and the Postural Origins theory of the evolution of primate handedness. He is a Fellow of the Acoustical Society of America and the American Association for the Advancement of Science.

**Alan Mann** (PhD University of California, Berkeley) is Professor of Anthropology at Princeton University and at the University of Pennsylvania (Emeritus). His primary interest is the fossil evidence for human evolution and in particular the origins of humanness. His current research focuses on the evolution of the Neanderthals and their relationships to modern peoples. He is also co-director of the excavation of a Middle Palaeolithic Neanderthal site in the Charente Department of southwest France.

**Steven Mithen** is a Pro-Vice-Chancellor at the University of Reading. His research interests concern early prehistoric communities and the evolution of human intelligence, language, and music. His authored and edited books include *After *the ice* (Weidenfeld & Nicolson, 2003), *The singing Neanderthals* (Weidenfeld & Nicolson, 2005), *The early prehistory of Wadi Faynan* (Oxbow Books, 2007), *To the islands* (Two Ravens Press, 2010), and *Water, life and civilisation* (CUP, 2011). He was elected a Fellow of the British Academy in 2003.

**Johanna Nichols** is Professor Emerita in the Department of Slavic Languages and Literatures and Affiliate Professor Emerita in the Department of Linguistics, University of California, Berkeley. She works on Slavic and other languages of the western steppe periphery, languages of the Caucasus, typology, and language spreads. She is the author of *Linguistic diversity in space and time* (University of Chicago Press, 1992), *Ingush-English dictionary* (RoutledgeCurzon, 2004), and *Ingush grammar* (University of California Press, 2011).

**Brigitte Pakendorf** obtained a PhD degree in Molecular Anthropology in 2001 and a PhD degree in Linguistics in 2007. She is a senior researcher at the CNRS lab Dynamique du Langage in Lyon, France. Her research focus is on the interdisciplinary investigation of prehistoric population and language contact.

**Irene M. Pepperberg** (S.B, MIT, 1969; PhD, Harvard, 1976) is a Research Associate and Lecturer (Harvard) and an Adjunct Associate Professor (Brandeis). She was a visiting Assistant Professor (Northwestern), tenured Associate Professor (University of Arizona), and visiting Associate Professor (MIT's Media Lab, Ecole Normale Superieure). She has received John Simon Guggenheim, Selby, and Radcliffe Fellowships, is a Fellow of AAAS and other professional societies, has published over 50 peer-reviewed papers, 60 reviews, and two books.

**Amy S. Pollick** received her PhD in neuroscience and animal behaviour from Emory University, where she conducted research on a variety of communicative behaviours in non-human primates. She was Director of Government Relations at the Association for Psychological Science in Washington, DC, and is now an adjunct professor at Gallaudet University.

**Camilla Power** completed her PhD under Leslie Aiello at the University of London. She is currently Senior Lecturer in Anthropology at the University of East London, specializing in Darwinian models for the origins of ritual and religion, and African hunter-gatherer gender ritual, having worked in the field with women of the Hadzabe in Tanzania.

**Paul T. Roberge** is Professor of Germanic Languages and Joint Professor of Linguistics at the University of North Carolina at Chapel Hill. He is also Extraordinary Professor of General Linguistics at the University of Stellenbosch. His research interests are historical Germanic linguistics, sociohistorical linguistics, pidgins and creoles, and Afrikaans. He teaches language evolution at UNC-CH in collaboration with his colleague, Elliott Moreton, and has written on the window potential of pidgins.

**Robert M. Seyfarth** graduated from Harvard University and received his PhD from the University of Cambridge, where his advisor was Robert A. Hinde. He was a post-doctoral fellow at Rockefeller University, working with Peter Marler. Together with Dorothy Cheney, he is the author of *How monkeys see the world* (University of Chicago Press, 1990) and *Baboon metaphysics* (Chicago, 2007). He is currently Professor of Psychology at the University of Pennsylvania.

**Peter Slater** is Emeritus Professor of Natural History at the University of St Andrews. Much of his work over the past 30 years has been on sound communication in birds and mammals and he is co-author, with Clive Catchpole, of the book *Bird song: Biological themes and variations* (CUP, 2nd edition 2008).

**Katie Slocombe** obtained a BSc in psychology from the University of Nottingham, and completed her PhD in chimpanzee communication at the University of St Andrews under the supervision of Klaus Zuberbühler. As a BBSRC post-doctoral research fellow she continued to investigate vocal behaviour in wild and captive chimpanzees. She became a lecturer in the department of Psychology, University of York, in 2007, where her research into chimpanzee communication and cognition continues.

**Kenny Smith** is a lecturer in the School of Philosophy, Psychology and Language Sciences, University of Edinburgh, with interests in the evolution of communication, human language, and the human capacity for language. He uses a mix of modelling and experimental techniques to address these questions.

**Michael Studdert-Kennedy** holds a BA in classics from the University of Cambridge and a PhD in experimental psychology from Columbia University. He is a former President of Haskins Laboratories in New Haven. His research interests include speech perception, hemispheric specialization for speech, and the development/evolution of speech. He is the author of many papers and the editor or co-editor of six books.

**Szabolcs Számadó** received his PhD in ecology and theoretical biology at the Eötvös Loránd University (Hungary) in 2004. His main research topic is the cost of honesty in animal communication, which he investigates by means of game theoretical modelling. He works with Eörs Szathmáry on questions surrounding the evolution of human language.

**Eörs Szathmáry** is the co-author with the late John Maynard Smith of *The major transitions in evolution* (Freeman, 1995) and *The origins of life* (OUP, 1999). His main interests include evolution in the origin of life and Darwinian approaches to brain dynamics. He is at Collegium Budapest and the Parmenides Foundation (Munich).

**Maggie Tallerman** has spent her professional life in northeast England, at Durham then Newcastle University, where she is currently Professor of Linguistics. Her edited and authored books include *Language origins: Perspectives on evolution* (OUP, 2005), *Understanding syntax* (Routledge, third edition 2011), and *The syntax of Welsh* (co-authored with Borsley and Willis; CUP, 2007). She started working on evolutionary linguistics in case a guy on a train asked her where language came from, though some think her real work is on Welsh.

**Marian Vanhaeren** is a Researcher at the French CNRS, specializing in the study of ancient personal ornaments which she investigates using technological and taphonomical analyses, reference collections, microscopy, GIS, and statistics. Her research focuses on the oldest traces of symbolic thinking in the European and African Palaeolithic as well as on ethnocultural diversity, exchange networks, and social inequalities among Upper Palaeolithic populations. She has co-authored more than 30 articles.

**Jacques Vauclair** is a Professor of Developmental and Comparative Psychology at the University of Provence (Aix-en-Provence, France) and a senior member of the Institut Universitaire de France. He is director of the Research Center in the Psychology of Cognition, Language and Emotion in Aix-en-Provence. His field of interest concerns the comparative study of the lateralization processes in object manipulations and communicative gestures in human infants and in non-human primates.

**Wendy K. Wilkins** is currently the Executive Vice President and Provost Emerita at New Mexico State University. Her PhD in linguistics is from UCLA. She has taught linguistics at UMass Amherst, the University of Washington, Arizona State University, Michigan State University, and at several institutions in Mexico City. With a primary research background in syntactic theory, most recently she has worked on the evolutionary neurobiology of language and comparative linguistic and musical cognition.

**Bernard A. Wood** is the University Professor of Human Origins at the George Washington University and Adjunct Senior Scientist at the National Museum of Natural History, the Smithsonian Institution. His research centres on increasing our understanding of human evolutionary history by developing and improving the ways we analyse the hominin fossil record.

**Thomas Wynn** is Professor of Anthropology at the University of Colorado, Colorado Springs, where he has taught since 1977. He has published extensively in palaeolithic archaeology, with a particular emphasis on cognitive evolution. His books include *The evolution of spatial competence* (University of Illinois Press, 1989) and *The rise of Homo sapiens: The evolution of modern thinking* (with F. Coolidge, Wiley-Blackwell, 2009).

**Klaus Zuberbühler** is a Professor of Psychology at the University of St Andrews and Professor in Biology at the University of Neuchatel in Switzerland. He holds an undergraduate degree in zoology and anthropology from the University of Zurich and a doctoral degree in psychology from the University of Pennsylvania. He conducts research on the primate roots of human language, focusing on the cognitive underpinnings of primate communication. His research has been published in major journals, including *Nature*, *PNAS*, and *Current Biology*.

# CHAPTER 1

····················································

# INTRODUCTION: THE EVOLUTION OF LANGUAGE

····················································

## MAGGIE TALLERMAN AND
## KATHLEEN R. GIBSON

## 1.1 ANIMAL COMMUNICATION SYSTEMS
### AND THE UNIQUENESS OF LANGUAGE

····················································

Most organisms communicate with conspecifics, whether intentionally or not, and such communication encompasses all conceivable mechanisms. Vocal and other sound-based signals, such as clicking wings or legs, are common. Visual signals are also widespread, including those most associated with humans and other primates: manual and facial signals, and bodily postures. Visual signalling with feelers or other body parts occurs in many species. Colouration is a common type of visual signalling: for instance, some species have distinct juvenile versus adult colouration, or special breeding plumages. Often, changes in colour occur according to context, for instance in some fish, in octopuses, and in chameleons; social cephalopods, such as squid and cuttlefish, deploy changes in skin colour and pattern to signal messages such as readiness to mate. Tactile signals are widely employed, such as touching with legs, trunks, or feelers. Communication via chemical signals is widespread; for example, moths use pheromones to attract conspecifics in the dark.

Electric organ discharge (for instance, in electric fish such as mormyrids) also occurs, but is much rarer. Numerous social insect species have highly sophisticated communication systems, such as the 'dance' used by honey bees, where complex movements produced by a returning forager indicate the distance and direction of pollen and nectar resources. Animal communication systems are thus immensely varied in form.

Some animals communicate not only with conspecifics, but also understand at least some of the signals produced by other species; for example, Diana monkeys learn the message conveyed by the alarm calls of neighbouring Campbell's monkeys (Zuberbühler, Chapter 5). Moreover, symbiotic relationships sometimes produce communication across unrelated species. The honey guide bird (*Indicator indicator*) leads honey badgers to bees' nests by making a sound that attracts the badger, which then breaks into the nest, allowing both animals to reap the rewards.

Mammals employ extensive vocal communication with conspecifics, often in addition to using visual display, chemical messages, and tactile communication. Humans are no exception here, and our ancient primate communication system encompasses many non-verbal signals, including laughter, crying, smiles, frowns, cries of pain, and postures of aggression and appeasement (Burling, Chapter 44). With a very small amount of cultural diversity, these signals are human universals. But all animal communication systems, including our own non-verbal signalling, share a (negatively-defined) property: these systems cannot combine signals to produce new meanings. In fact, they generally do not combine signals at all. For language, though, this property is fundamental. The combinatorial principle, exploited at different levels of organization, is a crucial, distinctive attribute of language. The overarching property, shared by no other animal system, is the open-ended productivity of language: humans combine signals to produce an infinite set of distinct meanings, and can convey to conspecifics any topic that can be thought of, including absent, hypothetical, and fictitious events and entities.

In every meaningful sense, language is an autapomorphy, i.e. a derived trait found only in our lineage, and not shared with other branches of our monophyletic group (say, the group of primates, or the group of great apes). We also have no definitive evidence that any species other than *Homo sapiens* ever had language. However, it must be noted straightaway that 'language' is not a monolithic entity, but rather a complex bundle of traits that must have evolved over a significant time frame, some features doubtless appearing in species that preceded our own. Moreover, language crucially draws on aspects of cognition that are long established in the primate lineage, such as memory: the language faculty as a whole comprises more than just the uniquely linguistic features. We do not know, though, if and how language has itself shaped properties such as memory (or vice versa), so the role of extra-linguistic factors is hard to evaluate.

We anticipate that both animal communication and animal cognition will shed light on the evolution of language, but in exactly what ways is hotly debated.

Biologists do not expect evolution to throw up a radically new complex system with no evolutionary precursors, so it is good scientific practice to look for relevant primitive features in closely-related species, i.e. phylogenetically ancient features that may have preceded language or been prerequisites for language; see Hopkins and Vauclair, Chapter 18; Wilkins, Chapter 19. Another established methodology is to search for examples of convergent evolution: functionally or formally similar features appearing in species that do not share a recent common ancestry. Unfortunately, for language such features are not easily detected. For specific traits, there are indeed both analogues (unrelated but superficially similar features) and homologues (features with a shared common ancestry) in other animal systems. These include such common features as vocalization and cultural transmission. But it seems clear that language *as a system* has no 'simpler' analogues or homologues in other animals. In fact, language is exceptional in almost all aspects.

Language obtains its unique expressive power by exploiting a few distinct formal principles that operate over numerous subsystems and at different levels of organization. These tools have little or no parallel in the animal kingdom. First, and perhaps most critically, language combines elements at all levels. Starting with sound systems (MacNeilage, Chapter 46), each language combines elements from an individual set of digitized sounds known as phonemes: discrete, contrastive sound segments. In turn, phonemes are often considered to be combinations of a discrete set of phonological features, such as [+/− voice] and [+/− sonorant] (though see MacNeilage, Chapter 46, for discussion). Phonemes combine in language-specific permutations to form syllables, and syllables combine to form morphemes and words; sign languages have equivalent manual systems (Goldin-Meadow, Chapter 57). Words are combined, both in morphology, to form compounds (*greenhouse, dog-house, icehouse, outhouse*), and in syntax, to form headed phrases.

Second, elements are ordered in predictable ways. Each language has its own set of phonotactic constraints, governing which sound sequences are permissible and which are not; English, for instance, allows word-initial sequences of /pl/ (*play*) and /kl/ (*clay*) but not */tl/. Morphemes are ordered in fixed ways (*un+afraid*, but *fear+less; hand+ful+s*, not *handsful*); see Carstairs-McCarthy, Chapter 47, on morphology. Words are also sequenced predictably, for instance by having a usual order of heads and complements across phrasal categories, though languages are not always dogmatic about this.

Third, language exploits hierarchical structure at several levels. Syllables are hierarchically structured, with a nucleus and coda combining to form a rhyme (say, vocalic nucleus /ɪ/ plus coda /ŋk/ forming *ink*), and then an onset, say *dr* or *sl*, combining optionally with the rhyme, forming *drink* or *slink*. Hierarchical structure also operates at the level of morpheme combinations: given the morphemes *un+friend+ly* we get the structure [*un*[*friendly*]] rather than *[[*unfriend*]*ly*], whereas with *untidily* (*un+tidy+ly*) the structure is [[*untidy*]*ly*]. Semantics exploits hierarchical structure, for instance by partitioning meanings into different levels of specificity: *spaniel, setter, retriever* are types of *dog, dogs* are a type of *mammal, mammals* a type of *vertebrate* and so on. Syntax exploits hierarchical structure by combining words into phrases, and phrases into larger phrases and clauses (Tallerman, Chapter 48). It is also widely argued that texts in discourse (e.g. conversations or stories) are hierarchically structured. In addition to these organizational principles, mappings occur between all linguistic levels, including most broadly between sound and meaning. This, then, is the formal basis of language.

Even at the lowest levels of organization, there are strikingly few parallels in animal communication systems. In human phonological systems, a relatively small, closed set of meaningless elements (sound segments and their visual equivalents in sign languages) combine to produce meaningful elements. Though bird song is sometimes described as having 'phonological syntax' (Marler 1977), the term is rather misleading. In bird song, discrete acoustic units also exist, and are combined and sequenced in rule-governed ways, but there is no compositionality; whatever the sequences of notes or motifs, the message never changes and no new information is produced (Hilliard and White 2009; Slater, Chapter 8). There is no productivity in the combinations. Bee dances display a limited compositionality (Kirby, Chapter 61) but again, no productivity. As we move up the levels of linguistic organization, we find fewer parallels still in animal systems. Hierarchical structure exists in some bird song and some whale song (Janik, Chapter 9), but it is always limited (Hurford 2011). There is no recursion (self-embedding) and no semantic compositionality.

A priori, we might expect that the natural communication systems of our closest living relatives, the great apes, would be nearest to language—perhaps rather like language, but with a smaller vocabulary and a simpler grammar. But this is absolutely not the case. Even at the most fundamental level, that of sound production, we have a different morphology of the supralaryngeal vocal tract from that of chimpanzees, with humans showing clear specializations for speech production (MacLarnon, Chapter 22). Moreover, humans have evolved far greater neurological control over their vocalizations than other primates. Although much is still unknown about the subtleties of communication systems in other primates, it is clear that there is really nothing analogous to human sound systems, lexicon, semantics, or grammar. Some call combinations do seem to occur in wild chimpanzees (Slocombe, Chapter 7) but as yet there is no evidence that these acquire a compositional meaning; see Tallerman, Chapters 48 and 51.

Certain animal systems have something that at first glance seems to resemble a primitive vocabulary. For instance, among other calls, some monkey species have a small set of distinct alarm calls, each produced in response to a different predator (such as the well-known vervet monkey calls, 'eagle', 'leopard', and 'snake'; Seyfarth and Cheney, Chapter 4). These have attracted much interest in the language evolution literature, doubtless because of the relatively close relationship between humans and monkeys. It should be noted, though, that domestic chickens also have distinct alarm calls for different predators, a system as sophisticated as those of monkeys, and, additionally, have referential food calls; moreover, prairie dogs (which are rodents) employ perhaps the most highly sophisticated systems of animal alarm calls (Gibson, Chapter 11). Are alarm calls or food calls parallel to words? They share one property—arbitrariness—with human vocabulary: they are non-iconic, meaning that they do not sound like the entities they represent; see Deacon, Chapter 43. Alarm calls are often described as having functional reference; that is, they are prompted by external events (such as the appearance of a leopard) rather than merely conveying an animal's internal state, such as fear or aggression. We might then assume that the leopard alarm in some way 'means' *leopard*. But this is not necessarily so—the leopard call may alternatively be associated in the hearer's mind with the leopard-specific escape route, climbing a tree; see Hurford, Chapter 40; Tallerman, Chapter 51, for discussion.

Alarm calls differ from words in all other respects; see Tallerman, Chapter 48. They are not formed from different permutations of a discrete set of sounds, but rather, are holistic. Both the calls themselves and the broad contexts that provoke them are innate. Conversely, words, both forms and meanings, are learned by human infants, and crucially, new words are learned by each speaker throughout life. Monkey alarm calls are primarily used when the particular predator is present, and sometimes to deceive conspecifics into thinking a predator is around. Even in the latter case, calls are wholly situation-specific; calls cannot be used predicatively to *discuss* a predator, past, present, or hypothetical. Alarm calls are indexical, meaning that they have a causal link to what they represent—normally, the presence of the predator induces the appropriate alarm call. Alarm calls thus also lack the property of displacement that is crucial in language: words are not tied to or produced in a precise context, but can be used whenever the concept they represent floats into our minds.

Words are thus true symbols, whereas animal calls, even if functionally referential, are not; symbolic reference, which must be acquired by learning, is explored in detail by Deacon, Chapter 43, and by Harnad, Chapter 42. Critically, word meanings are established between a community of speakers and agreed by convention. Part of what this entails is that the meaning of a word can change very quickly, providing other members of the language community adopt the new meaning (think of *net*, *web*, or *drive*). Alarm calls, in contrast, have a fixed meaning and essentially form a closed set. The total repertoire of calls in any animal species is tiny, numbering no more than a few dozen distinct calls, whereas the vocabulary of all human languages numbers tens of thousands of items (Tallerman, Chapter 48). The gulf between the small set of essentially innate and relatively inflexible calls found in all other primate species and the massive, open-ended, and learned vocabularies of human beings reveals one of the major innovations in language evolution that must be accounted for. This is no mere matter of degree—in vocabulary, something altogether different has evolved from anything seen in the natural communication systems of other animals (Burling, Chapter 44).

The evolution of a massive, learned vocabulary store (Tallerman 2009) is just one of the unique aspects of language. Only in language do we find the extensive categorization that, for instance, divides the lexicon into discrete categories such as noun, verb, adjective, each category with its own distinctive behaviour. The categories themselves are unlikely to be innate, since they differ from language to language, but the *ability* to categorize in this way, and on the basis of little data, appears to be uniquely human. Evidence of children's abilities in generalizing over categories has been well known at least since Berko (1958). In the *wug* test, children are told that a mythical creature in a picture is a *wug*; when asked what two such creatures are called, they have no difficulty in replying /wʌgz/, thus using the correct plural form of the noun.

Only language conveys propositional meanings ('idea units'; loosely, what we call sentences, such as *The bird flew past the window*), and of course these are unlimited in scope. Only language exhibits all the paraphernalia of syntax (Tallerman, Chapter 48), including headed phrases, recursion, long-distance dependencies, and expressions such as *each other* or *themselves* that can only be interpreted using other expressions (*Kim and Mel hurt each other*). Only language displays the property of duality of patterning (see Tallerman, Chapter 51), with combinations on two levels of organization: meaningless units (phonemes) are combined into meaningful morphemes/words, and words are combined into phrases. Other highly distinctive properties arise on each level of linguistic organization; even the speech signal itself displays significant adaptations both in production and perception (see Pinker and Jackendoff 2005 for an overview).

Given the limited nature of the evidence obtainable from studying animal communication systems, how do researchers hope to break into the evolutionary puzzle that is language?

## 1.2 WHAT COUNTS AS EVIDENCE IN LANGUAGE EVOLUTION?

The previous section introduced the major novelties of the language faculty, which includes notable discontinuities with animal communication systems. This gives rise to a fundamental dilemma in the field of language evolution. Language seems to display many features with no precursors, yet general evolutionary principles suggest that a complex trait like language, which is not under the control of any single gene or related group of genes, must have evolved in large part from simpler precursors. Frustratingly, we have no direct evidence for any aspect of language evolution, and no uncontroversial indirect evidence. Moreover, what is considered possible evidence differs from discipline to discipline, as we now discuss.

The comparative method is an obvious place to start; see chapters in Part I, also Fitch (2010a). There are two ways in which this method can be employed. The first involves comparing similar traits within a clade. For humans, the set of primates as a whole or the smaller set of great apes would be most relevant; for instance, tool use by other great apes is an established trait, so it seems likely that the last common ancestor of all great apes, including humans, was able to use simple tools. This trait is thus a homologue, involving a shared common ancestry. (See Wood and Bauernfeind, Chapter 25, for discussion of likely features of the last common ancestor between panins, i.e. chimpanzees/bonobos, and hominins, i.e. creatures that are on the human line of descent, though not necessarily direct ancestors to *Homo sapiens*.) Relevant here too are the natural communication systems of closely-related species, and also their latent language-related abilities, such as the ability to learn arbitrary symbols under human instruction (Gibson, Chapter 3). The alternative way of employing the comparative method involves comparing the convergent evolution of similar traits across a number of unrelated lineages. For instance, bipedal locomotion in humans, kangaroos, and birds is not due to common ancestry, so is an analogous trait across the three lineages. Analogues are useful because they may have evolved in different lineages under comparable selection pressures, such as a similar habitat, diet, or predation pattern. The problem, as noted above, is that homologues and analogues to essential properties of language are not easily established in animal systems, and no other species has a language faculty, so the comparative method is difficult to apply straightforwardly. For discussion in this volume, see especially Arbib (20); de Waal and Pollick (6); Gibson (3 and 11); Hopkins and Vauclair (18); Hurford (40); Pepperberg (10); Slocombe (7); Tallerman (48); Zuberbühler (5).

The discipline of palaeoanthropology examines the fossil record, and from skull endocasts may uncover anatomical evidence of brain structure of potential relevance to language, including brain size, external cortical reorganization, and hemispheric asymmetries (Wilkins, Chapter 19). Unfortunately, we cannot study past stages of brain evolution in any depth, since endocasts provide no evidence of internal brain structure. Similarly, with the exception of an occasional hyoid bone, we have no fossilized remains of the vocal tract (see MacLarnon, Chapter 22; Wood and Bauernfeind, Chapter 25). However, even if we had clear evidence of the emergence of modern vocal tract structure, we would not necessarily know how to interpret it. A broadly modern structure, for instance, could initially have evolved as a spandrel, that is, as a by-product, perhaps of bipedalism or changes in dental function (MacLarnon, Chapter 22). In that case, speech capabilities could still have been lacking if neural adaptations had not yet occurred. Even if we were certain that a modern vocal tract provided full speech capabilities, this would not necessarily imply the presence of a full language faculty, since this encompasses far more than speech.

Recently, molecular biology has provided another possible source of physical evidence: the use of genetic material from hominin fossils, and the tracking of changes in DNA in hominin populations (Cann, Chapter 24; Pakendorf, Chapter 59). Again, however, these methods are fraught with difficulties and controversies. For instance, which class of DNA (mitochondrial, Y-chromosome, or autosomal) should be considered the most reliable? This is as yet a young field, and new discoveries and constant developments in technology should provide more answers in future decades.

Another line of enquiry looks not at hominin fossil remains themselves, but at the artefacts left by our ancestors. Archaeologists have argued that inferences can be made about the development of symbolic communication and linguistic complexity by looking at tools and other implements, or personal ornaments such as beads, thus assuming some link between linguistic skills and cognitive sophistication, as evidenced in the material record. Moreover, if a certain level of cultural complexity is attested both in known societies and in prehistoric societies, it seems reasonable to assume that a similar level of complexity occurs in cognition too. In this volume, the chapters by Boeckx (52); Botha (30); d'Errico and Vanhaeren (29); Donald (17); Mann (26); Mithen (28); and Wynn (27) discuss the relevance of the archaeological record and the difficulties inherent in interpreting it; see also Cann, Chapter 24. There are many possible drawbacks to using technological advances to infer the presence of the language faculty, not least because crucial artefacts made of degradable materials may be absent from the record: for instance, early hominins may have utilized plant materials, including bark, leaves, wood, grass, and reeds, and animal soft parts, including hides, furs, and feathers. We only have to think of the exponential increase in the complexity of our own artefacts between 1850 and 2010 to realize that there is no simple chain of inference between sophistication in the archaeological record and the presence of language (see also Botha, Chapter 30). Moreover, new archaeological findings readily overturn previous conclusions. For example, it was once thought that art, beads, and some forms of stone-flaking appeared only in Upper Palaeolithic times, i.e. after about 35,000 BP. We now know that beads, other putative forms of symbolism, and advanced flaking techniques long predate the Upper Palaeolithic (Brown et al. 2009; d'Errico and Vanhaeren, Chapter 29; McBrearty and Brooks 2000). And until quite recently, tools comprising more than one component—such as harpoons or bows and arrows—were thought to have originated only within the last 20,000 years (Coolidge and Wynn 2009b; Wynn, Chapter 27) but a recent find suggests that arrows were being produced as much as 64 kya (thousand years ago) (Lombard and Phillipson 2010). Thus, the archaeological record requires us to frequently re-evaluate evidence and arguments.

Given the problems with the physical record, both of hominin fossils and associated artefacts, many have turned to other potential sources of evidence for language evolution. Jackendoff (2010: 65) suggests that reverse engineering provides the most productive methodology: 'We attempt to infer the nature of universal grammar and the language acquisition device from the structure of the modern language capacity'. Thus, one form of evidence comes from the study of normal language and its acquisition; in this volume, see in particular the contributions by Bickerton (49); Burling (44); de Boer (33); Falk (32); Goldin-Meadow (57); Graf Estes (64); Locke (34); MacNeilage (46); Studdert-Kennedy (45); Tallerman (48 and 51). However, the danger of confusing ontogenetic and phylogenetic processes must always be guarded against here. There is no reason to think that any specific evidence concerning the *origins* of language can be gained from studying the acquisition of modern languages. Moreover, infants learning language today have a full language faculty, which clearly is not the case for the earliest hominins.

Linguists often suggest that evidence can be obtained by extrapolating from other modern contexts; for instance, from observable 'language genesis' in adults and children, including the formation of pidgins and creoles (in this volume, see Bickerton, Chapter 49; Carstairs-McCarthy, Chapter 47; Roberge, Chapter 56), homesign, and emergent sign languages (Goldin-Meadow, Chapter 57). A very strong line of linguistic research (and one of the few areas widely considered to provide good evidence by practitioners of disparate linguistic theories) involves the study of *grammaticalization*. It is widely argued that putative prehistoric stages of language can be reconstructed by studying known linguistic trajectories of change—specifically, the ways in which grammatical elements are formed from lexical elements. In this volume, see especially the contributions of Bybee (55); Carstairs-McCarthy (47); and Heine and Kuteva (54). The importance of grammaticalization is also emphasized by Bickerton, Chapter 49; Corballis, Chapter 41; and Chater and Christiansen, Chapter 65.

There are also, however, applications of reverse engineering in spheres other than the narrowly linguistic. In the field of cognition, Coolidge and Wynn (Chapter 21) investigate the evolution of modern thinking, specifically the emergence of indirect speech acts. There are also applications of reverse engineering in evolutionary biology; in this volume, see in particular Számadó and Szathmáry, Chapter 14, who discuss the co-evolution of language and the brain. Since there must be some relationship between genes and language, it has sometimes been assumed that there are readily identifiable genes 'for' language, or aspects of language (for example, *FOXP2* was often carelessly reported in the popular press as the 'language gene'). Diller and Cann, Chapter 15, evaluate the evidence concerning genetic correlates for language, and conclude that language is highly unlikely to be associated with any single genetic mutation; see also Cann, Chapter 24.

Two related, relatively new applications of reverse engineering have become major fields of investigation in language evolution: computational and mathematical modelling, and robotics, including embodied agent models. Formal models allow the predictions of theories of language evolution to be tested empirically, by building in the assumptions to be tested and seeing if they indeed result from the model: if the model produces these results, the assumptions are borne out. In this volume, see especially Cangelosi (62); Kirby (61); and Smith (60); also de Boer (63); MacNeilage (46); Studdert-Kennedy (45). As both Kirby and Smith discuss, results and predictions obtained from the formal models can further be tested on human subjects in the laboratory.

In sum, though there will inevitably be much speculation in a field of this nature, we believe that serious advances have been made in the past few decades in terms of building an evidence-based discipline. In the next section we consider in more detail the properties of language as a biological system.

## 1.3 LANGUAGE EVOLUTION AND BIOLOGY

We start by examining the uniqueness of language in biological terms, in comparison with other animal communication systems. Language is a complex amalgam of lifelong learning (nonetheless including a critical period) and innateness; see Fitch, Chapter 13. Most researchers agree that both aspects are crucial to language, but many controversies arise over where the line should be drawn (see the following section). The aspects uncontroversially considered to be learned are, of course, vocabularies and idiosyncratic lexical properties of distinct languages, transmitted from generation to generation (a trait known as traditional transmission). Vocabulary is added beyond the critical period for language acquisition, a feature with few clear analogues in other animal communication systems.

Simple communication systems which combine vocal learning and innateness are found in some animals (notably, songbirds), but the contributions made by each aspect are easier to tease apart, since experiments can be performed which would be impossible with human subjects. Here we see a marked contrast with the communication systems of non-human primates, in which learning plays a minimal part—it is more a case of fine-tuning the acoustic properties of calls, and of learning the specific contexts in which it is appropriate to use each call. Vocal learning does play a vital role in the communication systems of some non-primates, however, especially in bird species (Slater, Chapter 8), in a number of marine mammals (whales, dolphins, sea lions etc.; Janik, Chapter 9), and in some bats. Among vocal learning birds, there are certain parallels to language learning:

song learning can involve a sensitive period, outside of which the learned system will either be incomplete or abnormal; song is traditionally transmitted (i.e. learned from adult models); and a stage analogous to babbling (known as sub-song) occurs. However, Gibson (Chapter 11) points out that language learning is actually very different from the learning of bird song, which often has a sensitive period followed by a long 'quiet' period, with song emerging only in adulthood; see Hurford (2011). Moreover, young birds raised without an appropriate adult model (e.g. solely female instead of male relatives) will nonetheless sing, even though the song is not adult-like. This shows that there is an innate stratum, some basis for the song which is not entirely learned.

In the case of language, the child undoubtedly brings crucial cognitive contributions to the learning process, yet without linguistic input, full language does not develop. Despite the necessity for learning, the language faculty (whatever it contains) provides such a powerful drive that in the absence of normal linguistic input, something language-like can emerge. A clear example comes from the deaf children of hearing parents: from the non-linguistic gestures that the parents make to communicate with the child, a structured system—known as homesign—develops spontaneously in the child's communication (see Goldin-Meadow, Chapter 57). This is not language, but has indisputable linguistic properties. And tellingly, when speakers of different homesign systems get together in a naturalistic setting, a shared system with more linguistic properties soon emerges, as in the well-known case of Nicaraguan Sign Language, also discussed by Goldin-Meadow. Over the course of a couple of 'generations' of schoolchildren, this sign system developed into full language. It is also well documented throughout the world that when contact occurs between groups with no shared language, restricted linguistic systems develop, known as pidgins (Roberge, Chapter 56), and these may in due course become full languages, learned natively by children. Given such evidence, it is difficult to conclude that language has no genetic component. We will assume, then, that there have been significant adaptations in our species with respect to a language faculty.

Strikingly, though, and unlike animal communication systems, language differs radically in its superficial form in distinct geographical locations—we have mutually unintelligible 'languages' in different regions, rather than distinct 'dialects', as is the case in some bird song and whale song systems. The superficial diversity of language systems has no discernible consequences for language learning; infants seem equally capable of learning any ambient language (or indeed, learning half a dozen or more languages in their environment), and take around the same amount of time to get to the same stages, whatever language they are learning. This fact alone suggests the presence of an innate predisposition for language learning.

Another biologically distinctive property of language concerns its function (see also below). If indeed language has biological 'function' at all, it is difficult to discern what the primary function might be, or might have been while language was evolving. The function of animal communication systems, on the other hand, typically revolves around reproduction, including mate attraction, pair bonding, and defence of territory. Even learned animal systems thus have a very limited message. There is a biological imperative for songbirds to learn their songs: birds that don't learn the species-appropriate song are less likely to be chosen as mates, and song quality is perceived by potential mates as a fitness indicator (Slater, Chapter 8). Song is, thus, an honest signal (Zahavi and Zahavi 1997), in a way that language is not. Song is 'costly', as it takes time to produce, and so reveals the quality of the singer: only a bird that is already in good condition can afford to spend time singing rather than feeding; song may also draw the attention of predators. Conversely, producing language requires virtually no calorific expenditure above and beyond that needed for overall brain growth and maintenance; it doesn't take up valuable time that could be used to forage and it doesn't require that the speaker be in good condition. One of the questions surrounding the origins of language is therefore how a 'cheap' communication system of this nature might have arisen; for discussion in this volume, see especially Donald, Chapter 17; Dunbar, Chapter 36; Falk, Chapter 32; Knight and Power, Chapter 37.

It is also notable that language involves developments on three distinct but interacting timescales (Kirby, Chapter 61; Carstairs-McCarthy, Chapter 47; Szá-madó and Szathmáry, Chapter 14). The first of these is biological evolution: whatever is in the language faculty (and its precursors in early hominins) must be genetically transmitted under selective pressures—the transition in hominins from no language to language is a biological fact, so must conform to known biological processes. Language in its earlier forms can therefore be assumed to have been adaptive, i.e. to have conferred fitness benefits on its users. At the very least, whatever neurological, physical, or other changes accompanied an evolving language faculty had to have no negative impact on selection.

Biological change thus encompasses all the phylogenetic changes in hominins which are prerequisites for language, including the evolution of crucial abilities not shared with other primates, or at best, only minimally developed in non-human primates. For the speech modality, these prerequisites include full vocal control (the ability both to vocalize and to suppress vocalization at will), vocal imitation, and vocal learning; see MacLarnon, Chapter 22; MacNeilage, Chapter 46. A certain amount of vocal flexibility is in fact attested in modern primates (see Slocombe, Chapter 7; Zuberbühler, Chapter 5), taking the form of acoustic modification of calls. It is now also known that some primates can both vocalize volitionally and suppress vocalization under certain circumstances. Slocombe also reports on some evidence showing that both vocal imitation and learning occur, for instance in different 'dialects' of vocalizations in chimpanzees; if there are novel vocalizations, they must be learned and must spread via imitation. But even before those traits emerged, our ancestors must have developed the ability to understand that conspecifics are communicating deliberately; to infer the mental states of other individuals (see Gibson, Chapter 3; Hurford, Chapter 40; Knight and Power, Chapter 37); and to engage cooperatively in all sorts of tasks, which eventually included discourse (Tomasello 2008). These traits are all expressed to some extent in modern apes, so probably existed in the last common ancestor of apes and humans. Language placed a premium on these abilities. For a protolanguage to emerge, hominins needed to develop expanded abilities in such domains, leading ultimately to the ability to learn, store, and retrieve a vast intersecting network of arbitrary symbols (words; Deacon, Chapter 43), and the crucial property of displacement (the ability to refer to entities remote in time or space; Hurford, Chapter 40); see also Tallerman (2009).

Using these conventional symbols relies in turn on the capacity to imitate, rehearse, and refine the practical skills required (Burling, Chapter 44; Corballis, Chapter 41; Donald, Chapter 17). The use of vocabulary also relies on a shared conceptual system, which probably developed directly from primate cognition (Hurford, Chapter 40), and requires 'the ability to associate gestures or vocalizations with concepts' (Burling, Chapter 44; see also Corballis, Chapter 41): this must be one of the critical first steps in language evolution. For full language, more is needed—the major development being the compositional syntactic abilities which are the main impetus in generative grammar for assuming an innate language capacity; see Bickerton, Chapter 49; Tallerman, Chapter 48, for an outline of syntactic processes.

The second timescale involves cultural transmission: individual languages are transmitted across generations, and within populations of speakers. This has led to proposals that languages themselves adapt to become more learnable (Christiansen and Chater 2008; Chater and Christiansen, Chapter 65). Many developments on this timescale are known from attested language change, in particular the processes known as grammaticalization, whereby lexical items evolve into functional items (auxiliaries, complementizers, demonstratives, determiners, and so on). Most linguists assume that similar processes were operative in the evolution of the full language faculty, so that the earliest protolanguages—simpler precursors to language—may well have distinguished no categories other than protonouns and protoverbs (Hurford 2003a; Heine and Kuteva 2007, Chapter 54; Tallerman, Chapter 51).

Cultural transmission involves not only vertical transmission, between parents and children, but also horizontal transmission of various kinds, both within and across communities. This includes transmission between speakers of different languages, in cases of language contact: see Pakendorf, Chapter 59. Such contact can lead to interesting mismatches between the genetic and linguistic heritage in a population, as Pakendorf outlines. Since population contact is likely to have been extensive throughout our evolution, language contact between linguistic groups has very likely contributed much to language evolution itself (Nichols, Chapter 58).

Horizontal transmission between groups of deaf children also occurred in the development of Nicaraguan Sign Language (Goldin-Meadow, Chapter 57).

The third timescale is that of individual learning—the growth of language in children. MacNeilage, Chapter 46, argues that there is one respect in which ontogeny recapitulates phylogeny, and that is in speech production; infants and early hominins must share the same biomechanical constraints on mouth movements, and these lead in both cases to initially simple syllable patterns (as seen in babbling; see Studdert-Kennedy, Chapter 45, for discussion). Even prelinguistic infants possess impressive statistical learning abilities which provide cues for segmentation, enabling the internal structure of words and phrases to be detected in the continuous stream of speech (Graf Estes, Chapter 64). Of course, these learning mechanisms also evolved (Számadó and Szathmáry, Chapter 14), thus relating back to the biological timescale.

As mentioned above, the complexity of the language faculty precludes any simple account of language evolution relying on a few, recent genetic mutations. The sequencing of the human genome (International Human Genome Sequencing Consortium 2004) revealed, rather surprisingly, that humans only have around 20,000–25,000 genes—far fewer than was anticipated. (A microscopic roundworm, *Caenorhabditis elegans*, has over 19,000 genes.) Since humans share approximately 99% of their genome with chimpanzees and bonobos, this suggests that relatively few genes determine all of the biological differences between humans and panins (Gibson 2002). Two factors may account for this. First, most genes are pleiotropic, which means that they have control over more than one trait. Second, many genes (such as *FOXP2*) are also regulatory in nature; that is, they serve as switches that turn multiple downstream genes on or off. Regulatory genes that are active early in development can have profound effects on developing phenotypes. Given the small number of genetic differences between panins and humans, it is likely that many of the phenotypic (i.e. observable) differences reflect functional differences in regulatory genes. The small number of total genes in the human genome—coupled with the small number of probable genetic differences between other apes and humans—also argues against views that each aspect of distinctively human neurology, behaviour, or language is controlled by a distinct gene (Gibson 2002; Diller and Cann, Chapter 15). Chater and Christiansen, Chapter 65, even doubt that the language faculty has genetic underpinnings at all, arguing that aspects of language fluctuate far more quickly than genetic changes could accommodate; but see Számadó and Szathmáry, Chapter 14, for an alternative view. We do not doubt that cultural transmission has shaped the language faculty to some extent; since the earliest forms of protolanguage must have been culturally transmitted (Nichols, Chapter 58), just as languages themselves are, then learnability seems likely to have played an important role in evolution. But we also see an evolving language faculty itself as clearly adaptive.

It is also important to acknowledge epigenetic factors in human evolution. Genes interact with their environment, so that the same genotype (i.e. the same DNA) occurring in two individuals does not necessarily produce the same phenotype (observable properties or behaviour) in both, a phenomenon termed phenotypic plasticity (Számadó and Szathmáry, Chapter 14). A simple example is height. The ultimate height reached by any individual is a product of interacting genetic and environmental effects, including intrauterine environment, postnatal diet, and overall health. As noted by Számadó and Szathmáry, and outlined in the introduction to Part II, phenotypic plasticity is built into mammalian, including human, brain developmental processes. It is possible, via the Baldwin Effect and genetic assimilation, for initially plastic phenotypes, including learned behaviours, to ultimately become genetically fixed (Fitch, Chapter 13; Gibson and Tallerman, Chapter 12; Számadó and Szathmáry, Chapter 14). Although an 'instinct' to learn languages has clearly been incorporated into the human genome, no specific lexical items or specific syntactic constructions are universal. This suggests that language, as opposed to most animal calls, is a specific adaptation for communicating about highly variable events.

## 1.4 Language: what are we trying to account for and (how) did it evolve?

Do we even agree what language is? Although we have written so far as if it is clear what the term 'language' refers to, the likelihood is that readers have quite disparate ideas on this topic. We started this introduction by comparing language as a communication system with animal communication systems, something that is controversial for those who do not regard language as primarily 'for' communication at all. If 'language' suggests different things to researchers from distinct fields, then we won't necessarily agree about what there is to account for in 'language evolution'. We therefore need to consider how various terms have been defined and used in the field.

A primary distinction often made in linguistics is that between E-language and I-language (Chomsky 1986). E-language ('external' language) refers to linguistic behaviours, also indicating an observable set of languages (living or extinct); E-language is in some sense 'out there' in a language-speaking community. I-language is a cognitive entity; it refers to the speaker's ('internal' and 'individual') knowledge of language, and is regarded by many linguists as the proper object of biological study. Broadly, I-language can be equated with the better-known term, competence; I-language is a property of an individual's brain, while E-language is the output of a set of I-languages. For evolutionary linguistics, the relevance lies in the distinction between the evolution of language as a human faculty, and the subsequent development of various languages (linguistic systems) over historical time, which is generally not thought to involve evolution in a biological sense.

There is, of course, no way to see I-language directly, and few methods are available for investigating the nature of the language faculty apart from studying the outputs of I-language, including interrogating native speaker grammaticality judgements: indeed, linguistics journals are full of papers investigating various aspects of (E-)'languages'. Whether or not these analyses shed light on the language faculty itself is often a matter of interpretation and of theoretical assumptions. Moreover, I-language itself is not transferred from parent to child, but must crucially pass through what Hurford (1990b) terms the 'Arena of Use'. Children, like linguists, have no direct access to their parents' language faculty, and their own I-language is in part the product of learning from incomplete linguistic data produced in a social setting. There seems little doubt that processes of socio/ cultural transmission play a role in shaping languages (Kirby, Chapter 61). An objection here might be that such transmission has shaped E-languages but does not affect I-languages. For instance, it is likely that traditional transmission is involved in forming vowel systems that keep segments as far apart as possible within the acoustic space available (de Boer, Chapter 63), and also involved in linearizing words and phrases in ways that aid processing (Hawkins 1994, 2004). But cultural transmission operating while the language faculty was still evolving may also have shaped I-languages themselves. The very fact of having to be learnable by human brains may determine structural properties of language (Anderson, Chapter 39; Chater and Christiansen, Chapter 65).

A second distinction (Hauser et al. 2002) is between FLN and FLB—the faculty of language in the narrow and in the broad sense. FLN is a component of the wider FLB, but refers to whatever is uniquely linguistic—'the abstract linguistic computational system alone' (Hauser et al. 2002: 1571)—and thus, uniquely human. FLB contains many additional capacities, including memory, respiration, and the auditory system; traits that are used in language but are not necessarily uniquely human. Jackendoff usefully (2010) refines this distinction. Some aspects of the broader language faculty are uniquely human, but have a wider function than the purely linguistic, such as a full theory of mind. Other aspects of the language faculty are both uniquely human and uniquely linguistic, yet have evolved directly from existing primate features; a clear instance is the specialized human vocal tract (MacLarnon, Chapter 22). In FLN remains whatever is radically new in the primate lineage—aspects of the language faculty that are so specialized or distinctive that they appear to have no primate precursors. From a biological perspective, as little as possible should be ascribed to this last category.

To step back a little, these distinctions also raise questions. What do we mean by a language faculty? Does it even exist? Most linguists, psychologists, and biologists assume, at a minimum, that humans have some genetic endowment for language acquisition; a biological trait which, in the presence of socially-presented linguistic data, ensures that language will develop in all children with normal biological endowments and normal socio/cultural experience. Briscoe (2009: 369) defines such an innate language acquisition device as 'nothing more or less than a learning mechanism which incorporates some language-specific inductive learning bias in favour of some proper subset of the space of possible grammars'. Linguists often refer to this biological endowment as universal grammar (UG). UG in this sense addresses the issue of the species-specificity of the language faculty; even when raised by humans, other great ape infants do not acquire language (though some may acquire rudimentary, protolanguage-like communications systems). Even if 'an innate, species-specific and domain-specific faculty for language' (Kirby, Chapter 61) is rejected, it is presumably impossible to deny some crucial involvement of our genetic code in language acquisition. As well as referring to the 'initial state' of the language faculty, for many authors UG also constrains the design of languages, providing 'restrictions on search space' (Chomsky 2010: 61). For instance, the infant language-learner can assume that syntactic processes are structure-dependent, so that, say, a fronting construction operates on a whole constituent rather than part of a constituent (*Whose book did you buy?* vs. **Whose did you buy __ book?*).

The concept of UG itself is frequently misunderstood (see Jackendoff 2002: ch. 4 for useful discussion and Goldberg 2008 for commentary on various interpretations). Although not everyone who uses the term UG has exactly the same conception of it, various aspects should be clear. UG is not 'what all languages have in common', nor a set of language universals (contra Tomasello 2009a). Nor is it an abstract semantic structure common to all languages. UG is often now seen as 'the "toolkit" that a human child brings to learning languages' (Jackendoff 2002: 75). Under this conception, UG provides a set of tools, or basic principles, for building languages, which each language customizes in specific ways; see also Culicover and Jackendoff (2005) for more details on the Toolkit Hypothesis. There is no expectation here that everything the toolkit can build is found in all languages (see Carstairs-McCarthy, Chapter 50), but it does constrain what *can* be built.

Many questions arise. A major issue concerns whether there is a specialized (domain-specific) language acquisition device at all. If a UG of this nature does exist, what aspects of the language faculty does it contribute to? Does it contain linguistically specific principles? As an alternative, can we do away with UG, so that every aspect of language learning is subsumed under more general learning mechanisms? There are probably two polarized extremes in this area. At one end of the spectrum lies the view that there is a completely specialized, innate language faculty, centring around—or even consisting solely of—a narrow syntactic core (see Piattelli-Palmarini 1989, 1994, 2010; Anderson and Lightfoot 2002). Much recent debate focuses on the content of 'narrow syntax' (Hauser et al. 2002).

Historically within generative linguistics, a great deal was attributed to an innate UG, including very specific autonomous syntactic principles such as subjacency and other island constraints, and numerous other filters such as the empty category principle or the specified subject constraint. Crucially, such properties were seen as highly abstract and arbitrary, rather than functionally motivated, and this arbitrariness was a central plank in the argument; if these domain-specific principles don't make language more 'useful' or usable—and may even be dysfunctional (Chomsky 1995)—then they can't be adaptive and thus can't have evolved by natural selection (see Lightfoot 1991, Chapter 31; Anderson, Chapter 39). Both Anderson and Lightfoot stress that it is extremely unlikely that natural selection accounts for every aspect of the language faculty.

Although UG is still a central concept in more recent Minimalist theorizing in linguistics, its role and hypothesized content is much reduced. The bulk of the machinery associated with the heyday of the Principles and Parameters framework is no longer considered part of UG (Hauser et al. 2002; Chomsky 2005, 2010; see Boeckx, Chapter 52). Chomsky (2005, 2010) proposes that the central syntactic operation is Merge, which takes items X and Y and combines them to form Z, thus building 'recursive' hierarchical structure; this, in Chomsky's view, is the main component of genetically-determined UG (see Bickerton, Chapter 49).

At the other end of the spectrum of views on UG lies a disparate body of work from various disciplines, including various 'usage-based' and 'emergentist' approaches to language (MacWhinney 1999; see Bybee, Chapter 55). Proponents of such approaches may deny that there is any UG: thus, no domain-specific properties pertaining to language, and no genetic endowment that is language-specific. In this vein, Tomasello (2009a: 471) comments that 'the idea that there is a biological adaptation with specific linguistic content . . . is dead'; see also Tomasello (2003a, 2005, 2008) and Christiansen and Chater (2008), who 'conclude that a biologically determined UG is not evolutionarily viable' (2008: 489); also Arbib, Chapter 20. This is not necessarily to deny that the child brings species-specific abilities to the language-learning task, but crucially, these are seen as *general* cognitive and pragmatic analytical capacities (Tomasello 2003a, 2005). Such factors constrain languages to conform to the patterns we find, but are not domain-specific to language. Bybee and McClelland (2005: 396) also 'view language structure as emerging from forces that operate during language use'; such forces include frequency effects, whereby common sequences of words come to be treated as a single unit and then undergo phonological reduction (e.g. *dunno* from *I don't know*). From a somewhat different perspective, Christiansen and Chater (2008) also argue that rather than 'language evolution' involving phylogenetic change in humans, language itself has adapted (literally) to fit the learner's brain: there are thus biological constraints, involving human learning biases, 'but these constraints emerge from cognitive machinery that is not language-specific' (2008: 507); see also Evans and Levinson (2009). Bickerton, Chapter 49, evaluates such 'cultural invention' accounts.

Common to these 'usage-based' approaches (also Croft 2001) is the idea that grammatical constructions themselves shape language and contribute to the appearance of design. Chater and Christiansen, Chapter 65, argue that human learning and processing capacities can account for many aspects of language structure. This view does not rule out the existence of linguistic universals (i.e. properties found in all languages), though of course these would have nothing to do with UG, but would be due to common 'aspects of human cognition, social interaction and information processing' (Tomasello 2009a: 471). Learners are sensitive to the communicative functions of language, which are the same across all human cultures, and stem from the fact that humans basically conceptualize the world in the same way (Tomasello 2008). Similarly, Christiansen and Chater 'adopt a non-formal conception of universals in which they emerge from processes of repeated language acquisition and use' (2008: 500).

Amongst those who support the UG hypothesis, a central tenet has been 'poverty of the stimulus' arguments, which claim that the language data which children receive as input are too limited, haphazard, and imperfect to allow them to infer the grammar of the ambient language without innate, language-specific learning mechanisms (Chomsky 1965, 1986; Piattelli-Palmarini 1989; Anderson, Chapter 39; Boeckx, Chapter 52). Much disagreement with the entire concept of 'poverty of the stimulus' has arisen. MacNeilage, Chapter 46, contends that arguments of this kind are inapplicable to phonology, since children 'hear all the sound patterns' they need to learn, though other phonologists may well disagree with this view. Extensive work has been undertaken on learning and other areas of cognition since UG was initially proposed, and undoubtedly indicates that there is less work for the child to do than was once supposed. Various kinds of 'head start' that do not involve language-specific principles are widely proposed. Goldberg (2008: 523) cautions against overlooking 'the power of statistics, implicit memory, the nature of categorization, emergent behaviour, and the impressively repetitive nature of certain aspects of the input' (see Graf Estes, Chapter 64, on statistical learning). Moreover, the input is likely not as unhelpfully degenerate as once assumed, and interactions between child and caregiver are probably highly significant in language acquisition (see de Boer, Chapter 33, on infant-directed speech; also Falk, Chapter 32; Locke, Chapter 34). To an extent, discoveries of this nature undermine arguments from the 'poverty of the stimulus', but they do not negate it: we are far from knowing all the methods employed by infants in learning any one of the world's 6000 or so languages, including the child's abilities to abstract beyond a limited set of data and to extrapolate the correct generalizations.

Tomasello's work (e.g. 2008, 2009b) also discusses the relevance of collaboration, cooperation, and shared intentionality in the evolution of human cognition, including language. He suggests that shared goals and collaborative actions arose in the service of new hunting and/or foraging techniques, under conditions not shared by other great apes (in this volume see Gibson, Chapter 35, on foraging; Knight and Power, Chapter 37; also see Bickerton 2009a). Specific behaviours which are undeveloped in other great apes, such as extensive pointing, establishing common ground, and joint attention are all highly relevant to language acquisition, especially acquisition of vocabulary (Burling, Chapter 44; Hurford, Chapter 40).

A large body of broadly 'functionalist' work within linguistics also suggests that grammars themselves are shaped by the functions they perform, lessening the need to posit arbitrary constraints in UG; see Newmeyer (1998, 2005) for extensive discussion. The most concrete of these proposals provide evidence from language processing. For instance, Hawkins (1994, 2004) demonstrates that the requirements of language processing link directly to the form of grammars themselves. In head-initial languages, such as English, short constituents generally precede long ones: normal English word order has Adj-Noun, as in *a yellow book*, but in *a book yellow with age*, the adjective phrase is 'heavy', so must follow the noun, hence the ungrammaticality in English of *\*a yellow with age book*. Head-final languages, such as Japanese, reverse the preferred order: long constituents precede short ones. Sometimes these principles are merely strong preferences, but they are also widely grammaticalized, meaning that a language disallows dispreferred orders. In a similar vein, Christiansen and Devlin (1997) show that the universally strong tendency for a word order that is fixed across all phrases within a language (head-initial vs. head-final) need not be due to an innate, language-specific principle, but instead may be accounted for by human sequential learning mechanisms. It seems likely, then, that processing requirements have been responsible for much language structure, thus obviating the need for many arbitrary constraints in UG.

The concept of UG is therefore subject to various lines of attack, including arguments that languages themselves adapt to learners' brains, that usage shapes grammar, that language processing shapes grammar, and that learning of grammar is aided by many domain-general cognitive processes. Does this mean that what we might broadly call performance factors, i.e. factors involving the use of language, can explain and predict all aspects of language structure, so that domain-specific principles and/or UG can be dispensed with entirely? For some, the answer is yes; Tomasello (2005) argues that poverty of the stimulus arguments are void, and that no language-specific principles need be postulated. But as Jackendoff (2002: 79) points out, 'if language is indeed a specialized system, one should expect some of its functional principles to be sui generis'. This debate essentially boils down to the question of whether general cognitive principles and domain-general learning mechanisms can 'buy' the kinds of language structure that recur cross-linguistically (Bybee, Chapter 55), as well as the child's ability to acquire these structures so readily, or whether domain-specific linguistic principles are required (see Anderson, Chapter 39; Boeckx, Chapter 52, for discussion).

In fact though, much recent work in linguistics draws on both traditions—on mainstream generative grammar and on cognitive/functionalist work. For example, the Construction Grammar approach (Goldberg 1995, 2006) influences not only the work of Joan Bybee and Michael Tomasello, working firmly within the usage-based tradition, but also the 'Simpler Syntax' of generative linguists Peter Culicover and Ray Jackendoff (2005). Chomsky (2010: 9) also notes that 'we need no longer assume that the means of generating structured expressions are highly articulated and specific to language'. Moreover, Chomsky's recent work explicitly proposes that language acquisition depends not only on genetic endowment (UG) and linguistic data, but also on 'third factor' principles not specific to the language faculty, such as the capacity for data analysis, and more general biological principles, including developmental constraints.

In conclusion, it is fairly clear that UG should no longer be conceived of as a large set of highly specific (and purely syntactic) principles, in the sense of the Principles and Parameters approach. But this does not entail that there is no specific biological endowment relating to the language faculty.

We turn next to the role of natural selection in the evolution of language, and the question of how, why (and if) a language faculty evolved at all. Clearly, if any domain-specific principles are required to account for the language faculty, then the appearance of such principles must be accounted for. There are, broadly, two views here, adaptationist and non-adaptationist (see Bickerton, Chapter 49; Chater and Christiansen, Chapter 65; Gibson, Chapter 35 for more discussion). Under the former view, the language faculty evolves gradually via natural selection; all stages are adaptive, so confer increased fitness on their possessors. The seminal paper here is Pinker and Bloom (1990); the target article and the following commentaries set out many of the important issues. Pinker and Bloom aim to counter the position that 'the evolution of the human language faculty cannot be explained by Darwinian natural selection' (1990: 707) by providing arguments from design, and by showing that language displays all the signs of adaptive complexity.

The non-adaptationist or exaptationist alternative (e.g. Piattelli-Palmarini 1989, 1990, 2010; Lightfoot 1999, 2000, Chapter 31) argues that natural selection may have played a minor role, or even no role at all, in the formation of the language faculty. Critical aspects of language may have arisen as a spandrel (an evolutionary by-product), for instance of increased brain size (Chomsky 2010), or via general physical or biochemical or developmental constraints ('laws of form') still dimly understood (see Boeckx, Chapter 52), or as a result of 'macroevolutionary changes that are caused by single point mutations in regulatory genes' (Piattelli-Palmarini 2010: 156). This view is essentially saltationist too, suggesting that the language faculty appeared very suddenly and without primate precursors, and denying that there has been gradual evolution of a language faculty under selective pressure. In part, this goes hand in hand with the view that the language faculty has not evolved 'for' (and hence was not shaped by) communication, but rather, involved a new kind of recursive thought process; see the discussion below.

The very existence of a language faculty is called into question by some. For instance, Tomasello (1990, 1999, 2008) argues that language is purely a human cultural invention, and is also acquired culturally, without help from an innate UG. Evans and Levinson (2009: 446) claim that 'The fact that language is a bio-cultural hybrid is its most important property'; this leads to what they see as extreme language diversity, rather than a homogeneous, but abstract, universal linguistic template. Supporters of this view also argue against a Pinker-and-Bloom-type of gradually evolving language faculty, but on the grounds that no domain-specific abilities have evolved: 'children learn language using general-purpose cognitive mechanisms, rather than language-specific mechanisms' (Christiansen and Chater 2008: 507). This is not necessarily to deny that there were adaptations, including biological adaptations, but these are for general human cognition (which includes language).

In large part, the answer to the question of 'what, if anything, evolved?' depends on what one thinks is uniquely linguistic; what the language faculty contains. As just noted, some recent work claims that general cognition handles everything linguistic, while other work (e.g. Culicover and Jackendoff 2005) regards the linguistic 'toolkit' as quite extensive, and certainly as containing more than just syntactic principles. For Hauser et al. (2002) and Chomsky (2010), FLN contains very little, perhaps only the operation Merge, which creates syntactic structure by combining lexical items (Bickerton, Chapter 49; Boeckx, Chapter 52). Thus, Chomsky can suggest that the 'simplest speculation about the evolution of language' (i.e. FLN) is that 'rewiring of the brain took place in some individual' to yield Merge (2010: 59). We should note, though, that to date there is no neuroanatomical evidence that any such rewiring occurred. In any event, this putative development is not intended to account for the entire language faculty—it doesn't need to: if FLN contains only one critical syntactic operation, then everything left over is regarded as part of FLB, which as noted above includes properties that are not even species-specific. If what is unique in language can be minimized in this way, then not much needs to be explained. Thus, Chomsky suggests that there may even have been a single 'genetic event' causing language (Chomsky 2010: 58; but see Diller and Cann, Chapter 15). Under this view, the role of natural selection in shaping the language faculty is also minimized (as noted by Pinker and Jackendoff 2005: 219). Chomsky (2010: 61) further suggests that 'solving the externalization problem' (i.e. getting I-language out of the brain into E-language, via phonology and morphology) 'may not have involved an evolutionary change—that is, a genomic change'. One problem with this approach is that numerous additional aspects of the language faculty apart from Merge appear to be not only uniquely human, but also domain-specific, and hence must be part of UG; crucial examples (two among many) are duality of patterning and the ability to learn and store a vast lexicon with highly specific linguistic properties; see Pinker and Jackendoff (2005), Jackendoff and Pinker (2005), and Jackendoff (2010) for extensive discussion and illustration; also Tallerman, Chapters 48 and 51.

In sum, we agree that it seems highly likely that many factors apart from 'mere' natural selection have shaped the language faculty, including some organizational principles that have nothing to do with genetic changes—but has anyone ever doubted this? Darwin certainly did not deny the existence of alternative evolutionary mechanisms, though of course he could not have known of such biological factors as random genetic drift or gene flow. In any case, natural selection crucially interacts with such factors, since selection pressures maintain or remove random mutations. Since the language faculty in its entirety is a complex collection of traits, not a single trait, the likelihood is that different factors shaped distinct parts. It is biologically—if not linguistically—feasible to argue that some single aspect is critical, and that this is not due to natural selection. But it is surely indefensible to propose that the whole language faculty is attributable to non-selective factors.

We turn next to the question of why language evolved, in other words, what selection pressures were involved. This of course also brings up the question of function, as mentioned above. Language is, as noted from the start, a collection of interrelated features, some of which are uniquely linguistic (either with or without obvious primate precursors), and others which have a broader application than the linguistic (see Jackendoff 2010). Discussion of function, selection, and adaptation may seem to suggest that we can disentangle all these factors, but this is almost certainly impossible.

One question regarding function that may be amenable to scientific investigation is why only one primate lineage developed a language faculty. To many, the answer seems clear: to enhance communication (in this volume, see especially Dunbar, Chapter 36; Falk, Chapter 32). But the issue is not whether communication has played *some* role in shaping the language faculty; there is probably near unanimous agreement that it has. What is at issue is what language evolved 'for' – communication or thought. The two main positions can be characterized thus: 1) language evolved as—and is uniquely adapted for—communication, therefore traits enhancing communication were selected for from the start; or alternatively, 2) language evolved in the service of internal thought and was only later 'externalized', therefore selective pressures for more efficient communication came later. Under this view, 'the earliest stage of language would have been [ . . . ] a language of thought, available for use internally' (Chomsky 2010: 55; see Boeckx, Chapter 52). Purely internal language would provide 'capacities for complex thought, planning, interpretation', etc. (Chomsky 2010: 59). Chomsky has consistently taken the view that communicative needs did not provide a major selection pressure (see Piattelli-Palmarini 1989, 2010; Chomsky 2005, 2010; Fitch et al. 2005), and language is not seen primarily as a communication system (Chomsky 2000a). Moreover, current utility (e.g. the use of language for communication) does not explain the functional origins of a trait (Fitch et al. 2005).

Although we do not share the view that the 'language of thought' came first, it is instructive to consider how 'inner speech' might nonetheless be adaptive (see also Coolidge and Wynn, Chapter 21). For example, Gary Lupyan's work (e.g. 2006) suggests how vocabulary might arise without communicative pressure. In experiments with adults, having mental labels for new concepts is shown to aid categorical learning; see also Harnad, Chapter 42. This is not inherently a communicative function, but it is adaptive; for instance, it would help a hominin to distinguish between two similar-looking mushrooms, one of which is nutritious and the other poisonous. Of course, labels (words) are now the prima facie instance of what is learned from the environment, but this need not (in fact, cannot) have been the case at the very start of the evolutionary process: the earliest arbitrary symbols did not exist in a community until someone put them out there. (See Harnad, Chapter 42, on the 'symbol grounding problem'; also Cangelosi, Chapter 62; Deacon, Chapter 43.) Others have proposed that critical selection pressures arise from the kind of thought which language makes possible; Penn et al. (2008) suggest that an ability to reason about higher-order relations would be adaptive, more so even than being able to communicate with conspecifics. On this view, some kind of simple pre-language, used for communication, might in fact have evolved first; subsequently, more complex linguistic constructions might arise in a 'language of thought', where they would be highly adaptive in terms of problem-solving.

The alternative view, that the primary adaptation was for communication, is held by many, including Pinker and Bloom (1990), Hurford (2002), Jackendoff and Pinker (2005), Pinker and Jackendoff (2005), Christiansen and Chater (2008), Levinson's contributions to Enfield and Levinson (2006), and Tomasello (2008). Pinker and Jackendoff (2005: 224) state that 'the key question in characterizing a biological function is not what a trait is typically used for but what it is designed for, in the biologist's sense—namely, which putative function can predict the features that the trait possesses'. The works cited argue that the design features of language are specialized to handle the mapping between meaning and sound, which is exactly what is involved in communication (i.e. rather than inner speech). As Pinker and Jackendoff note (2005: 231), 'the argument that language is designed for interior monologues rather than communication fails to explain why languages map meaning onto sounds and why they must be learned from a social context'.

In fact, languages are replete with features that only service communication, and play no role in mental representation. These features include (but are not limited to) speech production and perception; the entirety of the systems of phonology and morphology, including duality of patterning; devices that regulate the linearization of phrases and propositions, including unmarked word orders and 'movement' constructions such as focalization (e.g. *Beans, I like, but spinach, I hate*) and question formation; principles of interpretation of expressions with no

independent meaning, including pronouns and anaphors; the formation of grammatical functions such as 'subject' and 'object' and the ability to change these
functions by means of such processes as passivization, anti-passivization, dative
shift, and so on. More or less the whole point of syntactic operations is to express
different pragmatic effects; we wouldn't need constituent questions or a passive
construction unless we were trying to put a message across. Along with these
properties, all known languages have some set of purely grammatical or 'functional' elements (such as complementizers, auxiliaries, determiners, and pronouns; see
Carstairs-McCarthy on complexity, Chapter 50) and morphosyntactic features,
such as number and grammatical gender, case, and agreement. Some of these
elements have a clear role in terms of communication, such as complementizers
marking clause boundaries; and case and agreement, which mark grammatical
relations (thus showing who did what to whom). But none of them appear to play
any role in conceptual structure, though it might be argued that these functional
elements are relatively recent innovations in language (Heine and Kuteva, Chapter
54), thus played no part in the human 'environment of evolutionary adaptedness',
and are not part of the initial adaptation.

The issue of critical initial selection pressures relates to, but should not be
conflated with, the continuity issue. There are three distinct views of continuity
(see also Hauser et al. 2002). One, language is totally dissimilar both to animal
communication and cognition; there is thus no continuity at all with prior systems,
and the language faculty (or some subpart deemed essential) is a saltation (Piattelli-Palmarini 1989, 2010). Two, direct continuity with animal communication
systems is the only biologically feasible solution. Saltations giving rise to exceptional complexity are impossible. Our ancestors are primates, so language must
originate in primate call/gesture systems (Wray 1998, 2000). Three, language is
totally dissimilar to modern great ape communication, so cannot evolve from
similar ancestral systems, but instead its origins lie in primate cognitive/conceptual
systems (Bickerton 1998, 2000; Hurford 2002, 2007; Fitch et al. 2005; Newmeyer
2005; Pinker and Jackendoff 2005; for discussion in this volume, see Arbib, Chapter
20; Seyfarth and Cheney, Chapter 4; Wilkins, Chapter 19).

Proponents of the first view note that evolutionary novelties may arise, not by
gradual adaptation, but by apparently quite sudden shifts, a view drawing on the
punctuated equilibrium approach of Gould and Eldredge (1977); see Lightfoot,
Chapter 31. Not all changes are adaptive, though they may subsequently acquire
adaptive value and be selected for. (We note, though, that contrary to older
assumptions, natural selection is now known to produce some very fast adaptations; see Számadó and Szathmáry, Chapter 14.) Under this first view, the language
faculty (whatever it contains) may even be a spandrel, a feature not directly selected
for, but which originally arose for non-adaptive reasons, as a by-product of
evolutionary change (Gould and Lewontin 1979). Adopting this view, Piatelli-
Palmarini (1989) claims that looking for language precursors in other apes is

useless; once the gradualist/adaptationist view is discarded, biologists need not search for intermediate stages of language: none exist. But, of course, there is no way to test the validity of any hypothesis except by examining evidence. In this case, the only way to determine the validity of the 'no language precursors in apes' hypothesis is to study apes.

The remaining two views do assume some continuity with animal precursors, but cover a wide range of possibilities.

To an extent, we believe there is *some* evidence to support all three views. The problem is, which aspects of language are deemed to be critical? Since language is a complex system with crucially interacting subparts, it is unhelpful to promote one aspect at the expense of others. Some aspects of language may well be spandrels. For instance, Fitch (2000a) suggests that the lowered larynx may have evolved primarily for size exaggeration, and was only subsequently selected for with regards to speech sound production. But other aspects have been directly selected for, and have clear primate precursors with a similar function. There are certainly trivial senses in which primate communication systems give rise to language; for instance, we use a modified version of the same vocal tract, and the same auditory system, to produce and perceive sound (and mutatis mutandis for the gestural and visual systems in the case of sign languages). However, there are few similarities between language and the natural communication of other apes—not even in the sound system, which might be expected to show some traces of its evolutionary history. Therefore, the second view, if understood in any but the weakest sense, is unsupported. The third view, that (aspects of) language are rooted in primate cognition, seems to us to have empirical support (for discussion of evidence, see Hauser 1996; Hurford 2007, Chapter 40; Gibson, Chapter 3; Seyfarth and Cheney, Chapter 4). It also seems a promising line of further enquiry, since the cognitive capabilities of other modern apes can at least be investigated scientifically; we hope that this is not the biological parallel to the drunk looking for his keys under the lamp-post. In contrast, Penn et al. (2008) argue that there is a radical discontinuity between human and animal cognition, though they do not doubt that both human cognition and language 'evolved through standard evolutionary mechanisms' (2008: 129).

In the following section, we briefly examine relevant stages in hominin evolution.

## 1.5 HUMAN EVOLUTION AND LANGUAGE

Although all great ape species (Gibson, Chapter 3; see also Knight and Power, Chapter 37) have sufficient mental and communicative capacities to use rudimentary protolanguages, none do so in the wild. Hence, protolanguage almost certainly dates to a period subsequent to the hominin phylogenetic split from chimpanzees and bonobos, around 5–8 million years ago (mya) (Cann, Chapter 24). Language, then, is an innovation in hominins. Although a number of hominin and possible hominin fossils date to the lengthy period lasting from 2–7 mya (Wood and Bauernfeind, Chapter 25), we do not know for sure if any of these early hominins, such as *Paranthropus*, *Ardipithecus*, *Australopithecus*, or indeed early *Homo* were our direct ancestors. Moreover, we cannot tell whether any of these hominins had any form of protolanguage or anything we would recognize as speech. If they did, this is not obvious from fossil anatomy, as most species had brain sizes only slightly larger than those of apes, and at least one had an ape-like hyoid bone.

However, nearly all australopithecines and early forms of *Homo* had made definite strides in the direction of human-like adaptations. Although most retained some (ape-like) adaptations for an arboreal lifestyle, all were also bipedal to some degree; bipedalism is a trait often hypothesized to serve as a preadaptation to the descended larynx that characterizes modern humans (MacLarnon, Chapter 22). Most of these hominins also had enlarged molar teeth with thicker enamel layers than is generally present in apes (Wood and Bauernfeind, Chapter 25), suggesting dietary adaptations. By 2.6 mya, some were clearly manufacturing sharp-edged stone tools (Semaw et al. 1997) which were used for cutting meat and tendons (Mithen, Chapter 28; Wynn, Chapter 27). Finds of bashed long bones and crania indicate that hammerstones were used even earlier, and what are possible cut marks on bones suggest that manufactured or naturally sharp-edged stone tools may also have been used prior to 3 mya (McPherron et al. 2010). Taken together, this evidence suggests that by the period between 2–4 mya, early hominins had adopted some non ape-like foraging strategies (Gibson, Chapter 35). They had perhaps also begun the long evolutionary trek to a hominin feeding adaptation that was eventually characterized by cooking (Wrangham 2009), and by the exploitation of foods with high nutrient density, which were hard to acquire, largely extractive or hunted (Parker and Gibson 1979; Lancaster and Kaplan 2007). These altered dietary strategies both enabled and were accompanied by major changes in life history and social structure. For example, humans are less mature at birth than apes, have a longer period of growth and maturation, and live longer (Locke, Chapter 34). Also, human adults—unlike ape adults—form male/female food-sharing bonds, and routinely provision the young (Deacon 1997; Hrdy 2009). Possibly these dietary, life history, and social changes played a role in the selection of various aspects of protolanguage, babbling, or speech (Falk, Chapter 32; Locke, Chapter 34; Parker and Gibson 1979).

Dietary changes may also have helped provide the nutrients and energy necessary to sustain the brain enlargement which characterizes early *Homo*, with brain sizes of 500–725 cc, as opposed to 400–525 cc in australopithecines; Wood and Bauernfeind, Chapter 25. This was the initial step in a two-million-year-long period of continuing neural expansion. In a human adult, the brain uses 20% of the body's metabolic energy; in newborns the figure is closer to 60% (Aiello et al. 2001). Growing brains also have very high essential fatty acid requirements (Singh 2005). From comparative studies of animal tool users, Parker and Gibson (1979) hypothesize that the earliest hominin tool users would have acquired increased nutrients by practising omnivorous extractive foraging; that is, they would have adaptations enabling them to use tools to remove a wide variety of high energy, nutrient-dense foods from outer casings, including hard-shelled nuts, beans, tubers, embedded insects, honey, shellfish, brains, bone marrow, tortoises, burrowing animals, and meat that required extraction from tough outer hides (see also Lancaster and Kaplan 2007). Later work by Aiello and Wheeler (1995) provided a compatible, expensive tissue, hypothesis. Using evidence of relative gut and brain sizes in various animal species, they suggest that hominin brain evolution required increased consumption of high energy, easy-to-digest foods, such as animal products, nuts, or underground tubers. Both hypotheses appear to have been verified by findings of bones that are broken into to allow extraction of marrow, and stone tools that could be used to cut meat in early hominin times (Wynn, Chapter 27). Wrangham et al. (2009) also suggest that early hominins were exploiting water-based underground storage organs (see also Tobias 2001). Aiello and Wheeler (1995) further suggest that cooking may have been a critical adaptation for meeting the energy requirements of the brain, a hypothesis that has been greatly developed by Wrangham (2009). The cooking adaptation, however, almost certainly arose at a later time than the basic shift to a high quality, nutrient-rich diet.

By between 1.8 and 1.9 mya, we see the emergence of a new grade of *Homo*, generally referred to as *Homo erectus*, though African specimens are sometimes classified separately as *Homo ergaster*. These hominins are characterized by full bipedalism and greatly enlarged brains (900–1000 cc) in comparison to those of apes; see Mann, Chapter 26. Not only were *Homo erectus* brains absolutely large in comparison to those of apes or earlier hominins, they were also relatively large in comparison to body size, and they exhibited a hominin-specific enlargement ('reorganization') of the parieto-occipital-temporal region (Wilkins, Chapter 19). It has long been debated which factor has played the greatest role in the evolution of enhanced human intelligence: brain reorganization, absolute brain size, or relative brain size (Holloway 1968; Jerison 1973). *Homo erectus*, however, had them all. Perhaps this is not surprising since most postulated reorganizational changes in the human brain (such as increased numbers of gyri and sulci) increased neuronal connectivity, and proportionally greater increases in the size of some brain regions rather than others actually correlate with increased brain or cortical size (Jerison 1982; Passingham 1975). Of course, a postulated change in one parameter does not indicate that other changes lack relevance. Even if key changes in the brain that are not size-related have occurred in human evolution, this does not negate the potential cognitive importance of increased neural information-processing capacities (Gibson and Jessee 1999).

So the increased brain size and obligate bipedalism of *Homo erectus* clearly indicate an entry into a new, non-arboreal niche that was not ape-like, and that involved the exploitation of higher-energy foods than was the case for apes or earlier hominins, perhaps including increased quantities of animal foods such as scavenged (Bickerton 2009a) or hunted meat, along with tubers and/or cooked foods (Aiello and Wheeler 1995; Wrangham 2009). Whether this move into a new niche was propelled by climatic changes, population pressures, or simple opportunism is unclear. It is unknown whether the increases in brain size in *Homo erectus* had yet to result in the earlier births of their young (Falk, Chapter 32). It is also not clear whether dietary changes in this period had already necessitated social adaptations such as the adult provisioning of young, male/female food-sharing bonds, and cooperative foraging endeavours. Eventually, such social adaptations may have contributed to the supply of increased sustenance for growing brains (Marlowe 2010).

Evidence from the archaeological record may also provide indications of cognitive changes. Bilaterally symmetrical Acheulean handaxes (Mithen, Chapter 28; Wynn, Chapter 27) are produced by African *Homo erectus*, beginning about 1.6 mya. These indicate that in comparison to apes and earlier hominins, *Homo erectus* had increased spatial intelligence (Wilkins, Chapter 19), increased procedural learning capacities (Coolidge and Wynn, Chapter 21; Wynn, Chapter 27), possibly an increased tendency to practise new skills (Corballis, Chapter 41; Donald, Chapter 17), the ability to hold greater amounts of information in mind (Gibson and Jessee 1999), and greater social learning and imitative skills (Donald, Chapter 17; Mithen, Chapter 28). We cannot, of course, know for sure whether *Homo erectus* also had any form of language or protolanguage. Taken as a whole, though, evidence including the invasion of a new niche by this species, its expanded brain size, and its ability to manufacture spatially symmetrical tools do make it seem quite likely that *erectus* possessed a pre-syntactic protolanguage, though there is less agreement about the properties this might have had (Tallerman 2007, 2008a, Chapter 51). Dunbar (Chapter 36) argues on the basis of correlations between social group size and neocortical size that *erectus* also had enhanced vocal capacities in comparison to apes. MacLarnon, on the other hand (Chapter 22) argues that the narrow thoracic spinal canal of *Homo erectus* suggests an absence of enhanced breathing control for speech (though see Wood and Bauernfeind, Chapter 25.)

A further major transition occurred about 400 kya with the appearance of advanced hominins, which some palaeoanthropologists classify as archaic *Homo sapiens*—humans—and others as *Homo heidelbergensis* (Gibson and Tallerman, Chapter 23; Mann, Chapter 26). These hominins had an almost modern brain size of about 1200–1300 cc. Advanced lithic technology also emerges at this time, and we find the earliest clear evidence of hunting (not merely scavenging) in the form of carefully made wooden spears from Schöningen, Germany, dating to 380–400 kya (Thieme 1997); evidence also comes from the remains of hunted roe deer, horses, and giant elk from various English sites (Wynn, Chapter 27). From the same era, 400 kya, comes the first plausible evidence of deliberate interment of human remains, from the 'Pit of Bones' in Atapuerca, Spain, as well as the first evidence for the use of mineralized pigments, perhaps for body ornamentation (see Wynn, Chapter 27).

There are widely differing estimates of when language (let alone protolanguage) arose, depending on what evidence is considered relevant (see Gibson and Taller-man, Chapter 23). Some archaeologists, as well as some linguists, regard the emergence of the full language faculty as extremely recent; see, for instance, Tattersall (1998b, 2010) and Chomsky (2005, 2010). The works cited by Chomsky speculate that the language faculty is part of a broader 'human capacity' which only appeared around 50 kya, and certainly less than around 100 kya. The idea that language is not the product of a long and slow evolution, but rather, is a recent saltation ties in with the Minimalist assumptions discussed above. Chomsky consistently suggests that only one crucial step was required, the appearance of Merge, seen as the product of 'brain rewiring'. In Chomsky's view, this is incompatible with a gradual evolution of the full language capacity. However, the mere existence of the capacity to 'merge' information does not necessarily imply the presence of the expanded working memory capacities that would be needed to merge large amounts of information (Coolidge and Wynn, Chapter 21). It has also been argued that the 'merge' capacity is not unique to language, but is also necessary for the manufacture of constructed tools (e.g. hafted tools) and thus was present considerably earlier than 50 kya (Gibson and Jessee 1999).

What has been considered evidence for a very recent emergence of language is the massive increase in technological sophistication seen in the archaeological record in Europe, starting at around 35–40 kya, a period known as the Upper Palaeolithic. This technology led to composite tools such as harpoons and spear-throwers; highly adaptable, specialized stone blades and microliths, i.e. small blades used in backed tools; a wider variety of materials worked on, including ivory, bone, and antler; as well as an explosion in forms of art, including personal ornaments, an increased use of pigments, carvings in various materials, cave paintings, musical instruments, and grave goods, all of which have been associated with symbolic cognition (e.g. Tattersall 2010). According to this view, a 'human revolution' occurred within the last 50 kya, producing as a package advanced technology, symbolic thought, and language (Klein 1989, 1992, 1998; Mellars 1989a, b; Mithen 1996; Klein and Edgar 2002).

However, many recent archaeological discoveries, and more accurate methods of dating previous discoveries, have changed the picture radically; see d'Errico and Vanhaeren, Chapter 29; also Wynn, Chapter 27. What was once thought to be specifically European technology is now known to have been present in Africa, starting perhaps 300 kya, but in any case significantly pre-dating the European Upper Palaeolithic (McBrearty and Brooks 2000 is the seminal reference, but much work in the past decade also supports this view; see contributions to Mellars et al. 2007). The use of finely-made blades and points in the African Middle Stone Age dates to at least 280 kya (McBrearty 2007), as do grindstones for processing plant foods and pigments used in colouration. Since Middle Stone Age points were routinely hafted (McBrearty and Brooks 2000), it can no longer be assumed that composite *thought* is a recent innovation in our species. Personal ornaments such as beads date to between 70 and 100 kya, and abstract art, in the form of carved bone and ochre, dates to the same period. Brown et al. (2009) report on the controlled use of fire in the heat treatment of stones, in order to improve their flaking properties, apparently dating as far back as 164 kya in Pinnacle Point, South Africa. The authors point out that a sophisticated knowledge of fire is required to complete the process, which is cognitively highly demanding. This location also provides the earliest evidence for the consumption of shellfish (164 kya, $\pm$ 12 ky), argued to have been collected by predicting tides (Marean et al. 2007; Marean 2010a). And Lombard and Phillipson (2010) report on findings from Sibudu Cave, South Africa, showing that stone-tipped arrows were in use 64 kya, pushing the use of bows back at least 20,000 years from previous discoveries.

Interestingly, recent genetic findings support these lines of evidence. Behar et al. (2008) report that mitochondrial DNA (mtDNA—which is transmitted via maternal inheritance only) in the Khoisan peoples of South Africa diverged from mtDNA in the rest of the human gene pool between 90 and 150 kya, and remained separate for a long period: introgression from other lineages did not occur until about 40 kya. Since the Khoisan peoples have a normal human language faculty, this strongly suggests that full language was already in place at the time of the split. See also the discussion in Cann, Chapter 24.

In sum, the picture now emerging from archaeological, palaeoanthropological, geological, and genetic evidence (Cann, Chapter 24; Mann, Chapter 26) indicates that 'modern' human anatomy, behaviour, and cognition are significantly older than once believed, implying that far from being a recent innovation, symbolic thought and some form of language may have been in place 200 kya, or, indeed, significantly earlier.

## 1.6 ORGANIZATION OF THE VOLUME

The volume is divided into five parts. Part I, *Insights from comparative animal behaviour*, examines animal communication systems and cognitive capacities of potential relevance to the evolution of language and speech. Part II, *The biology of language evolution: Anatomy, genetics, and neurology*, offers various views of the physical components of a language faculty, including the evolution of a language-ready brain, the potential relevance of genetic changes in the hominin lineage, and the evolution of the vocal tract. Part III, *The prehistory of language: When and why did language evolve?*, centres on palaeontological and archaeological evidence of human evolution and presents current interpretations of the selective events that may have led to the evolution of language. Part IV, *Launching language: The development of a linguistic species*, presents the most immediately 'linguistic' chapters, dealing with central properties to be accounted for in language evolution, and issues surrounding the forces that shaped the language faculty. Finally, the chapters in Part V, *Language change, creation, and transmission in modern humans*, examine a number of putative 'windows' on language evolution; for instance, modern events involving language emergence or change, for which we have reasonably concrete evidence, might shed light on the evolution of the language faculty itself.

Chapters in Part I focus both on non-human primates and on other more distantly related species. In the case of non-human primates, the central question concerns homologous traits, that is, properties shared by humans and other primates by virtue of common ancestry. For instance, all apes (gibbons, siamangs, chimpanzees, bonobos, gorillas, orang-utans, and humans) lack tails, and apart from orang-utans, live in social groups. Hence, we can infer that the last common ancestor of these species (which probably lived 14–18 mya; Cann, Chapter 24) was also tailless and social. Similar methods can also shed light on changes within specific lineages. For instance, great apes apart from humans are all well adapted to tree-climbing and have air sacs, so we can infer with confidence that our distant ancestors were largely tree-dwelling and had air sacs, and it is the hominin lineage that diverged.

When it comes to cognitive characteristics, it is far harder to determine homologies, because unlike physical characteristics, these are not readily available for inspection in the fossil record and, indeed, it has often proven difficult to determine cognitive capacities in living species. Thus, in the case of language evolution, we have many more questions than answers concerning possible primitive traits, i.e. those inherited from a common ancestor. Nonetheless, progress is being made. From the chapters in Part I, it seems fairly clear that the common ancestor of great apes and humans, although almost certainly lacking protolanguage, would have possessed a number of protolanguage-pertinent cognitive and communicative skills, including the ability to create novel referential gestures and, if sufficiently motivated, to use such gestures in cooperative endeavours. It remains uncertain whether or not the common ancestor of all great apes and humans, or even the common ancestor of chimpanzees, bonobos, and humans (about 5–8 mya) had the capacity to create novel vocalizations. However, it now appears that extant great apes have more vocal flexibility than previously thought (Slocombe, Chapter 7).

Although great apes may have most, or even all, of the essential cognitive prerequisites for a protolanguage of some kind, they clearly do not possess the full complement of neural, cognitive, and physical characteristics (such as the uniquely human vocal tract) needed for fully developed language and speech, including syntax and extensive hierarchical capacities. In some cases, apes may possess cognitive or neural traits which they use in non-communicative contexts, but which were exapted for language; that is, traits that were co-opted for language at some point during hominin evolution, such as social cognition (Seyfarth and Cheney, Chapter 4). In other instances, essential components of language or speech lack any primate homologues at all, but rather evolved anew in the hominin line. Disentangling these issues is fraught with problems, but, nonetheless, stands as one of the most critical goals in the reconstruction of language evolution.

Examining communication and cognition in distantly related lineages such as birds and cetaceans (marine mammals) is unlikely to reveal relevant homologous traits, other than those that might be common to all vertebrates. However, it may shed light on analogous traits—functionally similar features that have evolved separately in more than one lineage, usually in response to similar environmental pressures, a phenomenon termed convergent evolution. For example, wings have evolved separately in birds and bats. Both types of wing permit flight, but because these lineages share no recent common ancestry, their wings are structurally very different. Although at least from the perspective of most linguists, nothing in the rest of the animal kingdom is remotely analogous to language, a number of animals do have vocal learning capacities that are far more sophisticated than those of non-human primates. What we can hope for from animal studies is to find out something about the selection pressures that led to the evolution of advanced vocal learning capacities and other traits absent in apes, but present in humans and some distantly related taxa. For example, what selective pressures led humans to a communication system that is fundamentally innate, since all normal infants clearly have a language faculty, yet which in all its fine details (all the specific elements of each 'language') is learnt, transmitted from parent to offspring, just like some bird song?

Turning now to Part II, *The biology of language evolution: Anatomy, genetics, and neurology,* we note that scientists from different disciplines ask different, but equally valid, questions. In doing so, as Fitch notes, they often ignore or 'black box' subject matter beyond their specific realms of inquiry and expertise. It is common, for example, for animal behaviourists to focus entirely on visible behaviours, while ignoring the genetic, physiological, and neurological mechanisms that make those behaviours possible. Similarly, many language evolutionary theorists treat genes and brains as black boxes. Black boxing often results in theories that make sense, until one examines the contents of the box. For example, on the basis of archaeological data, some have proposed that language arose from a sudden rewiring of the brain, perhaps caused by a specific mutation (see Klein and Edgar 2002; note also remarks above). Although such proposals may seem perfectly reasonable if viewed solely from the context of archaeological remains, to many geneticists and neurobiologists they seem untenable. Consequently, a full understanding of language evolution will require the opening of many boxes and the integration of their contents into comprehensive, synthetic frameworks. To aid in this endeavour, the chapters in Part II focus on biological aspects of language evolution primarily from the perspectives of anatomy, neurobiology, and genetics, but also to some extent on modern understandings of neural developmental processes and evolutionary mechanisms that can result in species-wide fixations of what were initially plastic phenotypes.

Part III is *The prehistory of language: When and why did language evolve?*. Chapters here address questions of language origins from genetic, palaeoanthropological, archaeological, and linguistic perspectives, and offer some selective scenarios for the evolution of language. Incontrovertible evidence for the existence of language dates only to the emergence of written scripts a few thousand years BP. Though it is certain that language arose long prior to that, the time period of its emergence is unknown. Widely diverse information drawn from a number of academic disciplines can, however, provide clues, which, taken in combination, may eventually yield plausible answers. Genes and fossils, in combination, help us chart phylogenetic pathways and times of origin of both early hominins and modern humans. From the fossils, we can also determine the size and external configuration of the brain of each hominin species, as well as the structure of the hyoid bone, oral cavity, thorax, and locomotor organs. From archaeological remains we glean evidence of hominin lifestyles, diet, technology, and art. From historical linguistics, we gain insights about language history as well as possible answers to key questions such as whether modern languages derive from single versus multiple early languages (see also Nichols, Chapter 58). The papers in Part III focus largely on two interconnected issues. First, when did the language faculty emerge? And when are protolanguages and languages likely to have initially appeared? Second, why did language evolve? Did language, for example, arise as a mere accident of genetic drift or as a spandrel (by-product) of some other evolved trait(s)? Alternatively, perhaps the language faculty, speech, or even particular linguistic features were the specific targets of selective agents; if so, what might those agents have been?

In Part IV, *Launching language: The development of a linguistic species*, the chapters deal with the various aspects of the language mosaic that must be accounted for in language evolution. Here, the cognitive capacities required as prerequisites for language are discussed, including the symbolic capacity, the development of linguistic meaning, and the ability to learn and store vocabulary. Questions surrounding the modality for language externalization are discussed: were the earliest pre-languages gestural or vocal? How did the uniquely human system of duality of patterning emerge? A central issue in evolutionary linguistics concerns the existence—and appearance—of what is generally termed 'protolanguage'; a putative pre-syntactic stage, which, like full language, depended critically on socio/cultural transmission, and thus involved learning. Protolanguage thus constitutes a radical break with the primate communication systems that must precede it: it is entirely volitional and (in its details) entirely learned. Whatever the actual form of such protolanguages was, how did they subsequently turn into fully syntactic languages? These issues are debated in Part IV.

Part V is *Language change, creation, and transmission in modern humans.* A number of chapters here discuss instances of observable language creation and change, including the formation of pidgins and creoles; homesign and emergent sign languages; the processes of grammaticalization, which occur in all languages; and the role of contact between individuals and groups in triggering language change and language shift. Plausibly, what is known about the way languages emerge and change in recorded history and in the present day may offer evidence for the trajectory of evolution in the earliest pre-languages and languages. Most of the chapters in Part V emphasize the critical role played by the socio/cultural transmission of language. Since the details of individual languages can only be transmitted in a social context, it seems highly likely that this mode of transmission has shaped the language faculty itself, and thus has shaped the way that languages are too. Some authors in Part V suggest that languages are themselves adaptive systems, akin to independent biological entities but residing in human brains. Evidence of a fairly new kind is offered to support the hypotheses in a number of chapters in Part V: work from computational, mathematical, and robotic modelling. As is the case with molecular evidence, modelling is a relatively young field, and it is certain that many advances will occur in this sphere in the coming decades.

# PART I

## INSIGHTS FROM COMPARATIVE ANIMAL BEHAVIOUR

CHAPTER 2

# INTRODUCTION TO PART I: INSIGHTS FROM COMPARATIVE ANIMAL BEHAVIOUR

KATHLEEN R. GIBSON AND
MAGGIE TALLERMAN

Which hominins first embarked upon the language evolutionary trajectory, why did they do so, and which modality did they use, gestural or vocal? Comparative studies of animal behaviour can shed light on these issues provided they follow proper scientific methods. For example, theoretical considerations rule out the possibility that any of our hominin ancestors was anatomically or behaviourally identical to any living species (Tooby and DeVore 1987). Even our closest relatives, the bonobo and chimpanzee, have almost certainly evolved since we last shared a common ancestor with them about 5–7 mya. Recent fossil finds confirm this theoretical prediction. The earliest probable hominin that is well represented in the fossil record, *Ardipithecus ramidus* (dating to about 4.4 mya), was clearly substantially different from the bonobo, the chimpanzee, or any other primate, at least with respect to locomotor and dental anatomy (White et al. 2009). Consequently, if we are to reconstruct the behavioural capacity of the earliest hominins, we must use more broadly comparative methods, as opposed to single-species analogies.

Parsimony dictates that any trait present in all descendants of a common ancestor is far more likely to have been present in that ancestor than to have evolved separately in each descendant species (Seyfarth and Cheney, Chapter 4). Consequently, by studying a number of descendants of a common ancestor, we can, with some confidence, determine what speech and language-related communicative, cognitive, and motor capacities may have been present in that ancestor, especially if the ancestral species had numerous descendents all of which share specific traits. While studies of non-human primates most often serve as the foci for ancestral behavioural reconstructions, studies involving a much wider range of animals have sometimes proven useful. For example, left–right brain asymmetries and functional lateralization, long thought to be uniquely human, have now been shown to exist in a wide range of vertebrates (animals with a backbone) including some fish, amphibians, and many birds and mammals. Even amphioxus, a small chordate (i.e. an animal related to vertebrates but lacking a true backbone) that burrows in seashore sands, has an anatomically and functionally lateralized nervous system (Andrew 2002). Hence, it now appears that brain asymmetry and functional lateralization is an ancestral feature of all vertebrates and not a hominin phylogenetic novelty. Similarly, in-depth studies of the genetics of *Drosophila* (fruit flies) led to the discovery of homeobox genes, now known to regulate body segmentation in a wide variety of animals including insects, crustaceans, and vertebrates, including humans. Given these findings it is possible that studies of almost any animal could shed light on the evolution of human language and cognition.

In practice, however, a volume of this nature cannot provide an exhaustive survey of the entire animal kingdom. Rather, we have chosen to focus primarily on the communicative and cognitive capacities of two distinct animal groups: (1) our closest phylogenetic kin, the non-human primates, especially those whose vocal and gestural capacities have been well studied, and (2) avian and cetacean species that are known to have well-developed vocal capacities or cognitive skills. Studies of our primate relatives are the most pertinent to the reconstruction of the behaviour of earliest hominins. Although studies of cetaceans and birds can, as noted in the lateralization studies cited above, provide insights into capacities likely to have been present in ancestral mammals or vertebrates, they are included in this volume for a different purpose. In addition to tracing the language evolutionary pathway, we need to know what selective pressures favour speech, protolanguage, symbolism, syntax, and other key linguistic features. Distantly related animals that face similar environmental circumstances often develop similar adaptations by a process termed convergent evolution: for instance, cetaceans have evolved a streamlined body shape similar to fish. Hence, a study of distantly related animals whose communicative systems may in certain respects resemble our own, for example, by involving considerable vocal flexibility or by utilizing displacement (as some insect communication systems do) can provide clues to the potential selective pressures faced by our ancestors.

The first chapter in this section, by Gibson, reviews the ape language literature. It concludes that human-reared and/or trained members of each of the great ape species, orang-utan, chimpanzee, bonobo, and gorilla, have learned to use gestures, tokens, or visual lexigrams referentially, and to combine limited numbers of these visual references in an apparently rule-based fashion. Virtually all referential gestures, tokens, and lexigrams used by the language-trained apes qualify as symbols in the sense that they are of an arbitrary, as opposed to an iconic, nature. According to Deacon (Chapter 43), however, genuine symbols are not necessarily lacking in iconicity. Rather, to qualify as symbolic, a visual, auditory, or other reference must be one whose meaning is derived contextually with respect to other symbols and clues. Few of the ape language studies tested their animals for these additional communicative skills. Deacon (1997), however, concluded that two lexigram-using chimpanzees, Sherman and Austin, and one lexigram-using bonobo, Kanzi, did meet his definition of symbol use. That great apes are capable of at least rudimentary symbolism (as defined by Deacon) receives further support from de Waal and Pollick (Chapter 6), who report that chimpanzees and bonobos interpret their own natural gestures with respect to the overall communicative contexts.

Gibson's review draws a number of other pertinent conclusions. Specifically, contrary to some reports, language-trained apes do often initiate their own gestural or lexigram-based communications; under appropriate circumstances, they do cooperate in the pursuit of common goals, and they do have some understandings of others' intentions and motives. In sum, they appear to have the basic capacities necessary to create a gestural protolanguage. Whether they possess sufficient vocal capacities for the creation of a vocal protolanguage is less clear. Moreover, although at least one bonobo, Kanzi, comprehended significant aspects of English, all of the apes appeared to fall far short of humans in their ability to create hierarchical communications. Given that apes also fall far short of humans in their abilities to construct complex tools, Gibson suggests that the ability to construct mental hierarchies is a critical factor distinguishing a range of human and ape cognitive capacities (see also Penn et al. 2008).

The following chapter, by Seyfarth and Cheney, complements Gibson's by focusing on baboon vocal and language-pertinent cognitive skills. From studies in which baboon vocalizations are first recorded and then played back in diverse circumstances and sequences, the authors conclude that baboon social cognition involves a number of cognitive processes essential for language, including, among others, understandings of causality, representational knowledge, and the ability to create hierarchical mental concepts by combining mental representations of ranked matrilineal lineages and of individual rankings within lineages. Hence, in their view, neural mechanisms for social cognition may have served as the initial templates for many aspects of language comprehension. These findings are intriguing and persuasive. They do raise questions, however, in light of Gibson's findings that great ape abilities to create mental hierarchies fall short of those of humans. One possible reason for the discrepancy is that Gibson focuses on the production of hierarchically-organized behaviours, whereas Seyfarth and Cheney focus on comprehension of social hierarchies. Gibson, does, for example, conclude that some apes at least are better able to comprehend hierarchical sentences than to produce them. Alternatively, hierarchies contain varied levels and the units that compose them comprise different degrees of discreteness. Neither chapter provides sufficient details on these issues to allow direct species comparisons. Finally, the baboon ability to mentally construct social hierarchies may be an adaptation to a specific social structure, present in some Old World monkeys, but not in apes. Specifically, baboons live in large multi-male groups with stable female-led lineages. Each lineage has a specific ranking within the group and each individual has a distinct rank within a lineage. (See Penn et al. (2008), though, for a critique of Seyfarth and Cheney's views of baboon hierarchical abilities.)

The Seyfarth and Cheney chapter also gives a general overview of the vocal capacities of Old World monkeys, especially vervets, baboons, and macaques. These monkeys can comprehend the vocalizations of other species, but they can neither create nor mimic novel vocalizations. Thus, the ancestral Old World monkey condition probably involved open-ended vocal comprehension but a small, inflexible, vocal repertoire. Since they accept traditional views that great ape vocal capacities resemble those of monkeys, Seyfarth and Cheney further postulate that flexible vocal production evolved subsequent to the phylogenetic split between hominins and chimpanzees/bonobos; hence it was not present in the common ancestor of great apes and hominins. If, however, further research corroborates Slocombe's views (Chapter 7) that great ape vocalizations are more flexible than previously believed, this hypothesis may require modification.

Zuberbühler's chapter (5) reiterates the view that non-human primate call comprehension is more flexible than call production. He notes, however, that chimpanzees, marmosets, and perhaps other species do have some vocal flexibility, as evidenced by the possession of dialects and group specific calls. Also, in contrast to older views, many primates modify their vocal production depending on the audience. Hence, they exert some volitional control over whether to vocalize or not as well as over the intensity and duration of their calls. Some primates also have calls that combine two separate calls, but which have distinct meanings separate from and unrelated to their individual components. For example, putty-nosed monkeys produce 'pyows' in response to leopards and 'hacks' in response to eagles and falling trees. Adult males also produce 'pyow hack' combinations, which have different meanings than either call produced individually. The significance of these call combinations for language evolution remains unclear. As Tallerman (Chapter 48) argues, since the ultimate meaning of the 'pyow hack' calls has no relationship to the meanings of either of its components, the combination does not qualify as grammar or syntax. Perhaps it best viewed as more akin to syllable combinations in human languages, such as *car + pet = carpet*, where there is no semantic compositionality.

De Waal and Pollick (Chapter 6), like Seyfarth and Cheney, accept traditional views that great ape vocalizations lack flexibility. In contrast, bonobo and chimpanzee gestural communications are quite flexible in terms of gestural form, meanings, and usage contexts. In turn, gestural usage and gestural meanings appear to be more flexible in bonobos than in chimpanzees. In both species, the meaning of a specific gesture can vary according to behavioural context and whether the gestures are used alone or in combination with other communicative signals. In light of these findings, they suggest that flexible usage of gestures preceded symbolization. Throughout most of their chapter, de Waal and Pollick reiterate common views that great ape vocalizations, unlike great ape gestures, are strongly tied to emotions and contexts. They do, however, note that bonobo vocalizations may be more flexible than those of chimpanzees. In particular, bonobos have soft peeps that they use in contexts involving unusual circumstances and events. De Waal and Pollick conclude that initial steps towards language may have been in gestural or in combined gestural and vocal modes, and they suggest that the communicative competences of the earliest hominins may have been more like those of bonobos than those of chimpanzees.

Slocombe breaks with tradition and challenges views that great ape vocalizations are entirely stereotyped and emotional. In fact, great ape vocal capacities have hardly been studied, and what we do know about them derives mainly from loud vocalizations used in emotional contexts, rather than from softer vocalizations used during relaxed social interactions, such as those in which flexible gesture use has been reported. Increasing evidence, however, suggests that ape vocalizations may be more flexible than previously thought. We now know that chimpanzees and bonobos have food grunts, which, in the wild, vary with food quality and quantity. In captivity, however, apes sometimes use specific grunts referentially with respect to specific foods. Moreover, although great apes lack the predator-specific alarm barks displayed by many monkeys, wild chimpanzees do give varied calls and produce call/drumming combinations in response to snakes. Some evidence reviewed by Slocombe also indicates that chimpanzees have dialects and group-specific pant-hoots, and in captivity a small number of orang-utans and chimpanzees have invented novel vocalizations. One orang-utan even imitated a human whistle. Hence, further study of the soft vocalizations that apes use in relaxed social interactions looms as a critically important endeavour for those interested in the possible vocal antecedents of speech and protolanguage.

Each of the remaining chapters focuses in part on vocal learning capacities in non-primates. Slater (Chapter 8) provides a broad overview of bird song features and usage contexts. He concludes that, although some bird songs are hierarchically structured, none has the referential capability of human speech, and that modern birds sing in such a wide variety of mating and territorial situations that it is difficult to determine the original selective pressures that led to song. The most elaborate cetacean songs, those of humpback whales, also occur during breeding seasons, and they are performed only by males (Janik, Chapter 9). The final chapter in Part I, by Gibson, compares animal songs to speech and concludes that differences overwhelm similarities. Hence, in her view, it is unlikely that human speech evolved from song (for a contrary opinion, see Mithen, Chapter 28). Some accomplished vocal learners, moreover, are not especially noted for their songs, including parrots (Pepperberg, Chapter 10), dolphins (Janik, Chapter 9), and bats (Gibson, Chapter 11). Instead, these animals either have learned, group-specific, contact calls (parrots, bats), and/or individual signature whistles (dolphins). Gibson suggests that vocalizations like these, or other social signals, such as the soft vocalizations of monkeys and apes—rather than song—may have provided the stepping stones to language. Alternatively, as Zuberbühler, Falk, and Locke all suggest in this volume, vocal learning may have first evolved in hominin infants who needed to attract the attention of adult caretakers.

In addition to discussing animal vocal capacities, the last chapters in this section (Pepperberg, Janik, and Gibson) focus on the cognitive, including language-pertinent, capacities of non-primate animals. Pepperberg summarizes the achievements of Alex, a language-trained, African Grey parrot. Although Alex was not tested on the full range of ape language-related capacities (Gibson, Chapter 11), he performed comparably to great apes on those capacities for which he was tested. In addition, unlike any of the apes, Alex could speak recognizable English words. Despite these impressive abilities, no wild parrots are known to use a referential communication system. Similarly, insofar as they have been studied, dolphins (Janik, Gibson) and sea lions (Gibson, Chapter 11), resemble apes in their abilities to comprehend and respond to some grammar-like constructions, especially those based on 'word' order. Unfortunately, neither dolphins nor sea lions have been extensively tested on their abilities to actually produce, as opposed to simply respond to, referential signals. Consequently, we lack sufficient data to determine whether they possess the full range of protolanguage capacities now known to exist in apes. Elephants have apparently never served as subjects of language-learning experiments, but Gibson (Chapter 11) concludes that their broad range of cognitive, vocal, and motor capacities suggest they would make good subjects. Corvids (Gibson, Chapter 11) have also performed extremely well on a number of cognitive tasks. To what extent, however, their intelligence is broadly-based or, alternatively, limited to specific contexts, remains unclear, and no corvids have served as subjects of language-training experiments.

In sum, although non-human primates have often been considered the most intelligent animals—as well as the animals most potentially capable of language learning—it now appears that many animals are quite smart, and some may rival apes in their language-learning capacities. To date, however, no animal has demonstrated the full range of ape cognitive capacities, and none stands out as a better animal model for language evolution.

# CHAPTER 3

# LANGUAGE OR PROTOLANGUAGE? A REVIEW OF THE APE LANGUAGE LITERATURE

KATHLEEN R. GIBSON

## 3.1 INTRODUCTION

Collectively, studies of the language capacities of the great apes (orang-utan, gorilla, bonobo, and chimpanzee) far exceed in numbers those of other animals, and for good reason. No matter how sophisticated the cognitive and communicative capacities of other animals may ultimately prove to be, comparative studies of our closest phylogenetic kin will continue to provide the strongest evidence of the probable behavioural capacities of the last common ape/hominin ancestor, and, hence, of the probable capacities of the earliest hominins.

From their inception, ape-language studies have been embroiled in controversies. To some extent, these controversies reflect the differing perspectives of those who hold Darwinian views of continuity between ape and animal minds versus those who adhere to Cartesian traditions of sharp qualitative mental differences between humans and other animals. Investigators also employ different working definitions of key aspects of language such as 'symbol' (Deacon 1997, this volume). Finally, researchers use differing criteria for evaluating the presence or absence of specific communicative capacities. Emil Menzel, a grandfather of great ape cognitive studies, considered the strongest test of an ape's signing capacity to be the ability of deaf human signers to understand the ape's intentions (E. Menzel 1978). Allen and Beatrix Gardner judged Washoe and other chimpanzees to have mastered specific gestural signs if, as judged by three independent observers, they made them correctly and used them appropriately on 15 consecutive days (Gardner and Gardner 1969). In contrast, the signing capacities of the chimpanzee Nim were evaluated on the basis of how often he repeated himself, how often he interrupted his trainers and what he most often used signs to express (Terrace 1979; Terrace et al. 1979). As a result of these contrasting philosophies, definitions, and criteria, investigators may interpret ape language-like achievements quite differently even when faced with nearly identical behaviours.

As much as possible, this review simply describes actual ape behaviours, without prejudging their linguistic nature. It does conclude, however, that a number of apes mastered essential components of protolanguage (Tallerman, Chapter 51), but none constructed hierarchically-structured sentences containing embedded phrases or clauses. Hence, the development of greater mental constructional skills may have been necessary for the development of full linguistic and syntactic capacities.

## 3.2 'LANGUAGE'-LEARNING APES

### 3.2.1 Talking/listening apes

Many apes have lived in human homes and/or trained for various aspects of the entertainment industry. Often, human owners have been convinced these apes understood English or other modern languages. Rarely have these reports been confirmed or negated. One exception was Gua, a female chimpanzee raised in a human home for nine months, from 7½ months of age (Kellogg and Kellogg 1933). Gua consistently responded correctly to 95 simple English commands, such as 'show me your nose'. At age eight, the bonobo Kanzi responded appropriately to 660 English commands, including unusual commands, such as 'hit the can opener with a rock' (Savage-Rumbaugh et al. 1993). Kanzi also distinguished English sentence meanings based on word order and/or on the prepositions used. For example, he responded appropriately to 'Make the doggie bite the snake', and also to 'Make the snake bite the doggie', as well as to commands to put objects in or on other objects. The gorilla Koko also appropriately executed English commands. Indeed, Koko's comprehension of English eventually became sufficiently sophisticated that her caretakers often took to finger-spelling in her presence (Patterson and Linden 1981).

In contrast to frequent, if mostly unconfirmed, reports that apes comprehend human speech, only a few apes have produced recognizable words of any human language, even when subject to intensive interventions and speech therapy (Miles 1999). This has led to the view that apes have no vocal learning capacities and are incapable of making novel vocalizations, a view that may not be entirely accurate (Slocombe, this volume). In particular, some great ape species have population dialects, and a few individual apes have created novel sounds and/or use some sounds referentially.

## 3.2.2  Signing apes

### 3.2.2.1  Signing chimpanzees

In the 1960s, Allen and Beatrix Gardner initiated studies of chimpanzee abilities to learn elements of the American Sign Language of the Deaf, ASL (Gardner and Gardner 1969). Washoe, their first chimpanzee, was housed in a trailer in the Gardners' yard from ten months to four years of age. Although the Gardners and their assistants avoided talking to Washoe or to each other in Washoe's presence, in an effort to ensure she was exposed only to sign, they were not themselves fluent signers. Washoe, who was initially taught to sign by hand-moulding techniques, eventually mastered new signs simply by observing her caretakers. At age four, Washoe and the Gardners' graduate student, Roger Fouts, moved to the Institute for Primate Studies (IPS), Norman, Oklahoma, where Fouts continued to train Washoe and also began training some IPS-owned chimpanzees. In 1980, Fouts and Washoe relocated to Central Washington University (Fouts and Mills 1997). At CWU, Washoe was joined by an infant chimpanzee, Loulis, from the IPS and by three animals also raised by the Gardners: Mojo, Tatu, and Dar. Unlike Washoe, Mojo, Tatu, and Dar were mostly trained by native ASL signers (Miles 1999).

Washoe eventually learned about 250 signs which she used to communicate various needs and desires, including requests for specific foods or preferred activities. She often made spontaneous comments, noting, for example, the presence of a dog, a toothbrush, or other items of interest, and, when alone, she was observed to sign to herself, especially when 'reading' books and magazines. On at least one occasion, she invented a new sign, 'bib', by making an iconic outline of a bib on her own chest. She also invented new sign combinations to refer to new objects. For example, she called a Brazil nut a 'rock berry'; the toilet 'dirty good'; and the refrigerator, 'open food drink' (Fouts and Mills 1997). It is unclear, however, if these sign combinations were permanently incorporated into her vocabulary. Once housed in groups at the CWU facility, Washoe and the other signing chimpanzees spontaneously signed to each other in situations involving play, social interaction, and reassurance, and, according to videotapes, they did so even in the absence of human observers. One infant chimpanzee, Loulis, learned several signs entirely through his interactions with the other apes (Fouts and Mills 1997).

Another chimpanzee born at the IPS, Nim, was loaned, shortly after his birth, to Herb Terrace, a Columbia University psychologist, who planned to teach ASL to Nim, but Terrace did not know ASL himself and had no fluent signers on his staff (Terrace 1979). Nim was initially housed with a large human family, the LaFarges, and later relocated to a country estate with varied caretakers. From 10 months of age, Nim sat at a desk in a Columbia University classroom several hours a day, several days a week, while a succession of instructors taught him signs. Shortly before Nim's fourth birthday, he was returned to the IPS. Later he moved to the Black Beauty animal sanctuary in Texas (Hess 2008). Reportedly, Nim learned 125 signs. In taped classroom sessions, however, Nim rarely signed spontaneously. Many of his responses to trainers' questions and cues were imitative, and he often interrupted his trainers (Terrace 1979; Terrace et al. 1979). Later, however, at both the IPS and the Black Beauty Ranch, Nim did sign spontaneously. Moreover, his signs repeatedly satisfied Menzel's criteria of being understood by native ASL signers (Hess 2008; O'Sullivan and Yeager 1989). Hence, Nim's classroom performances may not have fully reflected his abilities to use signs in spontaneous, communicative contexts.

By their very nature, spontaneous communications are unpredictable, often irreproducible, and unlikely to occur in structured testing situations. This point became quite clear to me in the early 1980s, when I frequently visited the home of Jim and June Cook in Conroe, Texas. The Cooks had raised Nim's full sibling, Tania, and were subsequently raising Tania's two offspring and another infant chimpanzee. According to the Cook family, Tania had mastered 60 signs prior to the move to Texas. During my visits, she routinely signed spontaneously. Once, she spontaneously signed 'pretty' when a female visitor appeared wearing a flowered dress. Another time, she became quite agitated when I was walking past her cage and she signed 'hurry, hurry, come here, hurt, hurry, come here, hurt' while staring intently at my calf and apparently trying to reach it. One family member stated, 'Oh, you have a huge mosquito on your leg'. No video camera recorded this event.

Nim and Tania were only two of many chimpanzees owned by and/or born in the IPS facility, a number of which received some ASL training including, among others, Ally, Bruno, Booee, Cindy, Lucy, and Thelma. Lucy is perhaps most notable as the first chimpanzee observed using signs to lie, specifically to blame her messes on others. She also invented novel sign combinations to refer to new objects, e.g. 'candy drink' or 'drink fruit' for watermelon and 'cry hurt food' for radish. By and large, however, the accomplishments of Lucy and other IPS animals resembled Washoe's and thus will not be detailed here (Fouts and Mills 1997; Hess 2008).

### 3.2.2.2 *Signing gorillas*

Penny Patterson and her assistants, including deaf, fluent ASL signers, taught signs to two western lowland gorillas, Koko and Michael. Currently, Koko is stated to have mastered over 1000 signs, and Michael mastered approximately 600 prior to his death in 2000. Reportedly, Koko and Michael often spontaneously signed to each other. In many respects, Koko's achievements are similar to those of the language-trained chimpanzees. She uses combined signs to refer to new objects, such as calling a ring a 'finger bracelet', and she regularly combines some signs in specific orders. Koko can also translate English words into her version of ASL signs (Patterson and Linden 1981).

### 3.2.2.3 *Signing orang-utans*

Chantek, an orang-utan raised by Lyn Miles and later housed at the Yerkes Primate Center and the Atlanta Zoo, learned approximately 150 signs, some of which he made with his feet as well as with his hands. The majority of Chantek's signs referred to objects and actions. Only about 25% pertained to food or drink. Chantek, like other apes, used sign combinations to refer to objects, e.g. 'car water' for bottled water, and he often referred to absent objects. For example, 76% of the time that he used the sign for the building 'Brock Hall' it was not visible. Approximately 3 times per week, Chantek used signs deceptively (Miles 1990, 1999).

Rinnie, a captive born orang-utan, was later rehabilitated to the wild at the Tanjung Putting National Park in Borneo. During her transition stage, Rinnie voluntarily maintained contact with humans and obtained some food from them. For a period of 22 months when she was 10 to 12 years of age, this contact incorporated training in ASL signs in a swamp forest environment (Shapiro and Galdikas 1999). Rinnie reportedly learned 32 signs, mostly related to foods obtained during her visits with human trainers. Rinnie invented signs for 'groom', 'scratch', and 'grab hair'. She reportedly called large edible ants 'pineapple nuts', and she routinely combined signs in attempts to obtain food, e.g. 'you food', 'give food', 'you more rice'.

## 3.2.3 Plastic token and lexigram-using apes

Rather than attempt to teach apes to speak or gesture, David Premack, at the University of Pennsylvania, and Duane Rumbaugh, at the Language Research

Center (LRC), Georgia State University chose to test ape cognitive and communicative capacities using visual symbols (Premack 1977; Rumbaugh 1977).

### 3.2.3.1  Sarah

Of his four initial chimpanzee subjects, only one, Sarah, mastered Premack's 'language'. Initially, Premack used plastic, metal-backed tokens and a magnetic board. Chimpanzee subjects and human investigators communicated by placing the tokens on the board. As Sarah became older and stronger, visual tokens were placed on a typewriter-style keyboard. The keys, when pressed, displayed on television screens. Ultimately, Sarah mastered the referential meanings of approximately 150 tokens referring to distinct objects, actions, adjective-like descriptors and other parts of speech. She could compose short grammatical sentences, such as 'Mary give apple Sarah'. Premack concluded Sarah could classify objects by colour, shape, and size, that she understood concepts of interrogation, same/different, and negation, and that she could comprehend *if/then* statements. Sarah used her token 'language' productively and often referred to absent objects (Premack 1977).

### 3.2.3.2  Lana

Lana, Duane Rumbaugh's first chimpanzee subject, spent much of her time in a room equipped with a computer screen and keyboard (Rumbaugh 1977). Each key contained a lexigram, that is, a visual sign composed of parallel lines, circles, Xs and other non-iconic shapes superimposed upon each other in seemingly random fashions. Lexigrams representing a variety of linguistic categories could be moved to new keyboard positions and/or removed and replaced by new lexigrams with different meanings. A computer grammar, Yerkish, was also devised. Lana's task was to press the proper lexigrams in the proper Yerkish sequence to receive rewards that were sometimes dispensed by the computer and sometimes by humans. If, for example, Lana wanted the computer to dispense M&Ms, she would press five keys in the following order: *please, machine, give, M&M, period*. Initially, Lana failed to comprehend this system, but after an assistant, Timothy Gill, demonstrated it, she made rapid progress. Ultimately, Lana routinely used grammatically correct Yerkish to request food, drinks, human visitors, and actions such as being allowed to leave the room, having the window opened, or having a malfunctioning computer (machine) fixed. Lana proved adept at learning lexigrams for colours, objects, and actions. When presented with new objects, with no known lexigram, she described them using combinations of familiar lexigrams. Thus, orange soda was described as the 'coke which is orange', while orange (the fruit) was described as the 'apple which is orange'.

### 3.2.3.3  Sherman and Austin

Sherman and Austin, two LRC chimpanzees trained primarily by Sue Savage-Rumbaugh, readily learned to use appropriate lexigrams for requesting items. Initially, however, they appeared not to fully comprehend the symbolic nature of the lexigrams. When others, for example, used the same lexigrams to request items from them, they appeared not to comprehend the request (Savage-Rumbaugh et al. 1978; Savage-Rumbaugh and Lewin 1994). Later, however, they learned to group lexigrams into classificatory categories, such as lexigrams for tools versus lexigrams for food. At that point, they were able to use individual lexigrams in more diverse contexts and also began learning them far more rapidly. Their most impressive accomplishments occurred when they were housed in adjacent cages, each containing a lexigram keyboard. When one ape pressed a key on his board, the same key would light up on the other's board. Thus equipped, the chimpanzees first used lexigrams to request food and other items from each other. (Unlike many captive chimpanzees, they had been trained to share and did so willingly.) They also used lexigrams to communicate information necessary for the achievement of joint goals. For example, a desired food would be locked in a box in one room, while the box-opening tools (e.g. screwdriver, wrench, money, key) were situated in a second room which afforded no sight of the food containers. One chimpanzee was allowed to enter the food-containing room, see the item housed in the box, and determine the tool needed to open the box, while the other animal remained in the tool room. To obtain the appropriate tool, the informed chimpanzee pressed the correct lexigram on his keyboard. The non-informed animal responded by sharing the appropriate tool. Foods obtained in this manner were shared between the informer and the tool-provider, thus providing motivation for continued cooperation. Sherman and Austin routinely communicated and cooperated in this way, even when roles of informer and 'tool-provider' were reversed (Savage-Rumbaugh et al. 1978).

### 3.2.3.4  Kanzi and other bonobos

Following her success with Sherman and Austin, Savage-Rumbaugh attempted to teach lexigrams to a mature wild-born bonobo, Matata (Savage-Rumbaugh and Lewin 1994). For two years beginning at six months of age, Matata's adopted infant, Kanzi, attended her language-training sessions, but was not directly trained himself. Matata failed to learn and was temporarily removed from their joint housing. During that time, 2½ year-old Kanzi demonstrated that he had mastered lexigram use, even though no attempts had been made to teach him. Specifically, on the very first day of Matata's departure, he used the keyboard to request items from the refrigerator and to announce his intentions, such as 'apple chase', i.e. intent to take apple and run, which he promptly did. After observing Kanzi's lexigram usage for several weeks, Savage-Rumbaugh abandoned direct drilling in lexigrams, choosing instead to create environmental conditions that would naturally result in 'conversations' and in motivations to learn names of places, objects, and actions. To this end, Savage-Rumbaugh and her co-investigators established 17 lexigram-named locations in a 55-acre forest adjacent to the LRC. Each location was associated with specific games, activities, and foods. Kanzi quickly learned to use lexigrams to announce his intentions to visit preferred locations. During these forest treks, Kanzi readily learned lexigrams for animals and plants that interested him. He also learned lexigrams for preferred games, preferred toys, and preferred foods.

About 90% of Kanzi's utterances were self-initiated, and he often combined two or three lexigrams in meaningful ways. Some of these combinations exhibited a stable lexigram order, even when the lexigrams themselves were different. For example, when requesting actions on people or objects, Kanzi usually put the verb first and the object of the action second, i.e. 'grab ball', 'chase Austin', 'hide ball', whereas when requesting actions by people or chimpanzees, the person/chimpanzee was normally first, e.g. 'Austin give', 'Austin go' (Greenfield and Savage-Rumbaugh 1990, 1993; see Tallerman, Chapter 51, for an alternative inter-pretation). Kanzi also invented rules for combining lexigrams and gestures and for combining two action gestures. Specifically, he pointed first to the lexigram for a desired action and second to the person designated to perform the action. Kanzi often put two action lexigrams together such as 'tickle bite' or 'chase hide'. In each case, Kanzi's self-imposed rule appeared to be that the first lexigram would refer to the more distant action, the second to the more proximal.

Nearly thirty years have passed since Kanzi first demonstrated competence with lexigrams. In those years, a number of other bonobos and some chimpanzees were born at the Language Research Center in Georgia. Several of these animals also mastered lexigrams. One chimpanzee, Panzee, demonstrated via lexigram usage what the investigators called episodic memory. Specifically, when Panzee observed a human demonstrator hide food in the forest outside her cage, she would later, sometimes days later, use lexigrams to direct naïve investigators to the hidden foods (C. Menzel 2005).

### 3.2.3.5 Summary of ape language studies

Although great apes do not mimic human speech, they occasionally create and possibly imitate other novel sounds (Slocombe, this volume). They also learn to make gestures by observing humans and other apes, both in captivity and in the wild (de Waal and Pollick, this volume). Indeed, Terrace and his colleagues were so impressed by the frequency with which Nim imitated his teachers, they concluded he could do little else (Terrace et al. 1979). Since then, scientists have come to recognize that there are different kinds and levels of imitation (Byrne and Russon

1998). The most sophisticated, production level imitation, requires parsing sequential actions into component parts, practising each component part, and then hierarchically reassembling the elements to reach an ultimate goal. Once mastered, each element can also be incorporated into other behavioural sequences. Great apes have demonstrated this capacity in some feeding and other object manipulation endeavours. It also occurs during human vocal learning. No investigators, however, have claimed that any of their subjects imitated complex gestural sequences via a parsing and hierarchical reassembly technique. Rather, they appear to have learned simply to copy individual gestures.

In the studies reviewed above, great apes of all species used manual gestures and/or lexigrams to refer to objects, places, people, and actions, including some not immediately present and visible. All apes also used gestures and/or lexigrams to request objects and actions. Most also made spontaneous 'comments' to themselves, their caretakers, and, when possible, other apes. Several, including Koko, Lucy, and Washoe were reported to sign to dolls and/or cats. Both lexigram-using and signing apes often invented sign combinations to refer to foods, animals, or other objects for which they had been taught no signs. Several invented new signs.

Many gestures and most lexigrams used in these studies functioned as non-iconic, arbitrary signs of specific objects or actions, and, thus, met classic definitions of symbol. Deacon (1997, this volume), however, maintains that true symbols function, not just in isolated labelling contexts, but also in relationship to other symbols. According to Deacon's (1997) analysis, at least three of the apes, Kanzi, Sherman and Austin, learned a set of logical relationships among lexigrams and, thus, were using symbols, as he defines them.

Great apes of all species also created action-oriented combinations, such as 'give apple', 'chase Sue', 'chase bite', or 'Mary give apple'. Two apes, Sarah and Lana, were trained to compose token or lexigram sentences of four to five words using proper English grammatical order. Others, however, including Washoe, Nim, Chantek, and Kanzi may have invented their own combinatory rules. Nim and Koko, for example, always placed the sign 'more' prior to the objects or actions requested. Washoe placed subjects first in 90% of her spontaneous combinatory utterances. She also made combinations of two to three signs to request items and used regular 'word' orders. For example, if an object was present and clearly visible she would sign 'object give'; if the object was absent, she would sign 'give object'. Greenfield and Savage-Rumbaugh (1990) proposed that some of Kanzi's combinatory rules qualified as grammar, because interchangeable lexigrams were assigned to specific places in the lexigram string depending on the function, e.g. actor, acted upon, action, etc.

Taken as a whole, it appears that at least some of these apes possessed all elements necessary for protolanguage (see Tallerman, Chapter 51). None of the signing or lexigram-using apes, however, spontaneously used regular rule-based combinations of more than a few signs/lexigrams. None of the apes in any experiments constructed hierarchical sentences containing embedded phrases and clauses. None used recursion, nor did any master duality of patterning. Possibly, these failings reflect the nature of their language environments. No signing apes were permanently housed with native ASL human signers. No evidence indicates that most human trainers used complex grammatical constructions in their own token/lexigram communications.

Great ape abilities to construct complex hierarchies, however, appear to fall short of human abilities across multiple domains (Gibson 1990, 1996a, 1997b, 2002; Gibson and Jessee 1999; Greenfield 1991; see also Penn et al. 2008). For, example, great apes do not make hierarchical constructions that require first constructing subcomponents such as stone points, shafts, binding materials, and fabrics and then putting them all together to make a variety of new objects such as spears, rafts, tents, costumes, or clothing. Nor do they construct complex dance sequences or rule-based games involving balls and other objects. Hence, the transition from protolanguage to language, as well as the transition from ape-like to human-like overall intelligence may both have primarily involved the emergence of increased hierarchical mental constructional capacities.

## 3.3 WHAT APES CAN DO VERSUS WHAT APES USUALLY DO: THEORY OF MIND, SHARED INTENTIONS

Despite abilities to master and use gestural signs, no wild ape population is known to use a gestural communication system that remotely approaches the protolanguage-like communications of language-trained apes. No wild apes, for example, have been reported using gestures to refer to absent objects or events, even though language-trained apes readily do so in captivity. Possibly, apes lack other capacities essential for the invention of protolanguage, such as theory of mind or the ability to develop shared intentions, or perhaps they simply lack the motivation or need to use protolanguages.

### 3.3.1 Theory of mind

Premack and Woodruff (1978) were the first to question whether chimpanzees possess a theory of mind, i.e. the ability to understand others' beliefs, desires, and intentions. For both human and non-human primates, the Sally Ann, or false belief test, has traditionally been the gold standard for determining the presence or absence of theory of mind. In the human version, three people are simultaneously present in a room. A child, say Sally Ann, and a human observer, say John, simultaneously watch a human experimenter hide an object, such as a pencil, under or behind another object, such as a cup. John then leaves the room. During his absence, the experimenter moves the pencil and hides it under a different cup. When John returns, Sally Ann is asked where John thinks the pencil is. Three-year-old children invariably respond that John thinks the pencil is where it actually is. Four-year-old children know that John thinks the object is where he saw it hidden.

Whether or not great apes also comprehend that others may have false beliefs has been a matter of some debate. Great apes perform poorly on Sally Ann tests. Consequently, some investigators have concluded that great apes lack a theory of mind and that this lack is a major factor accounting for their failure to develop language (see Call and Tomasello 2008). Human children, however, speak in grammatical sentences long prior to being able to pass Sally Ann tests. Moreover, wild chimpanzees sometimes engage in intentional intra-specific deception, and at least two of the language-trained apes, Lucy and Chantek, also engaged in frequent deceptive acts (Byrne 1995; Fouts and Mills 1997; Miles 1990). Sherman and Austin clearly behaved as if they were aware of each others' knowledge state, when they communicated about tools needed to open boxes (Savage-Rumbaugh et al. 1978). Laboratory chimpanzees also sometimes perform well on non-Sally Ann tests of others' knowledge and perspectives. Hence, irrespective of whether apes comprehend that others may have false beliefs, it appears that chimpanzees, '...understand both the goals and intentions of others as well as the perception and knowledge of others' (Call and Tomasello 2008; see also Byrne and Bates 2010). Consequently, inability to comprehend others' knowledge states does not appear to be a primary factor preventing apes from developing protolanguage.

## 3.3.2 Shared intentions, cooperation

Tomasello proposed that inabilities to share intentions and cooperate are major factors preventing great apes from developing language (Tomasello 2009b; Tomasello et al. 2005). This hypothesis drew support from a study that found juvenile chimpanzees were less likely than human infants to cooperate with human adults (Warneken et al. 2006). However, the 2005 publication ignored or discounted earlier studies that found chimpanzees sometimes cooperate with each other. Wild chimpanzee adult males, for example, sometimes engage in cooperative hunting endeavours which, according to some field workers, require individual animals to adopt specific roles in the hunt (Boesch and Boesch 1989). Sherman and Austin clearly cooperated and shared in their lexigram-mediated tool-using endeavours (Savage-Rumbaugh et al. 1978). In the early 1970s, a group of chimpanzees studied by Emil Menzel proved so adept at cooperating in the placement of logs to escape from a fenced compound that they had to be relocated to another study site (E. Menzel 1972). It has also long been known that chimpanzee males jointly patrol group boundaries and engage in lethal aggressive acts at group borders (Mitani et al. 2010). Further, recent studies from Tomasello's own laboratory indicate that laboratory chimpanzees do cooperate with selected partners and that bonobos may more readily cooperate than chimpanzees (Melis et al. 2006). None of these findings, of course, indicate that apes cooperate as readily or as often as humans, but they do indicate that given appropriate social circumstances and problem-solving tasks, apes can cooperate.

### 3.3.3 Summary

Chimpanzees and bonobos do have some understandings of others' minds and can cooperate. Hence, if they do not use protolanguage in the wild, the most likely reason is lack of motivation.

## 3.4 When did protolanguages and languages develop?

That members of all great ape species can master the essential components of protolanguages suggests that the cognitive capacities necessary for protolanguages were present in the last common ancestor of all great apes and humans some 14 to 20 mya (Steiper and Young 2006). Unless, however, ancestors of some modern great ape species once had protolanguages but later lost them, protolanguages must have arisen subsequent to the hominin–*Pan* phylogenetic split about 6–7 mya. Nothing in the archaeological or fossil records tells us precisely when. We do know, however, that by 2.6 mya, hominins were making simple stone tools with sharp cutting edges, and, thus, had entered a new non-ape-like environmental niche, which may have involved using stone tools to cut hides, meat, tendons, or vegetation (Wynn, this volume). Possibly, this new niche also selected for gestural or vocally mediated cooperative endeavours and/or for communication about absent objects/events? Alternatively, hominins may have invented protolanguage-like communications by 1.8 mya, by which time they had become fully terrestrial, expanded their brain size, and begun to manufacture hand axes, tools that are more complicated than anything made by apes. Whether initial protolanguages were gestural, vocal, or some combination of gestures and vocalizations cannot be definitively determined from current evidence, given that great apes, while known for their gestural capabilities, are proving more vocally adept than previously thought (Slocombe, this volume).

As noted earlier, great apes do not construct lengthy, hierarchical or recursive sentences. Nor do they construct tools of diverse components. Both Neanderthals and early anatomically modern humans, however, constructed hafted spears as well as dwellings of multiple subcomponents, such as poles and hides (Gibson 1996b; Wynn, this volume). Although we cannot be certain that mental constructional skills in technical and linguistic realms emerged simultaneously, it is quite possible they did. Hence, a hierarchical language, as opposed to protolanguage, could have been present in both Neanderthals and early modern humans. That this language could have been spoken or, at least, involved advanced vocal skills is suggested by the presence of the modern *FOXP2* gene in both Neanderthals and early modern humans (Diller and Cann, this volume).

# CHAPTER 4

# PRIMATE SOCIAL COGNITION AS A PRECURSOR TO LANGUAGE

ROBERT M. SEYFARTH AND
DOROTHY L. CHENEY

## 4.1 INTRODUCTION

The goal of phylogenetic reconstruction is to group similar animals together. One method is based on measures of distance, and arranges species into a phylogeny such that each is grouped with those with which it shares the greatest number of characters. Other methods rely on parsimony, generating the phylogeny that requires the fewest evolutionary changes in character states (Ridley 1993). Among primates, both methods yield a branching 'tree structure' in which humans are grouped most closely with apes, less closely with Old World monkeys, and progressively less closely with New World monkeys, prosimians, and non-primate mammals. This phylogeny is consistent with both distance and parsimony: for example, morphological and genetic evidence indicate both that there is less evolutionary distance between humans and chimpanzees/bonobos than between humans and any other primate and also that a phylogeny that groups humans and chimpanzees/bonobos together is more parsimonious (requires fewer evolutionary steps) than a phylogeny that does not (Boyd and Silk 2003).

As Ridley (1993) points out, the parsimony principle is reasonable because evolutionary change is improbable. Suppose we know, for example, that two modern species have the same character state. Parsimony suggests that all the intermediate, ancestral states in the continuous lineages between each species and their common ancestor possessed the same character state, and that the two species are alike in this character because they descend from a common ancestor. Parsimony, in other words, suggests that the two species are homologous in this character. Of course, an infinitely large number of changes could have occurred between ancestor and descendant; however, a change followed by a reversal of that change is unlikely.

For the characters shared between humans and chimpanzees, the argument is particularly powerful. Chimpanzees and humans share whole complex organ systems like hearts and lungs, eyes, brains, and spinal cords. The initial evolution of each of these characters required improbable mutations, and natural selection operating over millions of generations. It is evolutionarily improbable to the point of near impossibility that the same changes would have evolved independently in the two lineages after their common ancestor (Ridley 1993: 450).

The principle of parsimony allows us to identify homologous traits in humans and other primates that were likely to have been present in the ancestral systems of vocal communication and cognition from which language evolved. This makes it possible to specify those traits that may have served as precursors to language and to identify features that were most likely to have evolved only in the hominin lineage, after divergence from the common ancestor of humans and chimpanzees.

## 4.2 Reconstructing the prelinguistic ancestor

### 4.2.1 Vocal production

With a few exceptions, all modern mammals have a relatively small repertoire of call types (a variety of grunts, threatening vocalizations, alarm calls, screams, and so on), each of which has adult-like acoustic features when first produced and shows little modification during development. Mammals can control whether they vocalize or remain silent and make some limited modification in the acoustic features of their calls, but for the most part vocal production is highly constrained (for review see Hammerschmidt and Fischer 2008). The rare exceptions are some marine mammals (cetaceans, harbour seals) and humans (Janik and Slater 1997; Janik, this volume). The principle of parsimony dictates that flexible vocal production, once evolved, would be unlikely to revert to a system of fixed, unmodifiable calls. It follows that constrained vocal production was the ancestral mammalian condition and that flexible phonation is a derived characteristic. Because vocal production in the great apes (chimpanzees, bonobos, gorillas, and orang-utans) appears to be typical of that found in other mammals, flexible phonation in humans probably evolved during the last six million years, sometime after the divergence of human ancestors from the common ancestors of humans, chimpanzees, and bonobos (Enard et al. 2002).

## 4.2.2 Vocal usage

Non-human primates use acoustically different vocalizations in different social contexts, suggesting that the mechanisms underlying call usage have a strong genetic component, although perhaps not as strong as the mechanisms underlying call production.

For example, vervet monkeys (*Chlorocebus aethiops*) give acoustically different alarm calls to leopards, eagles, and snakes. Each call type elicits a different, adaptive response. Individuals on the ground run into trees when they hear a leopard alarm, look up in the air when they hear an eagle alarm, and peer into the grass around them when they hear a snake alarm (Cheney and Seyfarth 1990). Confronted with a wide variety of potential predators, adult vervets are highly selective, giving 'leopard alarms' to mammalian carnivores, 'eagle alarms' primarily to martial (*Polemaetus bellicosus*) and crowned (*Stephanoetus coronatus*) eagles, and 'snake alarms' to pythons (*Python sebae*). Infants and juveniles, by contrast, make many more mistakes, by giving alarm calls to species like warthogs or pigeons that pose no danger to them. Their mistakes, however, are not entirely random. They give leopard alarms almost exclusively to terrestrial mammals, eagle alarms to birds, and snake alarms to reptiles and snake-like objects. Vervet infants behave as if they are predisposed from birth to divide other species into broadly different classes: predator versus non-predator, and, within the former class, to distinguish among terrestrial carnivores, eagles, and snakes. With time and experience they sharpen the relation between each alarm call type and the stimulus that elicits it (Cheney and Seyfarth 1990).

Although rhesus (*Macaca mulatta*) and Japanese (*M. fuscata*) macaques both produce coo and gruff calls, individuals in the two species use them in different ways. In play, for example, Japanese macaques give coos whereas rhesus macaques give gruffs. In a 3-year cross-fostering experiment, two infant rhesus and two infant Japanese macaques were raised in a group of the other species. Despite their complete social integration, the cross-fostered infants showed little or no modification in call usage. They behaved as if the link between call and context was difficult to modify (Owren et al. 1993).

The mixture of innate mechanisms and experience found in these two studies is typical of vocal usage in virtually all mammals and birds (Seyfarth and Cheney 2010). Clearly, however, it differs from vocal usage in humans, who can learn to use any word in any context. If we assume that completely flexible vocal usage, once evolved, would be highly adaptive and unlikely to revert to a system with more fixed, innate links between call and context, it follows that the highly flexible call usage found in humans evolved relatively recently, after the divergence of the human lineage from the common ancestor of humans and great apes, and that the ancestral, prelinguistic condition was one in which vocal usage was partially innate and partially modifiable by experience.

## 4.2.3 Comprehension

In contrast to the data on production and usage, data on perception and comprehension reveal several similarities between human and non-human primates. Like human speech, primate vocalizations comprise a series of acoustically intergraded signals that are perceived, roughly speaking, as discretely different calls. In baboons, different call types are distinguished according to the placement of vowel-like formants (see Seyfarth 2005 for references). Non-human primate call perception also exhibits parallels with human speech in its underlying neural mechanisms (though see Wilkins, this volume). In macaques, for example, the left hemisphere is specialized for processing species-specific vocalizations but not other auditory stimuli (Poremba et al. 2004). This and other results (Ghazanfar and Hauser 2001) suggest that many of the neural mechanisms that underlie human speech processing are general primate characteristics, shared among humans, apes, and Old World monkeys. Once again following the principle of parsimony, the simplest explanation is that these traits are homologous, and were present in the common ancestor of all Old World primates.

Further parallels are evident in the development of call comprehension, which—in contrast to production and usage—is flexible, open-ended, and can be modified by experience. Infant vervet monkeys, for example, respond to playback of leopard, eagle, and snake alarm calls by running to their mothers or showing some other, often inappropriate, reaction. They require several months' experience before they respond to the different alarm calls in an appropriate, adult-like manner (Cheney and Seyfarth 1990). In their natural habitats, many primates learn to recognize the alarm calls of other species (see Zuberbühler, this volume) even though these calls are acoustically different from their own. In the cross-fostering experiments described earlier, cross-fostered subjects learned to recognize their foster mothers' calls—and the foster mothers learned to recognize theirs—even in contexts in which the two species used acoustically different vocalizations (Seyfarth and Cheney 1997). And throughout their lives, monkeys and apes must continually learn to identify the voices of individuals who join their group or are born into it. For group-living animals, it is clearly adaptive to learn these associations and to retain an open-ended ability to identify new sound-meaning pairs throughout one's life. Because the ability to form learned associations is widespread among birds and mammals, we assume that it has a long evolutionary history and was present in the prelinguistic ancestor of modern humans.

## 4.2.4 Summary: the prelinguistic ancestor had limited vocal production but open-ended comprehension

Modern monkeys, apes, and other mammals share an oddly asymmetric system of communication in which a small repertoire of relatively fixed calls, each closely linked to a particular context, nonetheless gives rise to an open-ended, highly modifiable, and cognitively rich set of meanings (see below; see also Seyfarth and Cheney 2010). Because these traits are widespread across so many taxonomic groups, it seems highly unlikely that they evolved independently in each case. Instead, we assume that relatively fixed production and open-ended comprehension are homologous traits, and were present in the common ancestor of Old World monkeys, apes, and humans. To illustrate the implications for theories of language evolution, consider the communication and cognition of modern baboons.

## 4.3 SOCIAL KNOWLEDGE IN BABOONS

Baboons (*Papio hamadryas*) are Old World monkeys that shared a common ancestor with humans roughly 30 million years ago (Steiper et al. 2004). They live throughout the savannah woodlands of Africa in groups of 50–150 individuals. Although most males emigrate to other groups as young adults, females remain in their natal groups throughout their lives, maintaining close social bonds with their matrilineal kin (Silk et al. 2006a, b). Females can be ranked in a stable, linear dominance hierarchy that determines priority of access to resources. Daughters acquire ranks similar to those of their mothers. The stable core of a baboon group is therefore a hierarchy of matrilines, in which all members of one matriline (for example, matriline B) outrank or are outranked by all members of another (for example, matrilines C and A, respectively). Ranks within matrilines are as stable as those between matrilines: for example, A1>A2>A3>B1>B2>C1, where letters are used to denote matrilineal kin groups and numbers denote the different individuals within them (Cheney and Seyfarth 2007).

Baboon vocalizations are individually distinctive (e.g. Owren et al. 1997), and playback experiments have shown that listeners recognize the voices of others as the calls of specific individuals (reviewed in Cheney and Seyfarth 2007). The baboon vocal repertoire contains a number of acoustically graded signals, each of which is given in predictable contexts. Because calls are individually distinctive and each call type is predictably linked to a particular social context, baboon listeners can potentially acquire quite specific information from the calls that they hear.

Throughout the day, baboons hear individuals giving vocalizations to each other. Some interactions involve aggressive competition; for example, when a higher-ranking animal gives a series of threat-grunts to a lower-ranking animal and the latter screams. Threat-grunts are aggressive vocalizations given by higher-ranking to lower-ranking individuals, whereas screams are submissive signals, given primarily by lower- to higher-ranking individuals. A threat-grunt–scream sequence, therefore, potentially provides information not only about the identities of the opponents involved but also about who is threatening whom. Baboons are sensitive to both types of information. In playback experiments, listeners respond with apparent surprise to sequences of calls that appear to violate the existing dominance hierarchy. Whereas they show little response upon hearing the sequence 'B2 threat-grunts and C3 screams', they respond strongly—by looking toward the source of the call—when they hear 'C3 threat-grunts and B2 screams' (Cheney and Seyfarth 2007). Between-family rank reversals (C3 threat-grunts and B2 screams) elicit a stronger violation of expectation response than do within-family rank reversals (C3 threat grunts and C1 screams) (Bergman et al. 2003).

A baboon who ignores the sequence 'B2 threat-grunts and C3 screams' but responds strongly when she hears 'C3 threat-grunts and B2 screams' reveals, by her responses, that she recognizes the identities of both participants, their relative ranks, and their family membership. Baboons who react more strongly to call sequences that mimic a between-family rank reversal than to those that mimic a within-family rank reversal act as if they classify individuals simultaneously according to both rank and kinship. In all of these cases, listeners act as if they assume that the threat-grunt and scream have occurred together not by chance but because one vocalization caused the other to occur. Without this assumption of causality there would be no violation of expectation when B2's scream and C3's threat-grunt occurred together.

Baboons' ability to deduce a social narrative from a sequence of sounds reveals a rich cognitive system in which listeners extract a large number of complex, nuanced messages from a relatively small, finite number of signals. A baboon who understands that 'B2 threat-grunts and C3 screams' is different from 'C3 threat-grunts and B2 screams' can make the same judgement for all possible pairs of group members as well as any new individuals who may join. This open-ended system of classification is, in at least one respect, abstract, because the categories of rank and matrilineal kinship persist despite changes in the individuals who comprise them (Cheney and Seyfarth 2007).

In addition to making judgements based on social causation, rank, and kinship, baboons appear to recognize other individuals' intentions and motives. Baboon groups are noisy, tumultuous societies, and an individual would not be able to feed, rest, or engage in social interactions if she responded to every call as if it were directed at her. In fact, baboons seem to use a variety of behavioural cues, including gaze direction, learned contingencies, and the memory of recent interactions with specific individuals when making inferences about the target of a vocalization. For example, when a female hears a recent opponent's threat-grunts soon after fighting with her, she responds as if she assumes that the threat-grunt is directed at her, and she avoids the signaller. However, when she hears the same female's threat-grunts soon after grooming with her, she acts as if the calls are directed at someone else and ignores the calls (Engh et al. 2006).

The attribution of motives is perhaps most evident in the case of 'reconciliatory' vocalizations. Like many other group-living animals, baboons incur both costs and benefits from joining a group. In an apparent attempt to minimize the disruptive effects of within-group competition, many primates 'reconcile' with one another, by coming together, touching, hugging, or grooming after aggression. In baboons, reconciliation among females occurs after roughly 10% of all fights, and typically occurs when the dominant animal grunts to the subordinate. Playback experiments have shown that, even in the absence of other behaviour, grunts alone function to restore former opponents' behaviour to baseline levels (Cheney and Seyfarth 2007).

In some cases, the behaviour of subordinates after aggression seems to involve more complex and indirect causal reasoning both about other animals' motives and their kinship bonds. For example, playback experiments have shown that baboons will accept the 'reconciliatory' grunt by a close relative of a recent opponent as a proxy for direct reconciliation by the opponent herself (Wittig et al. 2007). If individual D1 has been threatened by individual A1 and then hears a grunt from A2, in the hour that follows she is more likely to approach, and more likely to tolerate the approaches of, A1 and A2 than if she had heard no grunt or a grunt from another high-ranking individual unrelated to the A matriline. Intriguingly, D1's behaviour toward other members of the A matriline does not change. Subjects in these experiments act as if they recognize that a grunt from a particular female is causally related to a previous fight, but only if the caller is a close relative of her former opponent (see Wittig 2010 for similar behaviour in chimpanzees).

# 4.4 SOCIAL COGNITION AS A
## PRECURSOR OF LANGUAGE

Baboon vocalizations (and, by extension, those of other monkeys and apes) exhibit no properties that we would be tempted to call syntactic. Nevertheless, their social knowledge, assessment of call meaning, and parsing of call sequences display a number of features that we may think of as syntactic precursors.

First, knowledge is representational. When a monkey hears a vocalization she acquires information that is highly specific—about a particular sort of predator, or about a particular individual, her motivation to interact in specific ways with another, or the other animal's reaction.

Second, knowledge is based on properties that have discrete values (Worden 1998), such as individual identity, kinship, dominance rank, and call type.

Third, animals combine these discrete-valued traits to create a representation of social relations that is based on at least two relations—matrilineal kinship and rank—simultaneously, in a manner that preserves ranks both within and across families (Penn et al. 2008).

Fourth, knowledge is rule-governed and open-ended. Baboons recognize that vocalizations follow certain rules of directionality that must, for instance, correspond to the current dominance hierarchy. Threat-grunts are given only by dominant animals to subordinates, fear barks are given only by subordinates to dominants, but infant and move grunts can be given in either direction. Knowledge is open-ended because new individuals can be added or eliminated without altering the underlying structure, and because the set of all possible interactions is very large (Worden 1998; Seyfarth and Cheney 2007). Taken together, these properties lead to a cognitive system in which animals comprehend a huge number of messages from a finite number of signals.

Fifth, knowledge involves the recognition of motives and causality and is therefore propositional. Baboons evaluate the meaning of call sequences in terms of other individuals' identities and motives and the causal relations that link one individual's behaviour with another. That is, they represent in their minds (albeit in a limited way) the individuated concepts of 'Sylvia', 'Hannah', 'threat-grunt', and 'scream', and combine these concepts to create a mental representation of one individual's intentions toward another. In so doing, they interpret a stream of sounds as a dramatic narrative: 'Sylvia is threatening Hannah and causing her to scream'. Once we accept the notion of causality—and there would be no violation of expectation without it—call sequences resemble the words in a sentence in at least one respect: they are compositional. Individual calls preserve their meaning but the sequence as a whole conveys a meaning that is greater than the sum of its parts.

Sixth, knowledge is independent of sensory modality. While playback experiments allow us to explore the structure of primates' social knowledge and demonstrate that such knowledge can be acquired through vocalizations alone, social knowledge is also obtained visually. Indeed, we now know that at the neurophysiological level, visual and auditory information are integrated to form a multimodal representation of call meaning (Gil da Costa et al. 2004; Ghazanfar et al. 2005; Proops et al. 2008).

These properties of non-human primates' social knowledge, while by no means fully human, bear important resemblances to the meanings we express in language, which are built up by combining discrete-valued entities in a structured, hierarchical, rule-governed, and open-ended manner. This leads to the hypothesis that the internal representations of language meaning in the human brain initially built upon our prelinguistic ancestors' knowledge of social relations (Bickerton 1998, 2000; Cheney and Seyfarth 1998; Worden 1998). Indeed, as Worden (1998: 156) argues, 'no other candidate meaning structure has such a good fit to language meanings'.

We are not suggesting that all of the syntactic properties found in language are present in primate social knowledge. Such a claim would be entirely unjustified, given the many features of language—like case, tense, subject-verb agreement, or recursion—that have no counterpart in the communication of any non-human primate and that almost certainly evolved long after the divergence of the hominin line from the common ancestors of humans and chimpanzees. Instead, focusing on the early, prelinguistic stages of language evolution, we suggest that the precursor of the hominoid mind evolved in an environment characterized by social challenges and that such competition created selective pressures favouring structured, hierarchical, rule-governed intelligence. Because this social intelligence shares several features with language, many of the rules and computations found in human language may have first appeared as an elaboration of the rules and computations underlying social cognition.

Talmy (2007) argues that during the course of evolution, a crucial bottleneck was overcome when our ancestors' vocal communication changed from analogue to digital, and he poses the question: where did language get its digitalness from? The answer, we believe, lies in perception and social cognition. Long before they could engage in the computations that underlie modern grammar, our ancestors perceived calls as discrete signals, recognized individuals, and performed the computations needed to understand their societies. As a result, the discrete, compositional structure we find in spoken language did not first appear there. It arose, instead, because understanding social life and predicting others' behaviour requires discrete, compositional thinking. (See also Studdert-Kennedy, this volume.)

Similarly, Hurford (1990a) asks whether propositional structures (among other features) are 'elements of the structure of languages' or whether they 'somehow existed before language' in another domain. Here again, data on primate social cognition provide an answer: the propositions that are expressed in language did not originate with language. They arose, instead, because to succeed in a social group of primates one must understand an elementary form of propositional relations.

## 4.5 BEYOND PRECURSORS

At some point in our evolutionary history—probably after the divergence of the evolutionary lines leading to chimpanzees and bonobos on the one hand and humans on the other (Enard et al. 2002)—our ancestors developed much greater control over the physiology of vocal production. As a result, vocal output became both more flexible and considerably more dependent on auditory experience and imitation (P. Lieberman 1991; Fitch 2007). What selective pressures gave rise to these changes?

Vocal communication in non-human primates lacks three features that are abundantly present in human language: the ability to generate new words, syntax, and a theory of mind (defined as the ability of both speakers and listeners to make attributions about each others' beliefs, knowledge, and other mental states when communicating with each other; see Grice 1957). How might these traits have evolved: simultaneously, in response to the same selective pressures, or more serially, in some particular order? We propose that the evolution of a theory of mind came first, creating the selective pressures that gave rise to the ability to generate new words and syntax, and to the flexibility in vocal production that these two traits would have required (Cheney and Seyfarth 2007). We make this argument on both empirical and theoretical grounds.

Empirically, there is no evidence in non-human primates for anything close to the large vocal repertoire we find even in very young children. Similarly, non-human primates provide few examples of syntax. Recent work on the alarm calls of forest monkeys suggests that the presence of one call type can 'modify' the meaning of another (Zuberbühler 2002; Arnold and Zuberbühler 2006; Zuberbühler, this volume), and a study by Crockford and Boesch (2003) suggests that a call combination in chimpanzees may carry new meaning that goes beyond the meaning of the individual calls themselves, but these rare exceptions meet few of the definitions of human syntax.

By contrast, there is growing evidence that both Old World monkeys and apes possess rudimentary abilities to attribute motives or knowledge to others and engage in simple forms of shared attention and social referencing (see Cheney and Seyfarth 2007 for review). These data suggest that a rudimentary theory of mind appeared among primates long before flexible vocal production, the ability to generate new words, and syntax. More speculatively, we suggest that the prior appearance of a theory of mind acted as a prime mover in the evolution of language because, while it is easy to imagine a scenario in which a rudimentary theory of mind preceded and provided the impetus for the evolution of large vocabularies and syntax, any alternative sequence of events seems less likely.

Consider, for example, word learning in children. Beginning as early as 9–12 months, children exhibit a nascent understanding of other individuals' motives, beliefs, and desires, and this skill forms the basis of a shared attention system that is essential for early word learning (Tomasello 2003a). One-year-old children seem to understand that words can be mapped onto objects and actions. Crucially, this understanding is accompanied by a kind of 'social referencing' in which the child uses other people's direction of gaze, gestures, and emotions to assign labels to objects (see Fisher and Gleitman 2002 for review). Gaze and attention also facilitate word learning in dogs and other animals. Children, however, rapidly surpass the simpler forms of shared attention and word learning demonstrated by animals. Long before they begin to speak in sentences, young children develop implicit notions of objects and events, actors, actions, and those that are acted upon. As Fisher and Gleitman (2002: 462) argue, these 'conceptual primitives' provide children with a kind of 'conceptual vocabulary onto which the basic linguistic elements (words and structures) are mapped'. Moreover, in contrast to monkeys, apes, and other animals, 1-year-old children are highly motivated to share what they know with others (Tomasello and Carpenter 2007). While animals are concerned with their own goals and knowledge, young children are motivated to make their thoughts and knowledge publicly available.

The acquisition of a theory of mind thus creates a cognitive environment that drives the acquisition of new words and grammatical skills. Indeed, results suggest that children could not increase their vocabularies or learn grammar as rapidly as they do if they did not have some prior notion of other individuals' mental states (Fisher and Gleitman 2002; Tomasello 2003a).

By contrast, it is much more difficult to imagine how our ancestors could have learned new words or grammatical rules if they were unable to attribute mental states to others. The lack of syntax in non-human primate vocalizations cannot be traced to an inability to understand that an event can be described as a sequence in which an agent performs some action on an object (as already noted, baboons clearly do this). Nor does the lack of syntax arise because of an inability to mentally represent actions or signs that modify objects. In captivity, a variety of animals, including dolphins, sea lions, and African Grey parrots, can be taught to under-stand and in some cases even produce signs that appear to represent actions, modifiers, and prepositions (see Cheney and Seyfarth 2007 for review). Even in their natural behaviour, non-human primates and other animals certainly seem capable of thinking in terms of propositions, but this ability does not motivate them to speak in sentences. Their knowledge remains largely private.

This limitation may arise because non-human primates and other animals cannot distinguish between what they know and what others know, and cannot recognize, for example, that an ignorant individual might need to have an event explained to them. As a result, although they may mentally tag events as propositions, they fail to map these relations into a communicative system in any stable or predictable way. Because they cannot attribute mental states like ignorance to others, and are unaware of the causal relation between behaviour and beliefs, monkeys and apes do not actively seek to explain or elaborate upon their thoughts. As a result, they are largely incapable of inventing new words or recognizing when thoughts should be made explicit.

We suggest, then, that while our prelinguistic ancestors represented the world—and the meaning of call sequences—in terms of actors, actions, and those who are acted upon, a crucial step in the evolution of language occurred when these ancestors began to express their tacit knowledge and use their cognitive skills in speaking as well as listening. The prime mover behind this revolution was a theory of mind that spurred individuals not only to recognize other individuals' goals, intentions, and even knowledge—as monkeys and apes already do—but also to share their own goals, intentions, and knowledge with others. Whatever selective pressures prompted this change, it led to a mind that was motivated to make public the thoughts that had previously remained private. The evolution of a theory of mind thus spurred the evolution of words, grammar, and the vocal modifiability that these traits required.

# ACKNOWLEDGEMENTS

We thank Thore Bergman, Lila Gleitman, Mark Liberman, and Leonard Talmy for comments. Research supported by NSF, NIH, The Leakey Foundation, and the University of Pennsylvania.

# CHAPTER 5

# COOPERATIVE BREEDING AND THE EVOLUTION OF VOCAL FLEXIBILITY

## KLAUS ZUBERBÜHLER

## 5.1 INTRODUCTION

Primates communicate not only because they are biologically hardwired to do so, but also because they pursue specific goals during social interactions. This is well documented in the context of ape gestural signals, which have revealed a considerable degree of flexibility in psychologically interesting ways (de Waal and Pollick, this volume). In terms of vocal behaviour, however, both monkeys and apes appear to be much less flexible, which raises important questions about how and why vocal flexibility evolved in the human lineage. One purpose of this chapter is to review some of the current empirical evidence for vocal flexibility in non-human primates both in terms of production and comprehension; see also Slocombe, this volume. The emerging picture is that, across the primate order, flexibility is widespread in call comprehension but largely restricted to humans in call production.

Non-human primates, including the great apes, are curiously constrained by weak motor control over their vocal apparatus, resulting in limited vocal repertoires.

Initially, human infants differ little from the other primates in their vocal behaviour, but they soon gain increasing control over their vocal apparatus. Why humans have evolved relatively greater motor control remains largely unclear. One possible explanation lies in the highly cooperative nature of humans, which is particularly manifest during childcare. Humans are cooperative breeders, which exposes infants to a range of caretakers in addition to the mother. Although cooperative breeding provides mothers with significant fitness benefits, infants do not seem to enjoy any particular advantage. Instead, infants grow up in a social environment in which they need to compete with each other for resources as well as the attention of their caregivers, who are often not directly related to them. A basic primate repertoire of vocal and gestural signals may have been insufficient for this social challenge. Following the advent of human cooperative breeding, natural selection would have favoured individuals with advanced vocal skills if such individuals enjoyed a selective advantage over their peers in interacting with caregivers (Hrdy 1999, 2009; Locke, this volume). Much of this change must have built on the vocal flexibility already established in the primate lineage.

## 5.2 INTENTION IN PRIMATE COMMUNICATION

When chimpanzees produce visual gestures, they often position themselves in such a way that the targeted receiver is able to see the signal (Call and Tomasello 2007). Similarly, captive orang-utans modify their gestures depending on how well they have been understood by others. If completely misunderstood, they continue signalling, but elaborate the range and avoid failed gestures. However, if only partly misunderstood, they repeat previous gestures more frequently (Cartmill and Byrne 2007). Bonobos, playing social games with a human experimenter (e.g. rolling a piece of fruit back and forth), show signs of understanding the collaborative nature of such games. When the experimenter deliberately interrupts the game, subjects respond with a variety of gestures in an apparent attempt to re-engage the reluctant human partner with the game (Pika and Zuberbühler 2008). In an important parallel to human language, these examples illustrate how signal production is adjusted and controlled by the individuals, presumably the outcome of communicative intent, rather than being a hardwired response to an external stimulus or a mere expression of mood or another inner state (Call and Tomasello 2007; de Waal and Pollick, this volume).

In the vocal domain, evidence for such goal-directedness and intentionality is less strong, although there are a number of relevant findings. For example, work on free-ranging Chacma baboons' vocal behaviour has produced evidence that these monkeys are surprisingly aware of the social consequences of their calls (Cheney and Seyfarth 2007; Seyfarth and Cheney, this volume). Studies on audience effects in primate vocal behaviour have also revealed considerable degrees of social awareness and complexity (Zuberbühler 2008). In one study, male Thomas langurs continued to alarm call to a predator model until all other group members had responded with at least one alarm call, and the interpretation was that callers kept track of who had already seen the predator (Wich and de Vries 2006). In another example, male blue monkeys produced significantly more alarm calls if members of their group were close to the suspected eagle than if they were far away, regardless of the caller's own position (Papworth et al. 2008). Although there are alternative explanations, one interpretation was that these primates took into account the degree of danger experienced by other group members.

As mentioned above, chimpanzees are sensitive to whether the intended audience is in visual contact, but this is not limited to gestural signals. If a human experimenter is oriented so that there is no visual contact with a chimpanzee, then individuals are more likely to produce vocalizations as their first communication signals, in contrast to when the experimenter is oriented towards the individual, which triggers more gesturing (Hostetter et al. 2001). Equally relevant, wild chimpanzee females adjust the production of copulation calls depending on who is likely to hear the calls. In general, females are reluctant to produce vocalizations during mating, unless mating with a high-ranking male when other high-ranking males are nearby. Presumably the females seek to spread the likelihood of paternity more widely amongst the socially relevant males, because this will secure their support in the future when they are travelling with a vulnerable infant. If high-ranking females are nearby, however, then females usually remain silent during copulation, regardless of whom they mate with, suggesting that they are aware of the potentially severe social consequences of female–female competition in wild chimpanzees (Townsend et al. 2007, 2008). These examples demonstrate how high degrees of social awareness, present in many primates, not only affect the gestural domain, but also drive primate vocal communication.

## 5.3 REFERENCE AND INFERENCE

Although there is good evidence that primates attend to each others' vocalizations to make predictions about the event encountered by the caller, it is not clear whether this requires specialist comprehension skills beyond what is already handled by general cognition. According to one view, a receiver has simply learned that one thing predicts another, or even causes another, in the same basic way as many other everyday phenomena (Tomasello 2008).

Whether all empirical evidence is sufficiently explained by this associative account—and how human comprehension fits into this model—is not clear. There is empirical evidence that, when responding to alarm calls, primates not only attend to the peripheral acoustic features of calls but also maintain specific mental representations associated with these calls (Zuberbühler et al. 1999a). In one experiment, Diana monkeys were first primed with the alarm calls of Campbell's monkeys, a species often found associating with Diana monkeys. The Diana monkeys responded with their own corresponding alarm calls, for instance by producing their own eagle alarm calls when hearing the Campbell's monkey eagle alarm calls. After a brief period of silence the same monkeys then heard a second playback stimulus, either the growls of a leopard or the shrieks of a crowned eagle. If the predator vocalizations corresponded to the previously heard alarm calls (e.g. leopard alarm calls followed by leopard growls), then the monkeys no longer responded to the predator vocalizations, but they behaved as if they were already aware of the predator's presence. If the prime and probe stimuli did not match in their semantic content (e.g. leopard alarm calls followed by eagle shrieks), then the responses to the predator vocalizations were strong (Zuberbühler 2000a). This behaviour appeared to be driven by mental representations of different predator classes, which allowed the monkeys to equate another species' predator alarm call (e.g. to an eagle) with the vocalizations of the corresponding predator (e.g. eagle shrieks).

Primates share their habitats with a range of other species, and often respond to their alarm calls. In many cases the call referents are unspecific and often ambiguous. For example, Diana monkeys respond to the alarm calls of guinea fowl, a gregarious ground-dwelling forest bird, as if a leopard were present. Guinea fowl alarm call to leopards on a regular basis, probably because they fall prey to them (Zuberbühler and Jenny 2002). However, the birds also produce the same alarm calls to humans, suggesting that their calls indicate little more than the presence of a dangerous ground predator. This poses a problem for nearby monkeys, such as Diana monkeys, because the most adaptive response to humans is to remain still and avoid detection, while the most adaptive response to leopards is to behave conspicuously to signal detection and futility of further hunting (Zuberbühler et al. 1999b). In one playback study, Diana monkeys were led to believe that a group of nearby guinea fowl had encountered either a leopard or a human poacher before hearing a recording of Guinea fowl alarm calls. The monkeys' responses to the birds' alarm calls differed significantly depending on the priming stimulus, i.e. likely cause of the alarm calls. Overall, the results suggest that the monkeys took into account wider contextual cues when evaluating vocalizations, rather than responding to the calls themselves (Zuberbühler 2000b).

In sum, a relevant finding in primate communication is that the meanings of vocal signals vary with how signallers use them. Often, listeners cannot rely on simple stimulus–response associations, but need to retrieve meaning through inferential processes. Whether such inference-based comprehension is similar to or different from the one used by humans during language processing has not yet been investigated.

## 5.4  CREATING MEANING FROM
## A LIMITED REPERTOIRE

Non-human primates are profoundly constrained by the number of acoustic signals the different species can produce (e.g. Jürgens 1998; Owren and Goldstein 2008; Seyfarth and Cheney, this volume). Despite this limitation, fieldwork has shown that primate vocalizations can function as semantic signals. In one classic study, East African vervet monkeys produced acoustically distinct alarm calls to different predator types, which were meaningful to listeners (Seyfarth et al. 1980). This basic finding has been replicated with other primate species, suggesting that vocal 'labelling' of external events is a widespread feature of primate communication (e.g. Zuberbühler et al. 1997; Ouattara et al. 2009). In addition to producing a range of basic call types, some species have been observed to enhance their small repertoires by acoustic modifications of existing call types or by producing sequences of calls. Both means of increasing flexibility in a limited system are discussed next.

### 5.4.1  Acoustic modifications

Careful examination of the call repertoires of non-human primates typically reveals that some of the basic call types can be subdivided into meaningful acoustic variants (e.g. Crockford and Boesch 2003; Lemasson and Hausberger 2004). Crucially, some of these call types, particularly the ones used in social interactions, are acoustically modifiable even during adulthood (Snowdon and Hausberger 1997; Lemasson et al. 2003, 2005). This type of vocal plasticity is the source of local dialects, a phenomenon observed in various primate species. Most recently, dialects have been described in free-ranging pygmy marmosets (de la Torre and Snowdon 2009). Similarly, chimpanzee pant-hoot vocalizations are acoustically flexible, and dialects and group-specific call variants have been reported in different populations (Marshall et al. 1999; Mitani et al. 1999; Crockford et al. 2004). These and other examples illustrate that, for some of their calls, non-human primates are able to produce a considerable degree of acoustic flexibility, a behaviour governed by social factors.

Equally interesting are cases of short-term acoustic modifications performed by adult individuals. A chimpanzee attacked by another individual produces victim screams which reveal something about the nature of the attack (Slocombe and Zuberbühler 2006b). Playback experiments have shown that individuals are able to discriminate between different scream variants by responding more strongly to variants that indicated a severe attack (Slocombe et al. 2009). In addition, if high-ranking individuals are nearby, victims tend to produce variants that indicate a more severe attack than has actually taken place, probably as an attempt to recruit nearby high-ranking group members to intervene on their behalf (Slocombe and Zuberbühler 2007; Slocombe, this volume). One intriguing possibility, which requires further testing, is that chimpanzees are socially aware of the impact of their screams and strategically modify the acoustic structure in order to influence the audience to their own advantage, essentially by producing false information.

Taken together, these studies show that non-human primates can acoustically modify some of their calls, usually in response to social variables or some aspects of their environment. Further research will have to address how widespread such phenomena are in the primate order and how much active volitional control callers have in these circumstances.

## 5.4.2 Combinatorial signals

Another way in which non-human primates can circumvent the constraints of their limited repertoires is by combining different call types into more complex sequences of calls in context-specific ways. Examples come from Campbell's monkeys (Zuberbühler 2002), Diana monkeys (Stephan and Zuberbühler 2008), black-and-white Colobus monkeys (Schel et al. 2009), gibbons (Clarke et al. 2006), chimpanzees (Crockford and Boesch 2005), and bonobos (Clay and Zuberbühler 2009). In the great ape examples, it is not yet clear whether the different sequences carry any specific meaning. In putty-nosed monkeys, however, callers combine two of their alarm calls, the 'pyows' and 'hacks', into sequences, which serve as the main carriers of meaning (Arnold and Zuberbühler 2006a, b). Series of 'pyows' are given to leopards and a range of other disturbances, while series of 'hacks', or hacks followed by 'pyows', are given to crowned eagles and other startling events, such as falling trees. More intriguingly, however, males also produce a 'pyow'–'hack' combination, which consists of a few 'pyows' followed by a few 'hacks'. This call combination can precede or be inserted into other call sequences or be produced alone. The common feature in all cases is that 'pyow'–'hack' combinations reliably predict group movement, irrespective of context (Arnold et al. 2008; Arnold and Zuberbühler 2008). The ontogenetic pattern of this behaviour has not yet been studied and it is also unclear whether all populations of putty-nosed monkeys in sub-Saharan Africa produce the same calling behaviour. In Diana monkeys, ontogenetic experience is required for callers to assemble individual alarm calls into more complex sequences (Stephan and Zuberbühler 2008).

Since some non-human primates produce series of calls arranged in specific ways in response to discrete events, should this behaviour be considered as a 'syntactic' precursor and therefore be of relevance for theories of human language evolution? A key point here is that, for a call sequence to be syntactic, each individual call in the sequence should have its own stable meaning, but at present there is no good evidence for this.

## 5.5 Transitions to speech

Although non-human primates have comparatively limited motor control over their articulators, the basic vocal tract structures and mechanisms of articulation are the same as in humans. Diana monkeys, for example, can generate various vocal tract constrictions and articulatory manoeuvres which alter the formant frequencies of their alarm calls in communicatively relevant ways (Riede and Zuberbühler 2003a, b). Unlike in human speech, however, the primate tongue does not appear to play an important role during articulation (Riede et al. 2005, 2006). In human infants, the acoustic features of possible sounds also depend on the physical structure of the vocal tract (Smith and Oller 1981). Imaging work has shown that the infant vocal tract initially grows rapidly, until the age of about 15 months, but then growth rates decrease and the vocal tract develops at a slower pace (Vorperian et al. 2005). The relationship between these physical changes and the portfolio of vocal signals available to the infant has yet to be explored.

As infants experience increasing motor control over their vocal apparatus, they begin to produce consonant- and vowel-like sound sequences, or babbling, in a range of social situations, a behaviour not observed in infant chimpanzees. Prior to this babbling phase, infants communicate with a primate-like vocal repertoire, which consists of a few basic call types, such as grunts, cries, screams, or laughter (Wolff 1969; McCune et al. 1996). As with non-human primates, the different calls can be meaningful to others in the sense that listeners are able to infer the cause of calling (Zeskind et al. 1985). Which articulators are involved, and in particular the role of the tongue during such call production, is a topic for further research, but there is currently no reason to assume that this process of call production is fundamentally different from that of non-human primates.

## 5.6 COOPERATIVE BREEDING AND THE EVOLUTION OF VOCAL FLEXIBILITY

A key transition in the evolutionary origins of language may have been when early humans began to interact with each other collaboratively (Tomasello 2008). Collaborative behaviours require a high degree of social awareness, such as the ability to understand and share intentions. One context in which collaborative social behaviour is particularly evident is during childcare. Humans are cooperative breeders with large amounts of childcare undertaken by individuals other than the mother (Hames 1988; Hrdy 1999, 2009; Hewlett and Lamb 2005). Although cooperative breeding is relatively common in non-human primates, there are considerable inter-species differences in quantity and quality, with no species matching the degree of allocare observed in humans (Hrdy 1976; Solomon and French 1997; Ross and MacLarnon 2000). Clutton-Brock (2006) distinguishes four types of cooperative breeding: group breeding (multiple females breed together), communal breeding (multiple females breed together and share care), facultative cooperative breeding (non-breeding helpers can be present), and specialized cooperative breeding (non-breeding helpers are essential). Humans fall into the last category, while most cooperatively breeding primates are group breeders.

Another way of categorizing breeding systems is by looking at the care given by non-maternal caregivers. Non-maternal care, or allocare, can range from energetically costly behaviour, such as lactation or carrying, to less demanding activities, such as playing or grooming (e.g. Poirer 1970; Redican and Mitchell 1974; Hershkovitz 1977; Biben and Symmes 1986). Across species, there is a strong relation between the amount of allocare given and the reproductive success of the mother (Mitani and Watts 1997; Ross and MacLarnon 2000). Allocare is particularly prominent in New World primates, but this is usually due to fathers helping with infant carrying. In Old World primates, allocare is relatively rare (with the exception of the Colobinae, e.g. Poirer 1970) and infants typically avoid the proximity of other adult females and prefer to play with other infants or juveniles (Forster and Cords 2005). Great apes, in particular, provide conspicuously little allocare, although cases of adoption by older siblings have been reported (e.g. Goodall 1989). In humans, allocare is likely to have played a major role during evolution (Pavard et al. 2007). Modern humans are very unusual in the amount of effort they are prepared to devote to infants who are not their own, with grandmothers providing an unusually large contribution (e.g. Scelza 2009). In addition to kin, mothers often entrust non-relatives with looking after their offspring (Hewlett and Lamb 2005). For example, in the Efe, a forager people of the Ituri forest in Eastern DR Congo, children grow up in peer-groups often looked after by a non-relative, while their mothers are on foraging trips (Henry et al. 2005).

Ape childhoods are very different. In Budongo Forest, a habitat very similar to Ituri forest, young chimpanzees stay continuously with their mothers until about the age of 10 to form a small family unit that travels, forages, rests, and nests together, often separated from the rest of the group. If mothers are in almost continued contact with their offspring, a basic vocal repertoire and ritualized gestural conventions (Call and Tomasello 2007) are fully sufficient to regulate all social interactions. However, the challenges are infinitely greater in a human-type cooperative care system. Competition over resources and caregiver attention is likely to be considerable, and non-maternal caregivers may be more reluctant to provide care than the mothers, suggesting that natural selection will favour behavioural mechanisms that help the infant to overcome such obstacles. Communication skills are the obvious evolutionary target.

Vocal signals are particularly adaptive if direct visual interaction between individuals is difficult and the risk of attracting malevolent eavesdroppers is low, particularly violent neighbours, infanticidal males, or predators. Across all species of primates, humans probably have by far the most vocal infants, especially if compared with the great apes. This suggests that humans have been relatively unconstrained in evolving vocal behaviour. When comparing the vocal behaviour of human and ape infants, a major difference concerns the advent of babbling sometime in the first 12 months of life. It is relevant that babbling triggers positive social responses in human receivers, regardless of kin relations, suggesting that the behaviour may have evolved on a pre-existing receiver predisposition (Locke 2006). By producing signals that receivers find attractive as well as easy to detect, discriminate, and remember, human infants have evolved a communication tool that aids them with their species-specific social challenges (e.g. Guilford and Dawkins 1991; Locke, this volume).

Babbling is also found in some non-human animals, particularly songbirds (e.g. Goldstein et al. 2003; Aronov et al. 2008) but also in greater sac-winged bats (Knornschild et al. 2006). In primates, one intriguing example comes from the pygmy marmoset, a facultative cooperative breeder with bi-parental care (Elowson et al. 1998a, b; Snowdon and Elowson 2001). Pygmy marmosets are highly vocal as infants, producing over a dozen different call types at high rates. The different calls are assembled into sequences, which can last for several minutes. Some of the call types are specific to infants; others resemble the adult calls, or are acoustic variants thereof. Similarly to humans, the main function of infant pygmy marmoset babbling appears to be in increasing social bonding: parents are more likely to interact with a babbling than an otherwise active infant (Elowson et al. 1998a).

During puberty, babbling is still observed, although at lower rates, and the behaviour eventually disappears in adulthood (Snowdon and Elowson 2001). So far, the vocal behaviour of pygmy marmosets remains an isolated case in the primate literature. To what degree babbling is crucial for the development of adult vocal behaviour is also not explored, although adult pygmy marmosets possess considerable vocal flexibility, as evidenced by the presence of vocal dialects and other effects (e.g. Snowdon and Hodun 1981; Elowson and Snowdon 1994; Converse et al. 1995).

Once vocal control has evolved to help infants secure care, it is only a small step to producing utterances in context-specific ways. This may only be possible against a background of other psychological skills, such as the ability to share intentions and attention (Tomasello 2008), and well-developed comprehension. The key invention, however, is increased motor control over the articulators, and once this is established, vocal behaviour can become subject to learning and voluntary control.

At present, the proposed link between cooperative breeding and enhanced vocal control clearly requires further empirical investigation. Specifically, whether high degrees of allocare have had an effect on the evolution of vocal behaviour in human infants remains to be tested. It is interesting that high degrees of allocare have been linked with other types of infant signalling (Alley 1980). Using data from 82 primate species, Ross and Regan (2000) found considerable variation in the coat colour of newborn primates. Species with high degrees of allocare tended to give birth to infants that were brightly or conspicuously coloured, whereas species with little or no allocare produced very inconspicuous infants. If allo-mothering is essential, infants will benefit from advertising their need for care to attract the attention of conspecific caregivers at birth. The colobines, a group of Old World primates with the highest degrees of allocare (apart from humans), give birth to infants that are initially almost completely white, in stark contrast to the black coat of adults (Davies and Oates 1994).

Another prediction is that species in which infants are exposed to competition over non-maternal caregivers should be more likely to exhibit elaborate vocal behaviour than species in which infants are raised by their mothers only. Research on the communicative skills of other cooperative breeders, particularly communal breeders, may provide interesting empirical data to test this hypothesis. Hrdy (1999, 2009) recently made similar arguments, suggesting that human infants are equipped with especially powerful tools to solicit and secure care, not just from their mothers but potentially any involved bystander. Vocal control may have been the crucial component of this tool kit, subsequently paving the way to the elaborate and unique speech abilities of modern humans.

# ACKNOWLEDGEMENTS

Much of the reviewed fieldwork was funded by the Leverhulme Trust, the BBSRC, the European Commission (FP6, 'What it means to be human'), and the European Science Foundation ('Origins of Man, Language, and Languages'). I am grateful to the Wissenschaftskolleg zu Berlin for additional support, and to T. Riede, M. Tomasello, V. Kersken, M. Laporte, C. Hobaiter, D. Perrett, C. Cäsar, A. Whiten, R. Byrne, T. Fitch, R. Sprengelmeyer, J. S. McClung, J. C. Gomez, K. Gibson, and M. Tallerman for helpful comments.

# CHAPTER 6

# GESTURE AS THE MOST FLEXIBLE MODALITY OF PRIMATE COMMUNICATION

## FRANS B. M. DE WAAL AND AMY S. POLLICK

## 6.1 INTRODUCTION

An understanding of the complex issue of language evolution must be grounded in a range of disciplines, including linguistics, psychology, neuroscience, philosophy, archaeology, and primatology. The evolution of language is typically debated within a hypothetical framework, but we can look to extant non-human primate communication to help shape the discussion. While the vocal modality has seemed to be a naturally continuous one for complex communication, Corballis (this volume) and others (e.g. Arbib et al. 2008) have argued that hominin ancestors used manual gesture in a linguistic capacity prior to speech.

One of the most interesting and least studied forms of social communication in apes is gesture. All four species of great ape—bonobo, chimpanzee, gorilla, and orang-utan—use their hands to communicate, but gestures are difficult to study in the wild. A notable exception is one of the first reports on gestures in wild chimpanzees by Goodall (1968). The most detailed studies of gesture historically concerned human-reared individuals trained to use American Sign Language (Gardner et al. 1989).

In this chapter we will review gestures that we studied in two species of great ape, chimpanzees and bonobos. The gestural origin of language theory offers a tantalizing scenario for what human language may have looked like in its early stages, and we will review the data on ape gestures that support this theory, or rather, a suggested modified version.

## 6.2 Manual gestures in apes

Genetically equidistant from humans, chimpanzees (*Pan troglodytes*) and bonobos (*P. paniscus*) diverged from the line that produced our species approximately 6 million years ago (Patterson et al. 2006), whereas the two ape species themselves split apart approximately 2.5 million years ago (Sarich 1984). Studying similar types of communicative signals in closely related species allows one to determine homologies, i.e., shared evolutionary ancestry. A gesture that occurs in both of these apes as well as humans was likely present in our last common ancestor.

If we are going to draw any evolutionary comparison between ape gestures and human language, we need to narrowly define gesture as communication by means of hands, feet, or limbs (cf. Pollick and de Waal 2007). Restricting the study of gestures in apes to the limbs is crucial because the perception of manual activity in monkeys has been shown to be neurologically distinct. In humans, Broca's area, the neural region that is involved in speech production, is also active during the observance and performance of manual gestures but not other body movements (Rizzolatti et al. 1996b). Hence, a sharp distinction needs to be drawn (though not all primate gesture studies observe this) between manual gestures and any other non-vocal bodily-based forms of communication.

Another reason to pay special attention to manual gestures is that they seem to be a recent addition to primate communication. Whereas all primates regularly use vocalizations, orofacial movements, body postures, and locomotion patterns, gestures are typical of humans and apes (de Waal 2003). Descriptions of wild and captive apes' gestures span several decades, starting with chimpanzees (Goodall 1968; van Hooff 1973), followed by other anthropoid apes: bonobos (de Waal 1988;

Pika et al. 2005a, b), gorillas (Tanner and Byrne 1996), and orang-utans (Liebal et al. 2006). Facial expressions and vocalizations are common in all of the primates, but, with rare exceptions, monkeys lack free, ritualized hand gestures. As opposed to monkeys, chimpanzees and bonobos wave at each other, shake their wrists when impatient, beg for food with open hands held out, flex their fingers towards themselves when inviting contact, move an arm over a subordinate in a gesture of dominance, and so on (Pollick et al. 2008).

Beyond behaviour, gesture has certain indelible characteristics in the ape brain. Apes and humans gesture more with the right hand than the left hand (Hopkins and de Waal 1995), and because the right hand is left-brain controlled, this means that ape gestures share the same lateralization as human language (Hopkins and Vauclair, this volume). Another recent body of neurological work revolving around mirror neurons (see Arbib, this volume) intriguingly underscores the importance of gesture in the evolution of language.

## 6.3 FLEXIBLY DEFINED MEANING PRECEDES SYMBOLIC COMMUNICATION

The discontinuity between the Hominoidea and all other primates regarding the gestural modality suggests a relatively recent shift towards a more flexible and intentional communicative strategy in our pre-hominin ancestors (de Waal 2003). One mark of this shift is contextually defined usage—that is, a single gesture may communicate entirely different needs or intentions depending on the social context in which it is used. For example, a bonobo stretching out an open hand towards a third party during a fight signals a need for support, whereas the same gesture towards a possessor of food signals a desire for a share (de Waal and van Hooff 1981; Pika et al. 2005a, b; Pollick and de Waal 2007). Gestures are less closely tied to specific emotions than are vocalizations (Pika et al. 2005a, b; Pollick and de Waal 2007), which probably results from greater cortical control of the manual modality (Wiesendanger 1999).

Because many gestures do not seem tied to a specific social situation, there is a great deal of equipotentiality in these communicative signals, and we don't really understand how they acquire meaning, both ontogenetically and phylogenetically. Pollick and de Waal (2007), using context of usage as a proxy for meaning, found that gestures showed far looser contextual associations than facial or vocal signals. Two captive bonobo groups and two captive chimpanzee groups were videotaped for social interactions initiated by a gesture, vocalization, or facial expression. Chimpanzees used gestures 56% of the time to initiate exchanges, both facial and vocal signals 22% of the time, and combinations of gestures with facial/vocal signals 22% of the time. In the bonobos' repertoire, on the other hand, 78% were gestures, 14% were facial/vocal signals, and 8% were combinations. The most significant difference here is that chimpanzees combined their gestures with other signals more frequently than did bonobos (see separate data below).

For each communicative behaviour we calculated a Context-Tie Index (CTI), which is the percentage of interactions in which the signal occurred in its most typical context (e.g. affiliation, agonism, food, grooming, play, sex, and locomotion). We then compared the CTI for gestures with that for facial/vocal signals for each species. As predicted, the average gesture had a significantly lower CTI than the average facial/vocal signal in both bonobos and chimpanzees, meaning that facial expressions and vocalizations were more closely associated with specific social contexts than gestures. This was also clear if context-association was correlated between groups of the same species. Thus, the facial expressions silent bared teeth and relaxed open mouth showed extremely high correlations across contexts as did the vocalizations scream and pant hoot. None of the gestures, in contrast, reached high contextual correlations. Half the gestures even correlated negatively across contexts, suggesting dramatically different context-associations in each species.

Gestures showed greater contextual variation than facial and vocal displays between species as well. Comparing the two separate bonobo groups, facial/vocal signals showed significant overlap in context usage, but gestures did not. Thus, knowing how one species uses facial expressions or vocalizations allows one to predict how they will be used by the other species, whereas the same cannot be said for gestures, and sometimes not even how other members of the same species in another group will use them. For example, the facial expression silent bared teeth and the vocalization scream were almost always produced in a fearful, subordinate context in both ape species, yet the gesture arm raise was used mostly in play in bonobos, whereas in chimpanzees it was used mostly to solicit grooming.

This suggests that the meaning of a signal like arm raise, or any other manual gesture, is informed by other signals as well as by the situation, and that individuals need to interpret these signals in light of the entire behavioural context (de Waal and van Hooff 1981). The flexibility of this class of signals suggests that gestural communication may have been the means through which symbolic meaning was acquired in our hominin ancestors, perhaps alongside referential vocalizations (Corballis 2002; McNeill et al. 2008).

## 6.4 APE USE OF GESTURE

Characteristics that we share with apes but not monkeys likely evolved recently, hence may have provided a basis for the development of even more unique patterns found only in humans (de Waal 2003). In this context, the difference in gesture usage between apes and monkeys is highly relevant, and becomes even more intriguing if we consider that apes likely possess greater control over the production of gestures versus other signals (Wiesendanger 1999). This hypothesis is supported by several observations, and the case of cultural (meaning variations in behaviour between different populations of the same species) transmission of gestures is one example. Just as there are cultural variations of gestures in humans, population-specific communicative behaviours are also known to exist in chimpanzees, such as leaf-clipping (Nishida 1980) and handclasp grooming (McGrew and Tutin 1978). In chimpanzees and all other great apes species, gestures are more culture-specific than facial expressions, which tend to be relatively invariant. The tendency of cultural communication to be non-facial and non-vocal is probably due to the ape's limited control over face and voice. In humans, too, facial expressions seem universal (Ekman 1972b), whereas gestures often vary by culture (Kendon 1995).

That apes appear to have greater cortical control over limb movements than vocalizations is further supported by observations that while efforts to teach chimpanzees to modify their vocalizations have failed dismally (Hayes 1952), non-vocal paradigms have had more success. While apes do not employ consistent grammatical patterns, they can learn to use signs from American Sign Language appropriately in terms of meaning (Gardner et al. 1989). In fact, each great ape species has been successfully taught to communicate using visual and manual signals; see Gibson, Chapter 3, for review. Both chimpanzees and bonobos have learned to use a keyboard containing symbols, which they point to in sequence to deliver messages. Kanzi, a bonobo, spontaneously added gestures to this repertoire (Savage-Rumbaugh et al. 1998).

Greater control over gestures is further suggested by observations of deception, in which apes may use their hands to modify a facial expression (de Waal 1982), or a vocalization. This is no doubt why in so-called ape language studies the forelimbs have proven a more promising candidate for intentional communication than the voice. Goodall (1986) reported how a chimpanzee attempted to muffle his excited pant-hoot signalling the discovery of food by covering his mouth with his hand, presumably in an attempt to keep the food to himself. Note that monkeys also seem to have great difficulty producing vocal signals in the absence of a triggering situation (Goodall 1986).

## 6.5 MULTIMODAL SIGNALLING

Communicative signals such as vocalizations, gestures, and facial expressions are often produced in combinations, in both humans and apes. A deeper understanding of the evolution of communication and language must be based on comparative studies of vocal as well as other communicative abilities, and how the signals work in concert to convey information. Rather than gesture alone, it may be that multimodal communication was the springboard for the evolution of the almost infinite flexibility of human language.

There are many ways to characterize multimodal signalling, from the documentation of modalities involved to the description of complex temporal patterns. Of course, apes employ a battery of communicative signals, including head movement, posture, and gaze, but we are concerned here with three of the more distinguishable and easily observed signals: manual gestures, facial expressions, and vocalizations, and again, only those that initiated social interactions.

As noted above, our research (Pollick and de Waal 2007; Pollick et al. 2008) revealed that the multimodal signalling of bonobos included facial and vocal signals in equal numbers, whereas that of chimpanzees included more vocalizations. That is, chimpanzees more often combined their gestures with a vocalization, whereas bonobos exhibited no bias toward either a facial expression or a vocalization when combining their gestures with other signals. Chimpanzees aren't necessarily more vocal than bonobos; the discrepancy is likely the result of more combinations in agonistic situations, which usually involve vocalizing. Within a combination, the facial or vocal signal tended to occur first, before the gesture (cf. van Hooff 1973). It may be that facial/vocal signals are more easily triggered and more emotional, and the subsequent gesture informs or emphasizes the meaning of the first signal in a more deliberate manner.

While there was no overall difference in the production rates of the various signals, chimpanzees combined their gestures with facial and vocal signals more than bonobos did (22% vs. 8%, respectively, in a direct comparison; see Pollick 2006). Interestingly, though bonobos produced fewer combinations, these were more likely to elicit a response from the receiver than similar combinations did in chimpanzees. The combinations of gestures and facial or vocal signals we observed in bonobos were significantly more effective in getting the recipient to alter its behaviour (defined as any change in observable behaviour within 10 seconds of the signal). For example, an individual performs a reach out up gesture accompanied by a relaxed open-mouth facial expression, which results in the targeted recipient approaching the signaller and engaging in play (as opposed to the gesture alone, which the recipient ignores). Possibly, the relative scarcity of combinations in bonobos renders them more salient and more likely to affect behaviour.

## 6.6 Species differences

How the gestural patterns differ between chimpanzees and bonobos serves as interesting contrast. For example, when stretching the arm and hand out in a gesture, the palm can be facing upwards, downwards, or to the side (a distinction made for chimpanzees by van Hooff 1973). We did not observe the three being used interchangeably, however, with respect to social context: the reach out side gesture was more often made in food contexts, reach out up was made typically when requesting a grooming session, and reach out down was often produced in play (Pollick 2006). Of the 32 manual gestures we observed, bent wrist was rarely produced and when it was, it was never in an agonistic situation. This is a stark contrast with chimpanzees, who often use this gesture to ask for or provide appeasement (Goodall 1968).

There are several other differences between bonobo and chimpanzee communication that may make bonobos the better model regarding the prerequisites of language evolution. This has already been noted for vocal communication (Taglialatela et al. 2003), which appears more dialogue-like in bonobos, and includes soft peeps to draw attention to and 'comment' on novel items or environmental events (de Waal 1988), a characteristic shared with human infant language development (Tomasello and Carpenter 2007). Additionally, gesture patterns in one chimpanzee group allow one to predict the usage of the same gestures in another, which does not apply to bonobos, who are culturally more diverse in their gesture usage. Second, when bonobos combine gestures with facial/vocal signals, they are more effective at eliciting a response than when they use gestures alone (Pollick et al. 2008). That this contrast between multimodal and single modality utterances held only for bonobos is interesting, given that multimodal combinations are less common in bonobos. As noted above, this relative scarcity of multimodal signalling in bonobos may relate to a more deliberate combination of gestures with other forms of communication, perhaps in an attempt to add critical information to the message instead of merely amplifying it.

Although they are genetically equidistant to us, the question of which of our two closest relatives most resembles the last common ancestor of humans and apes remains unanswered. But we speculate that the bonobo's variable gestural repertoire and high responsiveness to combinatorial signalling characterized our early ancestors, and that these features in turn may have served as stepping stones for the evolution of symbolic communication.

## 6.7 CONCLUSIONS

Manual gestures play a significant role in great ape communication. The flexible nature of these gestures is underscored by the fact that facial expressions and vocalizations correlate to a much higher degree with specific contexts than do gestures. Gestures are also evolutionarily younger, as evidenced by their presence in apes but not monkeys, and are likely under greater cortical control than vocalizations. Unlike vocalizations, manual gestures have been repeatedly shown to be flexible signals that can be divorced from highly arousing contexts, although recent work has elucidated further nuances in primate vocal communication (Slocombe; Zuberbühler, this volume). This makes gesture a serious candidate modality to have acquired symbolic meaning in early hominins. While this supports the gestural origin hypothesis of language, it is impossible to rule out an alternative scenario (see Goldin-Meadow, this volume) in which gestures and early speech signals co-evolved.

# CHAPTER 7

# HAVE WE UNDERESTIMATED GREAT APE VOCAL CAPACITIES?

## KATIE SLOCOMBE

## 7.1 A NEGLECTED AREA OF RESEARCH

Considerable research effort has been dedicated to vocal communication in primates, and has revealed communicative and cognitive traits in non-human primates that have relevance for language evolution (see Zuberbühler, this volume). The vast majority of vocal communication studies to date have, however, focused on monkey species (Slocombe et al. 2011). In contrast both to research into monkey vocal communication and to research on other aspects of great ape behaviour, research into great ape vocalizations has been surprisingly limited.

This relative paucity of information on great ape vocal behaviour has serious consequences for our understanding of language evolution. First, given that apes outperform monkeys on many cognitive tasks (Tomasello and Call 1997), further research on great apes may reveal that they use their vocalizations in more sophisticated ways than monkeys, possibly demonstrating more commonalities with humans. Second, given the imbalance of research effort to date (Slocombe et al. 2011), current evidence appears to indicate that monkeys communicate in a more complex manner than great apes (Tomasello 2008). But if vocal traits are homologous, we would expect to find apes somewhere in between monkeys and humans in terms of complexity, just as we do for gestural communication (Tomasello 2008). If this is not the case for vocalizations, then the monkeys' sophisticated abilities may be the product of convergent rather than homologous evolution.

In what follows, I outline what we know so far about great ape vocalization.

## 7.2 FUNCTIONAL REFERENCE

Many different species of monkeys produce calls in response to specific external events (e.g. predator defence, food discovery, agonistic interactions) and these calls function referentially, conveying information about the ongoing event to listeners (see Zuberbühler, this volume). Comparable evidence for this ability in great apes had been absent until relatively recently. Great apes, in contrast to monkeys, do not face severe predation pressure. Consequently, the first evidence for functional reference in great apes came not from predator alarm calls, but from food-associated calls.

Chimpanzees often produce rough grunt calls in response to food (Marler and Tenaza 1977), and a study in captivity revealed that within their graded call system, chimpanzees produce acoustically distinct rough grunt variants in response to food of different quality (Slocombe and Zuberbühler 2006). Distinct rough grunt variants were elicited by high-, medium-, and low-preference foods and, in addition, food-specific calls were given in response to high-value foods (bread, banana, and mango). This high level of specificity for individual food types has not been found in monkey species. Food-specific calling was not, however, replicated using data from wild chimpanzees, indicating that this pattern of calling probably did reflect differences in the perceived value of the food; in captivity, the type of food is the main determinant of food value, as quantity, ripeness, and quality of food remain relatively uniform. A playback experiment showed that a listening chimpanzee was able to extract information about the value of available food from rough grunt calls and to use the information to maximize his own foraging (Slocombe and Zuberbühler 2005a). A young male, Liberius, heard rough grunts given to bread (high value) or apples (low value), and he then demonstrated significantly greater search effort for the food that corresponded to whichever grunts he heard. This represented the first evidence of functional reference in a great ape. It is still unclear what level of specificity was extracted from these calls: high- or low-value food, or apple and bread. The single subject also makes this finding difficult to generalize. However, these findings have recently been replicated at a different site (Slocombe et al., in prep).

Bonobos, like chimpanzees, have also been shown to give specific call types in response to foods of different qualities (Clay and Zuberbühler 2009). Bonobos commonly produce five call types in response to food, and calling bouts contain different proportions of these call types as a function of food quality. A recent playback experiment, similar in design to that conducted with chimpanzees, has shown that listeners can extract useful information from these call bouts (Clay and Zuberbühler 2011). Listening bonobos distinguished between call bouts given to kiwis (highly preferred) and apples (less preferred). Instead of attending to the individual calls, bonobos used the whole call sequence to make correct inferences about the kind of food that was available.

Chimpanzee barks are also produced in a context-specific manner, indicating they have the potential to function referentially. Crockford and Boesch (2003) found that wild adult male chimpanzees produced different bark variants in response to snakes, and whilst hunting. These barks were sometimes combined with other calls or drumming and when produced in conjunction with other signals they were highly context specific. Playback experiments are now required to assess whether recipients extract meaningful information from these context-specific calls.

Chimpanzees, like many other species, vocalize during agonistic interactions, and systematic examination of these screams reveals further examples of context-specific calling. Chimpanzees commonly scream as the victim of aggression, but they also scream in the role of aggressor, usually if attacking an individual of equal or higher rank. Victim and aggressor screams, although highly graded calls, have been shown to be acoustically distinct signals (Slocombe and Zuberbühler 2005b). A playback experiment performed in captivity showed that listeners understood the respective roles (victim and aggressor) of the protagonists in a simulated fight just by listening to the screams (Slocombe et al. 2010a). In this study, listeners heard two sequences of calls from an adjacent room into which they could not see. One sequence simulated an incongruous interaction that violated the dominance hierarchy, while the other simulated a commonplace interaction in line with the existing social order. Listeners showed significantly more interest in the incongruous sequence of screams, thus showing that they had understood the respective roles of the callers and thus the anomalous direction of the aggression. In addition to providing information about the role of the caller, agonistic screams also reflect the severity of aggression experienced by the victim (Slocombe and Zuberbühler 2007). The researchers found that the acoustic structure of victim screams varied systematically as the aggression experienced by the caller increased from mild to severe. A playback study conducted in the wild indicated that listeners could meaningfully distinguish between the screams given to mild and severe aggression (Slocombe et al. 2009). Although these calls meet the production and perception criteria for functional reference, it is a matter of debate whether the information they provide to listeners is truly external or an index of the caller's arousal and emotional state.

## 7.3 Flexibility in production

Primate calls have been dismissed by some as cognitively uninteresting, inflexible, involuntary reflexes that are not particularly relevant for understanding language evolution (e.g. Tomasello 2008). Recent findings challenge this assumption and show that great ape vocal production is flexible in a number of ways.

First, a number of studies have shown that calls are not just indiscriminately broadcast as a reflexive response to external stimuli. Call production in chimpanzees seems to be sensitive to subtle and complex social factors, including the composition of the audience. The production of copulation calls by females is influenced by the rank of the copulating partner and the identity of those in the immediate vicinity (Townsend et al. 2008). Females tend to inhibit calls when high ranking females are in the audience, probably as a result of high female–female competition observed at the study site (Townsend et al. 2007). Adult females also show flexibility in the production of pant grunt vocalizations which function as greeting signals directed at specific individuals of higher social rank (Laporte and Zuberbühler 2010). Females produced these calls in only 16% of encounters with other group members, showing they were not obligatory signals. Calls were produced across neutral, aggressive, and affiliative contexts, and if the alpha male was present, females were significantly less likely to greet a lower ranking male with a pant grunt. Males also display sensitivity to audience composition and preferentially produce rough grunts (food-associated calls) when a close social partner is in the vicinity to benefit from them (Slocombe et al. 2010b). In agonistic interactions, when the level of aggression faced by the victim is severe, the victim modulates the acoustic structure of their scream vocalizations if there is an individual in the audience who could help them (Slocombe and Zuberbühler 2007). More specifically, if an individual is present who outranks the aggressor, the victim will produce screams that are indicative of extremely severe aggression. By exaggerating the level of aggression experienced, callers may be more likely to receive help from high-ranking bystanders.

Orang-utans have also been shown to produce functionally deceptive sounds (Hardus et al. 2009a). When orang-utans encounter predators they produce kiss-squeak sounds, thought to function as a threat towards the predator. In situations of acute danger, orang-utans will create a leaf tool and hold this to their lips before producing a kiss-squeak. This lowers the frequency of their call, creating the impression of a larger bodied animal.

Secondly, the acoustic structure of existing vocalizations can be modified, likely through a process of vocal learning. There is some evidence for group-specific versions of a call, or dialects, arising in chimpanzees. The long-distance pant hoot has been shown to have subtly different acoustic parameters in different communities of chimpanzees, and although early studies found it difficult to exclude genetic and environmental differences driving the observed differences in call structure (Mitani et al. 1999), more recent work provides stronger evidence for vocal learning. In particular, studies of three adjacent communities of chimpanzees in Taï forest, Côte d'Ivoire, where the environment is shared and the groups are genetically similar, still found different pant hoot structures for each group (Crockford et al. 2004). Playback experiments have shown that these chimpanzees can distinguish between the pant hoots of neighbouring community members and strangers, indicating that group-specific signatures may be important for the quick identification of different non-group members in this territorial species (Herbinger et al. 2009). Further suggestion of vocal learning comes from Kanzi, the language-competent bonobo, whose peep calls for different events have certain structural similarities to the human words for these items (Taglialatela et al. 2003). The authors argue that these peep variants were unique to Kanzi, and have been formed through a process of imitating the human words in these contexts; however, more data on peep variants naturally produced by a representative sample of bonobos is needed to thoroughly evaluate this claim.

Finally, although the basic vocal repertoire of great apes appears to be largely fixed, some evidence shows that novel vocalizations and sounds can be produced. First, population-specific vocalizations have been identified in orang-utans, with seven call types present at some study sites, but absent at others (Hardus et al. 2009b). The authors suggest that these vocalizations may be local 'cultural' innovations; however, the identification of such population-specific calls relies on the absence of these calls in certain populations. It is difficult to conclude that something is definitely absent, given differing observation time and research foci across sites.

More robust evidence for the production of novel sounds comes from captive chimpanzee populations, who produce raspberry sounds, which have never been reported in the wild (Hopkins et al. 2007). These calls seem to function as attention-getting signals, and the authors argue they represent novel acoustic signals, challenging the assumption that vocal communication in primates cannot be generative (Tomasello 2008). In addition, a female orang-utan has been reported to spontaneously copy human whistling and is now proficient in producing this novel sound (Wich et al. 2009). The orang-utan's whistles don't seem to have a particular communicative function, but she does imitate the duration and number of whistles produced by human models. This study shows that novel sounds can be acquired in great apes and are likely spread through imitative processes. It is important to note, however, that the sound innovations discussed here do not engage the larynx, which is crucial for human speech (Fitch 2000a).

## 7.4 CALL COMBINATIONS

Important recent advances have been made in our understanding of call combinations in various monkey species (see Zuberbühler, this volume). Comparable systematic research has not been conducted in great ape species; however, one study has revealed that call combinations are a common aspect of chimpanzee vocal communication, with just fewer than half the vocalizations produced by the wild chimpanzees of Taï forest being produced in combination with other call types to form a sequence (Crockford and Boesch 2005). Call combinations seem to be an important part of chimpanzee vocal communication and as such deserve systematic research to investigate if the messages conveyed by calls in combinations are different from the constituent parts.

## 7.5 OUTSTANDING ISSUES

Although the research discussed here shows the potential of great ape vocalizations to demonstrate many interesting properties that are relevant for our understanding of language evolution, much work remains to be done. Compared to the wealth of studies conducted on monkeys in this modality, little is known about the great apes. Within the great apes, the vocalizations of gorillas and bonobos have still received virtually no attention.

Many issues need resolving, and numerous areas require more systematic investigation. In particular, the issue of the degree of volition and intentionality that drives call production in great apes must be addressed, as this currently represents a chasm between human and non-human primate vocal communication. Given that gestures seem to be produced intentionally (Tomasello 2008; de Waal and Pollick, this volume), great ape species appear to have the capacity for this kind of communication; whether it occurs in the vocal modality needs to be empirically tested. Call combinations provide an exciting and potentially fruitful area to explore, which may reveal high levels of complexity. Most vocal studies to date have focused on evolutionarily urgent contexts; great apes also produce vocalizations in relaxed social contexts, which are associated with highly flexible gesture production. If we examine vocal production in these contexts we may see a level of flexibility in vocal production currently associated only with gestures. More research on how great apes perceive each others' calls is also required: many of the great ape calls are highly graded, and if these continuums are perceived categorically by conspecifics, the repertoire sizes could be far bigger than we currently estimate.

# CHAPTER 8

...............................................

# BIRD SONG AND LANGUAGE

...............................................

## PETER SLATER

There are several reasons why bird song might be of interest to those studying human language. First, and most obviously, it is a system of communication. Birds use sounds to communicate with one another. We call the most elaborate of these sounds 'song', and songs are largely used by males in the breeding season to keep rivals out of their territories and to attract mates (Catchpole and Slater 2008). But there are many other simpler sounds, usually labelled as calls, which fulfil other functions and are often used by both sexes throughout the year. Contact calls help birds that move around in flocks to keep in touch with one another; alarm calls tell others when there is a predator about. These are just two examples, but a given bird species may have 20 or so different types of call, each with a distinct function.

A second similarity is that much of the complex communication that birds have, involving both songs and call notes, uses sounds. There is a good reason for this which also extends to the use of sounds by other animals, including ourselves. Sounds can be changed rapidly, so can convey a lot of information in a short period of time. Provided an animal is large enough, the sounds it produces can also travel long distances. Sounds can go round corners and are as useful by night as they are by day, both features that give them an advantage over visual signals. The third main modality, that of smell, has the advantage of persistence, as when the scent marks of one dog are sensed by another days later, but is certainly not appropriate for the transfer of a complex and changing stream of information. So it is not surprising that sound is the modality of choice in the signals of many animals, especially where the speedy transfer of complex and detailed information is required.

Beyond these two basic similarities comes a third, superficially more important, one: birds, like human beings, often have a huge repertoire of different sounds (Slater 2000). While they may only have a few different sorts of call notes that signal very specific things, some birds have a vast repertoire of different songs. A few, like the zebra finch from Australia or the white-crowned sparrow from North America, normally have one short and simple song. But in other species each individual may have hundreds or even thousands of different song types. The mockingbird in North America, the nightingale in Europe, and the lyrebirds in Australia are all examples here. The current record is held by the brown thrasher, an American relative of the mockingbird, in which each male has 1500 or more different song types. Furthermore, these birds are not just improvising and thus producing an endless stream of variations. Detailed analysis of the songs of individuals shows that their repertoires, even if huge, are limited, each song type being repeated again and again in identical form.

This could be mistaken for a complex language, but it is not. While our words convey different messages and have different meanings, in general the different songs that a bird has convey exactly the same message as each other but do it in a highly varied manner. Whichever song type the bird produces, the message may just be: 'I am a male robin in breeding condition on my territory'. In some species there are two different sorts of song, one mainly for interaction with other males, the other for signalling to females. But in most, regardless of how varied song is, the signal is the same and fulfils both of these functions.

Why then all the variety? There are perhaps two answers to this question. Where song is enormously varied it is likely to be the product of sexual selection, variety being favoured by female choice. Studies on various species show females to prefer to mate with males whose songs are more elaborate, and the ability to develop such songs may indeed be a good cue as to the health and vigour of a male. In the European sedge warbler, for example, each male has a repertoire of different syllables which he strings together to produce his song (Catchpole 2000). A syllable here is a single sound, or combination of sounds, which is used predictably and repeatedly. The sedge warbler can combine syllables in many different ways so that the exact sequence is probably never repeated. But the more syllables he has, the more varied sequences he can produce and this seems to be the important matter. Males set up their territories before the females return from wintering in Africa, and returning females then choose which male to pair with. The sequence with which males are chosen matches their repertoire sizes very closely, the first having many more syllables than the last. Clearly, having a more complex song pays as far as mate choice is concerned.

In other species, however, males have more modest repertoires of just a few song types. Here the benefit seems to be in interactions with neighbours. For example,

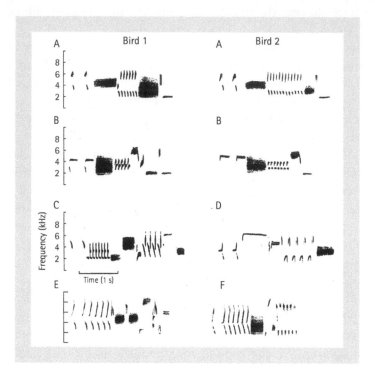

**Figure 8.1. Part of the repertoires as they might be sung by two different neighbouring song sparrows, the four songs on the left sung by one bird and those on the right by the other.**

Each song type is labelled by a different letter: A and B are shared by the two birds while C and D are not; E and F are a 'partial match', the two songs starting very similarly but being quite different towards the end. For further explanation, see text (sonagrams from Beecher et al. 2000 and Burt et al. 2002).

each male song sparrow has a repertoire of around 10 songs, each sung in exactly the same form whenever it is produced, so that the syllables are not shuffled around as they are in sedge warblers. A male song sparrow tends to share some but not all of his songs with each neighbour and the ones that are shared will differ between his neighbours. Birds often sing to each other across their territory boundaries, and song may help to delineate their borders and to settle disputes between them. The choice of song may indicate to whom they are signalling and, furthermore, the exact song used may be more or less aggressive. It is a strong threat to sing the same song back to a neighbour, but less so to sing another one that you share, and even less so to sing one that you do not share. Figure 8.1 shows what might be part of the repertoire of two male song sparrows.

If Bird 1 sings song A his neighbour might reply with the same song type, which is highly aggressive. But he might reply with song B, which they also share (so called repertoire matching), which is rather less aggressive. If he replies with song D, which bird 1 does not have in his repertoire, this is less aggressive still. A further complication is that birds may have song types that are similar but not the same, such as E and F, allowing a partial match. Thus, with a small number of song types birds may not only match particular neighbours but also raise or lower the stakes in their interactions (Beecher and Campbell 2005).

The similarity between the large number of song types a bird may produce and the large number of words in our vocabulary is thus a very superficial one which does not indicate great complexity in the messages their songs convey. However, a final point of similarity between bird song and language is one that may run deeper and help us to understand why language evolved. This is that both of them are learnt. Not all birds learn the sounds that they produce but three groups do so: the parrots (as is well known), less obviously the hummingbirds, and perhaps most strikingly the songbirds. This last group (the oscine passerines) amounts to nearly half of all known bird species, and includes virtually all the most elaborate singers: warblers, larks, wrens, thrushes, finches, and so on. That there is virtually no evidence for vocal learning in monkeys or apes means that something dramatic seems to have happened in our own lineage in the very recent past, but gives us little clue as to what this might have been. Perhaps the study of other groups, like the songbirds, in which song learning has also arisen, might give us some hints of the selective forces at work.

The development of song has now been studied in many bird species and, while there may be differences in detail, the overall pattern is often similar (Catchpole and Slater 2008). Young males that are isolated from others of their species develop songs that are usually rather simple and lack the detailed structure and phrasing of normal adult song. On the other hand, if they are played recordings of adult song, or even more so if they are raised in the company of a singing adult male, they will often produce a copy of that exact song that is precise in every detail. Copying is not always absolutely exact, however, and when errors are made, new song types arise. This process, of normally exact copying but with occasional errors, leads to gradual changes in songs in time and in space. At an extreme, the latter may lead to dialects, with all the birds in one area singing similar songs which differ from all those in another.

So why then do they learn? Among songbirds a number of suggestions have been made as to why vocal learning may be beneficial, though most do not seem applicable to more than a small number of species. The main ideas are as follows:

1. If males learn from their fathers, perhaps females might use song as a cue to choose mates that were most appropriate, for example, by avoiding mating with close relatives. This does seem to occur in some Darwin's finches, but these are among the few species in which father-to-son song transmission appears to be the norm (Grant and Grant 1996). Females, at least when they are over a year old, tend to mate with males that sing differently from their fathers. They are thus more likely to outbreed. As inbreeding is deleterious, this is to their advantage, and may be especially so in birds such as these where population sizes are small so

that inbreeding is all the more likely. It has also been argued that females of some species may do exactly the opposite: choose a mate that sings like their father did and thus choose one well matched to them. In birds that occur in many different habitats this might ensure that birds mate with others adapted to the same habitat so that that adaptation persists in their offspring. While a theoretical possibility, there is little evidence for this idea and it is certainly unlikely to be widespread given that father-to-son song transmission seems to occur in rather few species.

2. Song learning may enable birds to develop songs that are particularly appropriate to the acoustics of the habitat in which they live. As song degrades on its passage through the habitat, a young bird hearing song at a distance will only be able to copy sounds that transmit well, so that, with succeeding cultural generations, song will become progressively better adapted to that environment. Perhaps the best example of this is in the rufous-collared sparrow in South America (Handford 1988). The songs of these birds have a trill the speed of which varies with habitat. In open country it can be quite rapid, but in forest it tends to be slower. This is as one would expect, as rapid trills in forests become distorted by echoes off trees so that the notes run into one another in a way that is not the case when there are longer gaps between them. But again, while there are some excellent examples of habitat matching, there is little evidence of it in many other species so it is unlikely to be a widespread reason for vocal learning.

3. Song learning may also be a way of generating variety. In some species females have been shown to prefer males with the biggest song repertoires and learning may enable them to build these up. But some birds, like sedge warblers in Europe and catbirds in North America (Kroodsma et al. 1997), develop larger repertoires in isolation than when they are tutored, so that learning appears not to be essential to the generation of variety. Nor is learning only found where sounds are complex. Some simple calls, like the chink and rain call of the chaffinch, are copied from other individuals and vary from place to place.

4. Where males have small repertoires of songs which they use to interact with each other, perhaps the most likely benefit of learning is that it enables them to develop songs that match particular neighbours with which they can therefore countersing, as in the case of the song sparrows referred to earlier. But then, there are many cases where neighbours share songs rather little if at all.

The reason why songbirds learn the songs that they sing therefore remains something of a mystery. It may be that vocal imitation originally evolved in a quite different context to the one in which it now takes place and may now persist for quite different reasons. If territorial male birds did not learn their songs all would sing similarly and be able to match each other. But once they learn, mistakes will be made and different song types will arise. Small repertoires may become essential if birds are to match all of their neighbours, and any bird that loses the capacity to learn will be at a disadvantage compared with those that are able to do so.

Computer simulations also suggest that birds that learn their songs may be locked into doing so because they are more likely to attract mates. In a population where males learn, so songs are highly varied, females that will mate only with males with a narrow range of such songs are likely to be less successful in gaining a mate and thus in reproducing, so supporting the persistence of learning (Lachlan and Slater 1999).

These last ideas may account for why song learning is so widespread. They suggest that, once it evolved, it might be difficult to escape from. But they give no clue as to why it might have evolved in the first place. Its origin among the songbirds may pre-date the complexity of their songs, and be more associated with the simpler vocalizations that we refer to as calls. As mentioned above, these are sometimes learnt, and they may provide us with some clues about the advantages that learning has. The task is to tease apart consequences that are simply by-products of learning from those that are advantageous and may therefore have led it to be selected for. Dialects such as those shown in the songs and calls of many birds may come into the former category. Once birds learn, and sometimes make mistakes in copying, differences in song with distance are bound to arise unless birds learn before dispersal and the distances they move are very great. But as long as birds interacting with each other respond appropriately to the call or song of their area it may be of no consequence whether birds elsewhere use a different version which they would fail to comprehend.

A more likely benefit of call note learning is that it leads to adaptive differences between individuals in the area to which they belong. In some finches, the male and female of a pair home in on the same call as each other. In colonies of caciques in Central America all the individuals share a call, and this may act as a 'password' so that alien birds may be excluded. Something similar occurs in groups of budgerigars in captivity, so that their contact call takes on the same form within a group but differs from that of other groups. In another small parrot, the spectacled parrotlet, there is even evidence that birds may have different versions of their contact call for each of the other members of their group so that they can label them as the one they are signalling to, rather as if they were calling each other by name (Wanker et al. 2005). Call notes certainly deserve more study, but there is no doubt that vocal learning has an influence on many of them and that this has consequences for social relations within the group. It may be here that we need to look to understand the selective forces that led to the evolution of vocal learning in birds, and this in turn may give hints as to why it evolved in ourselves.

To conclude, it is clear that vocal communication is of prime importance in many birds as it is in humans. Some of the similarities, such as that between our vocabulary and the large song repertoires found in many birds, are superficial. But the fact that learning plays a role in the song development of many birds, as it does in language development, may help us to look back in time and think about the reasons why this crucial evolutionary step on the road to language took place (Doupe and Kuhl 1999).

# CHAPTER 9

# VOCAL COMMUNICATION AND COGNITION IN CETACEANS

## VINCENT M. JANIK

## 9.1 WHAT ARE CETACEANS?

The mammalian order Cetacea comprises all animals known as whales, dolphins, and porpoises, and is divided into two suborders, baleen whales (mysticeti) and toothed whales (odontoceti) (Martin and Reeves 2002). Instead of teeth, baleen whales have plates of baleen that filter small prey items from sea water. There are currently 14 recognized species of baleen whales. Their social structures appear to be simpler than those found in toothed whales (Tyack 1986). Most baleen whales are relatively solitary for most of the year but come together during the mating season when males often form surface-active groups around females. In many species, males also sing long and elaborate songs to attract females in what has been termed a floating lek. Given their size, these animals have rarely been studied in captivity and all our information on their cognitive and communication abilities comes from the wild.

Toothed whales are much the larger group, with more than 70 species. They tend to feed on larger prey items such as fish, squid, and marine mammals. Odontocete social structures are much more varied than those found in baleen whales (Tyack 1986). While some species occur mainly in very small groups of less than five, most delphinids live in larger groups and have complex societies. Fission-fusion societies are common among delphinids, while some species, like the killer whale (*Orcinus orca*), have a unique system in which both sexes stay in their maternal group for life. Toothed whales do not sing but use sounds in more direct social interactions.

## 9.2 COMMUNICATION SKILLS

Cetacean communication occurs primarily in the acoustic domain. Light scattering and absorption leads to very limited visibility underwater while the sense of olfaction is virtually absent. Sound travels with little loss of energy in water compared to air. Therefore many cetaceans use acoustic signals both for communication and for echolocation to explore their environment (Au 1993).

The males of most baleen whale species produce long, elaborate song sequences during the breeding season. These appear to keep other males away and attract females (Frankel et al. 1995; J. N. Smith et al. 2008). The song of the humpback whale (*Megaptera novaeangliae*) has a hierarchical structure and is the most complex one among whale songs. It consists of phrases that are made up of multiple elements. A phrase lasts for around 15 seconds and is usually repeated several times. Subsequent repetitions of one phrase are called a theme. Themes are presented in a specific order in a song, which is the same in all animals of a population. Occasionally, a specific theme can be omitted in a song. However, it is rare that themes are presented in an order other than the one commonly found in the population (Payne et al. 1983). One song consists of several themes and can last as long as 35 minutes. Singers repeat these songs and may sing continuously for more than 20 hours.

Patterns of change in the song of humpback whales demonstrate clearly that these animals are capable of vocal learning, a relatively uncommon trait in mammals (Janik and Slater 1997). All males in a population sing the same song at any one time, but the song of the population changes over the singing season (Payne et al. 1983). In one dramatic example, the population off the east coast of Australia switched its song to that of the west coast in only 2 years after invasion by a few males from the west (Noad et al. 2001). Without such an invasion small changes to elements occur throughout each singing season which lead to a complete change in the song structure within a population over a period of around 12 years (Payne and Payne 1985).

It is unclear why the animals change their song in synchrony. The most likely, albeit speculative, explanation is that males need to synchronize to instigate the necessary hormonal changes in females for mating, but also try to be sufficiently different to be chosen by individual females as a mating partner. These opposing pressures on song structure could explain the synchronous change in a population, where males would introduce subtle changes throughout the singing season which are then copied by neighbouring males. Even though the singing behaviour of baleen whales resembles bird song in many aspects, this pattern of synchronous change in a population appears unique to baleen whales. The bowhead whale (*Balaena mysticetus*) has a simpler song but changes song in synchrony similarly to humpback whales (Würsig and Clark 1993). The songs of other baleen whales are much simpler and often consist of only one to three elements that are repeated in long song sequences (Tyack and Clark 2000).

The study of toothed whale communication has concentrated largely on individual or group distinctiveness. Since these animals live in more individualized groups, they need to recognize each other and maintain contact at sea. Bottlenose dolphins (*Tursiops truncatus*) and several other dolphin species produce individually distinctive signature whistles that develop early in life (Tyack and Sayigh 1997). These can remain stable for at least a decade and, in the case of females, most likely for their entire lives (Sayigh et al. 2007). Signature whistle development is influenced by vocal learning, with dolphins copying and modifying aspects of other animals' whistles to develop their own unique frequency modulation pattern (Fripp et al. 2005). Playback studies demonstrated that this newly-created modulation pattern carries the identity information even when general voice cues are removed (Janik et al. 2006). Vocal learning is not limited to the early life stages of bottlenose dolphins but is also used in adulthood to copy the signature whistles of others, most likely in an attempt to address specific individuals at sea (Janik 2000c). Signature whistles within alliances of males that spend almost all their time in close associations tend to become more alike over time, departing from the pattern of long-term stability of signature whistles found for females (Watwood et al. 2004). Thus, vocal learning is used in a variety of contexts in dolphin communication.

Signature whistles contribute around 50% of all whistles produced at sea (Cook et al. 2004). Little is known about what non-signature whistles communicate. Furthermore, dolphins have many complex pulsed vocalizations which are used in social interactions. We know the communicative context of very few of these. A popping sound seems to be used as a threat (Connor and Smolker 1996) and bray calls appear to indicate food (Janik 2000a). Northern right whale dolphins (*Lissodelphis borealis*) produce long stereotyped sequences of burst-pulse sounds that can last around 1.5 seconds and are often repeated within a group (Rankin et al. 2007), but we do not know what information they carry. Repertoires of pulsed sounds can indicate group membership, as is the case for killer whales (Ford 1991) and sperm whales (*Physeter macrocephalus*) (Rendell and Whitehead 2003). These dialects, which are apparently learned, can be used to distinguish sympatric populations with different association patterns or foraging specializations. It seems likely that these dialects evolved as a consequence of social isolation between these groups, but may now be used to recognize group membership.

## 9.3 Cognitive skills

We know little about cognitive skills in baleen whales, since they are not easily accessible for experimental studies. Observations in the wild have provided evidence for social learning of song (see above) and also for lateralized brain specializations in foraging strategies (Clapham et al. 1995), but data for other behavioural domains are not available.

Much more detailed information exists on cognition in toothed whales, especially the bottlenose dolphin. Experimental work indicates that bottlenose dolphins have left-hemispheric dominance for the processing of visuospatial information (Kilian et al. 2000) and numerical tasks (Kilian et al. 2005). In social interactions, however, when looking at and rubbing conspecifics, bottlenose dolphins prefer to use the right brain hemisphere, as indicated by an asymmetry of eye and flipper use (Sakai et al. 2006).

Early studies demonstrated that bottlenose dolphins have both attribute memory and temporal memory skills equal to those of non-human primates and that they are capable of performing successfully in matching-to-sample tasks (Herman 1980). In a delayed matching-to-sample task, one dolphin retained attributes of novel samples for up to 120 seconds (Herman and Gordon 1974). The same animal could determine whether a probe sound was a match to any sound in a list of up to eight sample sounds (Thompson and Herman 1977). Dolphins also remember associations between objects and arbitrary signals over long periods of time (Herman et al. 1984).

To explore concept formation and communication skills, Herman and his colleagues trained two bottlenose dolphins with artificial communication systems (Herman et al. 1984). One received visual hand signals while the other one learned to react to acoustic signals. Each animal learned to associate a variety of arbitrary signals with different objects, actions, and modifiers. These were combined to form command sequences of the form 'direct object–action–indirect object' for one dolphin and 'indirect object–direct object–action' for the other. In order to perform correctly, the dolphins had to understand the rules underlying these sequences, since the same signals in a different sequence resulted in a different meaning of the sequence. For example, if one of the dolphins was given the sequence BALL–FETCH–HOOP the animal would have to bring the ball to the hoop while in HOOP–FETCH–BALL the hoop had to be brought to the ball. Both animals performed successfully in these tasks, even when presented with novel sequences that had not been used in training. Furthermore, Herman demonstrated that the dolphins had a very detailed understanding of the command rules by analysing their responses to incorrect or incomplete sequences (Herman et al. 1993). In later stages, the researchers added modifiers like 'left', 'right', 'surface', and 'bottom' and eventually one of the animals learned to respond correctly to novel sequences from a vocabulary of 40 items (Herman et al. 1984).

Kako (1999a) concluded that the dolphins' comprehension skills were comparable to that of language-trained apes. He also saw a greater syntactic competence in dolphins than in other language-trained animals, since the dolphins learned to use close-class items such as the words 'and' and 'that' (Kako 1999b). However, some authors have cautioned against calling such skills in marine mammals linguistic, concluding that the animals' performance in such tasks can be explained by complex association learning and the use of equivalence classes (Schusterman and Gisiner 1997). To date, studies teaching dolphins to actively use artificial communication signals have not progressed beyond simple conditioning to use specific signals for specific rewards.

However, dolphins perform successfully in a variety of other tasks that suggest complex cognition rivalling that of the great apes. Bottlenose dolphins understand the referential nature of artificial signals as demonstrated by their ability to report the presence or absence of named objects by pressing a 'yes' or 'no' paddle (Herman and Forestell 1985), and by their understanding of the human pointing gesture independent of the location of the target object (Herman et al. 1999). Captive bottlenose dolphins also spontaneously point at objects with their rostrum, seemingly to communicate with their caregivers (Xitco et al. 2001). The evidence from language-training experiments and the reporting on absent objects presents a convincing case that dolphins are able to form concepts. A study on cross-modal perception supports this further. Bottlenose dolphins immediately recognize objects they have previously seen but not perceived through echolocation when they are allowed to use echolocation but not vision to explore them, and vice versa (Pack and Herman 1995; Harley et al. 2003).

Many cetaceans are clearly capable of social learning in the vocal realm. In bottlenose dolphins, additional forms of social learning have been explored. They are capable of vocal learning (Richards et al. 1984), imitation (Herman 2002), mirror self-recognition (Reiss and Marino 2001), and emulation (i.e. the animal achieves the same end state as a demonstrator but develops its own strategy to get to it; Tayler and Saayman 1973). Both imitation (e.g. Meltzoff 1996) and mirror self-recognition can be seen as possible indicators for a theory of mind.

However, a study exploring belief attribution, usually considered the defining aspect theory of mind, was inconclusive (Tschudin 2006).

Some evidence exists for mental simulations as indicated by problem-solving skills that include advanced planning of actions (Kuczaj and Walker 2006). Smith et al. (1995) found some metacognition: specifically, bottlenose dolphins can report how certain they are about their choices in a forced choice task.

## 9.4 THE EVOLUTION OF COMMUNICATION AND COGNITION IN CETACEANS

Cetaceans have evolved in an environment that is as different from that of primates as one could imagine. Yet, they share many cognitive skills with the great apes. Their closest living relatives, the even-toed ungulates like hippopotamuses and deer, are not known for their communicative and cognitive complexity. Thus, it is safe to assume that in cetaceans these skills evolved after they had returned to an aquatic lifestyle. Some of the hypotheses brought forward for the evolution of complex cognition in primates (as summarized by Van Schaik and Deaner 2003) can be immediately discarded for cetaceans. Food processing or arboreal clambering certainly had no influence. Similarly, extractive foraging seems an unlikely explanation. However, spatiotemporal mapping or social strategizing are possible candidates. Some species migrate long distances and appear to be able to predict when and where foraging opportunities arise (Wells et al. 1999). However, others stay in the same area for their entire lives. Many toothed whales have complex social systems (Tyack 1986) and, entertaining the assumption that their communication and cognition skills have evolved in the context they are used in today, one could argue that social strategizing is the most likely origin at least for their cognitive skills. Improved sound transmission in the sea and low visibility, as well as the scarcity of landmarks, must have been major factors in the evolution of acoustic communication skills. In favourable conditions, dolphins can detect whistles of conspecifics over more than 10 km (Janik 2000b). Some baleen whales appear likely to detect each other over more than 1000 km (Clark 1995).

This large range leads to potentially wide communication networks (Janik 2005). Conspecific calls may be used to find large aggregations of whales at feeding or breeding grounds; however, it seems unlikely that whales coordinate their movements on a fine scale over such distances. Nevertheless, cetaceans are able to monitor and stay in touch with conspecifics over a larger range than most terrestrial animals.

This larger communication range has two main consequences. First, animals have to develop strategies to overcome considerable biological background noise if animal density is high. Some oceanic dolphin species can occur in groups of thousands which leads to a cacophony of constant vocalizations, a serious problem if an individual is trying to get a message across. Secondly, each sound is heard by many receivers, and addressing specific receivers or implementing strategies to avoid eavesdropping may be more important than in terrestrial species. Janik and Slater (1997) argue that the most likely context for the evolution of vocal learning was the need for individual recognition in social groups. This has led, at least in bottlenose dolphins, to a communication system that allows referential communication about the identity of conspecifics. Dolphins may be the only non-human mammalian species that introduces novel acoustic signals into its repertoire and then uses them in a referential way, although this vocal flexibility might also occur in parrots (Wanker et al. 2005).

Recent studies on language evolution have highlighted the importance of non-verbal sharing of information and joint attention in humans as a stepping stone to the evolution of language (Terrace 2005; Herrmann et al. 2007). There are no dedicated studies on this in cetaceans, but food sharing and cooperative hunting has been observed in several species (e.g. Hoelzel 1991; Gazda et al. 2005). This suggests that information is actively shared between animals since coordination by pure observation of conspecifics is often not possible in the marine environment. Dolphins are also capable of eavesdropping on the echolocation signals of conspecifics (Xitco and Roitblat 1996), which increases the potential for joint attention. Finally, the finding that dolphins spontaneously use learned artificial sounds that have been presented in association with novel objects, when they are allowed to manipulate these objects themselves (Reiss and McCowan 1993), is reminiscent of the first declarative use of language in human infants. The main question that remains is what aspects of a theory of mind are present in cetaceans and consequently how their impressive communicative skills are related to their mental representation of the world. Given their cognitive skills, the investigation of this question should be a high priority.

# ACKNOWLEDGEMENTS

I would like to thank Maggie Tallerman and Kathleen Gibson for their comments on an earlier draft of this chapter. The author was supported by a Royal Society University Research Fellowship while writing this chapter.

# CHAPTER 10

# EVOLUTION OF COMMUNICATION AND LANGUAGE: INSIGHTS FROM PARROTS AND SONGBIRDS

## IRENE M. PEPPERBERG

## 10.1 INTRODUCTION

Most language evolution research focuses on primates, positing a hominin transitional link with emerging learned vocal communication. Such research increased after apes, humans' closest genetic relatives, learned elements of human communication systems (Hillix and Rumbaugh 2003). Grey parrots (*Psittacus erithacus*), despite considerable phylogenetic separation from humans, acquire comparable human-like communication skills and, unlike present-day apes, can imitate human speech because they can learn novel vocalizations (Pepperberg 1999). Specifically, they acquire species-specific and heterospecific vocalizations by actively matching their progressive production of specific sound patterns to live interacting models or memorized templates. Research on selective pressures resulting in avian vocal learning and imitation could provide clues about pressures leading to similar human skills. To understand the ancestral hominin condition, language evolution researchers might thus use models based on both phylogenetic kin and birds.

## 10.2 PHYSICAL CAPACITIES: SPEECH PERCEPTION AND PRODUCTION

Many species, including non-human mammals, categorically distinguish various bits of human speech, for instance cleanly separating speech tokens such as /b/ – /p/ (Kuhl 1981; Dent et al. 1997; Patterson and Pepperberg 1998). Few, however, can produce human speech, and in some that do, speech-like reproductions may arise via mechanisms (such as sine-wave interference; Lieberman 1984) unrelated to those used by humans. Grey parrots, however, distinguish most human tokens (vowels, consonants) and also reproduce them accurately, including human-like formant structures (Patterson and Pepperberg 1984, 1988; Pepperberg 2007b, 2010).

## 10.3 IMITATIVE ABILITY

Imitation is likely involved in language acquisition, whatever the modality. Imitation is most stringently defined as purposeful, meaningful replication of an otherwise improbable, novel act (Thorpe 1963), distinguishing it from mimicry (meaningless reproduction of physical actions or vocalizations), social facilitation, stimulus enhancement, and other non-imitative, socially-mediated learning formats. Whereas the physical imitation abilities of parrots are limited (that is, they involve actions already in their repertoire; Mui et al. 2008), referential avian heterospecific vocal learning, demonstrated in my laboratory by Grey parrots, including Alex and Griffin (Pepperberg 1999), clearly fits Thorpe's definition. Alex, Griffin, and, to a lesser extent, the parrots Alo and Kyaaro learned to reproduce English speech sounds and use them meaningfully to interact with humans and to comment on items of interest in their lives.

Alex, for example, vocally identified over 50 objects. He labelled seven colours, five shapes, and quantities to eight. He also had concepts of category, and vocally reported on what attribute was *same* or *different* between two objects (i.e. colour, shape, material) or which was bigger or smaller. He stated 'none' if nothing was same or different, if items were of equal size, or if a designated quantity was missing from a collection. He used 'I want X' and 'Wanna go Y', where X and Y were, respectively, object or location labels. He combined labels to request, refuse, categorize, or quantify over 100 different items, including subsets in mixed-item collections (for instance, how many blue blocks in a collection of red and blue balls and blocks). Apes acquire comparable referential communication, using simplified American Sign Language (ASL), plastic chips, or computer symbols (see Hillix and Rumbaugh 2003); parrots, however, acquire a substantial vocal repertoire.

## 10.4 Untrained vocal practice, sound play, and referential mapping

Like children and songbirds, Alex privately vocally practised before acquiring targeted utterances (Pepperberg 1999, 2010, 2013), suggesting he actively matched memorized templates—a large number, given his repertoire. For example, early in training, Alex privately generated strings like 'mail chail benail' before producing the targeted 'nail' (Pepperberg 1999). Here, phoneme combination seemed less an intentional attempt to create a new label from specific sounds resembling the target than deliberate play within a range of existing patterns in an attempt to hit a pairing that matched some remembered template. Thus Alex recognized the combinatory nature of his utterances, but so far (however, see below) lacked knowledge of how to segment a novel targeted vocalization exactly, then match its components to those in his repertoire to create the trained label.

He apparently exhibited anticipatory co-articulation: that is, he separated specific phonemes from the speech flow and produced them, setting up his vocal tract to facilitate production of upcoming phonemes as the previous one was completed (for instance, /k/ in 'key' differed from his initial /k/ in 'cork'; Patterson and Pepperberg 1998). In humans, these abilities suggest top-down processing (Ladefoged 1982), necessary for segmentation and phonological awareness, discussed below.

Alex derived new speech patterns spontaneously from existing ones, with a format suggesting he abstracted rules for utterance beginnings and endings, consistently recombining label parts according to their order in existing utterances (e.g. 'carrot' from 'key' and 'parrot'; Pepperberg 1999). He constructed the novel label 'banerry' to refer to an apple (something tasting 'banana'-like, looking 'cherry'-like). He referentially produced and understood labels that form minimal pairs (Patterson and Pepperberg 1998), for instance 'Want corn' versus 'Want cork', or 'Want tea' versus 'Want pea' (and refusing the alternatives), again showing that he segmented phonemes from the speech stream (for non-human primate abilities, see Newport et al. 2004). He thus recognized these phonetic differences ('tea' vs. 'pea') as meaningful, though he may not initially have deliberately parsed those labels when learning to produce them.

New patterns not initially directed at novel items occurred via spontaneous play (e.g. 'grate', 'grain', 'chain', 'cane' evolving from 'grape'), and could then be referentially mapped: given relevant objects to which novel patterns could refer, Alex then used these labels to identify or request the items (Pepperberg 1999). Thus, spontaneous utterances initially lacking communicative value could, as they do for children, acquire such value if caretakers interpreted them as meaningful and intentional; Alex behaved as though human interactions 'conventionalized' sound patterns and sound-meaning connections toward standard communication. Comparable incidents for ASL-using apes—'water bird' for swan, 'cry hurt food' for radish (Fouts and Rigby 1977)—were not chereme combinations (comparable to phonemes) but rather whole signs, considered as descriptors of the entire situation, not as specific combinations to denote one element.

## 10.5 SEGMENTATION

Alex eventually demonstrated vocal segmentation—a special form of vocal behaviour—which implied that he understood that his existing labels consisted of individually separable morphemes or phonemes that could be (re)combined to create what were for him novel vocalizations, and he also demonstrated phonological awareness. Such behaviour is considered basic to human language development, and uniquely human: most non-humans, lacking speech, are never exposed to, trained, or tested on issues of phonological awareness, nor are they expected to have representations of phonemes to engender such combinatorial behaviour (Pepperberg 2007b). Alex, when learning 'spool' and 'seven', began by using combinations of existing phonemes and labels to identify, respectively, a wooden bobbin and the Arabic numeral. For 'spool', he started with /s/ (unvoiced, trained in conjunction with the alphabet letter, S) combined with 'wool', to form 's' (pause) 'wool' (/s/-pause-/wʊl/); for 'seven', he started with 's' plus 'one', thus forming 's' (pause) 'one' (/s/-pause-/wən/). Pauses provided space for initially absent /p/ and /v/ (difficult sans lips), preserving the number of syllables in targeted vocalizations and also prosodic rhythm. Alex retained these forms for months, despite learning other new labels having existing phonemes after only weeks of training (Pepperberg 1999). Eventually, he produced a perfect 'spool' (/spuːl/) and 'seben' (/sɛbɪn/).

Such behaviour requires understanding that labels consist of a finite number of sounds that can be recombined into patterns limited only by the phonotactic constraints of a given language; that is, understanding that existent complex entities (e.g. labels X and Y) can be parsed into pieces (their constituent phonemes) that can then be integrated into a new complex entity (label Z), which represents the imitated target. Non-human primates segment human speech sounds (Newport et al. 2004), but cannot produce sound-letter associations or (re)combine speech elements. Thus Alex, despite a limited combinatory rule system, showed intriguing parallels with young children's early label acquisition (Pepperberg 2007b).

## 10.6 OTHER LEARNING ISSUES: JOINT ATTENTION

Grey parrots learn human speech patterns best if training involves reference, pragmatic use, and considerable social interaction. The primary technique, the Model-Rival (M/R) method, uses three-way social interactions between two humans and a parrot to demonstrate targeted vocal behaviour (Pepperberg 1999). The parrot observes two humans handling and speaking about one or more objects; one trainer queries the other about targeted items (e.g. 'What's here?', 'What colour?'), giving praise and transferring the named object to the human partner to reward correct answers, thereby providing 1:1 correspondence between object and label. Incorrect responses are punished by scolding and temporarily removing items from sight. Thus the second human is both a model for the parrot's responses and its rival for the trainer's attention, and the consequences of errors are evident. The model must try again, speaking more clearly after a response was (deliberately) given incorrectly or garbled; thus the bird observes the model experiencing corrective feedback. The parrot is also included in interactions, being queried and rewarded for successive approximations to correct responses; training is adjusted to its performance level. Interestingly, apes that were most successful at acquiring communication skills were taught by comparable methods (Savage-Rumbaugh 1991). Removing reference, pragmatics, or social interaction causes learning to fail (Pepperberg 1999).

One social aspect, joint focusing of learner-trainer attention (Baldwin 1995), provides important comparisons with apes. In an M/R variant testing whether joint attention affects acquisition, a single trainer faced away from the bird (Kyaaro or Alo, in separate sessions), who was within reach of, for example, a key. The trainer talked about the item, emphasizing its label, 'Look, a shiny key!', 'You want key?' and so on, thus framing the label, and allowing repeated label use while

minimizing possible habituation. The trainer neither visually nor physically con-
tacted parrot or object (Pepperberg 1999). Both Kyaaro and Alo learned labels
trained simultaneously in standard M/R sessions, but never even attempted label
production with this variant, although Kyaaro tried to climb into the trainer's lap.
Possibly, Kyaaro sought the trainer's focus, to form a relevant object–label connection. Giret et al. (2009) also demonstrated some attention-following in Grey
parrots which experienced focused human interaction. Apes follow gaze, but do
not spontaneously understand gaze in terms of communicative intent; encultura-
tion (for instance, for apes acquiring Yerkish or simplified ASL) produces more
sophisticated understanding (Tomasello 2007).

## 10.7 THEORY OF MIND

Although no formal research exists on parrots' theory of mind (such as a Sally-Ann
test), one study provided indirect evidence for Alex (Pepperberg and Gordon
2005). The task involved labelling the colour of a targeted numerical set within
collections of simultaneously presented quantities (e.g. 4-, 5-, and 6-block subsets
of three different colours). After about a dozen correct trials with different item sets
(balls, keys, corks, etc.), Alex replied 'five' when asked 'What colour three?' for a set
of two, three, and six objects. Queried twice more, each time he inexplicably replied
'five'. The questioner finally said 'OK, Alex, what colour five?' He immediately
responded 'none'. Although he would respond 'none' if nothing (colour, shape,
material) was same or different for two proffered objects, and had spontaneously
used 'none' to answer 'What colour bigger/smaller?' for two identically-sized
objects, he had never been taught about absence of quantity nor how to respond
to a missing exemplar. Noteworthy, however, was how he manipulated the trainer
into asking the question he seemingly desired to answer, perhaps suggesting some
evidence for a theory of mind.

## 10.8 QUESTIONS OF SYNTAX

When non-humans are taught human linguistic systems, they acquire only simple
rule-governed behaviour; for instance, they can execute instructions given in a
particular order, such as 'Take X to Y', or produce sentence frames such as 'I want

X', where X and Y can stand for numerous items. In nature, however, both birds and non-human primates use certain combinatorial communication forms, which vary significantly across species.

In general, calls of monkeys and birds such as chickens lack what linguists consider syntax (see Tallerman, Chapter 48); these animals' vocalizations comprise some distinct sounds that can be repeated but are rarely combined. Chickens (Evans et al. 1993) and vervets (Cheney and Seyfarth 1990) both learn appropriate contexts for call usage, but calls themselves are innate. Even calls that are combined (Arnold and Zuberbühler 2006a) generally denote specific situations which are not directly related to the summed meanings of the individual calls.

Vocal communication in suboscine birds (e.g. flycatchers) parallels the un-learned ape systems: for both, vocalizations are more flexible and complex than those of chickens or monkeys in terms of meaning and context of use, though not in the sounds themselves. In addition to calls, flycatchers have simple innate songs of just a few notes, but learn the effect of context from social interactions, for instance how repeating innate signals or combining actions and innate vocaliza-tions extends meaning (Smith and Smith 1996; Leger 2005); such behaviour is much like that of apes (Pollick and de Waal 2007; Arbib et al. 2008). Flycatchers engage in very simple combinatory syntax by altering the number of repetitions of their utterances or by varying flight patterns or body postures while vocalizing (Smith and Smith 1996). These variant patterns signal differing levels of aggression or affiliation. Our ancestors may have similarly amalgamated grunts and gestures (Pepperberg 2007a; cf. Bickerton 2009a).

For oscines, avian vocal learners, song is more remarkable (Kroodsma 2005; Slater, this volume). Song repertoire size can vary from one to thousands; song 'syntax' can vary from a simple series of repeated notes to structures such as whistle-trill-buzz, or (at least to human ears) to endless collections of amorphous phrases repeated eventually but not often; birds learn which variations are used in given contexts. The extent to which birds can learn other species' songs seems constrained by combinatory rules of the songs in question (Pepperberg and Schinke-Llano 1991). The uniqueness of human syntax is best left to other entries (e.g. Bickerton, Chapter 49; Boeckx, Chapter 52; Tallerman, Chapter 48), but one controversial claim seems unfounded: Hauser et al. (2002) argued that a recursive syntax $A^nB^n$ (where A, B are specific elements) separates humans from all other species, based on its absence in monkeys. The monkey experiment used simple human syllables for the A, B elements. Interestingly, in contrast to monkeys, laboratory-trained starlings (*Sturnus vulgaris*) recognize this 'syntax' when spe-cies-specific warbles and rattles were used as the A, B elements (Gentner et al. 2006); no one has yet tested apes. Note that both monkeys and starlings might have learned the appropriate patterns by comparing the number of As and Bs in a string (e.g. AAAABBBB) given that both likely can, without counting, recognize quantity up to about four (Dehaene 1997); however, starlings succeeded and monkeys failed.

Although for humans such a recursive syntax generally involves embedded clauses, not simple syllables or their equivalent, the starling experiment supports the idea of using avian models for simple precursors to language.

## 10.9 LANGUAGE EVOLUTION

Bird 'song' thus may imply many things (Slater, this volume), but oscines' song must be learned. Bird song is a simpler communication system than human language, but important parallels exist between songbird and human vocal learning, which suggest birds as models for speech evolution (Pepperberg 2010, 2013). These parallels generally also hold for parrots. Both songbirds and humans have (a) a sensitive period during which exposure to the adult system allows development to proceed most rapidly, although later acquisition is possible, particularly if social interaction is involved; and some birds (such as parrots) are, like humans, open-ended learners; (b) a babbling-practice stage wherein juveniles experiment with sounds that will ultimately become part of their repertoire; (c) a need to learn not just what to produce but the appropriate context in which to produce specific vocalizations; (d) abilities to process hierarchically structured vocal sequences, which in humans must have been a precursor to syntax; and (e) lateralized brain structures devoted to acquisition, storage, and production of vocalizations.

Whereas behavioural correlates (a)–(d) are important, neurobiology is central for using birds as models for vocal learning and language evolution. Avian and mammalian brain structures responsible for vocal learning are thought to be derived from similar pallial structures (Farries 2004; Jarvis et al. 2005). Hence, behavioural parallels between avian and human vocal learners may be reflected in the presence of similar neuroanatomical systems. These systems may be absent or differently structured in non-vocal learning birds and mammals. Thus, birds can potentially provide models for how fully-developed vocal learning systems which include lateralization could evolve from pre-existing motor systems via addition, subtraction, or modification of projections between brain nuclei (Farries 2004; Perkel 2004; Feenders et al. 2008). Interestingly, a gestural theory of vocal learning/ language evolution has been posited for both birds and humans (Hewes 1973; Williams and Nottebohm 1985; see Corballis, this volume). Notably, avian beaks are often used like primate forelimbs. Motor control of the beak resides in neural areas separate from, but near to, the song system and these areas relate to those controlling human jaw movements (Wild 1997). Arbib (2008), for example, argues for expansion of the projection from F5 that controls vocal folds in monkeys to one that controls human tongue and lips (see Arbib, this volume). Although direct correlations such as those between human Broca's area and monkey F5 (Arbib 2008) are unlikely for avian–human brains, recent studies strengthen avian–human correlations, particularly possible mirror neuron systems (Prather et al. 2008; Keller and Hahnloser 2009) purportedly involved in producing and understanding gestural and vocal communication (Arbib 2008). Examination of additional avian brain areas co-opted for evolution of song learning and decoding might suggest parallel areas co-opted for human language evolution.

Birds may also provide models for neural mechanisms of primate co-development of gestural and vocal combinations. Young children begin combining objects (such as spoon-into-cup) and phonological/grammatical units (such as 'more+X' emergent syntax) almost simultaneously. Greenfield (1991) posited that control of such parallel development initially resides in one neural structure (roughly Broca's area) that differentiates as a child's brain matures into specialized areas for, respectively, physical combinations versus language, and she proposed that such competence is a critical aspect of language (i.e. human) development. Subsequent research on the physical combinatorial behaviour of non-human primates and combinatorial communicative acts by apes trained in a human-based code showed that ape combinations of physical objects and labels (such as 'more tickle') resemble, although are simpler than, those of young children. For monkeys, unlike apes, combinatorial behaviour develops only with intensive training and is even more limited (Johnson-Pynn et al. 1999). Greenfield (1991) thus proposed that non-human primate behaviour derives from a homologous structure just predating the ape/hominin evolutionary divergence. Whatever neural structures are involved, combinatorial behaviour is not limited to primates: my Grey parrot Griffin showed the same spontaneously co-occurring vocal and physical combinatory patterns (Pepperberg and Shive 2001).

But use of birds as models for language evolution really hinges on living avian species which apparently straddle the vocal learning/non-learning divide—possible avian models for similarly-behaving hominin ancestors. Specifically, a purported suboscine, the three-wattled bellbird (*Procnias tricarunculata*)—a close relative of flycatchers—seemingly learns its songs. The song is quite simple (a mixture of call-like notes and whistles, more suboscine- than oscine-like), but males have dialects, and can be bilingual with respect to these dialects (at least for several years). Moreover, a close relative, the bare-throated bellbird (*P. nudicollis*), learns songs of other species (Kroodsma 2005), thus providing indications of vocal learning in species once thought unable to learn even their own song. These facts, plus data that some bellbirds don't sound (or even look) like adults until about 5 years old (Kroodsma 2005), suggest a pattern radically unlike that of suboscines and oscines. Interestingly, bellbirds have more K-selected species traits than most suboscines and oscines: longer lives (possibly over 20 years), longer maturation periods, larger body size, fewer young, and intense male–male competition in which older, stronger males get the most matings and also lead changes in song patterns, thus forcing youngsters to follow (B. Snow 1977; D. Snow 1982; Powell and Bjork 2004; Kroodsma 2005). Such data strengthens parallels with great apes and hominins. Even oscines that learn songs throughout their lifetimes usually have a recognizable, characteristic song in their first adult year. Bellbird learning abilities seem similar to those of oscines, except for the extraordinarily long juvenile stage and their classification as suboscines. Might they, like oscines but unlike other suboscines, have brain areas for song learning? Is their prolonged babbling a consequence of brains 'differently' equipped for learning? No one knows. But, if so, might they have a primitive motor neuron system that is slow to mature beyond the babbling stage (Pepperberg 2007a, 2010, 2013)?

Such ideas support using bellbirds as a model system for what might have been the 'missing-link' hominin species (or multiple species) which bridged the gap between the communication systems of our non-human primate ancestors (vocal, but non-learning) and *Homo sapiens* (vocal learning); thus, bellbirds might provide a model of an intermediary brain system mediating early elements of vocal learning. Notably, these birds' vocalizations resemble those of vocal non-learners (suboscines with innate songs), but the vocalizations are indeed learned. Most likely, a continuum rather than a sharp break existed between innate and learned, with certain communicative elements shifting as flexibility provided evolutionary advantages. Conceivably, similar evolutionary pressures on brain structures responsible for vocalizations leading from the innate, simple song of true suboscines to the fairly simple but slowly learned bellbird song to the complexity of, for example, the brown thrasher's hundreds of songs may have been exerted on brain structures responsible for non-human-to-hominin vocal learning. If so, these evolutionary pressures were likely exerted on a motor neuron system, such that brain and corresponding behavioural complexity evolved in parallel, synergistically supporting the next evolutionary stage (Pepperberg 2007a, 2010, 2013). Articulatory gestures grounded in feeding behaviour and contact calls/cries that can be co-opted for other uses were as likely in birds as primates; possibly mirror neuron systems similarly shifted (Farries 2004; Feenders et al. 2008).

## 10.10 CONCLUSIONS

Birds, although diverging from the lineage leading to humans approximately 280 million years ago, can provide models for the evolution of vocal communication. Parallels exist at many levels: between vocal non-learning (calling) birds and monkeys, between non-learning suboscines and apes, among songbirds, parrots, and humans, and, most interestingly, possibly between an existent bird straddling the learning/non-learning line and the evolution of ancient hominins from non-learning to learning. Evolution is generally conservative; much can be achieved from studying birds.

# CHAPTER 11

# ARE OTHER ANIMALS AS SMART AS GREAT APES? DO OTHERS PROVIDE BETTER MODELS FOR THE EVOLUTION OF SPEECH OR LANGUAGE?

KATHLEEN R. GIBSON

## 11.1 INTRODUCTION

Great apes (orang-utans, gorillas, chimpanzees, and bonobos) possess virtually all motor, cognitive, and social abilities essential for the creation of a gestural proto-language communicative system (Gibson, Chapter 3). These include the creation and social transmission of novel gestures, the use of novel referential gestures to represent both present and absent items, and the combination of two to three gestures to create novel meanings. Great apes also understand that others have thoughts and intentions, and they manifest that knowledge in competitive, conciliatory, and deceptive actions (Call and Tomasello 2008). Under appropriate circumstances, apes cooperate with conspecifics in the pursuit of joint goals and may even use symbol-like lexigrams to do so (Menzel 1972; Savage-Rumbaugh et al. 1978; Melis et al. 2006). Great apes also have other capacities of possible relevance to language or to its cognitive base, including tool-making, imitation of complex manual manipulative tasks, and some elements of episodic memory. Given the breadth of language-pertinent abilities exhibited by captive apes, it is puzzling that no wild ape populations use gestural signs to refer to absent items (displacement) or to coordinate group behaviours. Perhaps, wild apes simply lack the motivation. Alternatively, perhaps, they lack critical, as yet unidentified, abilities.

Many other animals display high intelligence in some behavioural contexts. Indeed, especially accomplished birds, dogs, dolphins, and sea lions now challenge great apes' once seemingly secure intellectual throne, at least in certain behavioural realms. (See discussion below.) It remains unclear, however, whether other species possess the breadth of intelligence manifested by apes or whether any might serve as better models for the cognitive underpinnings of language. Quite a few animals, however, do exceed all primates in vocal learning capacities, and, thus provide potentially better models for the evolution of fine oral motor and vocal control. Song learning birds, in particular, have been proposed as especially good models for the evolution of speech (Fitch 2010a; Mithen, this volume; Pepperberg, this volume). Similarly, Bickerton (2009a) suggests that non-primates, especially some insects, may provide optimum models for the evolution of other protolanguage components, including displacement. With these considerations in mind, this chapter briefly reviews recent evidence for advanced, language-pertinent, cognitive capacities in birds and mammals and evaluates the potential suitability of song and other animal vocal behaviours as models for the evolution of speech.

## 11.2 Language-related cognitive skills in non-primate mammals and birds

Dolphins are extremely vocal, exhibit intelligence across a number of behavioural domains, are highly social, often cooperate to herd schools of fish, and, in some locales, routinely drive fish into fishermens' nets. Despite lacking hands, some dolphin populations use tools and socially transmit their tool-using techniques (Boran and Heimlich 1999; Bearzi and Stanford 2010). Dolphins can also recognize themselves in mirrors, coordinate body postures and swimming patterns with those of other dolphins, and imitate each others' vocalizations, including unique signature whistles which serve for individual recognition among adults and in the mother–infant dyad (Janik 1999). No evidence, however, suggests that wild dolphins communicate about absent animals, foods, or events (displacement).

Two dolphins, Phoebe and Akeakamai, demonstrated comprehension of sentence-like commands in artificial vocal (Phoebe) and gestural (Akeakamai) languages (Herman et al. 1984). Both could appropriately respond to commands containing semantic reversals such as 'bottom basket fetch surface hoop' (fetch a basket from the bottom and take it to a surface hoop) versus 'surface hoop fetch bottom basket' (take the surface hoop to the bottom basket). Nor are dolphins the only marine mammals that have demonstrated comprehension of sentence-like commands. A sea lion, Rocky, readily differentiated gestural commands such as 'bottle fetch ball' (take a bottle to the ball) from 'ball fetch bottle' (take a ball to the bottle). Moreover, his performance improved when modifiers were added to gestural sequences to yield commands such as 'large white ball small black cube fetch' (Schusterman and Gisiner 1988; Gisiner and Schusterman 1992). Although the dolphins and Rocky possessed smaller vocabularies than most ape-language subjects, their behaviours were sufficiently impressive to indicate that great-ape-like gestural and sentence comprehension may be more widespread than commonly thought. However, we do not yet know whether dolphins and sea lions can master productive gestural, vocal, or lexigram-based protolanguage-like communication systems, such as those evidenced by some great apes.

The only other non-primate mammals whose 'language' capacities appear to have been investigated are domestic dogs. One border collie, Rico, correctly fetched 200 different items in response to German commands spoken by his owner (Kaminski et al. 2004). In the popular press, Rico's comprehension of 200 spoken object names was widely compared to the ability of some apes to produce approximately 200 gestural signs and/or to appropriately point to approximately 200 lexigrams, but Rico never produced or pointed to signs or symbols of any sort. No captive apes have been tested to determine how many spoken words they can comprehend. The bonobo, Kanzi, however, appropriately responded to approximately 600 English commands. Many of these commands required executing actions on objects with respect to other objects, places, or people, as well as comprehending word order, and some prepositions such as *in* or *on* (Savage-Rumbaugh et al. 1993), and, hence, greatly exceeded in complexity and number the 200 simple fetching commands comprehended by Rico.

Some have also claimed that domestic dogs equal or exceed great apes in social intelligence (Hare and Tomasello 2005). In some studies, dogs did outperform chimpanzees in recognizing and appropriately responding to human pointing actions (Hare and Tomasello 1999). However, on more complex tests of social intelligence, chimpanzees outperformed dogs (Wobber and Hare 2009). Nonetheless, given that some dog breeds are natural pointers, dogs would seem appropriate candidates for training in lexigram-type 'languages' that rely on pointing rather than gestural skills.

It has also been suggested that both elephants and spotted hyenas are unusually intelligent (Holekamp et al. 2007; Irie-Sugimoto et al. 2008). Elephants remember and recognize by olfactory and visual means numerous conspecifics and classify them into social groups. They also sometimes cooperate to achieve joint goals and seem to understand others' intentions and emotions. Moreover, elephants have highly manipulative trunks, use tools for varied purposes, may recognize themselves in mirrors, and may have a stronger numerical sense than non-human primates. Finally, they have elaborate vocal, olfactory, tactile, and gestural communication systems and can imitate some sounds (Poole et al. 2005; Byrne et al. 2009). Given their broad cognitive and sensorimotor skills, elephants appear to have great promise as potential protolanguage learners. So far, however, they have not been subject to language-training experiments.

Spotted hyenas live in hierarchically-structured social groups similar to those of baboons, with the exception that hyena societies are female dominated. Like baboons, spotted hyenas can recognize individuals and hierarchically classify them into kin groups (Holekamp et al. 2007). These animals have complex vocal repertoires, hunt cooperatively in the wild, and may engage in deceptive behaviours. In captivity, they readily cooperate by jointly pulling ropes to obtain out-of-reach foods, as long as two dominant animals are not paired together (Drea and Carter 2009). However, spotted hyenas appear to lack imitative capacities, do not use tools, and have not been shown to recognize themselves in mirrors. Consequently, although they may equal or exceed baboons in many aspects of social intelligence, it is premature to claim that they are as bright as great apes or that they have the pertinent sensorimotor skills to master a protolanguage. Given that hyenas are scavengers, displacement (e.g. communication about absent foods) would appear advantageous for them, but it has not been reported.

Some of the strongest recent claims for high intelligence have involved birds, especially parrots and corvids. The most intensely studied individual bird, Alex, an African Grey parrot (Pepperberg 2000, this volume) could speak English words and combine them to create novel meanings. For example, when presented with an apple, a fruit for which he had no name, Alex combined the words for 'banana' and 'cherry' to create a new name, 'banerry'. Alex could also combine words to make requests such as 'give nut', 'wanna go back'. Pepperberg argues, rather persuasively, that Alex learned to speak phonemically. If so, Alex is the only non-human animal known to have mastered phonemes. Alex's use of English words and phrases indicated many additional cognitive capacities, including an understanding of object permanence to the level of Piaget's stage six, the ability to categorize objects based on colour, shape, or materials, and an understanding of the concept *same/different*. Alex could recognize and label quantities of six or less and could also add small quantities to six. Studies of Alex's word combinations, however, were just beginning at the time of his death, and he apparently was never tested on his ability to comprehend English grammar or on his ability to cooperate with other parrots to achieve common goals. Nor was he tested on his ability to use tools. Alex, thus, appears to have been by far the most accomplished non-primate language student yet studied, indeed, the most accomplished of all non-human animals, if speech and phonemic learning are considered language criteria. Possibly Alex also possessed all language-pertinent cognitive and social capacities found in great apes, but this is not certain.

Corvids, including various jays, crows, and ravens, and rooks are among the most versatile birds in their abilities to exploit diverse habitats and foods. Moreover, unlike great apes, some wild corvids cache food. In captive studies, Western scrub jays and some ravens have proven to have superb long-term memory for the type of food cached, caching locations, how recently the foods were cached, and whether others watched them cache (Emery and Clayton 2001; Bugnyar and Kotrschal 2002). On the basis of these findings, Emery and Clayton (2004) have claimed that Western scrub jays have theory of mind, tactical deception capacities and episodic memory, and that they may equal great apes in social intelligence. However, it has yet to be demonstrated whether jays and ravens cooperate in the pursuit of common goals. Unlike chimpanzees, however, the rooks always pulled strings immediately in lieu of waiting for a 'pulling' partner to appear, even when a partner was essential for success (Seed et al. 2008). Nor have any corvids been subject to 'language' training experiments.

Few, if any jays, use tools, but some corvids do. Wild New Caledonian crows, for example, fashion hooked and barbed probing tools from leaves (Hunt and Gray 2004). One crow, Betty, bent a wire into a hook-like shape for use as a tool (Weir et al. 2002). Four laboratory-housed rooks bent similarly-shaped wires, even though rooks do not use tools in the wild (Bird and Emery 2009). Both the tools of the wild crows and the hooks manufactured by Betty and the rooks exceed anything yet reported for apes in terms of the apparent manufacture of a tool to match a complex preconceived shape. This does not necessarily mean, however, that corvid tool-making and tool use is more intelligent than that of apes overall. New Caledonian crows manufacture one basic category of tools—probes to extract insects or small invertebrates from crevices or holes. Their tool use thus appears context specific, rather than broadly intelligent (Parker and Gibson 1977). Wild chimpanzees, in contrast, manufacture probing tools, sponging tools, and wiping tools. They also use hammers and anvils and possibly chopping tools (Pruetz and Bertolani 2007; Koops et al. 2010; McGrew 2010). In other words, chimpanzees have a diversity of tool-using and tool-making techniques which they use for a diversity of functions, including obtaining ants or termites from nests and mounds, cracking nuts and animal skulls, sponging up brains and liquids, probing for small animals or honey in tree cavities, and chopping large fruits. Hence, chimpanzee tool use, unlike New Caledonian crow tool use, requires knowledge of diverse foods, diverse environments, and diverse tool-using techniques.

In sum, a few animal species, most notably dolphins, elephants, and corvids, appear to have high intelligence across a variety of domains. A few dolphins and sea lions have demonstrated comprehension of some human gestural 'symbols' and symbol combinations, and one Grey parrot's language-like abilities matched or exceeded those of great apes. Overall, however, the data are insufficient to determine whether any bird or mammal truly matches or exceeds great apes across the entire range of capacities essential for protolanguage. Nor have any of those birds and mammals usually considered especially intelligent yet demonstrated a 'magic' intelligence ingredient, which, if added to the cognitive repertoire of the apes, would be expected to lead to the invention of a protolanguage. Indeed, all seem to be lacking a critical probable function of early protolanguages: displacement.

## 11.3 Types and functions of vocal communicative systems, sound combinations

All human spoken languages have a relatively small number of phonemes which can be hierarchically combined and recombined into tens, even hundreds, of thousands of referentially meaningful words. Words, in turn, can be flexibly and hierarchically combined into a virtually infinite number of novel, meaningful sentences and other complex utterances. These utterances can convey information about virtually any aspect of the physical or social environment. Spoken languages, then, are highly creative and potentially highly informative. Indeed, by about 2 years of age human infants already speak in creative sentences, each of which is composed anew to reflect whatever might be on the infant's mind. No animal vocal communication systems remotely resemble human spoken languages in creative communicative potential.

Nearly all birds and most mammals do, however, have well-developed call systems, which may include alarm calls, contact calls, food calls, signature or individual recognition calls, and the begging calls of the young. Many birds and a few mammals also possess well-developed singing capacities. Song, especially bird song, has drawn considerable attention from language evolution theorists, because it has some clear parallels with speech (Fitch 2010a). Both immature songbirds and human infants babble. Adult vocalizations of both humans and songbirds match at least some aspects of vocalizations heard when young; both humans and songbirds have sensitive periods, subsequent to which vocal learning becomes extremely difficult, and some songs exhibit hierarchical structure. In addition to these functional similarities, it is now known that bird song and human speech rely, at least in part, on homologous neural pathways (Jarvis 2004; Bolhuis and Gahr 2006).

It is questionable, however, how specific or meaningful some of the proposed parallels between speech and bird song really are. Sensitive periods occur in sensory, motor, and other behavioural systems across a wide variety of animals. Indeed, all mammalian and avian nervous systems develop epigenetically: that is, via gene–environment interactions; hence, experience in general, not just in the auditory/vocal realm, affects brain structure and development (Gibson 2005). Further, sensitive periods for bird song and speech are really quite different. In birds, sensitive periods often persist for a short period during development and are then followed by a relatively longer period in which no song occurs until adulthood (Hurford 2011). Even in adulthood, in many species, only males sing. In humans, a highly sensitive period for language development extends to puberty; there is no developmental period of vocal quiescence; and both sexes and all but the youngest infants talk. Nor are hierarchicalization abilities unique to bird song, speech, music, and language. Monkeys and hyenas comprehend hierarchical social relationships (Seyfarth and Cheney, this volume). Gorillas and chimpanzees construct hierarchical manual feeding sequences (Byrne 1995). Human tool-making, art, architecture, dance, gymnastics, and social structure are also hierarchical (Gibson 1996a; Gibson and Jessee 1999). Indeed, it has been argued that all of human cognition develops hierarchically (Case 1985).

Animal songs including the most complex songs of birds and humpback whales also differ profoundly from speech and language. Whereas in humans, the numbers of phonemes in any given language are dwarfed by the numbers of potential words and the virtually infinite variety of potential sentences, in many birds the syllabic repertoire matches or exceeds the number of songs (Hurford 2011). Many bird songs, as well as the songs of humpback whales, do involve some hierarchical combination and recombination of vocal syllables, but, with few exceptions (see Slater, this volume) these combinations result in a finite number of species- or population-specific songs, not in the essentially infinite variety of speech combinations critical for human language. Humpback whale song exhibits somewhat more flexibility than most bird song in that groups of adult males construct new songs each breeding season (Janik 1999). Nonetheless, each season all members of the group sing the same song.

The final and, from an evolutionary standpoint, perhaps the most important contrasts between song and speech are functional (Hurford 2011). Most animal songs function in territorial, mating, or pair bonding situations and have no referential meaning other than to announce the presence and condition of the singer. In contrast, human speech functions primarily within the context of referential human language.

Animal calls are far less elaborate than songs, are not organized hierarchically, and are mostly innate. Still, calls sometimes manifest interesting properties not found in song such as environmental reference. Specifically, those species whose optimal response to predation differs with the nature of predator may emit specific calls in response to specific predators or predator classes (Seyfarth et al. 1980). Vervet monkey alarm calls, for example, differ depending on whether the predator is a snake, a leopard, or an eagle. Each call elicits a different response. Many other mammals and birds have similar predator-specific alarms. Possibly the best developed are the alarm call systems of prairie dogs, small rodents that, along with bison, once dominated the Great Plains of North America (Kiriazis and Slobodchikoff 2006; Slobodchikoff et al. 2009b). These cooperatively breeding animals spend most of their lives in underground burrow systems, but emerge to feed on grasses and seeds during the day. Gunnison's prairie dogs' alarm barks and responses to them differ depending on whether the predator is a hawk, coyote, dog, or human. Barks may be given individually or in rapid succession in response to the speed of predator approach. In experimental conditions, prairie dogs also emitted readily distinguishable and reproducible alarm calls in relationship to differences in human body size and shirt colour, and alarm barks for domestic dogs are also thought to vary with colour and size of the dog (Slobodchikoff et al. 2009a). No animal songs remotely approach prairie dog calls in terms of referential capacity.

Most animal alarm calls, including those of monkeys and prairie dogs, are largely species-specific in that all members of a species use the same calls. As they mature, young monkeys, and possibly other animals as well, refine their calls and learn the appropriate contexts in which to use them. They may also learn to recognize and appropriately respond to the calls of other species. They do not, however, invent or socially transmit new calls. Although some cercopithecine monkeys do combine or, at least juxtapose, limited numbers of calls, these call juxtapositions appear to have different meanings for the monkeys than do the individual calls from which they are composed, in that they elicit different responses (Zuberbühler, this volume). Nor do the monkeys use novel and varied combinations of calls.

Many species of birds and mammals, including most primates, however, also have contact calls and/or food calls that help coordinate group movements and cement social relationships. Unlike alarm calls, contact calls may be learned. Bats, elephants, parrots, and some chimpanzee populations, for example, produce learned group or family-specific contact calls (Boughman 1998; McComb et al. 2000; Wright and Wilkinson 2001; Crockford et al. 2004). Learned calls are useful to species whose members routinely transfer between groups or live in fission–fusion societies. In bats, for example, such calls help coordinate group movements to feeding or roosting sites and determine which bats are permitted to remain at group-specific sites. Dolphins, bats, and some pinnipeds (sea lions, seals, walruses) also create individually-specific signature calls or whistles (Janik 1999; Schusterman 2008). In these taxa, mothers leave their young behind when foraging. Mother and young relocate via the calls. Dolphins also emit their unique signature calls in adult interactions (Janik 1999).

In addition to the rather loud contact calls described above, many mammals and birds, including great apes (Slocombe, this volume) have softer calls used between pairs or in small groups of individuals, including parent/infant contexts. These include the begging calls of altricial birds, and the soft grunts and coos that are used in close contact social-bonding situations by many primates. Marmoset infants also attract adult attention via babbling actions (Snowdon 1997). None of these close contact calls are known to involve the invention or social learning of novel vocalizations. Consequently, close contact calls, like alarm calls, louder contact calls, and animal songs, fall far short of fully-developed human linguistic vocalization. In human infants, however, speech is preceded by and develops from close contact coos and grunts (McCune 1999; MacNeilage 2008). Could not a similar process have occurred in language evolution? If so, why is it necessary to postulate that song, rather than contact calls, preceded speech?

In sum, no one vocal communication system contains all features of speech. Song may be learned, combinatorial, and hierarchical, but it is not referential, and songs are used primarily by adults in breeding or territorial situations. Alarm calls may be referential, but apparently are never learned, hierarchical, or composed of novel sound combinations. Contact calls may be learned, occur in 'friendly' social contexts, are used by both sexes and all ages as well as in mother–infant contexts, but are neither hierarchical nor combinatorial.

## 11.4 Motor communication channels

With the exception of olfactory communication, all animal and human communicative systems require motor channels of expression. Human language, which can be gestural, written or vocal, is possible only because humans are strongly manipulative animals. Humans can make voluntary, precise movements of fingers and hands and flexibly coordinate these movements with each other and with other body parts. Humans also have voluntary control of movements of the soft palate, lips, tongue, and cheeks, and the ability to make very precise movements of the lips and tongue. They create diverse phonetic sounds by coordinating precision movements of the tongue and lips with diverse positions of the teeth and soft palate and with laryngeal voicing.

Great apes have sufficient manual manipulative capacity and arm mobility to create novel manual gestures. With the possible exception of the elephant trunk, no other animal manipulative organs appear to have the motor precision and flexibility essential for the creation of novel visual gestures. The motor precision and flexibility to create and learn novel vocalizations appears somewhat more widespread in that it is found in a number of birds, cetaceans, pinnipeds, bats, and elephants as well as to a much lesser extent in great apes (Boughman 1998; Janik 1999; Poole et al. 2005; Schusterman 2008; Slater, this volume; Slocombe, this volume). A few animals other than parrots and some songbirds—most notably, pinnipeds and elephants—have sufficient vocal flexibility to sometimes imitate human speech (Ralls et al. 1985; Holden 2006).

Schusterman (2008) postulates that pinniped vocal flexibility reflects the need to communicate both on land and under water, as well as the possession of highly mobile oral structures that are used both in complex foraging endeavours and in vocalization. Elephants have extremely flexible, richly innervated trunks which are used in many contexts including sound production, social grooming and play, feeding, tool use, and both the sucking and squirting of water. When mimicking human sounds, elephants may place their trunks in their mouths (Holden 2006). This unusual flexibility of sea lion and elephant supralaryngeal filters may account for their occasional ability to mimic speech. Other mammals with vocal learning capacities include bats and dolphins, echolocators who use vocalizations in varied social, locomotor, and feeding contexts.

Most avian vocal learners possess fine neuromuscular control of the syrinx, their prime vocal organ. Parrots have less complex syringeal control, but they exceed most birds in their abilities to modify sounds via coordinated movements of their highly mobile, fleshy tongues and unusually mobile beaks (Beckers et al. 2004). Parrot tongue and beak mobility also function as foraging adaptations. In particular, parrots crack hard-shelled seeds and nuts using their mobile beaks and then extract the contents with their tongues.

The fact that in mammals and parrots, abilities to make and mimic novel sounds coexist with feeding-related oral or laryngeal modifications suggests that, in some species, fine motor control of the oral cavity may have evolved primarily as a feeding adaptation that was then co-opted for vocal learning. Could this also be true of human speech? Certainly, all great apes have extremely mobile lips and tongues which they use in both feeding and communicative situations. This suggests that, at the very least, great ape feeding adaptations served as pre-adaptations to speech. Moreover, early hominins dating to about 3 million years ago were eating more meat, and, possibly, more tubers, bulbs, and other underground storage organs than great apes (Wrangham et al. 2009; Wynn, this volume). Their dental anatomy had also changed profoundly from that of the apes in that they had relatively larger and more thickly enamelled molars, reduced canines, and more vertically-oriented chewing muscles (Wood and Bauernfeind, this volume). Possibly, then, additional hominin-specific dietary adaptations also served as pre-adaptations to the evolution of increased neural muscular control of the oral apparatus. That the motor capabilities of our vocal tract may be derived, at least in part, from predecessor feeding behaviours is, of course, not a new hypothesis (MacNeilage 2008).

## 11.5 CONCLUSION

Overall, it is clear that only humans evolved speech and language. No other animals, if studied alone, can tell us how it happened. By studying a broad range of animal social, cognitive, communicative, foraging, and motor behaviours, we may, however, eventually be able to solve the language evolution puzzle. Great apes, for example, appear to possess all of the cognitive and communicative skills essential for a gestural protolanguage, but in the wild, they do not use novel gestures or vocalizations to coordinate group actions or to discuss absent events or objects. Studies of other animals that exhibit behaviours that are lacking in apes may help determine the potential selective events that propelled an animal with an ape-like intelligence into the protolanguage domain.

Many other mammals and birds have also demonstrated impressive cognitive skills and one bird, Alex, performed comparably to great apes in many language-learning tasks. No other species, however, have been studied across as broad a range of language learning and cognitive tasks. Hence, whether any other animals possess an ape-like breadth of language-pertinent cognitive and social skills remains unknown. As of now, apes remain the best models of the probable cognitive adaptations of the earliest hominins.

A number of animals do exceed apes in vocal learning skills. In many cases, these skills manifest themselves in song. Song, however, differs from speech and language in critical structural and functional respects. Moreover, other animals, not necessarily known for their song, are more widely recognized for their overall cognitive capacities and, in some cases, appear more adept at mimicking human speech. Hence, it is suggested that an examination of oral/vocal behaviours other than song, such as contact calls or feeding behaviours, may also shed light on the evolution of the speech modality.

# THE BIOLOGY OF LANGUAGE EVOLUTION: ANATOMY, GENETICS, AND NEUROLOGY

# CHAPTER 12

# INTRODUCTION TO PART II: THE BIOLOGY OF LANGUAGE EVOLUTION: ANATOMY, GENETICS AND NEUROLOGY

KATHLEEN R. GIBSON AND
MAGGIE TALLERMAN

Some of us have long assumed that instinct versus learning controversies met their demise back in the 1960s with publications such as 'How an instinct is learned' (Hailman 1969) and the insightful behavioural analyses of Robert Hinde (1966). Not so. In Fitch's view (Chapter 13), these controversies continue, both because they reflect interdisciplinary gaps and because of the tendency of scientists to black-box issues not of their own immediate concern. Concepts of instinct and innateness are actually quite useful for describing behaviours that routinely characterize all members of species or at least all species members of specific sex and age classes. Thus, they tend to be favoured by scientists with a primary focus on the distinctive behaviours of individual species. To many developmental biologists and developmental psychologists, however, instinct and innateness are fallacious concepts because all behaviours develop through gene–environment interactions. The solution to this dilemma, in Fitch's view, is to abandon the terms 'instinct' and 'learning' in favour of other terms that more accurately describe the phenomena in question, such as 'species-specific' or 'species-typical' to describe behaviours routinely displayed by all members of a species, and 'canalization' (Waddington 1942) to explain the species-typical gene–environment interactions that produce behavioural regularities. From this perspective, language is a species-specific human behaviour that is developmentally canalized via interactions of genes and predictable environmental impacts such as typical adult–infant interactions.

Although all animals display species-specific behaviours, most also exhibit behavioural plasticity in response to learning and/or in response to environmental conditions that may directly impact on brain development or physiological status (West-Eberhard 2003). Some animals can even, if subject to unusual rearing conditions, develop behaviours not considered typical of their species. Great apes reared in human homes or subject to language-training experiments, for example, develop a number of behaviours not found in wild apes. In other words, dissimilar phenotypes (i.e. observable behaviours and characteristics) can develop from similar genotypes (i.e. genetic endowment), a phenomenon termed phenotypic plasticity. As Számadó and Szathmáry (Chapter 14) note, phenotypic plasticity plays important evolutionary roles. Specifically, those phenotypes which prove adaptive and the genes that facilitate their development are subject to positive selection, hence, increase in the population (see also West-Eberhard 2003). Ultimately, these phenotypes may become fixed in the population (Baldwin effect; Baldwin 1902). If the genes producing them also become fixed, genetic assimilation will have occurred (Waddington 1953).

Each species occupies physical environments that can change in response to numerous external events such as climate change, earthquakes, or volcanic eruptions. Species, however, also modify and create their own environments, and hence the selective pressures that impinge upon them, a process termed niche construction (Odling-Smee et al. 2003). Although external environmental events have undoubtedly influenced human evolution, niche construction has arguably played an even greater role in shaping the selective forces that help mould the modern human mind, and perhaps the human body as well, because our lineage has repeatedly created and adapted to new technological, cultural, and linguistic environments. It is sometimes thought that genetic change is too slow for our genes and brain to have adapted to selective pressures posed by ever-changing languages and cultures. Számadó and Szathmáry counter this argument by presenting numerous examples of rapid genetic change in humans and other species. They also argue that the pace of language change, like technological change, was probably considerably slower during Pleistocene times than it is today. The result of the combined processes of potentially rapid genetic change and an earlier, somewhat slower, pace of language change is that genes, languages, and the brain have co-evolved, and to some extent may be continuing to do so. On the one hand, genes and brains enable language; on the other, language change selects for further, linguistically-conducive, changes in genes and brains.

## 12.1  Developmental plasticity and genes

Számadó and Szathmáry (Chapter 14) also suggest that some biological systems, such as the immune system, are specifically adapted to enable rapid responses to environmental change. They suggest, for example, that the brain has been specifically shaped by selection to function as a rapid responder to linguistic change (and we would add cultural change as well). This postulate draws clear support, not only from our species' well-recognized learning and problem-solving capacities, but also from the plasticity that characterizes all developing and mature mammalian brains. First, during early developmental periods, all mammalian brains routinely overproduce neurons; those neurons that fail to achieve full functionality are subsequently pruned (Edelman 1987). In humans, neuronal production primarily occurs prenatally, as does much neuronal pruning. Similarly, all mammalian brains overproduce synapses during certain periods of development. Again, those that fail to achieve full functionality are later pruned. Our species typically overproduces synapses in the first several postnatal years and again just prior to puberty. One unexpected result is that the typical human adolescent has more synapses than most adults, at least in the frontal lobes (Blakemore and Choudhury 2006). Although the production and pruning of neurons and synapses is primarily a maturational phenomenon, these processes never truly cease. New cortical synapses continue to be produced and pruned throughout life, and a region of the brain concerned with declarative and episodic memory (Zito and Svoboda 2002), the hippocampus, continues to produce new neurons throughout life (Eriksson et al. 1998).

These processes have demonstrable functional effects. For example, in rats, final adult brain size as well as performance on laboratory learning exercises varies depending on experience during the maturational process (Bennett et al. 1964). Similarly, humans who practise particular skills such as piano-playing or taxi-driving develop enlarged neural structures pertinent to those tasks (Amunts et al. 1997; Maguire et al. 2000). Language-related functional reorganizations are also known to occur in humans in relationship to environmental inputs. For example, in congenitally deaf subjects who master sign language at a young age, regions of the temporal lobe that normally mediate auditory functions become more attuned to visual input, including visual gestures (Neville 1991). Similarly, the visual neocortex of congenitally blind subjects assumes tactile functions, if such individuals master Braille at a young age (Sadato et al. 1998). Even literacy changes brain functions, and may, in fact, sharpen the neural perception of phonemes (Dehaene et al. 2010). Recognition of the environmentally-induced developmental plasticity of mammalian brains helps explain why chimpanzees, bonobos, and other apes, reared from infancy in human homes, can, within limits, develop protolanguage-like behaviours, whereas wild apes and/or apes captured in adulthood usually cannot.

Brain plasticity, of course, has its limits. All brains of a given species strongly resemble each other in overall structure and function. This must reflect considerable genetic programming. As Számadó and Szathmáry note, numerous genes impact on brain development, and these genes appear to evolve at a rapid pace, thereby potentially impacting rapid evolutionary changes in behaviour. Diller and Cann (Chapter 15) focus on specific genes thought to influence the evolution of language and the brain. *FOXP2*, a regulatory gene, helps determine when and where other genes are expressed. In humans, certain *FOXP2* mutations produce orofacial dyspraxia (possibly by disrupting motor sequencing behaviours), some language deficits, and mal-development of several neural structures (Lai et al. 2003). In other animals, depending on the species, *FOXP2* may exhibit increased or decreased activity during periods of vocal learning. Hence, although no evidence indicates that *FOXP2* directly controls for vocal behaviour, the gene does, apparently, impact on the development and functions of neural structures that do. Specific human mutations in the *FOXP2* gene were once thought to have occurred in the last 120,000 years. Re-evaluations of the genetic data now suggest a much earlier date of about 1.8 to 1.9 million years ago (Diller and Cann, Chapter 15).

Diller and Cann also review variants of two additional genes that, when mutated in modern humans, result in microcephaly (*microcephalin* and *ASPM*). Dysfunctional mutations in these genes result in abnormally small brains. Hence, it has been suggested that both played key roles in the evolutionary enlargement of the brain. Brain development, however, is a complex process involving hundreds, possibly thousands, of genes. Functional disruptions in any of these can cause developmental neural pathologies. This does not mean that earlier, different mutations in the same genes caused increased brain size, only that normal, fully-functional genes are needed for brain development. Other evidence cited by Diller and Cann, however, indicates that certain variants of *ASPM* and *microcephalin* have increased in frequency in the last 37,000 and 5800 years respectively. Some have interpreted this to mean that these genes are currently experiencing positive selection for their roles in brain function or development, but after reanalysing the data, Diller and Cann conclude that the increased gene frequencies could equally well represent genetic drift. In their view, in-depth analysis also fails to support reports of correlations between the distribution of these genes and tonal languages. Ultimately, Diller and Cann conclude that language evolution is likely to have resulted from interactions of a multiplicity of genes, rather than from a single mutation in a 'magic' language gene. In sum, despite increasing research in this area, our understandings of the genetic basis of language and of human-specific neural developmental pathways remain vague.

## 12.2 Adult brains

Even though human children speak in full sentences by the time they are about 2½ years old, most research on the neurological basis of language focuses on the anatomy of the adult brain and, then, mostly on brain size or on the anatomy of neocortical structures, some of which reach full functionality only in adolescence or later. Brain size, both absolute and relative to body size, did increase steadily from about 2,000,000 to 300,000 years ago (Mann, Chapter 26). It is likely that these size increases were functionally adaptive; otherwise, they would have been selected against. Large brains, after all, are metabolically expensive (Aiello and Wheeler 1995). Specific language-related neural structures have also increased in size in human evolution, as delineated in a number of the chapters in this section. Consequently, increased brain size almost certainly contributed to the evolution of language. However, no one-to-one correlation exists between language and overall brain size, and no specific brain size Rubicon separates the linguistically capable from the linguistically inept. Indeed, given that microcephalics do not entirely lack linguistic abilities (Diller and Cann, Chapter 15) it is clear that overall brain size is not the sole determinant of language capacity.

Most investigators have worked on the assumption that language evolution primarily involved the neocortex, either the differential expansion of neocortical areas and connections already present in non-human primates and/or the addition of new neocortical structures. Gibson (Chapter 16) takes a somewhat different stance. Following on from Gibson and Jessee (1999) and P. Lieberman (1991, 2000, 2002), she reminds us that lesions in structures such as the cerebellum and basal ganglia often produce speech and language deficits. These areas have greatly expanded in human evolution and they mature earlier than many areas of the neocortex (Gibson 1991). In addition, a greater percentage of descending cortical fibres terminate directly on brainstem and spinal cord motor neurons in humans than in monkeys and apes, providing for finer control of lip, tongue, and finger movements (Kuypers 1958). Consequently, neural areas and connections other than those confined to the neocortex deserve far greater scrutiny from the language origins community.

Donald (Chapter 17) also emphasizes the role of neural circuitry involving the basal ganglia, cerebellum, and neocortical areas (especially the premotor and dorsolateral prefrontal cortex). These circuits enable procedural learning, that is, the acquisition of motor skills that require much practice, including those needed for mimesis and tool-making, both of which, in his view, preceded language evolutionarily (see also Arbib, Chapter 20). Donald further notes that although mimesis is, in large part, a sensorimotor function, the social contexts in which it is used are amodal. Hence, once mimesis became an integral part of human behaviour, through, for example, mime, it would have selected for enhanced amodal cognitive capacities, such as those needed for language and mediated by the inferior parietal and frontal lobes (see also Wilkins, Chapter 19).

Most vertebrate brains exhibit functional lateralization (Rogers and Andrew 2002). In humans, the left hemisphere controls the right arm and hand and, as Hopkins and Vauclair (Chapter 18) note, it is also dominant for language and speech in 96% of right-handed and 70% of left-handed individuals. Although it has long been known that individual primates prefer specific hands, until recently it was assumed that population-wide preferences for the right hand were a uniquely human trait. Indeed, the coincidence of two left hemisphere-controlled, largely species-specific human behaviours (right-handedness and language) has led to hypotheses that cerebral lateralization, language, and right-handedness evolved together in a causally interconnected manner (Corballis 1993; Crow 2004). Such views long received support from studies indicating that monkeys and apes fail to display population-level handedness in simple manual reaching tasks. More recently, however, Hopkins' group has found population-wide right-handedness in captive chimpanzees, when they were tested on complex manipulative tasks requiring that an object be held in one hand and manipulated in the other (Hopkins 1995).

In Chapter 18, Hopkins and Vauclair also report that captive chimpanzees, bonobos, gorillas, and baboons all exhibit population-wide biases for the use of the right hand for communicative gestures. In contrast, judging by asymmetrical facial expressions, the majority of vocalizations and facial expressions in non-human primates are controlled by the right hemisphere. The few exceptions, controlled by the left hemisphere, include marmoset twitters and the novel raspberry sounds and extended food grunts made by some captive chimpanzees. Hence, lateralization in non-human primates may be greater for communicative gestures than for manipulative behaviours, and for voluntary, as opposed to emotional, vocalizations. These findings suggest that left-hemisphere dominance for speech and language may have been preceded evolutionarily by left-hemisphere dominance for voluntary gestures and vocalizations in other primates.

In humans, language and handedness are usually thought to be accompanied by differential expansion of some left-hemisphere areas, in comparison to similar areas on the right. A literature review by Hopkins and Vauclair finds that Broca's area is somewhat inconsistently expanded in the left hemisphere in both apes and humans. In contrast, the left temporal plane is usually expanded not only in humans, but in apes as well. The left Sylvian fissure is also somewhat longer than the right in both apes and humans. This fissure, which separates the temporal lobe from the parietal and frontal lobes, is surrounded by neocortical areas known to have language functions. In sum, anatomical and behavioural data indicate that neural asymmetry is neither unique to humans nor a specific language specialization. That great apes and monkeys exhibit greater lateralization with respect to gestural usage and voluntary vocalizations may, however, provide clues to possible behavioural precursors to speech and language.

Wilkins (Chapter 19) addresses the anatomy and functions of Broca's area, the POT (parieto-occipito-temporal junction), the inferior parietal lobe, and tracts that interconnect these areas. Since one of her aims is the delineation of ape/human neural differences potentially visible in the fossil record, her primary focus is on those species differences that can be seen on the external surface of the brain. This is a critical point, because historically three different parameters have been used to identify neural regions: external anatomy, internal cellular architecture (cytoarchitecture), and function. The three do not always provide identical results. For example, a Broca's area homologue was identified in monkey and ape brains via cytoarchitecture as early as the 1940s (von Bonin and Bailey 1947; Krieg 1954), but most investigators continued to insist, based on external morphology, that Broca's area was unique to humans until the discovery, in the 1990s, of mirror neurons, in what many now accept as the monkey homologue of Broca's area (see Arbib, Chapter 20). Similarly, rhesus monkey and chimpanzee brains contain cytoarchitectonic areas that these earlier neuroanatomists considered homologous to the human POT. Externally, however, the anatomy of the POT region is quite different in apes and humans. In apes, the lunate sulcus separates the occipital lobe from the parietal and temporal lobes, while all three lobes merge in the human brain. Wilkins accepts that much of the parietal cortex and Broca's area have homologues in monkey and ape brains, but she considers the POT to be uniquely human. Nonetheless, she concludes from fossil evidence that the POT evolved early in our lineage, prior to speech. These findings present an evolutionary quandary. The so-called language areas of the human brain apparently evolved long prior to language. From this, she concludes that language evolution involved exaptation, that is, the re-appropriation of pre-existing functions to new uses.

For the most part, Wilkins focuses on the spatial functions of the parietal lobes and their interactions with Broca's and other motor areas in the frontal lobe. Specifically, she notes that that the human POT plays an active role in the formation of modality-free conceptual structures (see also Coolidge and Wynn, Chapter 21; Donald, Chapter 17). In her view, these functions represent a natural expansion of primate posterior parietal lobe functions, which include the construction of modality-neutral spatial concepts and the spatial orientation of arm and hand movements. In non-human primates, these posterior parietal functions are coordinated with motor functions of the frontal lobes to produce object-related actions. She hypothesizes that the expansion (or emergence) of the POT permitted the enhanced spatial analyses required for the coordination of arm, hand, and thumb movements with respect to tool use and throwing (see also Calvin 1985). Since many linguistic structures are spatially and thematically organized, POT expansion also provided the necessary conceptual structure for critical components of the language function; hence, in her view, spatial skills that developed initially in tool-using situations were later co-opted for language.

Arbib (Chapter 20) also pursues issues of primate/human neural homologues and neural exaptations. He accepts that the human Broca's area is homologous with similar areas in monkeys and apes, but notes that it has no obvious vocal functions in other species. In contrast, neural areas that do mediate primate vocalizations have no known linguistic role in the human brain. Rather, he posits that mirror neurons found in Broca's area of non-human primates served as the foundation stones upon which imitation, gesture, and language were built. These neurons fire when a monkey executes a particular manual action and when it observes another individual performing the same action. Mirror neurons thus provide an essential language function—parity; that is, assuring that communicator and recipient have similar perceptions. In Arbib's view, mirror neurons serve as essential components of language and imitation, but are not, by themselves, sufficient to mediate behaviours which require the hierarchical integration of multiple actions and concepts. Since the earliest mirror neurons to be identified were related to manual actions, Arbib adopts a gestural model of language origins and delineates how such a system may have evolved. More recent research indicates that mirror neurons are also found in the inferior parietal lobe; may represent oral movements as well as manual; and may also be of an audiovisual nature. Hence, the mirror neuron story continues to unfold.

Coolidge and Wynn (Chapter 21) focus on the neurological and cognitive correlates of indirect speech, that is, intentionally ambiguous utterances that must be interpreted with regard to social context and that are used primarily in situations that require diplomacy. In their view, indirect speech requires working memory, executive control structures, and theory of mind. Working memory, in turn, is composed of phonological storage capacity, a visual spatial sketchpad and an episodic buffer which allows the contents of phonological storage and the visuospatial sketchpad to be simultaneously held in conscious thought, manipulated, and combined and recombined with respect to each other. Hence, it facilitates the construction of complex plans and mental models. Executive functions monitor these activities via selective inhibition and attention. Since indirect speech is a product of multiple interacting cognitive components, it must also be a product of multiple interacting regions of the brain. In particular, Coolidge and

Wynn note the involvement of the inferior parietal and superior temporal lobes and the dorsolateral frontal cortex.

Taken as a whole, the chapters in this section indicate that nearly all higher neural processing centres play some role in the mediation of language or speech. The complexity of the neural interactions required for indirect speech, in particular, suggests that whatever neural changes may have been needed to initiate and sustain protolanguage and/or the language of human infants, fully developed 'diplomatic' language capacities reflect the interactions of much of the neocortex. In her paper on ape language (Chapter 3), Gibson notes that great apes fall short of humans in their ability to construct linguistic, technical, and other hierarchies, and it is widely accepted that many aspects of language, most strikingly syntax, are hierarchically structured. Consequently, it would seem of prime interest to determine which neural areas mediate hierarchical abilities. Greenfield (1991) assigned that role to Broca's area. Arbib (Chapter 20) follows her lead. Wilkins (Chapter 19) remarks that the POT is structured to automatically create mental hierarchies. Coolidge and Wynn (Chapter 21) do not use the term 'hierarchical', but they do suggest that the ability to hold multiple images in mind in order to combine and recombine them is mediated by the dorsolateral frontal lobe. That the various authors in this section assigned hierarchical processing or components thereof to different parts of the neocortex would appear to validate earlier suggestions by Gibson that the creation of linguistic and other hierarchies, like indirect speech, requires the interactions of multiple cortical processing areas (Gibson 1996a; Gibson and Jessee 1999).

## 12.3  THE VOCAL TRACT

Although changes in brain function almost certainly played central roles in language evolution, as MacLarnon notes (Chapter 22), other critical anatomical changes occurred as well. For example, the larynx is lower in humans than in apes and the oral cavity is differently structured. Together, these changes allow humans to produce sounds not readily produced by apes. This vocal tract reorganization may have been facilitated by bipedalism, diet, or a combination of the two. In addition, humans have far greater neural control of their breathing than do apes, and, unlike apes, they have no laryngeal air sacs. MacLarnon suggests that increased control of the respiratory apparatus involved expansion of the numbers of neurons in the thoracic spinal cord. While it is impossible to determine laryngeal position from fossils, the very few hyoid bones that have been found suggest that modern human laryngeal structure, including absent air sacs, may have been present in the common ancestor of Neanderthals and anatomically modern humans, but not in australopithecines. Similarly, fossil vertebrae indicate that both Neanderthals and anatomically modern humans had achieved the modern size of the thoracic spinal cord, but *Homo erectus* had not (see Wood and Bauernfeind, Chapter 25, for a contrary view on the thoracic cord).

## 12.4 SUMMARY

In sum, evidence indicates that language evolution probably demanded changes in multiple interacting genes and involved expansions in multiple parts of the brain, as well as changes in the vocal tract and thoracic spinal cord. Given our current understandings of exaptation, niche construction, the Baldwin effect, and neural plasticity, neural changes probably built upon precursor neurobehavioural functions in non-human primates and occurred over a lengthy period of time. In some cases both neural and vocal changes may have occurred in response to the selective pressures exerted by language and culture, as opposed to strictly external environmental circumstances; see also Bickerton (2009a). Nothing that we know about genetic or neural functions would suggest that language arose in response to a sudden mutation or the sudden appearance of a new neural module.

# CHAPTER 13

# INNATENESS AND HUMAN LANGUAGE: A BIOLOGICAL PERSPECTIVE

## W. TECUMSEH FITCH

## 13.1 INTRODUCTION

Nativism is the idea that some traits that an adult organism exhibits are caused not by postnatal interactions with the environment, but by virtue of biology, due to inborn or 'innate' factors already present when its life began. By this broad characterization, every biologist is a nativist. A congenital disease like cystic fibrosis is caused *not* by interactions with the environment (infection, toxins, injury, etc.) but by causal factors already present in the fertilized egg (namely, homozygosity for a rare recessive allele in the *CFTR* gene). Despite critics' frequent accusations, using the term 'innate' in such cases does not entail belief in 'pure' genetic causes (the environment necessarily plays a role), or in determinism (medical treatment can often ameliorate genetic diseases), or in preformationism (foetuses do not suffer from cystic fibrosis *in utero*). It simply picks out an important subset of traits that we observe in living organisms: those that have an important, ineliminable genetic basis.

Descartes argued, by analogy with hereditary diseases, that some *ideas* are inborn in a similar sense. Although most subsequent discussion of this 'doctrine of innate ideas' occurred among philosophers, in the 1950s Noam Chomsky put it at centre stage in linguistics, with his argument that crucial components of the mechanisms by which humans acquire language are innate, and that the 'general learning mechanisms' studied by behaviourist psychologists were inadequate for this task. Chomsky argued that language acquisition requires a more specialized set of innate propensities than the (innate) conditioned responses and analogical processes that Skinner (1957) claimed were sufficient. Despite intense debate, all parties agree that whatever systems underlie language acquisition must be biologically given, and following the critique of Chomsky (1959) few scholars have argued that the behaviourists' 'general learning mechanisms'—Skinner's 'tacts' and 'mands'—are up to the task.

Thus, despite oceans of partisan advocacy and rhetoric, this debate boils down to three substantive issues. First, what do we mean by 'innate' and how useful is this concept in biology? Second, what do we mean by 'cause' and how adequate are everyday conceptions for understanding biological causality (cf. Wagner 1999)? Finally, how specific to language are the innate mechanisms underlying language acquisition? This essay explores the first question, surveying the multiple uses of 'innate' and 'instinctive', and critiques thereof, by practising biologists, and aiming to delineate the useful concepts that underlie these usages. I argue that both mechanistic and evolutionary studies in biology demand a concept of 'heritable' or 'epigenetically determined' traits, and that nativist arguments remain a core component of biology, even for those who, perhaps wisely, avoid the term 'innate'. Nonetheless, both the word *and* the underlying concepts are inadequate to deal with the complexity of the developmental processes that generate such traits. The causally cyclical and interactive nature of ontogeny often leads developmentalists (both in biology and linguistics) to object to nativist arguments as 'preformation-ist', and to advocate some alternative '-ism' like constructivism (e.g. Quartz and Sejnowski 1997). I will conclude that the value of nativist concepts depends on the scientific question under investigation, and outline a pluralistic, Tinbergian explanatory framework to help delineate these valid usages.

## 13.2 BIOLOGICAL USAGES OF THE TERM 'INNATE'

Most nativists today use biology, and some notion like 'biologically given' or 'genetically determined' as their conceptual foundation. Critics of nativism just as often use biology, particularly developmental biology, to ground their attacks. This justifies limiting my discussion here to biology.

Biologists have long found useful the term 'innate', or the allied term 'instinct' (which I will use hereafter as a shorthand for 'innate behavioural patterns'). Darwin made free use of both words, which for him typically connoted 'partially unlearned' and 'having a heritable basis'. Darwin did not flinch from applying them to human behaviour: he argued that most aspects of human emotional expression are 'innate or instinctive', and used the close similarities between facial expressions in humans and other primates as strong evidence for our descent from an ape-like ancestor (Darwin 1872).

Darwin's heavy reliance on the notion that behaviours have an unlearned biological basis is unsurprising: heritability is one of the pillars of natural selection, and some instinctive component is thus logically necessary if behaviour is to evolve adaptively. A broad notion of 'innate' in the sense of 'having *some* genetic basis' has thus been central to evolutionary approaches to behaviour ever since. However, Darwin did not see instinct and learning as incompatible, opposing concepts. Darwin accepted that language is an 'art' rather than a 'true instinct' (because words and rules must be learned), but he also observed that language differs 'widely from all ordinary arts, for man has an instinctive tendency to speak, as we see in the babble of our young children; whilst no child has an instinctive tendency to brew, bake, or write'. For Darwin (1871: 55–56), language was not an instinct, but 'an instinctive tendency to acquire an art'.

The marriage of Mendelian genetics and Darwinian evolution during the modern synthesis of the 1930s (Fisher 1930; Dobzhansky 1937) put talk of heritability on a new scientific foundation. For founding ethologist Konrad Lorenz, an early student of instinctive behaviour, instincts could thus be denoted as acts with an adaptive, genetic basis (Lorenz 1965). Nonetheless, Lorenz's prototypical example of an instinct—imprinting in birds—requires an environmental trigger (the presence of a parent) to be of functional value. Genotypes do not generate phenotypes in a vacuum, and to mature properly, instincts may require inputs from the environment that are both permissive (adequate nutrition) and instructive (a moving parent). Like Darwin, Lorenz saw no incompatibility between learning and instinct.

Lorenz and other ethologists focused on the study of instinct for at least three practical reasons:

1. It justified the discussion and experimental investigation of the *adaptive function* of behaviour, in a Darwinian context.
2. It allowed ethologists to construct phylogenetic taxonomies of behaviour, and thus to explore the evolution of behaviour using the comparative method.
3. It signalled a research strategy focused on those aspects of behaviour that appear reliably in a species by the time of study, but which avoided the difficult problem of their developmental origins by treating them as a 'black box'.

The first two arguments are accepted, virtually universally, by biologists today. The third, though controversial, follows from the first two goals. Scientists cannot explore all questions simultaneously, and although evidence that a behaviour has *some* genetic basis is logically necessary for evolutionary investigation, such investigations do not demand any detailed specification of that genetic basis. 'Black-boxing' is the practice, common to all scientific endeavours, of focusing on certain aspects of the current problem, and taking for granted the (eventual) solution of others. Treating gravity as a black box gave Newtonian physics great explanatory power, even though (eventually) the 'gravity box' needed to be opened and understood. Similarly, neuroscientists can treat neurotransmitter binding coefficients as black-box variables without delving into the quantum physics that underlie them. When ethologist Niko Tinbergen investigated the adaptive significance of a nesting gull's removal of eggshells from the nest (a behaviour adults exhibit 'instinctively', without observation of others), he could safely treat this behaviour as genetically determined without knowing the specific genes or ontogenetic pathways involved. Black-boxing simply reflects one's current scientific goals. The early ethologists' core goals were to study function and mechanism, and their frequent black-boxing of development implied no denial of the importance or interest of developmental questions (Tinbergen 1963). Nonetheless, ethologists encountered sharp resistance focused around this point, particularly in the English-speaking world.

## 13.3 DEVELOPMENTALIST CRITIQUES OF 'INNATENESS'

Developmental psychologist Daniel Lehrman's famous attack on Lorenz and Tinbergen's ethology (Lehrman 1953) correctly noted that ethologists used the term 'instinct' in multiple different ways, and that this polysemy, and the subsequent tendency to conflate several different meanings, sometimes made their discussions of instinct slippery. In different contexts, the adjective 'instinctive' might mean that the behaviour in question is unlearned, inflexible, characteristic of a species, an adaptation, present at birth, or develops without practice. This basic charge of rampant polysemy has been developed by many subsequent critics of nativist explanations (e.g. Elman et al. 1997; Griffiths 2002; Mameli and Bateson 2006). While each implication above may be correct in certain contexts, they do not always co-occur. Thus, song is an adaptation typical of some bird species, but is neither unlearned, inflexible, nor present at birth. Species-typical courtship behaviours in waterfowl are adaptations characteristic of a species, but are not present at birth, and require practice to perfect. Ethologists recognized this polysemy, and pleaded guilty to both ambiguous and occasional sloppy use of the term 'instinct' (Lorenz 1965). But of course, most terms are polysemous, and it is not multiple context-dependent usages that are objectionable, but rather unwarranted slippage between these meanings in the same context. Thus this, by itself, is a weak criticism: careful thinkers who define what they mean by 'innate', and stick with that meaning, are immune to it. And substituting some new terms for 'innate' will not, by itself, guard against slippery reasoning.

The more telling criticism offered by Lehrman and subsequent anti-nativist biologists is that the term 'instinct' black-boxes precisely those processes and mechanisms that are of central interest to developmentalists. Any biologically-grounded notion of 'genetically determined' must ultimately be cashed out in terms of the developmental process that converts genotypes to phenotypes, and cannot ignore development. Lehrman, a developmentalist, assumes without argument throughout his critique that *the* scientific question for students of behaviour is the developmental question. This critique reflects the central importance of learning as *the* driving force of behaviour in Behaviourist psychology. But Lorenz's impassioned defence of the concept of instinct made it clear that ethologists' central interests were *evolutionary*, not developmental. Lorenz (1965: 31) correctly notes that, 'if the fact is forgotten that adaptedness exists and needs an explanation, [ethology] loses its character of a biological science'. Lorenz and his colleague Niko Tinbergen argued that evolved innate mechanisms could not be avoided in understanding behaviour, but that developmental, mechanistic, and evolutionary questions all have a role to play in ethology, which naturally embraces each of them (Tinbergen 1963).

Furthermore, Lorenz sharply rejected Lehrman's dichotomous view that instinct implies no learning or environmental influences. He denounced, as the central fallacy of his critics, 'treating the "innate" and the "learned" as opposed mutually exclusive concepts' (Lorenz 1965: 29). Much of the mischief caused by the term 'instinct' was based on the psychologists' interpretation of this as meaning 'wholly unlearned'. The ethological antidote to this misconception is nicely captured in the modern perspective on bird song as an 'instinct to learn' (Gould and Marler 1987; Marler 1999), and Lorenz provided many other examples where environmental input is necessary for instincts to mature correctly. As Lorenz noted, learning mechanisms must themselves be innate. More importantly, many of the 'teaching' mechanisms which guide the learning process must also be innate (Pavlov's 'unconditioned responses'). These mechanisms range from very simple (avoidance of pain) to quite complex (e.g. 'red underneath' signalling a rival to a male stickleback fish). For Lorenz the question was simply whether the particular items of adaptively-relevant information that inform a specific complex behavioural pattern were acquired via individual ontogeny ('learning'), or via evolution, and already present in the genome ('instinctive'). All complex behaviours, and indeed all aspects of the organism, require an environment to develop, of course, but this does not mean that the *specific information* reflected in a behaviour needs to be learned.

Lorenz concluded that learning is impossible without inherited information, but he denied the opposite claim, viz that all instincts entail learning: some behaviours are strikingly *resistant* to learning, resembling reflexes more than voluntary actions. To avoid discussion or exploration of these innate mechanisms is to 'black-box' precisely those components of behaviour that ethologists found centrally interesting. While rejecting as a false dichotomy innate versus learned, with one defined by exclusion of the other, Lorenz suggested it was perfectly reasonable to ask whether information used in behaviour derived from the genome or from individual experience. For the former case, Lorenz (1965: 2) claimed that abandoning 'innate' as a term 'leaves us without a word denoting an indispensable concept'.

Nonetheless, sensing that Lorenz was fighting a losing terminological battle, Tinbergen avoided using the term 'innate' in most of his later work. In contemporary biology the outcome is also clear: developmental biologists, and ethologists interested in development, rarely use the terms 'innate' and 'instinct', except in such dichotomy-denying phrases as the 'instinct to learn' (Marler 1991). This avoidance has been justified with vigorous, persuasive arguments (Oyama 1985; Griffiths 2002; Bateson 2004). But although evolutionary biologists tend to eschew 'innate', preferring 'genetically coded' or similar terms, they have certainly not relinquished the underlying concepts (Tinbergen 1963; Dawkins 1986; Marler 1999), because modern behavioural biology, behavioural ecology, and evolutionary theory rely upon the traits of interest having an ineliminable epigenetic basis. Lorenz's *concept* of 'innateness' is thus alive and well in biology, even if the term 'innate' is languishing.

## 13.4 THE DICHOTOMY THAT WOULDN'T DIE

Nonetheless, dichotomous views of 'innate' and 'learned' persist among non-biologists. For example, philosopher Richard Samuels rejects any concepts of 'innate' that have the 'highly implausible consequence that traits can be both learned and innate' (Samuels 2004: 138). Nor, as Pinker (2004) points out in an article entitled 'Why nature and nurture won't go away', has use of these terms diminished in modern cognitive science and linguistics. Evolutionary psychologists and linguistic nativists alike accept the explanatory centrality of an evolved genetic basis as adequate justification for considering 'innate' traits as a key part of human nature (Tooby and Cosmides 1990; Jenkins 1999; Laland and Brown 2002;

Maclaurin 2002). Many developmental psychologists disagree, and bridle when innate 'human nature' is rolled out as an explanatory concept (Elman et al. 1997). Scholars in the human-oriented sciences have not stopped exhuming what Bateson (2002) termed 'the corpse of a wearisome debate'.

In defence of continued usage, Samuels (2004) admits that the modern biological understanding of genetic determination fails 'to map smoothly onto the notion of innateness' used by cognitive scientists. Similarly, Pinker (2004: 12) claims that the term 'gene' as used by evolutionary psychologists 'is distinct from the most common use of the term "gene" in molecular biology'. Such divergent uses of an essentially biological term, among psychologists, seem a counterproductive hindrance to interdisciplinary communication.

Another traditional gambit is to see 'innateness' as a continuum, and to use genetic heritability, a technical measure borrowed from applied genetics, to quantify it. Some traits (like the number of fingers on a human hand) are 'mostly innate', while others (like one's taste in music) are probably 'mostly environmental'. Despite being a step in the right direction, this move does not solve the problem, because the assumption that the degree of innateness can be quantified on a simple line from more to less 'innate' is deeply problematic. In a trenchant critique, Lewontin (1974) showed that such attempts fail, because of the central, but typically invalid, assumption implicit in heritability measures: that genetic and environmental variance is additive. In reality, the natures of the causal forces underlying these two sources of variance are entirely different. Furthermore, experiments controlling genotype and phenotype can have many outcomes, and the 'norm of reaction' observed is highly dependent upon the range of environments, and also the range of the genetic backgrounds, explored. For most traits, there is no theoretical justification for using standard analysis of variance and heritability measures to determine how 'genetically determined'—and thus how 'innate'—a trait is. All traits indeed have both genetic and environmental bases, but these cannot be adequately conceptualized as x% genetic and (100 − x)% environmental. The 'heritability' gambit therefore fails to adequately resolve the issue.

Thus, contemporary cognitive scientists and linguists are left relying on terms and concepts that are essentially biological, but that many biologists vigorously reject. What gives? Are some of these biologists right, and others wrong?

## 13.5  A TINBERGENIAN DIAGNOSIS

The answer, alluded to by Tinbergen long ago, is simple: it depends on the problem at hand, or more broadly, the goals of the scientific research programme under discussion. I want to carry Tinbergen's allusion a bit further, using his famous 'four whys' as a basis for clarifying proper and improper uses of nativist concepts. Tinbergen observed that questions about why an animal exhibits some behaviour have multiple answers, each equally valid, and each important in any complete explanation. He specified four separate questions. Two concern individual organisms: the causal physiological MECHANISMS involved, and the ONTOGENETIC HISTORY of those mechanisms during development; and two concern the species to which the organism belongs: the ADAPTIVE FUNCTION of the mechanism, and the PHYLOGENETIC HISTORY by which it evolved in the species. Tinbergen's crucial insight was that, although all these questions are valid, and *complementary* components of a complete explanation, the answers are often misconstrued as *alternative* explanations. This was the central cause of the rancorous disputes between ethologists and behaviourists: evolutionists treated instinctive behaviour as a given, and inquired into its adaptive function, often using the term 'innate' to 'black-box' the specific genetic bases and development of such behaviours. Their developmentalist critics saw the latter as the central concerns, and typically 'black-boxed' evolutionary, adaptive questions about their ultimate origin. If I am correct in this diagnosis, it is no surprise that the biggest opponents of nativism have traditionally investigated developmental biology, development psychology, or language acquisition.

This observation allows us to draw a distinction cross-cutting the usual grouping of Tinbergen's questions into 'ultimate' (evolutionary) and 'proximate' (mechanistic) questions (Figure 13.1). Let us consider two of Tinbergen's four questions (mechanism and function) as *synchronic*: they treat the trait/mechanism/behaviour

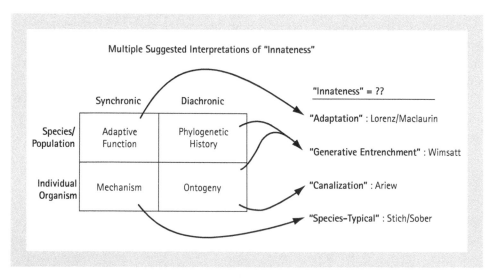

**Figure 13.1. Multiple suggested interpretations of 'innateness'.**

as fixed and functional at a certain point in time, and black-box its development. Depending on which question a given scientist is attempting to answer, it may be justifiable to treat the trait or behaviour under consideration as 'innately given' or instinctual, meaning that it reliably develops by a given time $t$. For a functional morphologist interested in how adult horses run, it is perfectly legitimate to black-box the genetic and developmental details by which the limb bones and musculature arose. Such mechanistic investigations are also directly relevant to questions of current adaptive function (are the horse's long limbs adaptations for running, swimming, or grazing in high grass—perhaps all three?).

The other two explanatory goals are *diachronic*: ontogenetic and phylogenetic questions take change through time as the basic explanandum. For the developmental neurobiologist interested in understanding how it is that horses can stand up and walk only minutes after birth, the answer that this capacity is 'innate' or 'genetically determined' explains nothing: the developmentalist wants to know how the neural circuits involved developed. Answering that 'the genes did it' or 'it is an adaptation' is not very helpful. Similarly, the palaeontologist seeking to understand the evolutionary history of horses' hooves will find little insight in the (correct) synchronic statement that hooves allow fast running: the crucial explanatory factors will be questions about precursor traits (hooves are essentially overgrown toenails) and species (horses are perissodactyls, with odd numbers of toes, and the single hoof is all that remains after a phylogenetic process of reduction and loss of the other four toes).

A notion like 'reliably developing' is unhelpful for the diachronic enterprise: it simply restates the central question of ontogeny, and begs the question of what causes this reliability. Similarly, the synchronic notion of current adaptive function may be less than relevant to questions of phylogenetic history, where notions of gene co-option or functional exaptation often play important roles. The mammalian middle-ear bones started their evolutionary career as gill bars in our fishy ancestors, and then served as jaw bones in early amniotes. This historical fact explains crucial aspects of their musculature and innervation, as well as many developmental and genetic facts (e.g. which genes they express). Such historical factors are part of any complete evolutionary explanation, and I suggest that their diachronicity helps explain why palaeontologists (e.g. Gould 1991) have often been less sympathetic to synchronic approaches, in contrast with those evolutionary biologists primarily interested in adaptation.

Thus, diachronic biologists (and psychologists) often reject nativist terminology, while synchronic biologists (evolutionary biologists, physiologists, and functional morphologists) typically find nativist concepts useful or indispensable. The same is true of nativists in the human sciences. For example, Noam Chomsky has adopted the abstraction of 'instantaneous acquisition' in his discussions of the biological bases of language, thus explicitly black-boxing questions of central interest to developmental psychologists (Chomsky 1965). Of course, Chomsky is well aware that children do not instantly develop language, and that both permissive and instructive environmental inputs are required. But for the mechanistic questions in which he is interested, he argues convincingly that such a strategy is justified. Indeed, he took his lead from ethologists like Lorenz and Tinbergen (Chomsky 2005).

For such scientists, probably the most satisfactory attempts to clarify innateness, and provide it with a biological grounding, are those like that of philosopher André Ariew, which ally the term with Waddington's concept of 'canalization'—the developmental robustness of the trait in the face of environmental variability (Ariew 1999). In this context, 'innate' really means 'reliably developing under normal circumstances'. A properly-conceived notion of 'epigenetically determined', along the lines Ariew suggests, is a necessary component of a scientific research programme aiming to answer the synchronic questions on the left of Figure 13.1. A virtue of this approach is that Waddington's 'epigenetic landscape' incorporates the notion of an ever-present environmental influence during development (denying any nature/nurture dichotomy). This model is also fully compatible with 'phenotypic plasticity': the adaptive development of different phenotypes from the same genotype under differing environmental conditions (cf. West-Eberhard 1989). Black-boxing further consideration of the genetic and developmental details is justified when pursuing these explanatory goals, if *any* degree of heritability is present in the trait.

# 13.6 CAN TINBERGEN'S FRAMEWORK SAVE INNATENESS?

Given its polysemy, and the rancour it evokes in developmentalists, can (should) the term 'innate' be saved? Numerous philosophers of biology have thought so, and have attempted to define the term 'innate' in various more circumscribed ways. These different attempts can also be insightfully understood within Tinbergen's pluralistic explanatory framework. For example, Maclaurin (2002) has attempted to define a useful sense of 'innate' in adaptive, functional terms: a trait is innate if it is built into a population by natural selection. This is closest to the usage that Lorenz (1965) defended. On a more mechanistic front, Stich (1975) and Sober (1998) have argued for a normative dispositional account, in which the mechanisms underlying the trait are 'normal to the species' in an abstract or statistical sense. Wimsatt's (1986) notion of 'genetic entrenchment' includes dual diachronic elements: innateness means that the ontogenetic mechanisms have been changed over phylogeny to increase their reliability. And finally, Ariew (1999) argues that 'innateness' entails robust, reliable development in the face of environmental variation, an ontogenetic interpretation. Only the last comes close to the most common use of 'innateness' among practising biologists: 'epigenetic robustness of outcome' or 'reliably developing'. Most biologists would simply use the term 'adaptation' for Maclaurin's version, and 'species-typical' for that of Stich or Sober.

Given this pervasive ambiguity of the terms 'innate' or 'instinctive', both as lay terms and as used in biology, how should those in the cognitive sciences proceed? Perhaps we should just define our current usage, be careful to stick to it, and get on with our empirical business? However appealing this solution may be, I believe it is dangerous. The mischief that the term 'innate' has caused is not due simply to the slipperiness of the term, but also to a pervasive, intuitive tendency to group together these different meanings, and treat them as different facets of 'the same thing' (Mameli and Bateson 2006). Griffiths (2002) has cogently argued that this reflects a deep 'folk biological' tendency to treat biological determination in terms of unchanging 'essences'. Children (and most adults) tend to reason about species deterministically, in terms of unchanging normative types. Griffiths suggests that such essentialism is a pervasive feature of our pre-theoretical reasoning about biological kinds, and it is quite difficult to escape these intuitions. Applying this intuition to 'human nature' thus leads us to see our biological nature as (a) 'genetically determined' (read, immutable), (b) the same for all humans (an 'ideal type'), and (c) normative (exceptions have negative connotations: 'malformations' or 'abnormalities'). If Griffiths is correct, this cluster of false assumptions surrounding the seemingly innocuous term 'innate' reflects deep-rooted pre-scientific intuitions about biology and nature.

All three of these are intuitions that biologists work hard to shed as part of their academic training. Modern biology since Darwin has forcibly rejected notions of biology as normative, typological, and deterministic. Ernst Mayr has argued that Darwin's replacement of typological thinking with population thinking was one of his most profound insights (Mayr 1982). Similarly, the growth of modern developmental biology required the rejection of simple, deterministic models like preformationism or instructivism (Medawar 1967), and entailed embracing the more complex metaphors of epigenesis, where effects at one timepoint act as causes later (Gottlieb 1992). Finally, biology provides no justification for the persistent human tendency to conflate 'natural' or 'adaptive' with 'normal' or 'good' (the so-called 'naturalistic fallacy').

I am therefore forced to concur with Bateson, Griffiths, and many others who advise avoiding scientific use of the pre-scientific terms 'innate' and 'instinct', particularly in popular or cross-disciplinary expositions, except in the dichotomy-defying phrase 'instinct to learn'. Continued use of the bare terms is typically counter-productive to accurate communication. This does not, of course, mean abandoning the several concepts denoted by these terms, any more than abandoning terms like 'weight' entailed abandoning the central concept of 'mass' in physics—that would be scientific suicide. But given the availability of clear, well-defined alternative 'terms of art', such as 'canalized', 'adaptation', or 'species typical' as given in Figure 13.1, we can afford to put aside pre-scientific terms and their excess baggage, and simply say what we mean.

## 13.7 SUMMARY AND CONCLUSIONS

I conclude that the central problem explaining the unproductive persistence of the 'nature/nurture debate' is that terms like 'innate' and 'instinct' on the one hand, and 'environment' and 'learning mechanisms' on the other, serve multiple different roles for different scholars, and that these quite different roles are often conflated (at least by readers, and sometimes by the authors themselves). A claim that some aspect of language is 'innate' may mean very different things to different people, and such claims often signal a broadly biological, synchronic evolutionary scientific strategy towards understanding language, rather than any particular empirically-testable claim. Those interested in the synchronic, mechanistic basis for language and/or its adaptive evolutionary function(s) tend to find nativist concepts useful, especially 'epigenetically determined', 'reliably developing', or 'canalized', and justifiably so. In sharp contrast, those mainly interested in the development of language in the child, or its phylogenetic history in our species, tend to find the term 'innate' obscure, and argue that it obfuscates, rather than clarifying, the diachronic problems in which they are interested. Both camps have valid points, and the apparent clash of their positions is caused by our intuitive tendency to cluster multiple separate empirical phenomena under the heading 'innateness', and then to confuse arguments for one as arguments for another (Griffiths 2002). Continued ambiguous usage of the term 'innate' in scholarly discourse is an obstacle to progress (contra Samuels 2004). The term finds its natural place as an intuitive, pre-scientific cluster of concepts, perhaps appropriate enough in folk biology, but often positively destructive in scientific discussions. Those interested in the role of biology and genes in language acquisition can use specific well-delineated terms, readily available to be borrowed from biology, and avoid further confusion.

But self-imposed terminological hygiene will not solve the empirical problems that face any eventual science of biological linguistics, which centrally include diachronic (developmental and phylogenetic) issues. What can we expect the genetic bases for language acquisition to look like? Taking a lead from the fields of developmental biology, molecular genetics, and their happy new marriage to evolutionary biology, we should abandon hope of simple unidirectional causal explanations, on the model of classical physics. Instead, we must embrace the biological notion of causal loops, and complex networks of interacting elements, as the unavoidable consequence of the contingent nature of evolution and development. Classical linear notions of 'heritability' assuming additive linear causality need to be jettisoned in favour of multiplicative, non-linear interactions (Wagner 1999). Fortunately, this does not entail abandoning the rigour and explicitness we envy in physics, but simply replacing older linear models with well-understood mathematical models of non-linear dynamics (Glass and Mackey 1988; Ball 1999). But this new framework requires new metaphors, and different notions of cause and effect, than those underlying traditional intuitive metaphors.

One justly popular metaphor is that genes are a recipe for a developmental process, rather than a blueprint. As stressed above, Waddington's *epigenetic landscape* seems the most appropriate and biologically up-to-date metaphor for development. Peter Marler's term *'instinct to learn'* is probably the only fully-justified use of the term 'instinct', precisely because the phrase denies the too-common notion that learning and instinct are mutually exclusive. I personally find the structural metaphor of the developmental tree valuable: every cell in the body (the twigs) derives from a single mother cell, the zygote (the root) via a process of differentiation (the branching points). Because cells influence each other in this process, the branches of this metaphoric tree curl back and contact one another, and some branches intertwine with one another, but these interactions can be conceptually disentangled. Furthermore, the reality of phenotypic plasticity must be recognized: many organisms have well-defined 'switches' that lead their development to different phenotypic end-states, sometime radically so (West-Eberhard 1989; R. D. Fernald 2003). None of these metaphors imply preformationism, or normative concepts, and all embrace the more interactive, constructivist perspective favoured by developmentalists, without denying the role of adaptation and evolutionary history in shaping development.

Fortunately, the deeply conservative nature of developmental genetics provides a previously unexpected justification for applying comparative biology very broadly to questions of language evolution, beyond the normal confines of primates or mammals (Carroll 2003). Furthermore, this new bounty of  relevant 'model organisms' means we can expect as many insights to come from fruit flies, zebrafish, or birds in the future as from our closer primate relatives, and thus confidently expect rapid progress in fleshing out these metaphors empirically.

Although I have only discussed 'language' in broad terms here, a successful future science of biolinguistics necessitates an explicitly multicomponent perspective on language (Fitch 2005, 2010a). Such a perspective views the language faculty as composed of multiple separable but interacting capacities, each component necessary, and no one sufficient, for language. Each of these components should be studied from all four of Tinbergen's modes of explanation (mechanism, function, ontogeny, and phylogeny), as well as encompassing cultural modes of explanation (Keller 1994; Laland et al. 2001), and it is safest to start by assuming each component of language may have different explanations at any of these levels. Taken together, this comparative, multicomponent approach, combined with the epigenetic perspective discussed above, holds out the exciting possibility that, in the next few decades, we can achieve substantial gains in understanding the biology of human language. Although the terms themselves may be best avoided in scientific contexts, the various biological concepts underlying the terms 'innate' or 'instinct' will play a central role in this endeavour.

# ACKNOWLEDGEMENTS

I thank Andrew Ariew, Patrick Bateson, Kathleen Gibson, and Maggie Tallerman for comments.

# CHAPTER 14

# EVOLUTIONARY BIOLOGICAL FOUNDATIONS OF THE ORIGIN OF LANGUAGE: THE CO-EVOLUTION OF LANGUAGE AND BRAIN

SZABOLCS SZÁMADÓ AND EÖRS SZATHMÁRY

## 14.1 INTRODUCTION

The main difficulty surrounding the evolution of human language is that the process involves an interaction of three major systems: biological evolution (and thus inheritance), cultural transmission (and thus inheritance), and individual learning. The problem is further compounded by the fact that different systems can evolve at different rates, with cultural change assumed to be much faster than biological change. Accordingly, scholars have argued that since linguistic conventions change more rapidly than genes can change via natural selection, any genetically encoded bias is likely to end up as incorrect, hence will be selected against

(Christiansen and Chater 2008; Chater et al. 2009; Chater and Christiansen, this volume). Culture, and hence human language, are thus said to provide a moving target that natural selection cannot keep pace with. Is this true? Here we explore this claim and its potential consequences for the evolution of human language and the brain.

## 14.2 ADAPTING TO A MOVING TARGET

There are many ways organisms can adapt to moving targets. The simplest case is genetic evolution, when natural selection acts on the variation in the population, selecting against those alleles that provide the least fit to the environment. The second way is by utilizing the phenotypic plasticity of a genotype. The third way is by means of systems and organs which have evolved to cope with fast-changing environments and which have genetic underpinnings as well.

### 14.2.1 Genetic adaptation

It is widely believed that if the change in environment is too fast then natural selection just cannot 'keep up' with these changes. However, this need not be so, as the ability of a population to keep pace with change depends on both the size of the population and the variation present. There are many examples both from nature and from controlled experiments showing that adaptation can be very fast if variability is there and can be inherited (Reznick and Ghalambor 2005; Carroll et al. 2007).

### 14.2.2 Phenotypic plasticity

While it is often conveniently assumed that one genotype codes for one phenotype, this need not be the case in nature. A set of genes can give rise to different phenotypes depending on the environment in which development takes place. This phenomenon, termed phenotypic plasticity, may be adaptive in species with variable environments. When natural selection acts to preserve adaptive phenotypes it can lead to genetic change and to the fixation of specific phenotypes within a population by several evolutionary processes, including the Baldwin effect and genetic assimilation; see Yamauchi (2004) for discussion and detailed review of models, and Számadó et al. (2009) for discussion of the potential role of these effects in language evolution.

### 14.2.3 Systems and organs evolved to track a fast-changing environment

A classic example is the vertebrate immune system in which basic building blocks are genetically encoded yet recombined and reassembled so that the organism meets the challenges presented by fast-changing pathogens. The convergent evolution of adaptive immunity in agnathans (jawless vertebrates) and in gnathostomes (vertebrates with jaws) (Cooper and Alder 2006) shows that similar selective pressures can select for similar solutions. Arguably the human brain itself is an organ designed to meet the biological, social, and linguistic challenges of a fast-changing environment. Of course the crucial question is, as ever, how can such organs evolve in the first place?

## 14.3 ADAPTATION BY MEANS OF NATURAL SELECTION IN NATURE

At one time ecological and evolutionary timescales were considered quite distinct. This is no longer the case. Numerous examples of rapid evolutionary change, now known from both laboratory and field studies, indicate that significant genetic and morphological change can occur in tens of generations, possibly faster (Reznick and Ghalambor 2005; Carroll et al. 2007). Accordingly, the traditional distinction between 'ecological' and 'evolutionary' timescales (a timescale usually based on the fossil record) is no longer thought to be correct (Carroll et al. 2007). Laboratory experiments and studies under natural conditions show that natural selection can produce fast adaptations with a rate of change much quicker than could be inferred from the palaeontological record. Examples include the adaptive radiation of soapberry bugs (both in America and in Australia) to new plants introduced into their range (Carroll and Boyd 1992; Carroll et al. 2005); adaptation of marine rotifers to fresh-water environments (Lee 1999); adaptation of yucca moths to new species of host (Groman and Pellmyr 2000); adaptation of Darwin's finches to the effect of drought and/or to the presence of competitors (Grant and Grant 2002, 2006); adaptation of guppies to low and to high predator-risk environments (Reznick et al. 1990); adaptation of Anolis lizards to new habitats (Losos et al. 1997); and adaptation of a Mediterranean lizard (*Podarcis sicula*) to new diet (Herrel et al. 2008). We will discuss these examples in some detail to show that rapid adaptation in nature is not as exceptional as was previously thought.

In the classic example, a major drought drastically changed the composition of the population of the finch *Geospiza fortis* during a single generation (Grant and

Grant 2006). Crucially, this change was adaptive and its direction depended, in part, on the presence or absence of a large-beaked, large-seed eating competitor, *G. magnirostris*. In the absence of the competitor, drought selected for large beak size in *G. fortis*. In sharp contrast, during the next drought this large-beaked competitor species was present and frequent, and the pool of large seeds was depleted. Drought then selected for small beak size in *G. fortis*. Consequently, it is possible to select for adaptations in opposite directions in the same population under natural conditions in a short time span (all the changes happened within 30 years) as long as heritable variation is present in the population.

Other examples also indicate rapid responses to selection. In experiments with guppies, lifetime characteristics of the populations changed in a few generations as a response to increased or decreased predation risk (Reznick et al. 1990). In a somewhat similar experiment conducted under natural conditions, Anolis lizards showed a similar capacity to adapt to new habitats within 10–14 years (Losos et al. 1997). Carroll and his colleagues found that beak size of soapberry bugs (*Jadera haematoloma* and *Leptocoris tagalicus*) evolved to fit the size of fruits of various introduced plants within 20–50 years in America (Carroll and Boyd 1992) and 30–40 years in Australia (Carroll et al. 2005); beak size is heritable (Carroll et al. 1997, 2005). Last but not least, Herrel and his co-workers (Herrel et al. 2008) found that lizards (*Podarcis sicula*) experimentally introduced into a small Mediterranean island 36 years ago shifted their diet significantly from invertebrate prey to plants. As a result, significant differences in head size and head morphology evolved compared to the founder population; moreover, a new digestive trait emerged: the so-called 'cecal valve' which is not usually found in this species but is charac- teristic of other herbivorous lizards. In other words, changes involve not just size differences in existing organs, but also the evolution of new structures over a short period of time.

All in all, these field studies demonstrate that natural selection is well capable of producing fast adaptations. Reznick and Ghalambor (2005: 459) conclude that 'These studies consistently reveal that the rate of evolution [ . . . ] can be many orders of magnitude faster than rates that are inferred from the fossil record'. They further argue that 'the reason that evolution is not usually seen is not because it is too slow, as Darwin assumed, but because it is too fast' (Reznick and Ghalambor 2005: 459). Since evolution can be very fast, we can observe the ongoing process only if we are looking for it—and in the right way. The reason it is rare to see rapid evolution in the fossil record is not the inability of a species to rapidly produce new adaptations, but rather that environmental changes fluctuate over time and rarely add up to consistent trends. Conversely, visible macroevolution in the fossil record requires consistent environmental trends in one direction (Carroll et al. 2007). Carroll et al. (2007: 389) conclude in the spirit of Dobzhansky (1937): 'Macroevo- lution may thus be nothing more than an aggregate of many small events, and is entirely explainable by events that we can observe and quantify over the course of our lives as investigators'. Can we expect this conclusion to hold up with regard to the evolution of the human brain? Our brain is a more complex organ than a bird's beak or a lizard's cecal valve. What evidence do we have about the role of natural selection in the evolution of *Homo sapiens*?

## 14.4 EVOLUTION IN HUMANS: THE ROLE OF NATURAL SELECTION

It is now well established that positive (natural) selection has acted on the human genome (see Vallender and Lahn 2004; Sabeti et al. 2006) and played an important role in the recent molecular evolution of our species (Bustamante et al. 2005). This conclusion is supported by a range of genetic studies carried out by different methodologies, including genome-wide scans (see Sabeti et al. 2006 for discussion). Moreover, recent studies show that the rate of recent genomic evolution (during the last 40,000 years), contrary to widespread belief, is more than 100 times higher than is characteristic for most of human evolution (Hawks et al. 2007), and that large chunks of the human genome (ca. 10%) are affected by linkage due to recent selective sweeps (within the last ~200,000 years; Williamson et al. 2007). This is due to the increasing size of human populations, since large populations can harbour more variation than smaller ones.

The list of genes and regions affected by positive selection is very long and involves at least the following broad functions: immune system, tumour suppression, dietary adaptations (e.g. lactase persistence in adults), reproduction (spermatogenesis), skin, hair, and eye pigmentation, and sensory systems (olfaction) (Nielsen et al. 2005; Voight et al. 2006; for reviews see Vallender and Lahn 2004; Sabeti et al. 2006). Moreover, genomic studies provide strong evidence that some adaptive changes occurred over a few hundred generations (i.e. under a few thousand years). Most notable examples are the origin and spread of alleles responsible for malaria resistance (Tishkoff et al. 2001; Sabeti et al. 2002) and lactase persistence (Bersaglieri et al. 2004). In both cases, alleles that confer an advantage in the given context rose to high frequencies in the past few thousand years (ca. 2500–6500 years in the case of malaria and ca. 5000–10,000 years in the case of lactase persistence).

Vallender et al. (2008) review several cases of genes that may have played a role in human brain evolution. *Microcephalin* (*MCPH1*) and *ASPM* affect brain size and cerebral cortical size respectively (Evans et al. 2004a, b). Accelerated protein evolution of *microcephalin* is characteristic of the primate lineage and started roughly 25–30 mya (Evans et al. 2004a); on the other hand, accelerated protein evolution of *ASPM* is characteristic of the human lineage and started after it diverged from chimpanzees some 5–6 mya (Evans et al. 2005b). Further studies provide evidence that this evolution is still ongoing both in *microcephalin* and in *ASPM* (Evans et al. 2005; Mekel-Bobrov et al. 2005). New genetic variants of these genes (arising 37 kya and 5.8 kya respectively) appear to have attained high frequency in some populations under strong positive selection (Evans et al. 2005; Mekel-Bobrov et al. 2005; for responses, some critical, see Currat et al. 2006; Mekel-Bobrov et al. 2006; Mekel-Bobrov and Lahn 2007; Yu et al. 2007; Timpson et al. 2007). Others argue that genetic drift (chance factors) could be responsible (Diller and Cann, this volume).

In sum, there is solid evidence that selection shaped important parts of the human genome and that human genetic evolution, including evolution of genes affecting brain development, is still an ongoing process. Indeed, the human genome may now be evolving even more rapidly than in the past. Hence, there is no a priori reason to exclude the possibility that the human brain adapted to the changing social and linguistic environment in the past; in fact the evidence strongly suggests that such adaptation has taken place.

## 14.5 HUMAN LANGUAGE: HOW FAST IS FAST?

In order to judge the ability of natural selection to track a 'moving target' (see Chater and Christiansen, this volume) it is a good idea to estimate how fast the target under consideration is actually moving. It is accepted that culture can change faster than genes and that aspects of human language may be amongst the fastest changing part of our culture. For example, recent language change-rate studies have found that the half-life of quickly-evolving words and rules is around 300–700 years (where 'half-life' refers to the time in which there is a 50% chance the word will be replaced by a different non-cognate form; E. Lieberman et al. 2007; Pagel et al. 2007). Hence it is tempting to conclude that human language presents a moving target that cannot be tracked by the brain. There are two reasons, however, why such a conclusion might not be correct.

First, even contemporary linguistic change need not be that fast. While it is true that the half-life of quickly-changing words is in the order of hundreds of years, the same studies show that the half-life of slowly-changing words is in the order of tens of thousands of years. This means that there is a 100-fold difference in the rate of evolution, where the rate depends on frequency of use: words and rules used more frequently evolve much more slowly. Lieberman et al. (2007) estimated the half-life of two irregular English verbs, *be* and *have*, at around 38,800 years, which is the rough equivalent of 2000 generations in humans—enough time for biological adaptive evolution. In general, E. Lieberman et al. (2007) argue that there is a square root relationship between the frequency of use and the rate of change. A verb that is used 100 times less frequently evolves 10 times as fast. So even today's 'fast' linguistic change is not universally fast.

Second, it might not be correct to extrapolate from the current rate of language change to past rates. Though the current rate of linguistic change appears to be much faster than the rate of gene change, it need not necessarily always have been so. There are several reasons why past rates of linguistic change could have been much slower:

1. *Smaller population size.* Larger populations harbour much larger variability which allows for faster rate of change. Human populations today are orders of magnitude larger than they were even in the Neolithic, and as a result both cultural and biological evolution are likely to be accelerated. Evidence shows that both cases hold. As discussed above, genetic studies show that the rate of recent genomic evolution (i.e. during the past 40,000 years) is more than 100 times faster than previously (Hawks et al. 2007). It is also well accepted that the rate of cultural evolution has accelerated in the last 40,000 years, so much so that the term 'Upper Palaeolithic revolution' is often used to describe the sudden explosion of cultural innovation. While it was arguably not the sudden revolution once depicted (as it started long prior to the Upper Palaeolithic; see McBrearty and Brooks 2000) it is clear that the rate of cultural change did accelerate during that period, and keeps on accelerating.

2. *Slower rate of technological innovations.* Innovations always result in a large influx of new words out of sheer necessity. Stable technologies and the relative lack of innovation could mean that this influx was mostly missing from the protolanguage state which probably characterized a large part of early human evolution. Acheulean tool-making technology was stable for more than a million years, and even after the end of the Acheulean, the rate of technological innovations was much slower than that of today.

3. *More limited contexts for language use.* This means not just that the influx of words from innovations was much smaller, but the context for language use itself was probably much more limited. A plethora of theories exist suggesting potential contexts for early language evolution (see Számadó and Szathmáry 2006 for review), but the majority of theories propose a *specific* context for language evolution. Whatever theory is correct, it is likely that early language evolution was highly context-specific. High context-specificity means a more stable linguistic environment, much smaller vocabulary, and a smaller influx of new words; hence, overall, a much slower rate of linguistic change.

4. *Much smaller vocabulary.* Arguably, whatever the context for early language, it was a much less complex protolanguage (Bickerton 1990), and its vocabulary

must have been orders of magnitude smaller than in today's full-blown languages. As we have seen, studies show that the rate of change inversely relates to frequency of use; thus, frequently used words and rules change the slowest. Small vocabulary means that frequency of use is much higher for all words. If we accept the square root relationship outlined above, then a 100-fold decrease in the size of the vocabulary (i.e. a 100-fold increase in the frequency of use) means a tenfold decrease in the rate of evolution. The slowest evolving words and rules currently have half-lives on the order of tens of thousands of years (E. Lieberman et al. 2007; Pagel et al. 2007); a tenfold decrease means that the slowest evolving words probably had half-lives of *hundreds of thousands of years*! This range is well within the range of biological adaptive evolution and well within the range of known adaptive changes observed in humans.

5. *Potentially high iconicity of early human language.* Many argue that gestural communication was an important first step in the evolution of early protolanguages (Hewes 1973; Corballis 2001, this volume; Pollick and de Waal 2007; Arbib et al. 2008). If true, then the iconicity of early gestural communication could stabilize the form of signals, for several reasons. First, iconicity is functional and it is easier to learn iconic than non-iconic signs; second, because of potential high iconicity the range of potential variation is more constrained; finally, iconicity is more prevalent and stable in sign languages—for example, many animal names are still recognizably iconic (even for naïve learners).

In sum, there are several lines of evidence that strongly suggest that the rate of change of linguistic evolution could have been much slower than today (by an order of magnitude). Even just 100,000 years means 5000 generations, which gives plenty of time for natural selection to work on the human brain if sufficient genetic variation is present in the population.

## 14.6 EVOLUTION OF THE HUMAN BRAIN

We have seen so far that natural selection has the potential to produce fast adaptations. How does this relate to the evolution of human language? According to Holloway (1995, 1996) there were three major reorganizations and four major periods during which brain size increased in the hominin line. Important for us is the fourth, which was a gradual non-allometric size increase (i.e. an increase that cannot be linked to the increase in body size) leading up to archaic *H. sapiens* from 0.5 mya to 0.075 mya (Holloway 1996). Both Holloway (1995) and Tobias (1995) argue that *H. habilis* (and thus *H. erectus*)—given the similarities of parietal lobe with modern humans—had some form of communication system which ranked in complexity between existing primate communication systems and modern human language. Holloway (1996) explicitly argues that 'I certainly believe that some form of primitive language was present in early *Homo*'. This would provide ample time for natural selection to adjust the human brain to the needs of language understanding and production. In this light, one could argue that the observed gradual but steady non-allometric increase of brain size leading up to archaic *H. sapiens* (Holloway 1996) is a result of this selection alongside the subtle reorganizations that may have taken place. This adaptive scenario is tempting because this period overlaps largely with the period of Acheulean tool-making technology, which implies that probably there was a long period of stable cultural and linguistic environment to which the human brain could adapt.

## 14.7 THE CO-EVOLUTION OF LANGUAGE AND BRAIN

The co-evolution of language and the human brain is not a new idea. Darwin (1871) himself proposed a co-evolutionary spiral of language and brain and some take his lead (Deacon 1997). While we do not want to propose a detailed scenario of co-evolution here, we note that in the light of the data discussed in previous sections, such a co-evolutionary spiral is not just feasible but in our opinion it is the likeliest explanation behind the current complexity of human brain, language, and culture.

On one hand, language variants that can be easily learnt and retained enjoy a fitness benefit in terms of cultural evolution and thus spread faster in a given population (Kirby et al. 2004; Brighton et al. 2005; Christiansen and Chater 2008; Chater and Christiansen, this volume); on the other hand, brains better able to cope with language varieties and with language change provide biological fitness advantages to their host; thus, the genes responsible for the adaptive differences will also spread in the population. As a result, languages become streamlined to the needs of the human brain, and brains adapt to language learning and processing. This is the same principle as host–pathogen co-evolution. Pathogens that are adapted to a host can reproduce quickly, while hosts adapted to cope with these pathogens enjoy a biological fitness advantage over non-adapted hosts. The crucial difference is that host–pathogen co-evolution is antagonistic while language–brain co-evolution is synergistic. In other words, humans actually benefit from this co-evolution; they have more streamlined, more efficient languages, better cognitive capabilities, and are able to learn and use language quickly and efficiently. As a result, they can perform a host of activities which benefit from more efficient language use (cooperation, tool use, maintenance of traditions, etc.); Szathmáry and Számadó (2008).

As we have seen, the arms race with pathogens left its signature in the human genome—for example, genetic adaptations to malaria. Do we have the same kind of evidence for genes involved in neural development? If there is indeed co-evolution between language and the brain then one might argue that the same kind of fast evolution of developmental genes or genes coding for neurotransmitters should be observed. The speed of this change, however, need not be the same, for several reasons. First, as noted, the speed of change of cultural evolution of human language need not be as fast as the biological evolution of pathogens, especially in the early stages of language evolution. Second, the development of the human brain is a fairly complex process; hence, tinkering with these genes is expected to be more difficult. In other words, neurodevelopmental genes are expected to be more conservative than, say, immune-defence-related genes. This does not mean that they cannot evolve; it just means that arguably it could take more time to hit upon the right kind of variant, even if selective pressure were there. All in all, one could argue that the change in genes involved in neural development should be fast compared to the evolution of the same genes in *other species* but not necessarily compared to the fastest evolving genes in humans (i.e. immune-defence- or spermatogenesis-related genes).

This is exactly what was found by Dorus and colleagues (Dorus et al. 2004), comparing genes involved in various aspects of nervous system biology. They found that such genes display a significantly higher rate of protein evolution in primates than in rodents. Moreover, in primates this accelerated evolution is more prominent in the lineage leading to humans. Finally, by comparing so-called developmental versus housekeeping genes linked to the nervous system, they found that genes related to nervous system development evolved faster than those related to housekeeping. However, this study has not escaped criticism. Nielsen et al. (2005) commented that Dorus et al. (2004) did not present direct evidence for positive selection. Nielsen et al. (2005), in their comparative study of the human and chimpanzee genome, found that genes expressed in the brain show little evidence of positive selection and in turn they argued that, owing to the conservative nature of these genes, direct evidence for positive selection in these genes is unlikely to be found. While it is true that Dorus and colleagues could not find direct evidence for positive selection in genes involved in neural development, they nonetheless built up a convincing case by providing a comparison of the rates of evolution of housekeeping genes in primates and rodents (where no differences were found, as opposed to genes linked to nervous system development) and by listing the effects of the mutations related to development, showing that they cause severe defects. The presence of these defects makes it unlikely that the relaxation of developmental constraints would have been the cause of the observed accelerated evolution.

Finally, Thompson et al. (2001), using dizygotic and monozygotic brain studies, found that broad anatomical regions are under significant genetic control, including the frontal lobe and Broca's and Wernicke's areas (which are heavily involved in language). They conclude that 'highly heritable aspects of brain structure may be fundamental in determining individual differences in cognition' (Thompson et al. 2001: 1). This is exactly what one would expect under brain–language co-evolution, where brain structures advantageous in language learning, processing, and production are heritable and selected for over many generations.

## 14.8 CONCLUSIONS

There are several ways in which natural selection can adapt to moving targets: genetic evolution, phenotypic plasticity, and specialized organs (systems) designed to track fast-changing parts of the relevant environment. Here we argue that all three played an important role in the evolution of human language and language capacities. We also argue that linguistic change was much slower during Plio-Pleistocene times, leaving natural selection ample time to adapt. This genetic adaptation was probably enhanced by phenotypic plasticity as well. Because of the nature of phenotypic plasticity its role can mostly be only indirectly inferred. This adaptation, however, has traces both in the human genome and in the structure of the brain. The human brain itself, we argue, is a very specific organ selected for the ability to track fast-changing parts of the relevant environment, which for hominins also included the linguistic environment. The human brain is highly efficient when it comes to language acquisition and production; in fact it is more efficient than any other known brain or artificial computing mechanisms. Thus the human brain today is well capable of tracking the fast-changing linguistic environment—much as the immune system is capable of tracking most of the pathogens—but this ability, just as in the case of the immune system, is the result of natural selection. Thus, we argue further that the very reason why linguistic change can be so fast today is that the human brain is well adapted to the task. However, unlike the case of host–parasite arms races, where the accelerated evolutionary rates of the parasites can hurt the host, here the accelerated evolutionary rates resulting from brain–language co-evolution actually benefit the host, opening up a range of potential biological and cultural adaptations unparalleled in any other species.

# CHAPTER 15

# GENETIC INFLUENCES ON LANGUAGE EVOLUTION: AN EVALUATION OF THE EVIDENCE

KARL C. DILLER AND
REBECCA L. CANN

It is commonly accepted by biologists that language is a defining characteristic of *Homo sapiens* and that the biological capacity for language was present in the earliest anatomically modern humans. Chimpanzees and bonobos, on the other hand—the species most closely related to us—have only limited linguistic capabilities, using manual, visual, and auditory modalities, and they have minimal conscious neuromuscular control of the vocal tract, not being able to speak or even mimic words. Now that both the human and the chimpanzee genomes have been sequenced, we can begin to ask seriously what the genetic changes were that gave humans the ability to speak and to use our grammatically elaborated languages. We are seeing that the answer is much more complicated than such simplifications as 'the grammar gene' or 'a mutation for language'.

We concentrate in this chapter on the three genes of recent interest in the literature on language origins: two genes that cause microcephaly when disabled (*microcephalin* and *ASPM*), and *FOXP2*, which, among other things, causes a severe speech and language disability when disrupted.

In evaluating the evidence, two important principles should be kept in mind: (1) many genetic processes which may interfere with normal language use are not related to the origin or evolution of language in any major way; and (2) the presence or absence of a large brain does not guarantee the presence or absence of language.

For an example of the first principle, the fragile X syndrome in humans can lead to a syndrome including delays in speech acquisition, repetitive speech, or problems with vocabulary, syntax, and labelling. In addition to communication difficulties, the children can show varying levels of mental retardation, distinctively large ears and testicles, and long faces, and they may suffer from excessive shyness, tremors, or seizures. In the disease state, the *FMR-1* gene cannot produce the FMRP protein that is necessary for proper development of neural connections in the developing brain. The mouse model of fragile X syndrome shows that this syndrome does not primarily target language, but targets underlying processes of neurodevelopment at a very basic level.

An example of the second principle, concerning large brains, is that microcephalics with a chimpanzee-size human brain can learn language at least to the level of 6-year-olds by the time they are 12, showing that the organization of the brain, not its size, is crucial for language. Note also that a human mutation in the *CMAH* gene about 2.7 million years ago stopped production of an enzyme that apparently inhibits brain cell growth (Chou et al. 2002). Releasing this brake on brain cell growth may have been a major factor in tripling the size of the human brain since that time. This growth may have been a prerequisite for the reorganization of the brain to give it the capacities for language, but it does not in itself explain this reorganization or the origin of language capabilities.

With regard to *FOXP2* and the microcephaly genes, discoveries have sometimes led to false hopes as well as premature and erroneous conclusions, but evidence is building up and is giving us leads for further study. Let us review this evidence.

## 15.1  *FOXP2*

In 1990 there was much excitement that the 'grammar gene' might have been found. Half of the members of a three-generation family in London, the KE family, had a severe speech and language disorder which showed the inheritance pattern consistent with a dominant autosomal gene (Hurst et al. 1990). Gopnik and Crago (1991) did a linguistic study on this family and found special difficulty with paradigmatic grammar. In the popular mind this translated to the notion of a 'grammar gene'. Noam Chomsky had been arguing for more than three decades that universal grammar was innate in humans, and here, finally, was possible genetic evidence.

Further studies of the KE family demonstrated that grammar was not the central issue; the core deficit was one involving sequential articulation and orofacial praxis (Watkins et al. 2002a). In affected members of the KE family we see disruption of normal brain development resulting in increases and decreases of a wide range of brain structures, including subcortical structures and the cerebellum (Watkins et al. 2002b).

By 2001 the gene was isolated, sequenced, classified as a member of the forkhead box family, and named *FOXP2* (Lai et al. 2001). The protein products of forkhead genes have forkhead DNA binding domains which bind to specified regulatory sequences in other genes, and regulate the expression of these other genes. More often than not *FOXP2* turns other genes off (Spiteri et al. 2007). *FOXP2* is expressed in the mouse brain during development, but is also expressed in a wide variety of mouse tissues; it has many essential roles in mammalian development and function that are totally unrelated to language.

Enard et al. (2002), in their study of the 'Molecular evolution of *FOXP2*, a gene involved in speech and language', found that there are three amino acid changes in human FOXP2 protein compared with mouse, and that two of these changes come in the human line in the 6 million years since our common ancestor with chimpanzees. Later work showed that the one difference between chimpanzee and mouse occurred on the mouse line. *FOXP2* is one of the most conserved mammalian genes, with no FOXP2 protein amino acid changes in chimpanzee, gorilla, or macaque going back some 90 million years since the common ancestor of primates and rodents. Yet there are two changes between humans and our common ancestor with chimpanzees. Enard et al. speculated that these relatively recent changes in the human line may have affected 'a person's ability to control orofacial movements and thus to develop proficient spoken language'. Then using computer simulation with a likelihood model they concluded that the most likely date for the fixation of these human mutations was zero years ago, that is, so unlikely, by their model, as to almost not have happened. They calculated a 95% confidence interval going back 120,000 years on a chi-square distribution highly skewed toward zero years ago. This, they said, was consistent with Klein's speculation that a mutation for language caused a cultural revolution 50 kya that led to art and to human migration out of Africa (Klein 1989).

McBrearty and Brooks (2000), in their article 'The revolution that wasn't' effectively refuted Klein's hypothesis of a cultural revolution. In a paper presented at the Cradle of Language conference in 2006, Diller and Cann showed that the date of zero years ago was based on a flawed and inappropriate model. Using genomic evidence, we proposed a date of 1.8 or 1.9 mya for the mutations in *FOXP2*, approximately the time when the genus *Homo (Homo habilis, H. ergaster, H. erectus)* emerged (Diller and Cann 2009). A year later, in 2007, a team including Enard sequenced the Neanderthal *FOXP2* gene and announced that Neanderthals have the same mutations in *FOXP2* that modern humans have (Krause et al. 2007). The date for the Neanderthal/modern human common ancestor is some 660–500 kya, so the mutations in *FOXP2* occurred some time before that split, consistent with our date of 1.8 or 1.9 mya. Hardly anybody believes any more that the human mutations in *FOXP2* occurred in the last 200,000 years, i.e. since the emergence of anatomically modern humans.

In several species, *FOXP2* is related to vocalization (see references in Diller and Cann 2009): it is upregulated in neurodevelopment during seasonal periods of song circuit growth for canaries, and during the time when zebra finches learn their song in infancy. In adult zebra finches, FOXP2 protein is downregulated during singing. In mice with only one copy of *FOXP2*, ultrasonic vocalization of infants is greatly decreased. In echolocating bats there is an unusually large number of mutations in *FOXP2* Thus it would seem likely that *FOXP2* is more important for developmental circuits for vocalized speech than for something as complex as grammar.

Speech and certain aspects of grammar, however, are closely related to each other from the standpoint of human neural function. The KE family with its disruptive *FOXP2* mutation has a disruption of both speech and certain aspects of grammar in the wider context of orofacial dyspraxia. Broca's aphasia, stemming from lesions in the motor association cortex for the vocal tract, involves both effortful, distorted speech and agrammatism. Grammar may have been dependent on speech for its neural origin, the neural mechanisms for grammar in Broca's area being elaborated on the motor association cortex for vocalization.

The date of 1.8 or 1.9 mya for the human *FOXP2* mutations is just at the time when the human brain began to triple in size, from the 450cc of australopithecine and chimpanzee brains to the 1350cc of modern human brains. If the elements of vocal speech began early in this evolution, then symbolic speech, grammatical language, and the spectacular brain growth would have evolved together, the type of co-evolution a biologist would expect.

Mutations in a single gene can cause disease and great disruption of function, as in the KE family, but biologists do not expect single mutations to cause complex innovations such as the origin of language; they expect long periods of co-evolution with many genetic changes.

## 15.2 TONE LANGUAGES, *MICROCEPHALIN*, AND *ASPM*

In 2005 it was announced that two genes essential for proper brain growth, *microcephalin* and *ASPM*, are currently undergoing a change: new variants of these genes have been gaining frequency in the last ~37,000 years (for *microcephalin*) or ~5800 years (for *ASPM*) (P. Evans et al. 2005; Mekel-Bobrov et al. 2005). Dediu and Ladd noticed a negative correlation between these new gene variants and tone languages (Dediu and Ladd 2007). They argued that tonality is phylogenetically older, and that these new gene variants give populations a bias towards non-tonality in language. Although Dediu and Ladd present statistically significant correlations, this is almost certainly a statistical artefact with speculation that goes far beyond the evidence, as discussed below.

We need some background on these two genes because of the controversies in the press about intelligence and race when it was announced in 2005 that the brain is still evolving, and that certain favourable new mutations are common in Eurasia but not in Africa. Bruce Lahn and the University of Chicago wanted to patent these genes for a potential intelligence test in case it could be shown that there was a cognitive advantage to these mutations (Balter 2005). No cognitive advantages have been found and the patent process was stopped. People with these mutations have no advantages on tests for general or social intelligence, and have no differences in brain size or head circumference. If Dediu and Ladd were right that these new mutations caused a bias against tone languages, this could actually be seen as a cognitive disadvantage.

The question of whether there was recent selection at the *microcephalin* and *ASPM* loci is a serious one. The original evidence came with comparison to simulated data. A Harvard group, noting wryly that 'detection of selection solely by comparison with simulated data has had a mixed record', compared *ASPM* with a number of other loci empirically, and found no evidence of selection (Yu et al. 2007). Population genetic models with population structure combined with population growth could also produce the patterns found at *ASPM* and *microcephalin* (Currat et al. 2006). That is to say, genetic drift without selection could explain the spread of these genes. If there is no selection at the *ASPM* or *microcephalin* loci, arguments based on selection would no longer be viable.

Defective versions of *microcephalin* and *ASPM* result in microcephaly, a genetic disorder in which people have small heads and small brains—brains the size of chimpanzee brains. With primary microcephaly, or microcephaly vera, there are no other physical signs except for the small brain and head and its attendant mental retardation. The structure of the small brain is grossly similar to the normal human brain, but there are subtle differences, and the cerebral cortex is somewhat smaller than in a perfectly scaled-down brain. Microcephalics can learn language (at least to the 6-year-old level) in spite of a chimpanzee-size brain, showing that it is the organization of the brain, not its size, that is important for language.

When it was discovered that mutations in *microcephalin* and *ASPM* caused microcephaly, the immediate speculation was that these genes might 'control' (P. Evans et al. 2004a), 'regulate', (P. Evans et al. 2005), or even 'determine' (Jackson et al. 2002) brain size, and thus be key to the evolution of the large brain in modern humans.

This trap of reverse thinking was present in the first major work on microcephaly, Charles Vogt's 1867 monograph *Memoire sur les microcéphales ou homme-singes* (*homme-singes* = ape men), which examined almost 200 known European cases (Vogt 1867). Vogt proposed that microcephaly involved an 'atavistic formation', or a winding backwards of evolution. Given modern genetic knowledge this argument is untenable. Nevertheless it is a common-sense trap that is easy to fall into even in the 21st century.

Microcephalin and ASPM proteins are crucial for proper brain development: microcephalin is involved in regulating the cell-cycle especially in relation to DNA repair before cell division. ASPM helps to align the mitotic spindles in the cell so that it divides symmetrically. It is not clear that these genes 'regulate', 'control', or 'determine' brain size any more than air pressure in a tyre regulates, controls, or determines speed—a flat tyre causes speed to plummet, but more air than normal doesn't do much, and if air pressure remains normal, something else determines speed.

The data on the global frequency of the *ASPM* and *microcephalin* variants (ASPM-D and MCPH-D, respectively), as presented in the maps of P. Evans et al. (2005) and Mekel-Bobrov et al. (2005), show that both mutations arose in Eurasia, with ASPM-D much more recent and not spreading as much to East Asia.

Dediu and Ladd (2007) present a figure which shows that in populations where there is a low frequency of both MCPH-D and ASPM-D, the ten languages sampled are all tone languages. This represents the reality of sub-Saharan Africa. In places with an ASPM-D frequency of at least 30% (western Eurasia) there are no tone languages. Elsewhere there are approximately equal numbers of tone and non-tone languages. The statistical algorithms used by Dediu and Ladd ruled out geography as a significant factor in the relationship between tone languages and these gene variants. But the mutations arose outside of Africa, and it is clear by inspection that if one eliminated Africa from the analysis the results would be quite different.

Dediu and Ladd exclude the Americas from their analysis because they were 'too poorly sampled for their genetic and linguistic diversity'. Of 1002 native American languages (Gordon 2005), there is genetic data for ASPM-D and MCPH-D for only five population groups. But Africa has an estimated 2092 indigenous languages (Gordon 2005) and there are only 11 in Dediu and Ladd's analysis—almost exactly the same low sample ratio as in the Americas. Australia and India have no representative languages in the analysis. Besides the low sampling of languages, the genetic sampling from each language population is very low. The typical language group analysed had only 19 people giving genetic information; a third of the groups had between 7 and 10 people in the sample. This statistical base is not adequate to test Dediu and Ladd's hypothesis.

An additional statistical problem is that the ASPM-D mutation originated so recently, an estimated 5800 years ago, that two-thirds of the samples in this analysis have a frequency of this variant of less than 30%, and only one sample is significantly over 50%. Is that small proportion of the population large enough to bias language change so strongly as to drive out tone languages in 5800 years? The frequency of ASPM-D 5800 years ago would have been 0%, and presumably it has been increasing at an exponential rate. This means that most of the increase has been in recent centuries in the historical period. Is there evidence that there has been widespread loss of tone systems in tonal languages during the historical period in populations where we find the ASPM-D haplotype?

Dediu and Ladd claim that the correlation of the distribution of tone languages with the distribution of ASPM-D and MCPH-D is not 'spurious', but the statistical base is not convincing. They do not present linguistic evidence that ASPM-D and MCPH-D have driven out tone systems in the historical period, and they do not specify any genetic or biological mechanism of causality.

## 15.3 GENE NETWORKS RELATING TO THE CAPACITY FOR LANGUAGE: *FOXP2* AND *CNTNAP2*

Although *FOXP2* does not have a simple direct causal role in the evolution of language, there is suggestive evidence of a role in vocalization and control of speech organs both in humans and other animals, in addition to a role in neurodevelopment. Since *FOXP2* is a transcription factor regulating the expression of other genes, two groups have looked for other genes important for speech and/or language by investigating the downstream targets of *FOXP2*, that is, the genes regulated in some way by *FOXP2* (Spiteri et al. 2007; Vernes et al. 2007). Vernes et al. (2007) suggest that they 'would expect a minimum of 1.5% of promoters in the human genome (i.e. at least several hundred genes) to be occupied by FOXP2' in their cell-based models. In turn, these genes would affect several hundred more genes downstream in various biochemical pathways.

One intriguing target of *FOXP2* is *CNTNAP2*, a gene involved in cortical development and axonal function (Vernes et al. 2008). High levels of *CNTNAP2* have been found in language related circuits. Polymorphisms in *CNTNAP2* have been associated with specific language impairment (as tested by nonsense word repetition), and with language delays in children with autism. Vernes et al. (2007) found that FOXP2 protein binds to and directly downregulates *CNTNAP2*, so that in the developing human cortex, the lamina that contain the most FOXP2 protein have the lowest levels of *CNTNAP2*. But if *FOXP2* and *CNTNAP2* are negatively correlated, how can high levels of both be important for language? This simple finding demonstrates the complexity of the gene networks regulated by *FOXP2*.

It is not likely that there was any single mutation causing the origin of language, or even speech, as seen by the complex relationship between *FOXP2* and *CNTNAP2*, and by the fact that *FOXP2* regulates several hundred genes, including many that have non-language related functions which are so important that there were no amino acid changing mutations in *FOXP2* for 90 million years, from chimpanzee back to its common ancestor with rodents. We are only at the beginning of understanding the role of genetic processes in building the neuroanatomical structures necessary for human language.

..................................................

# CHAPTER 16

# NOT THE NEOCORTEX ALONE: OTHER BRAIN STRUCTURES ALSO CONTRIBUTE TO SPEECH AND LANGUAGE

..................................................

KATHLEEN R. GIBSON

The term *cortex* derives from the Latin word for bark. Neuroanatomists use the term in reference to neural structures which have their cell bodies (neurons) arranged in layers along an outer surface of the brain; for example, the cerebellar cortex, neocortex, and paleocortex. Neocortex, by far the largest portion of human and ape brains, contains most structures visible from the lateral surface, including the frontal, parietal, temporal, and occipital lobes, and is distinguished from other cortical areas by containing six layers, as opposed to three for cerebellar cortex, and four or five for other cortical areas. As well as constituting by far the largest portion of the human brain, the neocortex has shown the greatest expansion in human evolution.

Although at one time, paleocortex and neocortex were thought to be unique to mammals, these structures are now thought to have homologues in other vertebrate brains. It remains the case, however, that regions of the avian brain now considered functionally homologous to human neocortex are nuclear, as opposed to cortical, in their cellular arrangements. The functional significance of nuclear versus cortical neuronal arrangements remains unknown.

Ever since the pioneering findings of Broca and Wernicke, demonstrating that neocortical damage can produce language deficits, language evolution theorists have focused primarily on neocortical evolution (see, for example, chapters by Arbib, Coolidge and Wynn, Hopkins and Vauclair, and Wilkins), and a similar singularity of focus has dominated the quest for the neural origins of intelligence. Some even suggest that intelligence is best measured by ratios that explicitly and/or implicitly discount other neural areas. The most extreme such measure is Dunbar's neocortical ratio: i.e. the ratio of the size of the neocortex to the size of the entire remainder of the brain (Dunbar 1992). This ratio, which is based on the explicit assumption that the neocortex is the primary seat of intelligence, also rests on the implicit assumption that enlargement of non-neocortical brain structures lowers intelligence. For example, gorillas have larger neocortices (and larger overall brains) than chimpanzees, but they also have a larger cerebellum, hence a smaller neocortical ratio.

In contrast to cortical areas, nuclei and basal ganglia contain neurons that are arranged in a non-layered fashion. Such structures may also lie entirely within the brain, and thus have no visible representation on the outer brain surface. Only a few lone voices have championed the possible roles of non-neocortical structures in the evolution of language and speech (P. Lieberman 1991, 2000, 2002; Gibson and Jessee 1999; Donald, this volume). Yet, lesions of the basal ganglia and cerebellum can disrupt speech, and other structures such as the hippocampus and amygdala play key roles in learning and memory. Cerebellar damage, for example, has long been known to produce slurred speech, and it is now known that cerebellar lesions can be associated with a much wider range of cognitive and sensory defects, including defects in working memory, procedural learning, syntax, word order, word choice, and autism (Silveri and Misciagna 2000; De Smet et al. 2007). Similarly, lesions in the basal ganglia can produce deficits in procedural learning, the production of oral (and other) motor sequences, and oral dyspraxia (P. Lieberman 2002). Deficits in both the basal ganglia and the cerebellum accompany the orofacial dyspraxia that results from *FOXP2* mutations (Lai et al. 2003). Both the basal ganglia and the lateral portions of the cerebellum are also strongly interconnected with the neocortex via an intermediary subcortical structure, the thalamus, and the basal ganglia also have direct neocortical interconnections. Hence, the basal ganglia and the cerebellum work together with the neocortex to enable language, speech, and other behaviours. Another key structure, the hippocampus, does not affect speech or language directly, but is essential for declarative (semantic) and episodic memory and, thus, for some language content, while the amygdala is critical for learning in situations which involve strong emotions, especially fear (Phelps 2004).

One reason these neural structures are often ignored is the common misperception that only the neocortex has enlarged appreciably in human evolution. Another is that these structures leave few or no traces on hominin fossil endocasts. Indeed, it would be impossible for the basal ganglia, hippocampus, or amygdala to do so, because, in primates, they are internal brain structures that have no projections to the external brain surface. Actually, however, the basal ganglia, cerebellum, and hippocampus are each two to three times larger in humans than in great apes. Moreover, the absolute size of each of these structures correlates very strongly (e.g. 0.91 to 0.99) with the absolute brain size in non-human primates (Gibson and Jessee 1999) and also in a sample composed of insectivores, bats, and primates (Finlay and Darlington 1995). Thus, although we cannot directly measure the size of these structures in fossil hominins, overall brain size serves as a useful proxy.

Animals also differ in spinal cord anatomy, including the amount of grey matter (cell bodies) innervating various anatomical structures. MacLarnon (Chapter 22) notes that humans have more spinal cord grey matter innervating the thoracic and abdominal respiratory muscles than do apes, and postulates that this was a critical evolutionary step in the direction of the enhanced respiratory control needed for speech. Neural tracts connecting the neocortex with brainstem and spinal cord structures also differ in size and in the precise details of their anatomical origins and terminations. Until recently, it was impossible to study such tracts in any detail except in deceased individuals. Hence, we have little information about the anatomy of subcortical tracts in great apes. It is known, however, that in most mammals, most tracts from the neocortex to the spinal cord and brainstem, although once considered motor in nature, actually terminate on sensory nuclei and/or on interneurons that modulate sensory and motor functions, rather than on those motor neurons that directly innervate muscles. In contrast, in mammals, which have fine motor control of specific body parts, many cortical motor fibres do terminate directly on spinal cord and brainstem motor nuclei (Nudo and Masterson 1990; Striedter 2005). This phenomenon, which also correlates with overall size of neocortical motor representation, permits greater direct neocortical control of fine movements than would otherwise be possible. For example, in humans many cortical fibres terminate directly on spinal cord and brainstem motor neurons which control movements of the fingers, hand, lips, and tongue (Kuypers 1958), but few directly terminate on spinal motor neurons controlling movements of other body parts. Similarly, animals with expanded fine tactile discrimination in specific body parts, such as the fingers or lips, have enlarged fibre tracts and cortical areas mediating those body parts (Nolte 2008).

Recent evidence indicates that in avian vocal learners, such as parrots, vocal motor nuclei in the pallium—a region of the brain considered homologous to mammalian neocortex—also directly innervate vocal motor neurons (Jarvis et al. 2005; see also Pepperberg, this volume). Moreover, avian vocal learning and imitation involves loops between pallial, basal ganglia and thalamic nuclei, similar to loops between neocortex, basal ganglia, and thalamus known to be critical for procedural learning in mammals. Perhaps, then, the most critical neuroanatomical resemblances between birds that can imitate vocalizations and human speakers lie in subcortical connectivity, rather than in the possible homology between avian pallial nuclei and mammalian neocortex?

The recognition that major reorganizations in extra-neocortical brain structures and/or in the anatomy of subcortical tracts contribute to human speech and language functions can possibly shed light on another issue. Microcephalics, despite their small brain sizes, can speak, and, possibly master language to the level of a human 6-year-old (Wilkins, this volume). In most instances of microcephaly, the major size defect is in the neocortex, not in the basal ganglia, cerebellum or, as far as is known, the subcortical circuitry. Perhaps microcephalics can speak, despite their small brain sizes, because speech is partially under the control of non-neocortical structures?

## 16.1 Conclusion

Structures other than neocortex help control speech and language. Hence, if we are ever to truly comprehend the neural basis of language origins, we must overcome neocortical fixation and begin focusing on the anatomy of the entire brain. Measures such as the neocortical ratio, which discount the potentially important contributions of non-neocortical structures to language, intelligence, and learning seem especially inappropriate, given current understandings of the functions of structures such as the cerebellum, basal ganglia, hippocampus, and amygdala.

# CHAPTER 17

# THE MIMETIC ORIGINS OF LANGUAGE

## MERLIN DONALD

This chapter focuses on one aspect—mimesis—of a comprehensive theory of human cognitive evolution (Donald 1991, 1993). Mimesis is an embodied, analogue, and primordial mode of representation, in the sense that it is not only a preadaptation for language, but also a self-sufficient cognitive adaptation in its own right, which accounts for some of the major features of human cultural and cognitive life.

A mimetic act is a performance that reflects the perceived event structure of the world, and is the purest form of embodied representation. It has three behavioural manifestations: (1) rehearsal of skill, in which the actor imagines and reproduces previous performances with a view to improving them; (2) re-enactive mime, in which patterns of action, usually of others, are reproduced in the context of play or fantasy (for example, a child pretending to act like a puppy); and (3) non-linguistic gesture, where an action communicates an intention through resemblance (for example, miming the proper way of greeting strangers, or demonstrating a specific way to strike off a stone tool). The contents of mimetic acts are observable by others, which makes them a potential basis for a culturally accepted 'mimetic' vernacular, enabling members of a group to share knowledge, feelings, customs, skills, and goals, and to create group displays of emotions and intentions that are conventional and deliberate (for example, shared aggression or grief). These types of shared representations seem quite limited, when compared to language, but nevertheless constitute a powerful means of creating culture and sharing custom, feeling, and intent.

Mimesis was conceived as a unified neuro-cognitive adaptation that formed the early foundation of a distinctively human mindsharing culture. In itself, it falls far short of language, yet this characteristically human capacity creates the rudiments of a community of mind. It was the first step toward the formation of shared cognitive-cultural networks that could accumulate culturally stored knowledge and skills. This development had major consequences for the future evolutionary trajectory of the hominin brain, and for the eventual shape of human culture.

Mimesis is a dimension of higher cognition that is usually left out of theories derived from symbolic logic or computational linguistics, but it accounts for many of the defining aspects of human culture, including not only refined skill, but also ritual, spectacle, conformity, and the performance arts, among others. Mimesis was also a necessary preadaptation for the later evolution of language. It established the neuro-cognitive foundation of the high-level skills needed before any species could become capable of generating a virtual infinitude of arbitrary codes, and it created a more complex communication environment, providing the social conditions that drove the evolution of a more powerful high-speed language capacity.

## 17.1 MIMESIS AND SKILL

The first hints of the presence of mimesis appear with early finished stone tools, about 2.6 million years ago (mya), and the subsequent appearance of more complex Acheulean tools approximately 1.8 mya. There is good archaeological evidence that early human ancestors became more skilled, not only in the manufacture of stone tools, but also in other areas.

Refined skills are direct evidence that the primate capacity for procedural learning and memory underwent significant modification early in human evolution. Non-human primates lack the ability to invent stone tools in the wild, and there is no convincing evidence that they can systematically rehearse skills in order to refine them. The ability to refine skills depends upon the deliberate and repeated rehearsal of previous actions in a purposive manner, toward an ideal end-state. The repeated practice of a skill amounts to a voluntary re-enactment of one's previous actions, or those of others, and the process of practising a skill is identical with re-enactive mime.

The underlying cognitive process can be broken down into a standard sequence: first, construct a plan of action by recalling a previous action, or by observing others perform the action; second, execute an approximation of the action; third, compare, in imagination, the performed act to the intended one. This sequence is repeated until a criterion is satisfied, typically after pedagogical interventions by others, in other words, by culture. Typically, the criterion for realizing an intended action is set relatively low at the start, and the bar is raised in stages, depending on the range of feasible achievement for the individual practising the action.

The strongest argument for the early appearance of mimesis in hominin evolution is that mime and non-linguistic gesture come free with skill, because the neuro-cognitive mechanism and computational logic are the same. Thus, the archaeological evidence of refined tools is also, ipso facto, evidence of a mimetic capacity in archaic hominins.

Evidence from human brain mapping and clinical breakdown indicates that the hypothetical space in the mind where this comparison occurs (the 'mimetic controller') involves the dorsolateral prefrontal cortex, which is richly interconnected with premotor regions known to contain mirror neurons (Arbib, this volume), as well as amodal parietal and temporal regions, known to be involved in social event-perception, and the basal ganglia. The lateral cerebellum, and thus, the fronto-cerebellar pathway, are also involved, especially in the acquisition phase. All of these structures are greatly enlarged in humans, relative to monkeys and apes. Young human children can execute skilled rehearsal from a relatively early age, but the capacity to generate a review-rehearsal sequence seems to be missing, or seriously limited, in other primates.

## 17.2 THE SOURCE OF MIMESIS IN SOCIAL EVENT-REPRESENTATIONS

Social events, such as grooming patterns, are crucial indicators of primate social structure, and for this reason, event-perception is highly evolved in social mammals. However, expression is not so highly evolved; primates are good at understanding social events but poor at expressing this knowledge in action. They do not engage in anything like the fantasy role-playing of human children.

Social events are typically amodal, or supra-modal, in their sensory impact on the nervous system, and mimesis is an amodal capacity. A typical social event, such as a dogfight, generates largely uncorrelated stimulation of the visual, auditory, olfactory, gustatory, somatosensory, and proprioceptive systems, and extends over several minutes. This amodal pattern must be integrated by the brain into a unified event-percept, and the event must be grasped as a unit, even though it is not marked by clear sensory boundaries. Most social mammals achieve this effortlessly. They not only understand events such as fights, but also remember specific details, such as place, agency, and outcome. In addition, humans are able to re-enact the event in various modalities of expression. Human children engage in complex role-playing and fantasy play from an early age. Such play is reversible in focus, inasmuch as children can play the role of any agent in the sequence, or choose to focus on any of the actions performed by those agents, or to invent new ones.

This underlines the unity of mimesis as an adaptation. The practice of a skill or the invention of a gesture are specific instances of mimetic fantasy play.

## 17.3 Relevance to language evolution

Language is a refined skill that must be practised for years, and is the most complex of all human skills. For this reason alone, any scenario for the evolution of language must assume that an amodal mimetic capacity was already in place (Donald 1999). However, mimetic capacity is essential not only for the acquisition and transmission of language, but also for generating a pool of conventional signifiers, from which language might be constructed. Thus, mimesis must have evolved, on its own, independently of language, and prior to it. Mimesis came first, primarily because of the adaptive advantages of improved tool-making.

In this scenario, prosody came long before phonology, because some limited capacity for voice modulation was already present in the voluntary motor repertoire of primates, and thus would have fallen under the aegis of an amodal adaptation, such as mimesis. Modern humans may be predisposed toward speech, but language is essentially amodal, inasmuch as it can take non-vocal forms (such as sign). This suggests that language came later in human evolution, scaffolded on mimesis, long after an amodal mimetic preadaptation set the stage for the further evolution of both culture and gesture (Donald 1998, 2009).

A massive modern cultural residue testifies to the importance and endurance of mimesis as a mode of expression in its own right. Mimesis dominates in many non-verbal domains of culture, such as theatre, dance, song, visual art, and body language. It is evident in popular culture, the behaviour of crowds, advertising, political propaganda, and the media. It is the most archaic and deepest foundation of human expressivity.

# CHAPTER 18

# EVOLUTION OF BEHAVIOURAL AND BRAIN ASYMMETRIES IN PRIMATES

WILLIAM D. HOPKINS AND
JACQUES VAUCLAIR

Hemispheric specialization refers to differential perceptual, motor, and cognitive processes performed by the left and right cerebral hemispheres. Two robust manifestations of hemispheric specialization in humans are handedness and language lateralization. Specifically, the majority of humans in most cultures are right-handed, hence, left hemisphere dominant for manual tasks (on average, 88%; Raymond and Pontier 2004). Among right-handed individuals, 96% are also left hemisphere dominant for language in comparison to 70% of left-handed individuals (Knecht et al. 2000).

The pronounced expression of population-level right handedness and left hemisphere dominance for language in humans has prompted some to hypothesize that these two functions co-evolved and are uniquely human (Warren 1980; Ettlinger 1988; Crow 2004). Indeed, a number of theoretical models of the evolution of hemispheric specialization are predicated on the assumption that the emergence of language in humans after the split from the common ancestor with chimpanzees was the driving force behind the eventual development of lateralized behavioural and neuroanatomical asymmetries. For example, in one of the most prominent genetic models of hemispheric specialization, it has been hypothesized that right-handedness in humans is a *consequence* of left hemisphere dominance for speech and language (see Crow 2004). Thus, in such a model, the existence of speech and language is a necessary condition for the presence of hemispheric specialization.

Certainly, other models of hemispheric specialization have been proposed, but in all cases, the assumptions are that it emerged as a consequence of evolutionary adaptations after the split from the common ancestor of human and chimpanzees (see Hopkins 2006). Early attempts to assess behavioural and cognitive asymmetries in non-human primates reinforced these models and views, because scientists rarely found evidence of population-level asymmetries. However, these early studies often used simple rather than complex tasks to assess handedness (Fagot and Vauclair 1993), used small sample sizes (Hopkins 2006), or failed to incorporate species-specific tasks and stimuli (Hamilton and Vermeire 1988) and this may have contributed to the largely negative findings. More recently, this view has begun changing, based on a growing body of literature demonstrating population-level behavioural and brain asymmetries in vertebrate species including rats, birds, fish, and non-human primates (Rogers and Andrew 2002; Hopkins 2007).

Nonetheless, parallels in lateralization in humans and non-human animals remain a topic of considerable debate, particularly in relation to communicative behaviours (Corballis 2002; Meguerditchian and Vauclair 2008). This chapter reviews evidence of behavioural and neuroanatomical asymmetries in non-human primates pertaining to the production of communicative behaviours. Specifically, we review studies of hand preferences in manual gestures and of asymmetries in communicative facial expressions. Finally, we present data on neuroanatomical asymmetries in non-human primates with specific reference to key areas that are considered the homologues to language areas of the human brain (i.e. Broca's and Wernicke's areas); see also Wilkins, this volume.

## 18.1 HANDEDNESS FOR MANUAL GESTURES

Population-level handedness in manual gestures has been found in captive populations of chimpanzees, bonobos, gorillas, and baboons. In two different cohorts of captive chimpanzees, Hopkins et al. (2005) reported population-level right-handedness for interspecies manual gestures associated with the request for food from a human. In a follow-up study, Meguerditchian et al. (2010) examined handedness for a variety of manual gestures during inter- and intra-species communication in captive chimpanzees and found that the apes were significantly right-handed for all gesture types.

In bonobos, three separate studies have examined handedness for manual gestures during interspecies communication (Hopkins and de Waal 1995; Shafer 1997; Harrison and Nystrom 2008). None of these individual studies found population-level handedness in manual gestures; however, the combined data of the three studies (n = 49) reveals significant population-level right-handedness in manual gestures by bonobos. In the only study on manual gestures and handedness in gorillas, Shafer (1993) reported a small bias toward preferential use of the right hand in a sample of captive lowland gorillas. Neither monkeys nor prosimians are known for their manual gesture abilities, but olive baboons (*Papio anubis*) often use hand slaps as threatening gestures. In a sample of 60 captive baboons, Meguerditchian and Vauclair (2006) found that the animals used the right hand significantly more often than the left to threaten both conspecifics and humans.

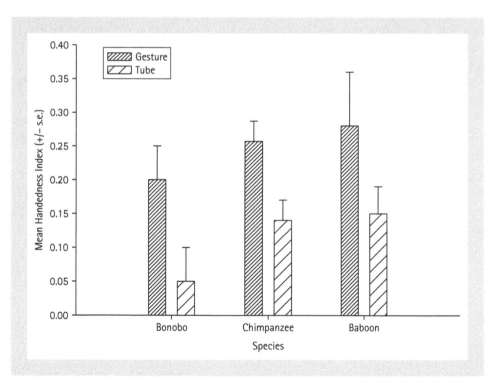

**Figure 18.1. Mean handedness indices (± s.e.) for chimpanzees, bonobos, and baboons for manual gestures compared to a task measuring coordinated bimanual actions (TUBE task).**
The handedness index is calculated following the formula [HI= (#R − #L) / (#R + #L)] where #R and #L represent the frequency of right- and left-hand use. Positive values indicate right-hand preference and negative values indicate left-hand preference.

Shown in Figure 18.1 are the mean handedness indices for manual gestures in chimpanzees, bonobos, and baboons in comparison to a task that measures coordinated bimanual actions. As can be seen, for all three species, subjects are significantly more right-handed for manual gestures compared to the non-communicative manual actions. These results suggest that lateralization in communicative signals is more pronounced than for non-communicative manual actions.

## 18.2 OROFACIAL MOVEMENTS

Other studies of captive monkeys and apes have attempted to quantify facial asymmetries in the temporal onset of orofacial movements or in intensity of expression of the mouth area (see Figure 18.2A, B).

Hauser (1993) reported that the left side of the face began to display facial expressions earlier than the right side for open-mouth threat and fear grimace in rhesus monkeys. Hauser and Akre (2001) examined onset of mouth-opening asymmetries in rhesus monkeys during the production of several types of vocalizations. Not all vocalizations led to asymmetrical patterns, but a consistent directional bias (left mouth opening before right) was reported for those that did. Hook-Costigan and Rogers (1998) showed that common marmosets displayed a larger left hemi-mouth during the production of fear expressions, including those that were or were not accompanied by a vocalization. Only one class of sounds produced by the marmosets, the 'twitter', which is a social contact call, showed a right orofacial asymmetry. In chimpanzees, Fernandez-Carriba et al. (2002) reported significant left orofacial asymmetries for several facial expressions including hooting, play, silent-bared teeth, and scream face. Losin et al. (2008) assessed orofacial asymmetries for four facial expressions associated with vocalizations in chimpanzees including hooting, food-barks, extended food grunts, and raspberries (see Figure 18.2C). The raspberries and extended food grunts were two classes of sounds that previous studies in chimpanzees have shown to be used as attention-getting sounds directed towards humans (Leavens et al. 2004; Hopkins et al. 2007b). Losin et al. (2008) found that food-barks and hoots were expressed more intensely on the left side of the face whereas extended food grunts and raspberries were expressed more intensely on the right side.

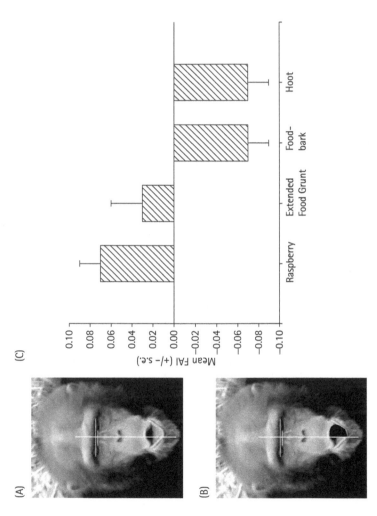

Figure 18.2. A) Example of the measurement of orofacial asymmetries in a chimpanzee. Note that a horizontal line connects the inner points of the eyes while a vertical line bisects the face at the midline. B) The regions of the mouth that fall on the left and right sides of the bisecting lines are quantified as an area measure. C) Mean FAI values (± s.e.) for different facial expressions of chimpanzees studied by Losin et al. (2008). FAI = facial asymmetry index. Positive FAI values indicate that the right half of the face is more expressive whereas negative values indicate that the left half is more expressive.

## 18.3 NEUROANATOMICAL ASYMMETRIES IN NON-HUMAN PRIMATES

Ever since 19th-century discoveries of language-related human cortical asymmetries by Broca, Wernicke, and others, scientists have wondered if similar asymmetries exist in non-human primates (Broca 1861; Wernicke 1874; Bailey et al. 1950; Geschwind and Levitsky 1968). Early studies from both cadaver brains and endocasts focused on left–right differences in sulci length and asymmetries in the shape of the skull (LeMay and Geschwind 1975; LeMay 1977; Cain and Wada 1979; Holloway and de Lacoste-Lareymondie 1982). With the advent of modern imaging technologies, more recent studies have quantified volumetric differences in cortical regions of interest, particularly in regions of the brain that are considered homologous to Broca's and Wernicke's areas, including: (1) the Sylvian fissure (SF), (2) the planum temporale (PT), and (3) inferior frontal gyrus (IFG) (see Figure 18.3).

### 18.3.1 Planum temporale

The PT is the flat surface of the superior temporal lobe that lies posterior to the primary auditory cortex of the human brain, Heschl's gyrus (see Figure 18.3A and B). In humans, the PT encompasses Wernicke's area, one of the main areas involved in speech comprehension, and therefore has been the focus of considerable research in the human neuropsychological literature (Shapleske et al. 1999).

Three different laboratories, using different methods and procedures, have reported leftward asymmetries in this brain region in chimpanzees. Gannon et al. (1998) measured the PT in 18 chimpanzee cadaver brains and reported that 17 of these individuals showed a left hemisphere asymmetry. Gilissen (2001) examined PT asymmetries in magnetic resonance imaging (MRI) scans of ten cadaver chimpanzee brains and found significant leftward asymmetries in seven of these individuals. Using MRI, Hopkins and Cantalupo (2004) traced the flat surface of the temporal lobe posterior to Heschl's gyrus and found significant leftward asymmetries in a sample of 66 living chimpanzees. More recently, Hopkins and Nir (2010) have added subjects to this sample and have now measured the PT in 106 chimpanzees from MRI, and a significant population-level leftward asymmetry was found (see Figure 18.4). In total, 72% of the sample (n = 76) showed a left hemisphere asymmetry, 17% (n = 18) showed a right hemisphere asymmetry, and 11% showed no bias (n = 12).

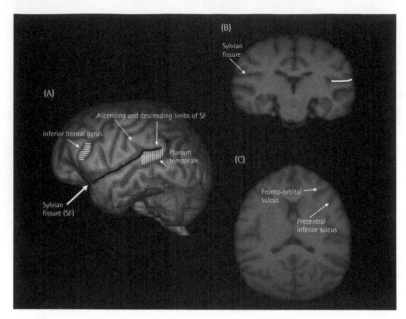

Figure 18.3. A) Three-dimensional MRI reconstruction of a chimpanzee brain with the lateral region corresponding to the planum temporale vertically etched on the image and the inferior frontal gyrus (IFG) horizontally etched. B) A coronal view of a chimpanzee MRI scan with the Sylvian fissure indicated on the right hemisphere. The white line in the left hemisphere indicates how the flat surface is measured on a single coronal slice. C) Axial view of a chimpanzee brain with the sulcal landmarks used to delineate the IFG indicated including the precentral inferior and fronto-orbital sulci. Note the distinction in grey and white matter within the IFG.

## 18.3.2 Sylvian fissure length

One challenge in comparative neuroanatomical studies is that sulci and the degree of gyrification vary substantially across species, and this often precludes direct measurement of some brain areas. The PT is one example of this challenge. The anterior border of the PT, Heschl's gyrus, is a very visible and reliable landmark in the human and great ape brain, but it is more difficult to visualize in lesser apes and monkeys. Thus, many investigators have needed to use more indirect means of measuring the PT. The most consistent approach has been to quantify the length of the Sylvian fissure either directly from cadaver brains and endocasts or from MRI scans.

The Sylvian or lateral fissure (SF) separates the temporal lobe from the frontal and parietal lobes of the brain (see Figure 18.3A and B) and constitutes the lateral border of the PT. Left–right differences in SF length are quite prominent, hence easily studied, in primate brains. Among great apes, chimpanzees have been

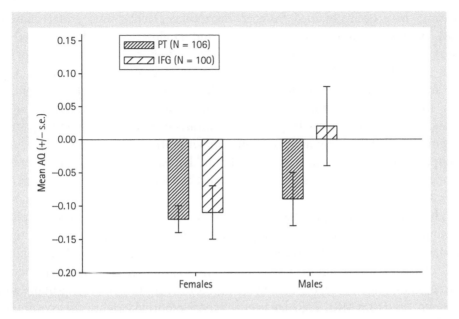

**Figure 18.4. Mean asymmetry index (AQ) ($\pm$ s.e.) for the PT and IFG measured from a sample of chimpanzee MRI scans.**
The AQ is calculated following the formula AQ= (R − L) / [(R + L) × **0.5**] where R and L represent the volume or area measures of right and left regions of interest. Positive AQ values indicate a rightward bias and negative values indicate a leftward bias.

studied the most extensively, and consistent leftward asymmetries have been found for the SF length on both cadaver specimens (n = 25) (Yeni-Komshian and Benson 1976) and from *in vivo* MRI measurements (n = 25) (Hopkins et al. 2000). Based on *in vivo* measurements, bonobos (n = 7) and gorillas (n = 5) also show leftward asymmetries in the SF length while the orang-utans (n = 10) show a rightward asymmetry (Hopkins et al. 2000).

Of the Old World primates, rhesus monkeys and related macaques have been by far the most extensively studied, but the results are not entirely consistent. In cadaver brains, Heilbronner and Holloway (1988) reported significant leftward asymmetries in 30 rhesus and 30 crab-eating macaque specimens but these same findings were not found in 18 subjects studied by Gannon et al. (2008) or 25 monkeys studied by Yeni-Komshian and Benson (1976). Measuring the SF from endocasts, initially Falk et al. (1986) reported a left hemisphere bias in ten rhesus monkeys but could not replicate this in a much larger sample of 335 monkeys (Falk et al. 1990). To date, studies using *in vivo* measurements of SF length in Old World monkeys have very limited sample sizes and therefore the existence of population-level asymmetries cannot be determined. Lastly, for New World monkeys, SF length measures have been obtained from 26 marmosets (Heilbronner and Holloway 1988), 28 squirrel monkeys (Heilbronner and Holloway 1988; Hopkins et al. 2000), 13 spider monkeys (Gilissen 1992), and 41 capuchin monkeys (Hopkins et al. 2000; Liu and Phillips 2009) using cadaver specimens, endocasts, and *in vivo* measurement. None of these species show consistent left–right differences, with the exception of the genus *Cebus*. In *Cebus capucinus*, Gilissen (1992) measured asymmetries in SF length from endocasts in 20 individuals and reported a significant leftward asymmetry. From *in vivo* MRI measurements, Liu and Phillips (2009) reported an overall borderline leftward asymmetry in SF length among 17 *Cebus apella* and a significant leftward bias within their sample of females (n = 8).

In humans and great apes, the posterior end of the SF often bifurcates (or splits) creating an ascending and descending branch (see Figure 18.3A). Some investigators have therefore separately measured the length of the ascending and descending rami of the SF (apes only). In cadaver brains, Gannon et al. (2005) reported a rightward asymmetry for the ascending limb of the SF in both orang-utans and chimpanzees. From MRI, Taglialatela et al. (2007) reported a rightward asymmetry for the ascending limb and no bias for the descending limb in chimpanzees. Taglialatela et al. (2007) also reported that female chimpanzees showed a significant rightward asymmetry in the length of the ascending limb of the SF compared to males. Finally, rather than focus on SF length, LeMay (1985) measured the height of the terminal point of the SF in several primate species. In the case of great apes, a bias was more often observed in the right compared to left hemisphere; however, in many of the species, there were simply too few subjects to make any meaningful interpretation.

### 18.3.3 Inferior frontal gyrus

In human and great ape brains, Broca's area is located on the inferior frontal gyrus (IFG) (Keller et al. 2009a, b) which lies between the precentral inferior and fronto-orbital sulci (see Figure 18.3A and C). While there is no question that Broca's area plays a critical role in a number of cognitive and linguistic functions in the human brain (Nishitani et al. 2005; Cooper 2006), the extent to which neuroanatomical asymmetries are found within this region in human and non-human primates is a matter of some debate. Some have reported that the left human IFG is larger than the right (Foundas et al. 1995, 1998) but others have not (Tomaiuolo et al. 1999). Similarly, some have found a leftward bias in the amount of grey matter within the gyrus, others have not (Good et al. 2001; Watkins et al. 2001; Keller et al. 2007).

Cantalupo and Hopkins (2001) found the volume of the left IFG to be larger than the right in a sample of 27 great apes, including 20 chimpanzees, five bonobos and two gorillas. In a follow-up study by Hopkins (unpublished data), the IFG was measured in a sample of 100 chimpanzees from MRI, following the procedures employed by Cantalupo and Hopkins (2001), and a sex difference was found, with females showing a significant leftward asymmetry, whereas no bias was found in the male sample (see Figure 18.4). As noted by Sherwood et al. (2003) there is considerable variability in the location and bifurcation patterns of sulci used to define the IFG in chimpanzees, and this has led some to question how reliably the entire gyrus can be quantified in apes. To address this issue, Hopkins and Cantalupo (2004) measured the length of the fronto-orbital sulcus (the landmark used to define the anterior border of the IFG) in a sample of 66 chimpanzees and found it to be significantly longer in the left compared to right hemisphere.

Rather than measure the entire IFG, Keller et al. (2009a, b) recently quantified just the grey matter volumes of the IFG in 30 human and 30 chimpanzee MRI scans and found no population-level asymmetries in either species. These results contrast with some existing findings on humans and chimpanzees that have quantified the entire volume of the IFG (including both the grey and white matter). This leads to an interesting possibility, namely that asymmetries within the entire IFG may be a consequence of white matter expansion rather than grey matter organization. White matter within the IFG would presumably reflect connectivity between the IFG and other brains regions, such as the posterior temporal lobe.

## 18.3.4  Microstructural asymmetries

Studies of human postmortem brains have reported significant leftward asymmetries in the volume, neuron number, neuron density and dendritic branching in Brodmann's areas 44 and 45, the major components of Broca's area (Scheibel et al. 1985; Amunts et al. 1999; Uylings et al. 2006). Recently, Schenker et al. (2009) quantified the cellular volume of BA44 and BA45 in 12 chimpanzees and found no strong evidence of population-level asymmetries in these regions. Overall, six of 12 individuals showed a leftward asymmetry for BA44 while five of the 12 apes showed a leftward bias for the BA45 cells. Interestingly, for BA44, there were sex differences with five of the six males showing a leftward asymmetry whereas five of the six females showed a rightward asymmetry. Gannon et al. (2008) examined cytoarchitectonic asymmetries in the posterior temporal lobe in rhesus monkeys and found a significant leftward asymmetry in five of the six monkeys.

Another cellular approach has been to quantify asymmetries in mini-columns within both the posterior region of the temporal lobe and inferior frontal gyrus. Mini-columns refer to vertically oriented cells with strong vertical connections between different layers of cortex. Schenker et al. (2008) examined asymmetries in Brodmann's areas 44 and 45 in a sample of 11 humans and eight great apes and found no population-level asymmetries in either taxonomic group for either mini-column density or grey-level indices. In contrast, Buxhoeveden and Casanova (2000) examined mini-column asymmetries in the posterior temporal lobe of 12 humans, seven chimpanzees and four monkey postmortem brains and found a leftward asymmetry in humans but not in chimpanzees and rhesus monkeys.

## 18.4 NEURAL CORRELATES OF BEHAVIOURAL ASYMMETRIES IN NON-HUMAN PRIMATES

Given the presence of laterality in manual gestures and orofacial expressions in monkeys and apes, as well as neuroanatomical asymmetries in the language homologues, there has been interest in whether significant associations exist between these two traits. Lesions in the posterior temporal lobe of the left, but not the right, hemisphere produce transient deficits in perception of species-specific vocalizations in Japanese macaques (Heffner and Heffner 1984). Similarly, using positron emission tomography (PET), Poremba et al. (2004) found rightward asymmetries in posterior regions of the temporal lobe and leftward asymmetries in the temporal pole when processing species-specific sounds in eight rhesus macaques, a finding somewhat at odds with the results in Japanese macaques using lesion techniques. Gil-da-Costa et al. (2006) did not find hemispheric differences in the processing of species-specific sounds in rhesus macaques, though the sample size was relatively small in this study (n = 3). In three chimpanzees, PET was used to examine processing of two classes of species-specific sounds (proximal and broadcast calls) and significant rightward asymmetries were found in the posterior temporal lobe (Taglialatela et al. 2009).

Very few studies have examined brain–behavioural relationships in the production of communication signals in non-human primates. Taglialatela et al. (2006) reported that chimpanzees that prefer to gesture with the right hand had larger leftward asymmetries in the IFG compared to non-right-handed individuals. Significant differences were not found between right- and non-right-handed chimpanzees for the motor-hand area, suggesting that the brain–behaviour associations were specific to the IFG. Significant handedness effects in relation to asymmetries in the IFG have also been reported in chimpanzees for tool use, with right-handed individuals showing greater leftward asymmetries compared to non-right-handed individuals (Hopkins et al. 2007a). Finally, Taglialatela et al. (2008) also conducted a PET study on three chimpanzees in which they measured metabolic activity during gesture-vocal communication compared to motor actions used when manually grasping objects. With specific reference to lateralized differences, significant clusters of brain activity were found in the left IFG, left caudate, left temporal pole, and right middle frontal gyrus.

# 18.5 DISCUSSION

Several conclusions can be drawn from the work on behavioural and brain asymmetries in non-human primates. First, there is good evidence of population-level handedness for manual gestures and orofacial communication asymmetries in monkeys (rhesus, baboons, marmosets) and apes (chimpanzees, bonobos, gorillas). In addition, lateralization for manual communicative signals is significantly more rightward than for manual actions associated with manipulation. Hence, neural substrates for manual communication may be dissociated from those for manipulative motor functions in non-human primates.

When considering orofacial asymmetries, the results overwhelmingly show that monkeys and apes show population-level asymmetries and, for the most part, expressions are lateralized to the right hemisphere. The fact that most facial expressions are right hemisphere dominant in monkeys and apes and that these expressions are often accompanied by vocalizations suggests that the signals are principally emotive in function. There are some exceptions in non-human primates, such as the 'twitter' vocalization in marmosets and the 'raspberry' and 'extended food grunt' in chimpanzees. Why these expressions are more intensely expressed on the right side of the face is unclear. One suggestion might be that they possess different emotional valences (i.e. some are positive and some negative). Davidson et al. (2004) have suggested that positive emotions are lateralized to the left hemisphere and negative emotions are lateralized to the right hemisphere. In chimpanzees, however, positive emotive expressions such as play and food-barks show leftward not rightward orofacial asymmetries and therefore are not consistent with the valence hypothesis (see also Hauser and Akre 2001). Alternatively, it may be that these sounds and vocalizations function differently than other expressions and vocalizations. At this point, attempts to quantify orofacial asymmetries in non-human primates should try to sample a wide array of expressions with different social and communicative functions.

Evidence for population-level brain asymmetries in non-human primates is less consistent than for behavioural lateralization, especially in monkeys. In chimpanzees, it seems evident that the surface area of the PT and length of the SF are larger in the left compared to the right hemisphere. These results have been observed in different laboratories using various techniques and materials and therefore seem to be replicable findings. Evidence of population-level neuroanatomical asymmetries in Old and New World monkeys are less consistent across samples and techniques. Specifically, for the SF, the procedures used, the sample sizes, and the type of specimen (*in vivo* versus postmortem brain) seem to yield different results.

For the IFG, the results in both humans and great apes are inconsistent. When considering the entire volume of the IFG, leftward asymmetries have been reported in humans and chimpanzees; however, when analyses are restricted to the grey matter, no population-level asymmetries appear evident in either species. Asymmetries in the IFG appear to be influenced by the method used to quantify the region and whether the analyses are restricted to grey matter or include all tissue within the gyrus. The evidence of population-level microstructural asymmetries for Broca's area is more apparent in humans than in chimpanzees. When considering the volume of BA44 and BA45, both male and female humans show a leftward asymmetry whereas male chimpanzees show a leftward bias but females show the opposite pattern. For mini-columns, neither humans nor chimpanzees show asymmetries in BA44 or BA45. Unfortunately, very little research has addressed the question of asymmetries in the homologue to Broca's area in monkeys and this seems like an important line of research for future studies, particularly in light of the observation that electrical stimulation of this region can induce orofacial movements (Petrides et al. 2005).

The recent use of *in vivo* functional imaging studies in monkeys and apes has laid the foundation for more direct assessments of brain–behaviour relationships in the domain of communication. Understandably, there were smaller samples of subjects in these studies and, pragmatically, *in vivo* studies are difficult to perform. Notwithstanding, their potential application for understanding the neurobiological substrates of communication in non-human primates cannot be overstated and the field will benefit tremendously from these advances.

In sum, the more one looks for continuities between human and non-human primates, not only in lateralization but in relevant areas of cognitive evolution, the more similarities one finds. At a minimum, in our view, it seems abundantly clear now that language and speech are not necessary conditions for the expression of hemispheric specialization in non-human primates and it is time to begin considering other variables or factors that influence individual and species differences in laterality. Perhaps Geschwind and Galaburda were right when they said, as early as 1985, that 'the recognition of asymmetry in the non-human nervous system is likely to lead to major conceptual advances in fields as widely disparate as human evolution, linguistics, psychology and psychiatry. If these suppositions are correct, it will also have major philosophical repercussions'. It appears, at the moment, that this prediction is coming to pass.

# ACKNOWLEDGEMENTS

WDH was supported, in part, by NIH grants NS-42867, NS-36605, HD-38051, and HD-56232. JV was supported by funds from the EC Sixth Framework Programme under Contract no. ERAS-CT-2003-980409 and from the ANR Programme, contract no. 08-3_311472.

# CHAPTER 19

# TOWARDS AN EVOLUTIONARY BIOLOGY OF LANGUAGE THROUGH COMPARATIVE NEUROANATOMY

WENDY K. WILKINS

## 19.1 INTRODUCTION: TAKING ANATOMY SERIOUSLY

Theories of the evolution of human linguistic ability, like theories of language function, must be biologically plausible. To be credible, a biolinguistic theory of language must work equally well in accounting for deep facts about linguistic cognition and in being executable in human neuroanatomy. The basis for this strong claim is that language has certain fundamental characteristics because the brain functions the way it does (cf. Chater and Christiansen, this volume). A further underlying assumption is that anatomy is relevant to function, and specifically, neuroanatomy is relevant to brain function. The facts of anatomy are directly relevant to the facts of normal physiology and function, and if the facts of basic anatomy were different, the theory of function would also have to be different.

By taking seriously both the biology and the linguistics, a truly biolinguistic approach to language can yield insights into the evolution of linguistic ability because evolution works on biology, ultimately at the level of the genome. Therefore, a good working strategy, to help us understand the emergence of linguistic capacity in humans, is to work backwards: first seeking to understand the current biological basis of language, and then tracing its development back through time. Ideally we would be working on tracing the genetic basis of language, but because much more is known about anatomy, we can more successfully look at the evolutionary development of the language-relevant brain structures. This means tracing the evolutionary development of the language organ, with the understanding that this 'organ' is a network of functionally interconnected parts: a mosaic (Wilkins 2009). Understanding the evolutionary biology of language involves working out the prehistorical development of each part of the mosaic. At the same time, it is important to recognize how unlikely it is that any of these parts were originally specialized for language. In fact, many of them may not be specialized for language even in the contemporary anatomical configuration. What is indeed apparently specialized for language is the system of interconnectivity. The neurobiological mosaic is, functionally, the language organ.

Too often, discussion of the evolution of language neglects the biology, and too little attention is paid to whether a proposed evolutionary scenario would be possible in a primate-type brain. Alternatively, proposals are made about the nature of linguistic precursors in primate or other mammalian species, with no attention paid to whether the anatomical structure underlying the behaviour in that species could have plausibly, or even possibly, evolved into contemporary human anatomy relevant to language. In order to address these shortcomings, work on a serious evolutionary biology of language can proceed in two ways: through examination of the fossil record and through comparative primate neuroanatomy.

## 19.2 LIMITS TO WORKING FROM
## THE FOSSIL RECORD

It is well known that structures in the peri-Sylvian region of the left hemisphere are necessary for language. These include Broca's area, the parietal-occipital-temporal junction or POT (Wilkins and Wakefield 1995a), and Wernicke's area (especially for auditory linguistic processing). Probably also critically necessary for language are the major fibre tracts, superior longitudinal fasciculus and arcuate fasciculus, which connect the anterior and posterior structures involved in language.

Substantial work has been done to determine whether there is evidence for these anatomical structures in hominin species ancestral to modern humans (e.g. Holloway 1978; Falk 1980, 1983). The most convincing analyses suggest that both Broca's area and the POT could be identified as early as *Homo habilis*, and some would argue even earlier (Wilkins and Wakefield 1995a, b). The work that has led to this claim involves the study of endocasts, moulds made from the interior of fossil skulls, which provide a way of reading the structure of the external surface of the brain that was encased in the fossil skull through study of the sulci and gyri visible on the endocast.

There is evidence that as early as 2.5 million years ago (or some would say even earlier), there was a Broca's area (roughly Brodmann's areas 44 and 45) and a POT. In earlier species there is less evidence of the left hemisphere asymmetry of the inferior frontal gyrus that would indicate the existence of Broca's area, and there is no POT. The lack of a POT is indicated by the existence of a major sulcal division, the lunate sulcus, at the terminus of the Sylvian fissure. In species exhibiting a lunate sulcus on the exterior surface of the brain, there would be no evident junction of the three posterior lobes.

The existence of a Broca's area and a POT are considered indicative of a hominin anatomical configuration rather than a great ape configuration (in contemporary species). The apes, even the great apes considered most closely related to humans, have a lunate sulcus on the lateral surface of the left hemisphere; anatomically modern humans do not. (Illustrations of the typical great ape and hominin neuroanatomical configurations are available in Wilkins (2005) and Wilkins and Wakefield (1995a).) The POT region in modern humans is essential not only to language but to basic conceptual structure (Geschwind 1965; Wilkins and Wakefield 1995a; Catani and ffytche 2005). It accounts for the modality-neutral character of concepts. Additionally, because the POT is connected to Broca's area (more accurately to Brodmann's areas 44 and 45) by the major fibre tracts, the modality-neutral concepts are hierarchically structured (like frontal lobe motor programmes) and, as necessary, are executable in real, linear time.

Returning to the matter of the fossil record, perhaps because of the scant number of available skulls to analyse, and the poor condition of many of the available specimens, there is much debate about the exact nature of what can be learned from them (compare, for example, Holloway 1978 and Falk 1980). Regardless of whether it can be determined when the hominin configuration first emerged, it is clear that the signature left-hemisphere anatomical features indicative of language capacity emerged in anatomical regions relevant for frontal motor and posterior somatosensory functions. It is also reasonable to assume that these regions, in ancestral species developing abilities associated with tool manufacture and throwing as well as preferential right-handedness, just as in contemporary humans, are intimately connected with neural control of the hand (specifically the right hand); see Hopkins and Vauclair, this volume.

Thus, from the admittedly scant palaeobiological evidence, we may say that the basic hominin/great ape distinction that is characteristic in posterior brain anatomy emerged very early in the ancestral line, and most probably far predated the anatomically modern human vocal tract. Not much can be surmised about language-relevant brain anatomy from the available fossil record, largely because there is so little available material to study and so little that can be said about neuroanatomy except what can be based on endocast maps from the cortical surface. Nevertheless, theories of language evolution should be consistent with what is known and plausibly connect to the information that can be gleaned from the available endocasts.

## 19.3 WORKING FROM COMPARATIVE ANATOMY

A richer line of investigation is based on comparison of human neuroanatomy with that of extant and closely related species. Such studies continue to corroborate that there is no POT evident in the great ape brain; in other words, there is no homologue of the POT even in the great apes. However, there are other potential homologues, indicative, for example, of Wernicke's area. There is evidence of a lateral asymmetry of the planum temporale in ape species (Gannon et al. 1998; Hopkins et al. 1998; Hopkins and Vauclair, this volume), and on many accounts the planum is a feature of Wernicke's area. Thus, such an asymmetry might be evidence of an incipient Wernicke's area in great apes. (Buxhoeveden et al. (2001a, b) distinguish microstructural differences between humans and great apes that might suggest a later development of Wernicke's area, so there may be a sort of mosaic effect in which macro- and microstructural developments differ).

If the planum temporale is a linguistically relevant part of Wernicke's area (researchers may differ on this point), and given that Wernicke's area is relevant for language, then it is important to consider the evolutionary development of this anatomical feature. This can be done by consideration of the homologous areas of human and non-human primate brains. Even while maintaining that language is a species-specific characteristic of humans, given the mosaic nature of the language organ, we should expect to find homologous structures in the ape brain (such as precursors to Wernicke's area). In fact, recent findings suggest that there may also be an incipient Broca's area, or at least an asymmetry of the left inferior frontal gyrus in the great ape brain (Cantalupo and Hopkins 2001). This is just what we would expect to find, considering both the mosaic nature of the language system and the need to take seriously the biological basis in exploring the origins of language.

The more sophisticated our understanding of the contemporary human neuro-biology of language, the more sophisticated will be the work on comparative anatomy. More simply put, the more we know about the anatomical basis and function of human language, the better positioned we will be to find relevant homologues in other primate species. It is undeniable that, minimally, human brains developed in such a way as to feature a POT and a Broca's area connected by a major fibre tract. It is therefore relevant to explore exactly what the precursors to these structures might have been through comparison with contemporary related species.

For this research strategy of comparative anatomy and the search for homo-logues to be fruitful, it is necessary to recognize that an account of language must be based on evolutionary mechanisms beyond simple adaptation. In the case of Broca's area and the POT, a part of the frontal lobe motor system co-evolved with a somatosensory posterior region due to adaptations, probably for better control of the hand and thumb, a feature necessary for tool manufacture and overhand throwing for predation at a distance (see, for example, Greenfield 1991 and other references in Wilkins and Wakefield 1995). But these anatomical features, so critical to language in contemporary human brains, most certainly did not originally support strictly linguistic cognition or behaviour, especially in light of how early they apparently emerged in the ancestral line. Once they were evolved, however, they were available for re-appropriation, or exaptation (Gould and Vrba 1982) for a new use.

Importantly, anatomical mosaic parts essential to language have not been shown to be homologous to anatomical structures that support vocal communication in related ape (or monkey) species. While it is possible in principle to do so, no one has yet developed an evolutionary biological story that would yield the Broca's area–POT complex, plus the relevant connecting fasciculi, from the anatomical structures that underlie strictly communicative behaviour in human close relatives—or, as a matter of fact, from the anatomical structures that underlie communicative behaviour in other more distant mammalian species. Instead, two recognized universals of language are arguably derivable from structures not directly or primarily related to communication. The system involving the POT (the convergence of the somatosensory, auditory, and visual association areas) and Broca's area (essentially motor cortex) is consistent with an account of why language universally features hierarchical structure and the expression of concepts not directly related to the sense modalities (for further detail, see Wilkins 2005, 2009 and Wakefield and Wilkins 2007 and references therein). Other aspects of language (see, for example, speculation below in the concluding section) would certainly be derived from other anatomical systems or structures.

It is also apparently universally true that linguistic expressions reflect spatial information. This is often described in linguistics in terms of 'thematic relations' or 'thematic roles.' The spatial structure concepts that are evidently necessarily expressed in some fashion or other in language involve motion and location (more or less concretely), as in (1), and are typically represented functionally in terms of source, goal, theme, and location, and involve places and paths, as in (2):

(1)   a. The horse trotted along the trail. ('Trot' = a particular type of spatial motion)
      b. Sue inherited the ring from her mom. (Possession, 'inherit' = go from 'mom' to 'Sue')
      c. Her mood changed from happy to sad. (Ascription of properties, 'change' = go from 'happy' to 'sad')
      d. The talk lasted from noon to 2:00. (Temporal duration, 'last' = go from 'noon' to '2:00')
      e. The road goes from Denton to Dallas. ('Go' in the sense of geographical extension)
      f. They circled the runway. (Verb + circular path)
      g. She pastured the horses. (Verb + path from 'out' of the pasture to 'in' the pasture)
      h. He shelved the books. (Verb + path from 'off' the shelf to 'on')

(2)   Theme = an entity GOing, BEing, or STAYing
     Location = the Place of the theme
     Source = the beginning point of a Path
     Goal = the end point of a Path

Many linguists have described how these spatial concepts are lexicalized and what sorts of roles they play in syntax and/or semantics. Also available for lexicalization in language are specific features of objects, such as orientation and shape (e.g. the distinctions between 'tall' and 'wide' or 'wide' and 'deep'), and many languages grammaticalize such features in classifier systems (e.g. counting long thin objects differently from round thick objects). Such spatial and object information forms part of human conceptual structure. Spatial structure is both relevant to conceptual structure and available to language (as for lexicalization and/or aspects of syntactic structure or categorization). This is neither accidental nor should it be surprising. Human cognition and language depend on neuroanatomical structures that lie adjacent to, and are intimately connected to, portions of the posterior parietal cortex that are responsible for spatial cognition. These brain regions, responsible for certain particular aspects of spatial cognition, comprise part of the posterior parietal cortex not only in humans but also in monkeys and apes.

Much is known about the anatomical basis of spatial cognition, and spatial information is broadly distributed in the brain. The posterior parietal cortex (PPC) is responsible for information involving the location of objects and their shapes. The PPC is also responsible for providing shape and orientation information, allowing the hand to effect the appropriate configuration to allow for grasping.

In humans, these PPC areas are typically referred to as Brodmann's areas 5 and 7. Especially relevant to the point being made here are areas that lie within the intraparietal sulcus, the major sulcal division lying above and posterior to the Sylvian fissure (Hamilton and Grafton 2006). These areas within the intraparietal sulcus are dedicated to actions involving the hand and forearm, and to motions and shapes necessary to perform a grasping action. (Other kinds of spatial cognition, such as colour, movement across the horizon, etc., are handled elsewhere in the brain.) There are precisely homologous areas of PPC in the monkey brain, both on the lateral surface of the posterior parietal lobe and within the sulcus.

An important point to remember is that the PPC, in fact the parietal lobe more generally, is not actually responsible, so to speak, for movement—it does not execute motor programmes. Therefore, by itself, it cannot accomplish a grasp. Real-time execution of movements is the responsibility of the motor areas of the frontal lobe. Not accidentally, the parts of the PPC that are involved in hand shape and forearm orientation are connected to premotor areas; each of the relevant areas of the intraparietal sulcus is directly connected to a corresponding area of motor cortex. This frontal-parietal circuitry is basic to the primate cortical motor system, is responsible for the ability of the primates to execute a grasp, and is exactly homologous in humans and non-human primates. (Many recent findings from the rapidly growing literature on motor neurons would be relevant here, but a discussion of the motor neuron system would be beyond the scope of this article. See Arbib, this volume.)

The region of the PPC involved in grasping lies right next to, and is closely connected to, the POT in humans. The premotor region involved in grasping is intimately connected to Broca's area. Notably, it was a great expansion of the parietal lobe in human ancestors, in approximately the region here called the PPC, which resulted in the POT (Wilkins and Wakefield 1995). The expansion in this area in human ancestors is what caused the disappearance on the lateral surface of the brain of the lunate sulcus, yielding the basic contemporary posterior hominin configuration and hence the basic hominin/great ape distinction.

Consider now the particulars of a grasping action. A limb that executes a grasp is necessarily a theme moving along a path. There is an initial configuration and an end point, somatosensorily defined. Further, the movement of the limb along the path to an object is visible. A very important aspect of primate spatial cognition, also relevant to human spatial and conceptual structure, is that the spatially coded information, whether represented initially by the somatosensory, visual, or auditory system is ultimately registered into a single spatial map. Thus, such thematic information is not unimodal—rather, it is modality-neutral. This, again, is a specialty of the POT region, to which the PPC is directly and intimately connected, and to which the premotor area is connected via its proximity and connectivity to Broca's area and the reciprocally connecting fasciculi (Wakefield and Wilkins 2007). Therefore, the aspect of the neurobiological mosaic that is responsible for spatial representations of the thematic sort (as distinguished from, for example, the thematic relations associated with event structure as in work by Bickerton and by Cheney and Seyfarth, see below) is homologous in humans and non-human primates, and in humans it is necessarily a component part of conceptual structure, and thereby an accessible input to language. Further, if Coolidge and Wynn (this volume) are on the right track, there may be an intimate connection, based in PPC anatomy, between the particulars of reaching and grasping and the ability to interpret the goals of others, so necessary to successful social interaction. The relevant areas of the PPC, with their indisputable homologues in the monkeys and apes, were most certainly characteristics of the neuroanatomy of the last common ancestor of humans and great apes.

The major point here is that the anatomical basis of spatial thematic relations is shared with non-human primates, even though the details of human-specific conceptual structure and language are not. Humans and the non-human primates share certain pieces of the language-relevant neurobiological mosaic, but not others. This is exactly what is to be expected in a plausible evolutionary account. Even though language is a unique species characteristic of humans, we should expect linguistic precursors to be evident in other species.

## 19.4 Conclusion

Ongoing research in comparative primatology can be expected to yield further insights about the prehistory of language. For example, primates have a very rich system of social relations, and are able to manipulate a complicated 'social calculus' (in the sense of Bickerton 2000, and also Cheney and Seyfarth 2005, although in somewhat different terms). A social calculus necessarily involves keeping track of who did what to, and for, whom; see also Seyfarth and Cheney, this volume. Such information is encoded in human conceptual structure, and therefore in language, in terms of such thematic relations as agent, patient, benefactee, etc. While the detailed research on the neurobiology of the encoding of social relations in primates is not nearly as advanced as, say, the research on grasping, it is probably the case that in humans and non-human primates, certain prefrontal areas are involved, possibly the same areas used to encode other information relevant to social relations. And if these areas are then also shown to have connectivity to the POT region, as seems likely, this would also be a piece of the neurobiological mosaic relevant to language. Further, if the involved anatomy can be shown to be homologous in humans and the other primates, then it would be fair to conclude that it was a feature of the last common ancestor of both.

More speculative yet, if the anatomical basis of action-event structure can be found, say within the system of social relations, allowing for the distinction between agent and patient, that is, the doer and the one who undergoes an action, this might be shown to allow for the most basic of syntactic (phrase structure) distinctions: the external-internal argument distinction (or in informal terms, the logical subject and object). Perhaps the basis of the prototypical subject-predicate characteristics, or at least the picking out of the prototypical subject/external argument (the agent), can be shown to reside in a bit of the anatomical mosaic shared with other primates and related to the social calculus (cf. Hurford 2003a). The neuroanatomical structure necessary for keeping track of who did what to whom would be ripe for reappropriation, evolutionary exaptation, into the biological mosaic system that underlies language in contemporary humans.

In conclusion, the findings and speculations reviewed here are intended to underscore the need for research on the origins of language to yield hypotheses that are biologically plausible. It is possible to assure such biological plausibility by being mindful of work on the contemporary neurobiology of language and considering the evolutionary trajectory of each of the involved parts of the system. It is highly unlikely to be the case that human language resulted from the simple adaptation of the communication system of an earlier species. Nothing we know about the language-relevant human neuroanatomy relating to the left hemisphere Broca's area–POT complex would lead us to expect to find homologues within the brain structures directly relevant to ape or monkey communication systems. Language does involve a complicated set of highly interconnected pieces, each of which is most likely to have a distinct evolutionary origin. Through review of earlier work on the POT and Broca's area, with the addition of more recent work on the PPC and spatial structure, and some speculation about directions that future work might take, a picture of biologically-responsible research into the origins of language emerges.

# ACKNOWLEDGEMENTS

The ideas discussed here were developed in collaboration with Jennie Wakefield over a decade-long period that began in the early 1990s. Her influence on my thinking about all things neuroanatomical is gratefully acknowledged, as is her painstaking work in reading and interpreting the anatomy literature for me. This chapter is closely based on a presentation given at the 2007 Linguistic Society of America Annual Meeting, in the Symposium, Language in the Light of Evolution, co-organized with Jim Hurford.

# CHAPTER 20

# MIRROR SYSTEMS: EVOLVING IMITATION AND THE BRIDGE FROM PRAXIS TO LANGUAGE

MICHAEL A. ARBIB

## 20.1 INTRODUCING MIRROR NEURONS AND LANGUAGE PARITY

There is something unique about the human brain which makes it *language-ready*. A normal human child will learn a language—an open-ended vocabulary, integrated with a syntax which supports the hierarchical combination of words into larger structures which freely express novel meanings as needed—while infants of other species cannot. The Mirror System Hypothesis of the evolution of the human language-ready brain emphasizes the *parity* requirement for communication via language—that what counts for the speaker must count approximately the same for the hearer (Liberman and Mattingly 1989). It gives key roles to mirror neurons for manual actions and the evolution of brain mechanisms for imitation of praxis (practical skills for, especially, manipulation of objects). But both imitation and language require integration of mirror neurons with diverse neural systems 'beyond the mirror'.

We start with neural mechanisms for visual control of hand movements. Visual data on shape and pose of an object are processed in parietal cortex and passed (in the macaque monkey) to an area of premotor cortex called F5. Many single neurons in F5 fire most strongly when the monkey executes a limited range of manual actions, with distinct neurons related to, for example, a precision pinch, tearing paper, or breaking peanuts. Tellingly, some of these neurons fire not only when the monkey executes these related actions but also when the monkey observes a human or another monkey execute a more-or-less similar action. These are called *mirror neurons* (Rizzolatti et al. 1996a).

Since single-cell recording is rarely available for humans, human brain imaging was used to seek a mirror *system* for manual actions, that is, a set of brain regions which, compared to some appropriate baseline, show significantly increased activity in the subject both when executing and observing some range of manual actions. Such a system was found (Grafton et al. 1996; Rizzolatti et al. 1996b) and the part of the mirror system so found in frontal cortex proved to be in or near Broca's area, an area traditionally associated with speech production. This accords with anatomical studies suggesting that the region of the human brain homologous to macaque F5 is Brodmann area 44, part of Broca's area.

These findings led Rizzolatti and Arbib (1998) to the view that the parity requirement for language in humans is grounded in the ability to recognize manual gestures, which in turn is grounded in the mirror property for manual actions. Their Mirror System Hypothesis holds that the brain mechanisms which support language evolved in part by elaboration of Broca's area atop the mirror system for manual action. The hypothesis thus provided a neurological 'missing link' for gestural origins theories of language evolution (see Corballis, this volume).

## 20.2 IMITATION EVOLVING

While many theories of language evolution have focused either on evolution of language as a separate faculty or internal to systems of communication, the present theory emphasizes that imitation of practical actions opened new possibilities that made language possible. In this respect, recall that Merlin Donald's theory of the origins of the modern human mind is centred on the introduction of a supramodal, motor-modelling capacity, *mimesis*, and its exploitation to create representations with the critical property of voluntary retrievability (Donald 1991; this volume). The Mirror System Hypothesis is broadly consistent with his general framework but is distinguished by its greater attention to parity, neuroscience, and primatology.

Here, imitation is a means for adding a new skill to an animal's repertoire in such a way that the details of the act depend on the specifics of the act as performed by the observed other(s). This is to be distinguished from momentary mimicking with no long-term effect, and from priming of the learning of a new behaviour by some small aspect of another's behaviour.

Monkeys have, at best, a limited capacity for imitation (Visalberghi and Fragaszy 1990), most of which can be viewed as *stimulus enhancement*, which changes the salience of certain stimuli in the environment, or *emulation*, which changes the salience of certain goals. As Byrne and Russon (1998) note, in such cases the way the observer responds to the enhanced stimulus or reaches that goal depends on individual learning or prior knowledge, rather than being directly influenced by the observed techniques. They unify such phenomena as instances of *observational priming*.

But the imitation exhibited by apes goes further. Richard Byrne and his colleagues (e.g., Byrne and Byrne 1993) showed that young gorillas learn complex feeding strategies but may take months of observation of adults to do so. Consider eating nettle leaves. Skilled gorillas grasp the stem firmly, strip off leaves, remove petioles bimanually, fold leaves over the thumb, pop the bundle into the mouth, and eat. The challenge for acquiring such skills is compounded because the sequence of 'atomic actions' varies greatly from trial to trial. Byrne and Russon (1998) see such behaviour as controlled by a learnable hierarchy of goals and subgoals. Basic actions may be iterated until some subgoal is reached. Short-term memory capacity may limit how deep a hierarchy a gorilla or human could expand 'without getting in a muddle'. Perhaps gorillas can only keep track of two embedded goals even with the aid of the 'external memory' present in physical tasks.

Byrne and Russon distinguish two levels of imitation. *Action level imitation* involves reproduction of the precise details of the manual actions another individual uses. In gorilla feeding strategies, these details seem to be learnt by trial and error rather than imitation. However, once low-level elements which achieve the same overall function are lumped together, the evidence suggests that gorillas can effectively copy the hierarchy of goals and subgoals, something Byrne has dubbed *programme level imitation*. Certain subgoals (for instance, nettles folded over the thumb) become evident from repeated observation as being common to most performances; action strategies for achieving them are then acquired by trial and error.

Human imitation differs from the capability of the great apes in three ways: (1) we can learn by programme level imitation more quickly than apes can. (2) We can learn deeper hierarchies than apes can. (3) We have a greater capacity for action level imitation—depending on circumstances, we may develop our own way of reaching a subgoal or, failing to do so, we may pay more attention to the details of the demonstrator's actions, and modify our actions accordingly. To mark this difference, I refer to what apes can do (but monkeys cannot) as *simple imitation*, using *complex imitation* to name the extended range of human abilities (Arbib 2002). In many cases of praxis (skilled interaction with objects), humans need just a few trials to make sense of a relatively complex behaviour if the constituent actions are familiar and the subgoals these actions must achieve are readily discernible, and they can use this perception to repeat the behaviour under changing circumstances (cf. the goal-directed imitation of Wohlschläger et al. 2003).

## 20.3 FROM IMITATION VIA PANTOMIME TO PROTOLANGUAGE

I posit that the mirror system for manual action was also present in the common ancestor of humans, monkeys, and apes (25 mya according to Steiper et al. 2004); and that the common ancestor of humans and chimpanzees (5–7 mya; Wood and Bauernfeind, this volume) had both a mirror system for manual action and a capacity for simple imitation.

Apes and monkeys cannot acquire true language. To elaborate the Mirror System Hypothesis, we must go beyond a monkey-like mirror system. First, a mirror system by itself does not support imitation. A monkey does not use observation of a novel action to add the details of that action to its repertoire—though its mirror system may well play a role in observational priming of goals and actions already in its repertoire. The first stages of the Mirror System Hypothesis posit embedding of a monkey-like mirror system in more powerful systems for imitation 'beyond the mirror'. In the version presented here, imitation is supported, first, by a simple imitation system for grasping, shared with the common ancestor of human and apes, and thereafter and increasingly by a complex imitation system which developed in the (proto)human line since that ancestor (Arbib 2005a).

Further stages embody hypotheses as to how our distant ancestors made the transition to protolanguage—a communication system supporting the ready addition of new utterances by a group through some combination of innovation and social learning. Protolanguage contrasts with the closed set of calls of a group of non-human primates but lacks any means, beyond mere juxtaposition of two or three elements, to put proto words together to create novel utterances (Bickerton 1995). Arbib et al. (2008) review data on vocalization and gesture in non-human primates, showing that monkey vocalizations are innately specified (though occasions for using a call may change with experience), whereas a group of apes may communicate with a small repertoire of novel gestures. This may rest in part on *ontogenetic ritualization* (Tomasello and Call 1997) whereby a communicative signal is created by two individuals shaping each other's behaviour in repeated interactions. For example, play hitting is an important part of chimpanzee play, and many individuals come to use a stylized *arm-raise* to indicate that they are about to hit the other and thus initiate play. Thus, a behaviour that was not at first a communicative signal would become one over time. Social learning may then aid the acquisition of gestures. The transition from small repertoires of ape-like gestures (perhaps ten or so novel gestures shared by a group) to protosign is then posited to exploit complex imitation for communication through pantomime of grasping and manual praxic actions and then of non-manual actions (such as flapping the arms to mime the wings of a flying bird).

Pantomime transcends the slow accretion of manual gestures by ape-like ontogenetic ritualization, crucially providing an 'open semantics' for a large set of novel meanings. However, pantomime is inefficient—both in the time taken to produce it, and in the likelihood of misunderstanding. Conventionalized signs extend and exploit more efficiently the semantic richness opened up by pantomime. Our hypothesis thus posits two further changes:

- Mechanisms to support 'early' *protosign*, a manual-based communication system breaking through the fixed repertoire of primate vocalizations to yield conventionalized gestures which provide the initial scaffolding of an open semantics opened up by pantomime.
- Cumulative developments in which the scaffolding provided by early protosign provided the basis for adding vocal gestures to yield protospeech, supporting an expanding spiral of conventionalized manual, facial, and vocal communicative gestures (Arbib 2006b).

## 20.4 GESTURAL VERSUS VOCAL ORIGINS OF THE LANGUAGE-READY BRAIN

The claim is that the flexibility of non-human primate communication in the gestural domain created the opening for greatly expanded communication once complex imitation had evolved for practical manual skills, making pantomime possible; see also de Waal and Pollick, this volume. This stands in opposition to theories that put the full focus on the evolution of speech alone, emphasizing elaborations intrinsic to the core vocalization systems (see MacNeilage and Davis 2005; Seyfarth et al. 2005; and MacNeilage, this volume).

It might be possible to develop a variant of the Mirror System Hypothesis that emphasizes speech rather than gesture, downplaying the evidence on the flexibility of ape gesture. Kohler et al. (2002) demonstrated that some mirror neurons for manual action are *audiovisual* in that if the action has a distinctive sound—such as that for breaking a peanut or tearing paper—the neuron could be activated either by hearing or seeing the action. However, these neurons are unrelated to recognition of monkey vocal productions. Closer to the mark, Ferrari et al. (2003) reported mirror responses for some F5 neurons coding orofacial actions. The majority of these 'mouth mirror neurons' become active during both execution and observation of mouth actions related to ingestion. Another neuronal population which discharges during the execution of ingestive actions has communicative mouth gestures such as lip smacking as their most effective visual stimuli. This suggests that macaque F5 is also involved in non-manual communicative functions. However, these orofacial movements cannot support an open-ended semantics as pantomime does, and they do not involve vocalization.

Jürgens (2002) found that monkey vocalizations are controlled by brainstem mechanisms, but that monkeys can be conditioned to vary their rates of vocalization. Such conditioning relies on medial cortex, including anterior cingulate cortex, rather than on lateral areas homologous to Broca's area. This involves initiation and suppression of innate calls, not the dynamic assemblage and co-articulation of articulatory gestures that constitute speech. By showing how proto-language could have evolved atop the mirror system for manual actions, with protosign scaffolding protospeech, the Mirror System Hypothesis offers a plausible explanation as to why Broca's area corresponds to F5 rather than the vocalization area of cingulate cortex—the area that might be expected to play a dominant role in a 'speech only' model of the evolution of brain mechanisms which support language.

However, stimulation studies in macaques *have* demonstrated a laryngeal representation in ventral premotor cortex (Hast et al. 1974), while anatomical studies showed connections of F5 with anterior cingulate cortex (Simonyan and Jürgens 2002). Coudé et al. (2007) trained two monkeys to vocalize (coo call) for a reward when food was placed on a table facing them. The researchers did find F5 neurons whose firing correlated with voluntary vocal production. However, both monkeys, when attempting to vocalize, often succeeded in producing the orofacial gesture which usually accompanies the coo sound, but not the sound itself. This suggests that voluntary control of vocalization in this case may have been an unreliable side-effect of orofacial control.

Such results show that the debate is far from over concerning gestural versus vocal origins of the language-ready brain. I propose that the demands of vocal expression of the open semantics opened up by protosign provided the adaptive pressure for the evolutionary extension of manual and orofacial gestural control to the speech apparatus and its neural control.

## 20.5 FROM PROTOLANGUAGE TO LANGUAGE

Greenfield (1991) posited that, early in human life, Broca's area supports the hierarchical organization of elements in the development of speech, as well as the capacity to combine objects manually, including tool use, but that subsequent cortical differentiation, beginning at age 2, creates distinct capacities for linguistic grammar and more complex combination of objects. Further, the performance of chimpanzees in both tool use and symbol combination matches that of the 2-year-old child. This view was formulated before the discovery of mirror neurons. It reminds us that the parity property cannot support language unless augmented by the ability for hierarchical structuring exemplified in programme level imitation. What we would add is the distinction between simple imitation shared by the ape and the 2-year-old child, and the human ability for complex imitation that develops in later years.

Complex imitation conferred a selective advantage to our distant ancestors for practical skill-sharing, but this was long before language entered the evolutionary picture. However, it is important to note its crucial relevance to modern-day language acquisition and adult language use. Complex imitation has two parts: (1) the ability to perceive in one or a few trials—though with more or less accuracy—that a novel action may be approximated by a composite of known actions associated with appropriate subgoals; and (2) the ability to employ this perception to perform an approximation to the observed action, which may then be refined through practice. Both parts come into play when the child is learning a language, whereas the former predominates in adult use of language as the emphasis shifts from mastering novel words and constructions to finding the appropriate way to continue a dialogue.

Complex imitation includes the ability to master reasonably complex hierarchical structures 'on the fly' rather than over many months of observation. For young apes learning feeding strategies, there is no further change in efficiency as measured by the time taken to prepare a handful of food after weaning at 3 years of age (Byrne and Byrne 1991). Thus, the time it takes young gorillas to learn feeding techniques is comparable to the time it takes young humans to learn to comprehend what a sentence is. However, the ape 'saturates' whereas the child has a vocabulary explosion and goes on to develop syntax (the hierarchical application of constructions) whereas the ape does not.

Empirical and computational studies of language acquisition have explained how modern children may acquire lexicon and grammar without invoking Universal Grammar. Hill (1983) showed that the child may first acquire what the adult perceives as two-word utterances as holophrases (e.g. 'want-milk') prior to developing a more general construction (e.g. 'want x' in which 'x' can be replaced by the name of any 'wantable thing'). Further experience will yield more subtle constructions and the development of word classes like 'noun' defined by their syntactic roles in a range of constructions rather than their meaning (Tomasello 2003a). Ontogeny does not recapitulate phylogeny. Adult hunters and gatherers had to communicate about situations outside the range of a modern 2-year-old, and protohumans were not communicating with adults who already used a large lexicon and set of constructions to generate complex sentences. Nonetheless, the present hypothesis is that similar mechanisms may have served both protohumans inventing language and modern children acquiring the existing language of their community (Arbib 2009). Complex imitation is the key.

## 20.6 THE SCOPE OF THE THEORY

The Mirror System Hypothesis has the following elements:

1. Language demands parity. Mirror neurons provide a basis for parity.
2. In hominin evolution, mirror neurons for manual actions preceded those for vocal actions, thereby lending support to gestural theories of language origin.
3. Ape gestures are flexible and learnable, in contrast to the mostly innate system of primate vocalizations, exemplifying processes whereby a practical action may become ritualized to serve as a communicative action.
4. Imitation is essential for language. Mirror neurons are essential for imitation but do not support imitation in and of themselves. The evolution and integration of both mirror systems and systems 'beyond the mirror' provided mechanisms for complex imitation, supporting a more open-ended style of skill acquisition than the programme level imitation exhibited by the great apes.
5. Pantomime could exploit complex imitation to yield an open-ended semantics for communication. Protosign emerged as more communicative acts became conventionalized, rather than directly understandable as pantomimes. This in turn supported the development of mechanisms which made protospeech possible.
6. The language-ready brain supports the ability not only to master a lexicon but also to employ constructions to hierarchically compose and parse novel messages. It is an open question as to whether a brain that could support protosign and protospeech was already language-ready; that is, whether the path from protolanguage to language required further biological evolution, or could be explained by cultural evolution alone. Some research on language acquisition offers support for the latter view.

Some of these claims—especially the gestural origins and cultural evolution theses—remain hotly contested. What is clear, though, is the challenge of developing an account of language evolution rooted in the comparison of brain mechanisms for both action and communication in the brains of diverse species, especially primates, and the need for sophisticated computational models in neurolinguistics which can make contact with the insights so gained (Arbib 2006). An expanded outline of the theory has been published as Arbib (2012).

# COGNITIVE PREREQUISITES FOR THE EVOLUTION OF INDIRECT SPEECH

## FREDERICK L. COOLIDGE AND THOMAS WYNN

Years ago, one of us (TW) applied in person for permission to study archaeological collections at an African museum. Toward the end of the interview the museum official made the following observation: 'The study area is very poorly lit'. From a simple transcript of the conversation, this phrase would appear to be a non sequitur. However, in the social context the intent was clear: a condition of receiving formal permission was that TW purchase lamps for the museum. Pinker et al. (2007), and others, refer to this kind of utterance as 'indirect speech'. What is most remarkable is that such intentionally ambiguous utterances are not exceptional. If anything they are the norm for many social interactions. Interpreting such utterances relies on much more than one's ability to decode a sentence. Pinker et al. also propose that the very existence of indirect speech suggests that there are adversarial dynamics in human communication and that most of the practical applications of indirect speech take place in 'arenas of conflict' (2007: 883). Pinker et al. also propose that human conversations are often the result of a target person anticipating what the other person in the interaction is thinking about the interaction, what the other person thinks that the target person is thinking about the interaction, what other humans think about the interaction and relationship, what people overhearing a conversation think, and so on. Ambrose (2008) has built on this suggestion to argue that indirect speech is the basis for diplomatic speech; it may have facilitated the mutual trust that was required to maintain reciprocal cooperation, presumably within a face-to-face group and/or with distant groups. The purpose of the present chapter is to speculate upon the cognitive requirements of such indirect speech.

## 21.1 Roots in primate social behaviour

Social dominance hierarchies appear to be an endemic and pervasive characteristic of most primate social interactions, and they have undoubtedly been characteristic for most of primate evolution. Dunbar (2003) has noted that physical grooming appears to foster social bonding and reduce interpersonal aggression in non-human primates, but that the evolution of the genus *Homo* required another grooming mechanism, language. Language, according to Dunbar, would serve the same initial purposes as physical grooming, but could be conducted on much larger scales, thus allowing an expansion of group size. In a highly structured social dominance hierarchy, reliance on direct forms of speech such as direct imperatives might suffice. However, even within a single group, indirect forms of speech might have been of great value. 'Get out of my way!' might suffice by those higher in the social dominance hierarchy, but 'Would you mind please moving over' might engender greater cooperation, trust, and positive feelings, and perhaps, reciprocal cooperation in future interactions, including the formation of alliances. Furthermore, successful social interactions between or among groups would have undoubtedly benefited from indirect speech.

## 21.2 The working memory model

We have previously used a cognitive model known as working memory to help explain aspects of the evolution of modern thinking (Coolidge and Wynn 2005). Working memory, first proposed by Baddeley and Hitch (1974), has been subsequently modified and substantiated by three decades of empirical research (e.g.

Miyake and Shah 1999; Baddeley 2000, 2001; Engle and Kane 2004; Hazy et al. 2006). As currently conceived, working memory is a multicomponent cognitive system, reflecting a capacity to hold and manipulate information in active attention consistent with short- and long-term goals and the inhibition of stimuli-irrelevant interference. The working memory model consists of a central executive, which manipulates two subsystems: (1) phonological storage, with vocal and subvocal articulatory processors, and (2) a visuospatial sketchpad. A third subsystem, an episodic buffer, integrates information from the other two subsystems and serves as a temporary store for this information and other material at the behest of the central executive. It is episodic in the sense that it can hold integrated scenes, stories, or personal episodes in temporary consciousness. Baddeley also proposes that retrieval from the buffer is the nature of consciousness, and its binding functions are assumed to be the principal biological advantage of consciousness. Furthermore, because the episodic buffer allows multiple sources of information to be considered simultaneously, it may allow the creation of models of the environment that can be used to solve problems and to make plans for future behaviours. Working memory capacity has been empirically demonstrated to predict a broad range of higher order cognitive tasks, such as attention, language comprehension and production, reasoning, and general and fluid intelligence (novel problem-solving abilities); see, for instance, Engle and Kane (2004).

## 21.3 ADEQUATE PHONOLOGICAL STORAGE CAPACITY

We propose that the first cognitive prerequisite for indirect speech might be adequate phonological storage capacity. The phonological store subsystem has been thought to play a critical role in language production and comprehension. Baddeley and his colleagues (Baddeley et al. 1998; Baddeley and Logie 1999) have proposed that phonological storage capacity 'might reasonably be considered' to form a bottleneck for language production and comprehension, and indeed recent empirical studies support this contention (Gathercole et al. 2004). Adults who have greater phonological storage capacity have also been found to score higher on verbal tests of intelligence (indeed, it is a subtest of the Wechsler Adult Intelligence Scale) and higher on measures of verbal fluency; they also do better on retroactive and proactive interference tasks (Kane and Engle 2002). In children who are matched on non-verbal intelligence measures, those with greater phonological storage capacity had a larger vocabulary, produced longer utterances, and demonstrated a greater range of syntactic constructions (Adams and Gathercole 2000).

Taken on the whole, these findings tend to support Baddeley's tentative contention that phonological storage capacity may have evolved primarily for the acquisition and comprehension of language.

Aboitiz et al. (2006) note that phonological storage capacity represents a short-term memory ensemble that can be phylogenetically tracked to earlier homologues in hominin evolution and to current primate brain systems. Further, they postulate that language has evolved primarily through the expansion of short-term memory capacity, 'which has allowed the processing of sounds, conveying elaborate meanings and eventually participating in syntactic processes' (2006: 41). They believe that an expanding memory system allowed more complex memories representing multiple items to be combinatorially manipulated, permitting 'the maintenance of a "state of mind" that captures attentional and memory resources' (2006: 51).

The neurological epicentre proposed by Aboitiz et al. (2006) for this expanded working memory capacity and generation of the phonological loop involves the evolutionary development of the posterior superior temporal lobe and the inferior parietal lobes. They also agree with Furster (1997), who noted that the dorsolateral prefrontal cortex plays an important role with reconciling short-term past and short-term future and cross-temporal contingencies. Thus, keeping track of what was said a few moments ago and ensuring that one's present speech is in accord with previous utterances are functions of the complex interactions of the prefrontal cortex, temporal, and parietal areas as well as their interconnectivity with other cortical area and subcortical structures.

Aboitiz et al. (2006) also note that empirical studies of short and long sentences suggest that short sentences do not impose an inordinate load on working memory capacity or short-term memory systems. However, longer canonical sentences, particularly those that present objects of the action first rather than subjects of the action, do impose a significantly greater load upon general working memory capacity and its phonological subsystem than do non-recursive and subject-first sentences. Furthermore, we have already noted empirical evidence in children and adults that those with greater phonological storage capacity produce longer utterances containing more complex syntax (Coolidge and Wynn 2009a).

# 21.4 RECURSION

Our second cognitive prerequisite for a language of diplomacy is recursive speech. It has been claimed that a hallmark of modern human language is recursion (Hauser et al. 2002), that is, embedding a phrase within a phrase, e.g. *Violet said that Sunny wants to escape.* Modern speech and thought are replete with recursive phrases, and theoretically, modern language, like natural numbers, is capable of infinite generative recursion, e.g. *Klaus said that Violet said that Sunny wants to escape.* Hauser et al. did not specifically address the natural selection advantages of human recursion, other than noting that it may have evolved for reasons other than language and offering a vague statement that recursion has 'limitless expressive power'. It is possible that in their thinking, recursion is simply the property of combinability (e.g. Reuland 2008). Thus, combinability gave rise to recursion, and its selective advantage over time would have been the ability to make more complex computations. This view of recursion, whose essential character is combinatorially manipulated complex memories, is also supported by Aboitiz et al. (2006), who, as noted previously, posit that recursion is highly dependent upon phonological storage capacity.

## 21.5 THEORY OF MIND

Our third cognitive prerequisite for indirect speech is theory of mind. Theory of mind refers to the ability to infer the thoughts, emotions, and intentions of others. Deficits in theory of mind have long been noted in psychological disorders such as autism, Asperger's disorder, and schizophrenia (e.g. Pennington 2002), and its causal role in these disorders has also been proposed (e.g. Kinderman et al. 1998). There is also an ongoing debate about the extent to which non-human primates may exhibit theory of mind (e.g. Focquaert et al. 2008). One of the more sophisticated conceptions of a multicomponent theory of mind is attributed to Baron-Cohen (1995). He hypothesizes that theory of mind consists of four independent skills: detection of the intentions of others, detection of eye-direction, shared attention, and the final component called the theory of mind module. The final component, whose onset in humans is thought to develop by the age of 4, contains a complex set of social-cognitive rules, and combined with the other three components, creates the full-fledged, adult-like theory of mind.

It has been proposed that a precursory theory of mind, if not full theory of mind, is founded upon the mirror neuron system (see Borg 2007 for a review of issues associated with this hypothesis). It was originally found that in macaques a set of neurons in the ventral premotor cortex were active when the subject individual observed conspecifics engaging in motor tasks like grasping. Strong evidence from functional magnetic resonance imaging and other sophisticated brain imaging techniques have confirmed the presence of a similar system in humans (e.g. Arbib 2005, this volume). Interestingly, the anterior part of the inferior parietal lobe has received much recent attention. Whereas theory of mind has traditionally been associated with prefrontal cortices, current neuropsychology and neuroimaging evidence points to the parietal cortex as the primary locus of category construction and concept formation (Medin and Atran 2004). It is the region where the brain integrates multiple sensory modalities into comprehensive models of the world (e.g. Lou et al. 2004; Wilkins, this volume). The ability to interpret correctly the actions, intentions, and goals of others may also be considered an important step in successful social interactions. It now appears that the epicentre for these latter abilities is the intraparietal sulcus (e.g. Hamilton and Grafton 2006).

Furthermore, we propose that indirect speech, particularly a language of diplomacy, is often internally debated (by quickly weighing alternative constructions) through subvocal articulation (i.e. inner speech) and posed by grammatical constructions with alternatives such as 'What if I were to state this communication in this manner? Or should I state it in this other manner?'. These statements appear to require adequate phonological storage capacity, recursion, and theory of mind. And yet, we would argue that these are necessary but not sufficient conditions for a language of diplomacy. We will now address our sine qua non condition, executive functions of the frontal lobes.


## 21.6 EXECUTIVE FUNCTIONS OF
## THE FRONTAL LOBES

Our fourth and sine qua non prerequisite for indirect speech is the executive functions of the frontal lobes. The origin for the metaphor of executive functions can be traced to Harlow, who, in 1868, published a short medical tract describing a young man, Phineas Gage, who suffered a partial frontal lobectomy as a result of a railroad construction accident. Harlow noted that Gage's use of language, his memory, and his general intellect appeared to be intact. He wrote, however, that Gage could no longer make and execute his daily plans of action. As Gage was the foreman of a railroad crew, these planning and execution skills were obviously critical, and although he recovered from his physical head wound, he could not regain his job. Approximately 100 years later, Luria (1966), a Russian neuropsychologist, helped to solidify and define the metaphor of executive functions, and his clinical work with brain-injured patients verified their neuronal underpinnings to the frontal lobes, particularly the prefrontal cortex. Empirical research in neuropsychology over the last five decades has further refined the nature of these functions. In Baddeley's working memory model, his concept of a central executive is completely synonymous with current definitions of the executive functions of the frontal lobes. (See Coolidge and Wynn (2001) for an extensive review of evidence for executive functions in the archaeological record.) Two abilities commonly associated with both working memory and central executive functions are the ability to maintain tasks in active attention while inhibiting both irrelevant stimuli and inappropriate prepotent (automatic) responses. In effect, one self-monitors one's own response in order to be able to evaluate and choose among alternatives.

We suggest that central executive functions are the sine qua non prerequisite for indirect speech, and furthermore, that they are critical to the expression of a full theory of mind. Our evidence for this contention comes from recent studies of the ontogenesis of children's expressions of executive functions and theory of mind. In a study of 122 English children from ages 2–4 years old, Hughes and Ensor (2007) explored the relationship between executive functions and theory of mind tasks. Partial correlations and hierarchical regression revealed stronger evidence for the hypothesis that executive functions are a prerequisite for theory of mind rather than vice versa. They concluded that 'children's growing competence in executive functions provides an important platform for their acquisition of a theory of mind' (Hughes and Ensor 2007: 1457).

As to the nature of the specific executive function that might be involved in theory of mind, Carlson et al. (2004) tested 49 American children aged 3 and 4 years old with two standard theory of mind tasks (Appearance-Reality and False Belief) and three inhibitory control tasks (ability to suppress automatic responses), three planning tasks, and two vocabulary measures. Multiple regression revealed that two of the inhibition tasks were significantly related to theory of mind (while co-varying with the effects of age and receptive vocabulary), whereas planning tasks shared no unique variance with theory of mind tasks. Their study reinforces the hypothesis that inhibitory processes underpin the relationship between executive functions and theory of mind. The authors further concluded that this relationship appeared to be especially strong for tasks measuring conflict inhibition rather than tasks measuring delay inhibition. Other studies (e.g. Carlson and Moses 2001; Perner et al. 2002) tend to support this contention, although the influence of general working memory capacity or its phonological and visuospatial short-term stores have not yet been investigated vis-à-vis theory of mind and inhibitory tasks.

In a provocative recent study of the nature of the relationship between executive functions and problem behaviours in childhood, with great relevance for our present contentions, Hughes and Ensor (2008), in a follow-up of the 122 children in their 2007 study, found that executive functions fully accounted for the relationship between early verbal ability (vocabulary and verbal comprehension) and later problem behaviours. It appeared that the children with unimpaired executive functions were using language as a tool for self-regulation, particularly of negative emotions (like anger and agitation) and impulsive behaviours. It has been previously hypothesized that children engage in 'private speech' as a means of solving problems, attaining goals, and regulating their behaviour (Berk 1999). Although this hypothesis was not tested directly by Hughes and Ensor, the notion that inhibitory executive functions help mediate inner speech in its regulation of outer speech and diplomatic speech remains an intriguing possibility.

## 21.7 SUMMARY

We have proposed that a confluence of at least four major cognitive factors, adequate phonological storage capacity, recursion, full theory of mind, and executive functions, may have been important prerequisites for indirect speech. We have also noted that there is growing evidence, both theoretical and empirical, that the inhibitory executive function may be the most critical component. As Hughes and Ensor (2008) note, language may serve as a mechanism for emotional regulation, and it appears that emotional regulation of prepotent behaviours (such as suppressing fear of strangers) would be of critical importance to communicatory success in many social interactions. Furthermore, debating through inner speech might also require the inhibition of a choice that, although prepotent and natural, would not serve the immediate social context as well as some other, counter-intuitive, choice. Thus, inhibitory executive functions might regulate emotional expressions in social interaction and be called upon to inhibit and to choose among alternative grammatical constructions in inner speech.

# CHAPTER 22

# THE ANATOMICAL AND PHYSIOLOGICAL BASIS OF HUMAN SPEECH PRODUCTION: ADAPTATIONS AND EXAPTATIONS

## ANN MACLARNON

The major medium for the transmission of human language is vocalization, or speech. Humans use rapid, highly variable, extended sound sequences to transmit the complex information content of language. Speech is a very efficient communication medium: it costs little energetically, it does not require visual contact with the intended receiver(s), and it can be carried out simultaneously with separate manual and other tasks. Although the vocal communication systems of some birds and other mammals, such as cetaceans, may resemble important aspects of human speech, none is as complex, nor as capable of transmitting information, as human speech-propelled language. Certainly, our closest relatives, the apes and other primates, demonstrate nothing close to this unique human form of communication. Human speech production involves a range of physical features which may have evolved as specific adaptations for this purpose; alternatively, they evolved as exaptations, commandeering existing features. Combining knowledge of the anatomical and physiological basis of human speech production, comparisons with other primate species, and information from the human fossil record, it is possible to form an outline framework for the evolution of human speech capabilities, the features concerned, the likely timing and sequence in which they arose, and the possible combination of adaptations and exaptations involved—the what, when, and why of speech evolution.

All mammalian vocalizations are produced similarly, involving features that primarily evolved for respiration or ingestion. Sounds are produced using the flow of air inhaled through the nose or mouth, or expelled from the lungs. Unvoiced sounds are produced without the involvement of the vocal folds of the larynx. They entail pressurizing the airflow by temporary restriction of the vocal tract at some point(s) along its length. The turbulence of the released air produces either an aperiodic noise, such as a burst or hiss, or, under special conditions, it may produce a periodic sound such as a whistle. For voiced or phonated sounds, the vocal folds at the glottis of the larynx (a structure which first evolved at the top of the trachea to prevent water entering the lungs in aquatic creatures) are held taut, and the air flow needs to be powerful enough to cause the vocal folds to vibrate. This cuts the air flow into a chain of 'air puffs', or a periodic sound wave, perceived by the ear as sound at a pitch equivalent to the air puff frequency; this is known as the fundamental frequency or $F_0$, and it varies with the length and tension of the vocal folds. Voiced sounds may be modified further by so-called gestural articulations of the supralaryngeal vocal tract produced by positions or movements of articulatory structures such as the tongue and lips, both primarily involved in ingestion. Mammalian vocalizations therefore require coordination of the articulation of the supralaryngeal vocal tract with the flow of air, in or out. For phonated sounds, an extensive series of harmonics above $F_0$ is produced by resonance. These series are filtered by the shape and size of the vocal tract, resulting in the retention of some parts of the series, and diminution or deletion of others, in the emitted vocalization. Unvoiced vocalizations generally have less structured acoustic features and broad bands of emitted frequencies. What distinguishes human speech from the vocalizations of other species is the extraordinary range of acoustic variation involved, produced by an enormous variety of gestural articulations of the vocal tract, together with intricate manipulations of the larynx and other respiratory structures. Rather than utilizing the air flow of both inspirations and expirations, human speech is also produced almost entirely on expired air, released in extended, highly controlled expirations.

More than 100 different sound units or phonemes found in human languages are recognized in the International Phonetic Alphabet, together with a further array of major variant types. Each sound unit is acoustically distinctive (Fant 1960), as depicted in spectrograms, in which emitted sound frequencies and their amplitudes are plotted against time. Phonemes vary with different relative timing of the start of phonation and of vocal tract constriction, different speeds of movement and combinations of vocal tract articulators, different intonation changes produced in the larynx or by the lungs; sounds may be breathy, creaky, nasal, or aspirated, and so the list goes on. Different languages use different subsets of phonemes.

Phonemes comprise consonants and vowels, which form the building blocks of syllables. Consonants, voiced or unvoiced, involve the complete or near complete obstruction and release of airflow through the vocal tract, which produces characteristic spectrum profiles or envelopes of sound frequencies emitted over time (Fant 1960). Vowels always involve phonation, and filtering through different vocal tract constrictions produced by gestures of the tongue, without complete obstruction. They are distinguished by their combinations of formants (Fant 1960), which are sharp peaks in the frequency ranges above $F_0$ emitted following filtration, known as $F_1$, $F_2$, etc.; typically, different vowels within a language can be characterized by the first two formants. The perception of vowels is not dependent on their absolute formant frequencies, but rather their relative values, normalized by the listener according to the typical frequency levels of a particular individual speaker, be they generally higher or lower pitched, the differences resulting from a shorter or longer vocal tract.

The range and variation of human speech sounds, the different subsets utilized in hundreds of languages, and how they are produced anatomically and physiologically, have been superbly documented in an extraordinary compendium by Ladefoged and Maddieson (1996). For consonants, they describe how nine independent, moveable, soft tissue articulators can be distinguished: lips; tongue—tip, blade, underblade, front, back, root; epiglottis; and glottis. These move to constrict or block the vocal tract at 11 main articulation points, or more accurately zones: lips, incisor teeth, different points along the palate, the velum or soft palate, and the uvula (the skin flap hanging from the velum), the pharynx or throat, the epiglottis, and the glottis. Together these produce 17 different categories of articulatory gestures, whose precise formation varies in different languages and dialects. Consonants are further differentiated into stops, nasals, fricatives, laterals, rhotics, and clicks, according to whether they involve, respectively, momentary complete stoppage of airflow by vocal tract obstruction, mouth closure and nasal-only airflow, a turbulent airstream, midline tract closure limited with lateral airflow around the partial obstruction, tongue trills and related movements, or two points of vocal tract closure trapping air with subsequent articulator movement increasing the trapped air volume and hence decreasing pressure prior to its sudden release. Vowel production involves subtle tongue-shaping in the oral or pharyngeal cavities, resulting in different points of vocal tract constriction, and hence different formant combinations.

It became evident early in attempts to teach apes to speak that our closest living relatives are not capable of the intricate articulatory manoeuvres of the upper respiratory tract which underlie the enormous range of human speech sounds. Recent evidence from Diana monkeys suggests that vocal tract articulation in non-human primates may not be as severely limited as previously thought (Riede et al. 2005). However, it seems improbable that capabilities so useful to human communication would not have been exploited more fully if they existed in other species, and it is therefore likely that the human capacity for the production of highly varied speech sounds is unique among primates.

Human sound sequences are also much more rapid than those of non-human primates, except for very simple sequences such as repetitive trills or quavers. Human vocal tract articulation is much faster, and humans are able to produce multiple sounds on a single breath movement, inhalation or exhalation. Most non-human sound sequences, such as chimpanzee pant-hoots and other vocalizations (Marler and Tenaza 1977), are produced on successive inspirations and expirations. Commonly each component sound of such sequences (e.g. the pant, or the hoot of the chimpanzee call) can only be produced on either an inhalation or an exhalation, which also restricts sound sequence combinations.

The laryngeal air sacs present in some non-human primate species enable them to produce slightly more complex sound sequences on single breath movements, either through additional breath movements in and out of the sacs, or by vibration of the vocal lip at the opening of the sacs into the larynx (e.g. bitonal scream of siamangs; Haimoff 1983). Humans do not possess air sacs, and instead produce complex sound sequences by the intricate manipulation of airflow within individual exhalations, freed much more than any non-human primate from the restrictions of vocalizations tied to breath movements (Hewitt et al. 2002). Overall, humans are able to produce sound sequences of up to about 30 sound units per second (P. Lieberman et al. 1992). Maximum sound production rates for non-human primates are typically only 2–3 per second, extending to 5 per second with the involvement of air sacs (MacLarnon and Hewitt 1999).

Human speech also demonstrates further flexibility through an enhanced ability to control breathing, the airflow itself, compared with non-human primates (MacLarnon and Hewitt 1999, 2004). First, humans speak on very extended exhalations, interspersed with quick inhalations, compared with much more even breathing cycles during quiet breathing; non-human primates appear not to be able to distort their breathing cycles so markedly. During normal speech, humans typically utilize exhalations of 4–5 seconds (Hoit et al. 1994), extending up to more than 12 seconds (Winkworth et al. 1995), whereas the longest calls given on single breath movements in non-human primates are only about 5 seconds (MacLarnon and Hewitt 1999). Calibrating these measures, taking into account the faster quiet breathing rates of smaller animals, the maximum duration of human speech exhalations is more than 7 times that during quiet breathing. In non-human primates, the normal maximum duration of exhalations during vocalization is only 2–3 times that during quiet breathing. The exceptions to this are species with air sacs, such as howler monkeys and gibbons, which can extend exhalations to 4–5-fold their duration during quiet breathing. Again, humans do not possess air sacs, an apparent alternative to control of pulmonary air release for extending call exhalation length, though one that does not enable the very subtle control of respiratory airflow of human speech (Hewitt et al. 2002).

## 22.1 SOUND ARTICULATION

The unique form of the tongue within the vocal tract in humans is considered to be a key factor in the speech-related flexibility of our supralaryngeal vocal tract (P. Lieberman 1984). In mammals, the tongue is typically a flat muscular structure lying largely within the oral cavity, anchored posteriorly by its attachment to the hyoid bone, which lies just below oral level in the pharynx, immediately above the larynx. The primary function of the tongue is to move food around the mouth for mastication, and posteriorly for swallowing. In humans, however, the tongue is a curved structure, lying part horizontally in the oral cavity and part vertically down an extended pharynx, where it attaches to a much lower hyoid, just above a descended larynx. The horizontal (oral) and vertical (pharyngeal) portions of the human supralaryngeal tract ($SVT_H$ and $SVT_V$) are equal in length, compared with other species in which $SVT_H$ is substantially longer. Greatly because of its curvature, movement of the human tongue, together with jaw movements, can vary the cross-sectional area of each of the two tubes of our vocal tract independently by a factor of approximately ten, providing a very broad range of articulatory gestures, and very variable resultant formants of emitted sound. The 1:1 ratio of $SVT_H$:$SVT_V$, with a sharp bend between the two, is notably important for the production of three vowels, designated phonetically [i], [u], and [a]. These vowels are particularly easily distinguished, with very low perceptual error rates, by their $F_1$, $F_2$ combinations, which lie at the outer limits of the acoustic vowel space, and [i], followed by [u], is the most reliable and commonly used sound unit for vocal tract normalization. The tongue positions for production of the three vowels utilize the angle at the midpoint of the human vocal tract to produce abrupt discontinuities in the cross-sectional areas of the tube. Because the angle is sharp, the articulatory gestures involved do not have to be performed with particular accuracy for consistent, distinctive acoustic results, making these vowels marked examples of the quantal nature of human speech sounds (Stevens 1972). Perhaps consequently, they are the most common vowels in the world's languages (Ladefoged and Maddieson 1996).

Humans are not completely unique in having a descended larynx; species including dog, goat, pig, and tamarin lower the larynx during loud calls (Fitch 2001b). Several deer have a permanently lowered larynx, which may temporarily be lowered further during male roars (Fitch and Reby 2001); large cats are apparently similar (Weissengruber et al. 2002). However, laryngeal descent is rarely accompanied by descent of the hyoid; hence the tongue remains horizontal in the oral cavity, and cannot act as a pharyngeal articulator (P. Lieberman 2007). Temporary laryngeal descent is also much less disruptive of other functions. In humans, because of marked, permanent laryngeal descent, simple contact between the epiglottis and velum is no longer possible, disrupting the normal mammalian separation of the respiratory and digestive tracts during swallowing, and increasing the risk of choking. Permanent laryngeal descent is thus a very different evolutionary development. Nishimura et al. (2006) have demonstrated that the larynx does descend to some extent during development in chimpanzees, followed by hyoidal descent. However, only humans have evolved permanent, major, laryngeal descent, with associated hyoidal descent, resulting in a curved tongue, and a two-tube vocal tract with 1:1 proportions. It is not laryngeal descent per se that is crucial to human speech capabilities, but rather a suite of factors in the shape and proportions of the supralaryngeal vocal tract and tongue (P. Lieberman 2007).

Considerable efforts have been made to determine when the two-tube vocal tract evolved in our ancestors, using indirect means, as its soft tissue structures do not fossilize. Reconstruction of the fossil hominin tract was first attempted by Philip Lieberman and Crelin (1971), using basicranial and mandibular characteristics, followed by Laitman and colleagues (e.g. 1979), who used the basicranial angle, or flexion of the skull base. However, Daniel Lieberman and McCarthy (1999) recently demonstrated, using radiographic series, that human laryngeal descent is not linked ontogenetically to the development of basicranial flexion. So, reconstruction of the supralaryngeal tract is not possible from basicranial form, and much previous work on the speech articulation capabilities of fossil hominins was therefore flawed, as P. Lieberman (2007) has fully accepted. In addition, D. Lieberman et al. (2001) showed that during postnatal descent of the hyoid and larynx in humans, the relative vertical positions of the hyoid, mandible, hard palate and larynx are held more or less constant. However, the ratio $SVT_H:SVT_V$ changes during development, as a result of differential growth patterns of the total oral and pharyngeal lengths, and only reaches 1:1 from about 6–8 years. Together these results indicate that the descent of the hyolaryngeal structures is primarily constrained to maintain muscular function in relation to mandibular movement for swallowing; speech-related factors are not maximized until well into childhood, matching the gradual ontogenetic development of acoustically accurate speech production (P. Lieberman 1980). Various possible exaptive explanations for why humans evolved their unique vocal tract configuration have been proposed. For example, obligate bipedalism required a more forward position of the spine under the skull, possibly reducing the space available in the upper throat, so squeezing the hyoid and larynx down the pharynx; increased carnivory in early *Homo* was associated with reduced jaw size and reduced oral cavity length, possibly requiring a compensatory increase in pharyngeal length (Negus 1949; Aiello 1996).

Recently, D. Lieberman and colleagues (e.g. 2002) have produced substantial new evidence on the integrated evolution of many modern human cranial features, providing a more comprehensive basis for exploring the evolution of the human vocal tract. They showed that a small number of developmental shifts distinguish modern human crania from those of our predecessors, including two—a more flexed basicranium and reduction in face size—which result in a shortening of $SVT_H$, contributing to the attainment of an $SVT_H$:$SVT_V$ ratio of 1:1. D. Lieberman (2008) suggested possible adaptational bases for these shifts, such as temporal lobe increase for enhanced cognitive processing including language, increasing basicranial flexion; increased meat consumption and technologically enhanced food processing including cooking, resulting in facial reduction; endurance running, building on obligate bipedalism, involving facial reduction for improved head stabilization; direct selection for speech capabilities, driving a decrease in oral cavity length, involving facial reduction and/or basicranial flexion, to produce a 1:1 $SVT_H$:$SVT_V$ ratio. In other words, a suite of factors may have affected $SVT_H$, and hence played a part in the evolution of the modern human capability for quantal speech. The other component in the evolution of a 1:1 ratio, an increase in $SVT_V$, may have been directly selected for enhanced speech capabilities, so counterbalancing the negative impact of increased choking risk. However, this would not have been advantageous prior to substantial decrease in $SVT_H$, because a long $SVT_V$ would require laryngeal descent into the thorax, producing muscular orientations that would compromise functional swallowing. Rather than major, coordinated shifts in both vocal tract parameters occurring with the evolution of modern humans, I think it more probable that other factors, earlier in human evolution, produced descent of the hyolaryngeal complex, and an increase in $SVT_V$. From this exaptive basis, final reduction in $SVT_H$, with the evolution of modern human cranial shape, could be adaptive for quantal speech. As outlined above, maintenance of functional swallowing is central to human developmental hyolaryngeal descent, which only becomes advantageous for speech articulation later in childhood. This, too, is congruent with the suggestion that hyolaryngeal descent resulted from earlier evolutionary change. The most likely candidate is the evolution of bipedalism, involving reconfiguration of neck structures, in *Homo erectus*. Jaw length also reduced in this species, associated with changing diet and food processing. The use of more complex vocalizations for communication may have begun to increase at the same time, alongside brain size and presumed social complexity (Aiello 1996).

As well as its curved shape, other features of the tongue have also been explored for their potential contribution to human speech articulation. Duchin (1990) drew attention to the greater manoeuvrability of the human tongue compared with apes.

Jaw reduction produces a shorter, more controllable tongue, and hyoidal descent angles the tongue, increasing mechanical advantage. Takemoto (2008) showed that chimpanzee and human tongues have the same detailed internal topology, a muscular hydrostat formation (Kier and Smith 1985), which enables elongation, shortening, thinning, fattening, and twisting of the tongue for moving food around the mouth and for swallowing. However, the overall curved shape of the human tongue, compared with the flat chimpanzee form, means the same internal structures are arranged radially in humans, compared with linearly in apes, which increases the degrees of freedom for tongue deformation (Takemoto 2008). Hence, the dietary and other changes from early *Homo* through to modern humans provided the potential for enhanced control of speech articulation gestures through exaptive realignment of both external and internal tongue features.

The lips are second only to the tongue in their importance as human speech articulators. They are particularly important for the production of two major consonant groups, stops and fricatives (the former being the only consonant type to occur in all languages), and also in vowel production (Ladefoged and Maddieson 1996). In typical mammals, the face is dominated by a prominent snout housing major structures of the highly developed olfactory sense, which extend onto the face, in the form of the rhinarium, or wet nose. Within primates, the evolution of the haplorhines (tarsiers, monkeys, and apes) involved a shift to diurnal activity from the typical mammalian nocturnal pattern retained by strepsirhines (lemurs and lorises). With this came increased specialization of the visual sense, and an associated reduction in olfaction. The snout reduced, and the rhinarium was lost. As a result, the facial and lip muscles became less constrained and were co-opted for facial expressions. Haplorhines evolved thicker lips (Schön Ybarra 1995), presumably to enhance this function. Hence, the evolution of mobile, muscular lips, so important to human speech, was the exaptive result of the evolution of diurnality and visual communication in the common ancestor of haplorhines. There is a lack of evidence as to whether there have been further adaptational developments in the lips during human evolution, or whether there have been changes in some other articulators, such as the velum or the epiglottis.

To date, there has been one attempt to investigate the comparative innervation of human vocal tract articulators. Kay et al. (1998) used the size of the hypoglossal canal in the base of the skull to estimate the relative number of nerve fibres in the hypoglossal nerve, which is a major innervator of the tongue. Their results suggested that Middle Pleistocene hominins and Neanderthals had modern human levels of tongue innervation, substantially greater than found in australopithecines and apes, and hence, they suggested, human-like speech-related tongue control had evolved by this time. However, DeGusta et al. (1999) demonstrated that hypoglossal canal and nerve sizes are not correlated, and Jungers et al. (2003) accepted that the canal size therefore offers no evidence about the timing of human speech evolution. Split second coordination between the highly flexible movements of the human speech articulators is required for human speech, as well as coordination with laryngeal movements affecting phonation. Different sounds result, for example, if the vocal cords start vibrating slightly before, at the same time, or slightly after an articulatory gesture. It seems likely that at least some increase in neural control has evolved in humans for speech articulation, even if empirical evidence is presently lacking.

## 22.2 RESPIRATORY CONTROL

Humans have enhanced control of breathing compared with non-human primates, which they use to extend exhalations and shorten inhalations during speech, as well as to modulate loudness. Humans are not constrained to produce vocalizations that fade as the lungs deflate. They can also vary the volume of air released through a phrase to emphasize particular words or syllables. In addition, variation in subglottal air pressure can affect intonation patterns. Enhanced breathing control therefore contributes to the human ability to produce fast sound sequences, and to generate a whole variety of language-specific patterns and meanings, communicated through the intonation and emphasis of phrases or specific syllables. Much of this needs to be tied to cognitive intention, involving complex neural communication and feedback (MacLarnon and Hewitt 1999).

Control of subglottal pressure is key to human speech breathing control. During speech breathing, intercostal and anterior abdominal muscles are recruited to expand the thorax and draw air into the lungs, and to control gravitational recoil and hence the release of air as the lungs deflate. This is similar to quiet breathing, except that the diaphragm has a very limited role in speech breathing. It also differs from muscle recruitment during non-human primate vocalizations, which does involve the diaphragm, and has only a limited role for intercostal muscles (e.g. Jürgens and Schriever 1991). The specific muscle movements required vary according to the volume of the lungs and other actions undertaken simultaneously (MacLarnon and Hewitt 1999). Overall, the fineness of control required of the intercostal muscles during human speech has been likened to that of the small muscles of the hand (Campbell 1968).

There is evidence, from an increase in spinal cord grey matter in the thoracic region, that humans have markedly greater innervation of the intercostal and anterior abdominal muscles compared with non-human primates (MacLarnon 1993). Spinal cord dimensions are well correlated with those of its bony encasement, the vertebral canal. Evidence from fossil hominins demonstrates that enlargement of the canal, and therefore the cord, was not present in australopithecines and

*Homo erectus*, but was present in Neanderthals and early modern humans (MacLarnon and Hewitt 1999). The function requiring enhanced neurological control therefore evolved in later human evolution. Of all the functions of the intercostal muscles, including maintenance of body posture for bipedal locomotion, vomiting, coughing, defecation, and breathing control, only enhanced breathing control for speech both requires substantial neurological control and fits the evolutionary timing constraints. It appears, therefore, that enhanced breathing control for speech was absent in *Homo erectus*, and present in the common ancestor of Neanderthals and modern humans, in the later Middle Pleistocene (MacLarnon and Hewitt 1999, 2004).

As outlined above, human breathing control is not aided by the presence of air sacs, which can provide additional re-breathed air for the extension of exhalations, without the risk of hyperventilation from excess oxygen intake (Hewitt et al. 2002). Larger ape species all possess laryngeal air sacs, so they were presumably lost at some point during human evolution. Air sacs abut against the hyoid bone where they produce characteristic indentions. The australopithecine hyoid from Dikika demonstrates the presence of air sacs (Alemseged et al. 2006), whereas hyoids from *Homo heidelbergensis* at Atapuerca, and a specimen from Castel di Guido dated to 400,000 years ago, as well as Neanderthals from El Sidrón and Kebara (Arensburg et al. 1990; Capasso et al. 2008; Martínez et al. 2008), show that air sacs had been lost by some point in the Middle Pleistocene. One possibility is that this occurred when the human thorax altered from the funnel-shape of australopithecines, to the barrel-shape of *Homo erectus*, as, in apes, air sacs extend into the thorax. It therefore quite probably occurred prior to the evolution of human speech-breathing control, and it may also have been a necessary prerequisite stage.

The mammalian larynx, which protects the entrance to the lungs during swallowing, comprises a series of three sets of articulating cartilages connected by ligaments and membranes. Some mammal species retain a non-valvular larynx, in which occlusion involves a simple muscular sphincter; other species have a valvular larynx, in which a mechanical valve provides for closure at the glottis. Based on the distribution of the valvular form, including its greatest development in primates, Negus (1949) proposed that the valvular larynx is a locomotor adaptation, enabling greater stabilization of the thorax in species with independent use of the forelimbs, through build up of air pressure below a closed glottis. Humans share with gibbons an extreme ability to close the glottis; other primates cannot completely close it off as the inner edges of the vocal processes of their arytenoid cartilages are curved, and when brought together, a small hiatus intervocalis always remains (Schön Ybarra 1995). Most likely humans lost the hiatus intervocalis independently from gibbons, as it is retained in living great apes. Gibbons may have evolved complete closure as an adaptation to brachiation. Bipedal humans use the capability of building up high subglottal pressure while lifting heavy objects with their arms, and in forceful coughing, which is particularly important with upright posture (Aiello and Dean

**Table 22.1 Summary of the evolution of human speech production features and potential speech capabilities**

| Species | Approx. dates | Mobile, thickened lips | Vocal tract proportions | | | Loss of air sacs | Loss of hiatus inter-vocalis | Enhanced breathing control | Membranous vocal folds | Potential speech capabilities |
|---|---|---|---|---|---|---|---|---|---|---|
| | | | Reduced face/jaws (increased tongue/jaw manoeuvrability) and $\downarrow SVT_H$ | Permanent laryngeal descent ($\uparrow SVT_V$) | Equal two-tube vocal tract [$SVT_H = SVT_V$] | | | | | |
| Ape ancestors | | E | | | [$SVT_H \gg SVT_V$] | | | | | Ape-like |
| Earliest hominins & australopithecines | 7–1.2 mya | E | | | [$SVT_H \gg SVT_V$] | | | | | |
| Early *Homo* (*habilis/rudolfensis*) | 2.4–1.8 mya | E | E | | e [$SVT_H > SVT_V$] | | | | | Some potential for limited increase in range of sound-types and speed of production |
| *Homo erectus* (including *ergaster*) | 1.8 mya–50 kya | E | E | e | e [$SVT_H > SVT_V$] | e | e | | ? | Potential for increased range of sound-types and speed of production, within short, relatively unmodulated sequences |
| *Homo heidelbergensis* (Middle Pleistocene hominins) | 800–200 kya | E | E | e | e [$SVT_H > SVT_V$] | E | e | A | ? | Significantly increased range of sound-types; potential for long, fast, modulated sequences |
| *Homo neanderthalensis* (Neanderthals) | 200–30 kya | E | E | e | e [$SVT_H > SVT_V$] | E | e | A | ? | |
| *Homo sapiens* (modern humans) | 200 kya–present | E | E | E | A [$SVT_H = SVT_V$] | E | E | A | A | Full range of modern, quantal speech sounds; efficient normalization capability; long, rapid, modulated sequences |

Character states: ■ Absent or primitive/ape form
■ Intermediate form
■ Present or modern human form

E = exaptation for speech production } lower/upper case = character inferred/known
A = adaptation for speech production }

1990). In addition, for human speech, substantial subglottal air pressure is required to fuel very long exhalations. Complete glottal closure enhances the ability to control the pitch or intonation (Kelemen 1969), something which gibbons use in their songs, and humans use in speech, although it is unclear whether subglottal air pressure, or movements of the laryngeal cricothyroid muscle are more important in human control of intonation (Borden et al. 2003). Overall, humans probably lost the hiatus intervocalis as an adaptation to bipedalism, providing an exaptation for speech. Further to this, the membranous part of the vocal folds of humans is less sharp-edged than in other primates (Negus 1929). This may be a direct adaptation for the production of more melodious sounds, selected for at some point after the locomotor-associated function of the larynx altered in humans, with the evolution of exclusive bipedality in *Homo erectus* (Aiello 1996).

## 22.3 EVOLUTIONARY FRAMEWORK

Diet and technology-related changes through human evolution, from the time of early *Homo*, have produced decreases in jaw and tongue length exaptive for the evolution of human speech capabilities. In addition to these, a three-stage framework for the major features of human speech evolution can tentatively be proposed: first, the evolution of obligate bipedalism in *Homo erectus* produced the exaptations of laryngeal descent, and the loss of air sacs and the hiatus intervocalis; secondly, during the Middle Pleistocene, human speech breathing control evolved as a specific speech adaptation; thirdly, with the evolution of modern humans, the optimal vocal tract proportions (1:1) were evolved adaptively. Further details are summarized in Table 22.1, together with suggested speech capabilities for each stage of the evolutionary framework.

## ACKNOWLEDGEMENTS

I would like to thank Kathleen Gibson and Maggie Tallerman for the invitation to contribute to this volume, and for their very helpful editing. My interest in the evolution of human speech was first stimulated by stumbling on evidence for the evolution of human breathing control working with Gwen Hewitt. This paper builds on a lecture prepared for the Language Origins Society, thanks to an invitation from Bernard Bichakjian.

# THE PREHISTORY OF LANGUAGE: WHEN AND WHY DID LANGUAGE EVOLVE?

# CHAPTER 23

# INTRODUCTION TO PART III: THE PREHISTORY OF LANGUAGE: WHEN AND WHY DID LANGUAGE EVOLVE?

## KATHLEEN R. GIBSON AND MAGGIE TALLERMAN

## 23.1 WHEN—A DIVERSITY OF CLUES

Traditionally, evidence for primate and human evolution has derived primarily from comparative anatomy and the fossil record, although since the 1960s, molecular and biochemical evidence have increasingly been used to delineate phylogenetic relationships among living species and diverse human populations. One of the most exciting current research frontiers involves analyses of the DNA of Neanderthals and other fossils (Green et al. 2010; Reich et al. 2010). These molecular findings are reviewed by Cann (Chapter 24) who reports that mitochondrial DNA and the fossil record roughly agree that the phylogenetic split between hominins and panins (i.e. bonobos and chimpanzees) occurred about 5–7 million years ago (mya). This, then, is the earliest possible date for the emergence of protolanguage.

Most interpretations of nuclear and mitochondrial DNA further suggest that Neanderthal and modern human lineages split somewhere between 270 and 480 thousand years ago (kya), and all modern humans shared a common maternal ancestor in Africa approximately 200 kya (Cann, Chapter 24; but for a contrary view see Templeton 2007). At a later date, possibly between 85 kya and 55 kya, some modern humans left Africa, while others remained behind (Forster and Matsumura 2005). Those who left dispersed throughout the Old World, and in the process of dispersal, replaced all archaic human populations, including Neanderthals. This model, often referred to as the replacement model, draws some support from putative modern human fossils from East Africa, dating to at least 160 kya and possibly 195 kya (McDougall et al. 2005; Millard 2008; Mann, Chapter 26). Since language is universal among modern populations, this model mandates the development of the full language faculty as occurring some time prior to the Out-of-Africa dispersal, i.e. prior to 55 kya. Other mitochondrial DNA data not reviewed by Cann (Behar et al. 2008) indicates a genetic split between the South African Khoisan peoples and other Africans sometime earlier than 90 kya. This finding would push the latest possible date for the emergence of the full language faculty back beyond 90 kya (Tallerman and Gibson, Chapter 1).

DNA-derived replacement models, however, are hotly disputed by many palaeoanthropologists (Mann, Chapter 26). For example, Milford Wolpoff (e.g. 1996) has long argued in favour of a contrasting multiregional model of human evolution (Mann, Chapter 26). This model posits that African and non-African populations maintained genetic contact throughout human evolution; on this view, no Out-of-Africa diaspora ever occurred; nor did ancestral Neanderthals and modern humans ever experience a complete phylogenetic split. Rather, Neanderthal and other archaic populations, both in and out of Africa, evolved together into modern humans. Multiregional and DNA-derived replacement models, of course, are only two of many possible evolutionary scenarios. Under a hybrid scenario, modern humans may have arisen in Africa, but interbred with populations elsewhere in the world, rather than replacing them. Indeed, recent nuclear DNA analyses strongly indicate that genetic interchange did occur between modern humans and Neanderthal populations, either directly or indirectly, and, thus, appear to completely negate the strongest versions of the Out-of-Africa model (Green et al. 2010). Moreover, a recent find of a putative modern human fossil from Zhirendong, China, dated to at least 110 kya (Liu et al. 2010) indicates that, even if a modified Out-of-Africa model should prove correct, the diaspora must have occurred prior to about 110 kya. Unfortunately, multiregional and hybrid models, unlike replacement models derived from DNA evidence, provide no firm estimate of a latest possible date for language emergence.

Chapters 25 and 26 concentrate on fossil evidence for human evolution. Wood and Bauernfeind review the earliest possible and probable hominin fossils, all of which come from Africa, and some of which date as far back as 6–7 mya. The most extensive of the very early hominin fossils are assigned to the species *Ardipithecus ramidus*, and date to about 4.5–4.3 mya (White et al. 2009). Ardi, as the fossils are called, appears to have been bipedal with some remaining arboreal adaptations, and its canines are less projecting than those of modern great apes. However, its molar (chewing) teeth suggest an ape-like diet, and it has an ape-sized brain. No evidence suggests that Ardi used tools or followed a lifestyle that had diverged sufficiently from that of apes to have required a protolanguage.

Many hominin fossils date between 4 and 2.4 mya. Wood and Bauernfeind (as splitters; see discussion below) classify these into three different genera (*Australopithecus*, *Paranthropus*, and *Homo*) and a number of different species. It is unclear which, if any, of these species qualify as direct ancestors of the human lineage. Almost all, however, have limb bones suggestive of bipedalism combined with some arboreal adaptations. Almost all, including the earliest of these post-Ardi species, *Australopithecus afarensis* ('Lucy'), also have molar teeth that possess thick enamel layers and are large by the standards of both modern humans and apes. Dental remains thus suggest that virtually all had diverged from ape-like foraging patterns, possibly relying more heavily on underground storage organs (Wrangham et al. 2009), brains, bone marrow, and meat (Mann, Chapter 26; Wynn, Chapter 27). Most of these fossils have ape-size or slightly larger cranial cavities (about 350–500 cc), but some had larger brains, about 510–725 cc, and are, thus, often classified in the genus *Homo*; these are referred to as habilines (e.g. *Homo habilis* and *Homo rudolfensis*). While it is often assumed that the larger-brained, possibly more intelligent, habilines made the stone tools, there is no clear evidence of this. Also, as Wood and Bauernfeind note, no definitive evidence indicates that any early hominins had language, protolanguage, or speech. Indeed, a hyoid bone assigned to *Australopithecus afarensis* is decidedly ape-like in structure, and thus suggests that *A. afarensis* lacked the ability to make the full range of modern speech sounds and may also still have possessed air sacs (MacLarnon, Chapter 22). Others, however, have hypothesized that these early changes in lifestyle provided motivation for some referential communication (Parker and Gibson 1979).

Chapter 26 (Mann) concentrates on the post-habiline fossil record. It is important, when reading this chapter, to realize that palaeoanthropologists tend to fit into one of two categories—lumpers and splitters—depending on how they view within-species anatomical variations. Lumpers, represented by Mann, assume that most species are highly variable, and thus tend to classify fossils with somewhat variable sizes, shapes, and anatomical features as single species. Splitters, who are less accepting of species variability, assign the same fossils to different species. By 1.8 mya, for example, a new hominin grade had appeared, characterized by somewhat smaller teeth and much larger brains (900–1000 cc). Judging by their vertebrae and limb bones, these hominins were fully bipedal, with no remaining arboreal adaptations (Mann, Chapter 26). Splitters have sometimes classified African representatives of this hominin grade as *Homo ergaster*, and Asian representatives as *Homo erectus*. Lumpers consider that they all belong to one species, *Homo erectus.*

By 1.6 mya, African *H. ergaster/erectus* populations were manufacturing new, mode 2 tools which differed from earlier stone tools in that they were bilaterally symmetrical (Mithen, Chapter 28; Wynn, Chapter 27). One mode 2 tool, commonly known as the Acheulean handaxe, continued to be produced in approximately the same form for one million years. The handaxe far exceeded any tools produced by captive or wild apes in terms of its spatial symmetry, and, possibly equally critically, in the amount of information that had to be held in mind in order to create it (Gibson and Jessee 1999). To make a standardized tool such as the handaxe would also have required enhanced procedural learning skills (Wynn, Chapter 27) and imitative capacities (Mithen 1999a). To the extent that spatial constructs (Wilkins, Chapter 19), working memory (Coolidge and Wynn, Chapter 21), hierarchical abilities, procedural learning skills, and imitative capacities (Arbib, Chapter 20; Donald, Chapter 17) are critical components of the language faculty, the handaxe lends support to hypotheses that *H. erectus* populations at least had full protolanguage capacities. On the other hand, the continuing manufacture of one specific tool tradition for a million years, coupled with a failure to invent new types of tools, suggests a distinctly non-modern mind, and an absence of fully modern cognitive and, hence, linguistic abilities. Some scholars argue that this technological stasis also supports theories that song (Mithen, Chapter 28) or mimesis preceded language evolutionarily (Arbib, Chapter 20; Donald, Chapter 17). If, however, MacLarnon (Chapter 22) is correct in her interpretation that *Homo erectus* lacked sufficient respiratory control to engage in extended speech, then it is equally unlikely that song was present during *Homo erectus* times.

By about 300–400 kya, hominins throughout Eurasia and Africa exhibited almost modern brain sizes (about 1200 cc as opposed to a modern human average of 1350 cc) and probably possessed modern thoracic canal diameters (MacLarnon, Chapter 22), but they still differed from modern humans with respect to cranial anatomy (Mann, Chapter 26). Some scholars lump these almost modern forms, which predated both Neanderthals and anatomically modern humans, into a catch-all category, archaic *Homo sapiens* (e.g. Mann). Others refer European and African, but not necessarily Asian, fossils from this time period to the species *Homo heidelbergensis* (Bae 2010). Whatever we call these hominins, in both Africa and Europe, they were using new, more advanced, technologies than their *H. erectus* predecessors, including wooden spears and prepared stone cores deliberately shaped to yield large numbers of stone flakes, each conforming to a pre-planned shape (Mithen, Chapter 28; Wynn, Chapter 27).

By about 200–250 kya, fossils considered to possess the full suite of Neanderthal anatomical characteristics had appeared in Europe (Wolpoff 1996) and by about 150–200 kya, fossils considered to be fully modern had appeared in Africa (McDougall et al. 2005; Millard 2008). Whether the two forms (Neanderthals and moderns) ever actually lived in the same place at the same time, as many popular scenarios assume, is unclear, as noted by Mann (Chapter 26). Both had brain sizes that equalled or exceeded those of modern humans, but Neanderthals still had a more archaic cranial form (Mann, Chapter 26), and they were far more physically stocky and robust than moderns. Both possessed modern forms of the *FOXP2* gene, possibly indicative of modern abilities to control sequential movements of the oral cavity (Krause et al. 2007). Both also possessed a modern diameter of the thoracic vertebral canal, possibly indicative of expanded neural control over the breathing apparatus (MacLarnon, Chapter 22). Philip Lieberman and colleagues long argued, primarily from observations of the cranial base of one Neanderthal fossil, La Chapelle-aux-Saints, that the Neanderthal larynx was situated high in the neck, as in modern chimpanzees, and, hence, that Neanderthals lacked the ability to pronounce certain vowels (P. Lieberman and Crelin 1971; Laitman et al. 1979). This argument is no longer accepted (MacLarnon, Chapter 22; Mithen, Chapter 28). For one thing, the La Chapelle fossil was found in a fragmented condition and critical portions of the cranial base were missing. An early reconstruction of the skull showed a flat, ape-like cranial base, but a later reconstruction showed a more modern cranial base (Heim 1989). More recent analyses indicate that indeed, not only Neanderthals, but a number of earlier hominin fossils had an essentially modern cranial base shape (Frayer and Nicolay 2000). In addition, it is now clear that laryngeal position cannot be determined from cranial base anatomy (Gibson and Jessee 1999; MacLarnon, Chapter 22). Finally, a Neanderthal hyoid bone has been found which is completely modern in anatomy (Arensburg et al. 1989). From these considerations, Mithen (Chapter 28) argues that Neanderthals had modern vocal capacities. Many theorists would interpret this to mean that Neanderthals could speak. Mithen, in contrast, argues that they sang.

Both Neanderthals and early modern humans continued and perfected prepared core techniques in what is known as the Mousterian archaeological tradition, and both groups hafted Mousterian stone points to wooden spear shafts (Wynn, Chapter 27). In Wynn's view, the manufacture of Mousterian tools required procedural learning skills, modern spatial intelligence, including control of three-dimensional space, and, possibly, an enhanced theory of mind. As Wolpoff (1996) notes, unlike preceding technologies, it also required that the entire tool-making sequence be visualized in advance. Gibson (1996b) argues that hafting required a distinctly human, rather than an ape-like, intelligence, as well as advanced hierarchical mental constructional skills; hence, in her view, hafting indicates the presence of fully modern intelligence in both Neanderthals and early modern humans. Still, as noted by Wynn, hafting was the only real technical innovation of the Mousterian, and neither early modern humans nor Neanderthals appear to have produced very much art or other forms of symbolism; at least they did not do so from materials that have been preserved to the present day. Complex multicomponent tools, such as bows and arrows, harpoons, and complex traps, which Coolidge and Wynn (2009b) consider the only indisputable evidence of modern working memory and executive functions, have long been thought to appear only much later in time, possibly as late as 18 kya. However, a recent find suggests that arrows may have been produced as much as 64 kya (Lombard and Phillipson 2010; also see Chapter 1).

Until recently, it was thought that the cave paintings and parietal art of the European Upper Palaeolithic, dating to about 30 kya, constituted the first evidence for symbolism. More recently, Henshilwood and Dubreuil (2009) have posited that 75,000-year-old engravings and bead work from Blombos Cave, South Africa, indicate the presence of a modern theory of mind, symbolic capacity, and syntax. D'Errico and Vanhaeren (Chapter 29) argue that a number of North and South African as well as Near Eastern archaeological finds of marine shell decorations and beadwork dating to at least 75 kya support the beads = language argument, because they required advanced social communicative skills and long-distance trading networks. Botha (Chapter 30) responds by delineating a series of logical criteria that, in his view, must be met if we are to assume the presence of symbolism, language, or syntax from beads or other archaeological remains. He concludes that current arguments based on bead work fail to satisfy these criteria. Botha's articulation of definitive criteria for inferring the presence of language from archaeological remains constitutes a major contribution to a field sometimes characterized by wildly speculative arguments. Neither Botha, nor anyone else, however, has yet provided a similar set of arguments for absent, as opposed to present, archaeological remains. One could postulate, for example, that if the absence of evidence for a particular behavioural attribute is to be used to indicate an absence of language in fossil hominins, it must be demonstrated that all modern linguistic communities do possess that attribute. Some absence-of-evidence arguments could not meet this criterion. For example, a number of modern cultures, such as those of Amazonia, have elaborate artistic traditions based on feathers, baskets, and bark paintings, but produce no art work from materials that could possibly survive for thousands of years.

It is evident from these discussions that no single piece of evidence can provide incontrovertible evidence for the presence of language in any fossil population. Rather, we must examine the preponderance of evidence. At the present time, arguments against the presence of language in Neanderthals and early modern humans derive largely from the presence of only minimal evidence for art work or complex tools prior to the Upper Palaeolithic. In addition, the pace of technological change clearly picked up about 30 kya (Wynn, Chapter 27; Mithen, Chapter 28). These absence-of-evidence arguments lead to estimates for emergence of the full language faculty sometime in the last 50,000 years or so (Klein and Edgar 2002). In contrast, a number of 'presence-of-evidence' arguments point to the existence of speech and even the possibility of fully syntactic language in both Neanderthals and early modern humans by 150–200 kya. These include modern brain size, constructed tools that require a host of cognitive capacities beyond anything yet demonstrated by any ape, modern hyoid bones, modern thoracic canal diameters, and modern *FOXP2* genes. Evidence for complex seasonal foraging endeavours, long-distance transport of materials, perforated beads, and advanced tool kits at 75–160 kya (McBrearty and Brooks 2000; Marean 2010a) provides additional support for probable modern cognitive and linguistic capacities in modern humans by at least 75 kya, possibly much earlier.

## 23.2 WHY DID THE LANGUAGE FACULTY EVOLVE? THE ROLE OF SELECTION

Determining when language evolved is child's play in comparison to determining why language evolved. Research of the last half century has demonstrated that many behaviours such as tool-making and tactical deception which were once thought uniquely human can be found in other animals. Yet, it remains clear that human behaviour, at all stages of the life cycle, does differ from that of the apes in many potentially language-related respects. Human but not ape infants, for instance, babble and routinely engage in social smiling. Humans are weaned at an earlier age than are apes (Locke, Chapter 34), and, for some years subsequent to weaning, the survival of human, but not ape, young depends on foods supplied by adults. Human adults establish long-term food-sharing pair bonds, cook food, and hunt big game; apes do none of these things. Quite a long list of such differences could be compiled, but doing so, much less explaining how each trait evolved, would be a daunting task. Instead, most language evolution theorists have built their theories around one or, at least a very few, of the ape/human differences. The result has been scores of single-cause language origins scenarios, none of which have yet succeeded in explaining all aspects of language evolution (Számadó and Szathmáry 2006). It is as if we language evolution theorists were the proverbial blind men, each of us seeing a part of the language-evolution elephant, none of us comprehending the entire beast.

Lightfoot (Chapter 31) leads the discussion of selective pressures with a cautionary tale. Language, as he notes, involved changes in the brain, some of them as yet unknown. What is known is that all neural changes, as well as the mutations that underlie them, must conform to basic rules of physics and chemistry, as well as to basic principles of growth and development. Language evolution, thus, is constrained by physical laws. Moreover, any change in one part of a complex system effects changes in others. Hence, many linguistic features are, no doubt, by-products of other evolutionary events (spandrels) that have never been directly selected for. Thus, those who seek selective benefits for each aspect of syntax or phonology and so on may be barking up the wrong tree.

Most, perhaps all, contributors to this volume would agree with Lightfoot that selection has not acted on each linguistic feature. Many do assume, however, that at least some aspects of the language faculty or speech evolved in response to selection, but they have widely varying opinions of what those selective factors were, or even whether language evolved with respect to natural selection, i.e. selection for specific individuals and their genes; kin selection (de Boer, Chapter 33; Hamilton 1964); sexual selection (Locke, Chapter 34); or various other scenarios somewhat akin to group selection (Wilson and Sober 1994), such as cooperative breeding (Hrdy 2009; Zuberbühler, Chapter 5), cooperative foraging and food sharing, or other co-operative problem-solving tasks. These, of course, are not mutually exclusive hypotheses: diverse selective agents may have acted simultaneously or at different times in hominin phylogeny. The chapters in this section represent some of the most prominent current theories.

Although parallels between ontogeny and phylogeny are often found in nature, no biogenetic law mandates that they must occur (Gould 1977). Consequently, we cannot begin with an assumption that the earliest stages in the ontogeny of language paralleled the earliest stages in language evolution. Nor can we rule such scenarios out (MacNeilage, Chapter 46; Studdert-Kennedy, Chapter 45). Indeed, a focus on infantile behaviours has some distinct advantages, because the vocalizations of human infants resemble the coos and grunts of many non-human primates, and thus, unlike complex song or syntax, were probably present in the earliest hominins, or even in the common great ape/human ancestor. For these reasons, a number of selective scenarios focus on infantile behaviours and/or mother/infant relationships. Most commonly these scenarios address babbling and motherese (de Boer, Chapter 33; Falk, Chapter 32; Locke, Chapter 34), although some have focused on a need for referential communication in human tool-using, food provisioning, and other adult/infant contexts (Parker and Gibson 1979; McCune 1999).

Falk and Locke (Chapters 32 and 34) both propose that infantile babbling arose to attract maternal care. In Falk's view, prior to the invention of slings, bipedal mothers would have put their babies down during two-handed endeavours. In such circumstances, babies would have vocalized to attract maternal attention in order to be picked up and fed. For Locke, babbling evolved in response to the reduced birth intervals in human evolution; hence, infantile competition for maternal attention. Falk expands her hypothesis to suggest that motherese is an evolved behaviour, which specifically functions as a means of fostering mother–infant bonds and encouraging the development of speech and language. De Boer (Chapter 33) reinforces Falk's motherese hypothesis describing the many ways in which motherese fosters language learning in infants. Although both Falk and Locke postulate that babbling and motherese evolved primarily in the context of mother-infant interactions, hence, natural selection, de Boer suggests they arose in response to kin selection (but see Tallerman 2011 for arguments against kin selection in language evolution). Hrdy (2009) and Zuberbühler (Chapter 5) propose yet another selective scenario: babbling arose in contexts of cooperative breeding; that is, resulted from an infantile need to attract the attention not only of mothers but of maternal helpers, such as older siblings, fathers, aunts, and grandparents. Although we cannot be certain when cooperative breeding first arose, Hrdy notes that its nearly universal presence in modern societies suggests it has long characterized our species, and possibly earlier hominins as well.

At the other end of the spectrum are sexual selection scenarios, which, in contrast to mother/infant scenarios, generally focus on linguistic competition between sexually mature males in pursuit of female mates. Since human females prefer males with lower voices (Locke, Chapter 34), sexual selection may explain the differential lowering of the larynx in adult males; also, why our language capacities (e.g. vocabulary size) sometimes seem to far exceed any communicative need, and even some of the more colourful aspects of language use, including poetry and metaphor (Miller 2000). In many respects, sexual selection scenarios are also compatible with views that language evolved from song (Mithen, Chapter 28). However, such scenarios cannot explain why humans of all ages and both sexes talk, and, indeed, are likely to do so at any time except when sleeping or engaging in periods of enforced quiet. Perhaps most importantly, it is difficult to explain the evolution of duality of patterning, object reference, complex syntax or other language fundamentals via sexual selection theories, except perhaps by circuitous routes that assume a prior development of complex song (Mithen, Chapter 28). Consequently it seems to us that sexual selection for advanced language capacities, if it occurred at all, must have been among the latest developments in the evolution of language.

Locke's proposal (Chapter 34) may partly resolve sexual selection and mother/infant language origin scenarios by positing that selection acts directly at each stage in human development, but acts on different aspects of language. In the mother/infant dyad, selection favours babbling. In childhood, in Locke's view, selection favours parent/child communications pertaining to potential hazards (also see Hart and Sussman 2005). Juveniles prepare for later sex and dominance encounters by developing more complex speech, such as gossip, joking, riddling, and storytelling. Finally, in Locke's model, sexual selection begins in adolescence, by building on and expanding the linguistic accomplishments of earlier developmental periods (Franks and Rigby 2005). Locke's scenario has the distinct advantages of pointing out that selection can operate at any stage in the life cycle. It is also compatible with views that simpler forms of protolanguage came first and subsequently served as foundations for later, more elaborate, syntactic and hierarchical languages. It ignores, however, other cognitive and behavioural developments that occur during human development, and thus implicitly assumes that cognition and language develop independently. Other scenarios not represented here, which also focus on development, adopt a strictly cognitive stance and postulate that language and cognition develop and evolve together (Gibson 1996a; Gibson and Jessee 1999). Under that view, the development of complex linguistic skills in late childhood and adolescence relates strongly to relatively late-maturing cognitive skills, such as hypothesis formulation, and arguing about and seeking evidence for facts; abilities that also appear to have been relatively late evolutionary developments. What is selected for in the developmental scenario are not specific language properties per se, but rather the overall cognitive (i.e. executive planning) capacities so essential to human problem-solving and long-term planning capacities (see also Coolidge and Wynn 2009b).

Questions of whether language first evolved in adolescents, mother/infant dyads, or older children and the extent to which language and cognition may have co-evolved are only some of the many currently irresolvable issues that face the language evolution theorist. Other hotly-debated points concern the selective pressures that led to language. Chomsky and other generative linguists argue that language evolved primarily as an aid to internal thought (Chomsky 2010; see Tallerman and Gibson, Chapter 1). Most evolutionary biologists, in contrast, assume that language evolved for its communicative potential, but they often disagree strongly about whether language was primarily selected for in social or instrumental contexts. Specifically, did we evolve language for social bonding and/or gossip (Dunbar, Chapter 36), or did we evolve it to exchange information about the material world, e.g. tools, foods, geography?

For a long time instrumental models held sway. Washburn (1960), for example, hypothesizes that tool-making, language, and bipedalism evolved together as one complex whole. For the most part, early advocates of the tool-making hypotheses assumed that tool-making selected for language capacities, because language facilitates the processes of learning to make and use tools. When studies clearly demonstrated that modern blacksmiths and others learn their skills primarily via imitation (Wynn 1993), most language evolution theorists dismissed tool-making hypotheses. This may have amounted to throwing the baby out with the bathwater. As Harnad (Chapter 42) points out, one of the key functions of language is that it helps people categorize, that is, to learn to do the 'right thing with the right kind of thing'. Calvin has also cogently argued that some kinds of tool use, mainly aimed throwing, demanded increased neural tissue that was then co-opted for speech (Calvin 1993). In this section, Gibson (Chapter 35) notes that human tool-making primarily evolved in foraging contexts and that human foragers talk about where animals, plants, and water are and whether they are available for consumption.

Donald (Chapter 17) hypothesizes that mime evolved prior to spoken languages, and that mime, in turn, may have evolved from tool use, since both utilize similar procedural learning and basal ganglia-mediated motor skills (see also Wilkins, Chapter 19). It thus appears that the tool-making hypothesis lives on, but in a somewhat different format than originally proposed.

Social bonding hypotheses draw inspiration from the alleged demise of tool-making hypotheses, from correlations between brain size and social group size (Dunbar 1992), from the amount of time that most humans spend gossiping (Dunbar 1996), and/or from a need to explain honest, as opposed to deceptive, communication (Knight and Power, Chapter 37). Dunbar (Chapter 36) has long argued that complex vocalizations first evolved as a form of social grooming in primates that were living in large groups. From these humble beginnings, language arose. Knight and Power's scenario is somewhat more complex than that originally proposed by Dunbar, but basically assumes that ritual and language evolved together, primarily as a form of social bonding among adult females in competition for food-provisioning by adult males. Another social hypothesis not covered in the volume is that of Deacon (1997), who suggests that symbolism evolved as part of the male/female food-sharing bond (see also Dunbar and Shultz 2007a). To the extent, however, that primate group size is partially determined by foraging strategies, and given that the hypotheses of Knight and Power, Deacon, and Dunbar and Shultz rely on social food sharing, even social theories of language origins assume changes in foraging strategies.

In sum, we are still a long way from a precise determination of when or why language evolved. Hopefully, however, the papers in this section will help point the way to eventual solutions to these complex issues.

......................................................

# CHAPTER 24

# MOLECULAR PERSPECTIVES ON HUMAN EVOLUTION

......................................................

## REBECCA L. CANN

## 24.1 INTRODUCTION

......................................................

If I were to describe the biology of our species as a distinct group of primates, I would emphasize how young we are, compared to other species. That alone accounts for a number of problems we have trying to understand the genetic basis of our big brain, bipedalism, and other anatomical features that allow complex behaviours and speech. Our history as anatomically modern people, *Homo sapiens sapiens*, traces back in time (Millard 2008) to African fossils found at Herto (dating to about 160 kya (thousand years ago)) and Omo Kibish (~98–192 kya). Yet, 200,000 years is only a small fraction of the entire time, estimated to be approximately 6 million years, since the divergence of the human and chimpanzee lineages (Cavalli-Sforza and Feldman 2003).

Historically, scientists have used various kinds of evidence to reconstruct human history. Only recently has molecular data—evidence from changes in proteins and DNA sequences of living humans—been used as evidence. If mutations arose that gave us our unique capabilities, when and where did they occur? The huge time span from divergence from a common ape ancestor to emergence of modern humans makes it difficult, even in the age of genome analysis when we can include some information from extinct Neanderthals, to identify the precise timing of changes in DNA sequences that underlie and facilitate uniquely modern traits and the sequences in which they occurred. In the words of three critics, ' . . . we are now trying to understand how 3 types of motor vehicle (e.g. a sports car, a van, and a truck) coming out of 3 different factories get to be so different just by looking at the parts' lists' (Erren et al. 2008: 5).

The problem is how to connect molecular evidence of evolutionary relationships between the various hominins (humans and their direct ancestral species) with fossil evidence from the Plio-Pleistocene times, a period covering episodes of immense swings in temperature and rainfall, beginning about 5.5 million years ago (mya) and ending only about 11 kya. New technologies, allowing analysis of trace amounts of genetic material from human fossils, may help determine these relationships (Noonan 2010). Mitochondrial DNA, for example, indicates that widely-dispersed human groups apparently split into at least two descendant populations in the late Middle Pleistocene, perhaps during the period of global climate extremes 480–425 kya (Endicott et al. 2010). One of these groups, Neanderthals, disappeared by 28 kya. The other is us, and we are the only humans left. What did we share with other species, what did we lose, and how can we know this?

New genetic evidence should help illuminate the problems we still face in understanding the tempo and mode of evolution. We now have the genome data from chimpanzees and gorillas, along with the 1000 Genomes Project, based on living people, which should help us distinguish the sequence changes in human DNA from those of more distant species. When we line up the human reference genome with the chimpanzee genome, a small subset of all mutations identified will be unique to the human lineage (Noonan 2010).

In our bodies we may have some 200,000 different proteins, and 20,000–25,000 genes that code for them (Scherer 2008). Slight differences in the way these genes are decoded can allow a cell to produce different proteins from the same gene. Scientists recently identified a single gene in the brain (*DScam*: Downs syndrome cell adhesion molecule) that can make over 38,000 different proteins from the same basic sequence block (Zipursky 2010). Thus there are many parts to analyse on our assembly list for the brain alone!

DNA, short for deoxyribonucleic acid, is the chemical polymer that encodes our genes. In a single cell, this polymer could be stretched out to over two metres. The DNA molecule is based on four different subunits, A (adenine), G (guanine), C (cytosine), and T (thymine), and a simple chemical language allows these bases to be arranged in variable linear sequences. DNA in animal cells is usually found tightly coiled in the nucleus, a separate compartment within the cell bounded by a membrane, and within the nucleus on chromosomes, which are usually portrayed as lines or x's in cartoon drawings. DNA is also found within the cytoplasm (on the other side of the nuclear membrane) of the cell, but is arranged there in a circular chromosome in the mitochondria. Around 2% of the total DNA content of our cells is mitochondrial, and because it is so abundant, found in most tissues, and likely to survive in bone and teeth after the death of the cell, mitochondrial DNA (mtDNA) is widely used in forensic analysis and ancient DNA studies.

Changes can occur in the DNA code, perhaps making more of a particular protein, changing its structure, or even eliminating it from a particular cell type. Mutations—changes to the code—can be removed by natural selection if detrimental to overall cellular housekeeping, or if beneficial they can spread into the population, sometimes getting fixed as an important trait for particular species.

My background in human population genetics constantly reminds me that, great as the new genetic evidence is, we still encounter considerable ambiguity when reconstructing the past on the basis of genes of the living. We measure what we can observe at the DNA and protein level in order to infer past processes that might have generated the patterns of gene and allele frequencies that encode them. Sometimes we can get very close to a good reconstruction, but in other instances arguments flare over individual preferences favouring one model over another. Are there historical links? Well-dated fossils? Is there evidence of a migration? Do we have strong corroborative evidence from analysis of shared cognate features? Are we inadvertently postulating false correlations? Comparisons of DNA in genetically interbreeding populations differ from comparisons in reproductively isolated species. Yet we are constrained to use some of the same methods, since computer models assume an ancestral sequence that continues to diverge in each generation. A model that employs a network rather than a diverging tree might be a better biological approximation of the problem, but is computationally more difficult from a mathematical perspective. Hence, we take shortcuts and use the tree when we know it isn't strictly correct.

## 24.2 MOLECULAR CLOCKS AND GENE PHYLOGENIES

Humans have 46 chromosomes, including 22 pairs of autosomes (non-sex chromosomes), one from each parent, numbered 1–22, and two sex chromosomes, X and Y. Women have two X chromosomes and men have one X and one Y. X chromosomes can be passed from parents to any of their children, but, during the processes of sperm and ova formation, they experience DNA recombination in each generation. In contrast, a portion of the Y chromosome passes directly from father to son without recombination, and mtDNA passes primarily from a woman to all of her children, probably without recombination. Molecular evolutionists can, therefore, study Y sequences which provide evidence of an individual's unbroken line of direct male ancestors (much like English surnames), mitochondrial sequences which are maternally transmitted and provide evidence of an unbroken direct line of female ancestry, or autosomal sequences on chromosomes 1–22, which constitute the greatest bulk of potentially available genetic evidence, but are almost impossible to trace through more than a few generations of specific parental lines.

Closely related individuals tend to share similar DNA sequences. So, the more closely related two individuals are, the greater the similarity in the particular stretch of DNA being compared. But a single DNA sequence can gradually change over time as mutations accumulate and are not repaired. If you can measure the mutation rate and count the number of mutations between two individuals, you have a 'clock' that helps predict when they could have last shared a common ancestor. As time passes and species adapt to new environments, DNA sequences diverge. The principle of a molecular clock underlies the use of DNA sequences or their derivatives as cellular fossils to aid reconstruction of speciation events (Avise 2005).

Estimating mutation rates for nuclear (chromosomal) DNA is difficult because chromosomes, and the DNA which composes them, recombine and homogenize DNA sequences in every new generation, in addition to undergoing single base substitutions, for instance putting a G where a C used to be. No single absolute rate of mutation characterizes all DNA, but on average, genes of the same functional class (i.e. those essential to the production of cellular energy or the maintenance of chromosome shape) tend to mutate at the same rate. For mitochondrial genes, the overall mutation rate is about 2% every million years. Genes that make redundant products or are not absolutely essential can change very fast, compared to those that must maintain essential cellular processes; thus, 'different rates for different traits'. If we find two species or two populations are 99% similar in a compared sequence, we infer that they shared a more recent common ancestor than two that are only 80% similar.

This general logic allowed molecular phylogenies to be built for many living primates, using individual nuclear genes like haemoglobins, but lineage reconstruction models are only crude approximations, because we do not fully understand the genetic processes that result in new combinations of DNA bases along a stretch of chromosome. Mitochondrial genes, with their own 37-gene circular chromosome, sometimes tell a different, simpler story from nuclear genes because they do not appear to recombine. Reconstructing from mtDNA how one person's sequence relates to their parents' sequence is therefore easy—one just needs to look at the maternal ancestor.

What we find, then, are different modes of inheritance, or transmission, of DNA. Mitochondrial sequences are inherited only from one's mother, whereas fathers pass their Y chromosome genes only to their sons. Nuclear DNA is inherited from both parents, with the possibility of genetic recombination, which can scramble DNA sequences and create whole new versions of old genes. Given these differing kinds of transmission, great uncertainty arises in considering the whole genome as an estimator of divergence within and between species. Do we take an average date of divergence based on all mitochondrial, Y-chromosome, and autosomal DNA, do we use only mitochondrial or Y-chromosome DNA, or do we use limited numbers of genes from each class of DNA? Which genes give the best, unbiased estimate of divergence time? Scientists can't decide, and so with whole genome sequences for at least 12 different humans, as well as the three Neanderthals from Vindija (Green et al. 2010), we are still struggling. Genomes from several chimpanzees, gorillas, an orang-utan, gibbon, siamang, macaques, baboons, and other non-human primate species are near completion as well. The finished genomes will give us a more sophisticated view of when we diverged from common ape ancestors and started on our unique trajectory as a new type of African primate, if we ask the right questions.

## 24.3 A MOLECULAR PERSPECTIVE ON HUMAN HISTORY, WITH REFERENCE TO KNOWN FOSSILS

Fossils belonging to the order Primates, which comprises humans, apes, monkeys, and prosimians, first appear in the fossil record near the end of the Cretaceous (a period lasting from 145–65 mya). Similarly, comparisons of mtDNA from 13 living primates and six mammalian orders suggest the primate order diverged from other mammalian orders about 77 mya (Steiper and Young 2006). Fossils from about 50 mya with long, dog-like snouts show resemblances to modern lemurs (the Adapids) and those with shorter faces look more like tarsiers and anthropoid primates (monkeys, apes, and humans: the Omomyids). The earliest fossils that have been attributed to anthropoids are from about 37 mya (Kay et al. 1997). After this time, two major groups of primates diverged into platyrrhine (flat-nosed) and catarrhine (narrow-nosed) primates. All extant New World monkeys (e.g. monkeys from South and Central America) are platyrrhines. All extant Old World monkeys (monkeys from Africa, Asia, and Gibraltar) and apes including humans are catarrhines. Molecular taxonomists believe the ancestors of both groups arose in Africa, and that those of the 'New World' rafted from the west coast of Africa at a point when the Southern Atlantic Ocean was much smaller and the continents of Africa and South America had not yet drifted to their modern positions (Takai et al. 2000). Molecular phylogenies of various monkey species show this divergence between catarrhines and platyrrhines to have taken place approximately 43 mya, and the divergence between hominoids and Old World monkeys to have occurred by at least 30 mya (Steiper and Young 2006). Molecular dates using nuclear gene data support an early Miocene divergence for Asian and African apes at 18 mya, but mitochondrial timescales are younger, by 4–5 million years (Steiper and Young 2006).

It appears that the African great apes—chimpanzees, bonobos, and gorillas—are the closest genetic relatives of humans, with estimated splits based on fossils between *Homo* and *Pan* (the chimpanzee and bonobo) dating from 6–7.5 mya (Benton and Donoghue 2007). Many palaeontologists and anatomists had long recognized the phylogenetic links, but it was not until the late 1960s and early 1970s that the recent common ancestry of these groups was recognized, forced upon the palaeo-anthropological community by the insistence of biochemists that the proteins in these species were too similar to have diverged 15–20 mya, as many fossil specialists claimed. Positions hardened around the placement of two particular groups of fossils from Pakistan and India, the ramapithecines and the sivapithecines, dating from 14–18 mya. Some specialists (Simons and Pilbeam 1972) believed that some of these fossils were hominins (directly related to humans) while others thought they were ancestral to some unknown ape. Molecular evidence, however, indicated that no fossils from this time period could possibly be hominins. According to the molecular clock, the human lineage separated from that of the African apes only about 4–9 mya. In other words, during the period 14–18 mya, no hominin had yet appeared (Sarich and Wilson 1967).

When molecular clocks were first applied to human evolution, the results were explosive (Gibbons 2006) and resulted in a major stand-off with respect to the relative validity of fossil versus molecular evidence. The debate over whether or not a molecular clock existed, or had been correctly calibrated, was notable for revealing the amount of hubris and ego demonstrated by protagonists on both sides (see Goodman 1996 for a detailed, first-hand account). By the late 1970s, however, new fossil discoveries and analyses had led to a universal acceptance of Sarich's claim for relatively late appearance of the hominin line, even among the palaeontologists. At the same time, more complete DNA sequence information, from both mitochondrial and nuclear gene sets, placed tighter limits on the timescale for human/chimp, chimp/gorilla, and gorilla/human divergence times. Molecular research confirmed that our closest relatives were indeed the two living chimpanzee species, *Pan troglodytes* and *P. paniscus*, which separated from human lineages approximately 5–7 mya (Kumar et al. 2005). This figure is, though, still hotly contested, because of questions about whether or not mutation rates have been properly calibrated.

A few fossils of possible hominin status date from 5–8 mya (see Wood and Bauernfeind, this volume). Specialists argue about which fossils fit on exactly which lineage—chimp, gorilla, or human. For this reason, specialists in molecular studies do not get heavily invested in arguments over which fossils fit directly onto the human tree (Wong 2010), but this may change if fossils are found with sufficient remaining organic material inside to warrant DNA extraction attempts.

## 24.4 MUCH ADO ABOUT NEANDERTHALS

I started working with human mtDNA over 30 years ago as a personal attempt to understand recent human history as reconstructed from modern human population genetics (Cann et al. 1987). At that time, we used mtDNA from modern humans to infer that our species arose in sub-Saharan Africa and last shared a common maternal ancestor ('Mitochondrial Eve') about 200 kya. But where did we fit as a new species coming out of Africa with the previously successful residents of Europe and Asia? It was a mystery then, as now, to understand why a well-adapted and long-lived archaic species of humans—the Neanderthals—died out about 30 kya in Europe, after successfully surviving for over a hundred thousand years in periglacial habitats. Were modern humans just more creative, was it climate change (Finlayson 2004), or did Neanderthals meet a violent end, as Shanidar 3, Ardeche, and other sites with butchered bones suggest (Churchill et al. 2009)? The 'lack of creativity' argument seems to be dying with recent analysis of a tool tradition, Uluzzian, from northern Europe, that is now attributed to Neanderthals (Riel-Salvatore 2010; also see d'Errico and Vanhaeren, this volume, contra Wynn, this volume). An alternative, that Neanderthals and early modern humans were never genetically isolated and/or that modern humans spreading out of Africa absorbed older populations, has always had various proponents (e.g. Wolpoff 1989; Mann, this volume) and that idea recently gained traction with the analysis of Neanderthal genomes.

Researchers led by Svante Pääbo at the Max Planck Institute for Evolutionary Anthropology in Leipzig have concluded that between 1–4% of the current Eurasian nuclear genome is derived from Neanderthals (Green et al. 2010). Modern Africans do not show this pattern, although molecular evidence points to sub-Saharan Africa as the ancestral homeland for our species' genome (Tishkoff et al. 2009). These results must also be reconciled with the observation that we also have 54 complete mtDNA sequences from modern humans and five from Neanderthals, with a most recent common ancestor estimated to have lived 315–538 kya (Endicott et al. 2010). Under normal circumstances, genetic divergence accompanies or even precedes population divergence. But if Neanderthals and anatomically modern humans were indeed once entirely separate lineages, they appear to have exchanged genes when they met again, this time in the Eurasian homeland of the Neanderthals.

Overall, 99.84% of our nuclear DNA is identical to that of the Neanderthals studied (Green et al. 2010). Given this level of divergence, the authors suggest that the two lines of humans, one which eventually led to Neanderthals and the other leading to modern humans, split off from each other between 270 and 440 kya: that is, nuclear DNA appears to provide a somewhat more recent date of divergence than suggested by the mtDNA studies reported by Endicott et al. (2010). Green et al. (2010) also consider that the acquisition of Neanderthal genes helped modern humans, migrating out of Africa towards more temperate zones, to adapt to these new climates and habitats. Humans may, then, have joined the ranks of animal hybrids, which include crosses of dolphins and whales; polar and grizzly bears; and donkeys and horses (mules).

While it is possible that Neanderthals did mate with anatomically modern humans who were spreading into temperate regions of the world from tropical zones, no evidence for this appears in the mitochondrial DNA. Nuclear genes from Neanderthals may have spread into modern humans, but their mtDNA did not. This is surprising if natural selection favoured the spread of genotypes common in cold-adapted populations, as suggested by Green et al. (2010), since mtDNA encodes 37 essential genes in the energy pathway that makes adenosine triphosphate (ATP), the root of cellular energy. Wallace (2007) suggests that mitochondria retain these genes because they are essential for rapid response to new adaptive shifts. People from the African tropics typically have long limbs for efficient heat transfer. As humans moved into the cold Northern hemisphere, the requirement to produce enough energy to maintain body heat would have shifted. If this view is correct, one might expect to see the incorporation of cold-adapted Neanderthal mitochondrial genotypes into the modern gene pool, precisely the opposite of what we observe. The mystery remains.

Analysis of new Neanderthal sequences hinges on the availability for study of more samples yielding high quality DNA, as well as better authentication of the sequences obtained from them. Until we understand how genetically different two Neanderthals were from each other, we will have a hard time connecting particular mutations in *Homo sapiens* to specific features such as language. A few mutations will be shared between Neanderthals and us but not found in chimpanzees, while some will likely be unique to either humans or Neanderthals. Right now, scientists are focusing on individual 'candidate genes', such as *FOXP2* for aspects of language and *MCPH1* for brain volume, to isolate important changes. This is akin to picking two shiny components off the parts list for making the power train of a vehicle and describing their width. Several thousand other pieces are missing in order to deliver power to the road surface! In the future, more comprehensive genetic information should be available.

..............................................................

# CHAPTER 25

# THE FOSSIL RECORD: EVIDENCE FOR SPEECH IN EARLY HOMININS

..............................................................

## BERNARD A. WOOD AND AMY L. BAUERNFEIND

This contribution reviews the fossil evidence for human evolution from the earliest hominins to the emergence of *Homo erectus*. We indicate the types of fossil evidence that can throw any light, no matter how dim, on the capacities for speech in extinct hominins, and summarize what these lines of evidence suggest about such capacities in the pre-*Homo erectus* taxa in the hominin clade.

## 25.1 THE HOMININ CLADE

..............................................................

Hominin is the vernacular for the tribe Hominini, which is the Linnaean term most researchers are now using for the twig, or clade, of the Tree of Life that contains modern humans but no other living taxon. So modern humans, and all the extinct creatures more closely related to modern humans than to any other living taxon, are called hominins, and chimpanzees and bonobos (hereafter called chimps/bonobos), and all the extinct creatures more closely related to chimps/bonobos than to any other living taxon are called panins.

## 25.2 CLASSIFYING HOMININS

Unlike a clade, which reflects the *process* of evolutionary history, a grade is a category based solely on the *outcome* of evolutionary history. A clade is analogous to a *make* of car (all Ford cars share a recent common ancestor, the Model

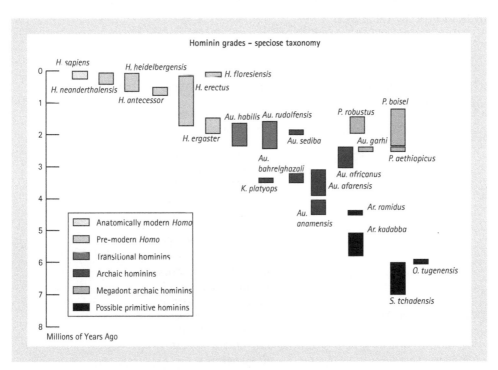

**Figure 25.1. Taxa recognized in a typical speciose hominin taxonomy.**
Note that the height of the columns reflects current ideas about the earliest (called the first appearance datum, or FAD) and the most recent (called the last appearance datum, or LAD) fossil evidence of any particular hominin taxon. However, the time between the FAD and the LAD is likely to represent the minimum time span of a taxon, for it is highly unlikely that the fossil record of a taxon, and particularly the relatively sparse fossil records of early hominin taxa, include the earliest and most recent fossil evidence of a taxon.

T, not shared with any other make of car), whereas a grade is analogous to a *type* of car (SUVs made by Lexus, Porsche, and Land-Rover are functionally similar, yet they have different evolutionary histories and therefore have no uniquely-shared recent common ancestor). Taxa in the same grade eat the same sorts of foods and share the same posture and mode(s) of locomotion; how they came by those behaviours is irrelevant. Because the pattern of relationships among fossil hominin taxa remains unclear we sort the hominin taxa into grades and not clades (Figure 25.1).

The grades we use in this review of pre-*Homo erectus* hominins are 'possible primitive hominins', 'archaic hominins', 'megadont archaic hominins' (hominins with larger than expected chewing teeth), and 'transitional hominins'. We use a relatively speciose taxonomic hypothesis, and we present the species within each grade in temporal order, starting with the oldest taxon. The hominin fossil evidence can also be arranged in fewer, more inclusive taxa, and these taxa are in bold type in Table 25.1.

**Table 25.1 Hominin species in a speciose taxonomy sorted into six grade groupings**

| Grade | Species included in a splitting taxonomy |
|---|---|
| Possible primitive hominins | *Sahelanthropus tchadensis* |
| | *Orrorin tugenensis* |
| | ***Ardipithecus ramidus*** |
| | *Ardipithecus kadabba* |
| Archaic hominins | *Australopithecus anamensis* |
| | ***Australopithecus afarensis*** |
| | *Kenyanthropus platyops* |
| | *Australopithecus bahrelgazali* |
| | ***Australopithecus africanus*** |
| | *Australopithecus garhi* |
| | *Australopithecus sediba* |
| Megadont archaic hominins | *Paranthropus aethiopicus* |
| | *Paranthropus boisei* |
| | ***Paranthropus robustus*** |
| Transitional hominins | ***Homo habilis*** |
| | *Homo rudolfensis* |
| Pre-modern *Homo* | *Homo ergaster* |
| | ***Homo erectus*** |
| | *Homo floresiensis* |
| | *Homo antecessor* |
| | *Homo heidelbergensis* |
| | ***Homo neanderthalensis*** |
| Anatomically modern *Homo* | ***Homo sapiens*** |

## 25.3 How do you tell an early hominin taxon from a taxon in a closely-related clade?

There are many differences between the hard-tissues of living modern humans and chimps/bonobos. However, scientists searching in sediments from 8–5 million years ago (mya) for fossil evidence of the earliest members of the hominin clade must consider a different question. What were the differences between the *earliest* hominins and *earliest* panins? These are likely to have been much more subtle than the differences between contemporary hominins and contemporary panins.

The common ancestor of the hominin and panin clades was almost certainly not like either a modern human, or a chimp or a bonobo. Nonetheless, most researchers agree that the last common ancestor (LCA) of the hominin and panin clades was probably more likely to have been chimp/bonobo-like than modern human-like. If this assumption is correct, then the skeleton of the LCA of chimps/bonobos and modern humans would most likely show evidence of still being adapted for life in the trees. For example, its fingers would have been curved to enable it to grasp branches, and its limbs would have been adapted to walk both on all fours and on the hind limbs alone. It would have had a snout, modestly-sized chewing teeth, prominent canines, and relatively and absolutely large upper central incisor teeth. Compared to the earliest panins, the earliest members of the hominin clade would most likely have had smaller canine teeth, larger chewing teeth, and thicker lower jaws. There would also have been some changes in the skull and postcranial skeleton linked with more time spent upright and with a greater dependence on the hind limbs for bipedal walking. These changes would have included, among other things, a forward shift in the foramen magnum (the aperture in the base of the skull where the spinal cord attaches to the brain), wider hips, habitually more extended knees, and a narrower, more stable, foot.

## 25.4 Possible hominins

This group includes four taxa, *Ardipithecus ramidus*, *Orrorin tugenensis*, *Sahelanthropus tchadensis*, and *Ardipithecus kadabba*, which might be hominins.

### 25.4.1 Taxon name: *Sahelanthropus tchadensis* (Brunet et al. 2002)

Temporal range: ca. 7–6 mya.

Source(s) of the evidence: known from localities in Toros-Menalla, Chad, Central Africa.

Nature of the evidence: a plastically-deformed cranium, mandibles and some teeth; no postcranial evidence.

Characteristics and inferred behaviour: a chimp/bonobo-sized animal displaying a novel combination of primitive and derived features. Much about the base and vault of the cranium is chimp/bonobo-like, but the relatively centrally-placed foramen magnum is hominin-like. The large ridge above the orbits, the lack of a muzzle, small, apically-worn canines, low, rounded molar cusps, relatively thick tooth enamel, and relatively thick body of the lower jaw suggest that *S. tchadensis* does not belong in the *Pan* clade. It is either a primitive hominin, or it belongs to a separate clade of hominin-like apes.

### 25.4.2 Taxon name: *Orrorin tugenensis* (Senut et al. 2001)

Temporal range: ca. 6 mya.

Source(s) of the evidence: the relevant remains come from four localities in the Lukeino Formation, Tugen Hills, Kenya.

Nature of the evidence: the 13 specimens include three femoral fragments, a fragmented mandible, and six dental specimens.

Characteristics and inferred behaviour: the femoral morphology suggests that *O. tugenensis* is bipedal, but the discoverers admit that much of the dental morphology is 'ape-like' (Senut et al. 2001: 6). *O. tugenensis* may prove to be a hominin, but it is equally likely to be part of the offshoot from great apes that included the common ancestor of panins and hominins.

### 25.4.3 Taxon name: *Ardipithecus kadabba* (Haile-Selassie et al. 2004)

Temporal range: 5.2–5.8 mya.

Source(s) of the evidence: Late Miocene fossils from the Middle Awash Valley of Ethiopia.

Nature of the evidence: six postcranial and 11 dental specimens.

Characteristics and inferred behaviour: the main differences between *Ar. kadabba* and *Ar. ramidus s. s.* (*sensu stricto*) are that the upper canine crowns of the former have longer crests, and that the $P_3$ crown outline of *Ar. kadabba* is more asymmetrical, and thus more ape-like, than that of *Ar. ramidus*. The proximal foot phalanx (AME-VP-1/71) combines an ape-like curvature with a proximal joint surface which is *Au. afarensis*-like and indicative of semi-arboreality. The ape-like dental morphology suggests that the case for *Ar. kadabba* being a primitive hominin is relatively weak.

## 25.4.4 Taxon name: *Ardipithecus ramidus* (White et al. 1994, 1995, 2009)

Temporal range: ca. 4.5–4.3 mya (but some specimens could be as young as 3.7 mya).

Source(s) of the evidence: the evidence for this taxon is a collection of ca. 4.4-million-year-old fossils, most recovered from a site called Aramis in the Middle Awash region of Ethiopia.

Nature of the evidence: the published evidence consists of two associated skeletons, one that includes a partial skull and especially good preservation of the hands and feet (ARA-VP-6/500), a piece of the base of the cranium, mandibles, associated dentitions, isolated teeth, two vertebrae, a first rib, fragments of long bones, and other isolated postcranial fossils.

Characteristics and inferred behaviour: the remains attributed to *Ar. ramidus* share some features in common with living species of *Pan*, others that are shared with the African apes in general, and several dental and cranial features that it is claimed are shared only with later hominins such as *Au. afarensis*. Thus, the discoverers have suggested that the material belongs to a hominin species (White et al. 2009). The new species was initially allocated to *Australopithecus* (White et al. 1994), but it was subsequently assigned to a new genus, *Ardipithecus* (White et al. 1995) which the authors suggest is significantly more primitive than *Australopithecus*. The body mass of the presumed female partial skeleton has been estimated to be ca. 50 kg (but there are reasons to believe that this may be an overestimate), the canines are less projecting than those of common chimpanzees, and the degree of functional honing is modest. The postcanine teeth are relatively small and the thin enamel covering on the teeth suggests that the diet of *Ar. ramidus* may have been closer to that of chimps/bonobos than to later hominins. Despite this specimen having ape-like hands and feet, the position of the foramen magnum and the reconstruction of the poorly preserved pelvic bone have been interpreted as confirmation that *Ar. ramidus* was an upright biped.

## 25.5 Archaic hominins

This group subsumes two genera, *Australopithecus* and *Kenyanthropus*.

### 25.5.1 Taxon name: *Australopithecus anamensis* (Leakey et al. 1995)

Temporal range: ca. 4.5–3.9 mya.

Source(s) of the evidence: Allia Bay and Kanapoi, Kenya.

Nature of the evidence: the evidence consists of jaws, teeth, and postcranial elements from the upper and lower limbs.

Characteristics and inferred behaviour: the teeth of *Au. anamensis* are more primitive than those of *Au. afarensis*, but they also show some similarities to *Paranthropus* (see below). The upper limb remains are like those of *Au. afarensis*, but a tibia attributed to *Au. anamensis* suggests that its owner was an accomplished biped.

### 25.5.2 Taxon name: *Australopithecus afarensis* (Johanson et al. 1978)

Temporal range: ca. 4–3 mya.

Source(s) of the evidence: Laetoli, Tanzania; White Sands, Hadar, Maka, Belohdelie and Fejej, Ethiopia; Allia Bay, West Turkana, and Tabarin, Kenya.

Nature of the evidence: *Australopithecus afarensis* is the earliest hominin to have a comprehensive fossil record including a skull, several crania, many lower jaws, and sufficient limb bones to be able to estimate stature and body mass. The collection includes AL-288, just less than half of the skeleton of an adult female, known as 'Lucy'.

Characteristics and inferred behaviour: body mass estimates for *Au. afarensis* range from ca. 30–45 kg and its endocranial volume is estimated to be between 400–550 cc. This is larger than the average endocranial volume of a chimpanzee, but if the estimates of the body size of *Au. afarensis* are approximately correct, then relative to the estimated body mass the brain of *Au. afarensis* is not substantially larger than that of *Pan*. It has smaller incisors than those of extant chimps/bonobos, but its premolars and molars are relatively larger than those of chimps/bonobos. The pelvis and the relatively short lower limbs suggest that *Au. afarensis* was not adapted for long-range bipedalism, and the hand and the shoulder girdle retain morphology that most likely reflects a significant element of arboreal locomotion. Footprints from Laetoli, Tanzania, suggest that the standing height of adult individuals in this early hominin species was between 1.0 and 1.5 m.

### 25.5.3 Taxon name: *Kenyanthropus platyops* (Leakey et al. 2001)

Temporal range: ca. 3.5–3.3 mya.

Source(s) of the evidence: West Turkana and perhaps Allia Bay, Kenya.

Nature of the evidence: the initial report lists the cranium of the specimen defining the species, or holotype, and the maxilla and 34 additional specimens, some of which may well belong to *K. platyops*.

Characteristics and inferred behaviour: the main reasons why KNM-WT 40000, the type specimen of *K. platyops*, was not assigned to *Au. afarensis* are its flat and wide face, and its relatively small but thickly enamelled molars. Its face is like that of the megadont archaic hominins (see below), but the chewing teeth of *K. platyops* are not enlarged. The new material bears some resemblance to *Homo rudolfensis* (see below), but the postcanine teeth of the latter are substantially larger than those of KNM-WT 40000.

### 25.5.4 Taxon name: *Australopithecus bahrelghazali* (Brunet et al. 1996)

Temporal range: ca. 3.5–3.0 mya.

Source(s) of the evidence: Koro Toro, Chad.

Nature of the evidence: the evidence is restricted to jaw fragments and an isolated tooth.

Characteristics and inferred behaviour: its discoverers claim that the thicker enamel of KT 12/H1 distinguishes it from *Ar. ramidus*, and that its smaller and more vertical mandibular symphysis and more complex mandibular premolar roots distinguish it from *Au. afarensis*. However, *Au. bahrelghazali* is most likely a regional variant of *Au. afarensis*.

### 25.5.5 Taxon name: *Australopithecus africanus* (Dart 1925)

Temporal range: ca. 3–2.4 mya.

Source(s) of the evidence: most of the evidence comes from two caves, Sterkfontein and Makapansgat, with other evidence coming from Taung and Gladysvale.

Nature of the evidence: this is one of the better fossil records of an early hominin taxon; the cranium, mandible and the dentition are well sampled, as is the post-cranium, but the axial skeleton is less well represented in the sample.

Characteristics and inferred behaviour: *Australopithecus africanus* was capable of walking bipedally, it had relatively large chewing teeth, and apart from the reduced canines the skull is relatively ape-like. Its mean endocranial volume is ca. 460 cc. The Sterkfontein evidence suggests that males and females of *Au. africanus* differed substantially in body size but probably not to the degree they did in *Au. afarensis*.

### 25.5.6  Taxon name: *Australopithecus sediba* (Berger et al. 2010)

Temporal range: ca. 1.977 ± 0.003 mya.

Source(s) of the evidence: Malapa, South Africa.

Nature of the evidence: The evidence consists of two partial skeletons, a juvenile (MH1) and an adult (MH2), plus other unpublished remains.

Characteristics and inferred behaviour: despite the late occurrence of *Australopithecus sediba* within the fossil record, the morphology appears to represent a mixture of primitive and derived traits. The cranial capacity of *Australopithecus sediba* is small (ca. 420 cm³) for the juvenile MH1 and aspects of the postcranium (e.g. the foot) are remarkably ape-like. However, the authors claim that some cranial morphology (e.g. more globular neurocranium, gracile face), mandibular morphology (e.g. more vertical symphyseal profile, a weak chin), dental morphology (e.g. simple canine crown, small anterior and postcanine tooth crowns), and derived aspects of pelvic morphology (e.g. reinforced hip joint, wide and short pelvis) are only shared with early and later *Homo* taxa.

## 25.6  MEGADONT ARCHAIC HOMININS

This group includes hominin taxa that some include in the genus *Paranthropus*, together with *Australopithecus garhi*. The genus *Paranthropus*, which subsumes *Zinjanthropus* and *Paraustralopithecus*, was reintroduced when cladistic analyses suggested that three of the species included in this section formed a clade. The term 'megadont' refers to the absolute size of the postcanine tooth crowns, but some individuals assigned to other pre-*Homo* hominin taxa (such as *Au. africanus*) have teeth nearly as big as the taxa (e.g. *Paranthropus robustus*) referred to here.

### 25.6.1  Taxon name: *Paranthropus aethiopicus* (Arambourg and Coppens 1968; Chamberlain and Wood 1985)

Temporal range: ca. 2.5–2.3 mya.

Source(s) of the evidence: Shungura Formation, Omo region, Ethiopia; West Turkana, Kenya; Malema, Malawi.

Nature of the evidence: the evidence for this species includes a well-preserved adult cranium from West Turkana (KNM-WT 17000), and mandibles (for example, KNM-WT 16005) and isolated teeth from the Shungura Formation, but no postcranial fossils.

Characteristics and inferred behaviour: similar to *Paranthropus boisei* (see below) except that the face is more projecting, the cranial base is less flexed, the incisors are larger, and the postcanine teeth are not so large or morphologically specialized. However, there is only one relatively complete *P. aethiopicus* cranium, and Smith's (2005) warnings about making taxonomic inferences based on small samples should be heeded.

## 25.6.2 Taxon name: *Australopithecus garhi* (Asfaw et al. 1999)

Temporal range: ca. 2.5 mya.

Source(s) of the evidence: Bouri, Middle Awash, Ethiopia.

Nature of the evidence: a fragmented cranium and two partial mandibles.

Characteristics and inferred behaviour: *Au. garhi* combines a primitive cranium with large-crowned post-canine teeth. However, unlike *Paranthropus* (see above), the incisors and canines are also large and the enamel lacks the extreme thickness seen in the latter taxa. An associated skeleton combining a long femur with a long forearm was found nearby, but it is not associated with the type cranium and these fossils have not been formally assigned to *Au. garhi*.

## 25.6.3 Taxon name: *Paranthropus boisei* (Leakey 1959; Robinson 1960)

Temporal range: ca. 2.3–1.4 mya.

Source(s) of the evidence: Olduvai and Peninj, Tanzania; Omo Shungura Formation and Konso, Ethiopia; Koobi Fora, Chesowanja, and West Turkana, Kenya.

Nature of the evidence: there are several skulls (the one from Konso being remarkably complete and well preserved), several well-preserved crania, and many mandibles and isolated teeth.

Characteristics and inferred behaviour: *Paranthropus boisei* is the only hominin to combine a massive, wide and flat face, large premolars and molars, small anterior teeth, thick enamel, a modest endocranial volume (ca. 480 cc), and a mandibular body that is thicker than that of any other hominin. The fossil record of *P. boisei* extends across about one million years of time during which there is little evidence of any substantial change in the size or shape of the components of the cranium, mandible, and dentition.

### 25.6.4 Taxon name: *Paranthropus robustus* (Broom 1938)

Temporal range: ca. 2.0–1.5 mya.

Source(s) of the evidence: Kromdraai, Swartkrans, Gondolin, Drimolen, and Cooper's caves, all situated in the Blauuwbank Valley, near Johannesburg, South Africa.

Nature of the evidence: some of the cranial remains and dentition are well preserved, but most of the crania and mandibles are crushed or distorted.

Characteristics and inferred behaviour: the brain, face, and chewing teeth of *P. robustus* are larger than those of *Au. africanus*, yet the incisor teeth are smaller. What little is known about the postcranial skeleton of *P. robustus* suggests that the morphology of the pelvis and the hip joint is much like that of *Au. africanus*.

## 25.7 TRANSITIONAL HOMININS

Some researchers have suggested that *Homo habilis* and *Homo rudolfensis* may not belong in the *Homo* clade, but until we can generate sound phylogenetic hypotheses about the relationships among these taxa and other hominins it is not clear what their new generic attribution should be. For the purposes of this review, these two taxa are treated as transitional hominins, for they combine some of the features of archaic hominins together with features seen in *Homo erectus* grade hominins.

### 25.7.1 Taxon name: *Homo habilis* (Leakey et al. 1964)

Temporal range: ca. 2.4–1.4 mya.

Source(s) of the evidence: Olduvai Gorge, Tanzania; Koobi Fora, Kenya; Omo (Shungura) and Hadar, Ethiopia, East Africa; perhaps also Sterkfontein, Swartkrans, and Drimolen, South Africa and Chemeron, Kenya

Nature of the evidence: mostly cranial and dental evidence with only a few postcranial bones that can with confidence be assigned to *H. habilis*.

Characteristics and inferred behaviour: the endocranial volume of *H. habilis* ranges from ca. 500 cc to an upper limit closer to 600 cc. All the crania are wider at the base than across the vault, but the face is broadest in its upper part. An earlier inference that *H. habilis* was capable of speech was based on links between endocranial morphology and language comprehension and production that are no longer valid (Holloway 1983; Corballis 2003).

## 25.7.2 Taxon name: *Homo rudolfensis* (Alexeev 1986; *sensu* Wood 1992)

Temporal range: ca. 2.4–1.6 mya.

Source(s) of the evidence: Koobi Fora and perhaps Chemeron, Kenya; Uraha, Malawi.

Nature of the evidence: several incomplete crania, two relatively well-preserved mandibles and several isolated teeth.

Characteristics and inferred behaviour: *Homo rudolfensis* and *H. habilis* show different mixtures of primitive and derived, or specialized, features. For example, although the absolute size of the brain case is greater in *H. rudolfensis*, its face is widest in its mid-part, in contrast to the aforementioned *H. habilis* whose face is widest superiorly. Despite the absolute size of its brain (ca. 725 cc), relative brain size (brain mass as it relates to estimates of body mass) of *H. rudolfensis* is not substantially larger than those of the archaic hominins. The more primitive face of *H. rudolfensis* is combined with a robust mandible and mandibular postcanine teeth with larger, broader, crowns, and more complex premolar root systems than those of *H. habilis*.

# 25.8 CATEGORIES OF HARD-TISSUE EVIDENCE RELATED TO THE GENERATION OF SPEECH

Holloway's (1983) classic review considered four categories of neuroanatomical evidence for spoken language: (1) brain size; (2) evidence for the reorganization, or enlargement, of Broca's area; (3) evidence for brain reorganization involving the temporal cortex and the enlargement of the parietal lobe at the expense of the visual cortex; and (4) petalial asymmetries.

Holloway admitted that with respect to providing evidence about speech capabilities '(brain) size is problematic and always has been' because intra- and interspecies comparisons do not yield a clear correlation between brain mass and speech production or cognitive functioning (1983: 111). Broca's area is located along the inferior frontal gyrus of the anterior prefrontal cortex and is thought to play a role in the production of spoken language (Damasio and Damasio 1989). Broca's area is generally enlarged in the left hemisphere of most modern humans (Amunts et al. 1999), and though present in apes, this lateralization occurs less frequently (Holloway 1996; see also Hopkins and Vauclair, this volume). A recent survey of extinct and extant hominins showed that asymmetrical enlargement occurs in

*Homo* taxa (*H. rudolfensis, H. erectus, H. heidelbergensis, H. neanderthalensis*), but it is absent in *Au. afarensis* (de Sousa and Wood 2007). However, doubt has been cast on the wisdom of using endocranial morphology as a proxy for identifying functional regions of the cortex (e.g. Holloway 2009). The evidence for brain reorganization is controversial because it focuses on a dispute about the location of the impression for the lunate sulcus on the endocranial casts of archaic hominins (see Wilkins, this volume). Lastly, petalias, or asymmetries in the cortical hemispheres of the brain, once thought to be peculiar to modern humans (and thus a sound way of imputing functions such as spoken language) have been identified in samples of higher primates other than modern humans (Hopkins and Marino 2000).

Since 1983, others have suggested that in addition to endocranial morphology, the fossil hominin record potentially provides other lines of evidence about the *production* of speech. These include hard-tissue evidence of: (1) 'extra' neurons in the thoracic spinal cord that would allow for fine control of the muscles of respiration; (2) 'extra' neurons that facilitate the type of fine control of the muscles of the tongue that is involved in speech; (3) the type of supralaryngeal vocal tract (including the form and location of the hyoid) that is suitable for the production of the types of complex sounds integral to complex spoken language; see MacLarnon, this volume.

Examination of the thoracic spinal cord across primates suggested that its cross-sectional area is correlated with the cross-sectional size of the vertebral canal in the thoracic region (MacLarnon 1995, this volume), and when the canal sizes were adjusted for body weight, only the relative size of the thoracic canals of modern humans and Neanderthals were larger than their body sizes would predict (MacLarnon and Hewitt 1999). However, experience with other systems suggests it is very unlikely that these types of broad across-primate allometric relationships are valid for a much narrower allometric context, such as that within the hominin clade. The initial results of attempts to infer the size of the hypoglossal nerve (the motor nerve to most of the extrinsic and all of the intrinsic muscles of the tongue) from the size of the hypoglossal canal (Kay et al. 1998) seemed promising, but closer examination (DeGusta et al. 1999) revealed flaws in this approach; see MacLarnon, this volume.

The supralaryngeal vocal tract (also called the SVT) is made up of two tubes. The horizontal tube is formed by the mouth and the oropharynx, and the vertical tube runs from the soft palate to the vocal folds (note the oropharynx is common to both tubes). Stevens' (1972) theory of quantal speech requires the tubes to be equal in length, and both need to have mechanisms capable of making substantial changes to the size of the lumen of each tube in order to produce the full range of sounds found in the speech of modern humans (P. Lieberman et al. 1972). However, reliable estimation of the length of the two components of the SVT from hard-tissue evidence alone is close to impossible. The hyoid bone is located above the larynx and is the attachment site for the strap muscles of the neck and for the stylohyoid ligament. The size and shape of the hyoid belonging to a juvenile *Au. afarensis* specimen from Dikika, Ethiopia is like that seen in African apes, prima facie evidence that this species was unlikely to be capable of modern human-like vocalizations (Alemseged et al. 2006).

Although each of these lines of evidence seemed to offer considerable potential as proxies for linguistic competence in extinct hominins, the reality is that for one reason or another none of them have lived up to their initial promise. Readers should refer to MacLarnon's chapter, this volume, for an in-depth review of the anatomical specializations connected with speech production.

Evidence related to the *perception* of speech in archaic hominins has also expanded beyond endocranial morphology to a consideration of the external and middle ears. The external ears of chimpanzees are both longer and smaller in cross-section (the external auditory meatus of modern humans [mean = 115mm²] is more than twice that of chimpanzees [mean = 45mm²]), and the longer canal may help amplify low-to-mid frequency sounds. What is known of the size of the external auditory meati of early hominins prior to *Au. afarensis* suggests that they are also chimp-sized. Middle-ear ossicles have been recovered at Swartkrans and Sterkfontein (an incus, SK 848 belonging to *P. robustus*, from the former, and a stapes, belonging to *Au. africanus* and *H. habilis*, from the latter). Moggi-Cecchi and Collard (2002) showed that there was a marked similarity in size between the footplates of the early hominin stapes and the stapes belonging to the living great apes, and that they were both substantially smaller than those of modern humans. But what, if anything, this implies about the speech capabilities of *Au. africanus* (and *H. habilis*) is unclear.

# 25.9 CONCLUSION

It is tempting to try to wring evidence about speech capabilities from the fossil evidence, but to cut a long and often confusing story short, the fossil evidence for archaic hominins contains little, or no, reliable evidence about the speech capabilities of these taxa. Even if it is possible to make broad functional inferences across a wide range of primates, it is imprudent to assume the same inferences can be made across a much narrower range of taxa such as those in the hominin clade.

# ACKNOWLEDGEMENTS

We thank the editors for their invitation to contribute this chapter. Amy Bauern-feind is supported by an NSF-IGERT Studentship and Bernard Wood's research is funded by George Washington University's Academic Excellence Initiative.

# CHAPTER 26

# THE GENUS *HOMO* AND THE ORIGINS OF 'HUMANNESS'

## ALAN MANN

## 26.1 DEFINING THE GENUS *HOMO*

Various authors have linked the evolutionary appearance of the genus *Homo* to diverse behavioural and biological attributes. Australopithecines presumably lacked these qualities, although we cannot be certain of this given the incomplete fossil record.

Wood and Bauernfeind (this volume) describe two possible 'transitional' hominins, *Homo habilis* and *H. rudolfensis*, which apparently evolved from late-in-time species of the genus *Australopithecus*, and which possess both primitive and derived anatomical features. *H. habilis* had narrower premolars and molars housed in a somewhat smaller face in comparison to the earlier australopithecines, but its brain size is only marginally larger than some australopithecine species. *H. rudolfensis*, in contrast, possessed a larger brain but also a larger, australopithecine-sized, dentition and face. Both are troublesome to place taxonomically and suggest it may be difficult to precisely recognize the earliest member of *Homo*.

## 26.2 Earliest indisputable representatives of the genus *Homo*

The earliest-in-time evidence suggestive of *Homo* is a fragmentary upper jaw with a partial dentition from the Hadar region of north central Ethiopia, dated to about 2.33 million years ago (mya) (Kimbel et al. 1996, 1997). This specimen, which possesses a number of facial morphological features similar to those in the *Homo habilis* sample, has been tentatively, but not conclusively, placed in that species.

The earliest fossils indisputably assigned to the genus *Homo* come from Kenya, Ethiopia, Tanzania, and perhaps South Africa and are currently classified as *Homo erectus*. African *Homo erectus* fossils, the earliest dated to about 1.8 mya, include cranial, dental, and postcranial specimens, as well as the almost complete skeleton of an adolescent. The combination of somewhat smaller, less projecting faces and smaller posterior teeth along with braincase volumes between 725–800 cc distinguish the *Homo erectus* sample from *Homo habilis* and *Homo rudolfensis* (Wood and Collard 1999; Kimbel 2009).

These latter species and *Homo erectus* were apparently contemporaneous in parts of East Africa (Kimbel 2009). Further, one *Homo erectus* skull (KNM-ER 3733) was found in deposits contemporary with specimens of the robust australopithecine, *Australopithecus boisei* (*Paranthropus boisei* in Wood and Bauernfeind, Chapter 25). Hence, at 1.8 mya, four species of hominin possibly coexisted in the same place (Grine and Fleagle 2009). These fossil and stone tool accumulations, however, resulted from various environmental and geological (taphonomic) processes that often transported materials some distance from their origin point. Consequently, it is difficult to determine if these diverse fossil species all coexisted in the same environment, and, if so, their possible differences in adaptation (Grine and Fleagle 2009).

A dried-up stream bed at Nariokotome, a locale west of Lake Turkana, North Kenya, has yielded the almost complete skeleton of an adolescent *Homo erectus* (KMN-WT 15000) (Walker and Leakey 1993). Apart from deliberate burials—a practice first known from about 115 kya (thousand years ago) in the Middle East— KMN-WT 15000 represents the most complete hominin individual ever discovered. Dated to about 1.6 mya, the specimen, around 11–12 years of age when it died, is notable for its stature. Whereas the earlier australopithecines were relatively small, the Nariokotome femur is similar in size to those of modern adults, which suggests that the boy, had he grown to adulthood, might have reached a height of as much as 185 cm. Whether this stature estimate represents the beginnings of increased body size or is a specific feature of this individual and/or its population requires confirmation from additional fossils.

The KNM-ER 3733 and the KMN-WT 15000 skulls possess large brow ridges, and low, flat braincases with their greatest width at the level of the external ear hole. In hominin evolution, brain size increases were accompanied by increasing height of the braincase. The faces are projecting, but less so than in the australopithecines. Braincase features are similar to those seen in the first *Homo erectus* ever found, by Eugene DuBois in Trinil (Java) in 1891. Many additional fossil specimens, possessing a similar suite of features, have subsequently been discovered in Java, other parts of Africa, and Eurasia.

Groves (1989) has questioned the attribution of the African specimens to *Homo erectus*. *Homo ergaster*, a species distinct from the later-in-time *Homo erectus* fossil samples from Asia, has been proposed to accommodate early African fossils such as KNM-ER 3733. However, most investigators consider the morphological differences between the two geographically separated samples insufficient to justify the establishment of different species, and thus place the African and Asian fossil samples in the same species, *Homo erectus* (Rightmire 1990; Gilbert 2008; Rightmire and Lordkipanidze 2009).

## 26.3 THE EVOLUTION OF BRAIN AND BEHAVIOUR

The earliest stone tools to have been discovered come from sites in East Africa, and are dated to about 2.6 mya (Wynn, this volume), more or less contemporary with the possible appearance of earliest *Homo*. Were the somewhat larger brain volumes associated with some early *Homo* specimens a necessary biological precondition for the conceptualization of a stone tool? Also discovered from this time are animal bones with cut or scratch marks produced by the sharp edge of a stone implement (Roche et al. 2009). These cut marks constitute the first evidence in human evolution of the use of tools to cut meat and tendons from bones. Whether animals were hunted or scavenged from predator kills is not known (Roche et al. 2009). The possible addition of meat at this point in human evolution represents a significant modification to early hominin diets, which may originally have been more focused on vegetable and insect resources (Sponheimer and Lee-Thorp 1999; Teaford and Ungar 2000; Ungar and Scott 2009; Gibson, Chapter 35). The additional fat in the meat, it has been suggested, provided the added calories necessary for the metabolic costs of a larger brain (Aiello and Wheeler 1995).

During the evolution of the genus *Homo* from these early beginnings to modern *Homo sapiens*, brain size gradually expanded, almost tripling in volume. Earlier australopithecines possessed brain sizes ranging from about 350 cc, in the range of chimpanzees, to about 500 cc; early *Homo* had an internal braincase volume of about 510–775 cc; later *Homo* possessed brain volumes from 1000 to over 1200 cc. Modern humans, *Homo sapiens*, range from about 1200 to more than 1500 cc, with most about 1250–1400 cc.

Various hypotheses have been proposed to explain this neural expansion, including climatic influences, the demands of the environment, and social competition (Holloway 1969, 1975, 1981; Alexander 1989). None are entirely satisfactory as single factors, but a combination, as suggested by Bailey and Geary (2009), may be the most reasonable model.

During the course of human evolution, increased brain size dramatically influenced cranial architecture. Skulls of later members of the genus *Homo* have an increasingly high and globular—dome-like—shape, with the maximum width of the skull, low and approximately at the level of the external ear canals as earlier described for *Homo erectus*, gradually moving higher on the vault, producing the strongly marked eminences on the parietal bones of modern humans. The forehead becomes more and more vertical, with the eventual diminution and loss of the projecting browridges. As brain volume increased, the face, projecting out front of the braincase in the first members of *Homo*, gradually rotates underneath, and the jaws and teeth become smaller.

# 26.4 EXPANSION OF RANGE

Sometime between 2.0 and 1.8 mya hominins expanded out of Africa. Why this expansion occurred at this time remains unknown, and indeed, there are suggestions that this time range may need to be re-evaluated (Dennell and Roebroeks 2005). Possibly, the development of stone tools allowed early *Homo* to exploit a greater range of habitats, eventually resulting in an expansion into Eurasia. Based on the approximately synchronous appearance in Asia of *Homo* and mammals previously limited to Africa, this may also imply an opening of a previously obstructed route out of Africa at Suez (Turner 1984). The duration of this 'Out of Africa' movement is uncertain, but it had begun by 1.8 mya, as evidenced by the presence of early *Homo* at Dmanisi in the Caucasus Mountains, Republic of Georgia.

The Dmanisi evidence includes at least four skulls, one with an associated mandible as well as other cranial and dental specimens, and stone tools similar to the Oldowan tools from East Africa (Wynn, this volume). These fossils have some features similar to those of African *Homo erectus* and some similar to the transitional species *Homo habilis*, perhaps indicative of a greater level of biological variation than the East African evidence suggests. Possibly as early as around 1.6 mya, *Homo erectus* fossils occur at various sites in Java (which at that time, because of the lowering of sea levels from glacial activity, was directly linked to the Asian land mass). Later-in-time *Homo erectus* has been found in the colder parts of Asia, at the celebrated site of the 'Peking Man' fossils at Zhoukoudian in north China (with occupation levels dated to between 800–400 kya) as well as sites in Central and south China (Shen et al. 2009).

Sites in Europe, particularly in southern Spain, have stone tools indicative of the possible presence of hominins earlier than 1.0 mya (Santonja and Villa 1990). The earliest indisputable occurrence of *Homo* in Europe, however, comes from cliffs and caves in the Sierra de Atapuerca, near Burgos, northern Spain. In one cave, the Gran Dolina, fragmentary hominin remains have been excavated in a level dated to about 780 kya (see contributions to the *Journal of Human Evolution* for 1999). Other fossil-bearing sites in Germany, France, Italy, and Greece are all 500 kya or later.

## 26.5 THEORIES OF MODERN HUMAN ORIGINS

After the initial movement of *Homo erectus* peoples from Africa, archaeological and fossil evidence documents hominin presence at sites throughout the Eurasian and African continents. As *Homo erectus* groups adapted to the various environments on these land masses, evolutionary changes occurred that would culminate in the appearance of modern humans. Two contrasting theories are proposed to explain the evolution of living peoples and their relationships to now extinct populations, like the Neanderthals. They mainly differ with respect to their views on the degree of isolation of Eurasian hominin populations. The 'Single Origins Model' (often called the 'Out-of-Africa Model') (Tattersall 1999; Stringer and McKie 1996) views this expansion as resulting in small, scattered, and isolated hominin groups that, lacking gene flow, underwent a series of speciation events. In Europe and Africa, perhaps as early as 700–500 kya, speciation resulted in the evolution of *Homo heidelbergensis* (named for the Mauer site in Germany), with a bigger brain than its ancestor, *H. erectus*. *H. heidelbergensis* populations in Europe, isolated from other hominin populations, evolved into a new species, *Homo neanderthalensis*, the Neanderthals. In sub-Saharan Africa, perhaps between about 200–100 kya, *Homo heidelbergensis* evolved into modern *Homo sapiens*. For reasons that remain shadowy, but perhaps are related to the emergence of 'humanness' (modern human symbolic and linguistic attributes), *Homo sapiens* groups began expanding out of Africa into Europe and Asia to witness or assist in the extinction of the descendants of the first out-of-Africa expansion. It is suggested that a number of critical modern human attributes such as language, symbolism, the use of ornaments, and the mastery of sophisticated tool kits of stone, bone, and antler implements evolved in Africa (McBrearty and Brooks 2000) and were beyond the abilities of these Eurasian peoples (Klein 2003; Mellars 2010).

The other major theory of human origins, the Multiregional Evolution Model (Wolpoff and Caspari 1997; Wolpoff et al. 2004) posits that with the expansion of *H. erectus* into Eurasia, hominin groups were continuously distributed over the continents and were in contact with other populations, sharing genes. Gene flow insured that hominins remained one evolving species. About 700–400 kya, *H. erectus* evolved into archaic members of *H. sapiens* (in the contrasting theory, these fossils are placed in *H. heidelbergensis*). Archaic *H. sapiens* continue to adapt to local environmental conditions while maintaining gene flow; they eventually evolve into living human regional populations (modern human 'races'). The theory of multiregional evolution stresses gene flow as a crucial factor in human evolution and in modern human origins.

Fossil and genetic data have been used to support both models. A number of fossils broadly ranging in time from about 450–250 kya have been uncovered in Europe, Asia, and Africa. All share similar anatomical traits. Although they possessed larger brain sizes than earlier *Homo erectus*, they resembled earlier hominins with large brow ridges, low braincases, and large projecting faces lacking a chin. These fossils are placed in archaic *Homo sapiens* according to the Multiregional model or *Homo heidelbergensis* in the Single Origins model. Fossil specimens from Europe possess morphological features in the face and skull that foreshadow the anatomy that will later characterize European Neanderthal populations. They provide evidence for the *in situ* evolution of the Neanderthals from earlier European ancestors (Hublin 1998).

The final 200 kya of human evolution are viewed very differently in the two models. Fossils from Africa appear to demonstrate the early evolutionary appearance of modern *Homo sapiens*, either contemporary with or earlier in time than archaic hominins in Europe. A partial skull recovered along the Omo River in southern Ethiopia has many anatomical traits typical of living humans, including a high, rounded skull with a vertical forehead lacking a projecting brow ridge and a marked chin. This Omo specimen has been dated to about 190 kya (Shea et al. 2007). From Herto (Ethiopia), an almost complete skull has been recovered that possesses similar features and has a date of around 165 kya (White et al. 2003).

Evidence suggesting long-term regional evolution comes from an almost complete skull, possibly dating to about 200 kya, from the site of Dali, central China (Wu 1981). The skull lacks facial projection (prognathism), the norm in other hominin specimens of this time period. This has been interpreted as evidence for evolutionary continuity with modern Asians, who possess similar facial anatomy. Fragmentary human remains from Zhirendong, China (Liu et al. 2010) include a portion of a lower jaw with a distinctive chin. Dated at more than 100 kya, the presence of a chin, usually associated only with living humans, also suggests regional evolution of modern Asians from earlier Asian ancestors.

## 26.6 NEANDERTHALS AND HUMAN ORIGINS

Neanderthals, the first fossil hominins recognized (in 1856), have been found across Europe. Hence, they have figured prominently in discussions of modern human origins. Questions focus on both their evolutionary relationships to living humans and their capacity for modern human behaviours.

Although Neanderthal anatomical features differ in some respects from those of anatomically modern humans, biologically both groups were extremely similar. In comparison with living humans, Neanderthals possessed a low, flat braincase, low, sloping foreheads, and large brow ridges. Viewed from the back, the Neanderthal skull is ovoid in shape, with the maximum breadth of the skull low in comparison to that of living humans. Brain size is a little larger than the average of living humans. Neanderthal faces projected markedly and there was an inflated or puffed-out cheek area, without the depression that occurs just above the canine tooth (called the *canine fossa*) in modern humans. The lower jaw lacked a prominent chin. The skeletons are strongly built and stocky, with a barrel-like chest, suggestive of a body morphology adapted to the cold conditions of ice age Europe.

Neanderthals have been discovered at many sites, from the Atlantic coast of Europe eastward to the Ural Mountains. Their presence elsewhere remains controversial. The earliest evidence for modern humans in Europe is a site in Romania dated to about 38 kya, while the latest Neanderthal find is from coastal France and is dated to about 36 kya (Vandermeersch 1993; Rougier et al. 2007). No convincing archaeological evidence indicates that modern humans and Neanderthals overlapped in time in Europe. Emerging data also indicate that the more complex Upper Palaeolithic tool industries found in Europe, beginning around 42–38 kya and traditionally associated with the movement of modern humans into Europe, are the result of *in situ* developments from earlier European Middle Palaeolithic industries and do not have African origins (Brantingham et al. 2004; d'Errico 2005; Zilhão 2006; Bednarik 2008; Teyssandier 2008).

In addition to fossil and archaeological evidence, genetic data has been employed in assessing human and Neanderthal relationships (Cann, this volume). While some comparisons of the DNA of living human populations support the idea that modern humans originated in sub-Saharan Africa, other research has pointed to a more complex scenario (Gutiérrez et al. 2002; Eswaran et al. 2005; Bazin et al. 2006; Rogers et al. 2007; Templeton 2007). The extraction of a virtually complete nuclear genome from a Neanderthal limb bone from Croatia shows that about 1–4% of the modern human genome is derived from Neanderthals, documenting a level of gene flow, possibly in the Near East and/or indirectly through intermediary populations (Green et al. 2010). The very recent extraction of the nuclear genome from a human fossil from the Denisova Cave in Siberia indicates gene flow between this population and modern Melanesians, thus providing additional evidence of genetic interchange between the ancestors of living humans and earlier non-African populations (Reich et al. 2010). However, there remains uncertainty about the intensity of this sort of gene flow, considering the accumulating data indicating that the modern human genome has undergone significant evolutionary change over the past 10 kya (Cochran and Harpending 2009).

Several earlier discussions of the Neanderthals and their evolutionary relationships to modern human populations stressed the idea that a clinal distribution might offer the most reasonable model (Howell 1951; Van Valen 1966; see also Wolpoff and Caspari 1997). The later phases of hominin evolution are viewed as a continuum from early *Homo* in Africa through the expansion of *Homo erectus* into the rest of the Old World and their subsequent long-term adaptation to local environmental conditions. Neanderthals, adapted to the glacial conditions of Europe, represent just one of a series of hominin populations scattered across Eurasia and Africa. They resemble their contemporaries anatomically but possess a number of distinctive features. Fossil finds in northern Israel, such as those from the Tabun and Amud caves and the skeleton lacking a skull from the Kebara cave, not only lack distinctive features which characterize European and especially western European Neanderthals, but also possess features similar to other Israeli specimens, the Qafzeh and Skhul samples, which have been termed early modern humans. Consequently, the morphology of these fossils is compatible with the hypotheses of Howell and Van Valen suggesting a cline of hominin groups from western Europe through the Levant and eastward into Asia and southward into Africa. Modern human-like features—high, rounded braincases with vertical foreheads lacking browridges, small faces tucked underneath the braincase with chins and a canine fossa—seem to develop earliest in sub-Saharan Africa, as evidenced by the fossils from Herto and the Omo Kibish Formation in Ethiopia. Human populations may have migrated into Europe and interbred with the Neanderthals. Or alternatively, their genes may have spread into Europe without population movements or direct contact.

# 26.7 SUMMARY

After the initial expansion out of Africa, Eurasian human evolution continued, eventually leading to modern humans. The evolutionary pathways to our present condition and our relationships to the Neanderthals, however, remain subject to differing interpretations.

The multiregional theory views the Neanderthals, not as a separate species, but as members of *Homo sapiens* who contributed significant genetic materials to modern Europeans and possessed behavioural abilities equivalent to other contemporary humans.

The Single Origins Model views the Neanderthals as having undergone a sufficiently long period of isolated evolution from the lineage leading to modern humans for speciation to have occurred, and for them to be placed taxonomically in their own species, *Homo neanderthalensis*.

Unanswerable at present, and perhaps forever, is the question of just how similar to us the Neanderthals were. During the course of human evolution, our ancestors underwent a series of biological and behavioural modifications which culminated in living *Homo sapiens*. Modern humans have a range of abilities in cognition, symbolic representation, speech and language, manipulative skills, and social complexity that might be summed up as 'humanness'. In this sense, were the Neanderthals human, non-human, or in the process of becoming human?

# CHAPTER 27

# THE PALAEOLITHIC RECORD

## THOMAS WYNN

## 27.1 INTRODUCTION

Archaeology studies the tools, structures, and refuse produced by individuals and groups who lived in the near and distant past. Most archaeologists concern themselves with historic and recent prehistoric time periods, roughly the last 12,000 years. But a small group of archaeologists investigates the behavioural and cultural developments that marked the evolution of humans from their split from other African apes to the advent of agriculture, an immense period of time known as the Palaeolithic or Old Stone Age. Using methods and techniques developed over the last century and a half, archaeologists of the Palaeolithic have been able to sketch an outline of some of the major developments in hominin technology, subsistence, social behaviour, and cognition.

## 27.2 THE EARLIEST EVIDENCE OF HOMININ ACTIVITY

The oldest known hominin archaeological site with stone tools is the 2.6-million-year-old site of Gona, in Ethiopia (Semaw et al. 1997). Earlier isolated finds of stone flakes stretch back perhaps as far as 3 million years ago (mya), and bones apparently cut by stone tools at Dikika, Ethiopia, date to 3.4 mya (McPherron et al. 2010), but Gona is the oldest well-dated site where artefacts have been little disturbed by natural forces of erosion and deposition. The Gona artefacts are the earliest examples of a technology archaeologists term Mode 1, or Oldowan; no actual tools have been recovered from the Dikika site.

## 27.2.1 Technology

Mode 1 tools consist of the three basic varieties of stone tool—hammers, cores, and flakes. The principle behind stone knapping is deceptively simple: breaking rocks produces sharp edges. In Mode 1 technology the knapper uses a hammer, which is a roundish hard stone, to strike the edge of another stone, termed a core (Figure 27.1).

If the knapper uses enough force and directs the blow to a spot near the margin of the core, a flake with very sharp edges suitable for a variety of cutting tasks breaks off. The core itself also now has sharp ridges, but initially, at least, the focus of Mode 1 technology appears to have been the production and use of sharp flakes (Toth and Schick 2009) (Figure 27.2).

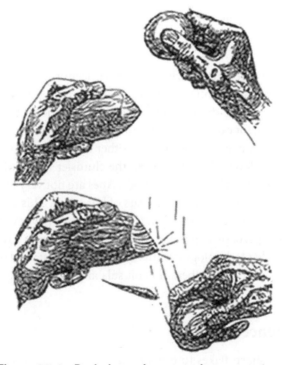

Figure 27.1. Basic knapping procedure or gesture.

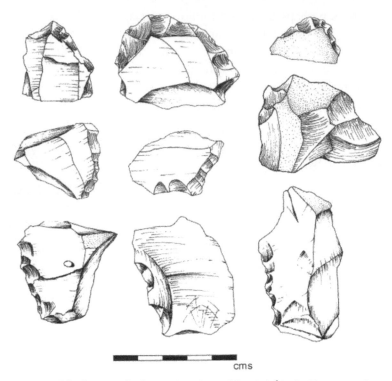

**Figure 27.2. Mode 1 tools from the site of Peninj (de la Torre et al. 2003).**

Basic knapping is not particularly difficult conceptually. There is nothing to indicate that the cognitive abilities of the earliest hominin knappers, such as those at Dikika (see above), were dramatically different from those typical of apes. The captive bonobo, Kanzi, for example, was able to pick up the basic idea fairly quickly in an experimental situation. Neither Kanzi, nor other bonobo knappers, however, have ever acquired the skill level achieved by even the clumsier Mode 1 knappers (Schick et al. 1999; Savage-Rumbaugh and Fields 2006). Apes are not very good at identifying optimal places to strike a core, even after years of knapping. This suggests that by the time of Gona, hominins had been knapping long enough to have evolved at least a few biomechanical, and perhaps cognitive, traits linked to stone knapping. Though initially African, Mode 1 technology eventually spread into Asia and southern Europe. By 1.8 mya it was present on the Iberian Peninsula and in the Caucasus mountains.

## 27.2.2 Subsistence

Hominins used the sharp flakes to butcher carcasses of medium (antelope-sized) and occasionally large (e.g. giraffe) mammals; cut marks on bones preserved at many Mode 1 sites provide direct evidence for this butchery. Hominins also used stone hammers and cores to smash long bones for marrow, and at some Mode 1 sites the presence of stones with crushed surfaces indicates that the hominins were pounding more than just bones (Mora and de la Torre 2005), possibly also roots or corms, though pounding meat itself would have rendered it easier to digest (Wrangham 2009). It is impossible to measure how significant meat was to the diet, at least from the archaeological evidence, but it was almost certainly more important than it is currently for modern apes.

### 27.2.3  Social behaviour

The archaeological evidence provides little direct evidence for social organization or behaviour. Most of the excavated sites cover small areas, at most a few tens of square metres, which in turn points to small size for the social unit active at the site. There is no way to tell if these were cohesive social units, or shifting fission-fusion groups similar to those typical for modern chimpanzees. By identifying sources of raw material used for stone tools, however, we can estimate territory sizes up to 150 mi$^2$, compared to 5–15 mi$^2$ for chimpanzees.

### 27.2.4  Summary

For almost two million years, 3.4–1.6 mya, early hominins relied on Mode 1 technology. It enabled them to exploit foods that apes rarely use, and adapt to life in more open tropical woodlands. It even enabled some of these early hominins to expand out of Africa into southern Europe and Asia. But in most respects these early hominins were apes. The first dramatic shift away from an ape way of life emerged about 1.5 mya with the appearance of Mode 2 technologies.

## 27.3  DEVELOPMENTS IN THE *HOMO ERECTUS* ERA

About 1.8 mya *Homo erectus* appeared in East Africa, and very soon after in western and eastern Asia. It was taller, had an almost modern locomotor anatomy, was less sexually dimorphic, and had a larger brain. *Homo erectus* was different enough anatomically that many palaeoanthropologists believe its appearance represented a new evolutionary grade that was much more human-like, and less ape-like, than the many hominins that preceded it. The archaeological record corroborates this assessment.

## 27.3.1 Technology

Initially *Homo erectus* produced a Mode 1 technology, and in many parts of Asia continued to make Mode 1 tools for hundreds of thousands of years. But in Africa, *Homo erectus* produced a new kind of lithic technology that archaeologists term Mode 2 (also known as Acheulean). All of the Mode 1 elements continue in Mode 2, but were augmented by a very different kind of stone tool termed a 'biface'. A biface is large stone tool (>10 cm in maximum dimension) made by trimming the margins of a core or large flake 'bifacially'; i.e. placing trimming blows onto both faces of the tool. Bifacial trimming resulted in two types of tool with sturdy cutting edges around most of their margins: cleavers with an unmodified 'bit' at one end, and handaxes whose sides converged to a narrow tip or point (Figure 27.3).

Experimental replication and use, and analysis of wear patterns, indicate that bifaces were multipurpose tools that were especially good at butchery (Schick and Toth 1993).

Bifaces embodied several 'firsts' in technical evolution. They were the first tools with an imposed overall shape, in this case bilateral symmetry. More importantly, they were the first 'tools' in the modern sense. Earlier Mode 1 tools resulted from a well-learned procedure: strike off a flake, use it, discard

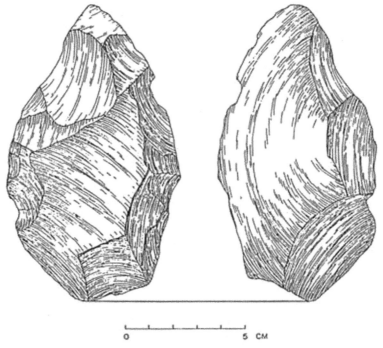

**Figure 27.3. A 1.4-million-year-old handaxe from Tanzania.**

it. They did not exist outside of the context of their use, but bifaces did. *Homo erectus* made them, used them, carried them around, and used them again, often for different tasks. They were continuously at hand, and continuously participated in *Homo erectus* life, suggesting a level of commitment to technology unseen in earlier hominins.

Fire also appears to have been a component of *Homo erectus* technology. The earliest possible evidence for fire consists of charred, butchered bones from the 1.4-million-year-old cave of Swartkrans in South Africa (Brain and Sillen 1988), but lack of any obvious hearths makes many archaeologists sceptical. The earliest generally accepted evidence for fire is considerably later, 790 kya at Gesher Benot Ya'aqov in Israel (Alperson-Afil et al. 2007). However, the rapid expansion of *Homo erectus* into many new habitats, including temperate climates, would certainly have been aided by use of fire for warmth, predator deterrence, and especially for cooking.

Mode 2 technology eventually found its way into the Indian subcontinent and Europe, but not until after 1 mya. Mode 2 has occasionally been described as 'changeless' or 'in stasis', but this is not quite true. Yes, the range of stone tools did not change for almost one million years, but the tools themselves did change—500,000-year-old bifaces were more regular in shape than 1.6-million-year-old bifaces, and had three-dimensional symmetry.

## 27.3.2 Subsistence

Features in anatomy, brain size, and teeth, suggest that *Homo erectus* relied more on meat than earlier hominins. Primatologist Richard Wrangham (2009) has argued that cooking was a key component to this shift. Unfortunately, as noted above, archaeology provides only minimal evidence for fire prior to 790 kya, and no solid evidence for hunting until even later. We know that hominins using Mode 2 tools butchered large animals, and we even have evidence that they used bifaces on wood, *perhaps* to make spears (Dominguez-Rodrigo et al. 2001).

## 27.3.3 Social behaviour

The size of Mode 2 sites suggests that *Homo erectus* face-to-face groups continued to be small, certainly fewer than 50, and there is no indication that these hominins congregated in larger communities. They did learn tool use and tool-making from one another. All appeared to have shared an idea of what a handaxe should look like. This suggests a socially learned standard that was more elaborate, with more components, than anything done by apes.

Bifaces present an unresolved enigma for palaeoanthropologists. As noted, hominins produced the same shape in Africa, parts of Asia, and Europe for hundreds of thousands of years. This shape was a cultural construct (unless there was a biface gene, which seems unlikely) with mind-numbing conservatism. Modern cultural constructs over the past 20,000 years have changed more or less steadily, for a variety of reasons. Something must have been very different about the role played by bifaces in *Homo erectus* life compared to the role of tools in the modern world.

### 27.3.4 Cognition

The archaeological record documents some significant developments in cognition. Bifaces required hominins to coordinate spatial cognition with shape recognition, something apes never do (Wynn 2002). Mode 2 knappers also had to attend to more things when making bifaces—not just knocking off flakes, but also attention to the overall shape of the core. Both of these developments indicate that *Homo erectus* could hold more in mind than earlier hominins (Gibson 1993), something cognitive scientists refer to as working memory capacity.

### 27.3.5 Summary

*Homo erectus*, many using Mode 2 tools, spanned the period of 1.8 mya–500 kya with little dramatic change. They possessed a successful, technically-assisted adaptation that enabled them to live in many different habitats. Still, their culture was very different from that of apes, and from ours.

## 27.4 THE SEEDS OF MODERN LIFE

Sometime about half a million years ago, hominins developed greater cultural complexity, as indicated by a greater variety of cultural activities, a greater number of steps involved in many activities, and more interdependency in the steps. Of course, 500 kya was much closer to the present than 2.5 or 1.5 mya, and many more sites have survived to be studied. Thus, some of this complexity reflects better preservation and better samples, but not all. Also, it is not as easy to generalize about the archaeological record of entire continents as it was for Mode 1 and Mode 2 times. Archaeological patterns in Africa, Europe, and Asia began to diverge from one another, and only one of these cultural trajectories led to ours. Nevertheless, there are enough similarities to provide an outline of important developments.

## 27.4.1 Technology

Although many hominins (in Africa and Europe this was a form known as *Homo heidelbergensis*) continued to make bifaces, the focus in Mode 3 knapping shifted to the production of flakes with a variety of working edges. Knappers developed techniques for managing the volume of cores so that they yielded either a

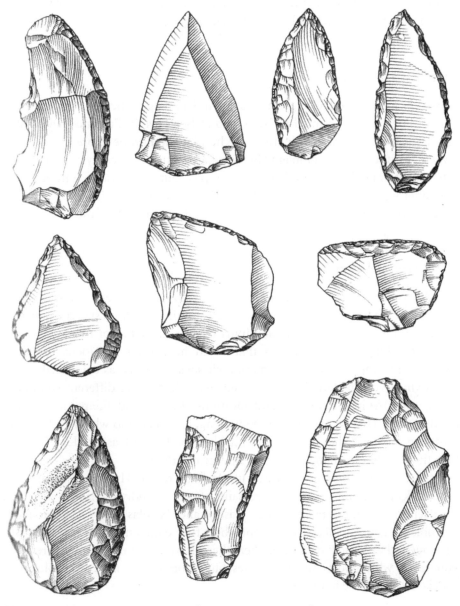

Figure 27.4.  Mode 3 flake tools (after Mellars 1996).

maximum number of large flakes, or even flakes with a particular shape (Figure 27.4). The most famous of these 'prepared core' techniques is known as Levallois.

Knappers then modified the flake edges into shapes and angles that best performed the task at hand. The result was a large array of slightly different edge varieties that performed a concomitant variety of tasks, yielding many different core management techniques and much regional variability.

The oldest hunting spears yet found date to about 400 kya from the German site of Schöningen. Hominins cut down small spruce trees and shaved the trunks into 2-metre long shafts pointed at both ends (Thieme 1997).

## 27.4.2 Subsistence

European hominins hunted large mammals. At Schöningen they hunted horses, at Hoxne in England they hunted roe deer, and at Boxgrove in England they hunted horses and giant elk. Archaeologists 'see' hunting in Europe more clearly than elsewhere because successful foraging in temperate latitudes generally requires greater reliance on animal products than in the tropics, but also because Europe is just much better known archaeologically. Plants do not preserve well in the archaeological record, but they were likely to have been an important part of the diet.

## 27.4.3 Social behaviour

About this time, the archaeological record begins to show evidence for a different kind of social life from that practised by earlier hominins. Group size continued to be small, and even though these hominins made regular use of fire, there is no evidence for long-burning hearths that could have been the focus of group interaction. But they had begun to mark their social identity, as evidenced by the site of Twin Rivers in Zambia, where residents collected five different colours of mineral, some from different distant locations, and ground them into powder (Barham 2002). They were colouring something, but what, and why? Most archaeologists suspect that they were colouring their bodies just as modern humans colour their bodies to change how they appear to others.

Another first was mortuary treatment. At Sima de los Huesos in Spain, also about 400 kya, hominins placed the remains of over 30 individuals into a vertical shaft deep in a limestone cave (de Castro and Nicolas 1997). The remains are jumbled together. This is clearly not where they died, and there is no obvious natural agent that could have carried them there. It would be an over-interpretation to equate this with modern mortuary rites, but it does suggest added complexity in the social lives of these hominins.

## 27.4.4 Cognition

Hominins who lived half a million years ago had brain sizes in the low end of the modern range (1200–1300 cc). Not surprisingly, the archaeological record documents changes in cognition. Spatial cognition achieved its modern scope at this time; core management techniques and bifaces with beautiful three-dimensional symmetry attest to a modern ability to conceive of and control three-dimensional Euclidean space (Wynn 2002). Technical cognition was also very sophisticated. Many of the core management techniques required flexible procedural cognition equivalent to that used by modern craft production, as well as an increase in working memory capacity (Wynn and Coolidge 2010). Use of pigments to alter appearance suggests developments in social cognition, especially an enhanced theory of mind, the ability to imagine what another sees and knows. Thus, these hominins were cognitively modern in some, though not all, respects.

## 27.5 NEANDERTHALS

Neanderthals were a population of European archaic humans whose evolutionary lineage split from that of *Homo sapiens* about 500 kya and who disappear from the archaeological record sometime after 30 kya. Culturally they were very similar to the African ancestors of modern humans who lived at the same time, but they did not acquire many of the features of modern life eventually associated with modern human behaviour. Their technology, known by archaeologists as 'Mousterian' or 'Middle Palaeolithic', continued the emphasis on core management and flake technology developed by their European ancestors, and showed little evidence of innovation. They did introduce hafting of stone points onto spears, but this was about the only significant technological innovation in their 200,000-year tenure. Neanderthals were very effective hunters, often focusing on the largest mammals available on the local landscape (including mammoth in Northern Europe). They lived out their lives in small face-to-face groups, and had little contact with other Neanderthals outside their local territories. Neanderthals practised a minimal kind of corpse treatment, placing bodies in protected places, occasionally scooping out shallow pits. They made extensive use of pigments, again probably for body decoration, but produced no depictive images and little or nothing resembling modern symbol use. Cognitively they were adept stone knappers, and had expert knowledge of their local territories, but their heavy reliance on well-learned procedural memories and failures to innovate may have put them at a disadvantage when modern humans arrived in Europe about 40 kya.

## 27.6 THE EMERGENCE OF MODERN CULTURE

The evolution of *Homo sapiens* can be divided into two phases. Modern anatomy first appeared about 200 kya in Africa (Shea et al. 2007), but for the next 100,000 years the archaeological signature of these 'anatomically modern humans' was decidedly archaic. Only after 100 kya did populations in Africa begin to acquire features of behaviour that clearly distinguished them from archaic humans. And after 70 kya, these behaviourally modern people began an expansion out of Africa that rapidly extended over the inhabitable world, including Australia and the New World.

### 27.6.1 Technology

Although developments in stone tools have often been touted as accompanying the emergence of modern behaviour, especially the manufacture of long, thin flakes known as blades, such techniques were no more difficult or complex than the techniques of Mode 3 knapping. Mode 3 technology, however, included only a few non-lithic tools (e.g. the Schöningen spears), whereas after 100 kya in Africa, *Homo sapiens* began producing a greater variety of tools in bone, including bone projectile points and bone awls. They, too, hafted points onto spears. These developments required no cognitive leap beyond what we know for archaic humans. The most significant change in technology left little direct evidence—the gradual shift from 'maintainable' to 'reliable' tools.

Reliable tools are ones that require more time and effort to make, but which are more effective when actually used. They are often multicomponent tools with complex linkages of elements. One example of such a system is a harpoon set, which includes a spear thrower, spear, detachable fore-shaft, and thin bifacial stone projectile point or barbed bone point. These are time-consuming to make, but very effective killing devices (Bleed 1986). The earliest such devices appeared in Europe only about 20 kya, but simpler antecedents appeared in Africa as early as 90 kya (Yellen et al. 1995). Equally reliable are traps, which are remotely operated hunting facilities. Traps are rarely found in the archaeological record, because, until the last few thousand years, they would have consisted primarily of wood and cordage, which do not preserve well. The oldest direct evidence is only about 10,000 years old, but indirect evidence extends much further back—75,000-year-old sites in South Africa have yielded remains of blue duiker, a small antelope that inhabits dense undergrowth and which is almost invariably captured by means of traps because it is extremely difficult to hunt using projectiles (Wadley 2010).

## 27.6.2 Subsistence

As with technology, the subsistence of modern humans was initially no different from that of archaic humans such as Neanderthals. One-hundred-thousand-year-old archaeological evidence documents two trends. The first was a broadening of the range of resources hunted and gathered. People began to adjust their foraging endeavours according to the nature of locally available resources, and they began to include foods rarely eaten by archaic humans, such as fish and shellfish. The second trend involved scheduling of foraging activities to optimize use of seasonally available resources. This included the use of fire to alter landscapes and change the foraging schedules of prey animals. And for the first time, the range of resources preserved in archaeological sites suggests a modern form of hunting and gathering with a marked division of labour by age and sex (Kuhn and Stiner 2006). In other words, the modern form of hunting and gathering evolved after 100,000 years ago, with *Homo sapiens*.

## 27.6.3 Social behaviour

The most significant behavioural developments associated with modern humans were in the domain of social behaviour. By the time of the European Upper Palaeolithic (ca. 40–12 kya) some archaeological sites were large enough to suggest face-to-face group sizes of well over 100, and there were more groups on the landscape. Even taking into account the better preservation of more recent sites, there were many more later Palaeolithic sites, over a shorter time range, than those of archaic humans. Finally, later Palaeolithic people were the first to establish and maintain long-range contacts between groups. Evidence for this comes from raw material, and occasionally artefacts, found hundreds of kilometres from their point of origin (Ambrose 2001).

Later Palaeolithic people developed material systems to mediate this larger-scale social world. Evidence for beads extends back almost to 100 kya in South Africa (d'Errico et al. 2005; d'Errico and Vanhaeren, this volume). Although interpretations of their significance have been controversial, most archaeologists agree that they must have been social markers of some sort, which in turn suggests interaction outside the daily face-to-face group (all of whom would already know someone's status). At the same time, the archaeological evidence includes the appearance of styles of artefacts, including stone tools that were distinctive for small regions, and perhaps tied to specific face-to-face groups.

Arguably the most famous developments of this time period are the traditions of depictive art. Though the archaeological record has yielded earlier, isolated, enigmatic, examples of possible depictions, the first convincing examples date to 50 kya

**Figure 27.5. Painted images of horses, cattle, and deer from Lascaux, ca. 17 kya.**

(d'Errico et al. 2003). The most spectacular examples are the cave paintings of the European Upper Palaeolithic (Figure 27.5), but examples of equivalent antiquity and sophistication occur in Africa, South Asia, and Australia. Interpretations of this art have ranged from the mundane to the fanciful. What is perhaps most telling is its resonance for anyone who sees it. It reminds us of ourselves.

## 27.6.4 Cognition

Consider several of the activities apparent from the archaeological record of modern humans:

1. Reliable, multicomponent tools and remotely operated facilities such as traps.
2. Diversified, seasonally scheduled and managed hunting and gathering with sex- and age-based division of labour.
3. Large social groups with long distance social networks.

What all of these activities share is a reliance on long-range planning ability, not just over hours and days, but over months and even years. It is often assumed that the emergence of symbolism and language are sufficient to account for these planning abilities. However, the findings of modern cognitive science indicate that planning and strategizing requires executive functions that have a clear neurological basis separate from the language-dedicated networks of the brain. A key component of executive functions is working memory capacity, the ability to hold information in attention and process it (Coolidge and Wynn 2005). Thus, though symbolic ability was clearly required for modern cognition, developments in executive reasoning ability were also necessary.

By the end of the Palaeolithic, roughly 12 kya, all of the components of modern culture were in place, and provided the foundation for the spectacular developments that followed.

# CHAPTER 28

# MUSICALITY AND LANGUAGE

## STEVEN MITHEN

Music and language are human universals, being found in all known communities of modern humans and in all individuals not suffering from cognitive or physical pathologies. Both can be vocal, gestural, and written down; both are hierarchically structured, being constituted by acoustic elements (words or tones) that are combined into phrases (utterances or melodies) which can be further combined to make language or musical events; and both languages and musical styles can be described as forming families within which patterns of descent, blending, and development can be reconstructed.

In light of such similarities, it is astonishing that music has received minimal attention in the literature on the origin of language. This neglect is one reason why progress in understanding the origin and evolution of language has been limited. It is surprising because previous scholars did not doubt that there was a co-evolution of music and language. In 1895, Otto Jespersen wrote that 'language began with half-musical analysed expressions for individual beings and events' (Jespersen 1983 [1895]: 365). He was not the first to associate the evolution of language with music; Jean Jacques Rousseau's 1781 *Essai sur l'origine des langues* was a reflection on both music and language (see Thomas 1995). More recently, the ethnomusicologist John Blacking (1973) argued that there had once been a 'nonverbal, prelinguistic, musical mode of thought and action'.

Communication with babies and infants has a particularly high degree of musicality. This is known as infant-directed speech (IDS) or 'motherese'; see de

Boer, Chapter 33; Falk, Chapter 32. The key characteristics of IDS are the extended articulation of vowels, heightened pitch, and exaggerated pitch contours. Research by Fernald (e.g. 1992) and others (e.g. Papousek et al. 1991; Monnot 1999) has shown that these are not simply used to facilitate the acquisition of language by infants; the musicality of speech has its own function in terms of its emotional impact on the infant. It would seem unlikely that infantile musical capacities could be a spin-off from language acquisition, while the musicality of IDS has been argued to be critical to the acquisition of language (Trehub 2003).

Further evidence indicating a close association between music and language comes from how the brain processes and generates language and music. Studies of those suffering from brain damage or congenital conditions show that music and language have significant degrees of independence in the brain, even a double dissociation. Hence some individuals who suffer from aphasia appear to have intact musical abilities (e.g. Luria et al. 1965; Miller 1989). Conversely those suffering from amusia appear to have intact linguistic abilities (e.g. Peretz et al. 2002)—although the evidence for this is more questionable. On the other hand, brain scanning has indicated that there are significant overlaps concerning which brain regions are recruited for music and language (Maess et al. 2001; Parsons 2003; Patel 2003). While the evidence from neuroscience remains open to various interpretations, such evidence will become increasingly central to our understanding of the relationship between music and language (Patel 2007).

A more usual and profitable way of drawing evolutionary implications from the modern world is by comparative primatology. Many studies document continuities in behaviour, perception, cognition, and neurophysiology between human speech and primate vocal communication (Seyfarth 2005). As such, it appears likely that human language evolved from a communication system that had strong similarities to that used by primates, although some scholars reject this idea (e.g. Bickerton 1990).

Primate calls are holistic utterances—they are not constituted by words combined with grammatical rules. They are limited in number and used in restricted contexts, the classic examples being the predator alarm calls of vervets (Struhsaker 1967) and the pant hoots of chimpanzees (Mitani 1996). Primate calls are thus more similar to human musical phrases than to spoken utterances. Indeed, they can have a significant degree of musicality (see Richman 1987 for geladas and Geissmann 2000 for gibbons). In general, the variations of pitch, rhythm, tone, and timbre of primate vocalizations—that is, their musicality—play an essential role in manipulating the emotional states and behaviour of other individuals.

All of these lines of evidence suggest that a reasonable hypothesis is that music and language co-evolved, or even that language was derivative of a musical form of communication. When evaluated against the fossil and archaeological record, this hypothesis is persuasive (see Mithen 2005 for detailed discussion). Studies of the fossil record indicate that breathing control in the common ancestor of Neanderthals and anatomically modern humans was sufficient to allow diverse and complex utterances (MacLarnon and Hewitt 2004; see MacLarnon, this volume). Reconstructions of the Neanderthal vocal tract indicate that this was not significantly different to that of modern humans (Morley 2002). Moreover, the complete bipedalism of *Homo ergaster* and all later hominins (Bramble and Lieberman 2004) indicates that the fully modern range of gestures and body postures, which are so often combined with spoken utterances by modern humans, may have been possible (Mithen 2005). While such fossil evidence suggests that the capacity for spoken language may have been present, the archaeological evidence provides no indication of such language-mediated behaviour, suggesting that a musical-like form of communication may have been present.

The archaeological record of pre-modern humans (i.e. pre *Homo sapiens*) is characterized by immense cultural stability. Oldowan, Acheulean, and Mousterian stone tool industries, lasting between 2.5 and 0.04 million years ago, change remarkably slowly, with limited technological progress within each industry. This is incompatible with a language-using species because spoken utterances provide a vehicle of cultural innovation and change (Mithen 2005). Wray (2000) suggests that this pattern of cultural stability in the archaeological record indicates communication by holistic rather than compositional utterances. Similarly, there are no unambiguous traces of symbolic behaviour in the archaeological records of pre-modern humans. This is again incompatible with the idea that such humans were communicating by the use of audible symbols (i.e. words)—if these were being used, so would visual symbols, of which there are no trace until the emergence of modern humans in Africa after 200,000 years.

Combining the fossil record for complex utterances and the archaeological evidence for an absence of language-mediated behaviour, the parsimonious conclusion is that pre-modern humans communicated by a form of 'music-language' (Brown 2000). This implies that language and musicality co-evolved, remaining as a single, non-symbolic, but emotionally potent form of communication until relatively late in human evolution. Only with the emergence of modern humans did this communication system bifurcate into the two separate systems that we today describe as language and music (Mithen 2005).

This particular evolutionary scenario may not be correct. But with the multiple lines of evidence coming from developmental psychology, neuroscience, primate studies, fossil and archaeological records, along with our knowledge of music and language themselves, it appears likely that the evolutionary histories of music and language are intimately linked.

# CHAPTER 29

# LINGUISTIC IMPLICATIONS OF THE EARLIEST PERSONAL ORNAMENTS

## FRANCESCO D'ERRICO AND MARIAN VANHAEREN

Until recently, the invention of personal ornaments was considered to be synonymous with the colonization of Europe by anatomically modern populations, some 40 thousand years ago (kya). Association of ornaments with other symbolic manifestations such as cave art and decorated objects has been used to support the hypothesis that modern language emerged abruptly at that time (Ruhlen 1994; Greenberg 2000). We know now that marine shells were used as beads in the Near East, North Africa, and Sub-Saharan Africa at least 35 kya earlier. Nine sites—Qafzeh and Skhul in Israel, Oued Djebbana in Algeria, Taforalt, Rhafas, Ifri n'Ammar, Contrebandiers in Morocco, Blombos Cave and Sibudu in South Africa—have yielded evidence of an ancient use of personal ornaments (d'Errico et al. 2009). Perforated shells from Qafzeh consist of *Glycymeris insubrica* bivalves, those from the next six sites consist of *Nassarius gibbosulus*, and those from Blombos are *Nassarius kraussianus*, marine gastropods common at present on

Eastern Mediterranean shores and in South African estuaries respectively. Analyses of these shells demonstrate that they were consistently used as personal ornaments, probably by modern humans, between 100 kya and 70 kya: shells used as beads from North African and Near East sites are not leftovers from human food because the animals were dead when collected. Three of the Moroccan sites yielding beads are located 40–60 km inland; the site from Algeria is 190 km from the sea. This suggests that the presence of beads at inland sites is the probable archaeological signature of well-established networks linking coastal areas and inland regions. Traces of manufacture and use-wear demonstrate that the shells were strung and the resulting beadworks worn for a long period of time. The presence of pigment residues on almost all well-preserved shell beads from these sites distinctly links bead and pigment use, further reinforcing the argument for their deliberate symbolic use.

This personal ornament tradition seems to disappear at the end of the last interglacial (ca. 70 kya) (d'Errico and Vanhaeren 2009), a disappearance that has been attributed to the impact of a 10,000-year-long cold climatic phase (Marine Isotope Stage 4) on demography and population dynamics (d'Errico et al. 2009; Powell et al. 2009). Around 40 kya, beads reappear almost simultaneously in Africa and the Near East, and for the first time in Europe and Asia. In Africa they take the form of ostrich eggshell beads and stone rings. In Europe the earliest ornaments are associated with both Neanderthals and modern humans and take the form of dozens of discrete, regionally patterned types (Vanhaeren and d'Errico 2006). The presence of personal ornaments at late Neanderthal sites has been variously interpreted as the consequence of acculturation of local Neanderthals by incoming Aurignacians, as independent cultural evolution of Neanderthals before the spread of the Aurignacian, or as cross-cultural fertilization of late Neanderthals and Aurignacian Moderns (Zilhão et al. 2006 and references therein).

Analysis of a geospatial database recording the occurrence of 157 bead types at 98 Aurignacian sites has identified a definite cline in ornament types, sweeping counter-clockwise from the Northern Plains to the Eastern Alps, via Western and Southern Europe, through 14 geographically cohesive sets of sites. The sets most distant from each other do not share any bead types but share personal ornament types with intermediate sets. It has been argued, based on the role that beadworks play in a number of traditional societies, that this pattern may reflect long-lasting ethnolinguistic diversity in the earliest modern human populations of Europe (Vanhaeren and d'Errico 2006).

The arguments put forward to link personal ornaments to the emergence of language are of various kinds. The most common extends to humans the principle of uniformitarianism that represents the foundation of the natural sciences: the cross-cultural analysis of historically known human societies can identify regularities that may help shed light on the way people communicated in the past (Tschauner 1996). Prehistoric societies which show in their social and cultural systems the same degree of complexity recorded in historically known societies must have had comparable means of communication (d'Errico et al. 2003; d'Errico and Vanhaeren 2009). A second argument seeks to link language and the symbolic function of ornaments. Since a key characteristic of all symbols is that their meaning is assigned by arbitrary, socially constructed conventions, a connection must exist between the eminently symbolic character of human language and the creation of the material expression of symbolic thought in human cultures (Donald 1991; Deacon 1997; Aiello 1998; Henshilwood and Marean 2003). Only a communication system like human language can transmit the symbolic meaning of signs and the structured links between them. According to some authors (Vanhaeren 2005 and references therein) this is particularly true when the physical body is used as a means of display. Beadwork represents a technology specific to humans which signals their ability to project social information to members of the same or neighbouring groups by means of a shared symbolic language (Vanhaeren and d'Errico 2006; Kuhn and Stiner 2007). Symbols applied to the physical body ascribe collectively-defined social status to the wearers that can be understood by the other members of the group only if the latter share the complex codes that establish a link between the worn items, the place and way they are displayed on the body, the social categorization they signal, and the symbolic meaning carried by the objects (d'Errico et al. 2003; Vanhaeren 2005; Vanhaeren and d'Errico 2006; d'Errico and Vanhaeren 2009).

Henshilwood and Dubreuil (2009) favour the ornaments-language equation on cognitive grounds: the capacity to represent how an object appears to another person (i.e. level-2 perspective-taking in developmental psychology, Flavell 1992) is necessary for the invention of symbolic artefacts like beads. Because recursion is essential to articulate in language the kind of meta-representations provided by level-2 perspective-taking and theory of mind, the authors predict that the presence of syntactic language can confidently be 'read' from complex symbolic material culture.

These arguments are not universally accepted and some scholars have countered that personal ornamentation is not conclusive with respect to language and, in particular, to syntax (Donald 1998). Wynn and Coolidge (2007) contend that early beads may only reflect attention to personal identity and do not necessarily stand for something else. They accept, however, that this requires a level of intentionality typical of modern human interaction.

By applying a deconstructivist approach, Botha (2008) contends that some inferential steps on which the bead-language equation is based are problematic, either because they are not underpinned by well-articulated theories of what 'fully syntactical language' is or because they do not fully explain why a complex language form is required for transmitting the symbolic meanings associated with the use of ornaments; see Botha, this volume.

In spite of these caveats most archaeologists accept that beadworks dated to 100 kya and 70 kya indicate a deliberate, shared, and transmitted form of symbolic behaviour and that to be conveyed over such a wide geographic area, this behaviour must have implied powerful cultural conventions. It can be argued that only beings in possession of language or language-like systems of representation could have created and maintained such conventions. This argument may also apply to Neanderthals. Beads found at late Neanderthals sites are more varied and complex than those produced in Africa and the Near East by early modern humans 80–70 kya, and comparable to those produced by Aurignacian moderns and historically known hunter-gatherers. Applying a uniformitarian logic, such facts suggest that Neanderthals must have had a communication system equivalent to the one we can infer for Aurignacian moderns (d'Errico and Vanhaeren 2009). This point of view is consistent with recent genetic evidence (Krause et al. 2007) indicating that human mutations in a critical gene known to underlie vocal praxis, and hence, articulate speech—namely *FOXP2*—were also present in the Neanderthal genome (see Diller and Cann, this volume). For anti-uniformitarianists (see Bickerton 2009c) the presence of the genetic basis for vocal praxis and a complex symbolic material culture do not represent enough proof that these populations had fully-modern language. Their argument is that since protolanguage may support the creation of symbolic codes, ornaments may just signal a form of 'speech' rather than language. This raises the question of how complex a symbolic material culture must be to unambiguously reflect the use of syntactic language. If the significance of ornaments was more precisely evaluated in this respect, as recently suggested by d'Errico (in his contribution to Számadó et al. 2009), the discovery of such artefacts could provide valuable information about the evolutionary steps that led to modern language. Correlates of functions integral to syntax, such as hierarchical organization, compositionality, recursion, and links between distant elements are found in complex symbolic non-linguistic codes. The discovery of symbolic artefacts displaying codes of such complexity may open the path to the identification of the earliest past populations with syntactic language.

# CHAPTER 30

# INFERRING MODERN LANGUAGE FROM ANCIENT OBJECTS

## RUDOLF BOTHA

## 30.1 INTRODUCTION

Inferences about facets of language evolution form a core component of important archaeological accounts of the emergence of modern human behaviour. Drawn stepwise from data or assumptions about properties of material objects, these inferences typically attribute a particular stage of language to some group of prehistoric humans. From properties of ancient shell beads, for example, it has been inferred that the humans who inhabited Blombos Cave in South Africa in the Middle Stone Age (MSA) had 'fully syntactical language' some 75 thousand years ago (kya) (Henshilwood et al. 2004; d'Errico et al. 2005). Such inferences owe their potential archaeological significance to two fundamental assumptions: (1) that the key criterion for modern human behaviour is the use of symbolism for organizing that behaviour (Wadley 2001; Henshilwood and Marean 2003), and (2) that 'fully syntactical language'—referred to also as 'modern language'—is required for organizing behaviour symbolically (Mellars 1998a, b; McBrearty and Brooks 2000; Henshilwood and Marean 2003). Clearly, then, the use of 'modern' or 'fully syntactical language' is held to be distinctive of modern human behaviour, also called 'human modernity' (Henshilwood and Dubreuil 2009: 65); see also d'Errico and Vanhaeren, this volume.

The line of thinking noted above cannot succeed unless the inferences attributing modern or fully syntactic language to groups such as the inhabitants of Blombos Cave are sound. And it is this need that gives rise to the four questions to be pursued in the present chapter: (1) What conditions must inferences about facets of language evolution meet to be sound? (2) How well do archaeological inferences about the emergence, use, and properties of modern or fully syntactic language meet these conditions? (3) What are the problems that detract from the soundness of such inferences? (4) How successfully have these problems been addressed in the literature?

In this chapter, I confine myself to the inference that the MSA inhabitants of Blombos Cave had fully syntactic language—henceforth the 'Blombos inference'— for two reasons. First, this inference represents an important class of archaeological inferences about language evolution. Second, the inference is believed to be of great potential significance. Blombos Cave—located on the southern Cape coast about 300 km east of Cape Town—is considered by some archaeologists to be ' . . . the most important currently known archaeological site for understanding the origin of modern thought and behaviour—and, by implication, language' (Mithen 2005: 250).

## 30.2 STRUCTURE OF THE BLOMBOS INFERENCE

It is not possible to assess the soundness of the Blombos inference without referring to its structure. The inference is composed of various non-compound inferences, each including a distinct inferential step. When reconstructed as in Figure 30.1— from accounts such as Henshilwood et al. (2004) and d'Errico et al. (2005)—the Blombos inference is seen to use three consecutive inferential steps as, from data about a number of material objects, it draws a conclusion about a facet of language evolution (Botha 2008, 2009b).

The inferential steps B, D, and F involve the following:

1. B represents the step by which it is inferred from data and/or assumptions about properties of a number of MSA tick shells that these shells were beads worn by the humans who inhabited Blombos Cave some 75 kya. The data and/or assumptions are about properties of 41 shells of the scavenging gastropod *Nassarius kraussianus*. These properties of the shells include: (1) their age, (2) their man-made perforations, (3) their flattened facets, and (4) their distribution

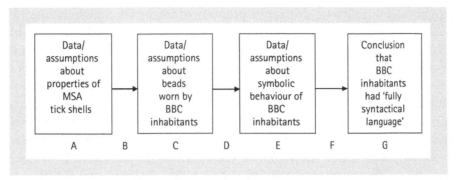

**Figure 30.1. Structure of the compound inference about the language used by the inhabitants of Blombos Cave.**
('Blombos Cave' is abbreviated in boxes C, E, and G as 'BBC'.)

in groups in the cave. (The properties at issue are more fully described in Botha 2008.)

2. D represents the step by which it is inferred from data and/or assumptions about these beads—or, more precisely, the beadworks of which they formed part—that these humans engaged in symbolic behaviour. One such assumption is that the beads were worn as personal ornaments.

3. F represents the step by which it is inferred from data and/or assumptions about this symbolic behaviour that these humans had fully syntactic language. It is assumed, for instance, that this behaviour involved the transmitting and sharing of symbolic meaning.

For compound inferences to be sound, each of their constituent non-compound inferences needs to be sound. To see what this involves in the case of the Blombos inference, we examine below its constituent represented by box E, arrow F, and box G in Figure 30.1, the symbols-to-syntax inference, for short.

# 30.3 SOUNDNESS OF THE
## SYMBOLS-TO-SYNTAX INFERENCE

To be sound, the symbols-to-syntax inference needs to meet a number of fundamental conditions, including the following one (Botha 2006a, 2008, 2009b):

(1)    The Warrantedness Condition
       The inferential step leading to some conclusion about language evolution needs to be suitably warranted or licensed.

This condition reflects a distinctive property of inferences drawn in empirical work about language evolution: the data or assumptions from which the inferential steps start out are always about one thing, whereas the conclusions with which these steps end up are always about something else. In particular, the conclusions are about language evolution, and the data or assumptions are about some phenonemon distinct from language evolution. In the Blombos inference, for example, inferential step F starts out from assumptions about MSA symbolic behaviour. This raises a question: why is it permissible or warranted to move, from assumptions about the Blombos Cave inhabitants' (presumed) symbolic behaviour, to the conclusion that they had fully syntactic language? Doubts about the existence of a simple link between symbolic behaviour and language evolution have been expressed by some archaeologists too, including Graves (1994), Chase (1999), Mithen (1999b), and Davidson (2003).

The Warrantedness Condition requires that the inferential steps should be underpinned by 'bridge theories' (Botha 2003, 2006a, 2009b). Such theories warrant the inferential steps by providing accounts of how properties of the phenomenon that the steps start out from—the 'departure' phenomenon—interlink with properties attributed to language evolution—the 'destination' phenomenon. To the extent that such theories have merit, they serve as the bridges over which to move inferentially from the 'departure' properties to the 'destination' properties. And to have some merit, bridge theories need to be made up of hypotheses that are explicitly stated, non-ad hoc, and supported by empirical evidence. It certainly would not do if the warrant for an inferential step were a mere stipulation: an arbitrary assertion to the effect that data or assumptions about some phenomenon other than language evolution bear on the correctness of claims about some facet of language evolution. This gives rise to the question, is the inferential step from symbolic behaviour to modern or fully syntactic language underpinned by an adequate bridge theory?

## 30.3.1 Transmitting and sharing symbolic meaning

Though the need for constructs such as bridge theories is recognized in earlier literature (d'Errico et al. 2003), that literature does not contain explicit proposals of a bridge theory which provides a warrant for the inferential step at issue (Botha 2008, 2009b). Only the core assumption of such a theory is alluded to in statements such as the following (Henshilwood et al. 2004: 404):

Fully syntactical language is arguably an essential requisite to share and transmit the symbolic meaning of beadworks and abstract engravings such as those from Blombos Cave.

Elsewhere, one finds similar formulations in terms of which fully syntactic language is claimed to be 'the only means of', 'essential for', 'necessary for', or a 'direct link to' the symbolic meaning or behaviour at issue (d'Errico et al. 2003: 6, 2005;

Henshilwood and Marean 2003: 636). The assumption that fully syntactic language is an essential requisite for aspects of symbolic meaning or behaviour cannot, though, by itself be a complete bridge theory warranting inferential step F. This theory—the 'transmission theory' for short—needs to be a theory which addresses questions such as the following: (1) What are the specifics of the meanings that were shared or transmitted? (2) Why was fully syntactic language rather than a less fully evolved stage of (syntactic) language needed for sharing or transmitting these specifics or specifics of this kind? (3) Why could these specifics not be shared or transmitted by some non-verbal means of communication? (4) How, in essence, do meanings whose transmission requires fully syntactic language differ from meanings transmissible by less fully evolved language or by non-verbal means? (5) What are the cognitive capacities or processes involved in the sharing and transmitting at issue? The required transmission theory should evidently meet the standards of adequacy adopted in empirical science. That is, rather than comprise ad hoc stipulations, the theory should express testable claims supported by empirical evidence or considerations (Botha 2009b). In the absence of such a theory the inferential step from symbolic behaviour to fully syntactic language cannot be considered sound.

## 30.3.2  Verbalizing or articulating meta-representations

Henshilwood and Dubreuil (2009) have recently admitted that syntactic language has been 'linked' to symbolic culture in a questionable way, agreeing with Wynn and Coolidge (2007) that beads, ochres, and engraved bones cannot stand as evidence for modern cognition, including language, unless it is specified what cognitive abilities these artefacts require. In proposing what the cognitive abilities at issue may be, Henshilwood and Dubreuil (2009) present what may be considered a bridge theory capable of warranting the inferential step from symbolic culture to syntactic language. In outline, they reason as follows:

(2)  (a)  The invention and maintenance of MSA symbolic culture – such as that attributed to the Blombos inhabitants – requires the higher-level cognitive ability of level-2 perspective-taking.

(b)  Level-2 perspective-taking involves the construction of hierarchical meta-representations.

(c)  Recursive syntax is required for verbalizing or articulating these meta-representations.

(d)  Recursive syntax is the defining feature of modern language.

(e)  Modern language, therefore, 'came along' with level-2 perspective-taking as part of modern cognition.

Turning to (2a), level-2 perspective-taking is said to be the ability to represent in the mind different—and even conflicting—perspectives of an object (see d'Errico and Vanhaeren, this volume). It involves a person's ability to reconstruct how an object looks from another person's perspective. This ability is claimed to appear in children at a relatively young age as the result of a change in their cognition. Henshilwood and Dubreuil (2009: 82) now contend that

...the emergence of artefacts such as Blombos beads and engraved ochres *could* indicate that a similar cognitive change occurred during the MSA. Beads *could* come to symbolize social statuses (e.g. one's position within a kinship structure), because people *would* have been able to recognize the stability of its meaning across contexts. [emphases added—R.B.]

It is clear from the words emphasized that, for claims made in empirical work, these claims are quite speculative. But let us accept for the sake of argument that the humans in question did have the ability of level-2 perspective-taking. And let us also accept the claim expressed in (2b), i.e. that level-2 perspective-taking involves the construction of hierarchical meta-representations.

We turn next to (2c), a claim crucial to Henshilwood and Dubreuil's reasoning about the way in which syntax is linked to the meta-representations at issue. Their unpacking of claim (2c) is instructive (2009: 88–89):

Imagine a language with a linear syntax, in which the meaning of a word changes with the position of the word in the sentence. The meaning of 'Bob hit Fred', for instance, would be different from the meaning of 'Fred hit Bob'. Such a language would be insufficient to verbalize the kind of meta-representations associated with level-2 perspective-taking and ToM [i.e. theory of mind—R.B.]. Meta-representations have to be articulated in a hierarchical way by embedding clauses, as in sentences like: 'Fred sees that I wear the beads' or 'Fred knows that I am the chief'. Without recursive syntax, it is impossible to articulate conflicting perspectives.

Though the expressions 'verbalize' and 'articulate' are crucial in (2c), their meaning is not clear, allowing at least two construals.

First, to say that clausal embedding is required 'to verbalize' or 'articulate' a meta-representation may be to claim that conveying the content of the meta-representation by means of language requires a particular kind of complex sentence. Such a claim would be false, however, since any unit of (cognitive) content or (semantic) meaning can be conveyed by using non-complex sentences, i.e. clauses, in juxtaposition—neither the whole nor its units being formed through recursion. This is illustrated by Newmeyer (2004: 4), who observes that the propositionally complex meaning conveyed by a complex sentence such as 'Mary thought that John would leave' can be conveyed just as fully by a juxtaposition of two clauses such as those in 'Here is what Mary thought. John was going to leave'. Similarly, to verbalize or articulate the content of a particular meta-representation, one can use either a complex sentence like 'Fred sees that I wear the beads' or a juxtaposition of the two clauses in 'Fred sees this. I wear the beads'. The clauses can even be used in the reverse order—i.e. 'I wear the beads. Fred sees this'—for conveying the complex meaning in question.

There is independent evidence that complex sentences are not necessary for conveying complex meanings such as those at issue. Thus, on various analyses, clausal embedding is not used by certain restricted linguistic systems, including: (1) the systems acquired by adults who learn a second language naturally (Klein and Perdue 1992, 1997), (2) homesign systems created by deaf children of hearing parents (Heine and Kuteva 2007), and (3) twins' languages (Bakker 1987, 2006; Heine and Kuteva 2007). In addition, early pidgins and creoles are claimed to have less subordination than their later developmental forms (Heine and Kuteva 2007). And, on some analyses, there are full modern languages such as Pirahã (Everett 2005; Parker 2005) that use recursion in a limited way only, if at all. (But see also Heine and Kuteva 2007: 272–273 in this regard.) That languages only need quite limited syntactic means for the purpose of communication is also shown by Gil's (2005, 2008) analysis of Riau Indonesian; see Carstairs-McCarthy, Chapter 50.

Second, on a less natural construal, 'to articulate' a meta-representation could mean to form or construct it by embedding clauses within clauses. On this construal, the claims cited would be questionable since they conflate two kinds of entities: meta-representations being units of cognitive content, and clauses being units of linguistic form. It would be no trivial exercise to show that the linguistic units are used here as components of the cognitive ones or to show that meta-representations of the kind in question are formed by means of a linguistic computation with the formal properties of recursive embedding.

Since (2c) is untenable, it does not follow that (2e) is true, i.e. that modern language came along with level-2 perspective-taking as part of modern cognition. (2e) would not even follow if (2d) (itself controversial; see Parker 2005) were accepted. In its present form, accordingly, Henshilwood and Dubreuil's account of the link between level-2 perspective-taking and recursive syntax falls short of being the bridge theory needed to warrant the inferential step from symbolic culture/behaviour to modern language. This does not imply that the MSA inhabitants of Blombos Cave lacked modern language. It means, more restrictively, that without drawing on an adequate bridge theory, amongst other necessities, it is not possible to infer from assumptions about the presumed symbolic culture/behaviour of these humans that they had modern language.

## 30.4 THE BIGGER PICTURE

The soundness of the Blombos inference, then, is jeopardized by the fact that the inferential step taken in one of its constituents, the symbols-to-syntax inference, fails the Warrantedness Condition. Some other difficulties, briefly noted below, also harm its soundness.

## 30.4.1 Further conditions

The symbols-to-syntax inference needs to meet, in addition to the Warrantedness Condition, two further fundamental soundness conditions. The first of these reads, in essence, as follows (Botha 2006a: 138, 2009b: 134–135):

(3)   The Pertinence Condition
      A conclusion needs to be pertinent in being about the evolution of one or more linguistic entities that are properly identified and characterized.

The conclusion of the symbols-to-syntax inference fails this condition: it is not clear what it is about since no empirically adequate characterization of modern language or (fully) syntactic language has yet been given by the archaeologists concerned (Botha 2009b). A recent attempt by Henshilwood and Dubreuil (2009: 61–62) to define 'modern language' fails in that it neglects to draw two basic distinctions: (1) that between language as a means or capacity for conveying ideas etc. and the ideas etc. conveyed by language; and (2) that between 'syntactic language', 'symbolic language', and 'phonemic language'. To be able to draw conclusions about the evolution of modern language or (fully) syntactic language, that entity—if real—needs to be properly characterized by drawing on a principled conception of language, an adequate theory of syntax, and a clearly articulated theory of the evolution of syntax. The latter theory, in turn, presupposes a general theory of what evolution (as opposed to other processes of change) involves in the linguistic domain (Botha 2009b).

The second additional condition to be met by the symbols-to-syntax inference requires the following (Botha 2006a: 134, 2009b: 148):

(4)   The Groundedness Condition
      In any inference about language evolution, the inferential step must be properly grounded in firm data or empirical assumptions about the phenomenon from which it starts out.

This condition is required since it is not possible to infer something about a facet of language evolution from a phenomenon about which little is known reliably or which itself is poorly understood. In the case of the symbols-to-syntax inference, that phenomenon is the presumed symbolic behaviour of the MSA inhabitants of Blombos Cave. Since that behaviour is not open to direct inspection, it needs to be characterized in terms of specifics by an empirical theory. To date, however, the behaviour in question has been referred to only in terms of generalities such as 'transmitting and sharing symbolic meaning' (Henshilwood et al. 2002: 1279; Botha

2009b: 148–150). Behaviour so underspecified is at best a poor basis for inferences about facets of the evolution of language.

### 30.4.2 Other constituents

The soundness of the Blombos inference is not dependent on the soundness of the symbols-to-syntax inference alone. Its two other constituents, the shells-to-beads inference represented by ABC in Figure 30.1, and the beads-to-symbols inference represented by CDE in Figure 30.1, need to be sound too, also being subject to the three soundness conditions, mutatis mutandis. Questions arise in this regard about, for instance, the warrant for inferential step D—the step from beads and other objects of material culture to symbols. For, as is widely recognized, there are difficulties in determining whether an ornament or artefact is or is not a symbol (Chase 1999; Wadley 2001; d'Errico et al. 2003; Wynn and Coolidge 2007; but see also Vanhaeren 2005). Questionable features of the shells-to-beads inference and the beads-to-symbols inference can, then, also detract from the overall soundness of the Blombos inference.

### 30.4.3 More structure

It is clear from the discussion above that non-compound inferences drawn in empirical work about facets of language evolution should have two layers of structure. The first is a relatively 'visible' surface layer that contains: (1) a conclusion about a facet of language evolution, (2) data or assumptions about some phenomenon other than language evolution, and (3) an inferential step that goes from these data or assumptions to the former conclusion. The other layer of structure is a deeper one that comprises the theories needed for underpinning these three components of the surface layer (Bickerton 2003: 79; Botha 2009b, 2009c). The two layers of structure are represented in outline by Figure 30.2.

In sum, many non-compound inferences about language evolution are flawed by an underdevelopment of their deeper layer: one at least of the theories necessary for underpinning their surface components is either inadequate or completely absent. This flaw has been shown above to also impair the soundness of the symbols-to-syntax inference—a building block of the archaeological inferences which the Blombos inference instantiates.

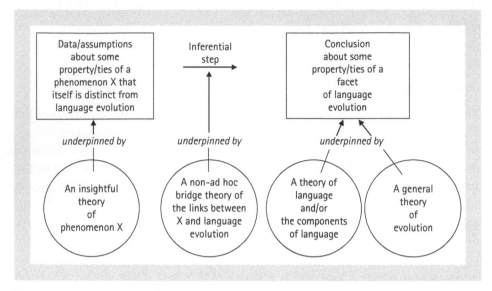

**Figure 30.2. Structure of non-compound inference about language evolution.**

# ACKNOWLEDGEMENTS

This article has benefited greatly from perceptive commentary by Walter Winckler, Kathleen Gibson, and Maggie Tallerman.

# CHAPTER 31

# NATURAL SELECTION-ITIS

## DAVID LIGHTFOOT

At the core of the cognitive sciences lies the toughest problem in all of science. Our most mature science seeks to understand matter and has developed rich theories that work in certain domains. However, physicists reckon that by far the greatest part of the universe is composed of 'dark matter', where we have no understanding. On a par with dark matter is brain matter. The great mystery here is to understand how the human brain, with its neurons, glial cells, electrical activity, etc., secretes (Darwin's word) the higher brain functions where we have some understanding: the faculties of number, language, and music.

We have learned about some neural mechanisms. In speech perception, we have been able to establish correlations between the firings of neurons in certain areas and distinguishing certain sound frequencies. That is progress but we do not understand how brain matter secretes consciousness and communication and we need the help of people who study matter; in fact, we need a new understanding of 'physiology', where the notion incorporates mental aspects (hence the 'cognitive physiology' of Anderson and Lightfoot 2002).

It is useful to bear this in mind when we consider the evolution of language. The language faculty does not show up in other species in anything like the same form, and every member of our species has it, except in extreme pathologies. It evolved and, when it evolved, there was a change in the brain: a new biochemistry, anatomy, or connectivity at the genomic level with corresponding new behaviours.

However, genes code for proteins, not behaviour. Work on neurogenetics shows that genomic variation in regulatory regions accounts for how much of a protein is made, when and where in the brain it is expressed. The brain links genomic sequence and behaviour: we will unravel how genomic variation influences behaviour by understanding how it influences neural circuitry. Brain function is specified by precise, interconnected regional circuits and all this is constrained by physical and biochemical laws.

As we learn about the physiology of the brain, construed more broadly than at present, we will discover limits on how a brain genome might mutate into another. Those limits constrain what may emerge in the next generation, what might evolve.

At a different level, Lightfoot (1999) depicts grammar change within recorded history as proceeding from generation to generation through a narrow range of options, defined by the parameters of the linguistic genotype (universal grammar, UG). Minor changes in environmental factors may trigger the growth of a grammar with different properties. The evolution of the language faculty may have proceeded in similar fashion. The similarity between language change over history and the evolution of the language faculty in the species is that change takes place in fits and starts, in a bumpily punctuated equilibrium, and within structural limits imposed by more general laws.

The fundamental properties of physical systems limit the mutations that organisms and specific organs might undergo—for example, the fact that organisms cannot transfer themselves instantaneously from Maryland to Cornwall or become invisible on demand (a property that would convey selective advantage, if it were possible). Similarly, biological systems are subject to particular principles. One thinks of the nature and behaviour of cells, the properties of exons and introns, and other fundamental aspects of the biological world that were not specifically selected for. In 1917 D'Arcy Thompson discussed constraints on the shape and functioning of biological forms, finding geometric forms recurring in many unrelated organisms: hexagons, spirals following the Fibonacci series, etc. (Thompson 1961). Constraints yielding these repeated forms hold independently of the effects of natural selection and sophisticated physical models explain Fibonacci series effects. Similarly the scaling laws of West et al. (1997) dictate that organisms as diverse as robins, redwoods, and rhinos obey the same mathematical laws governing the way size affects structure, physiology, and life history. Those laws—the 'scaling relations' that dictate how thick bones must be in animals of different sizes—are a near-universal feature of life (Lightfoot 1999: ch. 9 has discussion).

Since organisms are complex and integrated, any adaptive change must automatically spin off structural by-products. Our brain is a complex organ, and it may have evolved to its large size for adaptive reasons—for activities that our ancestors could perform only with bigger brains. But this doesn't entail that all attributes of human nature are adaptations. We can read and write, and these capacities are advantageous, but the mental machinery for them must have originated as an exaptation that was co-opted later.

Therefore it is an empirical matter whether any particular property of an organism evolved in the form it did because it was selected for. It might have arisen as a by-product of something else that was selected for, perhaps induced by physical or biological principles, or perhaps as a consequence of another change.

Some properties are not selected for and are not accidental by-products, but they emerge because of deep, physical principles that affect much of life. They reflect limits on the kinds of things that evolution can make, and they arise through the interaction of physical principles. Physical laws describe the limits to evolutionary change, in the same way that principles of UG prescribe the limits to grammatical change at the phenotypical level. They define the undulating terrain on which natural selection works, and they are part of a multifaceted approach to evolution, which goes beyond the working of natural selection.

This multifaceted approach to the evolution of the language faculty differs from the approach of people whom Gould (1997) called singularists. Singularists invoke just one factor to explain evolutionary development: natural selection. The result of natural selection is adaptation, the shaping of an organism's form, function, and behaviour to achieve enhanced reproductive success. In the context of the evolution of UG, singularists say that selective forces shaped individual components of UG, such as the Subjacency Condition, which permits elements to move only locally (*Who did you meet the boy who saw? *Who do you wonder whether John met?). For singularists, every element of UG is adaptive: the various principles of UG evolved by selective demands in a 'mosaic evolution' (Pinker and Bloom 1990; Newmeyer 1991). (This mosaic approach does not attribute to natural selection a single key innovation like recursion, which is the approach of Hauser et al. (2002), which I will not discuss here.)

The linguistic singularists have flourished at a time when others have articulated a conviction that every evolutionary change of any importance is due to the shaping effects of natural selection (Dawkins 1995; Dennett 1995). They have been joined by proponents of 'evolutionary psychology'; Wright (1994) has a deep faith in the power of natural selection:

If the theory of natural selection is correct, then essentially everything about the human mind should be intelligible in these terms. The basic ways we feel about each other, the basic kinds of things we think about each other and say to each other, are with us today by virtue of their past contribution to genetic fitness (Wright 1994: 28).

Natural selection has now been shown to plausibly account for so much about life in general and the human mind in particular that I have little doubt that it can account for the rest (Wright 1994: 383).

Returning to the evolution of UG, we might ask what would be involved in showing that some property is in fact due to the effects of natural selection. It is not enough to point to desirable functions that are served by that property, for that is to commit the 'Panglossian fallacy' of Gould and Lewontin's (1979) discussion of spandrels and by-products.

Modern Panglossians show that the Subjacency Condition constrains speakers to produce forms that can be understood ('parsed') in accordance with our apparent parsing capacity. However, to approach the question of why the Subjacency Condition evolved, one needs to have a notion of what evolved and how. Assuming that the Subjacency Condition is a condition on movement operations, one might show that organisms with movement constrained by Subjacency 'had an edge over' similar organisms that lacked Subjacency, other things remaining constant. Or did the condition evolve along with the possibility of movement operations? This makes a substantial difference for what is being attributed to adaptation. Needless to say, nobody has any idea of what properties the organism had when the Subjacency Condition evolved, and it is therefore hard to see how to address the question of why it arose.

Furthermore, to say that an organism with some property 'has an edge over' a similar organism without that property entails claiming that it had a better chance of having descendants, if one argues that the property is due to natural selection. One would need to show that an organism that solved its parsing problem by evolving a Subjacency Condition was more likely to reproduce than an organism that could not parse structures with long movement. An ability only to move elements locally would need to be shown to have increased the chances of repro-duction (Lightfoot 1991), unless we settle for Just So stories about what might have happened.

Dobzhansky (1973) said that nothing in biology makes sense except in the light of evolution. It may be that current attempts to formulate 'biolinguistic' analyses cannot yet make sense in the light of evolution, because we do not know enough to specify either the physical constraints on brain genomes that might have allowed the current genome to evolve from its predecessor, nor how that innovation might yield the new behaviour, nor the circumstances under which the evolution-ary development took place. As with the heart or upright posture, also with language; there are no principles that allow us to predict that from some organism some particular property must evolve. This is not to say that the developments are inexplicable, only that they are unexplained at the present state of knowledge. From that perspective, the evolution of the heart and mental organs are on a par.

It is misguided to seek natural selection accounts for every element of the language faculty, as it is currently understood; indeed natural selection has been overused, as the single driving force of evolution. As Darwin noted, natural selection is just one force and it operates only at the level of behaviour; the physical and biochemical constraints on the brain system are other forces that define possibilities.

## ACKNOWLEDGEMENTS

Thanks for helpful comments from Betty Tuller and Mark Weiss.

# CHAPTER 32

# THE ROLE OF HOMININ MOTHERS AND INFANTS IN PRELINGUISTIC EVOLUTION

## DEAN FALK

Selection for bipedalism was associated with a rearrangement of muscles and bony surfaces of the pelvis, which resulted in constricted birth canals in early hominins compared to quadrupedal apes. The conjunction of increasingly narrow pelvic outlets with ongoing selection for larger brains made giving birth excruciating and dangerous. Only the smaller, less-developed infants (and their mothers) survived the ordeals of birth. Consequently, hominin newborns were born relatively helpless and lost the ability to cling unsupported to the chests of their travelling mothers, an ability that contemporary monkey and ape infants very quickly develop. Before the invention of baby slings, prehistoric mothers would have carried their helpless babies on their hips or in their arms, and must have periodically put them down nearby in order to accomplish foraging tasks that required two hands. When separated from their mothers, babies would have fussed as contemporary ape and human babies do. At this point in prehistory, mothers would have begun to use their voices to soothe and engage infants, similar to today's universal use of lullabies and baby talk (motherese; see also de Boer, Chapter 33). According to the 'putting the baby down' (PTBD) hypothesis (Falk 2004), vocal interactions between early hominin mothers and infants sparked a sequence of events that led, eventually, to our ancestors' earliest words and, later, to the emergence of protolanguage.

Compared to adult-directed speech, modern motherese is more melodic, slower and more repetitious, has a higher overall pitch, uses a simpler vocabulary, and includes special words like 'bye-bye' and 'doggie' (Fernald 1994). Above all, contemporary motherese is known for its musical quality, or prosody. Prosody provides the melody or tone-of-voice in adult speech, colouring it with nuance and revealing emotions. Motherese, as defined in the PTBD hypothesis, is not just verbal but also encompasses facial expressions, body language, touching, patting, caressing, and even laughter and tickling. Of course, motherese itself would have evolved and changed during the long course of hominin evolution. Earlier forms would have been simpler than today's baby talk, and likely originated out of emotional vocalizations, mother–infant contact calls similar to those that occur among many animals, and may have been preceded by the first lullabies.

Although the extent to which motherese helps infants learn language has been controversial (Falk 2004), mounting evidence shows that it does so in a sequential, age-appropriate manner (Monnot 1999; Falk 2009): baby talk exaggerates vowels and highlights individual words and phrases. This helps infants learn to parse the speech stream into grammatically appropriate units and groupings. The clarity of motherese that normal babies are exposed to is associated with their development of speech discrimination skills (Liu et al. 2003), and infants who are best at perceiving speech sounds at 7 months of age score higher when they are older on language tests measuring the number of words they can say and the complexity of their speech (Tsao et al. 2004). Studies on French- and English-speaking parents and their 1- to 2-year-old infants show that the extent to which parents incessantly label objects and encourage repetition of names is associated with their babies' vocabulary growth, as well as their ability to manipulate and categorize objects (Poulin-Dubois et al. 1995). How quickly infants learn verbs depends on how often particular verbs occur when their parents talk to them (Naigles and Hoff-Ginsberg 1998).

By definition, language becomes grammatical as infants conform to conventional rules for constructing words and combining them into phrases and sentences (syntax) (Karmiloff and Karmiloff-Smith 2001). English-speaking mothers help their babies learn morphemes by repeating words back to them while adding the proper endings (such as -s or -ing) (Farrar 1990). As children increase their use of these morphemes over time, they become better at combining and moving words within sentences. Baby talk also influences the learning of grammar in languages such as Italian, Serbian, French, Russian, and Polish, where nouns are arbitrarily classified as masculine, feminine, or neuter (Kempe and Brooks 2001).

The premise in the PTBD hypothesis that motherese occurs universally has been questioned because of several studies done in the 1970s on Western Samoa; a small Kaluli society from Papua New Guinea; and a group of black working class Americans (Ochs 1992). Although these societies supposedly lack motherese, the literature suggests otherwise (Falk 2009). Take, for example, the Kaluli. When infants cry, mothers bounce them to soothe them, while repeating sounds of 'shh' (Schieffelin 1990). In the first few months of babies' lives, their mothers 'use expressive vocalizations' and:

Within a week or so after a child is born, Kaluli mothers act in ways that seem intended to involve infants (*tualun*) in dialogues and interactions with others. . . . Kaluli mothers tend to face their babies outward so that they can be seen by and see others who are part of the social group. Older children greet and address infants, and in response to this mothers hold their infants face outward and, while moving them, speak in a special high-pitched, nasalized register. . . . (Schieffelin 1990: 71).

Kaluli adults address 6- to 12-month-old infants with greetings, rhetorical questions, directions, and simple 'one-liners'. When babies babble, 'adults and older children occasionally repeat vocalizations back to the young child, reshaping them into the names of persons in the household or into kin terms' (Ochs and Schieffelin 1984: 291). Clearly, the Kaluli have motherese, although it is modified in keeping with cultural norms, which is true for the other cultures that are said to lack motherese (Falk 2009).

The hypothesis that prehistoric mothers and infants developed and propagated prelinguistic communications that eventually led to protolanguage is consistent with details regarding the appearance of proto-cultural behaviours such as wheat-washing and sweet potato-salting in Japanese macaque society (Kawai 1965), and the fact that females and infants were key players in transmitting these behaviours from generation to generation (Kawai 1965). Thus, innovations developed by one individual (usually an adult female) were initially spread horizontally among a population by infants who learned the behaviours from each other in play groups and then brought them back to their mothers. (Adult males were the last to acquire these innovations.) A second vertical phase of transmission occurred between generations as new offspring were born and learned the behaviours from their mothers and siblings. Similar horizontal and vertical transmission of new behaviours are entailed in the PTBD hypothesis. Horizontal and vertical transmission like that demonstrated for Japanese macaques emerged independently in simulations and mathematical models exploring the evolutionary emergence of vocabulary (Ke et al. 2002), and were instrumental in the development of a new sign language that was invented and transmitted by Nicaraguan children (Senghas et al. 2004). The PTBD hypothesis is consistent with the fact that, among the Hadza hunter-gatherers who live in northern Tanzania, mothers take nursing babies with them when they forage for food, and sometimes put them down next to them as they dig for tubers (Marlowe 2006; Falk 2009). Finally, the evolutionary loss of infants' ability to ride unaided clinging to their mothers was accompanied by changes in the hand representations of the primary somatosensory and motor cortices in the brain (Schultz 1969), which concurs (beautifully) with both the PTBD hypothesis and the independently developed hypothesis that language was 'tinkered' from networks in the brain that were originally important for reaching and grasping (for details see Preuss 2007; Falk 2009; Arbib, this volume).

# CHAPTER 33

# INFANT-DIRECTED SPEECH AND LANGUAGE EVOLUTION

## BART DE BOER

## 33.1 INTRODUCTION

Infant-directed speech is here defined as a set of speech registers that caretakers use to address infants. There are at least three different kinds of infant-directed speech: one that is used to get the infant's attention, one that is used to soothe the infant, and one that is used to address the infant with linguistically meaningful utterances. All have different characteristics, but there are also similarities, and they could be considered as points on a continuum. Nevertheless, it is unfortunate that in general no difference is made between the different kinds of infant-directed speech in the literature. The different kinds are used in different circumstances, and from an evolutionary point of view, they would make different contributions to the infant's fitness.

All kinds of infant-directed speech are characterized by slower speech rate and larger intonation contours (Fernald et al. 1989; Kuhl et al. 1997). Attention-getting infant-directed speech is characterized by higher volume and extreme intonation excursions, but it does not necessarily consist of meaningful utterances. Basically, caretakers use any speech-like means to get the infant's attention. Soothing infant-directed speech is characterized by lower volume, sometimes even whispered speech, and very flowing intonation contours. Lullabies could be considered part of this kind of infant-directed speech.

Although it can be argued that all kinds of infant-directed speech can serve adaptive purposes, for the purposes of this chapter, the meaningful kind of infant-directed speech is most interesting. It is characterized by short, syntactically simple utterances, generally about the direct context, exaggerated intonation contours, lower tempo, and clearer articulation.

Caretakers use infant-directed speech automatically when addressing infants, even without being aware of doing so. They also automatically adapt the complexity of their speech to the level of linguistic competence of the infant. In addition, infants prefer to listen to infant-directed speech over adult-directed speech (Fernald 1985). Infant-directed speech also appears to be nearly universal cross-culturally (Ferguson 1964; Fernald et al. 1989) and a similar register is attested in signed languages (Masataka 1992). Whether it really is universal cross-culturally is still an open question. It has been argued (e.g. Ochs 1983) that there are cultures in which no special speech registers exist for infants, or where speech in the presence of infants has very different properties from ordinary infant-directed speech, but these cases appear to be exceptional. There are even claims that in some cultures infants are not addressed by adults. However, in these cultures infants do receive linguistic input from older children, as is clear from the original sources (Schieffelin 1985).

Furthermore, it has been shown by computational experiments that it is easier to acquire vowel categories on the basis of infant-directed speech than on the basis of adult-directed speech (de Boer and Kuhl 2003; Vallabha et al. 2007). Other computational experiments have shown that infant-directed speech can help to preserve stability of vowel systems over time (de Boer 2003, 2005a). Experiments with infants have shown that they learn to distinguish speech categories from a second language when they are exposed to caretaker–child interactions in that language, but not when they are exposed to (adult-directed) speech from a television (Kuhl et al. 2003).

When a behaviour such as infant-directed speech is found to be almost universal across cultures, when it is engaged in automatically, and when it contributes to fitness, it becomes worthwhile to investigate how it could have evolved and how it could have influenced the evolution of language in general; see also Falk, this volume. Different theories exist concerning the adaptive purpose of infant-directed speech and its role in the evolution of language. It has been proposed that infant-directed speech serves an important role in acquiring speech and language, and that it is therefore part of what must be explained by a theory of language evolution. It has also been proposed that honest signalling, which is a necessary prerequisite for language to evolve, can most easily be explained as emerging from mother–child interactions in combination with kin selection (Fitch 2004; Locke, this volume). Finally, it has been proposed that language itself has emerged from mother–child interactions that have become more and more complex over time (Falk 2004, this volume; Locke 2006; Locke and Bogin 2006; for a critique of these theories, see Tallerman 2008b, 2011). Here the focus will be on the adaptive role of infant-directed speech, rather than on its role in the emergence of language.

## 33.2 THE ADAPTIVE VALUE OF INFANT-DIRECTED SPEECH

The properties of infant-directed speech, and more specifically, the kind that is used for linguistically meaningful utterances, facilitate acquisition of speech. Slower speed and more exaggerated intonation can help to divide the speech stream into its building blocks syntactically, lexically, and phonemically. Exaggerated articulation helps to separate the different categories of speech sounds. Using only simple, contextualized utterances also helps to facilitate acquisition of lexical and grammatical knowledge. It can be argued that an infant is not alone in the task of acquiring a language. The behaviour of caregivers helps in this task, and should therefore be taken into account when investigating the evolution of language.

A fact that is often overlooked when discussing the evolution of language is that the behaviour of the caregivers themselves needs an evolutionary explanation (Locke, this volume). Producing simplified language is not necessarily as simple as it might seem. It requires (subconscious) knowledge of the language and an ability to adapt one's utterances to the level of knowledge of the interlocutor. An ability to adapt one's utterances to the level of knowledge of the interlocutor is something that is also needed in adult-to-adult conversation. In the case of pragmatics this is well known, but it also occurs in other aspects of language, for instance when talking to foreigners or the hard-of-hearing. Being able to produce infant-directed speech therefore does not necessarily require extra adaptations than are needed for adult-directed speech. However, the fact that caregivers tend to use infant-directed speech automatically and almost without being aware of it indicates that some specialized mechanisms have evolved for adult speech to infants.

Given that linguistic input to infants is adapted to their linguistic abilities, the task of language acquisition becomes much easier for infants. Issues about the difficulties of acquisition sometimes raised on the basis of examples from adult-directed written language are most likely not relevant to acquisition of spoken language by infants. Complex syntactic constructions that would be impossible to acquire if presented to the infant directly are easier to acquire if complex examples are presented only when the less complex ones have been mastered. It might as a result turn out that the cognitive machinery necessary for acquiring language can be much simpler than sometimes assumed. Consequently there would have to be fewer biologically evolved and genetically coded adaptations in the brain for acquiring language. Potentially, co-evolution of infants' learning behaviour and caregivers' teaching behaviour is a more plausible evolutionary scenario than the isolated evolution of infant language acquisition would be (but this is still a topic for research). Part of this hypothesis is testable by investigating whether infant-directed speech really is more learnable than adult-directed speech (de Boer and Kuhl 2003; Kuhl et al. 2003; Vallabha et al. 2007).

There are also indications (de Boer 2003, 2005a) that in a system where caregivers use infant-directed speech, more complex linguistic systems remain stable over a longer time. Even though an infant would in principle be able to learn such a complex system without infant-directed speech, one would expect so many learning errors, and therefore variation in the population, that after a few genera-tions the system simplifies. This instantiates the fact that the class of learnable human languages is not the same as the class of human languages that can be stably transmitted over multiple generations (Brighton et al. 2005). In the presence of infant-directed speech, however, learning errors and variation diminish, and there-fore more complex systems can remain stable. The presence of more complex, culturally transmitted linguistic systems then makes biological, genetic adaptations to the existing complexity useful. In this way, the cultural presence of more complex linguistic systems can drive biological evolution of the language faculty. Thus, infant-directed speech can help to drive biological evolution.

This is of course something that is very difficult if not impossible to investigate directly in real human language. The results referred to here were achieved with agent-based computer models, based on the iterated learning paradigm (K. Smith et al. 2003b). In this paradigm, small computer programs (agents) model essential aspects of human behaviour. There is one parent agent and one child agent. After a number of linguistic interactions, the parent agent is removed, the child agent becomes the parent, and a new (empty) child agent is generated. In the case of de Boer (2003, 2005a) the linguistic interactions consist of the parent producing vowels, and the child learning them. The very first parent is initialized with a given five- or seven-vowel system. The system is run for a number of generations and then checked to see how well the structure of the original vowel system is preserved. In one condition, the infant agent has an innate mechanism to com-pensate for reduced speech; in the other it does not have such a mechanism, but the adult agent produces exaggerated examples of the vowels (comparable to the ones in real infant-directed speech). It is found that the five-vowel system remains equally stable in both conditions, but that for the seven-vowel systems both some kind of innate compensation and infant-directed speech are necessary. Although this project barely scratches the surface of the relevance of infant-directed speech to language evolution, it nevertheless provides an example of how computer models could be constructed. Experiments with (adult) human subjects are also conceivable. It is possible to create an experiment along the lines of the ones reviewed in K. Smith et al. (2008), where in one condition no teacher-learner adaptation occurs, while in another condition teachers must adapt to the level of the learners. However, as far as I am aware, no such experiments have yet been undertaken.

## 33.3 KIN SELECTION AND INFANT-DIRECTED SPEECH

A rather different perspective on caretaker–child interactions and the evolution of speech is taken by Fitch (2004). He observes that language is a system that requires cooperation because most of the information that is exchanged is honest. He also observes that speech is a relatively cheap means of communication: the metabolic cost of producing a speech signal is low. Fitch argues that such honest signalling systems with cheap signals are evolutionarily problematic. Signalling information to someone increases the receiver's fitness, but not necessarily the sender's. The temptation to give false information would then be great, but if signals are unreliable, receivers would evolve to ignore them. Honest signalling systems with cheap signals assume some degree of altruism between sender and receiver. Altruistic systems can evolve in two situations: if the altruism is reciprocal (that is, an individual can expect to benefit in return for its altruistic behaviour) or if an individual behaves altruistically towards its kin. According to Fitch, reciprocal altruism is rare and problematic in biology, whereas altruism towards kin is common. He therefore proposes kin selection as an evolutionary mechanism through which language can have started.

Fitch proposes that mother–child interaction is at the basis of language (his 'mother tongue' hypothesis). A mother shares half of her genes with her offspring, and therefore any gain in fitness of the offspring (that is not deleterious to the mother's own fitness) helps to spread the mother's genes. It is therefore in the mother's advantage to communicate to her offspring as much as possible of her knowledge and experience about survival. Thus a communication system could develop between mother and child, growing ever more complex, since the ability to transfer more and more complex information would increase the fitness of the offspring. In a later evolutionary stage, such communication systems could then be used to communicate with less-closely related kin and with non-kin.

Using the hypothesis that kin selection played a role in starting language evolution, Fitch derives a number of properties of language and compares these to the properties of language that would be expected if sexual selection (as proposed by some other researchers) played a role. Kin selection correctly predicts that language is acquired young. Sexual selection would predict an onset of language in puberty and also predicts that men would be better at production than women, which is not the case. Kin selection can also help to explain why language is learnt more accurately than is necessary for transfer of purely semantic information, and that the ability to learn language this accurately is lost before the age at which humans generally leave the place they grew up. In this way, linguistic accents can serve as reliable markers of kinship: speakers with the same accent are likely to be more closely related than speakers with different accents. This could also explain why people tend to be more favourably disposed towards people with the same accent than towards people with a different accent.

The theory of kin selection therefore gives a central role to mother–child interactions in the evolution of language. It should be noted, however, that Fitch only proposes kin selection as a selection mechanism, and does not provide a detailed scenario of how complex language would evolve, and why it would not have evolved in other species. Furthermore, as Tallerman (2008b) has pointed out, Fitch does not provide an explanation of how language would spread beyond a usage in immediate kin interactions.

## 33.4 CONCLUSION

Caregiver–child interactions and infant-directed speech might have played different roles in the evolution of language; see also Falk, this volume; Locke, this volume. As for kin selection, it could have facilitated the emergence of a cooperative system with cheap signals in the context of caretaker–child interaction. It is also possible that kin selection allowed this communication system to become more symbolic and more complex in nature. Once complex language was present, infant-directed speech could have helped make language easier to learn, and allowed complex language to remain stable for longer periods. This again could drive evolution for more adaptations to complex language. However, in none of these scenarios is there a compelling argument of how human language became semantically complex and symbolic in nature, while other primates' communication systems did not. Although caretaker–child interaction might therefore have been an important factor in language evolution, other factors (and likely historical coincidence as well) must also have played important roles.

# CHAPTER 34

# DISPLAYS OF VOCAL AND VERBAL COMPLEXITY: A FITNESS ACCOUNT OF LANGUAGE, SITUATED IN DEVELOPMENT

## JOHN L. LOCKE

## 34.1 Vocal control

Syntax is the centrepiece of modern linguistics, and it has also occupied pride of place in research on linguistic evolution. Recognizing that syntax presupposes the existence of vocabulary, some linguists have acknowledged the need to account for lexical capacity (Bickerton 1995; see Burling, this volume). Since words are made up of individual sounds or segments, other theorists have argued that the most basic change in linguistic evolution was the ability to particulate vocal behaviour into discrete elements that could be combined to construct massive vocabularies (Studdert-Kennedy 2005, this volume). What has gone largely unnoticed, or at least uncommented, is that none of these changes would have been possible without a degree of vocal or, more precisely, phonetic flexibility and control.

If one were to address this modality issue, however, a stumbling block would be encountered almost immediately. In many areas relevant to language, researchers have uncovered some measure of continuity between humans and the other primates. This has enabled cognitive, neurological, and social theorists to use ape and monkey data as a starting point. But when it comes to vocal and phonetic behaviour, there is an area of almost complete disconnect. Every hearing person in the world knows at least one language that is *spoken* (Locke 1998), none knows only a signed language. Within those vocal languages, individuals speak easily and often, even when there is little in the way of a discernible topic. They readily imitate vocal behaviours in speech and song, even unconsciously, and freely invent and modify spoken words. Infants do these things too, beginning before they are old enough to walk.

The apes vocalize under various circumstances, and derive indexical and affective information from each others' voices (Cheney and Seyfarth 2007; Seyfarth and Cheney, this volume). But apes appear to be more gestural than vocal, and there is little evidence that any primate species learns conspecific calls in the wild, produces more than a few distinctive signals, or is able to improvise new vocal behaviours or control existing ones (e.g. Hammerschmidt and Fischer 2008). An important consequence is that anyone wishing to explain the evolution of vocal and phonetic control in humans must start from scratch; and without such an account, anyone wishing to explain the lexical and grammatical components of language must take production, perception, and representation for granted.

My purpose here is to discuss factors related to the evolution of vocal and phonetic behaviours prior to, or in step with, the emergence of symbolization and reference. But I will also offer specific claims. The first is that at some point in evolutionary history, vocal complexity became a fitness cue, enabling selection to increase vocal ornateness; and that with increasing ornateness, the capacity to process—and possibly the ability to store and reproduce—patterns of sentence-length utterances also increased (Locke 2008a). The second claim is that vocal complexity built up a system for the mental representation and control of phonetic material, as well as a system for the evaluation of vocal material. I will suggest that the expanded time window required for the management of longer and more complex strings of phonetic behaviour, and the storage and other capacities required for their evaluation, conditioned the evolving human mind for syntax. In support of my claims, I will argue, first, that the necessary vocal, phonetic, and cognitive changes—like other modifications of existing traits—could only have occurred at critical moments in the development of individuals. Then I will review evidence that environmental changes produced new or modified developmental stages, and that these stages, in turn, produced new behaviours that were selected at the time of their appearance, and reselected in later stages, guiding our ancestors through a series of intermediate behaviours until they achieved fully-fledged human language.

## 34.2 EVOLUTIONARY RULES

Unless there is to be an entirely separate theory of evolution that works only for language, we must use the explanatory tools that are available; that is, linguistic theorists must play by the same (neo-Darwinian) rules that are used to explain the emergence of any new trait. At a minimum, evolutionary theories must identify the environmental changes that produced phenotypic variation and the modes of selection that reinforced certain of the variants, thereby increasing reproductive success, and they must specify the developmental stage(s) in which these actions took place (see below).

Since humans and the apes departed from their last common ancestor at least six million years ago (mya), it is possible that much or most of that period was required for the evolution of language. The primary task of evolutionary theorists is to identify the environmental changes, and the responses to those changes, that edged our ancestors closer to the linguistic capacity possessed by modern humans.

In the evolution of human language, there had to have been a number of prior stages in which precursory behaviours evolved. These not-quite-linguistic behaviours would have conferred benefits on their bearers, but these would not have been the advantages one associates with modern languages, nor would the mechanisms responsible for the production of these behaviours necessarily be the same. In the other primates, fitness information is carried by physical traits, such as size; or by behaviours, such as loud or low-pitched vocalization, which imply size and aggressiveness. The other apes engage in various displays in pursuit of rank and sex. I have suggested elsewhere that our own evolutionary ancestors used elaborate vocal and verbal displays to compete for equivalent resources (Locke 2001c). As we will see, the vocal traits that were displayed may have provided information as to the individual's health, strength, aggressiveness, virility, or social and cognitive ability.

## 34.3 EVOLUTIONARY DEVELOPMENTAL LINGUISTICS

An evolutionary account of a trait as complex as language is unlikely without an appropriate theoretical framework. Fortunately, a new paradigm is available. It is evolutionary developmental linguistics (EDL), a naturalization of human language (Locke 2009). Following on from recent developments in related fields—evolutionary developmental biology, and psychology—EDL is concerned with the evolution of developmental properties, processes, and stages (evo → devo) that independently, or in concert with other environmental changes, facilitated the emergence of language in the species (devo → evo). Here, I will attempt to demonstrate, first, that the stages of life history in which language now develops in the young were themselves the products of evolution and, second, that these developmental stages played a vital role in the evolution of language.

## 34.4 THE ROLE OF EVOLUTION IN DEVELOPMENT

It is obvious that the development of 'language' involves the activation of neural and vocal mechanisms that were designed by evolutionary processes to carry out linguistic operations. But this is only half of the relationship between evolution and development, since the stages in which these linguistic mechanisms develop also evolved. Unlike other primates, modern humans have four developmental stages: infancy, childhood, juvenility, and adolescence (see Bogin references in Locke and Bogin 2006).

### 34.4.1 Remodelling of infancy

Much of the linguistically relevant phenotypic variation originated in ancestral infancies, with selection by parents occurring in this stage, and, with persistence of selected behaviours, in later stages by peers and others. Infancy begins at (or before) birth and ends at about 30–36 months when, in traditional societies, the infant is weaned. This stage is characterized by rapid physical growth, provision of nourishment by maternal lactation, and eruption of deciduous teeth. Human infants are more helpless than ape and monkey infants, a 'deficiency' that requires a long period of continuous care. The associated interactions facilitate acquisition of socially complex behaviours, including language. One change that contributed to greater helplessness was bipedal locomotion (at least 4.4 mya), which eventually realigned the spine and narrowed the pelvis. Pelvic narrowing produced problems at birth for the mother and her large-headed foetus, a problem that would have been exacerbated by further increases in skull size about 1.8 mya. Infants with smaller heads at birth—and their mothers—were more likely to survive delivery. Over time, differential rates of survival caused a shift in skull and brain development from the prenatal to the postnatal period (Locke and Bogin 2006). In the final section, I discuss ways that this shift may have produced more complex and controlled forms of vocal communication.

## 34.4.2 Evolution of childhood

Childhood is a uniquely human stage that is thought to have entered the *Homo* line about 1.8 mya. At that time, there was an increase in population size and group size (Dunbar 2003). Early weaning may have contributed to both changes since this would have enabled women to bear more offspring in their reproductive lifetime. Bogin has argued that early weaning created a short childhood of about 2 years, which later increased to its present length of approximately 4 years, possibly because of communicative benefits associated with language (see references in Locke and Bogin 2006). Physical characteristics of childhood include slow and steady growth and relatively small body size, a large and rapidly expanding brain, immature dentition, and dependence on others for care and feeding. As childhood draws to a close, there are two important changes: a brief increase in the rate of brain development, which ends a period of steady deceleration in rate, and an improvement in the ability to eat, reflecting the presence of new teeth and increases in the strength of the lower jaw.

## 34.4.3 Remodelling of juvenility

Juvenility begins at 8 years, with the onset of adrenarche—a development of the adrenal system in which rising androgen stimulates secondary sexual characteristics in advance of puberty—and accompanying cognitive and social advances, and ends at 10 and 12 years in females and males, respectively. Individuals in this stage are sexually immature but much more independent of older individuals than are children. Following a remodelled infancy and new childhood, the juvenile stage could hardly have remained unchanged. In various species of mammals, juvenility provides additional time for the brain growth and learning required for reproductive success. In complex human societies, all of the juvenile and adolescent stages are needed for the social and linguistic skills required by sexual maturity to develop. In traditional societies, these skills include the ability to fluently manipulate elaborate and socially appropriate utterances (Locke and Bogin 2006). Modification of juvenility would naturally increase phenotypic variability and offer new bases for selection at a time when greater independence and sexual maturity were rapidly approaching.

## 34.4.4 Evolution of adolescence

Adolescence is the second stage that is uniquely human, the other primates proceeding directly from juvenility to adulthood. Adolescence begins at the end of juvenility and extends to 19 years, when adulthood commences. In modern humans, adolescence begins with puberty, when there is a surge in skeletal growth, and the development of new and stronger relationships. Imaging research now reveals a number of brain changes between childhood and adolescence (see references in Locke 2009). It has been argued that adolescence conferred reproductive advantages on our ancestors, partly by giving the young additional opportunities to acquire social and sexual skills before reproducing (Locke and Bogin 2006).

## 34.5 THE ROLE OF DEVELOPMENT IN EVOLUTION

Although theories of language evolution customarily propose a specific role for selection at sexual maturity (see Locke 2009), few proposals recognize the contributions of events that occur *before* that stage. But the fact is that no evolutionary account can be complete if it lacks a developmental component. The reason is that phenotypic variants that emerge in response to environmental changes, and which are reinforced by selection, *can only appear during an ontogenetic stage.* This was initially recognized by St. George Mivart in 1871 and argued by Walter Garstang in 1922, but arguments for a strong evolutionary role for development have increased in number and specificity in recent years (see references in Locke 2009). West-Eberhard has written that:

The causal chain of adaptive evolution begins with development. *Development,* or ontogenetic change induced by genomic and environmental factors, causes phenotypic variation within populations. If the phenotypic variation caused by developmental variation in turn causes variation in survival and reproductive success, this constitutes *selection.* Then, if the phenotypic variation that causes selection has a genetic component, this causes *evolution,* or cross-generational change in phenotypic and genotypic frequencies (2003: 141; italics in original).

Selection is still a vital process, of course, but as Lickliter (2008) said recently:

it is changes in development that are responsible for generating novel phenotypes, which must then pass through the filter of natural selection . . . Natural selection cannot serve as a creative generator of phenotypic form or phenotypic change. *Natural selection is simply the filter that preserves reproductively successful phenotypes, which are themselves products of individual development* (2008: 362; italics in original).

Earlier I referred to inter-specific continuity, but this evo-devo-evo process critically involves a second kind of continuity—the persistence of behaviours developing early in the lives of individuals into later stages. Because of this intra-individual continuity, new behaviours that emerged in early stages, when variability and plasticity are exceptional, would have persisted at some level, and in some form, in later stages. Then, selection would have automatically reinforced any precursory traits that facilitated the later ones.

## 34.5.1 Role of infancy

In several avian species, it has been found that physical features in chicks, e.g. feather and throat colour, are both indicative of health and predictive of parental feeding practices (Lyon et al. 1994; Saino et al. 2000). In songbirds, nutritional stress experienced soon after hatching impairs brain development and song learning. This affects the quality of songs that are produced later on, enabling females, who base mate selection decisions, in part, on song quality, to avoid unfit partners (Nowicki et al. 2002; Holveck et al. 2008).

Infancy is an important stage in our own species, too. Several years ago, I suggested that in evolution, babbling (the production of well-formed syllables) 'encouraged parental care and was therefore submitted to natural selection, providing infants with signalling systems and prospective caregivers with processing mechanisms' that would have been in place when our ancestors evolved the capacity for symbolic communication, causing languages to be vocal and syllabic (Locke 2001a; also see Locke 2001b). Later, I offered a formal ('parental selection') proposal according to which heightened competition, combined with unprecedented levels of helplessness, encouraged infants to explore clever new ways of using the voice to secure and maintain maternal proximity, and to monitor and 'read' maternal feedback. Infants who issued more effective care-elicitation signals, it was proposed, received more care and lived on to reproductive age. Mothers who were able to discriminate genuine from false expressions of need also stood to benefit (Locke 2006).

In foraging societies, infant care is provided by alloparents (relatives and other group members) as well as by parents (Hrdy 1999; Zuberbühler, this volume). This cooperative breeding practice, which presumably grew in response to increased care needs, may also have added to infants' motivation to vocalize more effectively, since individuals who are less closely related to infants may feel less obliged to take care of them.

If new levels of helplessness caused infants to work harder for care, so did increased numbers of siblings. When mothers began to wean earlier, they were able to bear more infants in their reproductive lifetime. This increased the number of competitors for care, intensifying the conflict between each of the siblings and its mother (Trivers 1974). In the early months, crying would have been sufficient to elicit care, but if infants continued to cry, or did so too noxiously, or too often, it could lead to withdrawal of care, or even abuse, neglect, or infanticide. Thus, when mothers began to divert their attention, according to my claim, infants were forced to invent new and more seductive forms of vocalization. This contributed to the 'emancipation', in development, of the voice for articulate use (Locke 2004; also see Oller and Griebel 2008a).

Consistent with the parental selection hypothesis are indications that infants who fail to engage in vocal play may be ill (Locke 1993), and that infants who do not babble may be less robust than others (Vestergaard et al. 1999; Oller 2000). Moreover, there is evidence that infants who produce few syllables are evaluated less favourably than their more syllabic peers, and that mothers also appear to interpret the use of reduplicated syllables (e.g. 'mama') as requests for parental attention (see references in Locke 2006).

### 34.5.2  Role of childhood

In the childhood that followed, any enhanced communication skills supplied by infancy would surely have proved beneficial, for if children are to avoid hazardous aspects of their environment, they must be warned or 'instructed'. According to Fitch (2004), hominin parents benefited by exchanging accurate information with their offspring, and with other kin who shared their genes. The better-informed young, according to Fitch, were more likely to survive into adulthood, passing on to their own offspring genes associated with the improved system of communication. But the evolution of 'language' went well beyond admonition and instruction. How did our ancestors get from a handful of words to voluminous vocabularies, ones that greatly exceed perceptible functionality, and from one- and two-word utterances to longer and more fluent stretches of speech?

### 34.5.3  Role of juvenility

Although childhood's physical and cognitive changes increased independence from family members, juvenility would have given the young opportunities to prepare themselves, while still sexually immature, for a stage in which vocal and verbal performance would play a prominent role in the quest for precious resources—particularly sex and dominance (Locke and Bogin 2006). It is relevant here to note that juvenility would have provided the context for a range of new socially relevant activities, ones that placed a premium on longer stretches of speech—from gossiping to joking, riddling, and storytelling—as well as the ability to display verbal behaviours in ways that would facilitate competition and courtship in the run-up to sexual maturity.

### 34.5.4  Role of adolescence

In modern societies, direct verbal aggression increases disproportionately in males in early adolescence (see references in Locke 2008a). In evolution, the relevant dispositions—in concert with endocrine changes—may have extended the functionality of vocal and verbal behaviour while also making it public, raising the probability that these skills would be sufficiently observable to be selected. There is anecdotal evidence for sexual selection of vocal behaviours in some species of primates, for example, the loud calls of sexually mature orang-utans (Delgado

2006), but natural selection may also have played a role in the evolution of vocal complexity; inter-male competition has much the same effect as female courtship (Locke 2001c, 2008a; Franks and Rigby 2005).[1]

In our own species, the speaking voice is an extremely rich repository of biologically relevant information. The fundamental frequency ($F_0$) is inversely correlated with a range of fitness indices in adolescent and adult males, males with lower $F_0$s having greater testis volume and levels of testosterone, which hormone is positively associated with coital frequency. Women prefer males with low voices, especially when these listeners are in the high oestrogen phase of their menstrual cycle (see references in Locke 2009).[2] Thus it seems reasonable to suppose that hominin females who chose a male with a low-pitched voice were likely to acquire a mate who was not merely competitive, but also fertile, protective, and provident (see references in Locke 2008a). Recently, Apicella et al. (2007) reported that in one traditional society, men with low-pitched speaking voices had significantly more offspring than other men. These and related findings favour speech- and song-based hypotheses. That speech may play an independent role is suggested by a study in which male voices that were favourably rated when played normally lost their attractiveness when played backwards (Vukovic et al. 2008) but it is possible that song quality or singing ability were also selected (see Locke 2008a).

## 34.6 DISPLAY OF VOCAL AND VERBAL COMPLEXITY

Vocal complexity may seem dissociated from larger linguistic issues, but it has never been clear why phonologies have more phonemes than their lexicons require, lexicons

---

[1] Most of the evidence on vocal fitness involves female preferences for male voices, but if males were more readily disposed to engage in vocal displays, it was undoubtedly because females also had a perceptual preference for these mating displays (see Locke and Bogin 2006; Locke 2008a). This leaves open the means by which enhanced vocal *expressivity* was transmitted to female offspring, and the capacity to appraise vocal complexity was transmitted to males. One obvious means would have been correlated response, or cross-sexual transfer, but males also have a stake in successful mating. Pipitone and Gallup (2008) have reported that young adult males appraise female voices more favourably if recorded during the high-risk phases of the menstrual cycle, and that the female voice is thus a key component of a 'fertility monitoring system'.

[2] An impediment to (sexual) selection-based linguistic theories has been the belief, based mainly on psychometric evaluations of written language, that females have 'better language' than males. Meta-analyses show this generalization to be false (Locke 2008b, 2010), but there is more evolutionarily relevant (anthropological) evidence, and it indicates that males display more playful, humorous, and creative uses of speech when competing with other males in public settings (Locke and Bogin 2006; Progovac and Locke 2009).

have more words than the average speaker needs to know, and grammars provide complex syntactic patterns that seem communicatively inessential. 'Many aspects of grammar', wrote Maratsos, 'are often more complex, often oddly so, than they need to be for straightforward communicative purposes' (1998: 461). This has posed a problem for functional accounts based on communicative efficiency. Premack suggested that it would be a challenge 'to reconstruct the scenario that would confer selective fitness on recursiveness' (1985: 281). He saw a number of grammatical devices as 'overly powerful . . . absurdly so'. Lightfoot (1991: 69) expressed difficulty in seeing the selective advantages of individual grammatical patterns. He was pessimistic about the possibility that subjacency, for example, would have increased communicative efficiency, or 'the chances of having fruitful sex'; see Lightfoot, this volume.

Under the circumstances, it makes sense to contemplate an alternative possibility—that an early benefit of vocal and verbal complexity lay in the information it gave listeners about the *speaker*. In the case of birds, the complexity of songs is frequently defined simply as the number of phrases per trill or notes per song. Selection may have operated here, for there is evidence that complex songs are preferred by male and female birds (Vallet and Kreutzer 1995; Ballentijn and Ten Cate 1999; Leitão et al. 2006; see Slater, this volume), and that males that are able to learn and use complex songs are of higher quality than males with simpler songs (Hasselquist et al. 1996; Ballentijn and Ten Cate 1999). In a recent study of male finches, vocal complexity was found to be associated with intelligence, as defined by the number of trials required to solve a foraging task (Boogert et al. 2008).

In evolution, vocal learning may have provided our ancestors with an indication of each others' physical or cognitive capabilities. For it is generally the case that the more complex the system, the harder it is to learn and manipulate, especially by unfit individuals. In Locke (2009), I suggested that in evolution, male listeners would have deferred to same-sex competitors who produced complex vocalizations, and females were attracted to males with unusually complex vocalizations. When our ancestors began to compete vocally, by adding new elements or by uttering familiar elements in novel sequences, communication systems would have diversified. These actions, I claimed, created the capacity for complexity at other levels of vocal production and processing, expanding cognitive support systems, and laying the groundwork for utterances that would eventually approach the rate, duration, and intricacy of sentences in modern languages.

There is evidence for this in the anthropological literature, which supports strong connections between verbal complexity on the one hand, and status and intelligence on the other. In traditional societies, group leaders are those who use an exceptionally broad range of words, and phrases that are 'ornamented' by material from outside the more limited repertoires of their listeners; and in members of modern societies, there is a positive relationship between vocabulary size and intelligence. A further relationship between vocabulary size and the use of rare words (see references in Locke 2008a, 2009) makes it possible for speakers to reveal their intelligence in brief social displays. I suggest that verbal complexity played a role in mate selection (Miller 2000; Locke 2009), intelligence being a trait that females seek in a mate (Buss 2003; Fisman et al. 2006). In Franks and Rigby (2005), young men reportedly produced more creative definitions of novel word constructions when tested by an attractive young woman, or in a competitive situation with other men. Recently, Rosenberg and Tunney (2008) found that young adult males used more low frequency words in a written exercise following an imaginary romantic encounter with a younger female, an effect not observed following encounters with older females, and in females who had a romantic encounter with males.

It is important to note that vocal complexity is, for the most part, manifested horizontally. That is, the elements that contribute to complexity tend to be spread out over a temporal plane. To fully appreciate vocal complexity, therefore, and to use it as a fitness indicator, the listener must have an immediate memory sufficient to accommodate the material that, in its totality, manifests the complexity. It is assumed that those who were able to sustain attention to long stretches of vocal activity, and hold onto them long enough to carry out the necessary appraisals, were able to make adaptive choices. Research over the last 20 years indicates that individuals with more robust working memories are better able to comprehend syntactically complex material than those with less adequate memories (e.g. Just and Carpenter 1992).

# 34.7 CONCLUDING REMARKS

To be complete, theories of linguistic evolution must identify the environmental changes that produced phenotypic variation and the modes of selection that reinforced certain of the variants, thereby increasing reproductive success. I have proposed a sequence of adaptive responses to environmental changes that increased vocal and verbal complexity, enhancing fitness and the perceptual, memorial, and control systems that support the speech of modern humans. Critical to the proposal is the insertion of new stages of development in human life history, and the extensive remodelling of pre-existing stages, each of these new and remodelled stages making a distinct contribution to the evolution of language.

In each stage, the basis of selection is assumed to have differed somewhat from preceding and following stages. In all four stages, according to the proposals offered, natural selection occurred, with sexual selection also occurring in adolescence. Both inter- and intrasexual selection would have increased vocal and verbal complexity, and ultimately the capacity for complexity at other levels of language. I suggest that increases in ancestral levels of vocal complexity and control were a step toward phonetics, phonology, and the combinatorial privileges that enable massive vocabularies (Studdert-Kennedy 2005, this volume).[3]

---

[3] Where fitness is concerned, it is assumed that the signals that evolved, and were later adopted (and adapted) for 'language', were highly functional from the start: one's mastery of the 'phonology' and 'syntax' of these complex signals would have implied some level of neurological, cognitive, and social functioning in infancy. On this one measure, at least, speakers unable to demonstrate vocal and verbal competence at sexual maturity would have fallen below the fitness standards of others.

# CHAPTER 35

# TOOL-DEPENDENT FORAGING STRATEGIES AND THE ORIGIN OF LANGUAGE

## KATHLEEN R. GIBSON

Human and great ape foraging strategies differ profoundly. Adults and older juveniles in some chimpanzee and orang-utan populations use tools facultatively to extract foods from embedded matrices (Parker and Gibson 1977). In human societies, however, the staple foods of all but the youngest human infants are acquired and prepared by means of tools. Humans also share food among family members and provision their young. Even the relatively simple technology of many human foraging societies facilitates access to a very wide range of extractive foods, including underground tubers, roots and bulbs, bone marrow, eggs, brains, embedded insects, shellfish, and turtles, as well as scavenged and hunted foods including burrowing mammals, big game, fish, and fowl (Parker and Gibson 1979; Kaplan et al. 2000). All societies use containers to gather, transport, and share larger quantities of food than would otherwise be possible (Tanner and Zihlman 1978), and all possess cooking and other food-processing techniques that permit the use of potentially toxic nuts and vegetables and ease the digestive process (Wrangham 2009). Human tool-dependent foraging strategies thus enable humans, in contrast to apes, to exploit a much wider range of environments, live in larger social groups at increased population densities, reproduce at shorter intervals, and have expanded lifespans and brain size.

Although humans can learn to make and use some tools primarily by observation and demonstration, language is integral to human tool-dependent foraging. Humans share information about locations of natural resources needed to make tools and about the physical properties and appropriate treatment of technical materials. Foragers also share information acquired during hunting and gathering expeditions. Much of this information is pertinent to future foraging success, for instance the state of ripening of plants, whether waterholes exploited by animal game are full, whether signs have been seen of migrating game, and whether certain travel routes have been impeded by floods (Marshall 1976). Much of this information-sharing demands a critical process, never observed in wild apes, but integral to language: displacement, that is, the ability to talk about absent objects and events. At some point, humans also began sharing critical food-processing information, such as which foods require leeching or heat treatment for toxin removal. Conceivably, some of this information could be transmitted in the absence of language via mime. Experiments have shown, however, that the comprehension of categorical information is greatly facilitated by language (Harnad, this volume).

Hominin ancestors embarked upon new non-ape-like foraging strategies by at least 2.6–3 mya. This included crushing bones to obtain marrow, using sharp-edged stone flakes to cut meat from bones, and, possibly, exploiting underground plant storage organs (Wrangham et al. 2009; Wynn, this volume). By 1.8 mya, hominins had expanded their geographic range into Eurasia and were manufacturing hand-axes which could have been thrown at prey and/or used to process a variety of plant and animal materials. At some point, hominins began using fire to cook, and containers to gather and transport food to home bases (Tanner and Zihlman 1978; Wrangham 2009). They also mastered new social foraging strategies, including male–female food-sharing bonds, and parental and grandparental provisioning of the young (Lancaster and Lancaster 1983; Hawkes et al. 1998; Kaplan et al. 2000). By 400 kya, hominins were using spears and hunting big game (Wynn, this volume). By 164 kya, in South Africa, modern humans were charting lunar cycles and predicting tidal fluctuations in order to improve the efficiency and safety of shellfish collecting (Marean 2010b). By Upper Palaeolithic times, Europeans were predicting and exploiting seasonal migrations of fish and mammals (Gibson 1996b). Indeed, with the exception of burials and pigment use at about 400 kya (Wynn, this volume), most pre-Upper Palaeolithic changes documented in the archaeological record pertain to foraging techniques and foraging technology.

Some have argued for the importance of specific foraging strategies in language evolution. Parker and Gibson (1979) proposed that tool-dependent extractive foraging by australopithecines started the language ball rolling by encouraging maternal–young referential communications in relationship to food provisioning. Deacon (1997) proposed that male–female, foraging-related pair bonds selected for symbolism. Bickerton (2009a) argued that power scavenging by *Homo erectus* populations led to protolanguage and displacement, and Wrangham (2009) considered cooking to be the key hominin adaptation propelling all further cognitive and social change. These hypotheses are not mutually exclusive. Each focuses on different aspects of the hominin dietary niche and different aspects of language facility, and each is likely to have been operable at some point in hominin evolution.

The evolution of spoken languages required increased capacities in a variety of motor and cognitive domains, including, among others, fine motor and procedural learning skills essential for fluid speech and gestures, declarative learning skills essential for the communication of factual knowledge, working memory, hierarchicalization skills, symbolism, and syntax (Gibson and Jessee 1999). These emerging functions reflected enhanced functioning of numerous brain regions, including the neocortex, cerebellum, basal ganglia, and hippocampus, all of which expanded in absolute size in human evolution. Dietary changes and cooking provided the increased energy needed for expanded brains, while at the same time permitting the decreased gut size demanded by Aiello and Wheeler's expensive tissue hypothesis (Aiello and Wheeler 1995).

Major changes in foraging strategy rarely occur in isolation. Rather, they are accompanied by altered strategies of environmental exploitation and altered social structures. Indeed, an examination of other hypothesized selective forces indicates that most assume the existence of non-ape-like foraging patterns. Falk (this volume), for example, explicitly argues that mothers placed their babies down in order to engage in manual foraging endeavours. Power and Knight's menstrual strike hypothesis (this volume) assumes female meat provisioning by males. Foraging theories are most often contrasted with 'gossip' or social group size theories of language evolution (Dunbar, this volume). Most ape–human differences in social structure, however, relate to altered foraging strategies, such as provisioning the young, male–female pair bonds, and group hunting endeavours. Moreover, gossip alone could not have provided the energy resources needed for brain evolution. In essence, then, nearly all language evolution scenarios presuppose that language evolved in an environment of expanded and changed foraging strategies. Expansions in tool-dependent food procurement and processing techniques may, thus, have jump-started the language evolution trajectory, kept it rolling throughout the evolutionary process, and provided the necessary fuel for brain expansion.

# CHAPTER 36

# GOSSIP AND THE SOCIAL ORIGINS OF LANGUAGE

## ROBIN I. M. DUNBAR

To the extent that language (and, particularly, in the grammatically structured form that we have it) allows us to exchange information, conventional wisdom has in the past invariably assumed that the kind of information involved is mainly either environmental (where to hunt, where to meet up at some future time) or instrumental (instructions on how to make a tool or how to hunt). The former would probably have been favoured by most anthropologists and psychologists, the latter by archaeologists. For this conventional view, language and speech (the articulatory mechanism that underpins it) are strictly functional in the instrumental sense, and hence any social uses that might arise are casual by-products of the capacities that underpin these instrumental functions. However, both social and instrumental functions involve the transfer of information (albeit of different kinds) and grammar itself is indifferent as to which kind of information it has to work with. Consequently, one could as easily argue the causal sequence the other way around: language evolved to support a social function, and the instrumental benefits are a by-product of this information-sharing capacity.

Language does not exist in a vacuum, but rather requires a community of speakers who can use it. One question we can ask is whether, in the course of human evolution, the size of the social community had any influence on whether or not language was necessary. The social hypothesis for language origins is premised on the claim that primates use social grooming to bond social groups, and the time available for grooming has an upper limit (at around 20% of total waking time) due to the demands of foraging and food processing (Dunbar et al. 2009). Because grooming time is a linear function of group size in both primates (Dunbar 1991; Lehmann et al. 2007) and birds (Radford and Du Plessis 2008), this sets an upper limit to the size of community that can be integrated using this conventional primate mechanism (Dunbar 1993, 2008). Dunbar (1993) suggested that language represented a phase shift in communication that allowed this partic-ular glass ceiling to be breached, making it possible for hominins to evolve significantly larger groups than those found among primates (see Aiello and Dunbar 1993). One reason for this suggestion is that, unlike grooming, language-based interactions (i.e. conversation) can be performed while one is engaged in other activities (e.g. feeding, walking, working), thereby permitting time-sharing and a more efficient use of time. In this sense, speech becomes a form of grooming-at-a-distance.

The key to this argument lies in the fact that group-living incurs significant costs that rise monotonically with group size, mainly because the time demands of foraging increase exponentially with foraging group size (Dunbar et al. 2009). Some additional form of bonding would have been required to allow hominins to break through this glass ceiling. One solution would be to use the vocal channel of communication that primates already have. Indeed, it seems that animals already exploit this opportunity. McComb and Semple (2005), for example, have shown that, across primate species, vocal repertoires become larger as social group size increases. Similarly, Freeberg (2006) showed (both observationally in the wild and experimentally in captivity) that the vocal repertoire of the chickadee becomes structurally more complex as group size increases. These findings suggest that the vocal repertoire can become more complex in order to provide a supplementary mechanism (that is, supplementary to grooming) for social bonding.

The correlation between brain size and group size in primates (Dunbar 1992; Dunbar and Shultz 2007b) implies that this first stage of vocal complexity must have occurred with the appearance of the genus *Homo* around 2 million years ago (mya) (Aiello and Dunbar 1993; Dunbar 2009). Note that a similar date would be implied by the tool-making hypothesis for language evolution, since manufactured tools emerge for the first time around 2 mya. In this case, however, the putative demands of instruction in tool manufacture would imply that full-blown language would have evolved at this stage, whereas the social hypothesis requires only an extension of natural primate vocal communication with full grammatical language evolving later.

However, it is unlikely that supplementing grooming with a more complex vocal channel would suffice to raise social group sizes from the maximum seen in primates (species averages of ~50) to the very large groups characteristic of modern humans (approximately 150; Dunbar 1992). The social bonding (or gossip) theory of language evolution argues that, ultimately, fully grammatical language evolved to bridge this gap. If language did replace grooming as a mechanism for community-bonding, we can ask when community size became large enough to demand such a phase shift. We can estimate this by interpolating hominin fossil brain volumes through a series of equations that specify neocortex ratio, then group size, and finally required grooming time, based on the primate relationships. We seek to identify the time at which grooming time requirement rose significantly above the upper limit of approximately 20% of total day time found in primates. The most recent analysis, using improved regression equations and better estimates of fossil brain volumes (Dunbar 2009), suggests that the crisis point probably emerged with the appearance of archaic humans (*Homo heidelbergensis*) around 500,000 years ago.

How does language break through the grooming glass ceiling? One important way it does so is by allowing time to be used more effectively by increasing the broadcast group size (the number of individuals we can interact with at any one time). Grooming is a strictly one-on-one activity, but, in naturally-forming conversations (as opposed to lecture-like contexts where turn-taking is formally regulated by social rules) language allows us to interact with up to three individuals at the same time (Dunbar et al. 1995). Language's information exchange capacities also allow us to use the social time we have available in ways that primates cannot: we can find out what has been happening in our social network while we have been away (monkeys and apes can only ever know about what they actually see), we can use conversation to manage both our own reputations and those of other members of the group (especially freeriders and 'social loafers'), and we can use it to identify group members (through social badges such as dialects or shared knowledge; Nettle and Dunbar 1997; Dunbar 2008).

If language is essentially social in character, then this should be reflected in the topics we prefer to talk about. Analyses of natural conversations suggest that around two-thirds of conversation time is devoted to social topics, but only about 10–20% is devoted to instrumental topics (work, technical know-how, etc.) (Dunbar et al. 1997). Conversations that are about social relationships (gossip in its generic sense) seem to be both intrinsically more interesting for us and easier to engage in than technical or work-related conversations, which tend to flag more quickly. Indeed, Mesoudi et al. (2006) showed, using a classic transmission chain experimental design, that the social content to a story (involving intentions and mental states) is significantly easier to remember and pass on than purely factual material (even if that factual information is about people's interactions).

Language, however, lacks one key ingredient that allows grooming to work as a bonding mechanism, namely endorphins (a neuropeptide involved in pain control as well as bonding in primates). One suggestion is that laughter (initially just synchronized chorusing) might have bridged the gap; later, this could have been developed into a more explicitly conscious process through the creation of language-based jokes once language came on-line (Dunbar 2008).

# CHAPTER 37

# SOCIAL CONDITIONS FOR THE EVOLUTIONARY EMERGENCE OF LANGUAGE

## CHRIS KNIGHT AND CAMILLA POWER

It might be imagined that social conditions are irrelevant to how language evolved, since humans everywhere use language independently of social complexity or political system. Yet despite cultural differences, all human societies have certain underlying features in common. Below a certain threshold level of cooperation and trust, not even the simplest form of language could evolve.

Language has emerged in no other species than humans, suggesting a profound obstacle to its evolution. What could this be? If we view language as an aspect of cognition, we might expect limitations in terms of computational capacity. If we see it as essentially for communication, we would anticipate problems in terms of social relationships.

To determine whether the constraints are fundamentally computational or social, let's begin with the simple activity of pointing. From a human standpoint, it seems surprising that wild-living apes don't use intentional gestures to point things out to one another. Why not? Possibly they lack the necessary mental machinery. Yet it turns out that an ape is quite capable of using a gesture analogous to pointing—the so-called 'directed scratch'—to indicate where it wishes to be groomed (Pika and Mitani 2009). If an ape can point for its own benefit, what stops it from doing so for others? The explanation is clearly social. Apes are not motivated to coordinate their purposes in pursuit of a shared future goal (Tomasello 2006). And if this obstructs so simple an activity as pointing, the chances of language evolving are slim to say the least.

The term 'mindreading' refers to the ability to infer others' mental states on the basis of direction of gaze, facial expression, and so forth. While all primates have significant abilities of this kind, in humans they have undergone extraordinary development. The differences can be attributed to contrasting levels of cooperation. Take two individuals, each seeking to reconstruct the other's thoughts. Either they compete or they cooperate. If they compete, each will seek to block the other's mindreading efforts while promoting its own. Only where both sides cooperate simultaneously will Darwinian selection favour what psychologists term 'intersubjectivity'—the mutual interpenetration of minds.

Apes cooperate, but only up to a point. They are eager to obtain information about one another's intentions, but much less willing to divulge comparable information about themselves. When a mindreading ape obstructs a companion from reading its own mind, or when it displays no intention of helping in this respect, it unavoidably deprives itself of a potential source of information about its own thinking—namely its companion's mental representation of that thinking. Neither simple pointing nor more complex referential signing can evolve under such circumstances. Language evolution will not get off the ground because such individuals cannot 'see' their own thoughts and intentions as if from another's perspective (Tomasello 1999).

The more primates rely on physical dominance to gain reproductive success, the less likely they are to assist one another's mind-reading efforts or to develop capacities for empathy or role reversal. Conversely, wherever individuals need coalitions to resist being dominated, we might expect them to encourage one another to participate in their feelings and plans.

Human psychology evolved in adaptation to a particular way of life, based on hunting and gathering. Evolving humans compensated for vulnerability to dangerous predators by developing unprecedented forms of social cooperation, material culture, and strategies for remembering, transmitting, and exchanging accumulated knowledge. One view—known as 'deep social mind' (Whiten 1999)—holds that distinctively human forms of cultural transmission necessarily co-evolved with cooperative mindreading together with increasing egalitarianism.

Unlike chimpanzee societies, which are hierarchical, hunter-gatherers living in societies most similar to those in which we evolved are committed egalitarians. Humans everywhere may share dispositions toward dominance as part of the inherited psychological package. But equally, humans have corresponding tendencies to resist being dominated—'counterdominance'. At a certain point in human evolution, the benefits of deploying Machiavellian intelligence to impose dominance over others became matched by the costs of overcoming the Machiavellian resistance of others (Erdal and Whiten 1994). The continual effort to prevent violence from paying produced broad and enduring structures of social collaboration. Strategies of collective counterdominance culminated eventually in what has been termed the 'reverse dominance' characteristic of extant hunter-gatherers, among whom the only approved form of violence is that of the ritually organized community enforcing its own egalitarian law (Boehm 2001). It was while this transition was being accomplished that selection fostered intersubjectivity—a willingness to share what I am thinking with you, and seek to know what you are thinking of my thoughts. Selection pressures for language were not a separate development but part of the same process.

But what concretely tipped the balance in favour of egalitarianism? Detailed evolutionary scenarios are always risky, but unless scientists are prepared to offer bold speculations, the hypotheses in circulation will remain abstract and untestable. One concrete scenario—the female strategic alliance model—goes beyond unisex accounts, factoring strategies of evolving human females into the story of modern human origins (Power and Aiello 1997; Knight 2008).

As human group sizes increased, this placed a premium on enhanced social intelligence—the ability to negotiate alliances—in turn driving selection pressures for neocortical expansion (Dunbar 1996). As offspring became more highly encephalized, they took longer to mature and became more energetically demanding, intensifying the costs to mothers of pregnancy, nursing, and childcare. Responding to these challenges, mothers could enhance their fitness by sharing childcare burdens and extracting greater energetic investment from males. Human hypersociality and intersubjectivity emerged initially under such selection pressures, with mothers increasingly willing to trust allocarers with their babies (Hrdy 2009; Zuberbühler, this volume). The most trustworthy helpers in this respect were women's own female kin: sisters, aunts, older daughters, and, above all, their own mothers (cf. O'Connell et al. 1999).

But what of males? Where females in a primate species can provision themselves and their babies, they may only require good genes. A single male may then suffice for a harem. Where, by contrast, a group of alloparenting females need time, energy, and food, they enhance their fitness by attracting into their extended family as many cooperative males as they can. But this implies strategies to prevent violence from determining the outcome of sexual competition. Extant human hunter-gatherers illustrate how such outcomes can be achieved, with males 'showing off' not through violence but by displaying prowess and generosity in hunting and sharing the meat (Hawkes 1990).

This brings us to the possible relationship between sexual signals, reproductive strategies, and conditions for the evolution of language. In primates, sexual displays such as chimpanzee oestrus, while not in themselves violent, regularly trigger violence (Goodall 1986). In the human case, ovulation has become effectively concealed, compelling males to spend more time with their partners to increase their chances of producing offspring. While we would expect this to reduce intermale reproductive differentials and associated conflicts, one distinctively human problem remains. The phasing out of external signs of ovulation leaves menstruation salient as the one remaining external cue of a human female's imminent fertility.

In any primate social system, the most damaging forms of violence are likely to reflect conflicts over sex. In marking out certain females as imminently fertile, menstruation might incite males to pick and choose between partners on that biological basis, abandoning former partners and struggling for additional mates in a sexual 'free-for-all'. In practice, in any functioning human social system, no such behaviour is likely to be tolerated. Hunter-gatherers in particular respond decisively to the threat before any damage can be done. By the time any male gets to know that a woman has begun menstruating, the female community will already have taken decisive countermeasures. Cultural anthropologists tend to explain the ensuing performances in terms of menstrual phobias or taboos, often with implications of irrational superstition. From a Darwinian perspective, the concerns and associated responses have a rational explanation.

We propose this specific context as the one triggering reverse dominance and the full transition to language and symbolic culture. Whenever a local female starts to menstruate, she is perceived as a threat. The danger is that some dominant male will take advantage of her condition, abandon his current partner, bond with his new one and—once she is pregnant—abandon her in turn. Those threatened by any such prospect (mothers and potential mothers, their male and female kin, subdominant males) need to take decisive action. They can do this by placing any female who has begun menstruating under strict supervision from the start, isolating her from male company. Through their physical solidarity, females, cycling and non-cycling, convey the message to males: 'violence will not pay'. Using blood-red cosmetics they present a united front. This is the crucial step into the 'rule of law' (Knight 2009), in turn establishing the conditions necessary for language to evolve.

# LAUNCHING LANGUAGE: THE DEVELOPMENT OF A LINGUISTIC SPECIES

# CHAPTER 38

# INTRODUCTION TO PART IV: LAUNCHING LANGUAGE: THE DEVELOPMENT OF A LINGUISTIC SPECIES

## MAGGIE TALLERMAN AND KATHLEEN R. GIBSON

In Part IV, we present the most immediately 'linguistic' chapters, dealing with the central properties to be accounted for in language evolution. The first chapter (39), by Stephen Anderson, asks why certain structural regularities become established in the world's languages, including universal properties such as structure dependence. Some have argued that languages are the way they are solely because the same functional pressures have shaped them (see Chater and Christiansen, Chapter 65). Other theorists see the evidence as necessitating a rich, species-specific cognitive capacity for language, though the precise contents of this are less certain. If the language faculty is genetically fixed, its contents must presumably be (largely) adaptive. But this is highly implausible, as both Bickerton (Chapter 49) and Lightfoot (Chapter 31) also argue: how could very specific aspects of syntax, for example, enhance an individual's fitness as the language faculty was evolving?

Anderson argues that there is no need to assume a dichotomy between a genetically determined language faculty and a language faculty shaped by external factors, such as functional pressures and the effects of grammaticalization. These are not alternative explanations for observed patterns, but rather, can be seen as part of the same process, once we take into account the Baldwin effect. This refers to a situation—an ordinary part of natural selection—in which a particular phenotype previously produced only in response to specific environmental influences subsequently becomes the norm in a population. (The trait selected for may subsequently go to genetic fixation, so that no phenotypic plasticity remains, a development known as genetic assimilation; Waddington 1953). The language faculty supports the learning of specific kinds of linguistic systems, and it would not be at all surprising if natural selection favoured those who were able to acquire language most efficiently. Grammars that are most easily learned will be the ones that are acquired, because generations of better learners also shaped grammars to be more learnable (a type of niche construction; Odling-Smee et al. 2003). As Anderson notes, this makes it harder for linguists to figure out what linguistic properties *have* to be attributed to the language faculty, rather than having external explanations. But an account along these lines also allows us to propose a language faculty that was shaped (at least in part) by natural selection, like other complex biological systems.

The next five chapters (40–44), by James Hurford, Michael Corballis, Stevan Harnad, Terrence Deacon, and Robbins Burling, investigate what cognitive capacities must have evolved before any kind of language could get off the ground. These capacities include the development of meaning (semantics and pragmatics), the origins of grounded symbols, and the ability to learn and store words. Hurford argues that other animals possess at least proto-conceptual categories, which form the basis for conceptual meaning. Many animals can think about things that are not in the here and now, as both laboratory experiments and observations in the wild show. Animals exhibit planning abilities, have mental representations of territory, and can make calculations based on their knowledge, such as transitive inference (e.g. X is higher ranking than Y and Y is higher ranking than Z, so X must be higher than Z). Moreover, there is evidence that our closest primate relatives are capable to some extent of knowing what conspecifics know, thus exhibiting at least some of the properties that constitute theory of mind. Why, then, do only humans have language? Hurford argues that one critical factor distinguishing humans from other primates is shared intentionality, but the theme of 'why only us?' recurs often in Part IV, and receives different answers from various quarters. Also, work cited by

Gibson (Chapter 3) indicates that apes do sometimes share intentions, so shared intentionality is not completely unique to humans.

Two chapters, by Harnad (42) and by Deacon (43), focus on the emergence of symbolic meaning. Like Hurford, Harnad argues that the first step is the ability to categorize—to distinguish between members and non-members of categories such as 'edible item' or 'predator', an ability that is clearly widespread in animals. However, whereas other animals can only learn categories by sensorimotor induction, humans also acquire categories directly from other people, perhaps initially in evolution via prelinguistic gestural communication (Harnad suggests). Category names—words—are a later development. Of course, not every meaning can be transmitted by what Harnad terms 'symbolic instruction': this is the 'symbol grounding problem'. Some core set of meanings can *only* be acquired by sensorimotor induction, and Harnad's research suggests that if about 10% of categories are acquired the hard way, by direct experience, and then given a label, this 'grounding kernel' of meanings can then be combined and recombined to define all remaining meanings in a lexicon.

Deacon's chapter (43) looks in depth at symbolic reference in language, arguing that the symbolic units of our mental lexicons construct a complex, interrelated network of indexical relationships, in which words always 'point' to each other: each morpheme is interpreted with respect to other entries in the network. Word-learning is a very special capacity in humans. It is not merely a matter of learning arbitrary associations, which a number of animal species can certainly manage; nor is word reference analogous to the referential alarm calls found in various animals. Deacon emphasizes, though, that there is no evidence of linguistically specialized neural apparatus (structures, processes, or regions) having evolved in humans. Rather, existing cognitive capacities form the foundation for language, using existing neural systems, and language systems are widely distributed in the brain, showing much neural plasticity; as other authors in Part II emphasize, there is no 'language module' in the brain.

The idea that the gestural modality came before the vocal modality, mentioned above in connection with Harnad's chapter, is treated in more detail by Corballis (Chapter 41); see also MacNeilage (Chapter 46). Corballis argues (in agreement with Deacon) that primate calls do not make a good model for language. Vocal learning is very limited in other primates, whereas we know from 'ape language' research that all the other great apes are capable of learning the rudiments of a protolanguage presented as a visual system of manual gestures or symbols on a keyboard. Thus, Corballis argues, the earliest forms of language were likely to be gestural. Corballis suggests that as the use of the hands for other purposes (such as tool-making) increased, so the use of facial gestures and eventually phonation would need to compensate, with the vocal modality finally taking over from the gestural, possibly quite recently. The idea that language had gestural origins is also supported by some of the authors in Parts I and II (see especially de Waal and

Pollick, Chapter 6, and Arbib, Chapter 20). However, it remains both controversial and a minority view amongst theorists in language evolution.

Burling's chapter (44) revolves around the lexicon, and the cognitive capacities needed to acquire it. Like Hurford, Burling starts with the importance of a rich conceptual system, and of shared intentionality—specifically, in the sphere of word-learning, the human ability to achieve 'joint attention' (where a child and an adult focus together on a third entity) without instruction; see also Hurford on the 'naming insight' in young children. Burling also emphasizes other central abilities which need to develop beyond the homologous capacities in apes—the capacity for imitation, without which no words will be learned, and the ability to perceive patterns (thus, tying in with Harnad's suggestions concerning categorization, which must also rely on pattern-finding). As for the lexicon, a uniquely human and uniquely linguistic trait, Burling proposes an explanation for why it would be advantageous to have a system that requires so much learning: it is highly flexible, since form-meaning pairs can be added throughout life; and, of course, flexibility is a highly adaptive trait in our species, since it enables us to adapt to (and indeed, to create) new environments and niches.

A frequent question concerns the apparent chicken-and-egg problem of how the first person with an advantageous linguistic mutation of some kind would benefit if no one understood them (see also de Boer, Chapter 63). Burling suggests an answer: it's not production capacities that are originally selected for, but comprehension. Even if there is initially no intention on the part of the signaller to communicate information, an animal that interprets a signal correctly will always benefit, whether the meaning is 'I'm about to attack you' or 'I want to mate with you'. It seems from ape language research (see Gibson, Chapter 3) that comprehension abilities are rather advanced in our closest relatives; Kanzi is the most impressive example. (See also Seyfarth and Cheney's discussion of comprehension in baboons, Chapter 4.) Yet these abilities have clearly not been followed by the production of protolanguage in the wild state. Also, production requires fine motor skills that comprehension does not, and these skills, both manual and vocal, are lacking in most animals. Apes, for instance, seem to lack vocal motor skills. Complex motor skills not only require a lot of brain power, they also necessitate specific changes in peripheral anatomy. Burling may thus be correct that comprehension came first, but production certainly must have been selected for.

The following three chapters (45–47), by Michael Studdert-Kennedy, Peter MacNeilage, and Andrew Carstairs-McCarthy, look at the origins of phonetic distinctions, phonological structure, and morphology. The critical event in the evolution of phonology is the formation of the 'particulate' system, whereby a small number of sounds are concatenated to form an infinitely large set of meanings. As Studdert-Kennedy points out, non-specialists often assume, largely on the basis of alphabetic writing systems, that consonants and vowels can easily be isolated in the acoustic and/or articulatory stream of speech—but they cannot.

What, then, are the atomic elements of sound systems? Consonants and vowels (known by linguists as segments) form the basis of all words in all languages, but they are in fact abstract, linguistic (i.e. cognitive) entities, rather than measurable physical entities.

MacNeilage (Chapter 46) starts off by outlining the standard view, that each speech segment consists of a bundle of *distinctive features*, such as 'voice' (e.g. distinguishing [p] from [b]) or 'nasality', though he subsequently suggests that phonological features are not innate entities, and may not even truly exist, but instead may merely be convenient categories adopted in linguistic description. Studdert-Kennedy (Chapter 45) adopts a different view; for him, the basic particle of speech is the phonological *gesture*, a constriction formed by one of six organs making up the vocal tract. He defends this view on the basis of child language acquisition and evidence from computational modelling. The regions of the vocal tract are differentiated by the child in response to cognitive pressure from an increasing vocabulary, and this, posits Studdert-Kennedy, is what also occurred in evolution. As vocabulary grew in our hominin ancestors, so particulate speech emerged—forming the requisite contrasts needed to keep words separate from one another. Computational modelling supports what would otherwise be mere conjecture, showing how segments and syllables emerge via the processes of self-organization, with conflicting pressures from speaker economy, on the one hand, and listener clarity, on the other, predicting just the kinds of systems we find in languages.

MacNeilage argues that the initial organizational unit of speech was not the phonological gesture, but the syllable, an essentially inevitable consequence of rhythmic alternations of the jaw from the closed to the open position, paired with phonation (sound). When the jaw is raised, we get consonants; when it is lowered, we get vowels. Initially (in ontogeny and phylogeny), protosyllable frames are very simple, relying on the inertial position of the tongue. This is the case in infant babbling and first words, and, like Studdert-Kennedy, MacNeilage thus regards infant vocalizations as providing a good indication of what the earliest speech of hominins was like, since the same kinds of biomechanical constraints operate in both cases. MacNeilage argues that the 'poverty of the stimulus' (see below) is irrelevant in phonology, suggesting that 'a listener hears all the sound patterns he/she needs to learn'.

Carstairs-McCarthy (Chapter 47) turns to a related, but distinct, area: morphology. Why should languages have complex words (combinations at morpheme and word level) at all? As Carstairs-McCarthy points out, the very existence of a morphological system separate from the combinatorial system used for syntax seems highly unlikely, yet it exists. One of the peculiarities of morphology is that it is the only part of the language faculty that appears to be virtually optional in realization—some languages have much morphological complexity, but others almost none. Although some scholars deny that there is in fact a separate system,

Carstairs-McCarthy argues that some features are more or less uniquely morphological: bound morphology (morphemes that can't stand alone), allomorphic variation (*baked*, but *taken* not *\*taked*), morphophonological alternation (*leave* but *lef-t* not *\*leav-ed*), and irregularity. Although most accounts seeking an explanation of the existence of morphology turn to grammaticalization (see chapters in Part V), Carstairs-McCarthy suggests an alternative: morphology was not a late development in the language faculty, but could have originated at the protolanguage stage, well before syntax. The basis for this account is that phonological processes of assimilation would inevitably occur between proto-words if they were frequently contiguous, and these could give rise to allomorphy and to morphophonological alternations.

The final five chapters (48–52), by Maggie Tallerman, Derek Bickerton, Andrew Carstairs-McCarthy, and Cedric Boeckx, look at the syntactic component of language. Three authors consider the properties of modern linguistic systems, thus asking which properties must ultimately be accounted for by a comprehensive theory of language evolution. Tallerman's chapter (48) on syntax introduces the central concepts and properties of syntactic systems in the world's languages, providing an overview for the non-specialist reader. Picking up on these themes, Bickerton (Chapter 49) evaluates existing scenarios for the origins of syntax, concluding that the main accounts are all flawed in various ways, and suggesting an alternative scenario.

Carstairs-McCarthy's chapter (50) on complexity asks whether all languages are equally complex in their syntax and morphosyntax. Linguists have traditionally regarded known languages (living and extinct, spoken or signed) as being commensurable in terms of complexity, but some recent claims have cast doubt on this view. Two languages in particular have been argued to lack complexity in significant ways: Riau Indonesian and Pirahã. Pirahã, for instance, has been claimed to lack recursion in its syntax. The concept of recursion came prominently to the attention of researchers outside of linguistics with the publication of Hauser et al. (2002), and is also discussed in the chapters on syntax by Bickerton (49) and Tallerman (48). Both Tallerman and Bickerton conclude that recursion is not the main explanandum in syntax.

The question of complexity with respect to creole languages arises in the chapters by Bickerton (49) and by Carstairs-McCarthy (50). Creoles are full natural languages (they have native speakers) but are claimed by many to exhibit exceptional simplicity in their grammars (see also Roberge, Chapter 56). Bickerton regards creoles as one specific type of 'window' on evolutionary processes (see also Botha, Chapter 30). Bickerton aims to determine an overall order in which the main processes in syntax must emerge from a simpler precursor system. These central processes (a) assemble words into hierarchical structures; (b) determine the boundaries of the resulting units; (c) displace elements from their normal position; and (d) determine the reference of phonetically unrealized elements. Bickerton suggests that since processes for marking clause and phrase boundaries are lacking in creoles today, ways of determining phrase boundaries may have been a very late (or even the final) property of syntactic systems to emerge.

Stepping back to pre-modern states, both Bickerton and Tallerman (Chapter 51) assume the existence of protolanguage, a non-syntactic pre-language. As a concept, protolanguage is broadly supported by researchers from most disciplines, though it is not regarded favourably from within the Minimalist programme (e.g. Piattelli-Palmarini 2010). However, the putative properties of protolanguage are disputed. The 'compositional' or 'synthetic' model of protolanguage, most widely associated with Bickerton's work (e.g. 1990), is strongly defended by Bickerton and by Tallerman on linguistic and biological grounds. Other models exist (e.g. holistic and musical protolanguage) but are shown to be highly problematic.

Boeckx (Chapter 52) returns full circle to the questions posed by Anderson's chapter (39) at the start of Part IV. Boeckx mounts a detailed defence of the concept of the 'poverty of the stimulus', or 'Plato's problem', from within the (Chomskyan) Minimalist Program. The idea is that children acquire their native languages with such ease, rapidity, and uniformity, despite receiving an incomplete and impoverished input, that they must have some kind of 'head start' in this process, an innate language faculty or 'Universal Grammar'. However, in line with Chomsky's recent work (e.g. 2005, 2010), Boeckx stresses the importance in language evolution of principles that are not specific to the language faculty, so called 'third factor' effects arising spontaneously as a result of generic principles such as laws of form; see also Anderson's contribution.

Boeckx argues that very little genuine evolutionary novelty is required to 'buy' the unique language faculty in humans, despite the fact that other animals are not close to having anything similar. He argues for a recent (occurring just in *H. sapiens*) and sudden emergence of the language faculty, with 'at most one or two evolutionary innovations'. The critical development bringing all the linguistic and generic properties together is the 'lexical envelope': the property that turns concepts into lexical items that can be combined by the operation 'Merge'; see Bickerton (Chapter 49) for discussion. The idea that a catastrophic event could give rise abruptly to the entire language faculty *ex nihilo* is criticized by Bickerton, who, as we have seen, favours the approach that sees full language as a development from a simpler protolanguage via a number of stages. Bickerton also proposes that Merge was a critical development in the evolution of syntax—in fact, the first in the sequence of events that transformed protolanguage into full language. Contrary to the Minimalist approach, though, Bickerton and Tallerman both argue for a prior protolanguage stage, in which words are simply uttered in short, unstructured sequences, not arranged hierarchically into phrases.

Linguists in general have been relatively slow to join the debates on the origins and evolution of language, but fortunately, that has changed quite rapidly over recent years. Interest is now widespread, and comes from many different theoretical perspectives, ranging from the 'biolinguistic' investigations (from a broadly

Chomskyan perspective) cited by Boeckx, to the perspective taken by (again, broadly) functional approaches, centring on the study of grammaticalization (see Part V). What is evident is that linguists must spell out clearly for researchers from other disciplines what exactly it is that biologists, neurologists, psychologists, and others have to account for: the observed properties of language-as-it-is (in all its forms) and the fact of its acquisition (or development) in real time by human children.

# CHAPTER 39

## THE ROLE OF EVOLUTION IN SHAPING THE HUMAN LANGUAGE FACULTY

### STEPHEN R. ANDERSON

A central question from a linguistic standpoint is: what aspects of language are hardwired, i.e. genetically endowed and therefore innate, and what aspects depend mainly on environmental factors? Heredity and environmental factors are intricately intertwined, and it is now clear that humans (and many other animals) possess far more developmental plasticity than was once assumed. Other possibilities exist too: some aspects of the language faculty might have emerged owing to self-organization (de Boer, Chapter 63), and language itself might also evolve (in some way) to be learnable (Chater and Christiansen, this volume).

Much theorizing about these matters assumes that any given property which we find in language is to be attributed *either* to a genetically determined cognitive faculty *or else* to the effects of external shaping effects such as functional pressures, the working of historical change, or other such non-inherited factors. I suggest in the survey below that this is a false dichotomy: that in fact, these two foundations for linguistic structure are not mutually exclusive, but rather that evolutionary considerations lead us to expect a duplication of foundation for much of the structure of language as we find it.

Broadly and uncontroversially, the field of linguistics is concerned with the scientific study of language and its structure. When we try to be more precise, however, the object of inquiry in the field is less obvious, and has changed considerably over time. I will assume, following the 'cognitive revolution' of the past half century, that we want to study not sets of sounds, or words, or sentences, or texts in themselves, but rather the knowledge or cognitive capacity that underlies our production and understanding of these things.

However we characterize this capacity, it seems clear that it is a species-specific property of us as human beings. Absent severe and obvious pathology, all humans acquire and use language spontaneously, without the need for explicit instruction. Furthermore, no member of any other species appears to have this capacity, with or without instruction.

When we examine the communicative behaviour of other species, we find that this is quite different in character from human language. Communication in all other species is based on a fixed set of discrete possible messages, essentially limited to matters of the here and now. This set cannot be expanded by combining elements to form new and different messages. In nearly all cases, animal communication systems emerge without the need for relevant experience, although in some instances either the conditions of use or the precise external form of a message may be refined by experience. In instances where the system is grounded in learning, of which song in oscine songbirds is by far the most robust example, the actual system acquired still does not go beyond the character of an essentially fixed list. Even a bird with a repertoire of hundreds of songs still conveys the same basic message in the singing of any one of them.

Human language, in contrast, provides an unbounded range of discrete and distinct messages. As opposed to the communicative behaviour of other animals, these messages are produced voluntarily under cortical control, and are not bound to the presence of particular stimuli. The mechanism behind the unboundedness of language is twofold: two distinct discrete combinatorial systems interact to allow for an unlimited set of messages grounded in a manageable inventory of meaningful symbols ('duality of patterning'; Hockett 1960). One subsystem combines members of a small set of individually meaningless sounds according to the phonological pattern of the language into meaningful words, which are in turn combined by a quite distinct subsystem, the language's syntax, into phrases, clauses, sentences, etc. (Although rarely included in discussion of these issues, the presence within the system that combines meaningful elements into larger constituents of two distinct subsystems, morphology and syntax, is a further remarkable property of human language, and one for which the functional motivation is at best obscure. See Carstairs-McCarthy (Chapter 47) for some discussion.) The recursive, hierarchical nature of such combination is the basis for the open-ended expressive capacity it provides.

No other system of communication found in nature has these essential proper-ties, and no non-human animal has—or has ever learned—a system with such structure. This should not be surprising, because language is grounded in our biology just as the often quite remarkable communicative systems of other animals are in theirs. Since we differ in these basic respects from even our closest relatives, chimpanzees and bonobos, the relevant capacity must have emerged in our evolu-tionary history since the time of the last common ancestor we share with them. The question is not whether this evolution took place, but how.

The re-emergence in the literature on linguistics of evolutionary discussion is largely due to the arguments of Pinker and Bloom (1990). They showed that human language has all of the basic character of an evolved system: a complex structure, with many specific mechanisms related to one another in partially arbitrary ways and collectively well suited to the function of expressing hierarchically organized propo-sitional structures in a linear channel from which they can be recovered. The clear adaptive significance of this function, which enables the cumulation and communi-cation of knowledge among members of a group, makes a strong case for an account in terms of evolution through natural selection. Subsequent discussion has made clear that the human language faculty meets the necessary conditions for such an account: a trait which is variable to at least some extent, where the variation is heritable such that phenotypic variation in the trait is plausibly associated with differential fitness.

While it is an article of faith among linguists that the human language faculty is completely uniform across the species, there is really no evidence for a conclusion as strong as that (see also Carstairs-McCarthy, Chapter 50). While it is undoubtedly true that a child raised in a community speaking any of the world's languages will acquire that language, regardless of the language of the child's biological parents, that does not mean there is no variation in the details of the acquisition of diverse languages by children of diverse ancestry. We do know that the language capacity has probably been relatively uniform for at least 40,000–50,000 years, since the settlement of Australia (whose indigenous languages are comparable in structure to those spoken elsewhere). While this suggests that there is not presently very much genetic variation in the language faculty, or at least that it has not been subject to much recent selection, the mere fact that any child can learn any language does not establish that there is no variation at all.

Evidence from a variety of sources for the heritability of variation in language abilities is surveyed in Stromswold (2001, 2010). An additional argument leading in the same direction is provided by Ladd et al. (2008), who note that specific alleles of two genes (*MCPH1* and *ASPM*) that have been subject to recent selection and that are involved in brain growth and development have a distribution that corresponds strikingly with the distribution of tonal contrasts in the world's languages. These authors do not at all claim to have found, as reports in the popular literature sometimes represented it, 'genes for tone'. Rather, they suggest that genetic differences, selected in this case for quite independent reasons, might result in a differential propensity to develop tonal contrasts in a language (though see Diller and Cann, Chapter 15).

We know that tonal distinctions come and go in the history of individual languages (see various papers in Fromkin 1978 for discussion). As a result, the observed asymmetry could result from a difference between populations in the predilection to make the kind of re-analysis that leads to the development of tone, with even very small differences showing significant effects over periods of thousands of years. The innovative alleles at issue here are associated with *non*-tonal languages, so their phenotypic effect seems to be to inhibit the emergence of tone and to facilitate its loss. There is no reason to believe that this effect on tone in language is at all the basis of the observed selection, but the observed effect does contribute to the demonstration that differences in the language faculty correspond to heritable genetic differences. See Diller and Cann, this volume, for further discussion.

The best evidence for the selectability of language, of course, would be the demonstration on the basis of molecular genetics that genes coding for language have in fact been under selection pressure. Unfortunately, with almost negligible exceptions, the relevant genes have not been established, nor a fortiori have we established the relevant relations between genotype and phenotype on the basis of which we could talk precisely about these genes 'coding for' language. As a result, arguments of this sort are quite impossible in our present state of knowledge.

Nonetheless, the human language faculty appears to have the characteristics of a system shaped by evolution. When we look at the communication systems of other species, we find that their biological nature is typically shaped in essential ways that provide privileged pathways for ecologically significant messages. For instance, the vomeronasal organ in mice is attuned to a limited range of odorants, primarily including pheromones that are the basis of much communicative behaviour in the species, and quite distinct both in its own physiology and in the brain region to which it projects from the more general olfactory system. The auditory systems of frogs, bees, and many other animals display particular sensitivities in exactly the frequency range in which energy concentrations are found in conspecific sound production. Given the centrality of language in human life, it would be quite remarkable if human biology had not been shaped evolutionarily by suitability for its functions.

Why, in fact, might we be tempted to believe otherwise? The treatment of these matters by Hauser et al. (2002) distinguishes 'FLN,' the 'faculty of language in the narrow sense' from 'FLB' or the 'faculty of language in the broad sense', and suggests that the only uniquely human component of a unique faculty for language (or FLN) might well be recursive combination in the syntax. Everything else relevant to language and composing FLB, on their account, either is not specific to language or else has analogues or homologues in other (non-linguistic) species.

Even if this narrowly drawn conclusion is valid, however, it does not follow that the role of evolution is negligible in shaping the language faculty in modern *Homo sapiens*. Much of FLB, in Hauser et al.'s terms, is distinctively structured in ways that at least suggest adaptation driven by increased utility for its use in supporting language. Those properties relevant to language that have analogues in other species, such as the capacity for vocal learning and imitation, must nonetheless have evolved (convergently) in *Homo sapiens*, because they are absent in our near biological relatives. Even language-relevant traits with homologues in closely related species show signs of having been shaped in humans by their role in language. Categorical perception, for example, may be characteristic of mammalian auditory systems broadly, but the specific range of categories which we find in humans are evidently grounded in the details of speech articulation and its acoustic/auditory effects. We now know (Fitch 2002) that the descended larynx is not a uniquely human characteristic, since members of other species lower their larynx to exaggerate size in competitive interaction, or more generally when phonating. Nonetheless, the permanently lowered state of the human larynx is surely a response to the utility of such a position for producing a wide range of speech sounds, and the prominence of speech in our behaviour.

One might well accept the broad role of evolutionary pressure in the emergence of a language faculty, while denying that the specific structural properties we attribute to that faculty were shaped in that way. There is a strong appeal to the notion that these details are to be seen as emergent, derived from general properties of computational systems. On that approach, the precise form taken by human language is inevitable and necessary, and could not have been otherwise given the overall computational task to be performed.

While this argument is tempting, consider the parallel between human language and bird song. Thousands of oscine species each learn their songs on the basis of models, usually ones heard in early life, and in most cases the range of songs that are (and indeed that can be) learned is rather narrow and species-specific. Surely it would be obvious to a nightingale scientist reasoning in an analogous way that the computational properties of song production necessarily lead to the consequence that a song must have a four part structure, with an $\alpha$ portion (selected from within a specific range) followed by equally specific $\beta$, $\gamma$, and $\omega$ sections (Todt and Hultsch 1998). Were the scientist a zebra finch or a white-crowned sparrow, however, he or she would completely disagree, insisting that a completely different structure was the inevitable consequence of the computational nature of song. And song sparrow scientists would be sure they were all wrong.

The point here is that humans are a single species, so we can only study a single language faculty. Evolution is clearly capable of producing many distinct and highly individual learning spaces in the many species of songbirds (though probably not all logically possible ones; Podos et al. 2004), and there is no obvious reason why what we find in the only species of language learners available should be any less a contingent outcome of the evolutionary history of that species.

Against this background, let us consider the basic goal of linguistic research. The object of inquiry in the field, the language faculty, supports the rapid and efficient acquisition and use of natural language, is a consequence of our biological nature as humans, and probably arose through natural selection. While much is often made of the extent to which aspects of this faculty overlap with other aspects of human cognition, the faculty as a whole is unique to humans, and investigating it is in principle independent of whether the relevant cognitive ability is based wholly, partially, or not at all on capacities domain-specific to language. But how do we infer the contents of this faculty, in order that we might ask how it arose in our evolutionary history?

The primary source of evidence comes from examination of the grammars of particular languages, considered as systems of knowledge that arise in the minds of speakers in interaction with their early linguistic experience. Whenever we can argue for the presence of some specific content in a grammar, it must have as its source one or another of the following (or their interaction):

- Input data: only systems corresponding to the evidence can be acquired.
- Learning process: only systems accessible through the available mechanisms of learning can be acquired.
- Language faculty [narrow sense]: only cognitively possible systems can be acquired.

The combination of the last two, the learning algorithm and the set of constraints on possible systems imposed by the overall nature of the mind and brain, is what is commonly described as the 'language faculty' (in a broad sense). The difference is significant: some cognitively possible systems might be inaccessible to the mechanisms by which language is acquired, and some of the outputs of the learning algorithm might be inconsistent with the way the mind is organized. We will not be concerned with this distinction here, however. What we wish to contrast is the contribution to the content of our knowledge of language that is due to properties of the input data, and the contribution made by the cognitive system(s) we call the language faculty.

In particular, an important strategy in the field is to argue that some of what we find in speakers' knowledge of language is *not* attributable simply to regularities in the 'primary linguistic data' on the basis of which that knowledge arose. Arguments of this sort are known as arguments from the 'poverty of the stimulus,' and would appear to provide a direct pathway to the structure of the language faculty. After all, if speakers come to know something for which the evidence in the data is not sufficient, it must be due to the properties of the system itself.

A number of arguments of this form have been offered, of which the argument from English auxiliary fronting (claiming that grammatical regularities are grounded in constituent structure rather than simple linear concatenations of words) is in some sense the poster child. Analysing specific examples would take us beyond the scope of this chapter, but the problem raised is that of proving a negative: how can we show that there is *no possible* way of deducing the property in question from regularities in the data?

Those who reject such arguments sometimes refer to them as arguments from the 'poverty of the imagination' instead. In the case of the structure-based nature of syntactic regularities, rejecting the claim that this is a property of the language faculty and assuming it could be learned from the data would make it remarkable that children always get it right, and we never find rules in any language that reflect an analysis of sentences simply as strings of words. Thus, even though it *might* be possible to learn that grammatical rules are structure-sensitive, it seems much more plausible to attribute this to the language faculty: learners only entertain structure-based hypotheses. But we cannot show that this *must* be the case, because of the difficulty of establishing that learning is absolutely excluded.

In spite of this problem, many linguists accept (and offer) arguments following the 'poverty of the stimulus' logic for the content of the language faculty. Much more general, however, are arguments of a different sort. When something appears to be true of all (or nearly all) languages, it is tempting to attribute it to the language faculty: either it is something assumed by the learning algorithm, or it is a characteristic of the space of cognitively possible grammars. In this case, however, it is even more important to bear in mind that the regularity we find might simply be a consequence of regularities in input data.

Of course, a property found in all languages could logically just be the residue of some contingent property of 'proto-World,' assuming human language originated only once in our history (see Nichols, this volume). To the extent such a universal is also characteristic of signed languages (Sandler and Lillo-Martin 2006), this is unlikely, since no existing signed languages have an origin in common with spoken languages.

More plausibly, a property found in all languages might be due to the constitutive characteristics of the language faculty; or else it might be due to (externally imposed) regularities in the input data available to learners around the world, and thus learnable. The tension between these accounts is roughly that between 'formalist' and 'functionalist' views of linguistic universals, and the two are generally posed as incompatible alternatives. The logical possibility also exists, however, that both might be true in a given case, if properties of the language faculty reflect recurrent regularities in the data. Looking at language from the perspective of evolution, in fact, it can be argued that this duplication is exactly what we should expect.

Arguments for the origin of universals in externally imposed properties of the data available to learners can be found in a number of domains. Blevins (2004) argues, for instance, that most if not all substantive universals in phonology are the product of independent mechanisms of linguistic change: the phonologies of languages are as they are not because they must be, but because linguistic change channels them into these patterns and not others. Mielke (2008) makes similar arguments about the most basic characteristics of phonological systems, the set of distinctive features defining dimensions of contrast and natural groupings of sounds. On this view, the Neogrammarians were right: the only way to understand why languages are as they are is to understand how they developed. In consequence, the regularities we find are regularities of the input data, and tell us nothing about the structure of the language faculty.

A similar result is suggested in syntax by Newmeyer (2005) on the basis of work by Hawkins (1994, 2004). On this picture, functional motivations lead speakers to choose particular structures whenever possible; later learners interpret the predominance of these structures in the data as a grammatical rule. When regularities become entrenched across languages, it is not because the language faculty requires them, but because external (functional) effects have conspired to make them properties of the available data.

We are left with a problem: on the one hand, there is reason to believe that a rich cognitive capacity for language is species-specific. But when we try to determine the substance of that capacity, there are alternatives to attributing specific aspects of linguistic structure to the language faculty. At least a possible hypothesis is that the two converge, and that attributing something to the language faculty and finding an external basis for it are not mutually exclusive.

To make sense of this, let us ask how the specific properties of the language faculty might have arisen, as part of our genetic endowment as humans. It is implausible to say that all the details have arisen through natural selection because they are adaptive: it is difficult to imagine how conforming to the principle of subjacency might have enhanced reproductive success in human history (Lightfoot 1991, this volume). But there is an alternative: that the genetic fixing of the properties of the language faculty came about through Baldwin effects.

The evolutionary effect associated with James Mark Baldwin has been given a variety of formulations and elicited a variety of reactions: for a survey and a spectrum of opinions, see Weber and Depew (2003). The logic involved can be outlined as follows. Certain behaviour that is learned (or culturally transmitted) may be selectionally advantageous under the conditions in which the organism finds itself. Selection may then operate to favour individuals who are able to learn the advantageous behaviour rapidly and efficiently. The learned behaviour may itself alter the characteristics of the environment within which selection occurs ('niche construction': Odling-Smee et al. 2003), favouring its acquisition even more. The eventual result may be to make the learning of such behaviour hardwired (the fastest and surest way to learn it). In these terms, there is nothing mystical (or Lamarckian) about the Baldwin effect: it is simply normal natural selection operating to favour learning mechanisms that contribute to enhanced fitness. Since the language faculty is a capacity to learn certain sorts of systems, this is just where we might expect such a principle to operate. Looking at language in this way, we expect the language faculty to favour the acquisition of grammars that have the properties most likely to characterize the ambient languages of learners.

Arguments such as those of Blevins and Mielke (for phonology) and Hawkins and Newmeyer (for syntax) show that historical change, based on auditory and other effects and functional pressures, is likely to converge on corpora of speech data that display certain recurrent properties. Computer simulations have suggested that structure sensitivity can plausibly be expected to arise in communication. But then the Baldwin effect should lead to the incorporation into the language faculty of these recurring regularities, so they don't have to be learned *de novo* by each new generation of speakers. If this reasoning is correct, properties of the language faculty are likely to duplicate, or at least closely reflect, regularities for which we can also find alternative explanations. The availability of those explanations is thus not mutually exclusive with attributing the properties in question to the language faculty. On the other hand, this often leaves us without a way to show that something that is true of all—or most—languages is in fact constitutive of language as a cognitive system.

The central task for linguistics is to devise ways to infer the properties of the language faculty from the available data. But in fact, very few aspects of language can be attributed *necessarily* to the biologically based language faculty. Some would argue that this shows there is not really much content to a species-specific language faculty. But that seems contrary to the available evidence for our capacity, unique in the animal world, to acquire and use systems with the properties of natural languages.

The human language faculty, like any complex biological system, has surely been shaped through evolution by natural selection. While directly adaptive explanations for the specific properties of natural language are not generally available, Baldwin effects in the context of the human cognitive 'niche' can be much more successful. This makes it possible to restore language to its place in the natural, biological world, but it makes our task as linguists much harder, because of the convergence of properties of the language faculty with ones for which external explanations are available.

# ACKNOWLEDGEMENTS

Some of the ideas in this introduction also appear in Anderson (2008). I am grateful to participants in EvoLang 8 for comments, especially Maggie Tallerman, Tecumseh Fitch, and Robert Berwick, although they certainly bear no responsibility for the consequences of my ignoring their good advice.

# CHAPTER 40

# THE ORIGINS OF MEANING

## JAMES R. HURFORD

## 40.1 MEANING BEFORE LANGUAGE

Generally, research in language evolution assumes some continuity between apes and humans. Despite the enormous gap between human cognition and communication and their ape counterparts, it can be shown that: (1) precursors to both sentence meaning (Conceptual Meaning) and speaker meaning (Pragmatic Meaning) are present in animals; (2) something other than the ability to comprehend such meanings was necessary to launch language, perhaps shared intentions; and (3) once language was launched it resulted in abilities to create new kinds of meanings.

### 40.1.1 Conceptual meaning

To see much of this, we must be prepared to concede that things other than linguistic expressions (e.g. words and sentences) can 'have meaning' in some sense for non-human animals. In this sense, the class of substances we call catfood is meaningful to my cat, the class of potential prey animals is meaningful to wild lions, and the alpha male gorilla is meaningful to the members of his harem. To be sure, these classes and individuals do not stand for anything other than themselves. Catfood is not symbolic of anything to a cat. So we are not yet speaking of a symbolic kind of meaning, such as the arbitrary relation between a word and its class of referents (e.g. the word *dog* and the class of dogs). But catfood plays a significant role in the mental life of a domestic cat. A cat behaves differently toward catfood, both in anticipation and in its presence, from the way it behaves toward doors, mud, birds flying overhead, and its owner's lap. An animal, virtually any animal, mentally carves up the world into distinct categories, and different behaviours are associated with those categories. Different categories of object have different affordances for animals. The affordances of objects (the potential actions that are typically associated with them, together with their perceptual qualities—size, colour, shape, smell, taste, texture, etc.) constitute complex mental representations in the animal's brain, presumably implemented by tangles of interrelated neural activation potentials. If we do not rule by fiat that the term *concept* be reserved only for linguistic creatures such as adult humans, the categories in terms of which an animal segregates its experiences can reasonably be called *proto-concepts* at least.

Proto-concepts exist in many animals, including primates and birds. Even frogs distinguish among prey objects, threatening objects, and obstacles. These are the seeds of one end of the symbolic relationship that, for humans, exists between words and objects. In human language, words stand for concepts, and concepts themselves (at least the concepts of concrete things) relate to entities in the external world in roughly the same way that non-human animal proto-concepts do. To oversimplify at this point, words are public labels attached by convention to mental categories rooted in perception and action. For this to start to happen, all animals in a group must have similar (not necessarily identical) proto-concepts. This is not too much to ask, as all members of a group contend with the same environmental challenges.

A distinguishing feature of language is our ability to refer to absent things, known as *displaced reference*. A speaker can bring distant referents to mind in the absence of any obvious stimuli. Thoughts, not limited to the here and now, can pop into our heads for unfathomable reasons. This ability to think about distant things necessarily precedes the ability to talk about them. Thought precedes meaningful referential communication. A prerequisite for the emergence of human-like meaningful symbols is that the mental categories they relate to can be invoked even in the absence of immediate stimuli. Thus, while the existence in animals of complex systematic responses to classes of object in the environment is necessary for the emergence of symbols (words) standing for those classes, it is not a sufficient basis for this emergence. What is needed is some capacity to entertain the concepts in the absence of any stimulus from the environment. There is evidence that some animals can think of things that are not present.

A phenomenon extensively researched in both developmental and comparative psychology is *object permanence*. Many animals and some very young infants seem not to know that when an object disappears behind an obstacle, it still exists. There are two forms of object permanence test, one harder than the other (Wynne 2001). The easier test, the *visible* object permanence test involves simply moving an object, such as a treat, behind a screen, where it is invisible to the animal or child subject, restraining the subject briefly, and then seeing if the subject moves to retrieve the object from behind the screen. In the harder test, the *invisible* object permanence test, the treat is placed into a small container in view of the subject, then the container is hidden behind the screen, where it is emptied out unseen by the subject; the empty container is then shown to the subject, who passes the test if he/she searches behind the screen. Here is a brief summary of the comparative results:

| Species | Visible/invisible | How long? |
|---|---|---|
| Domestic chicks | Neither | |
| Squirrel monkeys | Visible only | |
| Cotton-top tamarins | Both | |
| Parrots | Both | |
| Dogs | Both | Up to 4 mins |
| Chimpanzees | Both | Overnight |
| Humans over 3 years | Both | Very long times |

As can be seen, dogs' attention span to hidden objects is very brief. Yet for a few minutes the dog is indeed mentally attending to an object that is not present to its senses (Watson et al. 2001). The chimpanzee Panzee witnessed a piece of desirable fruit being hidden outside her cage, and next day spontaneously informed another researcher where it had been hidden. She had kept the hidden fruit in mind overnight, in the sense that memory of it and its desirability had not been lost to her (Menzel 2005). These non-human abilities differ in degree and in domain from human abilities. Humans can keep specific objects in mind for far longer than has been shown in any other species. Also, humans are much less restricted in the kind of objects that they remember. Panzee was motivated to remember the hidden fruit, and non-humans are generally not much interested in long-term memories beyond food and social relations, including sex.

Related to object permanence is episodic memory. This is a kind of memory for specific events that have happened to the individual subject. Loss of episodic memory shows up in amnesia, a condition in which patients cannot recall things that have happened to them, like where they woke up this morning, or how they got to be wandering this particular street. Such patients often have no loss of other kinds of memory, such as memory for piano-playing or bicycle-riding (procedural memory) or general knowledge of geography (Paris is the capital of France: semantic memory). Interestingly, amnesiacs typically don't lose their linguistic abilities—they still speak fluently and grammatically, albeit with signs of frustration at their loss of episodic memory. It has been suggested that episodic memory is unique to humans (Tulving

1999, 2005). Such claims challenge researchers to find counterexamples, and various animal species have been shown to display 'episodic-like' memory capacities.

Scrub jays cache their food for later retrieval. In experimental conditions, scrub jays have been shown to have a memory for the 'what', 'where', and 'when' of food-caching episodes. They revisit cache sites ('where'); they revisit sites where perishable food, such as grubs ('what'), was hidden, only within a specific time-period after caching it ('when'). Cache-sites for non-perishable food, such as nuts, are revisited even after longer periods (Clayton and Dickinson 1998; Clayton et al. 2001, 2003). Undeniably, scrub jays remember what food they have hidden, and where and when, within certain limits. Such abilities may represent convergent evolution in the bird lineage of the seeds of human-like episodic memory, but clearly there are large differences. The scrub jays were only shown to remember their own activities, and again food was the motivating factor. Squirrels who cache food 'for the winter' almost certainly have no mental picture of the circumstances of the future winter; evolution has just given them an adaptive instinct to cache food.

A gorilla, King, was shown images of various events not naturally of interest to his gorilla mind, and was able to tell, 15 minutes later, which events he had seen pictures of, given a choice from an array of images including events he had not seen (Schwartz et al. 2004, 2005). A 15-minute memory for events is not impressive by human standards, falling far short of the 'mental time travel' that we are capable of (Suddendorf and Corballis 1997; Suddendorf and Busby 2003a, b). But the difference between humans and non-humans is a matter of degree (the time periods involved) and domain (food versus other interesting things), and not an absolute difference. Note that experiments with animals only demonstrate the best that they can do in the specific experimental conditions, often involving quite unnatural tasks. By contrast, we sometimes take human abilities for granted, without experimental evidence.

It is likely that much knowledge of enduring features of their environment is common to all mature animals in a group. They all know where the waterhole is, which fruits taste good, and so on. Memory for such states of affairs has been termed *semantic memory*. (This is a usage of *semantic* different from linguists' use of the term, which involves the meanings of words and sentences.) If every member of a group knows the same enduring facts, there is not much for them to communicate about (apart from renegotiating social relations). But if a creature can recall an event which it alone has experienced, then, given 'altruistic' motivation, it has something potentially useful to tell its fellows about. Human linguistic communication is in large part the sharing of information about events, however trivial, e.g. gossip. The 'altruistic' motivation may well have ulterior motives, such as gaining prestige by imparting valuable information (Dessalles 1998; Scott-Phillips 2006). The evolution of developed episodic memory, for events worth telling others about, seems likely to have been a factor in the evolution of our capacity for informative language.

Memory is characteristically conceived as a relation to the past. It is clear, however, that there is substantial overlap between a capacity for recalling the past (retrospective memory) and planning for the future (prospective memory); see Cook et al. (1983). Rats exploring a radial maze showed parallel capacities in recalling which arms of the maze they had already visited (retrospective memory), and which arms they had yet to explore (prospective memory). Clearly, non-human animals can plan for the future to some limited degree. Their mental lives are not, as is sometimes asserted, absolutely bound by the here and now.

Animal planning is most evident in navigation. Some apparently impressive navigation is not actually very clever, not involving foresight or a mental map. Salmon return to their home river by swimming up the relevant coast until they smell its characteristic odour in the water (Hasler 1960). But many animals return to familiar places on the basis of a detailed map-like knowledge of the topography of their territory. When a tigress returns to her cubs after hours foraging, she is not merely following a present scent. It is inconceivable that she does not have some mental representation of where she is going, which might take her up to half an hour. Perhaps the most surprising evidence for map-like representations comes from insects. Several experiments show that honeybees learn the landmarks of their territory and can navigate to food sources and back to the hive even around obstacles, such as high hills or cliffs (Srinavasan et al. 2000; Menzel et al. 2005). Probably the proximate mechanisms involved in insect navigation are different from those used by mammals, as their brains and evolutionary niches are very different. But the commonness of some degree of planning in the animal kingdom, whatever the mechanism involved, shows that some mental representation of future goals, away from the here and now, is not surprising, especially in species closely related to humans. Again, it must be said that animal planning is more limited in time span than human planning.

In summary, many animals exhibit some capacity for entertaining concepts divorced from the here and now. Such proto-concepts are the stuff upon which the evolution of human semantic capacity has built. We humans can learn to attach public labels to our concepts. The capacity for fast learning of tens of thousands of arbitrary conventional mappings between private concepts and publicly uttered signals distinguishes us from other species. But some non-human species can learn lesser numbers of such mappings, given a captive artificial environment of association with humans. The language-trained bonobo Kanzi has mastered several hundred lexigrams, comparable to the vocabulary of a 3-year-old human child. It is presumed that when Kanzi signals, say, BANANA or TICKLE, something like human thoughts for these concepts go through his mind, although we have no neurological evidence. Of course, the subsequent progression to human gram-matical use of words is another matter. Merely knowing the meanings of words or lexigrams is less than knowing how they fit into grammatical sentences.

In the wild, no animal learns an arbitrary conventional signal for some concept. The well-known vervet monkey alarm calls are almost entirely innate, although there is some fine-tuning in infancy of the stimuli which trigger these calls (Seyfarth and Cheney, this volume). Bird and monkey responses to the alarm calls of other species are plausibly the result of symbiosis due to the species evolving in the same environment. Vervets learn to show extreme vigilance to the sounds of evolutionarily recent dangers, such as the cowbells of Masai herders, but they have not evolved any specific alarm call for this danger (Cheney and Seyfarth 1990). But even these innate calls reveal a disposition to attach public signals to private mental concepts. A contrary view, denying the involvement of concepts, would be that the vervets have separately evolved two mutually supportive reflex responses, one response to utter a bark on seeing a leopard (for example), and a second response to run up a tree on hearing a bark. On this view, the same kind of co-evolutionary story would have to hold for each of the other vervet alarm signals, for eagles and pythons. Attributing (proto)-concepts of leopards, eagles and pythons to the vervets, mediating between the alarm calls and appropriate evasive actions, accounts for the fact that the same evasive actions are taken when no alarm call has been given, but the presence of the predator concerned is detected. For instance, a solitary vervet encountering a leopard will still climb a tree. A solitary vervet spotting an eagle within swooping distance will still dive under the bushes. These are responses to the particular predators, not to alarm calls. An economical account of vervet behaviour needs to capture the coincidences between the evasive actions on hearing alarm calls and the same evasive actions when confronted with the predators themselves.

Experiments by Klaus Zuberbühler et al. (1999) on another alarm-giving forest monkey species, Diana monkeys, show that 5 minutes after hearing a call for one predator (e.g. a leopard), they are less surprised at concrete evidence for its presence (e.g. a leopard growl) than at evidence for the presence of a different predator (e.g. an eagle screech). A natural interpretation of the data is that the monkeys hold a representation of the particular predator in their minds for a few minutes, on hearing the call (see also Zuberbühler, this volume).

Many animals can be trained to make same/different judgements about stimuli, and to generalize these judgements across broad classes of stimuli which were not in the training material. Sameness and difference are abstract, relational concepts (Wynne 2001). Alex, an African Grey parrot, could make judgements of sameness and difference in the categories of colour, shape, and material. Alex plainly also had second-order understanding of some concepts. In answer to a question such as 'What colour is this?', when shown an object, he could answer with, for example 'blue'. This shows that, beside being able to make the first-order judgement that the object was blue, he also understood that blue is a colour, a second-order judgement, applying one predicate (COLOUR) to another (BLUE) (Pepperberg 2000, this volume).

A variety of laboratory and field evidence can be interpreted as showing that animals can do calculations involving transitive inference. Baboons live in troops of about 80, and yet seem to know the social dominance relations between any given pair of members of the troop. In a troop of 80, there are over 3000 pairs of animals. It seems unlikely that a baboon memorizes all pairwise dominance relations between troop members. An alternative is that the baboon generalizes by transitive inference from a smaller number of examples. The thinking attributed to the animal can be paraphrased as 'Fred is subordinate to Bill and Bill is subordinate to John, so Fred is subordinate to John'. We are not attributing verbal reasoning to the baboon, of course, but rather a private process manipulating mental representations of relations between individuals.

Humans are able, to some extent, to take a detached view of their own mental processes. We can come to realize, for instance, that a thought we have just had is mistaken. There is evidence that some animals are capable of this kind of 'meta-cognition', albeit to a much more limited degree than humans. Some animals have shown behaviour interpreted as 'uncertainty monitoring'. Dolphins and macaques, after training to discriminate between two classes of stimuli, are shown borderline cases and given the option of making an 'I don't know' response. When making such responses, they exhibit the same kind of hesitant behaviour as humans dithering about a choice (Smith et al. 1995, 1997).

Along with *concept*, the term *proposition* is reserved by some for human thought alone. It is assumed that, however much the mental processes of non-humans may resemble human thought, they do not entertain genuine propositions. Of course non-humans do not think in language, because they have no language. It has been argued, however, that the essential components of propositional thought are present in other species, including primates (Hurford 2003b). The core of the argument involves identifying the two essential components of a logical proposition, a predicate and its argument. If we become aware, in the night, of something flashing, and if our thought parallels this way of expressing it, then we have in mind both the 'something', whatever it is, and the thought FLASHING, which we apply to the 'something'. In this example, the FLASHING is a mental predicate, and the 'something' is its argument. It is not necessary that any words come to mind when we become aware of something flashing; what happens in our brain in such an instance is that something grabs our attention, and we make a judgement (e.g. FLASHING, possibly unverbalized) about it. Hurford relates the PREDICATE (argument) logical structure to the co-action of two separate neural mechanisms in humans and other mammals, known as the ventral and dorsal streams. The dorsal stream is responsible for our orientating response to attention-grabbing objects. The ventral stream, which operates later once focal attention is directed at an object, delivers judgements about the object, including its perceptual properties (e.g. redness, a face). Dorsal and ventral streams exist in macaques and all our close primate relatives. The claim is that some non-human thought is already essentially propositional in nature, despite the absence of language. Public language arrived on the scene later as a way of externalizing such propositional thought. Note that what is claimed has nothing directly to do with grammatical categories such as noun and verb, although there is a slightly closer connection to Topic/Comment structure.

To summarize this section, non-human animals form rich mental representations of the world, and are capable to some degree of having these representations in mind in the absence of immediate stimuli. They are also capable of some calculation or mental manipulation with these representations. It can also be argued that higher animal thought has the essential components of propositions, a type of theoretical entity sometimes denied for them. The obvious question arises why members of other species, with all this going on in their minds, don't communicate to each other about it. We turn to this question next.

## 40.1.2  Pragmatic meaning

All the mental activity mentioned above is private to the individual animals concerned. That section also focused on animals' representations of the world. Communication by one animal to another about some state of the world is triadic, involving three entities, the sender, the receiver, and the world-state described. Communication between animals starts more simply, with dyadic communication involving no reference to the world, but only involving the sender and the receiver of the message. In every human language, there are a few conventional expressions of this purely dyadic nature. The only meaning these expressions have is their illocutionary force, with no reference to any event or situation. The best example is the greeting *Hello*. This is just the conventional way in which English speakers greet each other; nothing is described or referred to. In every human language, utterances which do have descriptive content also have some illocutionary point; they are performed by speakers with the intention of causing some effect in receivers. The presence of 'objective' propositional content in sentences does not mean that humans do not also use them to *do* things, as Austin (1962) famously pointed out.

Dyadic communication is widespread among animals. Animals have ritualized signals, systematically interpreted by receivers, for doing things to each other. These include threat gestures, courtship behaviour, submission gestures, and grooming. (Interestingly, very few such signals among primates are vocal—they are mainly manual or facial actions; de Waal and Pollick, this volume.) The communicative acts thus carried out by animals resemble some of those carried out by humans in speech acts; greeting is the most obvious example. This basic kind of meaning, a pragmatic doings-things-to-each-other kind of meaning, is already amply present in non-human species.

Human linguistic expressions typically combine some illocutionary force with descriptive (propositional) content. We make statements about circumstances, we ask questions about the world, and we issue commands and requests for states of affairs to be brought about. This is achieved by reference, a conventional relation between words and the world. The most basic way in which words are used to refer to things is deictic reference (deixis). *Deixis* means pointing. Philosophers use *indexical* to convey the same meaning. Every language has a small set of pointing words, with little or no descriptive content beyond what can be found in the immediate situation of utterance. The best English examples are the demonstrative pronouns *this* and *that*, sometimes accompanied by a pointing gesture. If I say 'That's mine', the hearer identifies the referent of the pronoun by inference from the immediate situation of utterance. Usually it is some object which is salient at the time for both speaker and hearer. This basic form of reference thus involves joint attention, and the speaker directs the hearer's attention to the object concerned using a conventional linguistic expression. The same effect can be got without using the linguistic expression, simply by pointing. I can assert possession by pointing to an object and saying 'mine'. Humans, uniquely, often point to things without any simultaneous assertion about them, but just to draw attention to them as objects worthy of joint interest.

Strikingly, in the wild, non-humans do not point. In decades of field observation, no credible instance has been observed of an ape drawing the attention of another to some third object by a deictic gesture. In captivity, however, chimpanzees and bonobos do point, but almost exclusively to draw the attention of their human keepers to desired objects, i.e. to make requests. Captive ape pointing is a learned extension of a begging gesture (Gómez 2005), possibly partly spontaneously imitative of human pointing (Leavens et al. 2005). The capacity to use a deictic gesture is present, but the motivation for its use is severely limited in non-humans. In a few language-trained apes, such as Kanzi, deictic gestures are occasionally combined with conventionally descriptive signs (lexigrams on a board in Kanzi's case).

Hearers can pragmatically infer a speaker's intended meaning from context. What is going on here involves both mind-reading and manipulation, two factors which have been closely associated with animal communication (Krebs and Dawkins 1984). When humans choose what to say and how to say it, they calculate its effect on a hearer. In non-conventionalized behaviour, some animals also show a capacity for manipulating the state of mind of another. The most obvious example is tactical deception. Deliberate deception has been observed in many wild primates (Byrne and Whiten 1988, 1992; Byrne and Corp 2004). Deception involves anticipating the state of mind, or at least the behaviour, of another. There is disagreement among comparative psychologists on the extent to which animals are capable of a theory of mind, a capacity to recognize that another being has the same kind of thoughts (but not necessarily the very same thoughts) as oneself. Experiments by Hare et al. (2001) conclude that a chimpanzee can know what another chimpanzee can see, and perhaps know what the other knows. Other experiments in the same lab show that a chimpanzee can distinguish between some intentions of a human experimenter, whether cooperative or teasing. Thus some limited potential is present in apes to assess the intentions of others and to calculate the effect of an action on another. This capacity is not put to any positive communicative (i.e. cooperative) use by any species other than humans.

## 40.1.3 Why only humans?

Putting the quite rich private conceptual capacities of apes together with their capacity to read the likely intentions of others and to manipulate the attention of others, we are left with a puzzle. Given all this, what is lacking that keeps apes from benefiting from an evolutionary leap to full language, such as humans have made? Biological evolutionary theory gives plenty of reasons why individuals do not gain advantage from dispensing information to strangers, as humans do. So the non-linguistic state of non-humans is not so much a puzzle. It is humans who pose the puzzle. Why only us? And what were the factors that led us to take the extraordinary step of developing systems (languages) that facilitate disclosure of our private thoughts? A plausible partial answer has been suggested by Tomasello et al. (2005) in the shape of a theory of 'shared intentionality'. Only humans are disposed willingly to participate in helping to achieve the discerned goals of others. As Tomasello and co-authors write:

In general, it is almost unimaginable that two chimpanzees might spontaneously do something as simple as carry something together or help each other make a tool, that is, do something with a commitment to do it together and to help each other with their role if needed (Tomasello et al. 2005: 685).

This idea, of humans evolving into creatures innately disposed to shared intentionality, only pushes back the question of the evolution of shared cooperative language. In this view, shared intentionality came first, and this was a pre-adaptation on which a disposition to acquire and socially construct elaborate conventional communicative systems was built. But how did shared intentionality evolve, in just one species? Addressing this question is beyond the scope of this article. But a co-evolutionary story of parallel and mutually supportive gradual increases in language capacity and shared intentionality seems plausible.

A major hurdle, not always recognized, in the evolution of conventional signalling systems is the issue of 'signalling signalhood' (an appropriate term coined by Thom Scott-Phillips—see Scott-Phillips et al. 2007, 2008). Normal everyday actions, like walking, scratching, and eating, do not intentionally convey to another creature anything more than their intrinsic natural content, and whatever inferences can be drawn from them. If I scratch myself vigorously, do you automatically assume that I am trying to tell you something, or just infer that I have an itch?

Conventionalized signals need to be distinguished from non-signalling actions. The long elaborately structured noises that can be made with the vocal tract, distinct from a few natural functions like coughing and sniffing, have no obvious purely body-maintaining purpose. The vocal/aural modality provides a rich space in which distinctive intentional and conventional signals can be developed. Human babies naturally achieve a 'naming insight' (McShane 1979, 1980) after which vocabulary increases explosively. In children there is a steep transition from slow to fast acquisition of words effectively used, often together with a new delight in naming for naming's sake. Language-trained apes also appear to achieve a similar insight, but with much more limited post-insight explosion in learned vocabulary, and little or no apparent interest in naming for its own sake.

## 40.2 MEANING AFTER LANGUAGE

The evolution of a capacity to associate conventional public signals with concepts, in order to share one's thoughts, has had a subtle effect on the thoughts themselves. The advent of semantically compositional syntax has also affected the range of meanings which humans can entertain and express. Furthermore, we can do more things to each other using language than non-humans can using their ritualized signals.

Quine (1960) writes of 'the objective pull'. By this he means that when individual private concepts get associated with conventional signals used by other group members, the private concepts get trimmed to suit the average meaning of the public signal in the group. A child might form a private concept of dogs on the basis of a few family and neighbourhood pets, which might all be quite big for dogs. On encountering the wider world, with miniature and toy creatures which other people call 'dogs', the child adjusts its own concept associated with the word *dog*. There is psychological evidence that learning category labels for regions in a continuous space (such as colour) enhances any previously learned ability to make same/different judgements between examples drawn from the space. (For this and related work, see Katz 1963; Balaban and Waxman 1992; Goldstone 1994, 1998; Booth and Waxman 2002; Xu 2002.)

Syntax gives us the capacity for creative combinations of signals whose associated concepts may never have been simultaneously evoked by experience. Thus we can acquire concepts corresponding to *horse, white, horn,* and *forehead* by experiencing such things. Although we can never experience a unicorn, we can gain a concept of unicorns through the well-formed expression *white horse with a horn in its forehead*. If it be insisted that another component of the unicorn idea is the concept FICTIONAL, this, too, is a concept that takes linguistic construction, with something like a combination of negation and a concept of existence. Without syntactic language, it is hard to see how any concept of fiction could be acquired. Indeed, once productive compositional syntax is on the scene, allowing such combinations as negation and existence, then it becomes adaptive to have a concept of fiction, so that one can tell which expressions to believe in, or take seriously, and which not. Added to this is the extraordinary fact that some expressions which correspond to nothing in the physical world nevertheless prove to be extremely useful in making calculations about the world. Examples are *zero* and *the square root of minus one*. This last expression is clearly syntactically composed, and its meaning could not have been conceived by creatures without a conventional compositional syntactic system. Although *zero* is a single word, its meaning, like that of *unicorn* is usually inculcated in the young by means of some syntactic combination, such as *the number below one*.

Much of the material in this article is developed at greater length in Hurford (2007).

# CHAPTER 41

# THE ORIGINS OF LANGUAGE IN MANUAL GESTURES

## MICHAEL C. CORBALLIS

Language is gestural, in that it involves the use of the body to transmit information between individuals. Of course, many species communicate in this way, but human language has properties that other communication systems do not. These include ways of representing objects or actions that are not present in the immediate environment, grammatical structure, generativity, and the intention to communicate. But whether communication is language-like or not, there are different ways to use one's body to send messages, including using the limbs or the face to create visual signals, and the generation of sounds through the vocal tract.

In signed languages, hand and arm gestures serve as visual signals, which are then understood as gestures with symbolic meaning, rather than as visual stimuli per se. Similarly, according to the motor theory of speech perception, speech sounds are understood not in terms of their acoustic properties, but rather in terms of the articulatory gestures that led to their production (Liberman et al. 1967), and it is these gestures that are interpreted as having meaning. As Galantucci et al. (2006: 361) put it, 'perceiving speech is perceiving gestures'. Nevertheless language is seldom wholly spoken or wholly manual. People gesture manually as they speak, and their hand movements convey linguistic information (Goldin-Meadow and McNeill 1999; Goldin-Meadow, this volume). Lip-reading can serve as a proxy for speech perception, especially in the deaf, and in hearing individuals visual perception of mouth movements can even alter the auditory perception of speech sounds (McGurk and MacDonald 1976).

Since humans have the capacity to produce complex intentional gestures either vocally or manually, either system can serve as the medium for language. The question then arises, which came first in evolution—or could they have co-evolved? Some argue that language evolved from primate calls (see Cheney and Seyfarth 2005 for discussion), with the implication that manual language serves as an alternative when speech fails, or that manual gestures serve, at best, as a supplement to speech (e.g. Goldin-Meadow and McNeill 1999). Indeed, Goldin-Meadow (this volume) maintains that manual gestures are an essential supplement to speech in that they provide critical iconic information lacking in speech. Here, I argue that the priority lies with manual gestures; that is, language evolved initially from manual gestures with vocal elements gradually added, assuming dominance only late in the evolution of our species (cf. Corballis 2002; Armstrong and Wilcox 2007; Rizzolatti and Sinigaglia 2008).

## 41.1 INTENTIONAL SYSTEMS

One argument for the priority of the manual system is that language is intentional, and the primate vocal system, unlike the manual system, is poorly adapted for intentional production. Primate calls are for the most part under limbic rather than cortical control (Ploog 2002), and even in our closest relatives, chimpanzees and bonobos, are much more closely tied to specific contexts than are manual gestures (Pollick and de Waal 2007; de Waal and Pollick, this volume). In contrast to the inflexibility of vocalizations in primates, the communicative bodily gestures of gorillas (Pika et al. 2003), chimpanzees (Liebal et al. 2004), and bonobos (Pika et al. 2005b) are subject to social learning and sensitive to the attentional state of the recipient—both prerequisites for language. Vocal learning is especially critical to speech, and few non-human primate species appear capable of more than limited vocal learning. Studies suggest that primate calls show limited modifiability, but its basis remains unclear, and it is apparent in subtle changes within call types rather than the generation of new call types (Egnor and Hauser 2004; though see Slocombe, this volume and Zuberbühler, this volume, for new evidence of audience effects, call modification, and novel vocalizations). Attempts to teach great apes anything resembling human speech have failed (Hayes 1952), but reasonable success has been achieved in teaching them forms of visible language, either through manual gestures or using a keyboard containing visual symbols (e.g. Savage-Rumbaugh et al. 1998). This suggests that early hominins were better preadapted to develop an intentional, modifiable communication system based on manual gestures than one based on vocal calls.

The discovery of mirror neurons in area F5 of primate prefrontal cortex further supports the evolutionary priority of manual gesture (Arbib, this volume). In monkeys, these respond both when the monkey grasps an object and when it observes the same movement made by another individual—thus, perceived gestures are mapped onto gestures as produced by the receiver. As Rizzolatti and Arbib (1998) recognized, this system works essentially as proposed for the motor theory of speech perception, but applies to manual gestures, not vocalizations (though see comments in Chapter 12 above). Significantly, some mirror neurons in the monkey brain respond to the sounds of actions, such as tearing paper or cracking nuts, but not to vocalizations themselves, even though made by members of the same species (Kohler et al. 2002). Yet area F5 is the homologue of human Broca's area.

## 41.2 MIME

In bipedal hominins, the hands and arms would lend themselves naturally to mimed representation of events, and Donald (1991; this volume) suggests that 'mimetic culture' originated in the Pleistocene, coinciding roughly with the emergence of the genus *Homo*. This genus marked a switch from facultative to obligate bipedalism, suggesting freer availability of the hands. Further, brain size began to increase dramatically, reaching a peak at around 500 kya (thousand years ago), with the Neanderthals and forerunners of *Homo sapiens*, such as *Homo heidelbergensis* (Wood and Collard 1999; Wood and Bauernfeind, this volume).

Mime is fundamentally imitative, in that there is a mapping between the mimed action and what it represents. Even so, it may have at least some of the properties of language. For example, it permits representations of objects or actions not immediately present, so one can communicate about past or future events, or events in different locations. Modern signed languages retain a strong mimetic, or iconic, component. In Italian Sign Language some 50% of hand signs and 67% of the bodily locations of signs stem from iconic representations (Pietrandrea 2002). Emmorey (2002) writes that in American Sign Language (ASL) some signs are purely arbitrary but many more are iconic, yet signed languages are now widely recognized as true languages. Nevertheless, mime is not of itself sufficient to constitute language, but requires the addition of conventions.

## 41.3 CONVENTIONALIZATION

As languages develop, they become conventionalized in the interests of speed and efficiency, and so lose much of their iconicity. For example, the ASL sign for *home* was once a combination of the sign for *eat* (a bunched hand touching the mouth) and the sign for *sleep* (a flat hand on the cheek). Now it consists of two quick touches on the cheek, both with a bunched hand-shape, so the original iconic components are effectively lost (Frishberg 1975). Once the process of conventionalization is underway, signs can become arbitrary, and vocal signs can replace manual ones, to create speech. The transition may well have involved the face, and there are well-documented neurophysiological and behavioural interactions between manual movements, movements of the mouth, and speech itself (Gentilucci and Corballis 2006).

Conventionalization may well have extended to grammar. Christiansen and Chater (2008; Chater and Christiansen, this volume) have argued that grammatical language is the product, not of some innately-given universal grammar, as proposed by Chomsky (1975), but rather of a gradual process of 'grammaticalization' (Hopper and Traugott 2003) whereby communication, whether spoken or signed, is rendered more streamlined, and conventions are added to heighten precision or provide information not immediately available in pure mime. One possibility is that language evolved initially to allow communication about remembered events in the past or imagined events in the future, requiring conventions to represent times other than the present, as well as different locations (Corballis 2009). In ASL, for example, a notional time line runs through the body, with the body itself representing the present, and back and front representing past and future, respectively. In many spoken languages the verb is modified to signal tense, while in others, such as Chinese, there are no tenses and the time of an event is indicated by the use of adverbs or so-called aspectual markers (Lin 2005). These are conventions.

## 41.4 FROM HAND TO MOUTH

The transition from hand to mouth may have been prompted by increasing involvement of the hands in manufacture, leading at first to compensatory use of facial movement. The addition of phonation, perhaps through selection for a *FOXP2* mutation (Enard et al. 2002; see Diller and Cann, this volume), would allow non-visible gestures within the mouth, including movements of the larynx, velum and tongue, to be recovered from the acoustic signal, as proposed by the motor theory of speech perception (Galantucci et al. 2006; see also Goldstein et al. 2006). Other advantages of voicing include the capacity to communicate at night, the vastly reduced energy requirements of vocal relative to manual gesture, communication over larger distances, and the freeing of the hands for other activities such as the manufacture and use of tools.

These considerations may well explain the eventual dominance of *Homo sapiens* over the Neanderthals, an equally large-brained species, but one perhaps trapped in a communication system still dependent on use of the hands. Indeed, the hand-to-mouth switch may explain the extraordinary development of manufacture, artistic endeavour, music, that characterize our species (Corballis 2004). Precisely when human accomplishments began to diverge from those of Neanderthals is a matter of controversy; some have suggested that it was as early as 300 kya (McBrearty and Brooks 2000), but other evidence suggests that the critical burst of innovation may have been between 80 and 60 kya in Southern Africa (Jacobs et al. 2008), leading to the dispersal and subsequent dominance of *Homo sapiens* throughout the globe.

# CHAPTER 42

# FROM SENSORIMOTOR CATEGORIES AND PANTOMIME TO GROUNDED SYMBOLS AND PROPOSITIONS

STEVAN HARNAD

The adaptive success of organisms depends on being able to do the right thing with the right *kind* of thing. This is categorization. Most species can learn categories by direct experience (*induction*). Only human beings can acquire categories by word of mouth (*instruction*). Artificial-life simulations show the evolutionary advantage of instruction over induction; human electrophysiology experiments show that the two ways of acquiring categories still share some common features; and graph-theoretic analyses show that dictionaries consist of a core of more concrete words that are learned earlier, from direct experience, so the meanings of the rest of the dictionary can be learned from definition alone, by combining the core words into subject/predicate propositions with truth values. Language began when purposive miming became conventionalized into arbitrary sequences of shared category names describing and defining new categories via propositions.

In the beginning was the category. A category is a *kind* of 'thing': objects, events, actions, properties, states. Even individuals are kinds insofar as our brains are concerned, because to recognize an individual, we have to detect that all the different instances of that individual we encounter are instances of that same individual and not another, despite all the variation from instance to instance. So learning that this is a dog and learning that this is Fido are both cases of learning a category. In both cases, there are instances of members and non-members: with 'dog', there are instances of other members of the same category—other dogs—and instances of non-members, such as cats, trees, and rocks. With 'Fido' there will be other instances of Fido, seen near and far, in different positions, moving or stationary, awake or asleep, as well as instances of things that could be confused with Fido, but are not Fido, such as other dogs of the same breed.

It's important for organisms to get their categories right so that they can do the right thing with the right kind of thing: eat what's edible and not what's toxic, approach friend but not foe, etc. Most of cognition is the acquisition of categories and much of adaptive behaviour is doing the right things with the members and the non-members of those categories (Harnad 2005).

To be able to categorize correctly, one must be able to distinguish the members from the non-members: zebras have black and white stripes and giraffes are brown with long necks, but telling categories apart is not always that easy. It's always a matter of *detecting the features that reliably distinguish the members from the non-members*, but sometimes discovering those features is hard work. For some categories, the feature detector is inborn, as it is with the frog's bug-detector, with the hard work of detecting category-members done in advance by trial-and-error evolution during the prior history of the species. Most categories, however, have to be learned through trial and error during the lifetime of the organism. The process sounds simple, but achieving success might take a long time, and require a lot of trials: the organism encounters *positive and negative* instances (i.e. members and non-members) of the category, tries to do the right thing with them (such as eat them or avoid them), makes mistakes, which are then 'corrected' by feedback from the consequences of having done the right or wrong thing with the right or wrong kind of thing (eating toxic things and getting sick, passing up edible things and getting hungry). If all goes well, the organism will eventually learn how to tell apart the members and the non-members and what to do with what. Its brain, which contains powerful feature-learning mechanisms, will eventually detect the features that reliably distinguish one category from the other.

Notice that we have not said anything yet about words or language. We tend to think of categories as having names (and most do), but for species other than our own, 'doing the right thing with the right kind of thing' does not mean naming it, but doing something more concrete and practical with it, such as eating it, or fleeing from it. Nevertheless, the cognitive lives of many other species consist, as our own do, in acquiring new categories, except that they can only acquire them by direct trial-and-error sensorimotor experience, as just described, guided by the feedback from the consequences of correct and incorrect categorization.[1] Let us call this acquiring categories by 'sensorimotor induction'.

Our species has another way of acquiring categories, a better way, one that is freed from the delays and risks of trial-and-error learning by direct experience. We have shown in artificial-life ('a-life') simulations that simple virtual creatures in virtual worlds which must learn to do the right thing with the right kind of thing in order to survive and reproduce are able to do so through trial-and-error experience, with the help of neural nets that are able to learn to detect the features which reliably distinguish one category from another. So far that's not news. But then we showed that these creatures are out-survived and out-reproduced by creatures that can acquire categories in a much faster and surer way: through 'hearsay'. They are 'told'—by learners who have already learned them—which features distinguish the members from the non-members, hence they do not have to go through the time-consuming and risky process of learning the category through direct trial-and-error experience (Cangelosi and Harnad 2001). But this other way—symbolic instruction—is not autonomous: it can't be symbolic instruction all the way down. For how would you learn what the words in the instructions themselves stood for if all you ever heard was words?

This is the 'symbol grounding problem' (Harnad 1990). The best illustration is a dictionary. Suppose you had to learn what Chinese words meant, but all you had was a Chinese/Chinese dictionary. If you did not know any Chinese at all, looking up the definitions of words in the Chinese/Chinese dictionary would get you nowhere. It would just take you on a merry-go-round, from one meaningless definition to another. But if you already knew the meaning of some Chinese words, then that might be enough for you to learn the meanings of others via the definitions alone.

This was also how our a-life simulations had worked. In order to derive the adaptive advantage of hearsay over experience the creatures had to 'ground' some of their categories the old, hard way, via direct experience. But once they had done that, they could assign an arbitrary name to those categories, and the names could then be combined and recombined to 'define' further categories, whose descriptions could be conveyed to others, sparing them from having to acquire those

---

[1] Note that even if category learning is facilitated by watching and imitating kin or conspecifics who already know the category, as they are correctly categorizing, or even if they are deliberately pointing or miming to help us, the features distinguishing the members from the non-members must still be discovered by the brain through direct experience, by sampling a sufficient number of positive and negative instances, or we will never be able to categorize on our own.

categories the hard way.[2] That, we think, was the revolutionary advantage that language conferred on our ancestors: the advantage of symbolic instruction over sensorimotor induction, transmitting categories from those who already have them to those who do not by a means that has evolved in no other species.

Our a-life simulations were just in a toy world, with a few trivial categories, some of them being Boolean combinations of other categories. So 'edible' might be learned by induction, and 'markable' (i.e. location needs to be marked) might also be learned by induction. But then a third, higher-order category that is really just based on the conjunction of the features 'edible' and 'markable' might define the new composite category 'returnable' (i.e. return to this location for later eating) which would not itself have to be learned by trial and error in the way its two component categories were, if the creature were capable of learning through symbolic instruction. But a simple toy world and simple pairwise conjunctions do not yet show that this can scale up to full-blown natural language.

We have taken it a step further, with computer analyses of digital dictionaries. We used an algorithm to systematically reduce a dictionary to a 'grounding kernel' by eliminating every word that could be reached by definition from a combination of other words until we reached a subset of the words (it turned out to be about 10% of the dictionary) for which there was nothing left but the merry-go-round. If you did not already know what those kernel words meant, then the dictionary could not help you. But if you did already know that 10% somehow, then you could reach all the remaining 90% via definition alone (Blondin-Massé et al. 2008).

But where did the meanings of the grounding kernel come from, if not via definition? We hypothesized that these words were more likely to have been grounded by sensorimotor induction. We tested this by using the MRC psycholinguistic database to compare the words in the grounding kernel with the words in the rest of the dictionary in terms of their degree of concreteness/abstractness and their age of acquisition. The words in the grounding kernel turned out to be significantly more concrete (i.e. closer to the sensorimotor) and learned at an earlier age (Chicoisne et al. 2008).

We have also done human psychophysiological studies comparing category acquisition by sensorimotor induction versus symbolic instruction and found a

---

[2] As will be made clearer below, the crucial thing is not the 'naming' itself, for that is merely paired association. Language begins with being able to combine a name (a 'subject') with another name (a 'predicate') into a proposition with a truth value, asserting something to be the case (which is always equivalent to describing a new category). 'APPLE FRUIT' is asserting that an apple belongs in the category fruit, and 'CAT ON-MAT' is asserting that the cat belongs in the category, 'things on a mat'. We assume that the origin of arbitrary names is in instrumental actions and purposive miming associated with the category for which the action eventually becomes the name, once it is being used and understood as a component in a proposition intended to describe or define a category. Once it is being used as a component in a proposition, its resemblance to its referent (which is what connected the action to its referent) is no longer necessary or relevant, and the category names become arbitrary shared conventions.

late positive component of the event-related brain potential[3] that emerges during trial-and-error learning only if the subject is successful in learning the category; it is absent in those who fail to learn. But then when the unsuccessful learners are told in words what feature distinguishes the members of the category from the non-members, the component that accompanied successful induction learning appears in their brain activity too, as they are now able to categorize successfully using the verbal instruction, suggesting that instruction has produced an effect similar to that of induction (St-Louis et al. 2008).

Clearly, both our own species and others had and have the capacity to acquire categories by induction. Our closest cousins, the apes and simians, also have body structure and motor capacities similar to our own. We are all potentially equipped, for example, to both observe and (thanks to our mirror neurons; see Arbib, this volume) imitate and even mime 'doing the right thing with the right kind of thing'. None of this is yet linguistic, but it could certainly be useful. Now suppose that our species evolves a propensity toward this sort of non-linguistic gestural communication,[4] because of the adaptive benefits it confers in transmitting certain sensorimotor skills and perhaps even some help that it provides in the learning (by induction, not instruction) of some categories (Harnad 2007). Only two things are missing for a transition to language (in the gestural mode): (1) category-names and (2) truth-value-bearing propositions.

Prior to language, a 'name' is merely an arbitrary response associated with a category. If I first mime 'eating' and everyone recognizes that that gesture is associated with eating, then it is no longer necessary that the gesture should resemble eating in order to evoke that association. The 'iconicity' of the gesture, the resemblance that first made the associative link, becomes irrelevant, and the gesture can gradually become arbitrary and conventional, as long as everyone keeps making the association. But rote association is definitely not the same thing as linguistic reference. Perhaps pointing and making purposive gestures to evoke an association comes closer to reference, but not linguistic reference, for words are not

---

[3] The event-related potential is a brain wave that can be measured at the surface of the scalp. The wave, about 1–2 seconds long, is a smooth series of positive and negative oscillations, the earlier ones being more sensory and the later ones being more cognitive, and correlated with expectation, attention, and knowledge.

[4] Gesture is the natural modality for first establishing a functional association between objects and actions, through praxis (acting on the instrumental affordances of objects) and purposive miming (including pointing), but once the gestures are being combined into propositions to describe new categories rather than just to mime objects or events, their resemblance to their referent ('iconicity') or its instrumental affordances are no longer relevant, and their shapes can become simpler, conventionalized, and arbitrary, for speed and efficiency of communication in the transmission of categories. Propositional language having established its adaptiveness in conveying categories, the disadvantages of the gestural medium (speed, darkness, distance, visibility, need for free hands) and the advantages of the vocal medium could be discovered (perhaps as vocalizations accompanying manual gestures) and exploited. The vocal medium then evolves, resulting in a brain that is not only biased toward naming and describing categories, but toward doing so preferentially in the vocal modality (Steklis and Harnad 1976; Harnad 2000).

just category-names. Words can also be combined and recombined to form subject/predicate propositions that define new categories—and, most important, the proposition can be true or false. A name, 'X', cannot be true or false. Only a proposition—'This is an X'—can be true or false, and neither pointing nor naming is yet making a proposition; nor is purposive miming.

I do not, in point of fact, have a compelling hypothesis about what induced the transition from purposive pantomime to propositions (see also Donald, this volume), though I can spin a plausible Just-So story as well as anyone else (Harnad 2000). I would rather close by noting that once you can produce and understand a proposition at all, you can produce and understand any and every proposition (Katz 1976; Steklis and Harnad 1976). Propositions are all statements about category membership. (The foregoing sentence is as good an example as any!) So once you have made the transition from purposive pantomime to truth-valued propositions, you have the full power of language to define, describe, and explain any category at all: the full power of symbolic instruction, just as long as it is grounded, like the kernel of our dictionaries, in sensorimotor induction. In the beginning was the category; with propositions came the word.

# CHAPTER 43

# THE SYMBOL CONCEPT

## TERRENCE W. DEACON

## 43.1 INTRODUCTION

The term 'symbol' derives from the Greek stem of *ballein* 'to throw' and *syn* 'together'. This etymology characterizes the way that words are forced into correspondence with ideas and their physical referents irrespective of any natural affinities. Throughout philosophical history, the term 'symbol' is almost exclusively applied to spoken utterances, inscriptions, or other culturally generated meaningful artefacts and actions created specifically for representational purposes. These cultural phenomena include talismans, ritual performances, religious relics, military insignias, spoken words, and typographical characters, among innumerable other forms. In contrast, a cough is generally referred to as a *sign* of a respiratory infection, not a symbol, and portraits are generally described as depicting people, not symbolizing them. These latter are signs that represent by virtue of some 'natural affinity', irrespective of human cultural intervention.

Symbolic reference contrasts with two other categories of signs. *Iconic* reference is employed in pantomime and simple depiction. *Indexical* reference is employed in pointing and innate forms of communication such as laughter and facial expressions. Symbolic reference is a distinguishing feature of human language, in contrast with species-typical vocalizations and communicative gestures. Because of its arbitrary and conventional nature, symbolic reference must be acquired by learning, and lacks both the natural associations and trans-generational reproductive consequences that would make such references biologically evolvable. This is why language is distinguished by extensive reliance on social (as opposed to genetic) transmission. However, this absence of natural constraints also facilitates the capacity for distinct symbol combinations to determine unique references—another hallmark of language.

Despite superficial agreement on most points, there are significant differences in the ways that symbols and non-symbols are defined in the literature. Symbolic reference is often negatively defined with respect to other forms of referential relationships. Whereas iconic reference depends on form similarity between sign vehicle and what it represents, and indexical reference depends on contiguity, correlation, or causal connection, symbolic reference is often only described as being independent of any likeness or physical linkage between sign vehicle and referent. This negative characterization of symbolic reference—often caricatured as mere *arbitrary reference*—gives the false impression that symbolic reference is nothing but simple unmediated correspondence.

Consequently, the term 'symbol' is used in two quite dichotomous ways. In the realm of mathematics, logic, computation, cognitive science, and many syntactic theories the term 'symbol' refers to a mark that is arbitrarily mapped to some referent, and can be combined with other marks according to an arbitrarily specified set of rules. This effectively treats a symbol as an element of a code, and language acquisition as decryption. In contrast, in the humanities, social sciences, theology, and mythology, the term 'symbol' is often reserved for complex, esoteric relationships such as the meanings implicit in totems or objects incorporated into religious ritual performances. In such cases, layers of meaning and reference may be impossible to fully plumb without extensive cultural experience and exegesis.

This multiplicity of meanings muddies the distinction between symbolic forms of reference and other forms and also contributes to confusion about the relationship between linguistic and non-linguistic communication. Within linguistics itself, ambiguity about the precise nature of symbolic reference contributes to deep disagreements concerning the sources of language structure, the basis of language competence, the requirements for its acquisition, and the evolutionary origin of language. Thus, the problem of unambiguously describing the distinctive properties of symbolic reference as compared to other forms of reference is foundational in linguistic theory.

## 43.2 THE CODE FALLACY

The father of 20th-century linguistics, Ferdinand de Saussure, described language reference as a mapping between a *signifier* and a *signified* (see Saussure 1983). Many have described this as the linguistic code. Over the past century this approach has led to remarkable insights concerning the systematicity of language properties.

Computer 'languages' provide useful exemplars of simple signifier-signified relationships. The references assigned to bit strings in a computer 'language' directly correspond to specific machine operations or numerical values; hence, a code. A code is constituted by a one-to-one mapping between conventionally determined sign vehicles in two languages. Most familiar computer languages consist of terms and characters borrowed from English and mathematics. In order to control computer operations that lack the logical organization of a language, what amounts to a translation step is necessary. Software programs called interpreters and compilers substitute machine commands for certain terms and characters of programming language. A string of machine commands directly corresponds to operations to be performed. Computation is often described as 'symbol processing'. Of course, the only symbolic interpretation occurs in the minds of human users. Otherwise there is no more symbolic reference in a computer than in an internal combustion engine. That alphanumeric characters are not intrinsically symbolic becomes obvious when they begin to spontaneously appear on the screen due to computer malfunction. We interpret these as *indices* of an underlying functional problem, not symbolic of anything.

In a natural language, one-to-one mapping between elements of language and objects in the world is only characteristic of proper names (though the phonological mapping of letters to sounds in alphabetic writing systems offers an imprecise parallel). If a language consisted only of one-to-one correspondence relationships, it would consist entirely of something analogous to proper nouns. This could never produce anything other than lists. So clearly something is missing in this simplified account.

A close cousin to a code relationship is a translation. A completely literal translation between natural languages, such as that performed by a computer algorithm, is almost always seriously inadequate. Good translation is aimed at conveying meaning and reference rather than merely replacing words and their syntactic relations with counterparts from another language. The lack of simple counterparts inevitably forces the translator to deal with the complexity of the language-specific and culture-specific grounding of the symbols used in each language.

The symbolic reference that distinguishes language must instead rest upon a vast network of non-symbolic relationships that constitute the many nested contexts in which it occurs.

There are other serious consequences of adopting this simplified conception of symbolic reference. Codes are used for encryption because they add an additional layer of combinatorial arbitrariness between sign and reference. This astronomically increases the combinatorial possibilities. Even just provisionally assuming that language is code-like and made up of an arbitrarily structured set of components, arbitrarily assigned to correspond to another set of objects, gives the misleading impression that the domain of possible language structures is vast and unbounded. From this perspective, the problem of learning the particular system of principles for generating a given language is treated as analogous to a decryption problem involving a highly complex code. This requires either that children are genius code-breakers or else that they come equipped with the code-key from birth.

The code model is not, however, entirely irrelevant to language. It just may not apply to all aspects of language function, and particularly not to any aspects that depend on language reference. The rough correspondence between alphabetic characters of written languages and speech sounds, and between speech sounds and referents, exemplifies an independence from any 'natural' correspondence. Thus, a typographical character is often described as a symbol: it is an arbitrarily chosen marker that can be assigned to any one of an indefinite number of correspondence relationships to a speech sound. This openness to multiple forms of referential use demonstrates, however, a confusion of two quite different conceptions of the concept of 'symbol'—one pertaining to the sign vehicle and its properties and another to its mode of referring.

## 43.3 THE SEMIOTICS OF SYMBOLS

The question then, is this: how is the relationship between a written letter from the alphabet and the sound it represents different from the relationship between a spoken word or sentence and what it represents? As discussed above, both relationships are often described as symbolic. Both are arbitrary: the form of the sign vehicle (e.g. character or utterance, respectively) is not determined by any features of what is being represented. The letter-sound relationship is at least approximately code-like (even if it is seldom strictly rule-governed), but the word-meaning-reference relationship is considerably more complex. Unless we are willing to accept that there is a literal language of thought, we need to distinguish more carefully these conceptions of symbol.

The 19th-century philosopher Charles Sanders Peirce (1931) produced a taxonomy to account for the diversity and interdependencies of different sorts of sign relationships. His semiotic theory was never entirely completed, but it was sufficiently developed to provide distinctions that can help resolve this problem. Peirce's taxonomy is largely forgotten, and yet it differentiates many aspects of representational relationships that have since become confused. Specifically, it distinguishes the properties of sign vehicles, sign-object relationships, and the contextual basis for interpreting their relationships as hierarchically nested dependencies. To clarify these difficulties, I briefly re-introduce some of Peirce's terminological distinctions.

I reproduce only the relevant parts of his much more extensive taxonomic hierarchy in Figure 43.1.

In this taxonomy Peirce distinguishes those properties that characterize a sign vehicle, irrespective of any reference, from those properties linking a sign vehicle to its reference. A sign vehicle which exemplifies a general type by virtue of convention or rule of design is called a 'legisign'. This conventional property is distinguishable irrespective of whether these signs refer iconically, indexically, or symbolically. For example, stick figure drawings representing male and female bodies on restroom doors are iconic legisigns. However, a portrait of a famous person is iconic but not a legisign. Peirce would describe it as an 'iconic sinsign'. A sinsign is a singular instance taken as a sign, such as the individual portrait. A smoke alarm's sound is an indexical legisign because of its conventional creation and its physical linkage to smoke detection, whereas a particular smell of smoke is an indexical sinsign. The arrangement of furniture in a room indicating that a meeting recently took place is also an indexical sinsign, but for it to invoke this indexical reference it must first be recognized as an iconic sinsign due to its similarity to arrangements recalled from previous meetings. Written words are symbolic legisigns, since both the typographical sign vehicle and its reference to a general concept or type of object, property, etc., are conventionally determined. Notice, however, that a written word is first recognized as an iconic sinsign (an instance of a familiar form), then an indexical legisign (a type of sign vehicle contiguous with other related types), and then as a symbolic

| | Sign-vehicle itself | Sign to referent |
|---|---|---|
| 3 | Legisign | Symbol |
| 2 | Sinsign | Index |
| 1 | Qualisign | Icon |
| | 1 | 2 |

**Figure 43.1. C. S. Peirce's categorical scheme for a taxonomy of sign forms.**
Each sign relation is characterized by a combination of features involving the sign vehicle itself (left column) and the relation of sign features to features of the referent (middle column). There is an asymmetric dependency in both the vertical and horizontal dimensions of the chart, with positions designated by a **1** being more basic and **3** being most derived. The features of the sign vehicle must always be of an equal or higher rank than features of the sign-to-referent relationship. This chart omits a third column in Peirce's taxonomy consisting of a 'rheme' (**1**), a 'dicent' sign (**2**), and a 'delome' (**3**), which identify the relationship of the sign to its interpretant (essentially the semiotic context of a sign's interpretation).

legisign (a conventional type of sign referring to a conventional type of referent). In this taxonomy Peirce also recognizes that a mere abstract quality, a possibility, or a potentiality can serve as a sign vehicle. He calls these qualisigns.

In making this distinction between the way sign vehicles are determined and the way their referential relationships are determined, Peirce demonstrates an important and little-recognized constraint on this relationship. A qualisign can only be an icon. For example, the whiteness of snow (a qualisign) can be iconic of purity, but an instance of white snow (a sinsign), when contrasted to previous instances of dirty snow, can indicate that new snow has just fallen. Sinsigns can be either icons or indices. A face discerned in the clouds is an iconic sinsign, and dark clouds presaging an impending storm are an indexical sinsign. Finally, legisigns can represent in all three ways. A diagram is an iconic legisign, the position of a needle on a pressure gauge is an indexical legisign, and a military insignia is a symbolic legisign. This means that symbolic reference can only be supported by legisigns, which has almost certainly motivated the tendency to collapse these two facets of the symbol concept.

## 43.4 Hierarchic construction of interpretations

This asymmetric dependency is a consequence of necessary stages of constructing an interpretation. Consider the interpretation of the chevron insignia on a military jacket. Initially, it appears as a coloured shape, an iconic sinsign. As similar shapes are seen on other shoulders, it develops from an iconic sinsign to an iconic legisign (shapes of the same type). As it is understood to distinguish the individual wearing it, it becomes interpreted as an indexical legisign (pointing to something about this person). When its particular configuration is understood to designate that person's military rank it becomes interpreted as a symbolic legisign. The same sign vehicle thus is the locus for a sequence of interpretive phases in which both the relationship of the sign vehicle to other sign vehicles and the relationship of the sign vehicle to its reference are progressively developed.

The asymmetric relationship between features of the sign vehicle and features of the referential relationship explains why conventional typographical characters can refer both symbolically and non-symbolically. Consider for example, the text message use of the sideways 'smiley face' :-) created by punctuation marks. It is a combination of conventionalized sign vehicles that refers iconically. The combination of punctuation marks may be arbitrary in shape with respect to their canonical textual functions, but in this combination they refer to smiling faces by similarity. Thus, calling an alphanumeric character a symbol is shorthand for saying that it is the sort of sign vehicle *designed for* conveying its reference symbolically. But calling these marks 'symbols' confuses what they were created for with how they actually refer in a given context.

Even in this case, the interpretation can be layered. A smiling human face is a symptom of a happy state of mind—an index. Placed in a text field, this icon enjoins the reader to interpret it in two distinct framings. Its inclusion as a text entry *indicates* that it is to be interpreted as text (typically producing symbolic reference), but its non-phonetic function and its atypical combinatorial form deny this interpretation. It is also implicitly embedded in a larger, equally relevant, cultural context: a similar cartoon caricature of a smiling face is a popular contemporary sign. Since the character combinations of a text message are intended to convey thoughts and attitude, the initial iconic reference invokes an indexical reference prompting a symbolic interpretation—something like 'that thought makes me happy'.

Aristotle describes a related, classic example of a symbol (*On soul*, 1984): the impression of a signet ring in wax, to seal a note and verify the sender's identity. Aristotle argues that mental ideas need only capture the forms of things, not any other feature of their physical composition. Only the form of the ring transfers to the wax, not its material composition. Reconstructing the cognitive steps necessary to interpret a wax impression also demonstrates that symbolic function depends on more than a simple arbitrary correspondence. First, as Aristotle notes, the formal similarity between the impression and the ring is primary. This is *iconic*. But without the physical action of the ring-bearer pressing the ring into hot wax to produce this likeness, it would not *indicate* that this message, thus sealed, was produced by the bearer of that specific ring. The presumed connection between ring and bearer further *indicates* that a particular individual actually sealed the note. Typically, possession of such a ring is a mark of royalty, etc., this status being a mere social convention. To interpret the wax impression as a symbol of social position, one must also understand social conventions, because nothing intrinsic to the form or its physical creation supplies this information. The symbolic reference is dependent on already knowing something beyond any features embodied in this sign vehicle.

This dependency on an external system of relations within which the formal similarities and correlative aspects of the wax impression are embedded is a critical property of its symbolic reference. But without familiarity with this entire system of relationships, these non-symbolic components remain merely icons and indices. Indeed, if any link in this chain of referential inferences is broken, symbolic reference fails. So while the features comprising the sign vehicle are not necessarily similar in form or physically linked to what is symbolized, this superficial independence is supported by a less obvious network of other modes of reference, involving both iconism and indexicality.

Interestingly, Peirce's hierarchic analysis doesn't stop at one level of simple symbolism. A complex sign vehicle such as the diagram of an electronic circuit can serve as an icon even though it is composed of symbols. Once the many symbolic legisign components are interpreted, their collective configuration is seen as iconic of the organization of the physical circuit. This is relevant to language. Thus the combinatorial organization of symbolic legisigns comprising a phrase, sentence, or narrative may constitute a higher order iconic, indexical, or symbolic referential function. In this sense the logic of this constructive semiotic hierarchy is critically relevant to understanding the constraints of grammar and syntax, and the complexities of discourse or narrative. The same hierarchic dependencies underlying and supporting the interpretation of symbolic reference in the examples above impose analogous compositional constraints on word combination in sentence structure.

## 43.5 Semiosis and language structure

If this semiotic embeddedness of symbolic reference is relevant for language, then ignoring it will prevent access to a significant domain of explanatory principles. As we saw earlier, relationships between icons can generate indexical reference, and relations between indices can generate symbolic reference. So, do the combinatorial relationships between the symbolic units of language also function iconically, indexically, and even symbolically? We take for granted the way that combinatorial relationships among linguistic units affect language reference, but seldom consider this in semiotic terms. Nevertheless, relationships among sign vehicles and forms of reference are semiotic relationships, and this can generate higher order semiotic relationships. Let us consider to what extent the grammatical and syntactic regularities of language reflect and constitute these diverse semiotic functions.

Iconism is, of course, fundamental to writing using a phonetic alphabet or syllabary, and is essentially of the form of a diagram. Simple word repetition also has a syntactic function. Phrases like *very very difficult* or *millions and millions* utilize this, and repetitive superlatives are common in pidgins and child language. Literary use of repeated metaphoric images is a significant source of thematic complexity. Subtler forms of iconism are recruited for higher order structural organization. Agreement relationships (e.g. number or gender agreement) also link co-referring items not immediately adjacent (more below).

The effects of indexicality play a more elaborate, but often unrecognized, role in sentence structure. The importance of indexicality derives from the dependency of symbolic reference on indexical reference. As the examples above show, specific interrelationships between indices can prompt one to interpret their collective relationship symbolically. But whereas these indices each have specific referents, the symbolic reference that emerges from their reflexive relations to one another is abstract and general. This is another critical distinguishing feature of symbolic reference that is entirely absent from the code model: symbols refer to general types, not specific instances.

A *type* of thing is not something as neatly bounded and singular as a given occurrence of a word. Consider some extended uses of the word 'shadow'. Besides the particular light/dark phenomena that we term shadows, metaphorical usage in phrases like *shadow of a doubt*, *shadow of his former self*, and *living in his father's shadow* suggests that neither this thing in the mind nor its object of reference are simple singular *signifieds*. Yet when used in a sentence like *We watched the shadow cast by the Eiffel Tower as the sun set*, the same word has a precise, concrete, and singular physical reference. This is inherited from its relational locus in a higher-order unit—a sentence—which itself inherits further reference-fixing information from the larger context of the narrative it occurs within. A linguistic communication (along with its context of salient physical and social relationships) is also a composite sign vehicle that constructs specific symbolic reference from the iconic and indexical relationships of its ambiguous symbolic components.

Unlike the simple examples described earlier, however, the construction of symbolic reference in language is made possible by a vast network of inter-referring indices, rather than just a few. The thousands of symbolic units comprising the lexicon of a language (e.g. words and morphemes) effectively 'point' to one another as though comprising a complex interconnected network. This symbol-symbol indexicality is exemplified by the structure of a thesaurus, a network of one-to-many vectors. Thus, we can positively define symbolic reference as reference mediated by a closed system of indexical relations which, taken together, refer holistically to a system of relations in the world. Because of this holism, reference to anything specific outside this network of relations is necessarily ambiguous. This is why, except for the degenerate case of proper names, individual words cannot be mapped to any specific referents. They only map directly to specific positions in this implicit network. Moreover, these indicated positions are entirely relative to others, so their imprecise loci, which serve as something like category centres, are circularly defined.

This exemplifies an important difference between the symbolic reference in non-linguistic examples of symbolic reference above, and linguistic symbolic reference. The military insignia and the signet ring mark each stand on their own. Although embedded in a larger semiotic network, they are not components in the construction of higher order signs (whereas the smiley face text is). The systematic iconic and indexical relationships in each define a kind of reflexivity (by in effect pointing to each other and their opposites) that is critical to invoking the symbolic interpretation in each, but their relationship to some specific reference requires placing each in a context that indicates its place.

The primary meaningful units of language (e.g. words and morphological markers) have multivalent referential possibilities too (as the example of the word *shadow* demonstrates), but these are used in combinations that often provide highly specific reference. The basis of the symbolic reference of words is the systematicity that unifies the network of indexical relationships that they constitute and depend upon. But this network of indexical relationships is also reflexive, circular, and ultimately self-referential. Consequently, the use of linguistic symbols (e.g. words) to refer to specific objects, events, or properties of things inevitably requires indexical mediation. Indeed, in the absence of an additional indexical relationship, words only mark a relationship to other symbolic legisigns, and thus only refer to an ambiguously defined locus in this lexical system, not to anything in the world or even to a specific abstract referent.

This requirement of indexical mediation imposes a significant constraint, because indexical reference depends on immediate physical correlation: physical contiguity (adjacency), containment, temporal immediacy, and so on. The physical attributes of an indexical legisign are what matter. I postulate the following semiotic rule of thumb: every symbolic legisign must be immediately coupled with an indexical sign or else there is no specific symbolic reference (Deacon 2003). This index must itself refer to something in the immediate context, and is also subject to these strictures on indexicality. This coupling to another sign vehicle creates a transitive indexicality linking the symbolic legisign to something specific and particular in its context. So, uttering an isolated descriptive term like *smooth* offers ambiguous reference, but if uttered while running one's hand over a polished surface it refers specifically to this surface and that tactile experience by virtue of this indexical linkage. Substituting such phrases as *This table is...* or *The surface of the water is...* show that these noun phrases also indirectly provide indexical support for interpreting *smooth*. Without some immediate indexical linkage, explicit or implicit, the symbolic reference of *smooth* is unspecified.

The clausal structure of languages with constrained word order also reflects this limitation. An index refers by virtue of correlation, contiguity, and part-whole linkage. This means that temporal or physical separation undermines indexical reference. This proximity constraint is exhibited in certain syntactic rules. Consider the necessary immediate proximity of the quantifiers (e.g. *a*, *the*, *this*, *some*, *all*, etc.) to non-mass nouns and noun phrases. In English these quantifiers must immediately precede what they modify. Separation breaks the indexical link and renders their function ambiguous. This constraint is also reflected in *wh*-constructions in English, which respect the constraint of containment within the same clausal level. Even the agreement requirements of pronominal reference, which can span many sentences, reflect the constraints of immediacy to maintain indexical reference, because gendered pronouns point to the most recently mentioned gender-agreeing noun or noun phrase. All can be understood as reflections of the necessary constraints of indexicality. Only in highly inflected languages, where many of these indexical functions are incorporated into word morphology (and thus not splittable), word order within a sentence is comparatively free.

Peirce's analysis even suggests that we can attribute the dyadic structure of well-formed sentences (e.g. noun phrase/verb phrase, topic/comment, function/argument structure, etc.) to the dependency of symbolic reference on indexicality. The ability to replace noun phrases by pointing or other indicative gestures, or by indexical terms like *this* or *that*, demonstrates that noun phrases serve an indexical role, linking the predicate (as a symbolic core of the sentence) to some specific instance of reference. Even isolated expletives or commands, which lack explicit indexicality, implicitly indicate something immediately salient in the context. So uttering *Incredible!* in an appropriate context indicates a particularly salient and probably surprising feature of that context.

These indexical constraints are rigid, general, and universally required for explicit reference. Failure to respect them risks equivocal reference. They are not so much rules that must be learned, as constraints that can be discovered.

## 43.6 THE EVOLUTION OF LANGUAGE ADAPTATIONS

The above examples barely scratch the surface of the ways that the semiotic infrastructure of symbolic reference is integrated into the constraints affecting language structure. But they demonstrate how ignoring the non-symbolic basis for symbolic reference and assuming a code analogy can obscure functional principles relevant to explaining certain structural features of language. Additionally, ignoring this semiotic infrastructure impedes exploration of the neurological basis for the rapid acquisition of language in childhood, its inaccessibility to other species, and its evolutionary origin.

Despite its inadequacy, the code analogy has largely been assimilated into theories of language origins as an unquestioned fact. Thus, word reference has been analogized to the referential function of alarm calls for distinct predators, once thought special to vervet monkeys, but now recognized as widespread among birds and mammals. From this perspective the evolution of language is imagined to involve merely multiplying the number of distinct calls and referents and then superimposing combinatorial rules. It has also been argued that since many species (from pigeons to rats) can learn arbitrary associations, for instance between randomly chosen experimental stimuli, the capacity to learn the arbitrary referents of words cannot be in any way special. From this perspective what is in need of an evolutionary explanation is only grammar and syntax.

Since the code model of reference assumes that there are no constraints on the referential correspondences of the morphological units of language (e.g. words, prefixes, inflections) or on their combinatorial usage (i.e. grammar and syntax), it appears as though the identification of nearly universal grammatical regularities demands an explanation that is independent of referential functions. But the categories of grammatical functions only make sense in symbolic terms. They do not correspond to natural or social categories, and make no sense applied to non-symbolic communication such as facial expressions or non-linguistic manual gestures. This appears to require a separate evolutionary explanation for grammatical functions and categories, as well as for the syntactic rules that organize them. The question is whether these explanatory challenges are being posed by language or by the assumptions upon which our theories of language are based.

With respect to the neurology of language processing, the code model makes assumptions about specialized brain processes, structures, or modules, which are the presumed loci of language-specific grammatical functions. But though formal linguistic theories based on the code model make strong predictions about dedicated language algorithms and their neurological substrates, they have produced little by way of novel neurological findings. For example, no evidence has emerged that the brain structures involved in language are phylogenetically novel. Indeed, it is clear that those brain regions most critical for language processes have direct homological counterparts in other species (see review in Deacon 1997). Moreover, the number of brain systems involved in language is surprisingly extensive, and the way that diverse brain systems can be recruited to support language under pathological or atypical task conditions indicates considerable plasticity. These attributes don't easily fit with claims about language-unique brain processes unrelated to other forms of cognition.

If the symbolic reference of language is not, however, based on arbitrary correlation and a collection of human-unique mental algorithms, but is instead dependent on a higher order interdependency between iconic and indexical relationships, then we should not expect there to be an absolute boundary excluding non-human species from acquiring some aspects of language. Iconic and indexical functions are quite generic, and relevant to many sensory, mnemonic, and cognitive capacities. The challenge of understanding language origins thus becomes one of understanding why the critical juxtapositions and combinatorial analyses of non-symbolic relationships required to invoke symbolic interpretation are difficult for most non-humans to mentally construct. Similarly, the challenge of understanding which different brain systems contribute to the production and comprehension of language becomes one of understanding how the phylogenetically prior iconic and indexical analytic functions of those systems were recruited and modified to better suit this higher order synergistic use. Decomposing language functions into their contributing semiotic bases may also help explain how atypical brain regions can take on language functions and how supernormal symbolic processes, like lightning-fast calculation, can result from developmental abnormalities of brain function, such as autism.

By taking into account the semiotic infrastructure of language, the human neurological adaptation for language need no longer be viewed as a disconnected, anomalous cognitive module. It is just a special (though probably highly demanding and atypical) re-use of previously evolved mental capacities. If semiotic constraints can account for many of the robust regularities of grammar and syntax, we should not expect evolution to have produced any genetically specified neural instantiation of natural language grammar. Instead, the critical barrier crossed in human evolution must involve support for the special processing demands of symbolic interpretation. This suggests that an analysis of the cognitive operations and brain processes required to construct symbolic reference from systems of indexical relationships might yield important clues to the nature of the human language adaptation.

In conclusion, what at first appears to be merely a terminological difference in the definition of the word 'symbol' has profound consequences for explaining the production and origins of the distinctive features of language. Although formal descriptions of language structure may ignore this difference without loss of descriptive precision, efforts to explain how and why these language structures arise may lead to quite unrealistic predictions unless this semiotic complexity of language reference is taken into account.

......................

# CHAPTER 44

# WORDS CAME FIRST: ADAPTATIONS FOR WORD-LEARNING

......................

## ROBBINS BURLING

Language, as spoken by every reasonably normal human adult, is an enormously complex instrument. Every one of us must learn the meanings of tens of thousands of words, an intricate phonological system by which these words can be kept distinct from one another, and a complex syntax by which the words can be joined together into larger constructions. We learn all of this from the community in which we grow up, but we would learn none of it if we did not come to the task with the inherited capacity to learn the words, the pronunciation, and the grammar of whatever language happens to envelop us. For anyone who is interested in the origins of language, then, the central question has to be 'How did the capacity for learning a language evolve in the human species?'.

The question can be broken down into three major parts. First, how did the capacity to learn an enormous vocabulary evolve? Second, how did the capacity to learn and to use the kind of patterned phonological system that is found in all spoken languages evolve? And, third, how did we acquire the capacity to learn to organize our words according to the syntactic patterns of the language to which we are exposed? Of these, phonology and syntax have more often grabbed the fascination of linguists than words. We have tended to see the lexicon as a repository of messy details, an area that is less susceptible to generalizations and rules than is either phonology or syntax. Often, we have been content to leave words to the lexicographers. Nevertheless, as I will argue later in this chapter, it had to be with words that linguistic evolution began and, partly to compensate for the attention that others give to phonology and syntax, I will use the lexicon as an area in which to explore the circumstances that could have encouraged the launching, and then the continuing evolution, of our linguistic capacity. I will consider phonology and syntax more briefly, mostly to suggest that the same kinds of questions that can be raised for the lexicon can also be raised for phonology and syntax.

## 44.1 THE MIND

Even before our ancestors used anything that we would want to call 'words', they communicated by meaningful screams, grunts, postures, and facial expressions. We still use such vocalizations and gestures to communicate, but so do other mammals, and these signs belong to our mammalian heritage rather than to language. Our mammalian cries and gestures require little learning, because they are largely fixed by our inheritance, and they vary but little from one community to another. Smiles and sobs, scowls and sighs mean pretty much the same thing in New Guinea as they mean in New York (Ekman and Friesen 1969, 1971; Izard 1971, 1980; Ekman 1972a). It was only when our ancestors gained the ability to learn arbitrary associations between meanings on the one hand, and sounds or gestures on the other, that something that we would want to call 'language' got underway. It was only then that the symbols used in one community could differ from those used in another.

We can imagine a stage of early language when people could learn and use single words but could learn neither the kind of systematically patterned phonology that now distinguishes our words from one another, nor the kind of syntax that lets us combine words into larger meaningful constructions. Neither phonology nor syntax would have had any use when words were few and when they were used in isolation from one another. Isolated words could have usefully conveyed meaning without either patterned phonology or syntax. How, then, could our ability to learn and to use words have evolved?

The most crucial adaptations for word learning, just as for learning the rest of language, were cognitive, the way in which incipient speakers used their minds (Tallerman 2009). In the behaviour of apes, we can see minds that are more like ours than are the minds of more distantly related animals; see Gibson, Part I. Apes show us cognitive abilities that could have served as a launching point for language, but an ape mind is not able to learn or to use a language with anything that approaches a human level of complexity. Several essential cognitive capacities had to be developed before language could even begin.

First, language rests on a rich conceptual system. We perceive the world in complex ways. We see it as filled with objects, and we presume that these objects can persist through time. We recognize the intricate interactions among these objects. As far as we can tell, other primates share much of this cognitive understanding of the world (Hauser and Carey 1998; Gibson, Chapter 3), but we are much better than apes or monkeys at assigning symbols to the objects and events that we perceive (Hayes and Nissen 1971; de Waal 1982; Boesch and Boesch-Achermann 2000). We easily invent words, either gestured or vocalized, and we easily use these words to share our understanding of the world with other people.

When we use words, we expect other people to focus their attention on the objects and events that we have named. We expect, easily, to achieve what is known as 'joint attention'. Parents point out objects and events to their children, and even small babies eagerly hold up objects to show to their parents. Showing things to others would be pointless if we did not expect others to be able to attend to the same things that we do. Apes do not show things to each other, either to their babies or anyone else, and they do not come close to our ease at achieving joint attention (Baldwin 1991; Tomasello and Camaioni 1997; Hare et al. 2000).

Without being able to achieve joint attention so easily, we would find words much more difficult to learn. When we hear a new word in the context of a conversation we can often guess its meaning because we can grasp what the speaker is attending to. When we hear someone use a familiar word, we are directed to attend to an idea that the speaker is thinking about. Because we are so good at achieving joint attention, we find it easy both to learn new words and to communicate our ideas with familiar words. Human beings are very much better than apes at achieving the joint attention that language requires.

To learn a language we must also be skilful at imitation. An imitator needs to recognize the similarities between his own actions and the actions of others, so this is a cognitive skill. Students of ape behaviour have disagreed about how much apes can imitate, but we can have no doubt that we are much better at imitation than they are (Russon and Galdikas 1993, 1995; Tomasello 1996; Tomasello and Call 1997). We must be able imitate the words, the pronunciations, and the grammatical patterns that we hear others use.

To learn a word or to use one, we must be able to perceive patterns in the objects and events around us. If something happens regularly, we expect it to happen again. We recognize some things and some events to be similar enough to be considered the 'same', and this lets us name them by the same word. Nor could we learn or use a language without being highly adept at perceiving patterns in the language of others. Consciously or unconsciously, we must perceive and imitate the patterns in the language that we hear, both patterns that relate the parts of language to each other, and patterns that relate language to the ideas that we want to convey. We must perceive sounds or signs that others use, and detect their intended meaning. To understand or to use even isolated words, we must learn arbitrary associations between our vocalizations or gestures and our concepts. We must be able to associate the sound of the word 'no' with negation, to recognize a beckoning gesture as a request to approach the gesturer. Before language could get under way, all these psychological abilities—to achieve joint attention, to imitate, to find patterns, and to use symbols—had to develop beyond those that we can find in apes (Markman 1989; Marcus et. al. 1999; Bloom 2000; Tomasello 2003a).

These cognitive abilities converge to allow us to associate vocalizations or gestures with our ideas about the world around us. They let us give names to our concepts for objects, qualities, situations, acts, and behaviour. With my words I can call your attention to whatever I happen to be thinking about. By understanding my words, you can share my concepts. Am I thinking about bananas? All I need to do is to utter a conventional noise and you will think about bananas too, even when no banana is nearby. We can see hints, in apes, of many of the cognitive skills that are needed for language. These skills would have had to develop further before language could begin, but once started even the most limited language would have made these skills more valuable, and encouraged their continued improvement by natural selection. By now, of course, all these skills are far better developed in humans than in even our closest anthropoid relatives.

We don't know what environmental pressures selected minds until they reached the point where they could begin to share learned signs with other individuals in their group. Perhaps these skills were fostered by the new and increasingly varied environments into which our ancestors moved when they left our chimpanzee and bonobo cousins behind in the forest. As our ancestors moved out of the trees, and then out of the forest, their conditions changed radically. To cope with these changes, early humans would have been helped by an increasing cognitive and behavioural flexibility. They would have benefited by being able to form arbitrary associations between meanings and either gestures or vocalizations. Those who were best able to discern meaning in the behaviour of others, and then able to share their own ideas with others, must have had a selective advantage.

## 44.2 Words

The typical word in any human language that is used today is a conventional three-way association between a meaning, a distinctive sound sequence (or, in the sign languages of the deaf, a distinctive pattern of gestures), and a characteristic set of syntactic roles (Jackendoff 2002: 130). The earliest words, however, did not need to be so complex. At first, they would have had to be used alone, apart from other words, so they could have had no syntactic properties. Nor, as long as only a few words needed to be kept distinct, did they need the kind of patterned and structured phonology that we now find in all spoken languages. Even now, we use a few words that are exempt from both patterned phonology and syntax. A *tsk-tsk* of disapproval, an *oh-oh* after something goes wrong, or a *shh!* to ask for silence are difficult to spell because they do not fit the sound patterns of ordinary English, and since they are used alone, they have no syntax. Jackendoff aptly calls such words 'linguistic fossils' (2002: 240). In both phonology and syntax, the earliest words must have been more like *tsk-tsk* and *oh-oh* than like most of the words that we use today. Nevertheless, even noises like *tsk-tsk* and *oh-oh* relate a conventional sound to a conventional meaning so they deserve to be called 'words'. *Tsk-tsk* and *oh-oh* are 'conventional' in the sense of being both learned and shared by others in the community. Because they are used for communication, they must be shared with members of a community, but because they have to be learned, members of different communities can learn and use different words.

The ability to make arbitrary associations between meanings and either sounds or gestures is not quite limited to human beings. When coached by humans, dogs can learn to respond to several dozen hand signals or spoken commands, and apes can do much better than dogs (Savage-Rumbaugh et al. 1994), but no animal can learn words with the voracious ease of human beings. Many species of birds and some cetaceans such as whales are able to learn the particular forms of their songs from conspecifics in their neighbourhood, and it is entirely reasonable to refer to the local versions of their songs as 'dialects' (Marler 1970; Tyack and Sayigh 1977; Catchpole and Slater 1995; Payne 2000; Janik, this volume; Slater, this volume). Birds use their learned songs to regulate their relations with neighbouring birds, but the songs of birds and whales never convey anything that approaches the kinds of specific referential meaning that we convey so easily with words.

## 44.3 COMPREHENSION AND PRODUCTION

In speculating about the earliest stages of language, we risk a paradox. Let us suppose that you are the first person with a mutation that lets you speak just a bit more skilfully than anyone else. Someone, after all, has to be first, and in this case, you are the lucky one. But how could that help you? It takes two to communicate, and if no one can understand what you say, a new mutation would seem to be worthless. We can escape from this paradox by recognizing that natural selection works more insistently on comprehension than on production. It may confer no advantage to be able to share precious information with others, but it is always advantageous to understand. Any animal should be helped by understanding the noises and gestures of others, even when those noises and gestures were never intended to be communicative. As a result of selection for comprehension, all animals, including human animals, understand more than they can produce (Burling 2005). Animals can learn to understand human signals that they cannot produce. Small children understand much more than they can say. We often grasp people's intentions even when they try their best to conceal them. Comprehension must have preceded production at every stage of evolution.

Studying comprehension is considerably more difficult than studying production, but Sue Savage-Rumbaugh and her colleagues performed a careful experiment when they compared the comprehension of Kanzi, the famous bonobo, with the comprehension of a human child (Savage-Rumbaugh et al. 1993). Kanzi and the child (separately) were given instructions such as 'Put the ball on the pine needles', 'The surprise is hiding in the dishwasher', 'Take the [toy] snake outdoors', 'Go get the carrot that's in the microwave', 'Make the doggie bite the snake'. At the age of 8 years, Kanzi followed the instructions about as well as the child, who was not quite 2 years. Kanzi could understand the meaning of spoken words even when they were embedded in a string of other words, and he was even able to use word order to distinguish meanings. When asked to put the ball on the pine needles, he did not put the pine needles on the ball. Their age difference shows that Kanzi had been slower to learn than the human child, but we can no longer have any doubt that, under the right conditions, an ape can learn to understand a large number of English words and even sentences. Kanzi's comprehension, of course, was far ahead of his ability to use words of any sort productively, and the same must have been true of early humans.

As millions of astonished parents have discovered, sometimes to their considerable embarrassment, small children are often able to understand far more than they can say (Burling 2005: 5–8). They can understand words and follow quite elaborate instructions well before they use the words productively. Adults understand dialects that they cannot speak, and we all understand technical terms and the slang of other generations, ethnic groups, and professions that we would not be confident about using ourselves. For animals, for children, and for human adults, comprehension is always ahead of production. It must have taken the lead in evolution as well.

The importance of comprehension in the evolution of communication was shown in a classic paper by Niko Tinbergen (1952). The retracted lip of a snarling dog, he suggested, began with no threatening intent at all. It was simply a means of making sure that the animal did not bite its own lip as it captured its dinner or attacked an enemy. If animals regularly pulled back their lips in preparation for a bite, however, victims who could recognize what was coming had a better chance of escaping. Seeing the retracted lip told them to flee. The first step in this communication was comprehension, but once other animals began to flee, the ancestral dogs had a new opportunity. Even a dog that had no intention of biting might frighten off an enemy by pulling back his lip and, in that way, avoid any need to make a much more dangerous direct attack. Only at that point did the curled lip become a deliberate signal. It had already become communicative when it was first understood.

What is true of a dog's retracted lip was probably true for every stage of language. Only after others were able to understand did it become profitable to exploit that understanding by producing increasingly complex language. Because we generally think of language as active and productive, this focus on comprehension can seem backwards, but advantages must always have come to whoever could understand what a conspecific was up to. We should expect natural selection to work relentlessly to make us better at understanding. Before we could deliberately use gestures to communicate, we must have understood that the shape of the hand is an indication of another person's intentions—to pluck a fruit, to soothe a child, to give someone a poke. Perhaps the very first word-like signals were iconic, like the shape of a hand that reaches for a fruit, but once others could learn to understand those shapes, they could become increasingly conventionalized, and even lose their iconicity until they became fully arbitrary signals. Gestures and vocalizations could acquire meaning for those who listened and watched. Once their meanings could be perceived by others, they could be used with a deliberate intention to communicate.

When vocalizations or gestures became both deliberate and conventionalized they deserved to be called 'language', and at every subsequent stage of evolution, progress in producing language could only come after others had learned to understand. A good many conventional vocalizations or gestures might have been learned and used before any patterned phonology was needed to keep them distinct, and still more could have been used before they began to be organized into syntactic constructions. Words had to come first.

## 44.4 STORAGE CAPACITY

Language must have begun with the ability to associate gestures or vocalizations with concepts, and to use these vocalizations or gestures as a means of sharing our concepts with others. Selection for increasing skill with words has pulled us to the point where we can learn, and use, not just a few words, but tens of thousands. Our brains have evolved to make us ferocious word learners. We are able to store all those words somewhere in our heads, and then, sometimes years or even decades later, we can retrieve those words at high speed. If we are frustrated when we cannot remember a word, it is only because we so much more often remember them so easily.

In spite of much devoted research, we know only in the grossest of terms how the brain stores or processes language, and perhaps we will need to reach all the way down to its fine circuitry before we can really understand how the brain works. In the meantime, we need to recognize just how much we manage to store somewhere in the brain, and how dramatically our brains have evolved to let us store this material. Barring a handful of exceptional words like *tsk-tsk* and *shh!* that are used alone and so have no syntax, every one of our tens of thousands of words requires us to form an arbitrary association between a learned meaning, a learned pronunciation, and a learned syntactic role. A whole cluster of facts needs to be learned about every word in our immense vocabulary. Hundreds of thousands of lexical details about tens of thousands of words must be stashed somewhere in our brains.

Would it not be easier to gain control over a language if some of those words could be hardwired? If the sound and the meaning of laughs and cries can be built in, why not the sound and meaning of 'hot' and 'cold'? If enough were hardwired we might not need such a long childhood to learn our words. If most of our words required as little learning as our screams, sobs, chuckles, and laughs, we could mature more rapidly and get on with the serious business of life and reproduction.

The problem is how to build in such a huge amount of detail. Every word would need its own special circuitry and every circuit would require a long period of natural selection. To be sure, if too much were built in we would lose adaptability. When a talking species adapts to a new environment and a new technology, new words will be needed for new ideas and new things. Nevertheless, a large part of our vocabulary could have been built in without limiting our flexibility in any serious way. Everyone needs words for ordinary body parts, for example. Children could mature a bit faster if they did not have to learn words like 'hand', 'foot', 'ankle', and 'knee'. They could learn much faster if a large proportion of their words were built in. Learning words rather than having them built in speeded up evolution but slows down maturation.

The results of natural selection can seem astonishing, but building in tens of thousands of words with all their complex meanings, pronunciations, and syntactic idiosyncrasies would probably have been too much even for natural selection, at least within the mere five or six million years that have passed since we left our anthropoid cousins behind. Perhaps our chromosomes are not even large enough to hold all the information that would be needed for all of our words. At the same time, the flexibility that lets us learn an enormous number of words may have helped to give us the flexibility to adapt to different environments, and to create varied technologies and varied cultures.

In any case, large parts of our language, including many details of our lexicon, can only be acquired by learning. In this, our minds, or at least the brains in which our minds reside, are analogous to computer memory. Computer memory is built from many thousands of repetitious circuits. By comparison with a central processor, computer memory is deadly repetitious until it is filled, either by software or by strokes from the keyboard. Like a computer, the lexical storage of our brain may be constructed from many thousands, or millions, of repetitious circuits. It would surely have been far quicker for natural selection to build the DNA recipe for a brain with tens of thousand of repetitious but empty storage bins, than to construct the dedicated circuits for large numbers of individual words. The details—the syntax, the sounds, and the meaning of the particular words—had to be left for learning, even at the considerable cost of requiring each of us to have a long enough childhood to gain control over a massive vocabulary.

Linguists quarrel about how much of language is built in and how much has to be learned. Starting several decades ago, Chomsky pushed us to recognize that learning a language would not be possible without a dedicated, built-in, capacity. At the same time, the differences among languages show us that much remains to be learned, most obviously all those thousands of words. The complementary roles of inheritance and learning are somewhat easier to conceptualize for the lexicon than for other aspects of language. We could not learn any words at all without our built-in capacities, but the particular words that we store in our memory have to be learned. To ask whether language is inherited or learned is surely the most futile of questions, for certainly it is both. Rather than debating about which is most important, it is more reasonable, and much more interesting, to ask how heredity and environment interact to allow us learn a language.

# 44.5 Phonology and syntax

What is true for the lexicon is also true for phonology and syntax. Trills, velar fricatives, and all manner of phonological contrasts, as well as word order, systems of agreement, case and tense systems, and all the other phenomena that have traditionally been considered as belonging to phonology or syntax can be learned only because the ability to learn them has been built into us by natural selection. As with the lexicon, also, the more phonology and syntax that is built in, the more quickly we could learn the parts that remained. Because there was not enough time to build in everything, languages differ not only in their words, but also in their pronunciation and in the patterns by which they join morphemes and words in to phrases and sentences.

The need to learn so much requires a very long childhood, but the ability to learn so much also gives us unusual flexibility. Adaptability to varied circumstances is a great strength of our species. If so much were built in that it limited our flexibility, we might never have escaped from a life of hunting and gathering. We have evolved to be able to learn a language, and we have been pre-adapted for the ability to learn other skills, including the new technology and culture that lets us exploit such varied environments.

It is because so much is left to learning that languages can differ from one another in their phonology and syntax as well as in their lexicon. Much of our non-verbal communication—our laughs, screams, and sobs, along with our smiles, frowns, and angry looks—is much less variable from one community to another than is language. Because languages have to be learned, they can not only vary from place to place and from person to person, but they can also gradually change, even within a single community. To be sure, languages can change only within the constraints of the minds that learn them. Languages are by no means infinitely variable. The speed of change is also limited by the need to communicate with both grandparents and grandchildren. We are, nevertheless, sufficiently flexible to let our languages slowly change.

Like many of the gestures that we learn, such as our nods, our head shakes, or the thumbs up sign, and like our vocalizations such as *tsk-tsk*, and *shhh!*, the first learned vocalizations had to differ from each other, but they need not have conformed to a patterned phonology. If the number of words was to grow large, however, a more systematic means of keeping them distinct would become essential. The means that evolved was the system of phonological contrasts (Studdert-Kennedy, this volume). When our ancestors could learn to distinguish *p* from *b*, and *a* from *i*, they could use a single contrasting pair of sounds to distinguish hundreds of pairs of words.

Then, as words were used with increasing frequency, they would also have been used more closely together, and hearers would begin to perceive them as having related meanings. When a word meaning 'stone', was used just before or just after a word meaning 'hot', a perceptive listener might guess that it was the stone that was hot. Only as listeners began to infer connected meanings among a succession of words would it have become useful for a speaker to join them together deliberately.

Step by step, then, we can see that our capacity for learning both a phonological code and organized syntax would improve: the code to keep the words distinct, syntax to allow words to be used in increasingly intricate combinations. As with the lexicon, the capacity to learn to understand and to use both a patterned phonology and a complex syntax had to be built by the long process of natural selection, even while the details were left to be filled in by learning. Natural selection must have favoured those who could understand the most words and who were able to extract the most meaning from the combinations of the words that they heard. It is more difficult for us to conceptualize the complementary contributions of heredity and learning to phonology or syntax than in the case of the learning of words. We can imagine a bank of tiny cubby holes as a storehouse for words more easily than we can imagine some sort of storehouse for a phonological code or for a web of syntactic rules, but we know so little about the detailed circuitry of the brain that even a lexical storehouse has to be understood as no more than a metaphor, a way of thinking about the interaction of heredity and environment. Even a metaphor is more difficult to construct for the acquisition of phonological contrasts or syntactic rules than for the storage of words into waiting cubbyholes. Nevertheless, in whatever way they do it, our brains have unquestionably evolved so as to be able to learn a phonology of contrasting features, and an intricate syntax, as well as an enormous lexicon.

# CHAPTER 45

# THE EMERGENCE OF PHONETIC FORM

## MICHAEL STUDDERT-KENNEDY

## 45.1 INTRODUCTION

The unbounded semantic scope of spoken language rests on words. Words, as attested by the alphabet with which any spoken language can be written and read, are particulate combinations of consonants and vowels. Yet, paradoxically, neither of these phonetic units can be reliably isolated in either the acoustic or the articulatory record. The reason for this is that consonants and vowels, though they correspond to contrasting phases of a syllable, are not elementary units. They are intricate structures interleaved both within and between syllables: their formation is distributed across independently activated, though spatiotemporally overlapping, 'organs' of articulation. Similarly, face and hand configurations in sign language (hands alone in fingerspelling, the medium of Helen Keller) depend on rapid interleaved movements distributed across face, arms, wrists, and fingers.

Here I adopt, as the basic particle of speech, the gesture, a dynamic unit at once of phonetic action and phonological contrast, posited in articulatory phonology and its associated computational model of speech production (Browman and Goldstein 1992; Saltzman and Munhall 1989; Goldstein and Fowler 2003). A gesture is a constriction of variable location and degree (amplitude) formed and released by one of six organs of the vocal apparatus (lips, tongue tip/body/root, velum, larynx) to modify the flow of vibrating air through the vocal tract. The lips organ and the tongue organs are functional synergies that engage several articulators: a gesture of the lips, for example, engages a synergy of upper lip, lower lip, and mandible.

Unlike standard phonological theories which view consonants and vowels as bundles of features, linearly arrayed in time, articulatory phonology views them as emerging, in both action and perception, from the pattern of overlapping gestures that specify a word. Each word is entered in a speaker/hearer's lexicon as a gestural score: the score specifies the locus, degree, duration, and relative phasing of the word's gestures. How did human hands, face, and vocal machinery come to be so much more finely differentiated than those of other primates? Two areas of research illuminate this question: child development and computational modelling.

## 45.2 CHILD DEVELOPMENT

'Ontogeny does not recapitulate phylogeny: it creates it' (Garstang 1922: 82). Every evolutionary step is a change in development inherited by later generations; development itself evolves, and individual ontogenies are phenotypes over which natural selection operates (Locke, this volume). Development is thus a miniature record, or epitome, of evolution. Yet, despite the logic of growth from simple to complex, we cannot always be sure of the evolutionary sequence. The theory of recapitulation fell with the rise of Mendelian genetics, because evolutionary change could now supervene at any point in development, not only at the end as recapitulation requires (Gould 1977).

We may be tempted to see infant canonical babble as recapitulating a first evolutionary step towards speech, not only because its reduplicated syllables sound like and have the temporal proportions of adult syllables, but also because its mandibular oscillation resembles the rhythmic lipsmacking of affiliating macaque monkeys, thus opening an apparent path into speech by Darwinian 'descent with modification' (MacNeilage, this volume). Yet the habit did not descend the ape line: chimpanzees, our closest primate relatives, do not engage in rhythmic lipsmacking (Frans de Waal, personal communication, 2009). Moreover, several facts suggest that babble was inserted into the developmental sequence after speech had begun to evolve. First, babble, even though part of a broader bodily development of rhythmic movement, is imitative, as shown by its delay in deaf infants (Oller et al. 1985) and by its drift over time toward the ambient language (Jusczyk 1997: 177–199). Second, babble is motor practice: a child's first words typically draw on sounds most frequent in its babble; practice is unlikely to evolve before the behaviour that it practises. Third, and most important, babble, unlike monkey chatter, is not affiliative: infants babble alone or, if among others, with no evident communicative intent. Yet language surely began under pressure for communication, whether affiliative, instrumental, or referential.

None of this diminishes the possible importance of babble for normal development in the modern child or its value as an index of human phonetic proclivities (Locke 1983, this volume). And one aspect of babble may indeed correspond to an early evolutionary step toward speech, namely, vocal imitation, a capacity unique among primates to humans. Speech could not have spread across generations, let alone communities, if speakers had not been able to replicate what they heard. The capacity perhaps evolved from a system of facial mirror neurons, as observed in rhesus monkey (cf. Studdert-Kennedy 2002, 2005; Arbib, this volume).

We can follow the development of vocal imitation and concurrent differentiation of both the vocal apparatus and its basic output, the syllable, in a child's first words. For it is under cognitive pressure for increased vocabulary that particulate speech emerges in the child, as also, by hypothesis, in our hominin ancestors. Consider, for example, a child, aged 1:10, who had the idiosyncrasy of replacing difficult word-initial syllables with the low, back vowel [ɑ] (Studdert-Kennedy and Goodell 1995). For *cranberry*, [krænbɛɪ] she offered ['ɑ'buː 'di]. Here, she replaces the first syllable and its challenging initial cluster with [ɑ], she aligns lip-rounding for [r] with tongue raising for [ɛ] and [r] to give [u], but replaces approximant tongue retroflexion with full closure to give [d] for [r]. On another occasion, for *red lights* ['rɛd 'laɪts] she offered ['weː 'jaɪ], followed a moment later, without adult correction, by ['bɛt 'θaɪts]. In the first attempt she omits tongue tip retroflexion but retains lip-rounding to give [w] for [r]; she raises the tongue tip for [d], but fails to achieve full closure, giving [eː] for [ɛd]; for tongue tip grooving of [l] she offers the tongue tip palatal glide of [j], a common shift in early speech, and she omits final [ts]. In the second attempt, she again omits retroflexion, but replaces lip-rounding for [r] with lip closure to give [b]; she combines tongue tip closure for [d] with glottal abduction to give [t], and she fronts tongue tip action for [l] to give fricative [θ], the two gestures perhaps anticipating final [ts]. (For many further examples, usually described in the terms of traditional articulatory phonetics rather than of gestures, see Waterson 1971; Ferguson and Farwell 1975; Macken 1979; Menn 1983; Vihman and Velleman 1989.)

These examples illustrate several properties of a child's early word imitations: (1) imitation entails parsing a word into its component gestures and attempting to reassemble them in the correct order; (2) the model is the whole word or phrase, not the syllable or segment: the child combines gestures from different segments and syllables of the word in its errors; (3) gestures are somatotopically represented: the child often uses the correct organ, but makes an error of gestural locus, degree, duration, or phasing (for experimental support of this observation, see Goldstein 2003); (4) the child has a representation of her goal: she corrects herself without adult guidance.

As the child's vocabulary grows, her vocal tract differentiates more fully, and her imitative domain narrows from the word to the syllable to the segment. Implicit distributional analysis of her lexicon gradually converges on recurrent patterns of laryngeal, velic, and oral gesture, leading to their integration and encapsulation as segments (cf. Lindblom 1998). Thus the modern child develops in a few months the particulate speech that our hominin ancestors evolved over perhaps hundreds of thousands of years (see MacNeilage, this volume).

Infants imitate face and hand action as well as speech. All three modalities may share a common evolutionary path to organ differentiation through imitation. Facial imitation is unique among the three because infants can neither see the face they feel nor feel the face they see, so that imitation must be mediated by an intermodal representation. Meltzoff and Moore (1997) propose a model based on two decades of studying infant facial imitation. The key to the model is somato-topic organ representation; the metric of equivalence between imitating self and imitated other is organ relations, or organ configuration. The model can readily be extended to other modalities (Studdert-Kennedy 2002). Perhaps indeed the capacity to match manual, facial, and vocal tract configurations is a universal condition of language. Language, spoken or signed, evidently requires an integral anatomical system of discrete, independently activated parts that can be coordinated to effect rapid sequences of expressive global action. The only candidate animal systems seem to be primate hands, face, and vocal apparatus.

## 45.3 COMPUTATIONAL MODELS

The foregoing was largely verbal speculation. Quantitative support and further insight come from computational models of the evolutionary process. In a seminal series of papers, Lindblom (1998 and references therein) has shown how, given an evolved vocal tract under pressure for lexical growth, a discrete phonology may emerge from a continuous articulatory/acoustic space, as a result of sustained competition between a speaker's need for economy of effort and a listener's demand for clarity.

In his earliest papers, Lindblom developed an algorithm for predicting the vowels in a system of a given size by maximizing their dispersal (hence, perceptual discriminability) in a three-formant acoustic space. His predictions corresponded to the most frequent systems in languages with up to nine vowels, indicating that perceptual discriminability may be an important factor in shaping vowel systems.

Consonants, unlike vowels, cannot be described by points in acoustic space: they are specified by acoustic trajectories, formed by gestural combinations of varying degrees of complexity. The larger a language's consonant inventory, the more complex the consonants it is likely to contain (Lindblom and Maddieson 1988): languages, like children, evidently add consonants to their inventories in their order of complexity, or articulatory effort (cost).

Lindblom's next step was therefore a modified dispersal algorithm to predict consonant–vowel (CV) syllable trajectories by means of a cost/benefit ratio (articulatory cost/perceptual discriminability) summed and minimized over a system of syllable trajectories such as might appear in a small lexicon. In a recent formulation Lindblom et al. (2011) quantified articulatory cost as proportional to the distance between the tongue's position at rest and its position at syllable onset, plus the distance between the tongue's positions at syllable onset and offset. Also included in the algorithm was a term reflecting the reduction of articulatory cost due to repeated use of the same gestures. The modified algorithm accurately predicts both the typologically most frequent places of articulation in stop consonants and 'phonemic' segmentation of CV syllables. Segmentation arises automatically from repeated use of the same gestures at syllable onset (consonants) with different gestures at syllable offset (vowels), and vice versa. Lindblom comments on his original formulation of the cost/benefit ratio procedure: 'Two results are worth noting: (1) the derivation of gestures and syllables is *systemic* (presupposes the lexicon) and (2) phonological units are *emergents* of the developing lexicon rather than prespecified entities' [emphasis in original] (1998: 255).

Lindblom's work offers the most comprehensive computational model so far available of how systems of discrete gestures, phonemes, and syllables may have emerged by self-organization under perceptuomotor constraints from an evolved vocal tract. Notice that his model assumes equivalence between vocal action and perception in an individual speaker/hearer; other individuals are implied as sources of perceptual input, but do not appear as agents of social interaction. Other models posit mutually imitating agents as loci of evolutionary change (Goldstein 2003; de Boer, Chapter 63).

All the preceding discussion has assumed some form of Darwinian selective pressure toward increased communicative scope or efficiency. In an original and challenging series of simulations, too complex for summary here, Oudeyer (2006 and references therein) draws on dynamic systems theory to explore the process through which discrete, combinatorial gestures might arise, without selective pressure, by self-organization in a prelinguistic society of vocalizing agents who, though endowed with an adequate perceptuomotor link, neither imitate nor even endeavour to communicate. The key to the effect is a neural link between perception and action that might have evolved simply to negotiate the physical world.

How Oudeyer's work will stand up to neurological and genetic study remains to be seen, but computational modelling is likely to be a heuristic of choice in future study of phonetic evolution.

# ACKNOWLEDGEMENTS

My thanks to Tecumseh Fitch and Frans de Waal for useful comments. Preparation of the chapter was supported in part by Haskins Laboratories, New Haven, CT.

# CHAPTER 46

## THE EVOLUTION OF PHONOLOGY

### PETER F. MACNEILAGE

## 46.1 INTRODUCTION

Consonants and vowels, often described as segments, are the most basic units of sound in language. The *minimal* units or 'atoms' of phonology are considered to be the 'distinctive features'. Each segment of speech—each consonant and vowel—is considered to consist of a bundle of distinctive features. Features are called distinctive because they allow the listener to distinguish between two otherwise identical forms. For example, the English words *bill* and *pill* are distinguished by a 'voicing' feature (voicing is vocal fold vibration) in the first consonant whereby *bill* has a plus value of the feature and *pill* has a minus value. Consonants and vowels (at their most basic level called 'phonemes') are concatenated into syllables, which have, at a minimum, a single vowel and can have one or more consonants on each side of the vowel. Words consist of one or more syllables.

In addition, speech has a number of prosodic properties—properties that extend over more than one segment. Examples are particular rhythmic modulations of sentences, the phenomenon of stress or variable syllabic emphasis, and intonation, or pitch changes across all or a part of the sentence. As the focus here is on the segmental level of organization, these properties will not be considered.

This chapter focuses on a small number of topics. The first, a topic of obvious evolutionary interest, is whether there is an innate basis for the sounds and sound patterns of languages. The second will be a consideration of two attempts to sketch out a phylogeny of speech—a scenario for how speech might have evolved. Following this, the relation between speech production and speech perception will be briefly examined. Finally, two questions regarding the evolutionary implications for phonology of the existence of sign languages of the deaf will be considered.

## 46.2 INNATENESS AND PHONOLOGICAL THEORY

From an evolutionary perspective, the main thing to note about the modern discipline of phonology is that the most dominant concept in the field is one with evolutionary implications. It is the concept of innateness. A large number of properties of sound patterns of languages, particularly the possession of distinctive features, are considered to be *innate* by many researchers. What do such claims entail? The definition of the word 'innate' in *Merriam-Webster's Collegiate Dictionary* (2000) is:

1: existing in, belonging to, or determined by factors present in an individual from birth: NATIVE, INBORN <*innate* behaviour>
2: belonging to the essential nature of something: INHERENT
3: originating in or derived from the mind or the constitution of the intellect rather than from experience.

One can see that while this term (unfortunately) has a number of meanings (see Fitch, this volume), they all pertain to evolution in that they include, or at least imply, the transmission of specific biological capabilities across generations. Thus, the designation 'innate' means that certain *inherent* properties of sound systems have evolved. Braine has considered the question of why claims of innateness are so rife in linguistics in general:

The goal of linguistic theory is to describe human languages. Simplicity and generality are gained by a description that minimizes what is specific to each language; one tries to account for as much structure as possible by means of principles and facts that are universal to all languages, and one tries to account for as much variation as possible on the basis of variation along well specified parameters. The assumption that such universals have an innate basis is a natural one, and accounts for why so many linguists are nativists (Braine 1994: 14).

According to Braine there is a systematic tendency to attribute linguistic phenomena which are universal to innateness. But there is a problem here. It has recently been argued by Evans and Levinson (2009: 429) that, contrary to the impression gained from the phonological literature, 'there are vanishingly few universals of language in the direct sense that all languages have them'. Thus, there may be little scope for claiming innateness on the basis of universality in the first place.

More importantly, hypotheses regarding universal innate phonological phenomena can be tested. The most comprehensive investigation of the innateness hypothesis in phonology is that undertaken by Mielke (2008), regarding the common claim that there is a small finite set of universal innate distinctive features that can describe the sound patterns participating in what are called phonological processes of all languages. He points out that:

> ...multiple sounds often participate in the same sound pattern. When a group of these sounds exhibits the same behavior it is often the case that these sounds are phonetically similar to each other. This type of grouping of sounds has been termed a 'natural class' ...(2008: 2).

As an example he takes a set of Turkish non-nasal consonants which are voiced except when they occur as the final sound in a word, in which case they are devoiced. Mielke goes on to say that 'Because devoicing is something that happens to all these consonants in Turkish, it is claimed that the process applies not to segments but to the feature [voice]' (2008: 3). This tendency toward devoicing is an example of a prominent phonological process because it is observed in many unrelated languages, and this process is often taken as evidence that the feature of voicing is innate.

Mielke found, in an analysis of 6077 classes of sounds that are either targets or triggers of phonological processes in 628 language varieties, that even when jointly considering three different distinctive feature systems, all considered to be innate by their founders, almost a quarter of the observed patterns could not be accounted for. He concludes with the alternative view that:

> ...the natural classes and distinctive features found in human languages can be accounted for as a result of factors such as phonetically-based sound change and generalization, which can be described without reference to a feature system. A feature system can be constructed (by a language learner or a linguist) on the basis of the results, but the feature system does not critically need to be a driving force behind sound patterns.... [I]t follows that phonological distinctive features no longer need to be assumed to be innate (Mielke 2008: 4).

An even more radical conclusion than the one that features are not innate might be in order. Features might not even exist as functional entities that speakers and listeners have evolved to manipulate. This was the conclusion of Peter Ladefoged, perhaps the most important phonetician of the 20th century. After spending many years trying futilely to find, at the phonetic level, straightforward correlates of distinctive features (see, for example, Ladefoged and Maddieson 1996; MacNeilage 2008: 233–235), Ladefoged concluded that 'Phonological features are best regarded as artifacts that linguists have devised in order to describe linguistic systems' (2006:

12). The main type of result that led Ladefoged to this conclusion was that, across languages, the acoustic correlates of major speech features, such as those for voicing, and the place to which speech articulators such as the tongue moved to make a sound, seemed to constitute continua, without hints that there might be a subset of discrete categories underlying them.

Beyond the distinctive feature, the aspect of sound patterns most often called innate is one associated with the syllable. Syllabic 'sonority' is considered to be an innate mental principle, supposedly revealed by the fact that the loudest (most sonorous) sound in a syllable is the vowel, and sonority then tends to decrease as the distance from the vowel of a preceding or a following consonant in the same syllable increases (e.g. Blevins 1995). But this pattern can be attributable to peripheral biomechanics rather than mental structure. A more open mouth results in a louder sound, and vice versa, and the production of a syllable usually involves a progressive opening of the mouth until one reaches the centre of the vowel, followed by a progressive closure from then on.

The other main use of the innateness claim has been in dealing with the fact of variation, alluded to by Braine—the fact that some sounds and sound patterns are more common than others. The resultant concept of 'markedness' is considered to involve another innate mental principle, this time one that lies behind the hierarchy of sound and sound pattern preferences in language (Prince and Smolensky 1997). This concept is problematical from a logical standpoint (MacNeilage 2008). More frequent patterns are characterized as more unmarked, and vice versa, and then, via circular reasoning, the patterns are deemed to be explained in terms of markedness.

Perhaps the main causal factor behind the increasing tendency to regard universal phenomena as innate in the last half century is the contention of Noam Chomsky, the dominant figure in the recent history of linguistics, that all humans are endowed with an innate Universal Grammar (UG) (Chomsky 1965). This grammar, which takes the form of a language acquisition device (LAD) is considered to have a syntactic (sentence structure) and a phonological component. Chomsky himself feels quite strongly about the innateness issue: 'To say that "language is not innate" is to say that there is no difference between my granddaughter, a rock and a rabbit' (Chomsky 2000b: 50).

The main basis for Chomsky's contention that there is an innate universal grammar is the argument from 'the poverty of the stimulus'—the argument that there is not enough in the experience of an infant to allow language to be learned. This is a hotly debated contention in the area of syntax, but there is no basis for it in phonology, as some phonologists have pointed out (e.g. Blevins 2004). A listener hears all the sound patterns he/she needs to learn.

The discipline of phonology has contributed an enormous amount of valuable information about the sound patterns of language. All this has been done without much concern for the question of evolution. Nevertheless, I have focused on phonologists' use of the evolutionary concept of innateness here because I think it is important to correct the misleading impression, arising from the wide use of this concept, that we understand more about the evolution of phonology than we actually do.

## 46.3 THE PHYLOGENY OF SPEECH PRODUCTION

It is an inescapable conclusion that humans evolved speech by descent with modification from pre-speech capabilities—non-speech capabilities. This is so because speech perception has been superimposed on pre-existing auditory capacities, and speech production has been superimposed on pre-existing sound generation capacities of the lungs, larynx, and mouth; see MacLarnon, this volume. If our knowledge of the evolution of any other action capability is any guide, initial speech must have been relatively simple before it evolved into the amazingly complex phenomenon it is today. It is remarkable that in the history of thought concerning speech, no phonologist has presented a scenario regarding how our speech capacity actually originated and how it subsequently evolved from simple to complex. This is the central question of the evolution of phonology—the question of its phylogeny. Answering this question will provide an explanation of speech at the most fundamental level—the level of 'ultimate causes' (see Mayr 1982: 67).

There is a good consensus that the key initial event in the evolution of phonology itself was hominins' attaining the ability to concatenate a relatively small number of individually meaningless transmission units into a large number of packages, each with its own distinctive meaning. Studdert-Kennedy and Lane (1980) have described the probable scenario. Before phonology evolved, our ancestors were probably like our nearest primate relatives in having a relatively small set of holistic calls (often around 30), none of them sharing any single form of internal structure. Their holistic character is often indicated by the fact that they are given names with single auditory connotations. For example, terms used to describe gelada baboon calls by Dunbar and Dunbar (1975) include 'moan', 'grunt', 'vocalized yawn', 'vibrato moan', and 'how bark'. But as selection pressures increased for a larger set of meanings to be transmitted, it must have been increasingly difficult to keep individual holistic signals like these perceptually separate from each other. The solution was to change to a system with subunits and combinatorial rules, and today every spoken language, at least, has thousands of words, all sharing a single type of internal structure. As Studdert-Kennedy has described it: 'elements drawn from a finite set . . . are repeatedly permuted and combined to yield larger units . . . higher in a hierarchy and more diverse in structure than their constituents' (1998: 203).

In the absence of phonological conceptions of the phylogeny of speech, we must turn to conceptions centring on phonetics. The only comprehensive approach to the phylogeny of the organization of speech from this standpoint is the Frame/Content theory of speech production (see MacNeilage 1998, 2008). This approach asks the *functional* question required by the Darwinian approach; the question of how we evolved to be able to actually *do* speech (to speak). With regard to the origins of sound patterns of languages, MacNeilage has argued that the initial organizational unit to have evolved was the syllable, born of the very simplest, and most repeatable, movements of the hominin jaw (see also Jackendoff 2002). MacNeilage regards the rhythmic alternation of the mandible from the elevated position (associated with mouth closure for consonants) to the depressed position (associated with mouth opening for vowels) as the 'frame' for speech. He suggests that the frame originated in mandibular cyclicities (elevation/depression cycles) associated with chewing, sucking, and licking in early mammals, and was then exapted (co-opted) into the primate visuofacial communicative cyclicity of lip-smacks before being paired with phonation (voicing) to become the protosyllable.

The 'Frame/Content' theory proposes that an initial, very rudimentary frame stage was eventually followed by a frame/content stage involving the internal differentiation of frames. This culminated in hominins' ability to programme the internal structure of these frames with individual consonants and vowels, each with their own internal structures. The programme malfunctions when modern speakers make segmental speech errors such as spoonerisms, thus revealing the dichotomy between syllabic frames, which are not altered in these errors, and segmental content, which is misordered.

MacNeilage contends that the ontogeny of speech today reveals some details regarding what the first speech of hominins was like, because the first speakers shared the same biomechanical constraints as are revealed in the babbling and first words of infants. This is likely because hominins must have started to speak using the movement patterns most available to them, and those patterns must have been very simple ones, not unlike those of modern infants; see also Studdert-Kennedy, this volume. In infants, vocal babbling begins at about 7 months and is characterized by a rhythmic close-open alternation of the mouth, produced by mandibular oscillation, accompanied by very little capacity to actively move the other articulators—tongue, lips, and soft palate—during these alternations. This view of the relationship between phylogeny and ontogeny is consistent with that of the 19th-century school of Naturphilosophie (see Gould 1977) according to which phylogeny and ontogeny share common constraints such as biomechanical inertia, imposed by laws of physics.

This pattern of mandibular oscillation, accompanied by inertia in other articulators, is indicated by a number of properties of babbling. First, babbling tends to be reduplicative, meaning that successive consonant-vowel (CV) sequences are the same, as in 'bababa'. A good deal of evidence accumulated by MacNeilage and

Davis and others (e.g. MacNeilage and Davis 2000) suggests that nothing changes *within* a syllable in these forms except for the following of a closed mouth (elevated mandible) with an open mouth (depressed mandible). For example, a consonant with a closure in the front of the mouth such as [t], [d], or [n] tends to be accompanied by a front vowel such as [ɛ] or [æ], whereas a consonant with a closure in the back of the mouth, such as [k] or [g], tends to be accompanied by a back vowel, such as [o] or [u]. Both of these patterns could readily be achieved with the tongue in a single position in the mouth throughout the syllable. A third common consonant-vowel co-occurrence pattern is for consonants with lip closure to be accompanied by a central vowel, such as [a]. In this case, the tongue could be in its resting position throughout the syllable.

The fundamental nature of these three tendencies toward tongue inertia is suggested by the fact that they tend to be favoured in CV sequences in languages even today, according to a survey of a total of 24 languages by MacNeilage et al. (2000) and Rousset (2003).

While infants tend to produce the same syllable repeatedly (reduplication), languages tend to avoid repeating the same syllable (variegation). The main first step that infants make to move from reduplicative to variegated forms in their first words is to favour beginning a word with a labial or lip consonant (e.g. [b] or [m]) and then, after the vowel, produce a coronal or tongue-front consonant (e.g. [d] or [n]). For example, an infant is more likely to be able to say 'bado' for 'bottle' than to say 'dabo' for 'double'. Infants sometimes even produce the labial-coronal sequence mistakenly when the coronal-labial sequence is called for. MacNeilage and Davis (2000) suggest that this preference stems from a self-organizational process governed by ease of articulation and that a similar process may have been in operation when the first speakers were under pressure to produce an increasing number of vocal forms.

The fundamental nature of this sequence preference is further revealed by the fact that, like the consonant-vowel co-occurrence patterns, it is also characteristic of modern languages, according to the studies of a total of 24 languages by MacNeilage et al. (1999) and Rousset (2003). For example, in the MacNeilage et al. study of 10 languages there was a ratio greater than 2:1 of labial-coronal sequences to coronal-labial sequences.

How might the frame stage of speech have evolved by descent with modification? Van Hooff (1967) has suggested that lipsmacks may have evolved their communicative status from cyclical ingestive movements elicited during a manual-grooming event. Animals looking forward to finding a food item, such as a salt grain, in an individual instance of grooming, might have begun chewing movements in anticipation of such a discovery. Initial selection pressures for the protosyllabic cyclical forms (in effect, lipsmacks with voicing), may have come from *vocal* grooming. Perhaps, according to Dunbar (1996), vocalization may have been substituted for manual tactile contact as ancestral hominin group sizes increased enough to make the latter behaviour ineffective as a device for social cohesion; Dunbar, this volume. It's also possible that an evolving capacity to *learn* vocalization occurred when vocal grooming became important as part of a general-purpose mimetic capability, selected to enhance group solidarity, as suggested by Donald (1999, this volume). This capability to recreate the observed actions of others, almost as salient and unique in humans as is speech, and probably based, in part, on mirror neurons (see Arbib, this volume), is evident today in movements related to music, dance, opera, ballet, movies, games, sports, etc.—a capacity not present in other living primates. Monkeys can learn the appropriate contexts for vocalizations (Zuberbühler, this volume), but they do not invent and socially transmit novel vocalizations.

The Frame/Content theory is unusual among approaches to the origins of speech in having specific implications for the evolution of brain organization (MacNeilage 2008). According to the theory, the Frame/Content dichotomy is paralleled in the brain by a dichotomy of movement control systems, basically present in all primates. In addition, the specialization of the left brain hemisphere for right-handedness and for speech (and, as a phylogenetic consequence, language; see Hopkins and Vauclair, this volume) evolved from a specialization of that hemisphere for control of the whole body under routine (as opposed to emergency) conditions. The right hemisphere may have a complementary role in emergency reactions. Both specializations may have already been present in the first vertebrates, about 500 million years ago (MacNeilage 2008; MacNeilage et al. 2009).

MacNeilage's approach takes the increasingly influential 'embodiment' perspective, according to which the mind cannot be understood without acknowledging that the body is integral to it, and always has been (e.g. Clark 2008). This approach requires the following amendment to Descartes' famous aphorism: 'I *do*, therefore I am'.

A second approach to the evolution of spoken phonology, primarily by Studdert-Kennedy, is based on the concept of the 'gesture' (see Studdert-Kennedy 1998; this volume; Studdert-Kennedy and Goldstein 2003). A 'gesture' is defined as the making and release of a vocal-tract constriction. (The vocal tract is the air space between the larynx and the lips.) Vocal-tract constrictions are the main factor in the production of the various acoustic properties of speech sounds. There are considered to be six relatively independent 'organs' that make these gestures—'the lips, tongue tip/blade, tongue body, tongue root, larynx and velum' (Studdert-Kennedy and Goldstein 2003: 243). (The velum, or soft palate, controls the opening/closing of the airway joining the oral and nasal cavities). These gestures are considered to be the atoms of speech or the ultimate particles with which the particulate principle (Abler 1989) is implemented in speech. It should be noted though, that only two of these organs, the larynx and the soft palate, are truly anatomically independent of the others. Moreover, the assumption that the tongue, normally regarded as a single organ, consists of three independent organs, is highly unorthodox. Ladefoged and Maddieson (1996) have described 14 different positions that the tongue can adopt to constrict the airway as required for consonants, in the world's languages, and there is no evidence that this versatility is achieved by combinations of the three control elements that Studdert-Kennedy posits.

A major merit of the gestural approach is that it provides a realistic alternative to the distinctive feature concept in the characterization of the sub-segmental level of speech production at least. There is no question as to whether speakers make gestures. In the gestural approach, an attempt is made to characterize the physical basis of speech production in terms of time/space properties of movement of vocal tract components. This approach has proved useful in understanding various aspects of modern speech, such as how the components of successive segments co-articulate with each other, and how variation in speaking rate is accomplished.

Studdert-Kennedy believes that the crucial phylogenetic event underlying speech was to be able to separately control the positioning of the actions of the six organs in the time domain so that they could combine in a large number of ways to make many different segments. He concludes from a study of infant speech errors that this is also the main event in ontogeny. However, according to the Frame/Content theory there is also another problem that Studdert-Kennedy does not address. The three basic consonant-vowel co-occurrence patterns described earlier are indicative of biomechanical inertia—a tendency to not change the position of an articulator (beyond the mouth close-open cycle) during an utterance. This suggests that in addition to becoming able to position a gesture in the time domain with respect to a single segment, an infant must learn to restrict this gesture so that it does not affect the sound of adjacent segments as well as the one on which it is centred. Studdert-Kennedy does not consider this problem.

## 46.4 THE RELATIONSHIP BETWEEN SPEECH PRODUCTION AND PERCEPTION

So far we have only considered the production of speech. But speech must also be perceived. Perhaps the best generalization that can be made about the causal level of the phonological component is the one promulgated by Lindblom (e.g. 1998). He notes that a basic property of the sound transmission process in speech is that it is constantly being built and rebuilt by a process of interaction between a production system that tends toward a state of least effort and a perceptual system that strives to maintain perceptual distinctiveness between message units. In this context, sound change constantly occurs in the history of linguistic systems because of the continual occurrence of states of disequilibrium between the production system's tendency toward ease of articulation and the perceptual system's constant demand for perceptual distinctiveness. One of Lindblom's signal contributions was a simulation of the role of speech perception in the choice of vowel systems in the world's languages, in which he was able to predict the favoured vowel inventories of languages with up to nine vowels on the basis of the principle of maximal perceptual distinctiveness (Lindblom 1986). With this and other work Lindblom has put the causal basis of phonological evolution in self-organizational processes, where it should be, rather than in preordination of phonological forms and sound patterns. (For his conception of the evolution of phonology see Lindblom 2011.) An important theme of much recent work, building on Lindblom's approach, is the use of computer modelling of interactions between speakers and listeners in an attempt to understand the emergence of sound patterns (see in particular de Boer 2001, Chapter 63; Oudeyer 2006).

# 46.5 Phonological evolution
## and sign language

In the last half-century it has become clear that rather than being a degraded derivative of spoken language, sign languages of the deaf are independently in-vented and have all the major properties of spoken language except for the modality of transmission. Ideally, an attempt to understand the evolution of phonology should encompass the phonology of sign language. Two evolution-related questions with implications for sign language will be raised here. The first is whether phonology can be considered to be amodal; that is, to have a structure that is independent of whether language is spoken or signed. The second question is whether sign language evolved before spoken language (see, for instance, Corballis, this volume). If so, this raises the question of how phonology changed from a signed to a spoken basis (see Goldin-Meadow, this volume).

As to the first question, the putative innate module of Universal Grammar, which is supposed to be present in humans, is considered to be amodal. This means that the structure of the phonological level is considered to be fundamentally the same for speech and sign language.

Many people have argued that the fundamental phonological structures of speech and sign are different (e.g. Jakobson 1967). They point out, correctly, that speech is essentially strung out across the time domain, whereas information for a particular sign is presented simultaneously. As mentioned earlier, speech involves a time-dependent alternation between consonants and vowels, and syllables usually have at least two of these entities—though often, up to two or three consonants or even more, and these precede and/or follow the vowel in a syllable. On the other hand, in a sign, the basic location, handshape, and movement information are basically signalled at the same time.

But let us look more closely at the relation between the phonological structure of speech and that of sign language. Speech is thought by linguists to have three main units: the distinctive features, the phonemes, and the syllable. It was mentioned earlier that the proposed basic unit of speech phonology, the distinctive feature, may not exist. If that's true, then the question of whether distinctive features have an equivalent in sign language doesn't arise. Second, though a number of equivalences between consonants and vowels and the three basic formatives of sign language—locations, handshapes, and movements—have been suggested, this has been a very complex topic, marked by conflicting criteria and evidence (Sandler and Lillo-Martin 2006). Third, as was also pointed out earlier, the dominant concept regarding spoken syllables is that of sonority, which is related to loudness. But as Sandler and Lillo-Martin (2006) point out, the literal counterpart of this property in sign language is brightness, and signs have no such property.

As to the second question, there has been a relatively strong and continuing tradition of regarding sign language as the first form of language. Corballis (2002, this volume) and Arbib (2005, this volume) are recent proponents of this view. There are probably two main reasons why this view has persisted. One is that it offers a solution to the basic problem of how phonological symbols became attached to concepts in the first place. The solution is that the first signs could have been iconic—that is, related in a natural way to the concepts that they symbolize. For example, a pair of upraised hands flapping has a natural relation to the concept of *bird* in a way that the spoken word 'bird' or any other sound pattern signifying bird does not. The second reason is that while there has been little success in teaching great apes to speak, individual members of all the main species of great apes have been taught to make considerable linguistic use of visual signs, including those of sign language.

The possibility that sign language came first has received encouragement from the finding, by Giacomo Rizzolatti and his colleagues, that monkeys possess a class of neurons called mirror neurons—neurons which discharge when the monkey makes a hand movement as well as when the monkey sees another monkey making the same movement (Ferrari et al. 2003). These neurons have been thought to underlie the learning of the kind of input-output perception-production links necessary for a visual-manual language system to evolve. However, monkeys also have lipsmack mirror neurons, mirror neurons related to ingestive actions, and neurons related to sound-making activity, all perhaps relevant to the evolution of vocal communication. In fact, Rizzolatti's group has concluded that 'ingestive actions are the basis on which communication is built' (Ferrari et al. 2003: 1713).

To evaluate the basic claim of a hand-to-mouth sequence in language evolution we need to be clear about how we define language. The present contention, already mentioned, is that the key event in the evolution of phonology—namely, hominins' attaining the ability to concatenate a relatively small number of individually meaningless transmission units into a large number of packages, each with its own distinctive meaning—defines the beginning of language. Using this criterion, modern sign languages have the phonological structure of languages. But as the eminent linguist Charles Hockett observed some decades ago (1958), any earlier hominin signed communication systems could not have been like modern sign languages because, if they had been, they would have proved so indispensable that we would never have abandoned them as the primary mode of universal linguistic communication. The usual reasons given for the subsequent abandonment of any initial sign language—that sign is not omnidirectional, doesn't work at night, and doesn't leave the hands free—don't seem sufficiently substantial to have led to its demise.

It is fair to say that sign language has sown the seeds of an identity crisis in the discipline of phonology. Given that the phonology of sign language is very different from that of spoken language, it seems as if a second kind of phonology is called for. The most promising possibility is that, like spoken language, sign language will be best understood as a consequence of a modality-specific relation between ease of production and perceptual distinctiveness. But a key question is whether we need a phylogenetic conception of sign language phonology, or just one pertaining to the understanding of modern inventions of the form.

# CHAPTER 47

# THE EVOLUTION OF MORPHOLOGY

## ANDREW CARSTAIRS-McCARTHY

### 47.1 MORPHOLOGY AS A PUZZLE
### FOR LANGUAGE EVOLUTION

Syntax organizes words into phrases and sentences, in such a way that the meanings of these larger units are determined systematically by the meanings of the individual words that compose them. Thanks to English syntax, when we hear *Arsenal defeated Chelsea*, we know who won. By contrast, morphology deals with complex words. Some complex words contain more than one component, such as *baked* (consisting of *bake* with a suffix *-d*), *unhelpfulness* (consisting of *help* plus a prefix *un-* and suffixes *-ful* and *-ness*) and *headrest* (a compound with two elements). Other words are complex in that they are related to another word which is in some way more basic, as *sang* and *song* are related to *sing*, and *breathe* is related to *breath*. The two kinds of complexity can occur together: for example, *kept* contains an element *kep-*, related to *keep*, as well as a suffix *-t* that also appears in *lost*, *built*, *burnt*, and several other verbs.

It is easy to see why, as soon as some humans had acquired the biological underpinnings for syntax, this trait should have spread to all humans. In a kind of language that lacked syntax (such as a 'protolanguage': see Bickerton, Chapter 49; Tallerman, Chapter 51), *Arsenal defeated Chelsea* would be ambiguous; the intended meaning on any occasion would have to be gleaned through pragmatic clues. That difference would have been enough to allow the syntax-users within any human population to outbreed, over time, their syntaxless rivals. But it is less clear why all of us should have the capacity to learn natively languages whose complex units include not only phrases and sentences but also words that are complex in the ways that I have described. To impose order on the interpretation of strings of basic meaningful items, syntax alone would have been enough.

Some scholars have suggested that syntax is indeed enough—that is, that morphology as a distinct component of grammar does not really exist, being essentially just syntax below the level of the word (Selkirk 1982; Lieber 1992). Without going that far, other scholars use the term 'morphosyntax', implying that there is no crucial boundary between morphology and syntax (e.g. Hurford 2007). And indeed, if the boundary is fuzzy, this makes the existence of complex words, as distinct from phrases, seem at first sight less puzzling. Only at first sight, however. The unification of 'morphosyntax' does not explain why four complications are concentrated at its morphological end: (1) boundness; (2) allomorphy; (3) morphophonological alternation; (4) irregularity. I will illustrate each.

A form is 'bound' rather than 'free' if it cannot occur by itself. In English, open-class words—words that belong to word classes that are open to new members, such as nouns, verbs, and adjectives—are free. A closed-class word such as the definite article *the* is also arguably free because, although it seldom occurs by itself, it can do so (*'Did you say Bill is AN authority on trilobites or THE authority?' 'THE!'*). By contrast, the prefix *un-* and the suffixes *-ness*, *-d*, and *-t* are certainly bound. What's more, the suffix *-d* (in one of its meanings) competes with an 'allomorph' or rival form *-(e)n*, in the sense that, in wordforms where *-d* occurs, *-(e)n* cannot, and vice versa:

(1)  We have baked/*taked/sold/*stoled the cake already.

(2)  We have *baken/taken/*solen/stolen the cake already.

The allomorphs *-d* and *-(e)n* are entirely unlike one another. But some allomorphs are similar, such as *keep* (/kip/) and *kep-*, as in *kept* (/kɛpt/). These latter are therefore said to be morphophonological alternants. We use the term 'morpho-phonological' rather than 'phonological', because this is not a matter of pure phonology: that is, phonology alone cannot explain why the verbs *keep* and *seep* have divergent past tense forms, *kept* /kɛpt/ and *seeped* /sipt/ respectively. Finally, the contrasts between *kept* and *seeped* and between *-d* and *-(e)n* illustrate kinds of irregularity that are frequently encountered in morphology. One can easily envisage a similar sort of competition between rivals at the level of phrases rather than complex words; for example, the noun *cake* might have a synonymous rival—say, *bool –*, the two being distributed as in (3) and (4):

(3)  We will bake/*take/sell/*steal the cake tomorrow.

(4)  We will *bake/take/*sell/steal the bool tomorrow.

But this sort of arbitrariness just does not happen at the level of the phrase or the sentence. So morphology really does seem to behave differently from syntax, and the puzzle remains: why has the capacity for grammar evolved so as to make both available?

## 47.2 SOME PROPOSED SOLUTIONS

### 47.2.1 Different senses of 'evolution'

For proponents of the morphology-is-syntax view in its purest form, everything about morphological evolution is bound to be covered by an adequate account of the evolution of syntax and phonology. The rest of this chapter describes approaches by linguists who do not subscribe to that view.

It is helpful first to remind ourselves of three distinct phenomena to which the term 'language evolution' has been applied. These are:

  (i) Historical change in language over the last few thousand years.
 (ii) The cultural evolution of language, understood as long-term change in how the capacity for language is manifested, due to cultural rather than to biological factors.
(iii) The biological evolution of the language faculty.

The first two views that I will be discussing treat morphological evolution as coming under senses (i) and (ii) respectively, with perhaps some uncertainty (in respect of the second view) over whether (ii) is really distinct from (i). It is worth contrasting this range of views with those relating to syntax. Scarcely any serious linguist thinks that the origin of syntax can be accounted for solely by evolution in senses (i) or (ii). Thus, current views about the origin of morphology are skewed more towards culture and away from biology than are the corresponding views about syntax.

### 47.2.2 Morphology as 'yesterday's syntax'

Innumerable historical facts point towards non-morphological starting-points for many morphological phenomena; see also Heine and Kuteva, this volume; Bybee, this volume. Examples are:

(5) The French adverb-forming suffix -*ment* (as in *heureusement* 'happily') is descended from the Latin ablative singular form *mente* of the noun MENS 'mind'.

(6)  The Hungarian locative case suffix *-be/-ba* (depending on vowel harmony), as in *a házba* 'in the house', where it gives rise to the 'in' meaning, is descended from the noun *bél* 'entrails, innards' (Simonyi 1907: 366).

(7)  The suffix *-emo* of the Italian 1st plural future form *parleremo* 'we will talk' is derived from Latin *habemus* 'we have', as in the reconstructable Vulgar Latin collocation *parabolare habemu(s)*, literally 'to-talk we-have'.

Could it be, then, that all morphology originated this way? This subsection and the next discuss versions of this view.

Givón (1971) claimed that the order of the elements in complex wordforms reflects exactly the order of free wordforms at some earlier stage of the language. Morphology is thus 'fossilized syntax'. What was once a phrase may retain a syntactically obsolete ordering of elements, but only at the cost of ceasing to be a phrase and instead becoming a word; thus, when two constituents find themselves in the wrong order (so to speak), at least one of them must become 'bound', in the sense illustrated earlier by the affixes *un-*, *-ness*, and *-d*. So, for example, the stem-affix order in *parleremo* in (7) reflects a verb-final stage in the history of Italian, preceding the current subject–verb–object pattern. Morphological structure arises out of syntactic structure as the price for maintaining obsolete orderings of elements, and there is really no more to be said about its origin than that.

This raises the question, however, of why structures classified as 'obsolete' should be retained at all. Besides, one could argue that the very fact that a given structure is retained (even if it is used less widely than before) shows that it is not after all obsolete. In any case, the facts are not always so straightforward as they would need to be for Givón's account to be convincing. If Givón were right, then (for example) the stem-affix order in *heureusement* at (5) should indicate that, in Latin, adjectives consistently preceded nouns, whereas in French the order is consistently the reverse. Yet neither of these claims is correct; even in French, although most adjectives do usually follow their head nouns, there are some common ones (such as *grand* 'big', *vieux* 'old', and their antonyms) that consistently precede. Nevertheless, that pioneering work of Givón is one contribution to the development of 'grammaticalization theory', to which we turn now.

## 47.2.3  Morphology as due to 'grammaticalization'

Grammaticalization theory has over the last two decades become an influential current within historical linguistics (Heine et al. 1991; Heine and Kuteva 2002b, 2007, this volume; Hopper and Traugott 2003). Grammaticalization is the process whereby open-class lexical items develop over time into closed-class items with grammatical functions. There is said to be a uniform series of semantic changes involving metaphorical usage (for example, spatial terms acquire temporal meanings but not vice versa) and 'bleaching' (for example, more abstract meanings such as 'inside' may arise out of more concrete ones such as 'belly', as in (6)).

On the formal side, these new closed-class items often become reduced phonologically, so as to lose whatever in the language in question are typical phonological characteristics of an independent word. They may go so far as to cease to be words entirely. That is, grammaticalization often leads to 'morphologization': an independent marker of (say) tense or number becomes an affix rather than remaining a free wordform, and may even ultimately fuse with the root of the lexeme to which it is attached, as has happened in Germanic umlaut (e.g. English *feet*, the plural of *foot*, which originated as a form with a suffix *-i*, something like *\*foːt-i*).

This implies that morphology is a byproduct of syntax (even though less directly than was claimed by Givón) and thus subordinate to it. If so, it is reasonable to suppose that there was a prehistoric stage of grammatical development when morphology did not exist at all: there was only syntax (perhaps in some premodern form). Comrie (1992) proposes exactly this. There was (he suggests) a prehistoric stage of language 'before complexity', in which there were no affixes, no morphophonological alternations except of a transparent low-level kind, and certainly no fusion such as in *feet*. Similarly, Heine and Kuteva (2002a: 390) posit a prehistoric stage of grammatical development which they call 'Stage X', when there was some sort of distinction between nouns and verbs (denoting thing-like entities and non-time-stable concepts respectively), but no morphology.

The gap between Stage X and contemporary language is bridged in more recent work by Heine and Kuteva (2007, this volume). They now offer an account of 'the genesis of grammar' that projects the methods of grammaticalization theory into prehistory, to a point when grammaticalization processes 'took place *for the first time*, that is, when there were, for example, verbs but no auxiliaries—hence, when human language was less complex than it is today [their emphasis]' (2007: 32).

Yet most grammaticalization theorists recognize an important limit on what their approach can explain. Although grammaticalization processes may create morphology, this is not inevitable. It is always possible for grammaticalization to stop short of morphologization. This applies to most languages of east Asia, for example. But an awkward question now arises. Why does grammaticalization not always stop short of morphologization? What is it within the language faculty that allows the extra step to be taken? A simple thought-experiment demonstrates that this question is serious. Suppose it were the case that morphologization never occurred, and that morphology did not exist. In such a situation, a linguist who posed the question why morphology did not exist—a pattern of grammatical organization featuring bound affixes, allomorphy, morphophonological alternation and frequent irregularities—would be laughed out of court. 'Why on earth would the brain tolerate all that sort of complexity? No advantage, whether biological or cultural, would accrue from it! There is no way in which "morphology" (as you call it) could ever get established!'

Carstairs-McCarthy (2005, 2010) proposes an answer that challenges the usual assumption about the temporal order in which morphology and morphophonology arose. The grammaticalization approach takes it for granted that affixation would have become established after 'Stage X' without at first being accompanied by any morphophonological alternations such as we observe in *sing/sang* or *keep/kept*. The very word 'morphophonology' seems to imply a phenomenon that is secondary to, and thus later in origin than, morphology. But this may be wrong. Even without any syntax—that is, even in a kind of protolanguage (Bickerton 1990) in which sequences of 'words' are interpreted purely pragmatically—there could be phonological processes operating between regularly contiguous 'words', and some of these processes could in due course become opaque. This would give rise to situations where the same meaning was expressed by two or more forms in different contexts: that is, to instances of synonymy. Let me illustrate how this could happen and explain why it is important.

Even without syntax, some items could be regularly juxtaposed to express a consistent conventionalized meaning (a point made by Jackendoff 2002). This is like, in English, the juxtaposition of *head* and *rest* in a compound expressing the meaning 'pad or cushion to support the head'—a conventionalized meaning, inasmuch as it might equally well have acquired the sense 'period of rest from using the head in thinking', for example. Now, it so happens that *head* and *rest* do not much affect each other's pronunciation. But, in such juxtapositions, changes in pronunciation often arise: for example, *hand* is pronounced [hænd] in *handwork* but [hæmb] in *handbag* and [hæŋ] in *handcuffs*. We have thus arrived at a situation where the same meaning ('hand') is expressed by not one phonological shape but several synonymous ones.

This is important because of the evidence that the brains of not just humans (Clark 1993) but other mammalian species such as chimpanzees (Savage-Rumbaugh 1986) and at least one dog (Kaminski et al. 2004) abhor perfect synonymy between communicative calls or 'signs'. A functional explanation for this abhorrence is not far to seek: the learning task for the young animal is much simplified if it can reliably assume that each newly encountered sign means something different from all the signs that it already knows. The synonymy avoidance assumption is thus fundamental to the extraordinary speed with which young children acquire vocabulary. But how can this assumption be reconciled with the fact that phonological processes may yield not only minor differences in pronunciation such as in the *hand-* examples but also, through accumulated changes, such salient differences as in *foot* and *feet*—two forms that are synonymous in respect of the meaning 'foot'?

In such situations (Carstairs-McCarthy suggests), in order to mitigate obnoxious synonymy, human brains would naturally inject some differentiating information. In the *foot/feet* example, the differentiating information is clear: the first form is singular, the second plural. But the information need not have syntactic or semantic relevance. Rival expressions of a grammatical meaning (such as *-d* and *-(e)n* at (1) and (2)) may indicate membership of distinct inflection classes that an English-speaker keeps apart in the same way as an English–French bilingual keeps apart the synonymous rivals *dog* and *chien*. Alternatively, rivals may be differentiated by their phonological context, as with the English indefinite articles *a* and *an*: the former is used before consonants, the latter before vowels. The capacity for allomorphy and morphophonological alternation could thus have arisen alongside syntax or even before it, but at any rate independently of it. The fact that morphological constructs in contemporary languages are often traceable to earlier syntactic ones does not undermine this suggestion; it merely points towards one way in which the capacity for morphology has been exploited.

Carstairs-McCarthy's approach has yet to be evaluated by the linguistic and language-evolution communities. That said, it complements grammaticalization theory by focusing on those messy aspects of morphology that grammaticalization theory has least to say about. And by invoking characteristics of mammalian cognition, it asserts that not just syntax but also morphology has evolved in sense (iii), that is as a partly biological, not a wholly cultural, characteristic of language.

CHAPTER 48

# WHAT IS SYNTAX?

## MAGGIE TALLERMAN

## 48.1 INTRODUCTION

As the chapters in Parts IV and V show, syntax is not the only interesting part of language—but it is nonetheless central. Outside of linguistics, syntax is sometimes rather casually associated with rule-governed vocalizations (e.g. in bird song or whale song), or with rare examples of call combinations (occasionally reported in monkeys or apes), or with regularities in linear ordering (observed in ape language research). But these properties are far removed from the complex phenomena in the syntax of human languages. Here, I discuss the kinds of universal syntactic capacities that prompt many linguists to postulate that syntax is a separate, biologically-determined entity. We do not know whether syntax is simply an emergent property of advanced cognitive capacity, or, alternatively, is due to a discrete genetic or biological capacity. However, syntax cannot be reduced to or equated with any readily-identifiable alternative cognitive capacities. Nor does it have simpler analogues or homologues elsewhere in animal communication systems, even among our closest primate relatives. For this reason, linguists generally regard the evolution of syntax as a major challenge to researchers investigating language evolution.

## 48.2 SYNTAX AND THE LEXICON

I start with lexical items (fundamentally, vocabulary), since without these, there is no syntax (Burling, this volume). Lexical items are stored in the 'mental lexicon', an inventory of arbitrary form-meaning associations. These include single words and morphemes smaller than words (such as affixes), multi-word idioms, set phrases, and constructions of various kinds (e.g. *put up with X; high time; doing X's level best*). If learning vocabulary involved merely learning the sound-meaning (or handshape-meaning) correspondences of words—matching an arbitrary pattern with a concept—then great apes certainly display a similar property in captivity, since they can learn to produce and comprehend perhaps a few hundred such correspondences (Gibson, Part I). Various other animals, such as African Grey parrots (Pepperberg, this volume), display similar learning. But vocabulary involves far more than a set of learned associations.

In humans, vocabulary learning is sophisticated, involving a complex mix of grammatical properties, phonology, semantics, and cultural knowledge. Some aspects are universal, others language-specific. Vocabulary items belong to complex, structured semantic categories. For instance, the verbs *murder, kill,* and *assassinate* belong to the same semantic class, but aren't synonymous: for *murder* (but not *kill*) the act itself must be deliberate, and both parties must be animate, normally human; *assassinate* means to murder a socially prominent person, an elaborate meaning probably learned quite late. Both *kill* and *murder* have metaphorical senses (*My feet are killing me; I could murder a beer*), whereas *assassinate* apparently doesn't. Learning abstract nouns, e.g. *imagination, despair, sincerity,* must be even harder; they cannot be contextually demonstrated. And humans acquiring a word learn not just its pronunciation and lexical meaning, but critically, its syntax.

Universally, verbs fit into one or more 'subcategorization frames', which specify the number and type of obligatory dependents (known as 'arguments') the verb has. Universally, the number of arguments is limited, probably to four, as in [*He*] *sold* [*the book*] [*to the collector*] [*for fifty Euros*] (cf. Hurford's (2007) explanation, involving the inherited properties of a phylogenetically ancient visual system). Intransitive verbs have only one argument, a subject: *The unicorn disappeared.* Transitive verbs have two, a subject and an object: *The teacher corrected the child's work.* Ditransitive verbs have a direct object and an indirect object: *The teacher gave the work to the child,* and in some languages (but not all) this subcategorization frame alternates with a double-object construction: *The teacher gave the child the work.* Other verbs take a preposition phrase (PP) as a dependent: *She applied* [*for the position*], or a subordinate clause *She wondered* [*whether she'd get the job*]. There are more subcategorization frames for verbs, but crucially, not that many more, universally.

Syntactic knowledge is not limited to content words like verbs; speakers also know that *this* is followed by a singular noun (not necessarily directly, since adjectives may intervene) while *these* is followed by a plural noun; both can 'stand in for' a noun (*I like these__*), while *the* cannot. When apes or parrots learn a word, their knowledge is apparently restricted to basic sound-meaning and gesture-meaning correspondences. It does not encompass subtle and abstract lexical semantic distinctions, such as those in *kill*, *murder*, and *assassinate*. And critically, other animals appear unable to learn subcategorization frames—the lexical requirements of words—which humans (within a certain stage in development) manage effortlessly.

Perhaps, though, humans learn relatively easily that transitive verbs (like *assassinate*) differ from intransitive verbs (like *disappear*), and once a few such verbs are learned, then the properties of other verbs in these classes come, as it were, for free. But additional complexities abound. For instance, transitive verbs can passivize, as in (1), but some ostensibly similar verbs cannot:

(1)   a. Kim weighed the parcel.
      b. The parcel was weighed by Kim.

(2)   a. Kim weighed 120 pounds.
      b. *120 pounds was/were weighed by Kim.

Evidently, the *weigh* in (1) is not the *weigh* in (2), yet the distinction is quite subtle. In English, only 'true' transitive verbs passivize, but in German, intransitive verbs can also passivize:

(3)   Es wurde   getanzt.
      it  became dance.PAST-PARTICIPLE
      'There  was dancing.' (Literally, *It was danced.*)

When linguists talk of 'Universal Grammar', the term implies, among other things, whatever abilities children bring to the language-learning task that enable them to learn the intricacies of the ambient vocabulary with such apparent ease. Facts of this nature characterize all languages; they aren't taught, yet children acquire them. No other species has ever mastered such complexities.

The human lexicon displays at least three further unique characteristics. First, its sheer size is staggering: speakers probably store at least 50,000 entries for each of their native languages. Interestingly, even our own 'primate' calls, such as cries of pain, aren't wholly innate but are overlaid by learning, differing from language to language. Second, though the learning of syntax, phonology, and morphology is subject to critical period effects, new lexical items are learned throughout life; there is no critical period for vocabulary acquisition.

Third, the human lexicon crucially contains two major classes of items: content words, known as lexical categories, and grammatical elements, or functional categories (lexical and functional elements also combine, forming idioms and other multi-word entries). The lexical/functional division occurs in all languages, including supposedly 'simple' languages, such as Riau Indonesian (see Carstairs-McCarthy, Chapter 50), although functional categories in particular vary greatly cross-linguistically. Lexical categories are typically, though not always, open-class words, so new exemplars can be added, both by a speaker, as new words are learned, and by the language (think of the vocabulary of the electronic revolution). Nouns and verbs are the central lexical classes, and are probably universal; additionally, there may be some lexical adpositions (prepositions/postpositions), and adjectives and adverbs if the language has these classes.

Functional categories include 'small' grammatical words, such as pronouns, determiners, auxiliaries, complementizers, conjunctions, noun classifiers, and 'grammatical' prepositions such as *of*; also vital are sub-word morphosyntactic markers, such as noun and verb inflections, expressing grammatical categories like case, definiteness, tense, aspect, etc. These are mostly closed-class items; new exemplars arise slowly, mainly through historical change (see Bybee, this volume). Functional elements perform crucial work in grammars; even languages like Chinese, which lack inflectional morphology (e.g. verb and noun 'endings'), have vital functional elements such as aspect markers (see Heine and Kuteva, this volume). Furthermore, grammatical rules involving functional elements operate over specific syntactic categories; for instance, case typically applies to nouns, tense to verbs, and comparison to adjectives. Thus, knowledge of the lexical classes that words belong to is critical for syntactic competence.

Not all functional items even have a meaning. 'Dummy' subjects like English *it* and *there* illustrate: *It's certain he'll leave* or *There was a problem*. (These differ from 'referential' *it* in *You ate it* and *there* in *You went there*.) In *Did you go?*, auxiliary *do* has a grammatical function, expressing tense, but adds no meaning. So the ability to learn form-meaning pairs is only part of the human 'vocabulary' story. An equally important evolutionary novelty is the functional/lexical distinction, unlike anything in animal communication systems. Moreover, functional elements are rarely reported in 'animal language' labs. It may be, then, that only humans can learn functional vocabulary.

## 48.3 WHAT DOES SYNTAX INVOLVE?

Syntax begins, in ontogeny as it must have in phylogeny, with single words bearing high semantic content. Until words are obligatorily combined, both in ontogeny and in phylogeny, we cannot truly speak of 'word classes': there are no 'nouns' or 'verbs' in protolanguage until words from these semantic classes co-occur in predictable ways with their dependents; when this happens, syntax is born. Apes under 'language' instruction produce noun-like and verb-like words, but they never *systematically* combine these words with their dependents, as do children beyond about 3 years old. The formation of distinct word classes is the basis for syntax.

Over time, single content words accrue modifiers—words placed next to them which modify their meaning. For instance, in ontogeny, *milk* becomes *more milk.* In language evolution, as Jackendoff (2002: ch. 8) suggests, the earliest principles grouping words together were most likely purely semantic/pragmatic (Tallerman, Chapter 51). Elements frequently co-occurring in sequences start to form meaning chunks (see Bybee, this volume). In a short linear sequence, one content word will be obligatory, bearing most of the meaning: this is the basis for the lexical *head* of a phrase in modern syntax. The next step occurs when a head *requires* some co-occurring word, as outlined above; then a phrase is formed. Phrases in full language consist of a syntactic/semantic head plus its obligatory and optional dependents, such as a verb plus its object plus an adverb (e.g. *devoured the bread quickly*).

Combining a head and a dependent produces a phrase; combining the resulting phrase with another head produces a larger phrase, resulting in hierarchical structure. So *this + hill* form a noun phrase [this hill]; when combined with *over*, a preposition phrase is formed which contains the noun phrase [over [this hill]]. Sentences are not mere linear strings of words, or even linear groups of words, but consist of phrases within larger phrases. Hierarchical structure is easily demonstrated using examples containing structural ambiguity. In (4), the same words occur in the same linear order, but are organized hierarchically in two different ways: the brackets indicate distinct constituent structures, and thus, distinct meanings. In (4a), the girl has the feather and Sue tickled her, while in (4b), Sue used the feather to tickle the girl:

(4)   a.  Sue tickled [the girl [with a feather]]
      b.  Sue tickled [the girl] [with a feather]

In (4a), the preposition phrase (PP) *with a feather* is contained within the larger phrase *the girl with a feather*; the PP modifies the head word of that larger phrase, which is *girl.* In (4b), *the girl* forms a separate phrase from *with a feather*. Thus, we can insert the adverb *relentlessly* after *the girl* in (4b), at a major constituent boundary, but an adverb can't occur in that position in (4a), where it would disrupt the larger noun phrase *the girl with a feather*. Crucially, the two different meanings in (4) are expressed by two distinct hierarchical structures: we use the syntax to manipulate the meaning.

This is why syntax exists: it produces meanings we need to express by manipulating the structure of phrases and sentences. The different constituents in (4) can be reorganized in various ways: *The girl with a feather was tickled by Sue* only corresponds to (4a), while *The girl was tickled by Sue with a feather* only corresponds to (4b). Syntax is clearly more than mere regularities in the linear ordering of words. Languages are structure dependent: they exploit hierarchical structure to express different meanings.

Consider next the following sentences:

(5)    The jury believed the defendant.

(6)    The jury believed the defendant to be a liar.

Both contain the same linear string of words, *the jury believed the defendant,* but they have different meanings. In (5), *believe* has a direct object, *the defendant,* but what the jury believe in (6) is the entire proposition, *the defendant to be a liar* (alternatively expressible as a finite clause *the defendant was a liar*). In (6), *the defendant* is the subject of a subordinate clause. Partial structures are given below, showing that the sequence *believed the defendant* is a constituent in (7) but not in (8):

(7)    The jury [believed the defendant].

(8)    The jury believed [the defendant to be a liar].

Again, what's crucial isn't linear order, but how words group into hierarchical structures.

As well as hierarchical structure, syntax involves *dependencies,* relationships contracted between elements in a sentence. One dependency, discussed above, is the lexical relationship between heads and their arguments. A second type is agreement: sharing or copying grammatical features such as person, number, and gender between heads and their dependents. Some agreement is very local; for instance, sharing the feature 'number' in *this book* vs. *these books.* Agreement dependencies are, though, often long distance. Subject–verb agreement in English matches the number (singular/plural) of the verb with that of the subject: *the girl likes swimming* vs. *the girls like swimming.* An unlimited number of words can intervene between the head noun *girl,* which controls the agreement, and the singular verb *plays:*

(9)    That <u>girl</u> with the red swimming cap in the outdoor pool today <u>plays</u> tennis with me.

If we assume, though, that the head noun *girl* passes its singular feature to the whole subject noun phrase, *that girl with the red swimming cap in the outdoor pool today,* then the distance between the agreeing elements (subject and verb) is not arbitrary, but is regulated by hierarchical structure.

Dependencies also arise via syntactic displacement (sometimes considered 'movement') of heads or phrases. In the passive construction *The opera singer was assassinated,* the verb's 'agent' argument is suppressed, and the subject position is filled by a noun phrase interpreted as being displaced: in an active sentence it is the object (*The gunman assassinated the opera singer*). Co-indexing indicates the dependency between the grammatical subject position and the understood object of the verb, the 'gap':

(10)   [The opera singer]$_j$ was assassinated__$_j$.

Displacement also occurs in (11), a complex sentence containing two clauses: the main (*say*) clause and a subordinate (*works*) clause. The asterisk means 'ungrammatical':

(11)   [Which woman]$_j$ did your friends say [__$_j$ works/*work in our office]?

Two distinct dependencies interact here. First, the displaced phrase *which woman* forms a dependency with the gap indicated: *which woman* is 'understood' as the subject of the bracketed lower clause, and speakers recover the meaning *which woman works in our office*, though *which woman* actually appears at the left edge of the upper clause. This is an *unbounded* dependency, potentially crossing any number of clause boundaries (*Which woman did you think your friends said __ works in our office?*).

(11) also contains an agreement dependency, a non-local dependency between *which woman* and *works*. Note that the overt subject noun phrase nearest the verb is *your friends*, but this doesn't control the agreement. Instead, we interpret the displaced *which woman* as if it were the subject of the *works* clause; the gap shown in (11) stands in for the displaced phrase, and controls the agreement.

Other dependencies involve no displacement, but involve restrictions on the interpretation of elements within a specified syntactic space. The dependency between anaphors (such as reflexive -*self* forms) and their antecedents illustrates:

(12)   a. Sue loves herself.
       b. Sue's brother loves *herself.
       c. Sue's brother loves himself.
       d. Sue's brother says she loves herself/*himself.

Anaphors need an appropriate antecedent (a preceding noun phrase with matching features, such as gender). But the structure is crucial too: in (12b), the anaphor can't 'see' *Sue* inside the larger phrase *Sue's brother*, so *Sue* cannot be an antecedent. Instead, the antecedent is the whole subject noun phrase, (12c). Moreover, the antecedent must be local to the anaphor, in fact in the same clause—it can't be the subject of a higher clause, as *Sue's brother* is in (12d). Though the specific facts differ, similar complexities characterize the syntax of all languages.

I have emphasized both hierarchical constituent structure and dependencies between elements. However, it is sometimes argued that whereas all languages exhibit dependencies, not all languages have hierarchical constituent structure (e.g. Evans and Levinson 2009). *Non-configurational* languages have very free word order, typically with no syntactically neutral order of subject, verb, and object.

Words in a phrase are freely split up rather than having to be adjacent. From Warlpiri, an Australian language, (13) illustrates a discontinuous noun phrase: the modifier meaning 'small' is separated from the head, the word meaning 'child' (Austin and Bresnan 1996: 235). The meaning here is ambiguous:

(13)   <u>Kurdu-jarra-rlu</u> *ka-pala*     maliki wajili-pi-nyi       <u>wita-jarra-rlu.</u>
       child-DUAL-ERG PRES-3DU.SU dog     chase-act.on-NONPAST small-DUAL-ERG
       a) 'Two small children are chasing the dog.' *or*
       b) 'Two children are chasing the dog and they are small.'

However, when the words in the phrase are linearly adjacent, the meaning is fixed; (14), with a continuous noun phrase constituent, has only the 'merged' meaning:

(14)   <u>Kurdu   wita-jarra-rlu</u>     *ka-pala*       maliki  wajili-pi-nyi
       child    small-DUAL-ERG    PRES-3DU.SU dog       chase-act.on-NONPAST
       'Two small children are chasing the dog.'

It seems, then, that constituent structure plays a role even in non-configurational languages, since it disambiguates the meaning here. Note also the long-distance agreement dependency in (13): the number/case markers *jarra-rlu* (DUAL-ERGATIVE) appear on *each* element of the discontinuous noun phrase (underscored), indicating the shared role that these dispersed words contribute to the meaning. Conversely, in (14), the case marker occurs only on the final element of the continuous phrase; in fact, this is one test for noun phrase constituency (Austin and Bresnan 1996).

Moreover, non-configurational languages often display syntactic restrictions on word order. In Warlpiri, the verbal auxiliary (italicized in (13)/(14) above) must be either the second word in the clause, as in (13), or else the second constituent, as in (14). The auxiliary cannot break up a constituent, for instance by being the third word in a four-word phrase. Again, constituent structure plays a role even in non-configurational languages.

Example (13) also illustrates the identification of grammatical functions: in Warlpiri, case markers identify the dispersed elements constituting the 'subject' of the clause. All languages distinguish between *grammatical functions*, such as 'subject' and 'object', and semantic roles (sometimes called thematic, or theta roles). Grammatical functions are purely syntactic, and often interact syntactically with other elements in a sentence; in English, for instance, subjects control verb agreement in the present tense (e.g. *I was* vs. *we were*). The underscored phrases in (15) all have the grammatical function *subject*:

(15)   a. <u>The burglar</u> broke the window.
       b. <u>The kids</u> broke the window (with their ball).
       c. <u>The ball</u> broke the window.
       d. <u>The window</u> broke.

But each grammatical function bears numerous different *semantic* roles. Archetypal subjects are semantic 'agents' (volitional actors), as in (15a). In (15b), the subject *the kids* bears the 'actor' role: the kids probably didn't deliberately break the window. In (15c), the subject (*the ball*) is an 'instrument', while in (15d), the subject (*the window*) bears the role 'theme' (here, what got broken). Subjects can bear various other semantic roles, including 'experiencer', as in *Lill* hates spiders, and 'stimulus', as in *Spiders* frighten Lill. Evidently, then, grammatical functions and semantic roles are distinct. The passive construction in (10) also illustrates: the grammatical subject bears a semantic role generally associated with objects. Grammatical functions such as 'subject' and 'object' are identifiable in most languages, though not necessarily as simply as in English, where their position in the clause is fixed. Why these purely grammatical entities should have evolved is unclear, but languages frequently display phenomena that we can only characterize by referring to grammatical functions. They are therefore central to syntax.

## 48.4 WHAT ABOUT RECURSION?

The concept of recursion has a long history within linguistics, but has received widespread attention since the publication of Hauser, Chomsky, and Fitch (2002; henceforth HCF). This hypothesized that the crucial component of language—and possibly the only property both uniquely human and uniquely linguistic—is recursion. Extensive criticism soon followed, then various clarifications and extensions (e.g. Fitch et al. 2005; Jackendoff and Pinker 2005; Pinker and Jackendoff 2005; Bickerton 2009a, 2009b, 2010; Kinsella 2009; Chomsky 2010; Fitch 2010b; Hauser 2010). Rather than summarizing this sizeable literature, I offer a brief overview; Bickerton, this volume, discusses further issues.

Unfortunately, HCF do not define the term 'recursion', leaving scholars to interpret it in various ways, even within linguistics. Recursion traditionally means self-embedding, for instance embedding a noun phrase within a noun phrase ([NP [NP my father]'s brother]) or a clause within a clause ([s Jill said [s she was fine]]). This process potentially produces infinitely long strings: *my father's brother's wife's . . . cat*, or *Jill said Kim thought Mel claimed . . . she was fine*. Recursion is thus a specific kind of hierarchical structure, involving a constituent embedded within another of the same category.

Further controversy arose over claims that Pirahã, an Amazonian language, has no recursion in the sense of self-embedding (Everett 2005, 2009; see Carstairs-McCarthy, Chapter 50). The implication was that HCF were wrong about the privileged status of recursion. Intriguingly, however, Everett's own earlier analyses indicate the existence of recursion in Pirahã. Nevins et al. (2009b) reassess the data, and argue that recursion occurs widely, both at clausal level (equivalent to English *He wants* [*me to leave*]), and also within the noun phrase, though here only one level of recursion occurs (e.g. *sister's son*, but not *sister's son's daughter*). It is fairly clear, though, that HCF are *not* using 'recursion' to mean self-embedding, but rather, to refer to the formation of hierarchical structure generally: the phrase-building capacity, or 'the capacity to generate an infinite range of expressions from a finite set of elements' (2002: 1569), otherwise termed 'Merge'; see Chomsky (2010). Whatever the correct analysis of Pirahã, there are no implications for the language faculty. If Pirahã has no self-embedding, this does not entail that it has no hierarchical structure: as noted above, some languages make relatively little use of hierarchical structure. Under the 'toolkit' conception of Universal Grammar (Jackendoff 2002; Culicover and Jackendoff 2005), each language 'chooses' its own set and custom settings of the general tools made biologically available by the language faculty; a language may happen not to instantiate part of the toolkit, such as self-embedding.

Additionally, Bickerton (2009a, b, this volume) indicates that recursion—in the traditional sense of self-embedding—is not involved in phrase-building using 'Merge'. Essentially, Merge (Chomsky 1995) takes two words and forms them into a phrase, then merges the resulting phrase with another word, forming a larger phrase, and so on. Each phrase is the projection of its syntactic head: as outlined above, a preposition (P) merged with a noun phrase forms a PP with P as head; if PP is merged with a verb, V projects, and a VP is formed, and so on. Hierarchical structures are formed by repeated applications of Merge; self-embedded phrases have no special status.

The implications for language evolution are interesting (Bickerton 2009a). If a simple 'merge' operation was already available in other cognitive domains, then the critical *syntactic* development was using that operation to join words, as Bickerton (2009a, b) outlines. The emergence of syntax requires a lexicon, where words are stored along with their dependencies, and also the ability to fulfil those dependencies by 'merging' words into headed phrases. This replaces the protolanguage mode of delivery, in which proto-words are uttered singly, in unstructured sequences. In biological terms, this seems plausible.

What, then, of recursion? Recursion (in the sense of self-embedding) is not the critical property separating language from animal communication systems, and recursion in the looser sense of phrase-building is one amongst many specialized features of language. What is unique, as HCF note, is that 'no species other than humans has a comparable capacity to recombine meaningful units into an unlimited variety of larger structures, each differing systematically in meaning' (HCF: 1576). The remaining question concerns the existence of latent syntactic abilities in other species.

## 48.5 Do other animals manifest any syntactic properties?

This section considers whether any syntactic properties exist either in natural animal communication systems, or under 'language' instruction in captivity; see Gibson's chapters, Part I. Various experiments also investigate the 'syntactic' abilities of monkeys, starlings, and dolphins, but since all train animals to recognize abstract patterns involving no meaning, their relevance to the evolution of syntax is tangential. To appraise the complete canon of work would require an entire volume (Anderson 2004; Hillix and Rumbaugh 2004; Hurford 2011; see also Kako 1999a); what follows is a necessarily brief sketch.

Researchers in animal communication systems often talk about 'song syntax' (e.g. Okanoya 2002). Rule-governed combinations of notes, forming larger units termed 'songs', occur widely in bird song (Slater, this volume), whale song (Janik, this volume), and also gibbon song; see Hurford (2011) for review. Animal song is somewhat analogous to phonological processes in language, where elements from a finite set of meaningless units (phonemes) combine into syllables, also inherently meaningless (of course, syllables may be used as meaningful units, i.e. morphemes and words). Limited hierarchical structure also occurs in some bird song and whale song, though no recursion. Local dependencies between elements in a song are common: for instance, note or phrase A precedes note/phrase B, which precedes note/phrase C, and so on; each element may be internally complex, and may be repeated several times, but their order is fixed rather than random. Long-distance dependencies of any meaningful kind do not occur. Animal song carries a (limited) message, rather than a meaning, always centring on reproduction, including defence of territory and mate attraction. Combining elements—units or phrases—does not change that message.

Human syntax differs crucially: it is *semantically compositional*. The meaning of a sequence is assembled from the meaning of its individual parts; distinct combinations produce distinct meanings. The 'syntax' of animal song lacks semantic compositionality. As the individual elements have no inherent meaning, assembling them in different ways cannot modify meaning. Alarm calls, however, are different: calls are often associated with distinct predators; thus, each has (a type of) meaning. Recent monkey studies claim that two alarm calls are sometimes combined, producing distinct meanings. One study of putty-nosed monkey calls has generated particular interest (Arnold and Zuberbühler 2006b, 2008; see Zuberbühler, this volume). A 'pyow' vocalization is basically a leopard alarm call, and a 'hack' vocalization basically an eagle alarm call; since different predators require different avoidance strategies, these calls elicit distinct behaviours. However, a 'pyow-hack' sequence, either spontaneously produced by a monkey or artificially composed by the researchers, elicits another response entirely: the group starts to move off. Interesting though this behaviour is, the 'pyow-hack' is not semantically compositional. The meanings of each individual call do not combine to produce a new, 'move off' message.

Zuberbühler (2002) argues that monkey calls are sometimes modified, producing a distinct meaning from the basic alarm call. Campbell's monkeys produce 'boom' calls in contexts involving a disturbance, but no imminent danger. When nearby Diana monkeys hear a Campbell's leopard or eagle alarm call, they normally respond immediately. But if the alarm call is preceded by a boom, no predator-avoidance strategies occur. Perhaps the boom 'modifies' (here, attenuates) the meaning of the basic alarm call, and thus constitutes embryonic syntax. Even if this interpretation is correct, the behaviour is extremely limited, since the 'vocabulary' of alarm calls is small, and the modification is not productive, so not extended to new contexts.

I finally turn briefly to ape language research, i.e. attempts to teach (aspects of) language to apes in captivity; see Gibson, Part I, for more detail. The star pupil is undoubtedly the bonobo Kanzi (Greenfield and Savage-Rumbaugh 1990, 1991; Savage-Rumbaugh et al. 1998). In production, Kanzi uses combinations of lexigrams (abstract symbols indicated on a keyboard) and gestures, such as a 'chase' gesture, and a demonstrative point towards a person, or some food. The data show significant tendencies in ordering, such as action-object (*hide peanut*, *grab head*) and action-agent (*hide Austin*, meaning that Austin is hiding; or *chase* [*point to Mary*], meaning that Kanzi wanted Mary to chase him). Clearly, the action-agent order doesn't derive from the English ordering used by Kanzi's human caregivers. However, the major ordering principle in Kanzi's output is 'place lexigram first' (Greenfield and Savage-Rumbaugh 1990: 560), which typically means a lexigram followed by a gesture. As Kako (1999a) observes, a modality-based rule of this kind is interesting, but utterly unlike human language. Though Greenfield and Savage-Rumbaugh argue that Kanzi has acquired productive grammatical rules, it is difficult to draw conclusions from Kanzi's output, because his utterances are mostly restricted to lexigram plus gesture, or occasionally lexigram plus lexigram. Because of the limited nature of Kanzi's output, the authors concentrated on word order as an indication of his syntactic ability. But human syntax is far more than regularities of word order. At most we can agree that Kanzi has learned a productive proto-grammar (Greenfield and Savage-Rumbaugh 1990: 572).

In comprehension, Kanzi's abilities are impressive. He understands many instructions such as *Put the raisins in the shoe* or *Go get the balloon that's in the microwave*, but, contra Savage-Rumbaugh et al. (1998: 72), we cannot show that he understands the relative clause in the second example. Such instructions only require comprehension of salient lexical items: *put—raisins—shoe* and *get—balloon—microwave*; all the rest is reconstructable from context. Kanzi's comprehension of English is explicitly used 'as an index of his syntactic capacity' (Savage-Rumbaugh et al. 1998: 66), and he certainly differentiates between distinct word orders (as can dolphins: Kako 1999a; Gibson, Chapter 11). But Savage-Rumbaugh's conclusion (Savage-Rumbaugh et al. 1998: 74) that Kanzi has acquired language massively overstates the case, and underestimates what human syntax involves.

Notably, Kanzi was not tested on distinctions such as *a raisin* vs. *the raisins*, which crucially require comprehension of grammatical information. Savage-Rumbaugh et al. mention (1998: 70) that Kanzi has trouble with certain words, such as modal auxiliary *can* and conjunction *and*; both are functional categories. She attributes the problems with modal *can* to its homophony with the noun *can*, though Kanzi easily distinguishes *hot* and *dog* from *hotdog*. Crucially, though, modal *can* carries little meaning, and is mostly used for pragmatic purposes (avoiding a direct imperative). Kanzi understands instructions starting *Can you put the . . . ?*, where the salient part follows *put*, and the content-free start of the sentence can be ignored. He is confused by instructions such as *Can you use the can opener to open a can?*; humans are predisposed to distinguish lexical from functional vocabulary, whereas other species home in on the content words alone. And when Kanzi is asked to *Give/show/bring X and Y*, he mostly only brings one item; Savage-Rumbaugh attributes this to memory failure, rather than failure to understand the conjunction. Kanzi also has trouble with conjoined clauses, such as *Go to the group room and get the ball* (Hillix and Rumbaugh 2004: 178). Memory problems cannot be the explanation, since these instructions are no longer than many that Kanzi gets right. More likely, the problem centres on Kanzi's inability to understand either functional *and* or the syntax of conjunction itself.

Do other animals display any syntactic comprehension? Alex the parrot (Pepperberg 2005, this volume) performed better on comprehension of conjunctions, such as *What shape is blue and wood?*, where the correct answer (say, *square*) demands attention to both conjuncts. Kako (1999a) reviews a study by Herman (1987) which suggests that dolphins correctly interpret prepositions, such as *under, over, through*, but Kako concludes that the dolphins have not acquired closed-class vocabulary. By comparison, even at the two-word pre-grammatical stage (analogous to Kanzi's proto-grammar), English-speaking children produce numerous functional items, including modal *can*, modifiers like *more*, pronouns like *I, my, it*, prepositions like *off, on, away*, demonstratives like *this/that*, and negation markers *no/not*.

In sum, certain properties that we might call proto-syntactic are attested in animal language research. Words can be meaningfully combined, especially in novel ways, by animals of various species (see Gibson, Part I). Semantic distinctions reliant on different word orders can be understood, as when Kanzi distinguishes correctly between *Pour the coke in the lemonade* and *Pour the lemonade in the coke*. Simple category-based rules can be learned, as shown by Alex's extension of a pivot like *Want/Wanna + Noun* to new productions (*Want cork, Want cracker*), and new rules can even be invented, such as Kanzi's lexigram-first rule; of course, the categories an animal produces are not necessarily those employed in language.

Other syntactic properties have either not been demonstrated, or not been investigated, in the animal language research lab. Dependencies between items, either local or long-distance, appear to be absent. Structure-dependent rules (such as subject-auxiliary inversion in English *yes/no* questions: *You can leave ~ Can you leave?*) do not occur, nor is hierarchical structure (as opposed to word order) exploited to make semantic distinctions. Displacement of constituents is absent. Functional vocabulary is rarely explicitly taught, or looked for, and to date hasn't been successfully demonstrated. Such properties are the hallmarks of syntax. Natural languages are often very different superficially, but never fail to display properties of this type.

# Acknowledgements

Many thanks to Jim Hurford for excellent advice on an earlier draft.

# CHAPTER 49

........................................................................

# THE ORIGINS OF SYNTACTIC LANGUAGE

........................................................................

## DEREK BICKERTON

### 49.1 INTRODUCTION

........................................................................

Syntax is, on the face of things, the most clearly distinguishing mark of human language. The nature of syntax should first be briefly discussed. To the lay person, syntax is essentially a matter of word order, i.e. of linearization. But linear relationships tell us very little about relationships between words. Take for example these two sentences:

(1)  a. Bill says he agrees.
     b. Somebody who talked to Bill says he agrees.

In (1a), *Bill* and *says* are adjacent and *Bill* is the subject of *says*. In (1b), *Bill* and *says* are also adjacent but *Bill* is no longer the subject of *says*; in fact, there is no direct relationship between them. Real relationships can only be understood if the sentence is presented as a hierarchical tree structure, since most significant relations are vertical rather than horizontal. Linearization is epiphenomenal, arising from the fact that we have only one communicative channel.

The basic processes of syntax may be regarded as falling under four main heads:

(2)  A process for assembling words into hierarchical structures.

(3)  Processes for determining the boundaries of segments within such structures; that is, determining where units such as clauses and noun phrases begin and end—for example, determining that a clause boundary falls between *Bill* and *says* in (1b) but not, of course, in (1a). One process involves insertion of specialized word-classes like complementizers and conjunctions; another involves case-marking—if you hit a second nominative, you know you must be in another clause.

(4)  Processes for moving segments within such structures (for example, question-words such as *What* in sentences like *What does he want?*, where *what* is absent from its 'expected' position as object of *want* (cf. *He wants what?*).

(5)  Processes for determining the reference of elements that are not phonetically expressed (for instance in the sentence *She needs someone __ to talk to__*, the two gaps indicate, respectively, the unexpressed subject and object of *talk to*).

All human languages exhibit all four classes of process. However, while in all languages (2) is fully developed and strikingly uniform, the level of development of the other three varies considerably across languages, both in the types of process employed and their degree of richness/complexity. For instance, in some languages (e.g. creoles and some Southeast Asian languages such as Vietnamese) mechanisms for (3) are relatively few and poor, since case systems and specialized boundary-marker words have not (yet) developed, while with respect to (4), movement processes like the question-word movement in *What does he want?* that are hyper-developed in some (e.g. Slavic) languages may be rare or completely absent in others (e.g. Chinese; Cheng 1997).

While syntax characterizes all languages, whether signed or spoken, in a highly developed form, it is entirely absent both from the productions of 'language-trained' animals and the natural communication systems of other species. In part due to this lack of any apparent antecedent, its origins remain highly controversial, and scenarios of its possible development fall into several mutually-incompatible types.

## 49.2 SCENARIOS FOR THE ORIGINS OF SYNTAX

### 49.2.1 Cultural invention accounts

A number of authors (e.g. Donald 1991; Deacon 1997; Tomasello 2003 amongst others) have expressed doubts as to whether any system of rules and/or principles could have been absorbed into the human genome. The most recent expression of this viewpoint is that of Kirby et al. (2009) (see also Christiansen and Chater 2008;

Chater and Christiansen, this volume), who note what they regard as three serious problems for any biologically-based theory of syntax: (i) the dispersion of human populations, leading to divergent systems; (ii) the abstract nature of the proposed biological universals, whereas 'natural selection produces adaptations designed to fit the *specific* environment' (original emphasis), hence more superficial properties of language at the time of selection; (iii) the rapidity of linguistic change, providing a constantly 'moving target' for selection. However, all three of these objections depend on two assumptions that are themselves questionable: that syntax was still evolving at the time of the human diaspora, and that the unique road along which it evolved was by bootstrapping from contemporaneous production phenomena to the genome via some kind of Baldwin effect (a process by which changes in a species' behaviour can select for hitherto neutral or unutilized genes).

In fact it is likely, indeed probable, that universals evolved prior to the diaspora of ca. 90,000 years ago; if they had not, then segments of the world's population would have different 'universal' grammars, and a language from one segment might be unlearnable (or would at least present serious obstacles to successful learning) by speakers from another segment.

Moreover, Kirby et al., like most authors regardless of their persuasion, suffer from both a serious omission and a dubious assumption. The omission is any consideration of empty categories: these are referents that are 'understood'— phonetically unexpressed, like the subject of *open fire* in *I gave John an order to open fire on the mob*—but which can be identified by any native speaker. The rules that determine the reference of empty categories are both highly abstract and highly unlikely to be either inventable or learnable by induction. The assumption, admittedly tacit, is that the brain, prior to language, was a tabula rasa that not only had no means for processing words but did not even have any mechanisms that could be adapted for processing words. An alternative approach to this issue is developed below.

## 49.2.2 Catastrophic accounts

Others in the field of language evolution (e.g. Bickerton 1990—but see subsequent work—Jenkins 2000; Hauser et al. 2002; Chomsky 2010) hold both that syntax is biologically instantiated and that its emergence was quite abrupt, via either mutation or the exaptation of some pre-existing faculty. According to Hauser et al., the unique human contribution was the capacity for recursion, normally described in linguistics as the insertion of a unit of one structural type—NP, S, etc.—into another unit of the same type, as in [s *The boy* [s *you saw yesterday*] *is here*] or [NP [NP *Bill's*] *nephew*]. All other components of language could be found in other species, and perhaps even recursion had been developed by other species for non-linguistic purposes.

Biologists remain sceptical of any 'hopeful monster' mutation, and talk of a task-specific, purpose-built 'language organ' has faded as imaging techniques have shown the extent to which linguistic operations are distributed across the brain. The Hauser et al. thesis has emerged as the leading contender among those who wish somehow to reconcile language's uniqueness with Darwinian continuity. However, that thesis is seriously flawed. For one thing, the status of recursion itself is dubious (Bickerton 2009a: ch. 12). Recursion, if defined as the insertion of one structural type into another of the same type, is no more than an artefact of nowadays-abandoned generative formalisms which are superseded by the Minimalist Program's Merge—a process that consecutively attaches constituents to one another in order to build complex structures, rather than inserting one structure within another. If as a fallback a broader definition is adopted—a process that takes the output of one step as the input to the next, as suggested by Rizzi (2009)—then many activities of other species, from nest-building by birds to the making of hand axes by *Homo erectus*, involve recursion, and the 'unique to humans' claim evaporates.

But a much broader problem arises when we take a cross-species perspective. Not just syntax, but language itself, is unique to humans. To hold that virtually all prerequisites for language are found among other species, particularly among closely-related primates (a view shared by many outside the Hauser–Chomsky school) makes it hard to explain why other species, sharing those prerequisites and under similar environmental pressures, did not also develop language. This problem, severe enough in itself, is compounded by the fact that whereas in humans, language is developed to a high degree of complexity, the communication systems of other species show not the slightest sign of developing in the direction of language.

## 49.2.3  Adaptive accounts

More in line with mainstream evolutionary biology would be a scenario in which language evolved gradually, through natural selection, as other complex adaptations, such as the eye, evolved. The arguments are similar, whether specific rules and/or principles were being selected for (Pinker and Bloom 1990) or whether progress involved a series of discrete stages (nine, in the model proposed in Jackendoff 1999, 2002). But whether the steps were many or relatively few, the same two problems arise with any account that relies on natural selection.

The first problem concerns selective advantage. A behavioural trait will not go to fixation unless it confers an enhanced level of fitness on its possessors. But how exactly would a rule like Passive or a principle like Subjacency enhance anyone's fitness (Lightfoot 1991, this volume)? The second is basically one of the problems raised by Kirby et al. (2009), but it can be expressed in more specifically evolutionary terms. Natural selection cannot, by itself, create novelties; it can only select from variation in existing traits (or in this case, behaviours).

However, syntactic universals are not only (by definition) novelties, but also tend to be highly abstract generalizations across multiple examples (many of which differ superficially from one another). Consequently, how could they be visible to selection? These problems have not yet been fully confronted by advocates of an adaptive history for syntax; it is not easy to see, even in principle, how they could be resolved.

## 49.3 THE SEQUENCE OF SYNTACTIC EVOLUTION

Do the distinct processes of syntax shown in (2)–(5) above provide any clues as to the order in which different aspects of language evolved? It was noted that while process (2) (hierarchical structures) was uniform across languages, there was variation in the extent to which, and the ways in which, the remaining processes are instantiated in languages. Such phenomena accord with the logical relationships between the processes concerned. It is possible to conceive of languages (even though no pure forms exist today) that exhibit (2) but not (3) through (5), while a converse relationship is logically impossible. From this we can draw the following tentative conclusions:

- (2) preceded (3) through (5) phylogenetically.
- (2) may have a stronger genetic basis than (3) through (5).

The latter conclusion may require some degree of qualification; see below. It would be premature to draw further conclusions before considering, first, the basis from which syntax developed, and second, the role that pre-existing types of process within the brain may have played in going beyond that basis.

### 49.3.1 The origins of hierarchical structure

I am assuming here that in protolanguage, symbolic units (proto-words or proto-signs) were dispatched singly to the organs of speech (Calvin and Bickerton 2000: ch. 8), as appears to be the case in early-stage pidgins (Bickerton and Odo 1976). There is also good reason to believe that in natural language, words are assembled in the brain into roughly clause-sized units prior to being dispatched. The best evidence for this may be found in sentence-pairs like the following (an asterisk indicates an ungrammatical sentence):

(6)   a.  Who do you wanna meet __ today?
      b.  *Who do you wanna __ meet John?

The contexts in which *want to* can, in casual speech, be reduced to *wanna* include all cases where no lexical material intrudes between *want* and *to*:

(7)  a. I wanna meet John.
　　 b. I want you to meet John too.
　　 c. *I wanna you meet John.

In other words, the presence of *you* blocks the reduction. On the face of things, this makes the ungrammaticality of (6b) seem mysterious. The only possible explanation is that when *who* in (6b) is moved from its 'natural' position, it leaves behind, not a vacuum, but a real, albeit unpronounced, replica of itself—a replica that can be made to surface in 'surprise-questions' like (8):

(8)  You want *who* to meet John?

It is hard to see how the speech organs could be inhibited from producing the contracted form in (6b) if they did not receive a specific prohibition from higher processing areas, or how such a prohibition could be issued if the brain did not preform the sentences concerned. Unfortunately, it appears that neuroimaging techniques are not yet adequate to determine the processes that preformation utilizes.

However, we know that preformation must build hierarchical structures. These can be produced by any process that progressively merges outputs—that links units A and B to produce a single unit C, then C and D to produce a similar unit E, and so on. In other words, the Merge process central to the Minimalist Program (Chomsky 1995), which progressively merges words to form first phrases, then clauses and sentences, is the expression of (2) above, hence the most basic and universal of syntactic processes. Moreover, this process must have existed before language, not as a specialized operation for a particular non-linguistic function, but as part and parcel of the brain's normal machinery for merging its own outputs.

In that case, why is it necessary to hypothesize an initial, unstructured protolanguage? Because a potential capacity to build hierarchical structure was a necessary but not a sufficient prerequisite for syntax. Words were total novelties, and however the brain represented them, there is no reason to suppose that the neurons involved were linked with one another any more closely than any randomly-chosen set of neurons. Until direct links between them were established, no signal representing their merger could be generated. Such links could be formed in only one way, by the Hebbian method of repeated simultaneous firing (Hebb 1949), and such firing could only be generated by repeated protolinguistic uses of words in unstructured strings. Note that this sequence is the exact opposite of that envisaged in Chomsky 2010, where Merge appears in the brain prior to any form of language and only subsequently achieves 'externalization', i.e. use in the act of speaking. Missing from Chomsky's picture is any account of what, in the absence of externalization, would have selected for Merge in the context of language.

### 49.3.2 Merge and its application

Constraints on Merge would at this stage have been exclusively semantic. Merge would, however, have been subject to a problem pointed out by Calvin (Calvin and Bickerton 2000): that, in order to transmit reliable signals, larger groups of neurons relaying the same signal would have been required. The reason for this is as follows. We are assuming that protolanguage utterances were assembled, not by Merge, but by a process that adds individual units in a string, rather than arranging them hierarchically—A + B + C, rather than A + B → C, C + D → E, etc., so that there would be no way in which we could say that B was more strongly linked to A than to C (whereas with Merge, B is clearly linked much more strongly to A than it is to C). The simplest explanation for this absence of closer links would be that, unlike true language, protolanguage does not assemble utterances in the brain and send them pre-formed to the organs of speech, but transmits each word separately to those organs. Pidgin speech is on average three or more times slower than non-pidgin speech (Bickerton 2008), the likely reason being the difficulty (for pidgin speakers) of rapid lexical retrieval. Thus any message takes longer to deliver, and the longer a message takes to deliver, the greater the possibility that interference from other brain processes or simple leakage of electrical current will distort that message *if the speaker is attempting to preform it in the brain*. If, however, words are dispatched singly to the organs of speech, the risk of distortion can be significantly reduced.

The problem faced by pidgin speakers must be similar to the problem faced by the earliest speakers of protolanguage. Pidgin speakers are slow because they do not have full and automatic access to a new vocabulary; early protolanguage speakers would have been slow because they did not have full or automatic access to *any* vocabulary. Even at subsequent stages of protolanguage development, it seems likely that the time taken to preassemble utterances in roughly clause-sized chunks (perhaps corresponding to the 'phases' of Chomsky 2001, which are assumed to be fully preassembled before transmission to PF (phonetic form), i.e. to the organs of speech) would have substantially raised the level of sentence distortion. In other words, even when the possibility of Merge had developed, the protolanguage strategy of individual dispatch of single words would have remained a more trustworthy means of transmitting information than the syntactic strategy of Merge. In consequence, the onset of syntax might have been further delayed until the brain could undergo the changes—changes both in wiring patterns and numbers of neurons available for linguistic tasks—that were necessary before rapid and automatic speech could become possible.

We still do not know enough about the nature of meaning-bearing signals in the brain to fully confirm the foregoing account. However, the hypothesized difference between language and protolanguage—that the former employs an [[AB] C]-type processing strategy and the latter an A + B + C-type—is potentially testable by means of neuro-imaging techniques.

The question naturally arises as to what constraints might have limited the Merge process, other than semantic coherence constraints. The answer would appear to be, none. It will be assumed here, in conformity with most current thinking on the topic (Rizzi 2009), that Merge is a strictly binary process, attaching A to B to form [AB], C to [AB] to form [[AB]C], and so on. In modern language, Merge is constrained by a variety of factors, including agreement, anaphoric reference, and others that are unlikely to have been present in the earliest stages of syntax. However, rather than assuming that ascending orders of Merge for three, four, five, etc. constituents had to be specifically licensed in some kind of progressive expansion, it seems reasonable to suppose that Merge was in principle unlimited from the start, and that performance factors alone limited the number of modifiers that could be attached to nouns and verbs respectively.

The developments listed above would suffice to produce a language adequate for the speaker but less than optimal for the hearer. As sentence length and complexity increased, there would be increasing difficulty for the hearer in determining where units of structure began and ended, and what precise relationships existed between them. In modern language, grammatical items, bound and unbound (i.e. those that must attach as affixes to other words, as well as those that are words in their own right) exist in order to make boundaries and relationships explicit, and many of these have been produced, even in historical time, in what represents the only way in which the first grammatical items could have been produced—by processes of grammaticalization, the semantic bleaching of pre-existing referential items (see Heine and Kuteva 2002, this volume; Bybee, this volume; Carstairs-McCarthy, Chapter 47). These processes still operate, and can be seen at work in contemporary languages: for instance, a verb of saying can be downgraded to a complementizer, first introducing reported speech and later spreading to factive clauses of all types; a verb of motion can be downgraded into a directional preposition. Such developments naturally raise the question, to what extent can observable phenomena in the modern world serve as 'windows' on the early stages of syntax?

## 49.4 WINDOWS ON EARLY SYNTAX?

The notion that modern phenomena can shed light on language evolution has come under some criticism and should not be approached without caution. Obviously, the circumstances under which phenomena develop in the modern world are very different from those obtaining perhaps some hundreds of thousands of years ago. However, language of any kind offers only a limited set of structural possibilities, and contemporary phenomena may serve as some indication of which were likeliest to have been developed early. At least three potential 'windows on early syntax' are available: child language, creole languages, and historical change. All three will be rather briefly considered here.

## 49.4.1 Child language

It is tempting to take a recapitulationist stance and argue that the ontogenetic development of language mirrors its phylogenetic emergence. Children first acquire nouns, then a few verbs, and only later begin to add other word classes. The acquisition of grammatical items (except for a preposition or two, such as *up*, which is probably interpreted as a verb with the meaning 'lift') follows some time after the emergence of recognizable syntactic structures, even if (as suggested here) those structures do not normally begin to appear until age 2 or thereabouts, and the earliest stages of development constitute an example of protolanguage, rather than full human language. The emergence of these structures is typically quite rapid (especially when one considers the preceding 6–12-month period of mostly asyntactic utterances) with several types of both simple and complex sentence appearing within a few weeks. Moreover, some work (e.g. Crain 1991) shows that forms more complex than a child normally produces can be elicited experimentally, therefore must fall within the child's competence.

However, it must be borne in mind that the behaviour of children may simply result from the fact that they are children. Since we still know next to nothing about how the brain actually produces language in adults, let alone children, we do not know what connection if any there is between the typical stages of child language development and stages of brain maturation (including processes such as myelinization). Moreover, it is quite impossible to determine the relative contributions of adults and children to the earliest stages of language evolution. While we may reasonably suppose that the relative plasticity of children has always given them a leading role, the extent and nature of that role remain matters for speculation.

## 49.4.2 Creole languages

Creole languages are really a special case of child language development, representing what is produced by the language faculty when structured input (an early-stage pidgin, in this case) is severely reduced (Bickerton 1981). However, a reduction in the contribution of input makes it correspondingly easier to assess the contribution made by the child's own mind/brain.

Attempts to support the hypothesis that particular creole structures are invariably inherited from pre-existing language invariably founder when the data base for the hypothesis is extended; it is always possible to find a creole that contains a particular structure even though none of the languages that contributed to its birth exhibit that structure.

For instance, if we look only at English-related creoles, we might assume that double-object constructions (*I gave Mary the book*, as opposed to *I gave the book to Mary*) were present simply because English has them. However, French and Portuguese do not have double object constructions, yet these are also present in French-related and Portuguese-related creoles.

More telling still is the case of serial verb constructions (in which clauses are merged without benefit of either coordinating or subordinating conjunctions, and the distribution of phonetically unexpressed items differs from that found in embedded or coordinated clauses). Such constructions are found in most creoles and many West African languages, and since most creoles that have them also have historical West African connections, their presence in creoles seemed to be explained. Unfortunately Seselwa, the French-related creole of the Seychelles islands, which never had any input from any language with serial constructions, also contains a wide range of these constructions (Bickerton 1988).

In terms of the processes listed as (2)–(5) in section 49.1, creoles appear to be fully developed with respect to (2), (4), and (5). However, with respect to (3)—processes for determining the boundaries of clauses and phrases—they are markedly deficient. This suggests (while falling, naturally, far short of proof) that if process (2) was the initial step in language evolution, (3) was the final step. Certainly, at a first approximation, variation between languages in (3) seems to be more widespread and diverse than variation in the other categories, which is what the suggestion predicts. It may well be that a creole like Saramaccan, which has had less contact with other languages than most creoles, may be closer than other languages to the state of human language at a fairly late stage of evolution.

### 49.4.3 Language change

Scholars from Givón (1979a) to Heine and Kuteva, this volume, Bybee, this volume, have argued that diachronic developments may be indicative of earlier stages in language evolution. Such developments provide abundant evidence for the process of grammaticalization, mentioned above, which forms grammatical items from semantically-bleached lexical items. Other inferences drawn from diachrony are less firmly based. For instance, it is frequently argued that hypotactic constructions (constructions that join clauses without overt grammatical markers of coordination or construction, but also without the distribution of phonetically unexpressed items and other features characteristic of serial verb structures) are found with much higher frequency in earlier texts of existing languages, and from this an evolutionary progression from hypotaxis to subordinating and embedding constructions is sometimes inferred. Before accepting such claims, two things have to be borne in mind. First, the frequency or infrequency of certain types of construction is irrelevant. What is at issue is what the mind/brain could or couldn't do with language at any given period. A single example of complex embedding is all that is needed to show that complex embedding already lay within human competence; even the absence of such examples tells us little, since surviving texts represent only a minuscule percentage of the language actually produced in any given period.

Second, the written record of language goes back only a few thousand years. Are we then to assume that language reached its present stage only within historical time? This seems implausible. What could then have caused language to become more complex? Writing is often blamed, but the languages of preliterate groups typically show a highly elaborated syntax. It is much more likely that cultural forces are at work, and languages merely cycle through the various possibilities that the language faculty leaves open.

A similar argument applies to the claim that, since historical changes from SOV to SVO surface order are more frequent than changes from SVO to SOV, then earlier languages were predominantly or wholly SOV. Granted that if we project current rates of change backwards, in a few thousand years we would reach a stage where all languages were SOV. But since language may have been in existence for an order of magnitude longer, what happened before that? Did word-order change only happen in recent times? It seems likelier that some kind of pendulum process occurs, so that in an earlier period the opposite direction of change could easily have prevailed (see also Nichols, this volume).

## 49.5 ORDERING OF DEVELOPMENTAL STAGES

In sum, evidence from the three windows is, while short of probative, broadly self-consistent and consistent with the model of syntactic development presented here. To give just one concrete example, creole data suggests the presence of serial verb constructions in early syntax, and logical considerations point in the same direction. If Merge was initially unconstrained (that is, did not have to satisfy the lexical entries of particular items), [V V] merges would have been licit. If vocabulary was initially limited, it would have been natural to use strings of more primitive verbs—common in creole languages, such as *take X carry come*—to express meanings like *bring X*. If few or no grammatical items were present, verbs may have been recruited to introduce non-subcategorized arguments, as in common creole expressions such as *take knife cut bread* for *cut the bread with a knife*.

Further implications for the ordering of developmental stages come when we consider the conflicting interests of speakers and hearers. Speakers are benefited by anything that makes speech faster, easier and/or more automatic. Accordingly, process (2) plus extensive use of phonetically unexpressed constituents provides most of what speakers need. Hearers, on the other hand, are benefited by anything that makes the stream of speech more easily divisible into its structural units and generally more comprehensible. Accordingly, the means offered by (3) of marking structural boundaries and by (5) for identifying the referents of phonetically unexpressed items are strongly in the interests of hearers. These considerations reinforce the evidence from 'windows' suggesting a sequence of (2) followed by (3), while (5) may have been intermediate.

Processes under (4), permitting the movement of items such as question words and emphasized constituents to positions of prominence, would appear to be of equal benefit to speaker and hearer. The speaker wants to ensure that the main point of the utterance is grasped, and the hearer, equally anxious to grasp it, is benefited by having a fixed point in the utterance where it is expected to appear. There appears to be no evidence for hypothesizing a stage of language where word order was rigidly fixed and thus no constituent could be moved to a position of prominence. To the contrary, there seems reason to suppose that the movement rules of syntax may be no more than a formalization and restriction of an unordered (or very loosely ordered) protolanguage that allowed free repetition of semantically or pragmatically important constituents (McDaniel 2005). Certainly such loose ordering and repetition is a feature of protolanguage as expressed by trained apes, for example an utterance such as the following from the chimpanzee Nim:

(9)    Give orange me give eat orange me eat orange give me eat orange give me you (Terrace 1979).

It may even be the case (as McDaniel suggests) that the copy theory of movement (which holds that movement is the apparent result of copying a constituent, usually to sentence-initial position, and then erasing the original) is equivalent to a literal historical account of how movement processes originated.

Returning to (3), it is tempting to claim that these processes were the final additions to syntax, a faculty not yet hard-wired at the time of the human diaspora, and hence subject to a much higher degree of variation than other processes. It is true that we find a wide range of devices for signalling structural relations: case markers, focus markers, prepositions, postpositions, each category with its own range of variation. However, while the means of marking categories and structures may vary widely, the categories and structures that are marked are strikingly consistent across languages.

## 49.6 CONCLUSION

The origin and development of syntax remains a contentious and controversial field. However, most of the controversy has arisen through contention between the two rival paradigms within which most previous thinking on syntax has been trapped. Either there was a universal grammar that depended on task-specific adaptations yielding some kind of syntactic module, or the creation of a universal grammar was biologically impossible and syntax must derive from human interaction and/or general cognition. These paradigms, over the last half-century, have fought one another to a stand-off. But neither paradigm has taken into account the possibility that a primate brain, once inseminated with symbolic units, would find itself already equipped with ways to process them and to lay the foundations for a universal syntax.

But this third course is what is proposed here. The primate brain reacted to the first words just as earlier brains reacted to the first sights, the first sounds, the first smells. It reacted by processing this new source of data in an orderly and automatic fashion so as to make it usable, just as it had done earlier with sense data. And as with sense data, in order to perform the new tasks, the brain had to develop more cells and more connections between cells. And since words demanded not just some physical reaction but a *reaction in kind*, an output in the form of words, a development with immense potential significance followed.

The brain had always been potentially capable of creating hierarchical structures— one of its most basic operations is to merge outputs from different neurons. It was only when it became apparent that dispatching words singly to the organs of speech would not support word-sequences of more than a few units that the brain applied its merging powers to words so as to create process (2), a process for assembling words into hierarchical structures. Subsequent use of process (2) served as a selective pressure for the other processes. Thus language bootstrapped itself into existence, and the brain produced language universals through its own modes of activity.

# CHAPTER 50

# THE EVOLUTIONARY RELEVANCE OF MORE AND LESS COMPLEX FORMS OF LANGUAGE

## ANDREW CARSTAIRS-McCARTHY

### 50.1 INTRODUCTION

Linguists long ago gave up expecting to find any equivalence between the grammatical complexity of a language and the technological or cultural development of its speakers. Earlier legends about 'primitive' tribes with languages whose grammars could be written on a postage stamp were based on prejudice rather than fact. As Edward Sapir put it (1921: 22, 234): 'The lowliest South African Bushman speaks in the forms of a rich symbolic system that is in essence perfectly comparable to the speech of the cultivated Frenchman. . . . When it comes to linguistic form, Plato walks with the Macedonian swineherd, Confucius with the headhunting savage of Assam'. Sapir's attitude to non-European cultures may sound patronizing to modern ears. However, that does not weaken his point about the independence of culture and grammar.

More recently, the pendulum has swung towards the opposite extreme: the view that, fundamentally, all contemporary natural languages are equally complex (or equally simple). This fits in with an opinion often expressed by Noam Chomsky, as for example in an interview with Tim Halle (1999): '[I]f some Martian was looking at us, the way we look at mice or something, we'd all look identical, we'd all seem to be talking the same language with little variations here and there which are sort of fine-tuned by experience'. We would all be 'talking the same language', in Chomsky's view, because of our shared language faculty, assumed to be essentially identical in all normal humans at birth.

If Sapir and Chomsky are right, then differences in the complexity of contemporary languages (however complexity is measured: see Dahl (2004) on that issue) will shed no light on language evolution. Yet some scholars now take a different view. The following sections deal with various manifestations of language, all in some sense 'simple', that could be regarded as evolutionarily relevant; the first three sections consider natural languages, while the following two sections deal with artificial or imaginary ones that supply material for evolutionary-linguistic thought-experiments. Alongside the works cited below, Miestamo et al. (2008) and Sampson et al. (2009) offer compendiums of new research.

# 50.2 CREOLES

The term 'creole' has been used in a variety of ways (Roberge, this volume). One usage links its definition to that of 'pidgin'. A pidgin has been defined as a rudimentary even if to some degree institutionalized form of language used between speakers whose mother tongues are mutually incomprehensible. A creole is then a pidgin that has acquired native speakers—for example, children surrounded by adults that belong to different speech communities and therefore talk to each other most of the time in pidgin. According to intriguing suggestions by Bickerton (1981; this volume), creoles (in this sense) may shed direct light on language evolution.

Bickerton shares Chomsky's view that the innate language faculty (or 'bioprogram' for language) must be tightly structured. But when a child acquires as a mother tongue a language with stable grammatical norms that are shared throughout a speech community, those norms overlay or mask the contribution of the bioprogram. On the other hand, when a child is among the first generation of children acquiring a particular pidgin natively, stable grammatical norms are absent. In this unusual situation, the bioprogram will get a chance to influence directly the grammar that the child acquires. We should therefore expect (Bickerton says) that, irrespective of the mother tongues of the parents, newly developed creoles will display common grammatical features worldwide, reflecting the bioprogram's influence when it is not skewed by any ambient linguistic norm.

Is Bickerton's prediction correct, then? Yes, he argues. In creoles there is a strong tendency for grammatical distinctions of tense (such as [±anterior]), mood (such as [±realis]), and aspect (such as [±punctual]) to be signalled by markers in that order, preceding the lexical verb. And this may reflect language evolution (he argues) inasmuch as there is reason to think that the order of the markers reflects the evolutionary sequence in which the cognitive antecedents of these grammatical distinctions were acquired (see Heine and Kuteva, this volume). The punctual–non-punctual distinction may reflect the phenomenon of habituation, already manifested in the nervous systems of molluscs, while the realis–irrealis distinction may reflect dreaming, first manifested in mammals. The grammatical nesting [tense [mood [aspect [verb]]]] may thus recapitulate our cognitive ancestry (Bickerton suggests), the more deeply nested categories being incorporated earlier into grammar as it evolved.

Bickerton describes this account as 'no more than a rickety bridge' towards a possible 'handful of relative certainties' in the future (1981: 288). Bickerton's account of the tense-mood-aspect system is not widely accepted by other creolists, and some of his later writings on language evolution (e.g. 1990) emphasize it less. There is wider acceptance, however, of Bickerton's view that creole languages are, in some important sense, unusually 'simple' (e.g. McWhorter 2005). McWhorter claims that no languages other than creoles combine three characteristics:

- Absence of inflectional affixation;
- Absence of lexical tone in monosyllables;
- Absence of opaque or non-compositional derivational morphology.

However, David Gil, cited by McWhorter (2005: 68–71), has suggested Riau Indonesian as a counterexample. We will consider this language next.

## 50.3 RIAU INDONESIAN

Riau Indonesian (RI) is spoken by a few million people in east-central Sumatra and neighbouring islands (Gil 1994). What is unusual about it in comparison with most varieties of Malay or Indonesian is the absence of affixes and particles that encode, for example, relativization, nominalization, and changes in verbal valency (such as from intransitive to transitive). Thus an expression such as (1) has not only an obvious reading such as in (1a) but also less obvious ones such as in (1b–d):

(1)   orang   Amerika   beli   anjing   itu
      person   America   buy   dog     that

  a. 'The Americans bought that dog.'
  b. 'That dog that the Americans bought.'
  c. 'The Americans' purchase of that dog.'
  d. 'The place where the Americans bought that dog.'

These different readings could be ascribed to differences in syntactic structure. Thus, in sense (1b), the expression could be analysed as a head-internal relative clause (that is, a relative clause in which the noun that the clause modifies, *anjing* 'dog', is inside the clause itself); in sense (1c) it could be analysed as a nominal expression; and in sense (1d) it could be the modifier of a locative noun that is syntactically present but has no phonological shape (an 'empty' element of a kind that is familiar in contemporary syntactic theorizing). However, Gil suggests that this is wrong. He argues that RI is just as simple syntactically as it looks. Instead of having a range of phrasal categories, such as the traditional S (sentence), NP (noun phrase), and VP (verb phrase), it has only one open syntactic category, which Gil calls 'S'. This 'may be associated with any interpretation belonging to any of the major ontological categories: event, state, time, place, thing, and possibly others' (1994: 188). Example (1) may perhaps be semantically vague but it is not syntactically ambiguous.

If that were all there were to say about RI syntax, it would be a perfect example of what Gil (2005) calls an 'Isolating-Monocategorial-Associational' (IMA) language, that is, a language with extremely simple grammar: only one syntactic category, purely compositional semantics, and no bound morphemes (so that every individual meaningful item can potentially stand on its own). In fact, RI also has a closed class of bound morphemes (or words) with meanings such as 'from', 'but', and 'Agent' (Gil 2000). It also has structures which are 'headed' in the sense that they contain one item (the 'head') which identifies what the expression refers to, while the other items modify the head; moreover, in RI, the head is usually at the beginning. Thus, the expression *makan ayam*, made up of *makan* 'eat' and *ayam* 'chicken', is most plausibly interpreted in English as 'The chicken is eating' or 'Someone is eating chicken', the head being *makan*. Less likely are interpretations such as 'a chicken for eating' or 'a chicken that is eating', which would require *ayam* to be the head and which would therefore tend to be expressed as *ayam makan*. So, even though in Gil's analysis RI has only one phrasal category, the possibility of choosing different elements as heads means that RI grammar goes beyond IMA grammar to some extent.

Gil claims that IMA language has a role in linguistic phylogeny as an antecedent of fully modern language. He sees it as essentially similar to Bickerton's 'protolanguage' (Bickerton 1990; Tallerman, Chapter 51). What RI illustrates, then, according to Gil's analysis, is the stable and successful functioning in the modern world of a kind of language whose syntax is in only in a few respects more elaborate than 'protolanguage'.

## 50.4 THE 'BASIC VARIETY' USED BY
### SECOND-LANGUAGE SPEAKERS

Many adults, such as immigrants and 'guest workers', find themselves in the position of trying to communicate in an alien speech community, without the benefit of any explicit language instruction. Such a person in an English-speaking context, wanting to say that a girl had stolen some bread, might produce an utterance such as (2):

(2)    Steal girl bread

One way of characterizing (2) is as an example of 'bad English'. On this view, the speaker who produces (2) is assumed to be trying to speak 'proper' English, but failing; moreover, there is no point in treating (2) as an illustration of some language variety that is independent of English. An utterance such as (2) may be of interest to an applied linguist (an expert on second-language acquisition, say), as an example of a kind of 'error' that the learner needs to correct, but it is of no interest to the theoretical linguist.

   Klein and Perdue (1997) argue that this attitude is wrong. The 'mistakes' that speakers make in guest-worker-like situations (they argue) are to a considerable extent independent of both the source language (the speaker's mother tongue) and the target language. This testifies to the existence of a general 'Basic Variety' (BV) whose vocabulary is drawn from the target language but whose structure is governed by a set of universal principles, such as:

(3)    The NP-referent with highest control comes first.

(4)    Focus expressions come last.

In virtue of (3), 'agents' (denoting who or what is acting) will tend to precede 'themes' (denoting what or who is acted upon).

   Klein and Perdue argue that the BV shows more clear evidence of structure than Bickerton posits for protolanguage. Indeed, they do not see BV as fundamentally unlike most contemporary languages. They do not question the relevance to the BV of traditional categories such as 'noun phrase' and 'verb', and they see the BV as consistent with the mid-1990s version of Noam Chomsky's Minimalist Program: it exploits 'Merge' but it shows little or no evidence of 'Move' only because it lacks 'strong features' of the kind that trigger 'Move'.

   Even though the structure of the BV is (according to Klein and Perdue) less strange than that of RI as seen by Gil, they raise explicitly a question of central concern from a language-evolutionary point of view: 'Why are "fully fledged" languages more complex than the BV?' (1997: 304). They do not discuss this question at any length, but they do suggest that various grammatical elaborations may arise as a result of conflicts between the structural principles that govern BV. Case-marking on nouns, for example, may supply one way of indicating that a noun phrase that is utterance-final by virtue of (3) may nevertheless be higher in the control hierarchy than an earlier noun phrase, despite (4). This, however, provokes a further question: how is it that RI, a 'fully fledged' language, can get along without these elaborations?

Klein and Perdue's concern is not with language evolution, any more than Gil's is. It is therefore not fair to criticize them for saying so little about it. What is clear is that (as Jackendoff (2002) argues) the BV deserves the attention of anyone looking for clues in the contemporary world to how grammar evolved.

# 50.5 PIRAHÃ

Hauser et al. (2002) compare human cognitive and communicative capacities with those of animals. They attempt to identify what is contained in the 'faculty of language in the narrow sense' (FLN), that is those characteristics or capacities that are both peculiar to humans and peculiar to language. They suggest that the FLN may turn out to be limited to a sole characteristic, namely recursion (exemplified in the embedding of sentences inside larger sentences; see Tallerman, Chapter 48).

The centrality of recursion to human language has been emphasized in generative linguistic theory since the earliest days. Yet there is a language in Brazil (Pirahã) that allegedly lacks any mechanism for recursion (Everett 2005). As Pinker and Jackendoff (2005: 216) put it, replying to Hauser et al.:

All semantic relations conveyed by clausal or NP embedding in more familiar languages, such as conditionality, intention, relative clauses, reports of speech and mental states, and recursive possession (*my father's brother's uncle*), are conveyed in Pirahã by means of monoclausal constructions connected paratactically (i.e. without embedding).

If Everett's analysis of Pirahã is correct, then the existence of this language would seem to be at least as embarrassing for the Hauser–Chomsky–Fitch view of FLN as Riau Indonesian is (according to Gil) for McWhorter's view of creole grammars as uniquely 'simple'. Surprisingly, however, Fitch et al. (2005: 203), replying to Pinker and Jackendoff, take Pirahã in their stride:

The putative absence of obvious recursion in [Pirahã] is no more relevant to the human ability to master recursion than the existence of three-vowel languages calls into doubt the human ability to master a five- or ten-vowel language.

Their view is, then, that, even if some property of the language faculty is peculiarly human, a language may perfectly well exist whose acquisition exploits only other properties that are either not peculiarly human or not peculiar to language.

# 50.6 MONOCATEGORIC

Superficially similar to RI is a kind of language that Carstairs-McCarthy (1999) labels 'Monocategoric'. Carstairs-McCarthy devised Monocategoric as a thought-experiment, to illustrate a direction in which language might have evolved but did not. This was to prepare the ground for a discussion of why language has evolved in the direction it has.

The vocabulary of Monocategoric contains two classes of items: 'simple expressions', such as *snake, you, John, Mary,* and *story,* and 'operators'. Operators may be one-place (such as YESTERDAY, DISAPPEAR, SEEM), two-place (SEE), three-place (TELL) or in principle *n*-place for any $n > 0$. A well-formed 'expression' in Monocategoric is any simple expression or any complex expression formed from one or more other expressions (whether simple or complex) followed by an appropriate operator.

Examples of well-formed expressions in Monocategoric are the following:

(5)  you snake SEE
   a. 'You saw a snake'
   b. 'The snake you saw'
   c. 'Your sight of a snake'

(6)  you snake SEE YESTERDAY
   a. 'You saw a snake yesterday'
   b. 'The snake you saw yesterday'
   c. 'Your seeing a snake yesterday'

(7)  you snake SEE YESTERDAY DISAPPEAR SEEM
   a. 'The snake you saw yesterday seems to have disappeared'
   b. 'The apparent disappearance of the snake you saw yesterday'

(8)  John Mary you snake SEE YESTERDAY TELL
   a. 'John told Mary that you saw a snake yesterday'
   b. 'The snake that John told Mary you saw yesterday'

The range of English glosses for these Monocategoric expressions resembles the range of glosses supplied for the RI example at (1). Also, Monocategoric resembles RI in having only one syntactic category to which free well-formed items, simple or complex, belong: in RI it is 'S', in Monocategoric it is 'expression'. Yet Monocategoric differs from RI in important ways, as we will see.

Carstairs-McCarthy claims that Monocategoric would be perfectly serviceable as a means of communication and expressing complex ideas. So, inasmuch as all actual languages distinguish between nominal and clausal expressions, the reason why they possess this distinction—a superfluous one, in the light of Monocategoric—is a central puzzle for investigators of language evolution. Carstairs-McCarthy (1999) suggests a partial answer to that puzzle. But an important issue for present purposes is the light that RI may shed on his claims.

The serviceability of Monocategoric is supported by the fact that RI gets along fine as a natural language with only one syntactic category. On the other hand, the existence of RI appears to show that the distinction between nominal and clausal expressions is not after all universal. In that case, this distinction presents no evolutionary puzzle after all, one could argue.

This may be an over-hasty conclusion, however. In Monocategoric, one cannot create a well-formed expression by simply combining two expressions without an operator, as one can in RI, where two members of the sole category 'S', such as *makan* 'eat' and *ayam* 'chicken', can be combined simply as either *makan ayam* or *ayam makan*. Yet, in accordance with the head-initial bias of RI, only *ayam makan* will ever be suitably rendered with a nominal expression in English, such as 'chicken for eating' or 'chicken that is eating'. So the nominal-clausal distinction seems to return by the back door, in virtue of the possibility that either *ayam* or *makan* may be the head of an expression containing both. In Monocategoric, by contrast, no such back door is available because there is no counterpart of the notion 'head'. Instead, any well-formed expressions that are plausible counterparts to *ayam makan* and *makan ayam* (with EAT as a two-place operator) can be glossed in either nominal or clausal fashion, as (9) and (10) illustrate:

(9)   someone chicken EAT
    a. 'The chicken was eaten'
    b. 'The chicken that was eaten'
    c. 'The eating of the chicken'

(10)   chicken something EAT
    a. 'The chicken was eating'
    b. 'The chicken that was eating'
    c. 'The chicken's feeding'

A possible reaction is: 'Perhaps the fact that nothing in a Monocategoric expression can be picked out as its head means that Monocategoric grammar cannot after all express as much as the grammar of actual human languages'. But this criticism is not valid. One can easily envisage a single-place operator such as FOCUS which could be used (if desired) to indicate whether it is the chicken or the activity of eating that is the focus of attention. Thus, for example, *chicken* FOCUS *something* EAT would be glossable only as in (10b), not as in (10a). The important point is that this narrowing of the range of possible interpretations would be achieved not by any grammatical device comparable to the head-modifier distinction (much less the distinction between sentences and noun phrases), but by purely lexical means, in virtue of the meaning of the operator FOCUS. Yet nothing like this operator seems to appear in natural languages.

There is more that could be said in comparing RI with Monocategoric and other imaginable 'simple' languages. For now, what is clear is that imaginary 'simple' languages, as well as actual ones, have a considerable potential—so far underexplored—to shed light on why the human language faculty as it has evolved seems to make available only some kinds of grammar and not others.

## 50.7 ARTIFICIAL LANGUAGES SUCH AS ESPERANTO AND LOGLAN

Esperanto is an invented language, just as Monocategoric is. However, the purpose for which Esperanto was invented is different, namely to serve as an international auxiliary language. The same applies to Volapük, Interlingua, Interglossa, and numerous others. It may seem that such languages are of no interest to researchers on language evolution. However, even those artificial languages that consciously borrow lexical and grammatical features from actual languages, as Esperanto does, are 'experiments of nature' in the sense that it may be of interest to observe whether any features of actual languages are consistently absent from them.

Esperanto is clearly Indo-European in flavour, with verbal tense, nominal number and case, unmarked subject–verb–object order, fronting of question words, and so on. But one thing that is absent from Esperanto, unlike any European language, is allomorphy (see Carstairs-McCarthy, Chapter 47). Every root and every affix appears in only one shape. It is like a language in which a considerable amount of grammaticalization has occurred, leading to morphologization, but no phonological processes have disrupted the one-to-one relationship between forms and meanings. This reinforces the point that morphologization does not inevitably entail allomorphy. Why the brain tolerates allomorphy is therefore a genuine puzzle.

Many invented languages differ from those mentioned so far in that they are consciously designed from first principles, usually with the intention of being more 'logical' or 'consistent' than natural languages (Libert 2000). These are traditionally referred to as '*a priori* languages' to distinguish them from '*a posteriori*' artificial languages such as Esperanto. Few of them have grammatical characteristics that would reward study on the part of an evolutionary linguist. A possible exception, however, is Loglan (Brown 1966) and its variant Lojban, both of which have a small but enthusiastic following and a considerable presence on the internet. Loglan, which is based in part on principles derived from predicate calculus, has been judged 'a creation of great complexity and subtlety' by a serious linguist (Zwicky 1969).

## 50.8 Conclusion

If some natural languages really are significantly simpler than the majority, how and why has the brain evolved so as to support unnecessary grammatical complication? Or is the simplicity of those languages really only apparent? And what about simpler imaginable outcomes of language evolution, as represented by Monocategoric and perhaps Loglan, for example?

Creoles have been brought into the language evolution debate by Bickerton, and the Basic Variety by Jackendoff. On Pirahã there has been much recent discussion (Everett 2009; Nevins et al. 2009a) but little meeting of minds. Yet Riau Indonesian, despite Gil's thought-provoking discussions of it, has not received the attention it deserves in this context. So there is scope for the complexity debate to contribute more on language evolution than it has so far.

# CHAPTER 51

·······································································

# PROTOLANGUAGE

·······································································

## MAGGIE TALLERMAN

## 51.1 WHAT IS PROTOLANGUAGE AND WHEN DID IT EMERGE?

·······································································

Most researchers suggest that early hominin communication involved some form of pre-language, or *protolanguage*. Protolanguage is seen as simpler than full language, with a proto-lexicon, i.e. storage for learned, meaningful signals, but no syntax (Bickerton 1990). Protolanguage may have utilized vocal, gestural, and mimed components (see Arbib; Corballis; Donald; Harnad, this volume). However, I assume for brevity that the primary—and dominant—modality was vocal. A gestural protolanguage predicts sign as the dominant modern language modality, obviously incorrectly. Scenarios for a switch from manual to vocal can easily be invoked (for instance, speech frees up the hands for increased tool use), but all lack evidence.

We have no idea when protolanguage evolved, though many proposals link the *Homo* genus with the first protolanguage, perhaps 2 million years ago (mya). Suggested evidence comes from the archaeological and palaeoanthropological records. Stone tools appear around 2.6 mya (Wynn, this volume), including sharp-edged cutting tools, a kind of tool that is apparently beyond the capability of modern great apes. The fossil record indicates hominin brain growth and a developing vocal tract (MacLarnon; Mann; Wilkins; Wood and Bauernfeind, this volume) but provides only indirect evidence. Selective pressures for vocal tract changes doubtless come from the emerging speech capacity, but even dating speech would not date language: language could occur without speech (i.e. sign), and the speech capacity could merely indicate a limited protolanguage.

On selective pressures specific to hominins, Bickerton (2009a) suggests a scenario involving construction of new niches: early *Homo* is postulated to employ cooperative scavenging, vocally recruiting aid to protect large carcasses. This builds in the evolution of cooperation, changes in diet leading to morphological changes in brain and body, and the beginnings of protolanguage. It appears consistent with the archaeological and fossil record: early hominins split animal bones to extract marrow using stone tools. Scavenging constitutes novel behaviour in the hominin lineage, thus might be the novel selection pressure needed for the development of new communicative behaviour.

Lacking any definitive way to date protolanguage, I assume it emerged within the last 2 million years or so, roughly coincident with early stone tools and with brain growth beyond the size of other primate brains. Full language must already be in place by the time of the human diaspora, around 85 kya (thousand years ago), since all modern populations have the same language faculty (i.e. can learn any natural language); at the latest, the full language faculty must be fixed before Australia was settled, around 50–60 kya. Possibly, full language is linked to the speciation of *Homo sapiens*, around 195 kya (McDougall et al. 2005). We cannot tell whether other species had (any form of) language; for instance, there is debate over the linguistic capacity of Neanderthals (e.g. Mithen 2005; P. Lieberman 2006), which became extinct around 30 kya.

## 51.2 COMPOSITIONAL PROTOLANGUAGE

A *compositional* or *lexical* protolanguage consists of single proto-words, initially uttered separately and slowly, and subsequently joined in short, fairly random sequences (Bickerton, this volume). It has no hierarchical structure, no syntactic combinatorial principles, and only a loose pragmatic relationship between proto-words. What meanings might proto-words express? Bickerton (1990, 2009a), Hurford (2003a), and Tallerman (2007) suggest noun-like and verb-like words, while Heine and Kuteva (2007, this volume) suggest that noun-like words appear first, with all other categories deriving from these, including verbs.

The term 'proto-word' reflects significant differences between proto-vocabulary and true words. Modern vocabulary items (almost) all fit into a structured semantic network, and contract obligatory relationships with other words. For instance, transitive verbs and prepositions require syntactic objects with specific semantic properties. No *subcategorization* relationships (Tallerman, Chapter 48) would occur in protolanguage—proto-words did not obligatorily select other words. Modern 'defective' vocabulary items are similar, having phonology and meaning but no syntax; examples include *yes/no, hello, ouch, oops, wow, hey, shh, psst,* and words for animal calls, like *oink* and *woof.* Jackendoff (1999, 2002) regards these as living linguistic fossils. Unlike ordinary words, defective words are used alone as meaningful utterances, and cannot be combined (except in quotatives: *She said 'ouch'*). Some are largely involuntary, apparently under right hemisphere control, and some even survive aphasia; such features are suggestive of primate calls. However, unlike primate calls, they are crucially culture-specific, and thus *learned.*

A crucial development occurs when words are first combined: stringing proto-words together, still without hierarchical structure, brings an advance on a single-word stage (Bickerton, this volume). Jackendoff (2002) suggests compounding as a pre-syntactic principle, involving mere concatenation. Consider some English compounds: *penknife, breadknife, table knife, butter knife.* The relationships between the semantic head (*knife*) and the modifier are idiosyncratic: penknives sharpen pens, breadknives cut bread, table knives are used at the table, and butter knives spread butter. Compounding forms around twenty distinct semantic relationships, potentially producing quite an expressive protolanguage. Spontaneous compound-like (signed) utterances occur in captive apes, such as the chimpanzee Washoe's 'water bird' for duck (Fouts 1975), but we cannot know if chimpanzees intend one sign to modify another, or understand that for the observer, concatenations generate meaning.

What is the evidence for an unstructured word + word (+ word . . . ) protolanguage stage? Bickerton (1990, 1995) argues that the protolanguage capacity is retained by modern humans, emerging in child language and in pidgins (Roberge, this volume), in adults learning a second language naturalistically, in homesign (used by the deaf children of hearing adults; Goldin-Meadow, this volume), and in linguistically-deprived children, who lack adequate input within the critical acquisition period (see Curtiss 1977 on 'Genie'). Moreover, protolanguage may not be species-specific: trained apes can produce sign or symbol 'utterances' with short sequences of proto-words, lacking syntax (e.g. Gardner and Gardner 1969; Patterson 1978; see Gibson, Chapter 3). Though non-human primates never acquire protolanguage in the wild, their abilities in captivity suggest some phylogenetically ancient pre-linguistic capacities.

Examples of various putative forms of modern protolanguage are given in (1)–(3); Roberge, this volume, provides samples of pidgins:

(1)   Ape protolanguage (Kanzi (bonobo), using a combination of lexigrams on a keyboard and gestures; data from Savage-Rumbaugh et al. 1998)
water chase        water balloon
food childside     childside orange
Matata bite        chase water

bad water        chase you
juice raisins     Austin carry
childside carry   hide peanut

(2) Child language (Tom, 23 months)
doggie fall     I get that
want hat        there birdie
put sock off    more milk
where gone      Tom cup

(3) Genie (Curtiss 1977)
Paint. Paint picture. Take home. Ask teacher yellow material. Blue paint.
Yellow green paint. Genie have blue material. Teacher said no. Genie use
material paint. I want use material at school.

Protolanguage exhibits the following properties (e.g. Bickerton 1990). First, the ordering of elements is relatively random. No hierarchical syntactic structure constrains surface order, and different word orders have no link to information structure (e.g. given vs. new information). The bonobo Kanzi illustrates this, producing *Austin carry* when asking to be carried to see Austin (Savage-Rumbaugh et al. 1998: 62), but *Matata bite* when Matata (his mother) bites him. Savage-Rumbaugh reports definite ordering regularities in Kanzi's output (Greenfield and Savage-Rumbaugh 1990, 1991), but these differ significantly from the spoken English input that Kanzi receives. Pre-grammatical utterances in young children typically reflect closely the word orders of the ambient language, specifically by being consistently head-initial or head-final; Genie's utterances in (3) also share this characteristic. Simple word order regularities do not, though, necessarily indicate syntax. Ancestral protolanguage putatively contained various 'purely semantically based principle[s] that map into linear adjacency without using anything syntactic' (Jackendoff 2002: 248). 'Fossils' of these principles, such as Agent First and Focus Last, still occur: Agent First produces the subject-initial constituent order found in 90% of languages today. Another principle, Grouping, ensures that in *dog brown eat mouse*, the dog is brown, while in *dog eat brown mouse*, the mouse is brown; Agent First ensures that the dog is eating. Yet no constituent structure is assumed here. Pre-syntactic principles of this nature in protolanguage could start to tie information structure to ordering.

Next, consider the subcategorized arguments of verbs and other syntactic heads. In full languages, these are often phonetically null, but are systematically related to overtly present categories. Below, *e* stands for 'empty', an element understood, not pronounced:

(4) Kim is too mean [*e*] to make supper.   (Here, [*e*] = Kim)

(5) Kim is too mean [*e₁*] to make supper for [*e₂*]. (Here, [*e₁*] is *not* Kim, but [*e₂*] = Kim)

The meanings of null elements are not random, but are syntactically regulated. Contrast the protolanguage utterances from Genie: *Paint picture* (where the agent is missing) or *Take home* (where the agent and patient—the item to be taken—are both missing); null elements in Kanzi's utterances appear similarly unconstrained. Bickerton notes that 'in protolanguage... any item may be absent from any position' (1990: 124); null elements are randomly distributed, so subjects or objects of verbs often get omitted. In ancestral protolanguage, a major rubicon is crossed when words start requiring co-occurring words with specific syntactico-semantic properties.

However, some full languages also exhibit few syntactic restrictions on null elements. In Chinese, 'He saw him' translates as in (6), with an overt subject and object, but is also expressed (in an appropriate pragmatic context) as (7a), (b) or (c):

(6)   ta kanjian ta  le
      he see       he ASPECT
      'He saw him.'

(7)   a. [*e*] kanjian ta le
      b. ta kanjian [*e*] le
      c. [*e*] kanjian [*e*] le

Of course, Chinese is not protolanguage, but a full language with regular subcategorization requirements: *kanjian* 'see' is a transitive verb with an animate agent and a visible patient, just as in English. But the principles regulating null elements in English are not universal, so cannot form a model for how protolanguage became language.

Ancestral protolanguage putatively lacked a mechanism for assembling words into structural units (Bickerton 2009a, 2010, this volume): initially, there were no syntactic relationships between proto-words. For Bickerton, the crucial development is the appearance of 'Merge' (more precisely, the novel linguistic use of an existing cognitive ability), which combines two words to form a phrase, then combines that phrase with another word, forming a larger phrase, and so on. Under this view, clausal subordination is not special; it is simply due to repeated applications of Merge. (Modern) protolanguage sometimes exhibits apparent subordination, such as Genie's *I want use material at school*, but these are merely prefabricated routines, consisting of *I want* + *state of affairs*; they are not productive. Bickerton suggests (2009b) that protolanguage-speaking children may not yet know the kinds of verbs that require subordinate clauses.

Finally, protolanguage lacks a distinction between lexical elements (primarily verbs, nouns, adjectives) and functional elements (grammatical items, including determiners, auxiliaries, and sub-words such as affixes). Modern protolanguages lack grammatical markers (for instance, Genie's *ask teacher yellow material*, or Kanzi's *ball slap*), while in full languages, functional and lexical elements occur in roughly equal proportions in utterances. There is widespread agreement that ancestral protolanguage would contain at most two categories, the precursors to nouns and verbs. The transition to language involved the gradual accretion of other word classes via the same processes of *grammaticalization* that occur in all recorded languages: see Bybee; Heine and Kuteva, this volume; Hurford 2003a; Tomasello 2003b. Some grammatical elements mark phrase and clause boundaries, so presumably by the time these appear, speakers have passed the item-by-item stage of protolanguage production, and instead pre-form phrases before they are uttered.

Of course, modern peoples all possess a full language faculty; thus, Bickerton's proposals to model ancestral protolanguage on modern child language or on restricted linguistic systems are controversial. Modelling protolanguage on ape 'language' capacities is also controversial: the last common ancestor of chimpanzees and humans, around 6 or 7 mya, need not possess any specifically 'linguistic' characteristics, since there is plenty of time since the split for the full suite to evolve. In sum, using modern reflexes of 'protolanguage' as evidence for ancestral protolanguage is contentious. Nonetheless, the models of protolanguage presented by Bickerton and by Jackendoff—together with pathways of grammaticalization outlined by Heine and Kuteva—go a long way towards elucidating likely processes in language evolution.

## 51.3 PRIMATE VOCALIZATIONS AND PRIMATE COGNITION

Under the compositional view of protolanguage, the earliest development is the creation of arbitrary signals connecting sounds to simple meanings—a proto-vocabulary of symbols, lacking word classes. Proponents of this view reject the idea that protolanguage emerged from a primate communication system, though it may have utilized essentially the same mechanical means of sound production. Proto-vocabulary thus represents a major discontinuity with primate communication. The evidence draws on known features of vocabulary, which show little overlap with features of natural vocal or gestural communication in other primates. In this scenario (e.g. Burling 2005) primate gesture-calls are not precursors to words; instead, the critical continuities are cognitive.

The primate literature certainly provides increasingly sophisticated evidence concerning primate vocalizations and gestures (in the wild and in captivity), indicating a network of similarities and differences between human and non-human primates (see the contributions in Part I). But there is no straightforward pathway via which primate vocalizations and/or gestures could 'turn into' linguistic utterances. Below, I focus on comparison of words (or proto-words) and primate calls.

Human (proto-)words differ from primate calls in major ways. The first concerns symbolic reference (see Deacon, this volume). Some primate vocalizations have functional reference: they refer to events or entities external to the caller, and not merely the animal's own emotional state. This applies both to monkey and ape vocalizations (see Slocombe and Zuberbühler 2006; Slocombe, this volume), but prime examples are monkey alarm calls. Vervets produce different calls in response to each main predator, eagles, leopards or snakes (Cheney and Seyfarth 1990, this volume; Zuberbühler, this volume). Conspecifics clearly associate each alarm call with specific dangers, taking appropriate avoidance action for each predator type. But alarm calls are not word-like. They are more like propositions, rather than 'referring' to specific predators. As Bickerton (2009a: 200) points out, alarm calls may simply mean 'threat from the ground', 'threat from above', and so on. Unlike vocabulary items, each alarm call is tied to one specific context, with no flexibility or nuances of meaning (monkeys can't indicate a particularly mean leopard). Primate calls never form part of an interconnected network of related symbols, as words do. And critically, alarm calls cannot be used merely to mention the concept of a leopard.

Thus, a second distinction between human (proto-)vocabulary and primate calls is displacement. Using words in the absence of their referent is a novel feature in primate communication, though limited tactical deception (uttering an alarm call when no predator is visible) occurs in some monkeys (Wheeler 2009), and perhaps in chimpanzees too. The earliest hominin vocabulary likely had no displacement. For instance, a word indicating an animal is initially uttered when the animal is visible to both speaker and addressee. Later, the speaker sees the animal while his companion is distracted, and uses the animal's name, since he can see it. If the companion is smart, he understands. The ability to *comprehend* displacement thus plausibly emerges before it is used deliberately in *production*, to refer to entities not present; see also Burling (2002). Displacement must be a highly adaptive feature of protolanguage (Bickerton 2009a).

A scenario like this reveals a third major difference between human use of vocabulary and primate communication: only the former exhibits *shared intentionality* (Tomasello et al. 2005; Tomasello and Carpenter 2007), the mutual commitment to collaboration found in human interactions. Before 1-year-old, human infants can triangulate between themselves, an adult, and external objects, by pointing, gaze-following, or offering objects for inspection: they establish *joint attention*. Thus, unlike primate calls, words can be used merely to mention, or to point something out. Other primates use vocalizations and gestures to draw attention to *themselves* (e.g. to initiate play, or beg for food). But only humans engage spontaneously in triadic reference: two people attend to some external object, and agree on a convention for referring to it. Such collaboration is an absolute prerequisite for protolanguage (Tomasello 2003b).

Shared intentionality gives rise to a fourth distinction: human vocabulary involves cultural transmission and learning, unlike non-human primate vocalizations. Moreover, though language has a critical period, vocabulary learning does not atrophy in adults. Learning also brings the prospect of innovation. Other primates are reported to produce some novel vocalizations (in Part I see Gibson; Slocombe), but in the wild their call repertoire is basically fixed, whereas vocabulary is productive and open-ended.

Fifth, vocal learning requires both vocal control and vocal imitation. Researchers originally assumed that non-human primates only produce 'affective' (i.e. emotionally-driven) vocalizations, and couldn't vocalize at will, suppress, or modify vocalizations. This is now known to be inaccurate. Audience effects and call modifications occur both in monkeys (Cheney and Seyfarth 1990) and great apes (Slocombe and Zuberbühler 2007; see Slocombe; Zuberbühler, this volume). This, along with tactical deception, suggests elements of vocal control. On the other hand, primate vocalizations *are* essentially driven by an internal state, rather than being volitional. And vocal imitation is a novelty in the human lineage.

Such distinctions between words and primate calls might all appear in the earliest proto-words. Full language displays yet more differences. Duality of patterning is pivotal: a small, discrete set of sounds combines in different ways (phonology), giving rise to open-ended sets of morphemes and words, which themselves combine productively to form phrases and clauses (syntax). We assume protolanguage to lack this duality, and primate calls have nothing analogous (and nothing homologous). Ancestral protolanguage would not yet have a generative phonological system: for instance, Lindblom (1998) demonstrates that pressure for phonological complexity only comes from increases in vocabulary (see MacNeilage; Studdert-Kennedy, this volume).

In sum, the earliest words had little in common with primate calls, apart from probably using the vocal/auditory modality (inconsequentially, since nearly all mammals vocalize). Protolanguage most likely did not develop from primate calls.

An alternative is that primate *cognition* played a crucial role; see Seyfarth and Cheney (this volume); Hurford (2007, this volume). Hurford argues that human conceptual structure derives from primate perceptual structure. The fundamentals of modern cognition (concepts such as object permanence) probably evolved before the split from the *Pan* genus; see Tallerman (2009), also Coolidge and Wynn, this volume. Bickerton (1990: 91, 101) notes:

In all probability, language served in the first instance merely to label protoconcepts derived from prelinguistic experience. [ . . . ] Protoconcepts which could serve as referents for nouns and even verbs – nouns and verbs being the basic units from which other linguistic categories are derived – were in place by the time the higher primates had developed.

Strikingly, however, Bickerton (2009a) denies that any species other than *H. sapiens* had genuine concepts. Unlike mere *categories*, which other animals do have, concepts involve offline thinking (thinking about an activity or entity you are not currently engaged with) and displacement (e.g. imagining a leopard that's not present). Concepts have permanent storage in the brain which can be accessed voluntarily (a lexicon). True concepts are triggered, in Bickerton's view, by the emergence of the earliest words (see also Boeckx, this volume).

Discussion of these two extremes—the idea that conceptual structure is in place well before protolanguage emerged versus the view that concepts are impossible without language—cannot be pursued here. However, researchers constantly invent subtle ways of examining animal cognition, producing new data to further the debate.

## 51.4 HOLISTIC PROTOLANGUAGE

I emphasize critical distinctions between primate vocalizations and human vocabulary, because some recent speculation links primate calls directly to protolanguage. Mithen (2005, 2009) and Wray (1998, 2000, 2002a) assume that primate calls are ancestral to human vocabulary:

Protolanguage would...be a phonetically sophisticated set of formulaic utterances, with agreed function-specific meanings, that were a direct development from the earlier noises and gestures, and which had, like them, no internal structure (Wray 1998: 51).

Primate calls are not compositional, but *holistic*: the entire call is the entire message. Wray and Mithen, also Arbib (2005) and Fitch (2010a), propose that protolanguage was also holistic. They reject the compositional account of protolanguage starting with discrete proto-words representing concepts, and then forming short, unstructured proto-word strings. In holistic protolanguage (HPL), each utterance represents an entire proposition, with arbitrary form and a complex meaning agreed by the community. Wray's toy examples are *tebima* 'give-that-to-her' and *kumapi* 'share-this-with-her'; 2000: 294). The idea is that form/meaning correspondences occasionally occur fortuitously; here, *ma* occurs in each string, and the meaning 'her' also occurs in each. A speaker might assume that *ma* means 'her', and a 'word' for 'her' then 'fractionates' out of the non-compositional sequence. Utterances are thus broken apart to form proto-words.

The HPL idea is highly problematic. First, for fractionation to succeed, holistic calls must contain phonetic break-points (Studdert-Kennedy and Goldstein 2003), and early hominins must notice them. But just like our own innate vocalizations (laughter, crying, shrieks of fear, etc.), holistic primate calls contain no discrete phonetic units. One element of proposed continuity thus disappears. HPL must be physically very unlike primate calls, and proponents of HPL don't explain how a presumed complex phonetic system originates; how do holistic primate calls *turn into* a discrete segmental system?

Tallerman (2007) also questions the assumption that calls would be long enough to fractionate: instead of *tebima*, for instance, a signal in HPL might be simply *ma*—far more likely, given the protosyllable account of MacNeilage (1998, 2008, this volume). If each signal is short, there's no material to break down, and the account fails. Moreover, the HPL account requires early hominins to possess a sophisticated compositional semantics (Johansson 2008), which, on the basis of comparative biology and the archaeological record, seems improbable. On the compositional account, semantics simply evolves in tandem with words. On physical properties alone, then, HPL is unsupported.

Second, the processes turning a putative HPL into compositional language differ completely from observed processes of language change; see Bybee; Carstairs-McCarthy; Heine and Kuteva, this volume. The bundle of effects termed 'grammaticalization' create syntactic constructions (such as the passive), produce new word classes (such as adjectives), and form grammatical elements from content words (for instance, creating auxiliaries and complementizers out of verbs). Heine and Kuteva (2007, this volume) argue that grammaticalization is the *only* process that could produce words of distinct classes from a protolanguage consisting initially of noun-like items. As Bybee (this volume) notes, grammatical constructions are overwhelmingly formed by composition when adjacent elements fuse, not by breaking complex elements apart (cases like back-formation of *edit* from earlier *editor* are much rarer). The large-scale deconstruction presumed in accounts of HPL is unsupported by historical linguistics. Nor do language deficits support HPL: grammatical breakdown in agrammatical aphasia has entirely different properties.

Third, consider the problem of counterexamples. Discussing Wray's HPL examples above, Tallerman (2007) surmises that many utterances might contain *ma* but mean nothing to do with 'her', or might pertain to a female recipient but not contain *ma*; the number of counterexamples would overwhelm positive examples. This intuition is confirmed via computational modelling (Johansson 2008; K. Smith 2008). Johansson's models vary the parameters of a toy HPL by various factors, including total inventory of utterances, number of sound segments, number of meaning elements etc., and:

For all parameter combinations, the number of counterexamples were found to outweigh the number of positive examples by a considerable margin. For no parameter combination did the fraction of all predicates with more positive examples than counterexamples exceed 2% (Johansson 2008: 175).

Fourth, some accounts (Mithen 2005, Arbib 2005) suggest that highly complex meanings could be inferred from holistic utterances. A. Smith (2008) observes that meanings in HPL must be reconstructed purely from context, and while humans can conceptualize simple, cognitively salient meanings, associated with basic-level categories such as 'dog' and 'chair', it is hard to learn general categories such as 'animal' or 'furniture' contextually. Moreover, if we show a child a picture of a 'dax', a mythical creature dancing on a table, she doesn't assume that 'dax' means *This-is-a-dax-dancing-on-a-table*, but rather, she associates the novel creature with the label *dax* (Tallerman 2008a). The intricate, very specific, multi-propositional meanings suggested by some proponents of HPL (see Tallerman 2007 for discussion) thus cannot be reconstructed from context in the first place, let alone transmitted successfully between further individuals. A. Smith concludes that 'Unitary, unstructured meanings can only reliably be associated with highly salient, *relatively simple* meanings, as they must be reconstructable without any linguistic cues' (2008: 109). Complex propositions are thus unlikely to be associated successfully with holistic utterances.

Fifth, consider the use made of HPL. For Wray, its function was not informative, but social and manipulative, like animal communication systems (adding further continuity with primate calls). HPL delivers 'subtle and complex social messages' (Wray 2002a: 117), covering threats, greetings, and commands; a primitive compositional protolanguage, lacking grammar, would, Wray suggests, be too ambiguous to function properly. (Though potential ambiguities in complex holistic message strings are not seen as problematic.) However, Bowie (2008), in experiments using restricted language systems, shows that a small compositional system (containing just a few words) significantly enhances communication in novel situations; conversely, a semantically-fixed set of holistic signals is highly inflexible.

Moreover, early hominins don't need a new system to deliver the kind of social messages Wray suggests (Bickerton 2003, 2009a; Tallerman 2007). Our ancestors had, as we still have, all the primate vocal and gestural features necessary: tears, laughter, sighs, snarls, shouts of joy, cringing, plus biochemical signals; see Burling (1993, 2005). HPL adds nothing to this innate repertoire (nor does language). Language doesn't replace primate signals, but adds an entirely different system alongside them (sometimes literally: cries of pain are involuntary, yet often expressed using language-specific vocalizations; cf. English *ow!* but French *aïe!*).

Finally, proposals for HPL entirely disregard typical communicative attempts made by apes in the lab. Far from being holistic, whole propositions, ape utterances are typically short, perhaps two proto-words, crucially revolving around content 'words'. Apes trying to communicate with humans produce the elements with most meaning (noun-like and verb-like items), and ignore the rest. Their ancestors are our ancestors too, and this strategy—concentrate on producing maximum meaning with minimum effort—likely utilizes the type of cognition early hominins brought to protolanguage. HPL is thus too complex for our ancestors; instead, protolanguage comprised short proto-word sequences of one or two items bearing high meaning.

I conclude, then, that holistic protolanguage is linguistically untenable, and does not achieve continuity with primate communication systems anyway. Primate cognition is more relevant in the continuity debate than primate vocal communication.

## 51.5 MUSICAL PROTOLANGUAGE

Some recent publications suggest a musical protolanguage as a precursor of HPL (Mithen 2005, 2009, this volume; Fitch 2010a); see Botha (2009a) for critique. Fitch focuses on 'complex vocal imitation' (vocal imitation, control, and learning; 2010a: 340). In other primates, few homologues to these vital features of spoken language occur. However, complex vocal imitation occurs widely elsewhere. If the selection pressures giving rise to learned 'song' in songbirds, seals, whales etc. also applied to hominins, then novel vocal capacities in speech are a case of convergent evolution.

Problematically, though, sexual selection drives the evolution of animal song: learned song is mostly produced by males, in courtship and defence of territory. But both males and females possess *speech*. So how would 'musical protolanguage' spread from males to females? Fitch emphasizes social bonding or group cohesion, as in other species where both sexes display complex vocal imitation. But there is no evidence that learned vocalization evolved first in males and later spread to females. Secondly, as is expected with sexually-selected characteristics, song arises at puberty, thus highly unlike learned vocalization in humans. Moreover, learned song shows seasonal peaks and is hormonally driven, again unlike speech (see Gibson, Chapter 11). The biological perspective offers little evidence that sexual selection drove human vocal learning.

From a linguistic perspective too, musical protolanguage is dubious. Fitch suggests that a musical protolanguage contained 'meaningless sung phrases of complex phonological structure' (2010a: 496), and that 'the generative aspect of phonology might have emerged before it was put to any meaningful use' (2010a: 471). Fitch's musical protolanguage is 'bare phonology', like non-lyrical song, and initially lacked meaning entirely. But as noted above, selective pressures for contrastive phonology come from an expanding vocabulary; complex phonology cannot evolve before vocabulary exists. Even allowing that Fitch really means *phonetic* structure, this scenario still entails a massive evolutionary leap, as other great apes have nothing comparable. More plausible scenarios are outlined by MacNeilage; Studdert-Kennedy, this volume. Both stress the importance of vocabulary (i.e. of meaning) as a selection pressure in learned vocalization.

Fitch suggests that meaningless melodies subsequently become associated with whole events, hence meanings are paired arbitrarily with musical 'phrases' (forming a holistic protolanguage). These utterances have complex, hierarchical structure (Fitch 2010a: ch. 14), subsequently exapted for syntax. But phrases in music or animal song differ radically from syntactic phrases, which start with a semantic/syntactic head that gains dependents—in evolution (Jackendoff 2002) as in child language acquisition; see Tallerman, Chapter 48.

Musical protolanguage is thus an evolutionary cul-de-sac (since the musical aspects must ultimately be abandoned for a word-based protolanguage), and moreover, does not provide any observed features of full language.

# CHAPTER 52

# THE EMERGENCE OF LANGUAGE, FROM A BIOLINGUISTIC POINT OF VIEW

## CEDRIC BOECKX

## 52.1 BIOLINGUISTIC APPROACHES

Biolinguistics is the most transparent term I know of to characterize the research focus of modern linguistics-as-cognitive-science, a focus which has been constant since the mid-1950s. The goal of this discipline is to shed light on the human language faculty, and thus, given the latter's species-specificity, on human nature as a whole. Biolinguists seek to do for what Darwin called our 'instinctive tendency to speak' what ethologists do for animal instincts generally: figure out as precisely as possible the nature of the instinct underlying behaviour, study its development, its functions, and its evolutionary history (compare Chomsky 1986 and Tinbergen 1963). No phrase sums it all up as well as the title of Eric Lenneberg's 1967 classic: biolinguistics aims to uncover the 'biological foundations of language'.

Needless to say, biolinguistics is a fairly broad research programme, and allows for the exploration of many avenues of research, including the following: formalist;

functionalist; nativist, and insisting on the uniqueness of the language faculty; or alternatively, nativist about general (human) cognition, but not about language per se. In practice, though, the term biolinguistics is now generally more narrowly construed as a label for generative-oriented studies (see Jenkins 2000, but see Givón 2003 for an important exception). This narrower characterization is in part due to the fact that the term biolinguistics was successfully established in the context of the generative enterprise (Piattelli-Palmarini 1974), the research programme assumed in the present overview (for additional remarks, see Boeckx and Grohmann 2007).

Until recently it was often said that the generative enterprise lacked an interest in evolutionary questions (see, among many references, Pinker and Bloom 1990; Calvin and Bickerton 2000), meaning that generative practitioners (most prominently Chomsky) failed to address the issue of language evolution, let alone formulate specific evolutionary scenarios. Turning to the textual record reveals this to be nothing more than a crude caricature. Generative linguists, and Chomsky in particular, have not infrequently raised phylogenetic issues regarding the language faculty (see Otero 1990 for an excellent collection of excerpts from Chomsky's writings; see also Jenkins 2000, especially ch. 5), but it is true that Chomsky and others have consistently resisted facile adaptationist stories of the sort that populates the evolutionary psychology literature. It is also true that, though phylogenesis was not completely ignored, the major focus of generative grammarians was, until recently, what Chomsky has called 'Plato's Problem'. Since the very beginnings of generative grammar, the question on everyone's mind was how a child uniformly and seemingly effortlessly develops into a mature native user of one of the world's possible languages, despite the obvious fact that much of her knowledge of language cannot come from the input she receives, the latter being so fragmentary, ambiguous, etc. (the essence of 'Plato's problem'). Short of a miracle, this state of affairs requires a fair amount of innate knowledge/biological endowment (call it Universal Grammar, UG) to supplement what the external input cannot provide (the essence of Plato's solution in *Meno*).

As linguists learned more and more about the richness of our tacit linguistic knowledge, it appeared reasonable to take this biological endowment to be very specific to the task at hand. The highly specific richness attributed to UG reached its height in the 1980s, the first period of the so-called Principles and Parameters approach, which many dubbed the Government-and-Binding model (Chomsky 1981). In those days UG was hypothesized to contain not only a set of rules/ principles underlying the grammar of all languages, it was also said to contain a set of rules/principles that were parametrized. Such parametrized principles (parameters for short) were rules whose workings were relativized to the specific languages acquired by the child; they contained options from which the child had to choose on the basis of the input she received. The combination of universal principles and parameters marks an important achievement in modern linguistics. For the first time linguists were able to break through the paradox of unity and diversity, by embedding points of (limited) variation inside universal constraints.

Having reached this important epistemological landmark, a few of those who had contributed to this picture of UG stepped back, and pointed out that if all of this is true, the challenge for proponents of selectionist/adaptationist accounts of language evolution is very large indeed (see especially Piattelli-Palmarini 1989). None of the principles and parameters entertained in the technical literature seemed amenable to a 'survival of the fittest'-type construal, especially when fitness is, as is almost always the case, defined in terms of communication. (Although our understanding of principles and parameters has changed, Piattelli-Palmarini's conclusions regarding the limitations of adaptationism still hold; see Uriagereka 1998; Lorenzo and Longa 2003).

Other linguists took a different approach, and asked how much of this picture of UG could be given a 'deeper' explanation (see Chomsky 1995). This marked the beginning of the Minimalist Program in linguistics, which, as we will see, is intimately connected to the revival of biolinguistic concerns, especially as they bear on evolutionary questions. I do not intend to survey the minimalist literature here (I have done so elsewhere; see Boeckx 2006, 2010). Suffice it to say that minimalists subject Government-Binding-style UG to constant constructive scepticism. I say constructive because minimalists do not question the idea that previous generative models captured something accurate about the human language faculty, but minimalists cast a sceptical eye on the richness and specificity assumed in previous models, and seek to replace these by more minimal, fundamental, and not necessarily linguistic-specific principles. That is to say (to borrow a metaphor from Chomsky 2007) minimalists approach UG from below instead of from above (the traditional way to proceed in generative grammar): instead of asking how much one should attribute to UG to capture the richness of linguistic knowledge and diversity, minimalists ask how little one could attribute to UG while still accounting for all that richness and diversity.

## 52.2 THE EVOLUTION OF THE LANGUAGE FACULTY IN A NEW LIGHT

By insisting on a minimal UG, minimalists have helped renew linguists' appreciation for evolutionary issues. I will assume here that the language faculty arose in *Homo sapiens*, and fairly recently, i.e. within the last 200,000 years.[1] Let me stress that because this event did not leave many traces in the fossil record, we can't know

---

[1] Interestingly, recent genetic data suggest that *Homo sapiens* split into two subpopulations around 150,000 years ago, which remained separated for about 100,000 years (Behar et al. 2008). If this interpretation of the data is correct, it suggests that the language faculty was already in place 150 kya, further reducing the window of time during which it evolved.

for sure, but several pieces of evidence conspire to suggest that this is as good a guess as any: emergence of new tools, cultural artefacts, signs of trade, paintings, and so on, in the archaeological record, first in Africa and then in Europe (see McBrearty and Brooks 2000; Mellars et al. 2007) point to a significant evolutionary transition. I tend to agree with Diamond (1991), Tattersall (1998a), and many others that it is hard to imagine the emergence of these artefacts and signs of modern human behaviour in the absence of the language faculty (see also d'Errico and Vanhaeren, this volume, and compare Botha, this volume). My favourite piece of reasoning along these lines involves the use of knots in tools and other artefacts. Camps and Uriagereka (2006) seem to me to be correct in arguing that the sort of mental computation involved in tying and untying knots is on a par with the kind of system required by human languages. It's hard to imagine having one without the other, just as it is hard to imagine our mathematical capacity in the absence of our linguistic capacity.

If this conjecture concerning the archaeological record is correct, it suggests that the human language faculty emerged a few seconds ago by the evolutionary clock (which runs much more slowly than our perception imagines). This means that our linguistic capacity did not have the time to evolve the sort of highly-specific properties that most linguistic theories (including Government-Binding) ascribe to it. The recent emergence of the language faculty is most compatible with the idea that at most one or two evolutionary innovations, combined with the cognitive resources available before the emergence of language, delivers our linguistic capacity pretty much as we know it today. This picture, in turn, prompts the following research programme well-articulated in Hauser et al. (2002): to describe the prelinguistic cognitive structures that yield UG's distinctive properties when combined with the one (or two) specifically linguistic features of the language faculty.

The prelinguistic cognitive structures form what Hauser et al. call the Faculty of Language in the Broad Sense, and the minimal novelties are what they call the Faculty of Language in the Narrow Sense. This research programme meshes well with the minimalist trend in linguistic theory, which strives to keep the core properties of UG to a bare minimum. It also encourages comparative studies which aim to identify computational primitives in other species that could have been recruited for linguistic purposes. Such comparative studies effectively move away from the standard, but sterile question of whether other species have (human) language (see Anderson 2004)—they don't; they have their own modes of communication—and focuses more on computational properties that may assume an interesting (possibly novel) function when placed in a 'linguistic' context (a context where sound and meaning interface). This is the sort of descent with modification scenario that Darwin insisted upon. For research along these lines, see Fitch and Hauser (2004); O'Donnell et al. (2005); Hauser et al. (2007). This type of research will undoubtedly lead to a greater appreciation of the cognitive capacities of other animals (see Cheney and Seyfarth 1990, 2007; Hauser

2000; Carruthers 2006: ch. 2; see also the collection of papers in Parker and Gibson 1990), and to a more sober look at our own capacities (see Samuels 2009a, 2009b, on the non human-specific character of most of our phonology). I would not be surprised in the least if 5 or 10 years from now most of the properties of the systems with which our linguistic faculty interacts (sensorimotor and conceptual systems) will have been shown to have evolutionary precursors, conserved in other species alive today.[2] Those who think otherwise have simply not yet assimilated Darwin's 200-year-old basic lesson.

Before turning to the one or two key innovations that may have given human language its specific character, let me pause to note the conceptual similarity between biolinguistic reflections on phylogeny and ontogeny. Here it is in a nutshell: given the richness and complexity of our human knowledge of language, the short time it takes for children to master their native languages, the uniformity displayed within and across languages during the acquisition process, and the poverty of the linguistic input to children, there doesn't seem to be any way out of positing some 'head start' in the language acquisition process. I will assume that this comes in the guise of an innate component called Universal Grammar. This head start not only allows linguists to make sense of the speed at which (first) languages are acquired, but also why the acquisition process takes the paths it takes (as opposed to the paths it could take). By minimizing the role of the environment, UG allows us to solve 'Plato's problem'. Similarly, in light of the recent emergence of the language faculty, the most plausible approach to the question of the evolution of language (what I like to call 'Darwin's problem') is one that minimizes the role of the environment (read: the need for adaptation), by minimizing the structures that need to evolve, that is, by provided pre-adapted structures, ready to be recruited.

In addition to computational properties that may have been recruited, biolinguists, especially those of a minimalist persuasion, have explored the possibility that some of the properties of our language faculty may have emerged spontaneously, by the sheer force of biophysics (a possibility mentioned as long ago as Chomsky 1965: 59). The type of principles by which minimalists seek to reanalyse the data captured by previous models (principles that guarantee economical derivations and representations, ensuring efficient computations, and so on; see Boeckx 2006 for a survey of specific examples) are, quite plausibly, reflexes of computational laws that go well beyond the linguistic domain. They are some of what Chomsky (2005) calls the third factor effects that enter into the design of organisms, the sort of principles that are gaining importance in systems biology, dynamical/complex systems sciences, and biophysics (Kauffman 1993; Mueller and Newman 2003; Forgacs and Newman 2005; Kirschner and Gerhart 2005; Alon

---

[2] For example, reviewing the literature on *FOXP2*, Piattelli-Palmarini and Uriagereka (2011) suggest that its hypothesized computational role in the process of linearization/externalization is on a par with the role played by *Foxp2* in songbirds.

2007; among others). Such principles are sometimes called generic (or epigenetic), as opposed to genetic, because they are the inevitable results of elementary physico-chemical interactions that need not be coded in the genome, nor need they have been selected for (this, of course, leaves open the possibility that some of these properties, once emerged, have been stabilized by genetic means).

Much of the explanatory weight in minimalism is placed on the action of such generic principles. To the extent that this proves empirically adequate, it gives minimalism-inspired biolinguistics its special character, where most of the biological foundations of language are seen not as the result of selective pressures, or historical contingencies, but as the ineluctable workings of computational, developmental, and physico-chemical laws. Arguably this sort of emphasis reflects the deep rationalist commitment that pervades the generative enterprise (see Chomsky 1966), and accounts for the numerous references in the minimalist literature to the growing body of contemporary work in biology that returns to early attempts to formulate laws of form by Goethe, Geoffroy, Owen, D'Arcy Thompson, and Turing (for a survey of such contemporary work, see Piattelli-Palmarini 2006; Fodor and Piattelli-Palmarini 2011).

Still, at the end of the day, for all the precursors that may have been recruited to make the language faculty work, in the sense of connecting it to sensorimotor and conceptual systems, and for all the generic properties that minimalists claim characterize the faculty of language in the narrow sense, something must have provided the crucial spark to set all of this recruitment and spontaneous generation going, something that in effect brought together this cluster of properties we might call the 'language organ'. To date, I think the best hypothesis we have in this regard is what I call the lexical envelope, by which I mean simply the property that turns concepts into lexical items that can be combined via Merge (set-formation). (What I call the lexical envelope, Chomsky (2008) calls the 'edge feature'.)

The motivation for this specific hypothesis is twofold, or comes from two domains: theoretical linguistics and comparative psychology. On the one hand, all the linguistic models, no matter how minimalist (that is, no matter how much they manage to explain away the specific character of linguistic computations), rely on the existence of lexical items. Without lexicalization there would be no material for third factors/computational principles to work on. On the other hand, numerous comparative studies in psychology reveal that mature linguistic creatures transcend many cognitive limits seen in animals and prelinguistic infants (infants whose linguistic capacity has not matured yet). Such limits are the signature limits of what Elizabeth Spelke has called core knowledge systems, which correspond to primitive knowledge modules in roughly the sense of Fodor (1983). Such systems (for space, numbers, actions, objects, social interactions, and perhaps a few more) suffer from informational encapsulation and quickly reach combinatorial limits (see Spelke (2003) for a survey). By contrast, linguistically mature individuals regularly go beyond the computational boundaries of core knowledge systems to yield markedly different modes of conceptualization. As Spelke stresses, such new modes of thought often correspond to what would result from the combination of otherwise encapsulated concepts; for example, the ability to think of sets of individuals plausibly results from the conjunction of thinking about sets and thinking about individuals in the same conceptual space.

Spelke is, I think, right in taking language to provide the key combinatorics to make this possible.[3] But it would be a mistake in my opinion to conclude from this that the key evolutionary event was combinatorial in nature. The combination in question (what minimalists call Merge) is as primitive as one can get: it boils down to set-formation. The key event, rather, must have been the ability to combine virtually any concept (from whatever (core) knowledge system) with any other concept (from the same or another knowledge system).[4] This is what lexicalization does; it provides a uniform format for all concepts: it mixes conceptual apples and oranges in virtue of them all being word-like things. Lexicalization in this sense is what enables the language faculty to function as the lingua franca of the mind, to function as the bridge across core knowledge systems, to be our distinct language of thought, going well beyond the confines of what in other species and prelinguistic infants amount to (isolated) dialects of thought-modules (see Bickerton, this volume; Tallerman, this volume, on protolanguage).

Since Descartes, it has been clear that human thought is quite distinct from what other animals and machines can ever hope to achieve. Summarizing numerous experiments with animals, Hauser (2009b: 192–193) observes that humans alone can 'detach modes of thought from raw sensory and perceptual input', 'create and easily understand symbolic representations of computation and sensory input', 'apply the same rule or solution to one problem to a different and new situation', and 'combine and recombine different types of information and knowledge in order to gain new understanding'. Such a characterization of what Hauser dubs 'humaniqueness' fits snugly with the conclusions reached by the Cartesians. But I think that Hauser (2009a, b) has not gone far enough: the four ingredients just mentioned are clearly reflexes of one and the same key innovation: the lexicalization function and the unlimited range of combinations it makes possible.

If I am right, the emergence of lexicalized concepts was the sort of perfect storm that gave us, *Homo sapiens*, our niche. Once concepts are dissociated from their conceptual sources by means of a lexical envelope, the mind truly becomes algebraic, and stimulus-free. As one might expect, once the language faculty is in place, there will be collateral modifications of cognitive systems that were already in place. For

---

[3] Spelke is not the only one to have speculated along these lines. See Carruthers (2006), Pietroski (2008), Ott (2009), and, to some extent, Mithen (1996) and Tattersall (1998a). See also Chomsky (2005) on the evolutionary importance of edge features (which makes lexical items mergeable).

[4] I have argued for this position in Boeckx (2011). My hypothesis is very close to the views entertained by Pietroski (2008) and Ott (2009).

example, a sensorimotor system with ancient roots, of the sort Samuels (2009a, b) suspects underlies our phonological system, may get 'boosted up' by the appearance of recursive syntax, with non-trivial repercussions in the domain of lexical entries (underspecification), prosody, etc. In the conceptual realm, it is quite plausible that primitive capacities of mind-reading (theory of mind) may acquire a novel character once they interface with syntax (the unique 'recursive mind-reading ability of humans' which Tomasello (2008) discusses can, I submit, be plausibly interpreted in this light). The same is true for other systems such as number cognition, music cognition, space cognition, and, no doubt, more. There is no need (nor is there evolutionary time!) for all of these distinctly human capacities to have emerged independently of one another. As Darwin (1871: 126) suspected:

If it could be proved that certain high mental powers, such as the formation of general concepts, self-consciousness, etc., were absolutely peculiar to man, which seems extremely doubtful, it is not improbable that these qualities are merely the incidental results of other highly-advanced intellectual faculties; and these again mainly the result of the continued use of a perfect language.

One would, of course, like to know how the lexicalizing function (this 'edge feature') emerged in the species: was it a case of random mutation, or an inevitable spandrel? (Adaptationist scenarios are of no help here, since at best they would account for why this property, once it emerged, was preserved, not how it arose in the first place.) Perhaps we will never know (Lewontin (1998) thinks this is very likely), but it is tempting to connect this event to brain growth (see Chomsky 1975; Gould 1994), which may have affected the patterns of connectivity of brain cells, allowing for uncharacteristically long-range connections.

It seems to me that the emergence of the lexical envelope, coupled with conceptual and sensorimotor precursors,[5] and the workings of generic computational properties of the sort minimalism continues to uncover, goes a long way toward accounting (in principle, of course, since all of this is informed speculation) for the core properties of the language faculty, including its plasticity (variability, parametrizability). As I have discussed elsewhere (Boeckx 2008), if UG is as minimal as minimalists make it out to be, many features of the language faculty are left underspecified[6] (UG, for example, does not code for a rigid word order in the present picture), and as such offers various ways in which such 'coding' gaps may get filled in by experience (all the attested variations in word order boil down to different solutions to the same problem: linearizing in some way the hierarchical structure generated by syntax). It is true that a very minimal UG predicts the range

---

[5] Among the precursors I do, of course, allow for the very real possibility of important modifications that took place after the disappearance of the last common ancestor we share with our closest living relatives. It is very plausible that bipedalism radically restructured the sensorimotor domains with which syntax later interfaced.

[6] As opposed to overspecified, as in the classic parametric approach. Overspecification would not be what one would expect given the recent emergence of the language faculty.

of options among which the language learner will have to choose to be quite large, much larger than what early proponents of the Principles and Parameters model suspected, but fully in line with the number of parameters currently entertained in the literature. From the present perspective, linguistic diversity is the inevitable outcome of the very recent emergence of the language faculty—there simply wasn't enough time to genetically code for each and every detail of UG.[7]

## 52.3 CONCLUSION

Let me conclude this brief survey of current biolinguistic thought on Darwin's problem by stressing a few important points. First, biolinguists are concerned with the evolution of the language faculty, the computational mental organ that Chomsky (1986) called I-language. It is emphatically not about the evolution of 'language'—a concept that is not amenable to rigorous scientific inquiry. Since Hauser et al. (2002) it is clear that investigations into the evolution of the language faculty must begin with a fragmented view of the language faculty, minimally a distinction between the faculty of language in the broad sense and the language faculty in the narrow sense. Furthermore, evolutionary studies should resist the temptation to conjure up adaptationist stories: for reasons discussed in detail in Lewontin (1998), it is quite likely that we will never know what led to the stabilization ('selection') of the language organ in the species. It is certainly very plausible that once in place, the language organ was so beneficial to the individuals possessing it that selective pressures made sure it got maintained, but this is probably as much as we will ever be able to say about this. Instead of focusing on questions about natural selection, the focus should be on questions about computation. There are likely to be many computational primitives that enter into the language faculty in the broad sense, and maybe even in the narrow sense. We should try to design experiments that uncover these. We should also stress the existence and importance of generic (as opposed to genetic) 'third factors' that may account for many properties of the language faculty that were once thought to be *sui generis*. Clearly, the biolinguistic perspective outlined here demands that we adopt a pluralist view of evolution, of the sort advocated by Gould (2002). Some properties of human language will have followed the path of descent (with modification

---

[7] The fact that virtually all parameters seem to have to do with the externalization of language may be used as suggestive evidence that the recruitment of sensorimotor systems to bring out the structures generated by syntax was a late addition to the architecture of the language faculty, taking place after the syntax-conceptual structure interface was established (see Chomsky 2005, 2007 for speculations along these lines). If correct, this suggests that the initial function of language was devoted to internal thought, and not communication, contrary to most adaptationist scenarios in the literature.

perhaps); some will have arisen spontaneously, by virtue of the dynamical character of linguistic computation; some properties will be spandrels, others accidents; some will be generic; some will be genetic; all of these will be intertwined along the lines articulated in Lewontin's (2000) image of the triple helix, where genome, environment, and epigenome interact and determine one another.

I have suggested that very little genuine novelty is required to account for the rather unique character of our language organ, and our mode of cognition. I firmly believe that the Minimalist Program in linguistic theory has contributed to this interesting conclusion. In previous stages in the development of biolinguistics, properties attributed to UG consistently failed to receive plausible selectionist justification, but at the same time, UG was seen as so rich, specific, and complex that only the work of natural selection could account for such a system.[8] Approaching UG from below has cut through this paradoxical situation. By viewing UG as considerably more minimal, generic, and simple, it de-emphasized the possible role of natural selection, and enabled interdisciplinary studies to focus on the origin of (linguistic) form. Not surprisingly, this focus on form has brought biolinguists in line with recent trends in biology that emphasize the explanatory gap in the modern synthesis pertaining to the origin (generation) of form, such as evolutionary-developmental biology (Evo-Devo) (Carroll 2005), systems biology (Kirschner and Gerhart 2005), and other attempts at an expanded modern synthesis (see Gould 2002; Pigliucci 2007).

In sum, by fragmenting and minimizing UG, biolinguists have begun to move beyond sterile, unfalsifiable discussions, and begun to formulate hypotheses with enough commensurability to engage experts in other fields and enough biological plausibility to convince the remaining sceptics that linguistics is biology at a suitable level of abstraction (even if the biology it requires is more subtle than the modern synthesis anticipated).

# ACKNOWLEDGEMENTS

The views expressed here and in related publications have been influenced by illuminating discussions I have had over the years with Marc Hauser, Dick Lewontin, Noam Chomsky, Massimo Piattelli-Palmarini, Juan Uriagereka, Norbert Hornstein, and Paul Pietroski. I have also benefited greatly from the work of my students, especially Bridget Samuels, Dennis Ott, and Hiroki Narita, and from the comments of the editors of this Handbook.

---

[8] On why complex design virtually requires natural selection, see Dawkins (1996) and Pinker (1997).

# LANGUAGE CHANGE, CREATION, AND TRANSMISSION IN MODERN HUMANS

# CHAPTER 53

# INTRODUCTION TO PART V: LANGUAGE CHANGE, CREATION, AND TRANSMISSION IN MODERN HUMANS

MAGGIE TALLERMAN AND
KATHLEEN R. GIBSON

The chapters in Part V move beyond the core features of the language faculty that are the focus of Part IV, discussing the processes of (modern) language creation and change, and the role played in language evolution by socio/cultural transmission. Another factor affecting language change is population movements, since contact between different populations can result in massive structural changes to languages, and indeed, can trigger language shift. Authors investigate what light these modern 'windows'—creation, transmission, and contact events which can be directly examined—shed on language evolution itself. A number of chapters discuss a type of evidence that is relatively new to evolutionary linguistics: computational, mathematical, and robotic modelling.

Various themes recur in both Part IV and Part V of the volume. How much of the human language faculty should be ascribed to a putative Universal Grammar (i.e. a genetic endowment for language learning)? How much can be accounted for by other mechanisms, including sophisticated statistical learning? How much of observed language structure should be ascribed to natural selection, in other words what properties of (proto)language were adaptive as hominins started along the trajectory towards linguistic communication? Alternatively, how much structure arises spontaneously as a result of processes of self-organization, including linguistic changes that adapt to the learning mechanisms best suited to the human brain? Our view is that there are really no dichotomies here, and that in all cases, complex gene–environment interactions give rise to linguistic behaviours and structures. For instance, it is likely that external functional pressures have, in part, shaped linguistic structure; a well-studied example concerns principles of linearization of phrases and sentences (see Chapter 1 for some discussion). However, such functional pressures are of course not 'external' in any way: they arise from the way humans process the world and learn about its properties, and are, in most cases, phylogenetically primitive. We would expect the types of learning mechanisms occurring in our hominin ancestors to have directly shaped the way that languages developed, and in turn, assuming that an evolving language faculty is adaptive, we expect that early humans evolved in ways that would better enable them to learn ambient languages quickly, and making the most of a fragmented input.

Chapter 54, by Bernd Heine and Tania Kuteva, uses well-known processes at work in observable language change to reconstruct a plausible scenario for the development of the earliest languages. 'Grammaticalization', a concept also discussed by Joan Bybee (Chapter 55), refers to a bundle of processes causing diachronic change that are known to occur in all languages. Over time, lexical forms (such as nouns and verbs) turn into grammatical forms (such as auxiliaries), and grammatical forms turn into forms that are even more grammatical (morphosyntactic items, such as tense markers). These developments are directional—for instance, an auxiliary is not expected to become a lexical verb. Since these processes are ubiquitous in observed language change, linguists propose that they also played a vital role in the initial stages of language evolution. The earliest (proto)languages thus were probably simple concatenations of lexical (proto)words, lacking exponents of grammatical categories such as tense and aspect, case and agreement, passive, and so on. Many propose that nouns and verbs are the two word classes from which all other classes develop (or rather, proto-nouns and proto-verbs, since these categories would not initially have the fully-modern set of properties), but Heine and Kuteva suggest that noun-like words were the first category, and that all other classes, including verbs, derive from nouns. Grammaticalization is posited as a critical driving force in the evolution of language, and grammaticalization theory gives us a scientific tool for reconstructing earlier linguistic states.

Bybee's chapter extends this theory to constructions. Once words start to be grouped together in sequences that are repeated, 'chunking' occurs; units are formed in the memory that can be accessed directly. Novel constructions sometimes involve grammaticalization, meaning that a new grammatical morpheme arises (for instance, the future *gonna* construction, deriving from (literal) *going to*), but not all constructions create new grammatical elements (an example is the *drive X crazy* construction). Bybee argues that capacities for acquiring and processing language are mostly not domain-specific, but rather, are domain-general processes, applying to other types of learning. Moreover, language change mostly occurs in language use by adults, and not during language acquisition by children, as has often been proposed.

Paul Roberge also argues against the prevailing view concerning the role of child learners in language change, here in connection with the formation of creoles. He argues that native acquisition of pidgins (which are restricted systems, not full languages) is not necessary to form creoles, which are full linguistic systems. Roberge compares the factors leading to the evolution of full language from protolanguage with the factors involved in the formation of pidgins and creoles. Modern instances of language creation should shed light on language evolution itself—in Botha's terms, they form a 'window'. Certain 'primitive' linguistic features typify pidgins, such as free concatenation of words, and pragmatically rather than syntactically regulated word order; these are also posited as properties of protolanguage (see also Tallerman, Chapter 51). Creators of pidgins seem to resort to the pre-grammatical mode of protolanguage, thus putatively reflecting the earliest hominin use of language. However, as Roberge notes, modern speakers already all possess full language; does this influence (pidgin) language creation?

The theme of language creation also appears in Susan Goldin-Meadow's chapter (57) on gesture. She first explores the role of the manual modality when used (as it is in all cultures) alongside speech, then investigates what changes occur when this modality fulfils all the functions of language, without speech. This situation arises in existing and newly emerging sign languages. Sign languages are fully-fledged languages, but more primitive gestural communication occurs in homesign systems. These ad hoc creations are used between deaf children and hearing (non-signing) parents—thus, they are pidgins of a sort. Like pidgins, they are not full linguistic systems, but they exhibit some intriguing language-like properties, including segmentation and combination. Also like pidgins, homesign systems may become fully-fledged languages, if conditions for socio/cultural transmission are met. A well-documented example is the emergence of Nicaraguan Sign Language, which became a full sign language when deaf children with different homesign systems were brought together in a school, and had to communicate for the first time outside of their families. In evolutionary terms, Goldin-Meadow argues that the vocal and manual modalities may have evolved simultaneously, complementing each other as they do today.

The next two chapters further examine the role of contact (and lack of contact) between groups of speakers in creating language diversity and language change. Johanna Nichols (Chapter 58) notes that the principles of historical reconstruction only allow linguists to go back to around the last 7000 years, whereas language itself is assumed to have arisen at least 100,000–200,000 years ago, and pre-language (what is elsewhere in this volume termed 'protolanguage') had probably been evolving for at least a million years. What, then, can examination of modern situations tell us about the origins of language? Nichols shows that, given the plausible size and dispersal of early human populations in Africa, extensive linguistic diversity must always have been the norm, just as it is today in New Guinea and in Northern Australia. There is no single ancestral language or, indeed, protolanguage. Nor does any evidence indicate that all non-African languages descend from a single ancestral language, as might be expected had there been a single, fairly recent Out-of-Africa diaspora.

Brigitte Pakendorf (Chapter 59) looks at instances of language change via contact, but rather than contact between small, relatively isolated groups of individuals in pre-history (Nichols), or of the kind that occurs today in emerging sign languages (Goldin-Meadow), her chapter investigates what happens when population-based contact occurs. In the most extreme case, the result is language shift: a population formerly speaking one language will switch to a new language entirely. Intriguingly, if linguistic studies of contact situations are married with molecular anthropology, then as Pakendorf's work shows, prehistoric language shifts can be detected via genetics. Pakendorf outlines details of a case study from Siberia, showing how evidence from language and from genes in a modern population—and the mismatches between the two types of evidence—can reveal prehistoric population contacts resulting from immigration.

The next four chapters (Smith, Kirby, Cangelosi, and de Boer) all investigate language creation and transmission, particularly the role played by social interaction. All four chapters discuss the evidence that can be obtained from mathematical, computational, and robotic modelling in evolutionary linguistics. Kenny Smith (Chapter 60) argues that verbal reasoning can only take us so far in working out the predictions of a theory, and that formal models can test assumptions in a scientific manner. This is particularly useful in language evolution theory, where direct evidence is almost non-existent. Smith explains how formal models are used, and why it is that the results themselves are built into the models; this is not a drawback, but the entire point of using a model—it allows the researcher to *test* assumptions by varying the parameters of interest, then seeing what results from the model.

Simon Kirby (Chapter 61) uses formal modelling to examine the way that language is passed on via socio/cultural transmission. Kirby assumes that a genetically-specified language faculty exists (i.e. there is some innate capacity for language). Of course, individual languages do not emerge spontaneously from this language faculty, but rather are transmitted between generations of a speech community. To understand language evolution, we must consider the interaction between three distinct systems: biological evolution of the language faculty in the species, socio/cultural transmission of languages in populations of speakers, and individual learning in the child, which involves building a grammar on the basis of language data received. An interesting extension to computer modelling involves cultural transmission in the laboratory, using real human subjects and a simplified artificial 'language' that participants transmit. Kirby's results show that the very process of transmission (iterated learning) can lead to the *appearance* of design in language-like data, without either natural selection (or an intelligent designer) having intervened. Kirby concludes that languages have themselves evolved to be learnable in this way: they are in fact adaptive systems.

Angelo Cangelosi's chapter (62) on the use of robots and embodied agents (i.e. simulated agents) in modelling considers the implications of these experiments for the evolution of signalling behaviour and coordination, the lexicon, reference, and syntactic compositionality. Central questions involve the initial capacities for social coordination and prelinguistic communication before any specific communication channel evolved; and also the emergence of a shared lexicon in a situation where the agents initially share no meanings. The results show that limited verbal communication can arise under these circumstances, via social interaction. Thus, the importance of socio/cultural transmission is once again emphasized.

These themes of interaction between population-level and individual learning, and the spontaneous emergence of order in a system are also taken up by Bart de Boer (Chapter 63), in his contribution on self-organization. As de Boer notes, if certain complex linguistic structures can be shown to result from self-organization, then we need not ascribe to them a genetic basis. Many factors must still be explained by biological evolution, but these generally involve simpler behaviours, more likely to be dependent on widespread cognitive capacities also found in other animals. Reducing the involvement of biological evolution is desirable, and helps to explain how language may have evolved relatively rapidly from simpler cognitive precursors. Once a system emerges from self-organization, then the usual biological mechanisms select for adaptations which enable the user to handle the resulting system. Impressive results concerning self-organization come from investigations of sound systems, as de Boer describes; for instance, the structure of small to medium vowel systems can be explained on the basis of acoustic distinctiveness. Self-organization also occurs at population level, and can help explain what aspects of language structure emerge during transmission from one generation to the next, as both de Boer and Kirby discuss.

A process with similarities to self-organization is statistical learning, the process of detecting existing structure by tracking patterns in the input. Of course, this process also involves socio/cultural transmission, since infant learners receive language input from competent speakers. Katharine Graf Estes (Chapter 64) discusses how, via statistical learning, humans of all ages can track regularities in sounds, words, and grammars on the basis of distributional information. For instance, how are words segmented by infants from the incoming speech stream, where word boundaries are not explicitly flagged up? How is it that adult speakers of a language generally share grammaticality judgements on syntactic data? At 8 months, infants are capable of tracking the statistical cues that enable them to start to detect words. One-year-old infants can distinguish grammatical from ungrammatical word orders. And infants of 18 months can learn non-adjacent dependencies. Graf Estes concludes that '[h]umans readily learn regularities that commonly occur across human languages, but have greater difficulty learning regularities that do not'. If linguistic structure of various kinds can be acquired on the basis of statistical learning, the role played by an innate universal grammar may be reduced or eliminated. However, the learning abilities discussed by Graf Estes must all have evolved in their turn, and many of them may well be species-specific. Thus, the predisposition to acquire linguistic structure on the basis of statistical regularities can itself be seen as a central component of the language faculty; see also Anderson; Boeckx in Part IV.

The kinds of learning mechanisms discussed by Graf Estes are brought to centre stage by Nick Chater and Morten Christiansen (Chapter 65), who propose that abstract and arbitrary features of language (for instance, agreement, or case-marking) are shaped entirely by the processes involved in socio/cultural transmission, rather than by a genetically specified universal grammar. They develop Graf Estes' view that features which are common cross-linguistically are easily learned. The idea is that properties which humans cannot learn readily or which hinder communication will be discarded by languages, whereas features that are easily learned and processed, and which are communicatively effective, will be retained and expanded. Thus, languages themselves evolve to fit the kind of learning best suited to the human brain. A central theme in this chapter is that language change is too fast for genetic change to keep up with, thus eliminating the possibility that abstract linguistic features are shaped by natural selection; see, however, Számadó and Szathmáry (Chapter 14) for a different view. For Chater and Christiansen, since language is shaped by socio/cultural transmission, the same processes of language change and creation which are explored in other chapters in Part V also underpin language evolution. However, there is in addition a central role for biological and cognitive constraints in this model: 'the processes of cultural transmission that have shaped the creation of natural languages [are] grounded in prior human neural and cognitive capacities'. This also means that natural selection can be involved in shaping *functional* aspects of language (for instance, duality of patterning).

In conclusion, specific human learning and processing capacities (which, of course, have themselves evolved) are the ones that languages must adapt to, and in turn, human learning biases guide the rapid acquisition of languages (this last property being the main impetus in generative grammar for proposing a dedicated universal grammar). The construction of the human niche (see Gibson and Taller-man, Chapter 12, for some discussion) has undoubtedly required adaptations to an evolving language faculty, and the extreme phenotypic plasticity which charac-terizes humans in particular has also undoubtedly played a critical role. The investigation of ongoing processes of language creation and change, both in the field and in the computer lab, is becoming an increasingly important subfield, and should hopefully lead to a deeper understanding of the processes involved in language evolution itself.

CHAPTER 54

# GRAMMATICALIZATION THEORY AS A TOOL FOR RECONSTRUCTING LANGUAGE EVOLUTION

BERND HEINE AND
TANIA KUTEVA

## 54.1 INTRODUCTION

This chapter aims to show the potential that studies of grammaticalization offer for reconstructing earlier phases in the evolution of language, that is, phases not within the scope of classical methods in historical linguistics. What distinguishes grammaticalization theory from other linguistic approaches is that it has a diachronic foundation, and the hypotheses proposed rest, firstly, on regularities in linguistic change and secondly, on comparative observations across languages.

Building on reconstruction work proposed by Heine and Kuteva (2002a, 2007), we discuss the methodology used within grammaticalization studies and present some findings relevant to language evolution.

## 54.2 GRAMMATICALIZATION AND THE RECONSTRUCTION OF GRAMMAR

Grammaticalization theory offers a tool for pushing linguistic reconstruction back to earlier phases of linguistic evolution, that is, to phases where human language or languages can be assumed to be different in structure from today's languages. We define grammaticalization as a process involving the development from lexical to grammatical forms, and from grammatical to even more grammatical forms and constructions (on constructions, see Bybee, this volume). Underlying this is a cognitive mechanism whereby concrete and salient concepts serve as vehicles or structural templates to conceptualize less concrete and less readily accessible concepts—so that linguistic expressions for concrete concepts, such as physical objects or actions, are recruited to express more abstract concepts. Thus, visible and tangible objects such as body parts or physical landmarks serve to express non-physical relations, such as spatial relations, and concrete actions serve as conceptual vehicles to express more abstract concepts describing the aspectual, temporal, or modal contours of events.

We illustrate the process of grammaticalization with the following example. In many languages across the world, demonstrative deictic words (such as 'this', 'that') have developed into definite articles ('the'); and numerals for 'one' have developed into indefinite articles ('a'). Languages such as English, Dutch, German, French, and many others exemplify this: the (masculine) Latin demonstrative *ille* 'that' gave rise to the (masculine) definite article *le* 'the' in modern French, and Latin *unus* 'one' to the indefinite article *un* 'a' of modern French. Conversely, there are no languages where a process in the opposite direction took place—as far as we know, articles never develop into demonstratives or numerals. Demonstratives and numerals have fairly concrete meanings: the former typically express distinctions of physical space ('near' versus 'far') and the latter denote concrete number values. Articles, on the other hand, are more abstract and context-dependent: their use requires information about the linguistic discourse, and on what the speaker knows as opposed to what the speaker assumes the hearer knows. Thus, we are dealing with a unidirectional process from more concrete to less concrete concepts and more context-dependent grammatical forms.

Such unidirectional processes form the backbone of grammaticalization theory and provide the basis for linguistic reconstruction. Moreover, the methodology of grammaticalization theory is based on such processes: since definite and indefinite articles can almost invariably be traced back to demonstratives and to the numeral 'one', respectively, we hypothesize that there must have been a stage in the earlier history of human languages when there were demonstratives and numerals for 'one' but no articles.

Underlying the methodology of grammaticalization theory are the assumptions and observations in (1) (Heine and Kuteva 2007: 14–15):

(1) Assumptions and observations underlying the methodology of grammaticalization theory

    a. The development from early language to modern languages involved linguistic change. Accordingly, in order to reconstruct this development, we need to know what is a plausible linguistic change and what is not.

    b. An important force driving linguistic change is creativity.

    c. Linguistic forms and structures have not necessarily been designed for the functions they currently serve.

    d. Context is an important factor determining grammatical change (this concerns both the linguistic and the extra-linguistic context).

    e. Grammatical change is directional.

Much work on the genesis of grammar relies on generalizations concerning synchronic language structure and does not take into account findings on how languages change, in particular which changes are plausible and which are not. Our concern here is with language change as modification of individual properties or structures of languages. There is no indication that the principles of language change in early language were significantly different from the ones we observe in modern languages; hence, in accordance with (1a), we assume that early language can be studied on the basis of the same principles as modern languages. Conversely, a hypothesis on language evolution that is not in accordance with observations concerning change in modern languages is less plausible than one that is.

We assume that creativity is a factor of central importance to many kinds of grammatical changes; accordingly, (1b) is an important assumption underlying our methodology. Creativity must not be confused with productivity, that is, with the use of a limited set of taxa and rules to produce a theoretically unlimited number of taxonomic combinations or structures. Rather, creativity is about modifying rules or constraints by using and combining existing means in novel ways, giving new meanings and structures. In accordance with (1c), we are interested less in the current utility of words or constructions and much more interested in what these entities were designed for. Thus (1c) concerns the following issue: do categories serve the purpose for which they were designed? The answer can be based on the general observation, made independently in numerous studies, that language change is a by-product of communicative intentions not aimed at changing language (see especially Keller 1994; Haspelmath 1999). Rather, when a new functional category is created, nothing suggests that this is what speakers involved in this process really *intend* to happen.

The following example, involving the French negation marker *pas*, shows that linguistic forms and structures need not have been designed for the functions they presently serve. In (2), *pas* is a negation marker; but previously, *pas* was a noun meaning 'step', used not for negation, but rather for efficiently supporting a negative predication (cf. *He didn't move a step*), and it is only with the gradual decline of the erstwhile negation marker *ne* that *pas* assumed its present-day function as the primary or only marker of negation. The French negation marker thus serves a function it was not designed for by earlier speakers. Its original function—reinforcing another word—has little in common with its current usage.

(2)  Je    (ne)    vais    pas
     I     (NEG)    go      NEG
     'I'm not going.'

Likewise, the grammaticalization of demonstratives as described by Greenberg (1978) shows that functional categories may change in such a way that they bear little resemblance to their original design. The first step in this process is from demonstrative to definite article; subsequently the element may develop further to be used for indefinite reference, and in a final stage the erstwhile demonstrative may turn into a semantically largely empty marker of nominalization. Again, the current use of functional categories need not have anything to do with the motivations speakers had when they 'designed' them.

The example of the French negation marker *pas* also illustrates (1d): it may be, and frequently is, the context which determines semantic and syntactic change. Nothing in the meaning of the French noun *pas* 'step' suggests the meaning of negation; rather, the use of this noun in one particular context shaped the development from noun to 'emphasizer' and finally to negation marker; elsewhere, *pas* remains what it used to be, a noun meaning 'step'.

(1e)—unidirectionality—is a cornerstone of grammaticalization theory. For example, lexical verbs commonly develop into auxiliaries for tense, aspect, or modality, but it is unlikely that a tense auxiliary would develop into a lexical verb (Heine and Kuteva 2002b). Similarly, demonstratives give rise to definite articles, and numerals for 'one' to indefinite articles, or body part nouns may give rise to adpositions (prepositions or postpositions), but it is unlikely that articles will develop into demonstratives, adpositions into nouns, or auxiliaries into lexical verbs.

Using the above observations as a starting point, our procedure of reconstruction is outlined in (3):

(3)   Reconstructing language evolution (Heine and Kuteva 2007: 20)

   a. X and Y are phenomena that are interrelated in some way.
   b. Hypothesis 1: X existed prior to Y.
   c. Hypothesis 2: there was a change X > Y (but X continues to exist parallel to Y).[1]
   d. There is evidence in support of (3c).
   e. There are specific factors that explain (3c).

---

[1] It may happen that X is lost and only Y survives. This situation is not considered here since it is not relevant to the kind of phenomena examined here.

Over the past decades, the study of language genesis has been approached from a wide range of different angles, many of which are not primarily linguistic. Our approach, founded on the basis of (3)—i.e. grammaticalization theory—is linguistic in nature: it relies on regularities in the development of linguistic forms and constructions.

We illustrate this approach with an example from English. In (4) there are two instances of the item *used*; in (4a), it has the function of a physical action verb (a lexical verb), while in (4b) it is an auxiliary verb expressing the aspectual notion of past habitual action:

(4)   a. He used all the milk.
      b. He used to play the piano.

From the history of English we know that the lexical sense of *used* as in (4a) is older than the auxiliary usage in (4b), and that the latter has developed historically out of the former, in accordance with (3a) through (3c). So at some earlier stage, there was a lexical item *use* but no habitual marker *used to* (on the phonological as well as morphosyntactic details involved in this auxiliation, see Heine and Kuteva 2007: 21).

As shown in Heine and Kuteva (2007: 21–22), one comes across examples like this in hundreds of both genetically and geographically related as well as non-related languages all over the world (see especially Heine 1993; Bybee et al. 1994; Kuteva 2001; Heine and Kuteva 2002b). The relevant general properties are listed in (5):[2]

(5)   Generalizations
      a. There are two homophonous items A and B in language L, where A serves as a lexical verb and B as an auxiliary marking grammatical functions such as tense, aspect, or modality.
      b. While A has a noun as the nucleus of its complement, B has a non-finite verb instead.
      c. While A is typically (though not necessarily) an action verb, B is an auxiliary expressing concepts of tense, aspect, or modality.
      d. B is historically derived from A.
      e. The process from A to B is unidirectional; that is, it is unlikely that there is a language where A is derived from B.
      f. In accordance with (5d) and (5e), there was an earlier situation in language L where there was A but not B.

Of these, properties (5d) through (5f) are central to grammaticalization theory in general, and in particular to the methodology used in grammaticalization studies. They allow us to use techniques of linguistic reconstruction, with the

---

[2] Our reconstruction is based on attested cases of grammatical change, where we have written records and where these generalizations seem to hold. So we assume that these generalizations can be used for reconstructing cases where written records are missing.

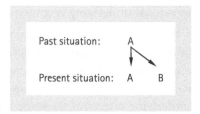

**Figure 54.1. Basis of reconstruction.**

situation depicted in Figure 54.1 as a basis. Thus, given a current situation where there are phenomena A and B (as presented in (5a–e)), we hypothesize that (5f) applies.

Applied to (4), this means that in Modern English there are functional categories, exemplified by *used to*, not present at some earlier stage in English; moreover, it is possible to reconstruct this earlier stage on the basis of (4), even in the absence of any historical evidence.

As we have argued elsewhere (Heine and Kuteva 2007: ch. 1), this technique can be traced back to the well-established method of internal reconstruction used in historical linguistics. However, unlike internal reconstruction, our technique is not restricted to the analysis of language-internal processes; rather, it is comparative in nature and allows for reconstructions across languages. Argumentation in line with the present approach is found in some of Greenberg's works (Greenberg 1992: 154; see also Greenberg 1966; Croft 1991).

Crucially, this approach makes it possible to use observable phenomena involving the development of concrete linguistic structures in historically attested time to extrapolate on the genesis and evolution of language forms in pre-historic time. Thus, the technique outlined above has been recruited—implicitly or explicitly—to deal with earlier situations in language evolution (e.g. Sankoff 1979; Comrie 1992; Aitchison 1996). Common to these works is the assumption that languages reveal layers of past changes in their present structure. Thus, Comrie (1992; 2003) argues that certain kinds of attested linguistic alternation, such as that between oral and nasal vowels, can be reconstructed back to earlier states without that alternation.[3]

In the spirit of the works just cited, the methodology of grammaticalization can be applied to stages in the development of language that are inaccessible to other methods in historical linguistics. The assumptions and observations underlying our reconstruction work are summarized in (6):

---

[3] It might be argued that this approach works in cases where appropriate historical evidence exists, but not necessarily in other cases. In other words, our claim that the presence of two structures A and B can be traced back to an earlier situation where there was A but no B cannot be generalized. It is a common analytic procedure, we argue, to describe the unknown in terms of the known, given appropriate correlations between the two, and not much would be gained by rejecting such a generalization.

(6)    Assumptions and observations underlying reconstruction

    a. Grammaticalization theory offers a tool for reconstructing the rise and development of grammatical forms and constructions. It rests on generalizations about language change in modern languages.

    b. There is no intrinsic reason to doubt that language change and the functional motivations underlying it were of the same kind in early language as observed in modern languages; as Comrie (2003: 256) notes: 'We propose no processes that are not attested in the historical period'.

    c. Accordingly, grammaticalization theory can be extended from modern languages to early language by extrapolating from the known to the unknown.

    d. Human language was structurally less complex at its earliest stage of evolution than modern languages are (for detailed discussion of the controversial nature of some of these points, see Heine and Kuteva (2007: 24ff.).

Applying the methodology of grammaticalization to a sizable body of data from over 500 languages across the world (e.g. Lehmann [1982]1995; Heine and Reh 1984; Heine et al. 1991; Bybee et al. 1994; Heine and Kuteva 2002b; Hopper and Traugott 2003; see also Dahl 2004), Heine and Kuteva (2007) argue that it is possible to reconstruct some major regularities in the development of functional categories. We turn next to the network of grammatical developments emerging from these reconstructions, leading step-by-step—or rather, layer-by-layer—to the full set of grammatical categories in modern languages.

## 54.3 THE LAYERING MODEL OF THE GENESIS AND EVOLUTION OF GRAMMAR[4]

The layering model of the genesis and evolution of grammar (Heine and Kuteva 2002a, 2007: 111) represents several steps—six layers—leading to full-blown, modern grammars, each successive step adding more to what existed already. See Figure 54.2 (Heine and Kuteva 2007: ch. 2, presents the main evidence for this reconstruction).

The layers in Figure 54.2 constitute clusters of categories that show the same relative degree of grammaticalization vis-à-vis both the categories from which they are derived and those into which they develop. For example, Heine and Kuteva (2002a, b) observe that aspect categories (ASP) can further develop into tense categories

---

[4] The term 'grammar', as used in this article, refers essentially only to the morphosyntactic structure of a language or of languages in general.

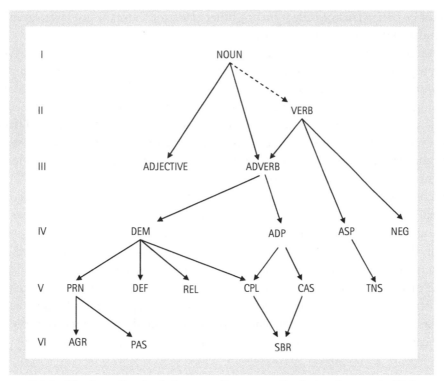

**Figure 54.2. Six hypothesized layers of grammatical development (Heine and Kuteva 2007: 111).**
(Abbreviations: AGR = agreement marker; ADP = prepositions and other adpositions; ASP = (verbal) aspect; CAS = case marker; CPL = complementizer; DEF = marker of definiteness ('definite article'); DEM = demonstrative; NEG = negation marker; PAS = passive marker; PRN = pronoun; REL = relative clause marker; SBR = subordinating marker of adverbial clauses; TNS = tense marker. The dotted line indicates that there is only indirect evidence for reconstructing this development.)

(TNS); therefore aspect and tense each represent a different layer. Thus, in this example we reconstruct three distinct layers.

In accordance with the reconstructions summarized in Figure 54.2, we hypothesize that there are six main layers of grammatical development. At the earliest layer I there were only nouns or noun-like items; the appearance of verbs at layer II enabled the speakers concerned to form simple sentences. Subsequently, language became increasingly more complex: the emergence of adjectives, adverbs, and other categories at the next two layers made it possible to form more complex noun phrases and verb phrases, and sentence subordination sets in at layer V, eventually leading at layer VI to complex language structures as we know them today. Thus the first layer in our model of the genesis and evolution of grammar, layer I, represents the least grammaticalized categories, that is, categories that cannot be derived historically from any other categories, and the last layer, layer VI, the most highly grammaticalized ones.

Several caveats must be borne in mind when discussing the layering model. First, the categories we select to illustrate the layering model are not necessarily completely uncontroversial. Selection was determined partly by particularly common patterns in the languages of the world—irrespective of whether these patterns are defined in terms of syntactic, morphological, or semantic criteria, or any combination of these. However, we also aim to select the most inclusive categories available; for instance, we have chosen a more comprehensive category 'pronoun' (PRN) instead of less inclusive categories such as 'personal pronoun' or 'indefinite pronoun'.

Second, we describe language evolution in terms of a set of grammatical categories typically distinguished in modern languages. Very likely, in the earlier development of language, these categories were not the same as today. For example, modern nouns usually have syntactic properties such as taking adjectives and demonstratives, or markers for number, gender, and/or case—properties which were presumably absent in the earliest stages of language evolution. The reader must therefore be aware that reconstructions we propose are based on the application of grammaticalization theory and can be accounted for with reference to this theory, but these are not necessarily the same categories that may have characterized the structure of early language.

## 54.4 THE LAYERING MODEL AND THE CLAIM FOR UNIVERSALITY

One possible critical rejoinder to our layering model concerns our proposal for its universality. Thus, languages like Chinese, traditionally considered to have very little morphosyntax, could be regarded as problematic: either one has to claim that these are comparatively 'primitive' languages or else one must abandon the layering model.

We now outline two versions of our response to this critique, a weak version and a strong version.

### 54.4.1 Universality of the layering model: the weak version

Grammaticalization theory leads us to hypothesize that language was simple before it became complex; however, the layering model applies universally to individual grammars and not to individual languages overall. This—at first sight—might seem confusing. The confusion, however, disappears once we recall that (i) individual languages encompass both lexicon and grammar (i.e. morphosyntax), and

(ii) the layering model presented in Heine and Kuteva (2002a, 2007) should be considered as a pathway leading to full-blown, modern language *grammar* (more precisely: morphosyntax), which is also what the title of Heine and Kuteva (2007, *The genesis of grammar: a reconstruction*) indicates.

One can argue—along with a growing number of typologists—that languages differ in terms of complexity of their grammar, or morphosyntax (see Carstairs-McCarthy, Chapter 50). Accordingly, languages manifest a different 'division of labour' between lexicon and morphosyntax: some languages rely a lot on grammar (i.e. they have an elaborate morphosyntax), whereas others rely on lexical means and/or pragmatics, and have simple grammars. It is the former group of languages that the layering model captures, for obvious reasons: the latter group of languages have only very simple—or next to zero—grammar, and the layering model is a universal model of the development of grammar (or morphosyntax).

## 54.4.2 Universality of the layering model: the strong version

On the strong version, the layering model claims universality of development of linguistic structure overall. The model does not assume a priori that all languages manifest overtly-marked morphosyntactic structure, based on the accretion of overt expressions of underlying semantic and pragmatic distinctions. On the contrary, nothing in the model rules out the possibility of languages where only a small number of explicit morphosyntactic markers develop, and even these few markers need not be bound and/or obligatory forms. In other words, in addition to languages with overt morphosyntax (such as familiar European languages), the model allows for a second group of languages, namely languages with 'covert' morphosyntax, based on pragmatics and hidden distinctions; see Bisang (2009) on pragmatics-based languages in East and mainland Southeast Asia; see also Kuteva (2010) on languages 'without grammar'. Such covert systems have only a small set of markers, with the following properties:

(i) A broad functional range: the concrete function of a marker can only be inferred from context; much of the grammatical complexity of a covert system remains hidden. One reason for this is that an individual marker carries a number of different distinctions, and the distinction involved in a particular utterance must be inferred from context, both linguistic and non-linguistic.[5] (Note that even in such languages, where context plays a crucial role, context is—nonetheless—not everything: if it were, then we would communicate only through context, and no language would develop.)

---

[5] Bisang (2009) exemplifies this by means of the way a classifier is used in Thai: depending on a complex interaction between the speech situation and the construction in which the classifier occurs, it can express no less than four functions: individuation, definiteness, singulative, or contrast.

(ii) Lack of obligatoriness: the markers allow for the inference of highly grammaticalized concepts such as tense or number but their expression is not compulsory. Depending on context, the same concepts can be inferred without the presence of a marker. Thus, a seemingly simple sequence may represent a vast number of different constructions: in this case—again—the construction intended by the speaker must be inferred by the hearer from linguistic and non-linguistic context. This observation about Chinese was made at least as early as von Humboldt's time (von Humboldt 1826[2005]: 133).

(iii) No phonetic reduction, or if there is reduction it is mostly limited to tonality.

The layering model is entirely compatible with the above distinction between languages with overt morphosyntax and languages with covert morphosyntax. Accordingly, it does not regard languages like Chinese, with little morphology, as 'primitive'. There are at least two reasons for this: one concerns boundedness of form; the other, obligatoriness of linguistic expression. Let us take a closer look at each.

### 54.4.2.1 *Boundedness of form*

The layering model does not imply that only bound, inflectional morphology 'counts'; the lack of boundedness of form does not mean lack of grammaticalization. Grammatical categories can be expressed by non-bound forms; in fact, this is the general tendency in earlier stages of grammaticalization. This work views phonological erosion—which leads to cliticization and ultimately to affixation—as a possible (but certainly not necessary) phenomenon accompanying grammaticalization (on the non-intrinsic status of phonological erosion in grammaticalization processes, see Heine and Kuteva 2002; Wiemer 2002, 2004; Bisang 2004).

It is, indeed, true that Chinese does not use verb affixes to provide information on the time of the occurrence of the event; instead it uses adverbs of time, or lexical time-point words. Thus in the following examples the same verbal form *gongzuo* 'work' is used and it is the adverbs *xianzai* 'now', *zuotian* 'yesterday', and *mingtian* 'tomorrow' that mark the relation between the speech time and the time of the occurrence of the event; in the corresponding English sentences, on the other hand, the verb *work* takes different tense forms to express present, past, and future activity (our Chinese examples lack diacritics because we have followed our sources verbatim):

(7)    Chinese (Yang 2007: 3)

    a. wo   xianzai   zai   zhe li   guongzuo
       I    now      at    here    work
       'I am working here now.'

    b. wo   zuotian   zai   zhe li   guongzuo
       I    yesterday at    here    work
       'I worked here yesterday.'

c. wo   mingtian   zai   zhe li   guongzuo
   I     tomorrow   at    here    work
   'I will work here tomorrow.'

Even though Chinese has no grammaticalized tense system,[6] the widespread belief that Chinese has a simple (or next to zero) grammar overall seems to be based on equating grammar, i.e. morphosyntax, with inflectional morphology: linguists are more ready to identify a structure as grammaticalized if it involves inflectional morphology, and Chinese happens to be a language with little inflectional morphology.

From a non-Eurocentric perspective, Chinese can be regarded as a language with an extremely complex morphosyntax: one must know the rules for combining lexical-to-lexical morphemes—in addition to the, allegedly, very few grammatical rules—in order to express lexical as well as grammatical notions. As Heine and Kuteva (2002b) show, Mandarin Chinese has many more grammaticalized/ grammaticalizing patterns than usually recognized. In our world lexicon of grammaticalization, Chinese is represented with no less than 49 instances of grammaticalization, whereas Russian—a language traditionally thought of as having a highly complex grammar in both the domain of the noun and the verb—has only eight instances. One reason why these patterns are easy to miss in Chinese, we believe, is the analytic nature of the language.

Soon after Heine and Kuteva (2002b), there appeared the first corpus-based study of Mandarin Chinese usage (Xiao and McEnery 2004), which showed that in the area of the verb at least, Mandarin Chinese has developed a highly sophisticated, fine-grained grammatical system of expressing aspectual distinctions, even though the marking of these distinctions is not obligatory. The richness of the Mandarin Chinese aspectual system is manifested by no less than four perfective and four imperfective aspects. The perfective aspects are (i) the actual aspect -*le*; (ii) the experiential aspect -*guo*; (iii) the delimitative aspect marked by verb reduplication; and (iv) the completive aspect marked by resultative verb complements. The imperfective aspects encompass (i) the durative aspect -*zhe*; (ii) the progressive aspect *zai*; (iii) the inceptive aspect -*qilai*; and (iv) the continuative aspect -*xiaqu*.

Xiao and McEnery (2004: 227) point out that of these, only the last two, namely the inceptive -*qilai*, and the continuative -*xiaqu*, are not fully-fledged aspect markers. Nevertheless, they analyse them as grammaticalizing patterns, whereby the directional verb *qilai* ('upward movement') is becoming an inceptive marker as in (8), and the directional lexical verb *xiaqu* indicating downward movement is developing into the aspectual marker -*xiaqu* for the continuative as in (9):

---

[6] Notice that there is some evidence for incipient grammaticalization of markers for the future, for instance, in Mandarin Chinese (Heine and Kuteva 2002b).

(8)    Mandarin Chinese (Xiao and McEnery 2004: 217)

| zuo | zai | ta | shenbian | de | Liu | Xiaoqing | hahadaxiao- | **qilai** |
|-----|-----|-----|----------|-----|-----|----------|-------------|-----------|
| sit | at | he | beside | GEN | L. | X. | laugh.heartily- | INC |

'Liu Xiaoqing, who sat beside him, started to laugh heartily.'

(9)    Mandarin Chinese (Xiao and McEnery 2004: 228)

| ruguo | rang | zhe- | zhong | shitai | fazhan- | **xiaqu**[ ... ] |
|-------|------|------|-------|--------|---------|------------------|
| if | let | this- | kind | situation | develop- | CONT |

'If this situation is let to continue developing [ ... ]' (i.e. 'If this situation is allowed to continue')

The development of the actual aspect *-le*, the experiential aspect *-guo*, the durative aspect *-zhe*, and the progressive aspect *zai* represents well-established grammaticalization paths across languages (Heine and Kuteva 2002b), which fully supports the network of the layering model in Figure 54.2. The delimitative aspect, which is marked by verb reduplication, and the completive aspect, marked by resultative verb complements, on the other hand, show (a) how important syntax and semantic verb class are for the functioning of grammatical categories, and (b) that the expression of grammatical categories need not involve bound forms.

### 54.4.2.2 *Obligatoriness of linguistic expression*

In the layering model, a particular morphosyntactic structure does not need to be obligatory, in order for it to 'count' as grammaticalized/grammaticalizing: in many cases grammaticalized structures are only optional. Obligatoriness should not be equated with grammar; optionality is also a property of grammar. Even though in a number of languages it might signal incipient grammaticalization processes, optionality may just as well be a relatively stable property of grammar.

To return to our discussion of the aspectual distinctions in Mandarin Chinese, what is most unusual from the perspective of European language speakers is the fact that the marking of these distinctions is not obligatory. Thus, even though Chinese has abundant aspect markers, many sentences are aspectually unmarked. Nevertheless, Xiao and McEnery (2004: 236) point out that in their corpus they did not find a single instance of an aspectually unmarked sentence that was neither perfective nor imperfective. The key to this 'mystery' seems to be that Chinese avoids redundancy of expression. Thus, C. Smith (1997: 280) observes that 'LVM [lack viewpoint aspect marker] sentences', i.e. aspectually unmarked sentences, occur in different contexts and genres, and two very general conventions can be stated: 'LVM sentences' are possible when (a) the 'viewpoint' [= aspect; Heine/ Kuteva] information of an 'LVM sentence' would be redundant, because it is conveyed by other means in the sentence or context; or (b) the information conveyed by an 'LVM sentence' is backgrounded rather than foregrounded.

Thus it turns out that aspectually unmarked sentences in Mandarin Chinese typically occur in a limited number of contexts, where it is not hard to infer either their perfective or imperfective nature (Xiao and McEnery 2004: 236–240). First, stative situations normally do not take an aspect marker because they do not have to be marked aspectually anyway. Dynamic situations are either irrealis—that is, future, habitual, conditional, or negative—or the aspectually unmarked sentence will be perfective.

Second, the actual aspect marker -le tends to be omitted in discourse segments in which a series of events is presented; in this case the explicit marker -le is used only for the peak event in the discourse segment, though it applies to the whole series:

(10)    Mandarin Chinese (Xiao and McEnery 2004: 237)
        yi-ge[ . . . ]  bairen qingnian  chuangru [ . . . ]  yi-ge    jiaji
        one-CLF    white youngster  rush-into         one-CLF  family-planning

        zhensuo,  yong  buqiang  xiang  limian de  ren      saoshe,  ranhou
        clinic,   use   rifle    at     inside GEN  people   strafe,  then

        taozou-  le
        escape-  ACTL
        'A white youngster rushed into a family-planning clinic, and strafed people there with his rifle, and then ran away.'

Third, when a sentence ends with the sentence-final particle le, which denotes change-of-state, and which, historically, gave rise to the actual aspect marker -le, the latter marker can also be left out.[7] This again can be interpreted as a tendency to avoid (i) repetition of the same syllable, and (ii) redundancy of marking meaning: change-of-state entails perfectivity.

Fourth, Xiao and McEnery found that the presence/absence of explicit aspect markers may well involve purely phonological factors. They conclude that 'with most monosyllabic verbs, -le cannot be omitted, though most disyllabic verbs do not have such a requirement' (2004: 238).

The above discussion shows that, should we choose to change our perspective, instead of claiming simplicity for Chinese (aspectual) grammar, we could just as

---

[7] According to Xiao and McEnery (2004), historically, the perfective marker -le and the change-of-state sentence-final particle le developed at different stages in the evolution of Chinese. The sentence-final particle le is derived from the verb liao 'to finish, to come to an end' (the same syllable with a different pronunciation) which is still current in modern Chinese. 'When its sentence-final function was well-established, it also developed a use in which it appears directly after the main verb (whether or not it is sentence-final) signalling actuality' Xiao and McEnery (2004: 92).

well say that Chinese speakers have developed a highly sophisticated (aspectual) grammatical system, but they make full use of pragmatic (contextual) means before they take recourse to that redundant, 'decorative' grammatical system. It may well be that from the perspective of a Chinese speaker, European languages, employing obligatory grammatical structures, actually use unnecessary, redundant decorations (though these are now essential)—to the extent that we may have lost much of our ability to anchor our languages in context. That is, from a Chinese speaker perspective, our natural sense for the embeddedness of language in the discourse-pragmatic situation may well be regarded as 'atrophied'. In other words, on the layering model, languages like Chinese are languages with a covert morphosyntax.

In sum, the layering model claims universality of the evolution of grammatical markers in all languages where such markers take explicit shape, regardless of whether they are obligatory or optional, bound or non-bound, and regardless of whether they are polyfunctional or not; in other words, in both overt and covert morphosyntactic systems.

# 54.5 Conclusions

We have tried to show the role played by grammaticalization in shaping the grammatical categories found in modern languages. On the basis of observations of regular processes of language change in historic times it is possible to identify a network of crosslinguistically common grammaticalization pathways, leading from lexical to grammatical, and to even more grammatical categories.

Applying the grammaticalization method—which deals with comparison of grammaticalization developments across phyla—we have argued that it is possible to use observable phenomena involving the development of concrete linguistic structures in historically attested time to extrapolate on the genesis and evolution of language forms in pre-historic time. Accordingly, grammaticalization represents one of the most reliable scientific tools for the reconstruction of earlier stages of language. We have proposed particular sequences of the evolution of grammatical structures. These sequences lead, in a principled way, from concrete lexical items to abstract morphosyntactic forms. Grammatical forms such as case, agreement, voice markers, etc. are regarded as the result of gradual evolution, so that the earliest stage of human language—reconstructable by the methodology of grammaticalization theory—must have lacked grammatical categories such as case, agreement, voice.

# ACKNOWLEDGEMENTS

Bernd Heine wishes to thank Tom Givón, Hyun-Jung Koo, Heiko Narrog, Kyung-An Song, as well as the Korean Ministry of Education, Science and Techonology for having generously sponsored the research leading to this paper within its World Class University Program (Grant No. R33-10011).

Tania Kuteva thanks the A. v. Humboldt Foundation and SOAS, University of London, for their generous support.

# ABBREVIATIONS

| | |
|---|---|
| ACTL | actual aspect marker -*le* |
| CLF | classifier |
| CONT | continuative |
| COS | change-of-state |
| GEN | genetic |
| INC | inceptive |
| PASS | passive |
| PRT | particle |

# CHAPTER 55

# DOMAIN-GENERAL PROCESSES AS THE BASIS FOR GRAMMAR

### JOAN BYBEE

## 55.1 INTRODUCTION

An emerging view of grammar sees it as evolving from the application of domain-general processes over many instances of language use; this has profound implications for an investigation into the evolution of language. While the generative theory of grammar, with its postulation of certain innate language structures, has been most visible to observers outside the field of linguistics, long-term research traditions in typology, discourse analysis, historical linguistics, and corpus linguistics have converged on a view of grammar, termed 'usage-based', that explains the properties of human languages as a product of the way cognitive mechanisms apply to a language-user's experience with language in context.

In this chapter I present this view of grammar and its implication for language evolution. I focus primarily on what is known about the dynamic processes that create grammar, as documented in many studies of language change; it follows that processes of language evolution which can be documented in the present should guide our proposals about the past. I demonstrate that many aspects of grammar can be derived from domain-general cognitive processes, especially those of neuromotor automation, chunking, categorization, inference-making, and cross-modal association (Bybee 2010).

## 55.2 Constructions as the
## basic unit of grammar

Rather than conceiving of the syntax of a language as being generated by abstract rules with no connection to meaning (as proposed in the transformational-generative tradition), Construction Grammar (Fillmore et al. 1988; Goldberg 1995, 2006) posits a direct connection between the conventionalized constructions of a language and their meanings. According to Goldberg (1995, 2006) all form-meaning pairings are constructions. This includes single morphemes, words, morphological formations such as VERB + PAST, idioms, and word sequences with schematic slots. This chapter concentrates especially on the latter type of construction.

Examples of constructions that include groups of words or morphemes with schematic positions can be both very specific and very general. On the specific end of the spectrum we find constructions such as (1) and (2); here, the verb *drive* is used with a category of adjective (roughly synonymous with *crazy*) in a range of tenses and with an animate object and a wide range of subjects. (Examples (1)–(4) are from the Corpus of Contemporary American English.)

(1)    It's been <u>driving me crazy</u>.

(2)    For one thing, the isolation here <u>drives men mad</u>.

A more general or abstract construction is the ditransitive construction, as in:

(3)    I'm gonna <u>give you</u> an option.

(4)    Hey, Jimmy, Mac, <u>throw me</u> the ball.

This construction can be used instead of the *to*-dative (as in . . . *throw the ball to me*) with some main verbs (Goldberg 1995). Note that almost all constructions have some *specific* lexical or grammatical material in them. It is rare to find a well-documented construction that is purely abstract and schematic, consisting only of categories such as noun phrase or verb phrase; instead, specific nouns, verbs, prepositions, pronouns, and inflections occur in constructions. Construction grammar, then, emphasizes the interaction of the lexicon with the syntax (Langacker 1987).

The two constructions exemplified above have well-defined meanings, partially independent of the particular items that participate in them. We know this because the schematic slots of constructions are productive: a new item can be inserted and the meaning still comes through. For example, *bananas* (in the sense of 'crazy') can be substituted for *crazy* in (1) and *fax* or *text* can be substituted for *give* in (3). Thus we conclude that the conventionalized sequence of words has meaning attached directly to it via the domain-general process of cross-modal association—the ability of humans to associate temporally contiguous percepts from different modalities with one another. Having experienced utterances such as (1) and (2) in circumstances where their meaning can be inferred, one learns the meaning of this particular construction.

The other domain-general processes involved in construction formation and use are sequential processing and categorization. Sequential processing or chunking is the process by which repeated sequences of experience (words or other events) come to be grouped together in memory as units that can be accessed directly (Anderson 1993; Ellis 1996). Thus *drive* X *crazy* may become a sequential unit in memory (despite the interruption of the schematic slot for the object of *drive*). We know that such processing occurs independently of meaning from experiments in which infants and adults hear sequences of nonsense syllables and learn to recognize recurrent three-syllable sequences (Saffran et al. 1996; Graf Estes, this volume).

Categorization is necessary to the cognitive representations of constructions in several ways. First, categorization is necessary for the recognition that an element or sequence is the same as one previously experienced. Second, categorization is used to develop the schematic slots of constructions; semantic similarity to *crazy* is a criterion for an adjective to occur in the *drive someone* ADJ construction. In the ditransitive construction, several semantic classes of verbs appear: related to *give* are *hand* and *pass* and related to *throw* are *toss* and *flip*. Thus the productivity and creativity of language derive from the use of the conventionalized form-meaning associations with novel elements chosen for their ability to fit in certain categories.

## 55.3 WHERE DO CONSTRUCTIONS COME FROM?

### 55.3.1 Grammaticalization

Constructions are created through the repetition and thus conventionalization of useful sequences of elements; their meanings arise from associations with the context and implications that are present. The most pervasive process by which new constructions are created is grammaticalization, in which a new construction is created along with a new grammatical morpheme; the latter evolves from a lexical morpheme or combinations of grammatical and lexical morphemes (see Heine and Kuteva, this volume). An accessible example is the periphrastic future in

English, SUBJECT *be going to* VERB. The source of this construction is evident from the morphemes that compose it, but the meaning 'intention to do something' or 'future' is not directly derivable from the meanings of the components. At the same time, there is considerable phonetic reduction of *going to*, often produced as *gonna*. Thus, a new grammatical morpheme—a future marker—arises.

It is instructive to see how a new grammatical morpheme arises, as cross-linguistic evidence confirms that the same factors are involved in the development of almost all grammatical morphemes in the languages of the world. Four centuries ago, when Shakespeare was writing, *be going to* VERB was just an ordinary instance of a more general purposive construction used with motion verbs (and perhaps other verbs), as in (5):

(5)    . . . the kings
       and the princes, our kindred, <u>are going to</u> see the queen's picture.
       (*Winter's Tale V.2*)

As *go* is a frequent verb with a very general meaning, instances of this construction with *go* occurred more often than with other verbs. As with other highly practised behaviour, repetition leads to certain changes. First, sequences of words repeated together tend to form chunks that can be accessed directly. Second, inside such chunks phonetic reduction is more likely, as the sequences of articulatory gestures composing such chunks tend to overlap and reduce. Third, higher frequency words and phrases are easier to access, and thus their frequency spurs even more repetition, leading to a snowball effect. Finally, certain meaning shifts within contexts of use can occur if inferences from the context are repeated with the construction.

An illustration of how meaning change via inference-making occurs in language use can be found in the following dialogue from Shakespeare (Hopper and Traugott 2003):

(6)    <u>Duke</u>    Sir Valentine, whither away so fast?
       <u>Val.</u>    Please it your grace, there is a messenger
              That stays in to bear my letters to my
              friends,
              And I <u>am going to</u> deliver them.
       <u>Duke</u>    Be they of much import?
       (1595, Shakespeare, *Two Gentlemen of Verona III.i.51*)

This dialogue is interesting because the Duke asks Valentine where he is going (*whither* means 'to where') but Valentine does not actually say where he is going; rather he says what he is intending to do. This response seems appropriate in the context—apparently that is what the Duke wanted to know anyway, especially given his next line, which is about the letters, not about the location Valentine is headed to. Thus the *be going to* construction, which is on the surface about movement in space, is used in contexts in which there is a strong implication of the subject's intention to complete the action described by the following verb. If such inferences occur commonly, they can become part of the meaning of the construction (Bybee et al. 1994; Traugott and Dasher 2002). Thus one important use of *be going to* in contemporary English is to signal intention, as in this example.

(7)    <u>I'm going to</u> do everything I can to pay off that obligation.

It is this intention meaning that eventually gives rise to the future meaning, again by inference.

Other changes can also be related to the increased frequency of use of the phrase *be going to*. As a grammaticalizing phrase becomes more frequent and more frequently accessed as a chunk, the parts from which it was originally composed become less identifiable (Haiman 1994). This has not happened completely with *gonna*, but it can be seen in a grammaticalized sequence such as *would have*, where the second component is sometimes misidentified as *of* (Boyland 1996). Related to the loss of analysability is the loss of internal constituent structure. Rather than functioning like a main verb with a complement, *be going to* now functions more like an auxiliary with the verb following it functioning as the main verb, as evidenced by the fact that restrictions on what can be the subject are determined by that second verb rather than by *go*. Thus, in *it's going to rain*, *it* is the subject of *rain* and no movement is implied. Loss of constituent structure also occurs in complex prepositions that become simple ones: *before* and *behind* each consisted of a older preposition *be* and a noun, *fore* 'front' and *hind* 'back', but they have become simple prepositions with no internal structure.

A final important point is that grammaticalizing elements often move from being separate words to being attached to other items as affixes. For example, the subject agreement suffixes on verbs in the Altaic language Buriat are clearly derived from personal pronouns (Poppe 1960). Compare the suffixes in (8) to the first and second person subject pronouns in (9). The third person singular has no suffix and the third plural is derived from a demonstrative.

(8)    jaba- 'go' + -na- Present Tense
       1s jabana-b    1p jabana-bdi
       2s jabana-s    2p jabana-t
       3s jabana      3p jabana-d (cf. ede 'these')

(9)    Personal pronouns, nominative case
       1s bi    1p bide
       2s si    2p ta

There is only space here for these few examples, but recent research shows that these same mechanisms of change operate in other grammatical domains than tense, including modality, aspect, definiteness, voice, and so on. Moreover, grammaticalization occurs in all languages. In fact, the paths of change in unrelated languages are remarkably similar to one another (Bybee et al. 1994; Heine and Kuteva 2002b, this volume). The following just sample the many cross-linguistically verified paths of grammaticalization ((10)–(13) from Bybee et al. 1994; (14)–(16) from Heine and Kuteva 2002b):

(10) Future from movement verbs ('go': Margi, Cocama, Maung, Atchin, Abipon, Krongo, Mano, Bari, Zuni, and Nung; 'come': Margi, Tucuno, Guaymí, Danish, Krongo, Mwera, Tem, Mano, Tojolabal, and Cantonese)

(11) Progressives from locative constructions (Basque, Island Carib, Cocama, Jívaro, Alyawarra, Tahitian, Motu, O'odham, Abkhaz, Baluchi, Mwera, Ngambay, Shuswap, Haka, Lahu, Cantonese, Dakota, and Tok Pisin)

(12) Perfects from 'have' or 'be' auxiliaries plus non-finite form of the verb (Basque, Tigre, Maithili, Baluchi, Modern Greek, Danish, English, Spanish, Mano, and Buriat)

(13) Perfects from 'finish' (Bongu, Temne, Lao, American Sign Language, Tok Pisin, Palaung, and Sango)

(14) Definite articles from demonstratives (Romance and Germanic languages, Bizkaian Basque, Vai, Hungarian, Haitian Creole)

(15) Indefinite articles from the numeral 'one' (English, Albanian, Turkish, Hungarian, Greek, Lezgian, Easter Island, Tamil)

(16) Middle and passive voice from reflexive (Oneida, South !Xun, North !Xun, Danish, Spanish, Teso, Russian)

This is only a small sample of grammaticalization changes found cross-linguistically. The fact that grammaticalization occurs in all languages at all stages indicates that grammaticalization is the main process by which grammar evolves. Note further that the process is directional—lexical items become grammatical but rarely does the opposite occur. Thus, there is good reason to suppose that whatever the 'original' grammar of human language was, it evolved in the same way (see Bybee 1998; Heine and Kuteva 2007, this volume).

Grammaticalization, then, creates a new construction with a new grammatical morpheme in it. As mentioned, the domain-general processes at work are sequential processing, neuromotor automatization, categorization, and inference-making. Historical evidence shows that grammatical constructions and complex words are formed by composition—the fusion of two elements that frequently occur side-by-side, not by the decomposition of complex items, as in the speculations of Wray (2000) and Kirby (this volume).

## 55.3.2 New constructions without grammaticalization

Every language has thousands, perhaps tens of thousands, of specific constructions that are concatenated and overlapped one on another to produce fluent speech.

These constructions also arise out of other, more general constructions and take on special meanings because of use in specific, repeated circumstances (Bybee 2006b). Some of the same mechanisms apply to the creation of these constructions as apply in grammaticalization, but these constructions do not create a new grammatical morpheme—no particular lexical item undergoes the phonetic and semantic/pragmatic changes characterized above. The difference is that some constructions do not reach the frequency levels necessary for extreme phonetic reduction and semantic change. A good example is the construction discussed above, exemplified by *drive someone crazy*. The essential components of this construction are all lexical items, though pronouns can occur in the object position and the verb can be inflected.

Despite being very specific, this construction is part of the general grammatical repertoire of native speakers. It apparently arose in the 19th century: the first attestation of *drive* with an adjective listed by the Oxford English Dictionary is in 1813. It is used there with the adjective phrase *raving mad*. This usage was apparently an extension of the already metaphorical use of *drive* with a prepositional phrase attested since the 14th century, in phrases such as *drive to scorn, driven into dumpes of doubtfulnesse*, and *to drive one out of his senses*. In these uses, what one is driven into is rather negative, so the appearance of *drive mad* could be based on semantic similarity to one of these prepositional phrases. The combination *drive mad* has apparently spawned a new productive construction. In the Time Magazine Corpus, which begins in 1923 and covers all issues of the magazine to the present, *drive* was used in the 1920s with *mad* and *insane* and one other more creative adjective, *rumour-frantic*. It appears with *crazy* in the 1930s and begins a steep increase in frequency. The construction changes from expressing literal meaning of *mad* or *crazy* 'clinically insane', to more hyperbolic uses; it also expands to a wider range of adjectives, including *nuts, batty, wild, loony*, and *half-mad* (Bybee 2010).

Languages are full of such conventional pairings that show productivity. Just as in grammaticalization, the processes that create them are sequential processing, repetition leading to chunking and conventionalization, and categorization, which creates a set of adjectives that can be used in the schematic slot. In this case we also see how closely the word choice is associated with the particular grammar of the construction.

## 55.4 IMPLICATIONS FOR A THEORY OF GRAMMAR

The evidence from language change and from current variation indicates that grammar is emergent, not static (Hopper 1998). As just demonstrated, the mechanisms used in everyday interaction make subtle changes in the language that can be conventionalized and expanded with repetition. These facts point to a rich memory representation for language as language users keep track of the range of variation in the phonetics, semantics, and form of the utterances they process. In a rich memory (or exemplar) representation, each instance of language use has an impact on cognitive representations (Pierrehumbert 2001; Bybee 2006b, 2010). The specificity of memory for language means that what makes a language a language is not just the abstract patterns but also (or perhaps instead) the very specific word combinations or constructions that are conventionalized; these specific word sequences increase fluency as several words can be accessed at once (Pawley and Syder 1983; Erman and Warren 2000; Wray 2002b).

In this view, language is a complex adaptive system: no structure is given in advance, but various mechanisms applying iteratively as language is used give rise to structure (Ellis and Larsen-Freeman 2009). The similarities and differences among languages arise because the same dynamic processes occur during usage in all languages (Greenberg 1969). That is why the same grammaticalization paths are repeated across languages and why it is easier to identify cross-linguistic patterns of change than to find cross-linguistic similarities in synchronic states.

The present discussion of change has emphasized that change takes place during language use; that is, change can occur in adult grammars. I emphasize this because there is a general misconception among linguists and others that language change takes place during language acquisition, or 'cultural transmission' (Lightfoot 1979; Janda 2001; Kirby, this volume). However, the empirical record is completely clear on two points: (1) the types of innovation found in child language are missing from the record of language change and (2) the social status of children makes them unlikely to exert sufficient influence on adults as to change language (Croft 2000; Bybee 2010). Even in those cases where an adult model is not available, as in the recently-formed Nicaraguan Sign Language (Senghas et al. 2004) and Al-Sayyid Bedouin Sign Language (Sandler et al. 2005), the variability among age cohorts or generations of speakers is consistent with change taking place during language use.

## 55.5 IMPLICATIONS FOR EVOLUTION

As a general research strategy, it is preferable to assume that the ability to acquire and process language is based on domain-general abilities and to postulate abilities specific to language only when domain-general abilities cannot be identified. Thus I have identified here at least some of the abilities necessary for the construction of a grammar, where I take grammar to mean the cognitive representation of language. To review, in the previous discussion I have identified the roles of neuromotor automation, chunking, categorization, inference-making, and cross-modal association. All of these abilities are present in non-human primates and many other mammals as well, although to be sure, the human cognate capacities are much richer, both in detail as well as degrees of abstractness. Thus the human capacity for fine motor control, as well as complexity of units that can be processed together, far exceeds that of other primates. At the same time, the levels of categorization and the abstractness of inference-making also are well beyond the abilities of non-humans.

Other abilities that are prerequisites for language, such as complex imitation (Bates et al. 1991; Arbib 2003) joint attention, and social learning (Tomasello 1999) are particularly well developed in humans, but note that these are domain-general abilities that are applied to language as well as other types of learning and cultural activity. Thus I would argue that the acquisition and evolution of grammar is not based on special skills necessarily, but rather depends in large part on many domain-general capacities. Only after a thorough examination of domain-general abilities should we consider that the acquisition and use of human language requires abilities specific to language.

Thus, a plausible scenario for language evolution begins with the assignment of meaning to certain vocal and/or manual gestures through cross-modal association. These meaningful gestures are in essence 'words'. Using these words in sequence is an important step that increases the power of communication but also sets up the prerequisites for the development of grammar. Once two words can be strung together, the process of grammar creation can begin. When one word is used in combination with other words yielding a set meaning, a construction is born. The frequent use of the construction can lead to the development of a grammatical morpheme, as described here. The conclusion of this chapter agrees with Heine and Kuteva—the earliest language was one of words only; grammatical morphemes and grammatical constructions developed in much the same way as we can observe them developing today. Moreover, grammaticalization relies heavily on domain-general processes.

CHAPTER 56

# PIDGINS, CREOLES, AND THE CREATION OF LANGUAGE

## PAUL T. ROBERGE

A number of linguists have sought to identify phenomena that can be observed in (or deduced from) actual instantiations of language, and propose that these are of probative value for studying the evolution of human language. Three types of modern situations are thought to preserve modes of expression that emerged among our immediate hominin predecessors and/or to mirror processes underlying the subsequent development of language in our species: (1) situations in which full language has not developed or is disrupted; (2) situations in which people have created a language or part of a language, availing themselves only of certain minimal requirements for linguistic development, such as the existence of a lexical component prior to a syntactic one (Givón 1998, 2009; Bickerton 1990; Comrie 2000); and (3) the development of overt markers that encode syntactic organization out of lexical and discourse organization (Heine and Kuteva 2002a, 2007; Hurford 2003a). The thesis of this chapter is that 'modern' instances of language creation have properties that offer an 'analogue window' (in the sense of Botha 2006b, 2009c) on aspects of language evolution.

## 56.1 DEFINITIONS

A *pidgin* is the linguistic creation of a new contact community that has need for a medium of interethnic communication (MIC) for specific purposes (such as in trade or labour settings) but does not share a pre-existing language that can fulfil this function. Typically, this community comprises groups of people who speak mutually unintelligible and typologically different languages. Pidgins are restricted linguistic systems; that is, their range of lexical and structural means is limited in comparison to the resources available in full languages. Because pidgins arise in situations that require interethnic communication only in specialized domains by people who retain their heritage languages, they are not the native or primary language of any of their users. Botha (2009b: 106) discerns a tendency in the literature to ignore the fact that pidgins can develop a considerable degree of complexity. Pidgins represent dynamic phenomena that show qualitatively different developmental stages, ranging from unsystematic, ad hoc jargons, to more systematic but still highly restricted MICs displaying structural norms (pidgins *sensu stricto*), and to more elaborated MICs (extended pidgins) that come to be used in a variety of functions in a complex multilingual society.

The related concept, *creole language*, represents a class of vernaculars that emerged from the 17th through the 19th centuries under similar geographic, demographic, and economic conditions, viz in colonies settled by Europeans who typically spoke non-standard varieties of metropolitan languages and who put in place plantation economies that utilized non-indigenous slave or indentured labour (Mufwene 2008). Like pidgins, creoles formed in contact situations in which no group had the need, motivation, or opportunity to acquire the language of another group as a complete system. A labour force drawn from geographically different areas and representing heterogeneous linguistic backgrounds would have created a basic MIC to suit its immediate communicative needs. Speakers subsequently adapted and expanded the MIC, drawing on the linguistic resources at hand and also innovating (Baker 1990, 1997). Creoles differ from pidgins in that the former serve as the primary language of a speech community and are acquired as native languages (typically with concomitant language shift); once created, they are appointed with a wholly developed lexicon and grammatical system, like any other full human language. Additionally, they fulfil an indexical function, as mediums for community solidarity that are emblematic of locally born, labour-caste identity (Baker 2000).

## 56.2 BICKERTON'S HYPOTHESIS

Derek Bickerton is a creolist who has concentrated on the question of how language evolved (see Bickerton, this volume). Roughly 1.5–3 million years ago,

*Homo erectus* developed what Bickerton calls protolanguage, which designates a form of communication that contained arbitrary, meaningful symbols but lacked any kind of syntactic structure (Bickerton 1990, 2000, this volume; Calvin and Bickerton 2000; Jackendoff 2002; Tallerman, Chapter 51). The next stage in the evolution of language came about due to strong selective pressure for the development of a social calculus that would allow individuals to keep track of behaviours within their networks. At different times and on different occasions, the self and other could be performers of actions, the acted upon, or recipients of something that is acted upon. The exaptation of these abstract categories, which correspond (respectively) to the thematic roles of Agent, Theme, and Goal, provided a basis for syntactic structure. A predicate, its arguments, and appropriate thematic roles are the elements out of which phrases and clauses are built (Bickerton 1995, 1998, 2000, 2003; Calvin and Bickerton 2000). A third evolutionary stage saw the production of and competition among devices which, by a series of Baldwin effects, would enhance the efficient parsing and automatic comprehension of strings. Shared elements of human language (Universal Grammar) must have been in place in *Homo sapiens* not later than approximately 90,000 years ago (Bickerton 2007: 520).

In Bickerton's view protolanguage has left 'living linguistic fossils' in restricted systems, such as homesigns created by deaf children of hearing parents (Goldin-Meadow, this volume), untutored adult L2-acquisition, and early-stage pidgins (1990; cf. also Jackendoff 1999, 2002; Comrie 2000; Heine and Kuteva 2007; and contributions in Botha and De Swart 2009). A first cohort of pidgin speakers is forced to revert to a protolinguistic mode of communication, even though its users have full competence in existing languages. On plantations in European colonies, for example, the immigrant labour force, lacking a common lingua franca, drew lexis primarily from the superstrate (European) language, to which most members had little or no access. Such rudimentary codes are not true language but protolanguage, characterized, as they are, by sound-meaning correspondences that are strung together without phrase structure.

The formation of creoles is in essence an abrupt transition from protolanguage to full language. In the 'interesting' cases, at least, a pidgin—created by adults—has not existed for more than a generation and constitutes the primary linguistic data for their children (Bickerton 1990; Calvin and Bickerton 2000). While plantation children could have acquired the heritage languages of their parents, there was little incentive for them to do so in such a diverse milieu. Instead, they compiled a full-fledged language on the basis of input that is mixed, internally inconsistent—both across the speech community and within the output of individual speakers—and virtually structureless (Bickerton 1995, 2007; similarly, Givón 1979b: 224). Moreover, it is striking that the grammar of a creole bears the closest resemblance not to grammars of indigenous and/or immigrant (substrate) languages, nor to that of the dominant (superstrate) language, but rather to the grammars of creole languages in other parts of the world (Bickerton 2007). Bickerton has sought to explain these (in neither case undisputed) facts by appealing to a 'bioprogram' for language (1984) or what in more recent work he has called a 'biological template' (2007) that harks back to the emergence of *Homo sapiens*: 'Creole grammar constitutes a kind of "inner core grammar" from which more complex and varied grammars may have evolved' (1984: 188). Creole languages stand closer to the 'archetypal pattern of human language than older and more established languages do' (1995: 37); as such, they form 'an unusually direct expression of a species-specific biological characteristic, a capacity to recreate language in the absence of any specific model from which the properties of language could be "learned" in the ways we normally learn things' (1990: 171).

# 56.3 ASSESSMENT

The idea that a first generation of children on plantations quickly created creole languages, with all the basic features of human language that antecedent pidgins lacked, still holds currency in some work on language evolution (e.g. Pinker 2003). But contemporary theory has distanced itself from the view that creole formation requires the special intervention of children (e.g. Thomason and Kaufman 1988; Baker 2000; Mufwene 2008), and it has consistently resisted the proposition that children resourced a primeval grammar in extreme circumstances or that creole grammar reflects Universal Grammar in a direct or privileged way (Marantz 1983; Kihm 2002; Slobin 2002; Lightfoot 2006). Nativization is not a prerequisite for structural expansion, nor is creolization necessarily abrupt. Complex linguistic systems can arise out of long-term encounters between adults in contexts of increasing use of a restricted but developing MIC. Child language learners level out variability and produce more regular grammars, but they do not appear to be the innovators (Slobin 2002; Mufwene 2008). A case in point is Tok Pisin, a creolizing extended pidgin of Papua New Guinea in which features of complex syntax have arisen before there were native speakers.

The idea that restricted linguistic systems provide windows on certain facets of language evolution is taken quite seriously in evolutionary linguistics. Jackendoff (1999, 2002) claims to show not just that earlier stages of language are still present in the brain, but that their 'fossils' are present in the grammar of modern human language itself. These parts of language are not subject to critical-period limitations and are immune to degradation when the transmission of language is disrupted. Fossil phenomena include the following:

- The acquisition of vocabulary.
- Single-symbol utterances that are interpretable as propositions (holophrasis), e.g. Cape Dutch Pidgin (spoken ca. 1658–1800) *tabackum* 'tobacco' (in context 'Give me tobacco', 'I want to barter for tobacco').

- Free concatenation of words (*Hottentott brukwa* 'Hottentot piece', i.e. 'Give this Khoikhoi a piece of bread').
- Simple, semantically-based principles of word order (cf. also Mufwene 2008) such as Agent First and Focus Last (the natural mirror image of which is Topic First); Grouping ('modifiers tend to be adjacent to what they modify', Jackendoff 2002: 248), and
- Nominal compounding (e.g. Cape Dutch Pidgin *bacaleij booij*, 'fight boy', i.e. 'Khoikhoi warrior').

The survival of these features—and not others (such as the details of phonology, phrase structure, and especially inflectional morphology)—in 'degraded' forms of language may serve as evidence for their 'evolutionarily more primitive character' (Jackendoff 1999: 276). Those subcomponents that *are* particularly prone to disruption are the same ones in case after case, the remnant of which is protolanguage (Jackendoff 2002: 264). Jackendoff portrays grammar as a collection of simpler systems, many of which are built up as refinements of pre-existing interfaces between components. We can extrapolate from modern human language a sequence of partially ordered evolutionary steps or stages in the emergence of language in our species. Some of these stages are prior to protolanguage in Bickerton's sense, and some later; each is an improvement in terms of expressive power and precision. Hence, the evolution of the human language faculty can be seen as 'deeply incremental' (Jackendoff 2002: 264).

Givón (1979b, 1998, 2009) characterizes incipient pidgins as instantiations of what he has called the 'pragmatic' or 'pregrammatical' mode of communication. They conform to several 'rules' that reflect cognitively 'natural' (i.e. transparent, iconic) meaning-form pairings, such as 'Information chunks that belong together conceptually are kept in closer spatio-temporal proximity'; and 'predictable—or already activated—information will be left unexpressed' (Givón 2009: 244). Jargonized communication exhibits properties that are characteristic of a pregrammatical evolutionary stage. In addition to the regularities of 'pregrammar' or 'protogrammar', these properties include mostly concrete vocabulary, lack of inflectional morphology, typically short clauses (1–3 words), clause chaining rather than embedding, and heavy reliance on the lexicon and context. Critical steps in the evolution of grammar, which is the last major developmental phase in the evolution of language, would entail a progression from one-word, mono-propositional communication, to the appearance of protogrammar and multi-propositional discourse (akin to the pregrammatical pidgin mode), and then to the integration of protogrammar into the more 'arbitrary' (i.e. symbolic) encoding of the emergent grammatical mode.

# 56.4 PIDGIN FORMATION AS
## LANGUAGE CREATION

As for what pidgins might actually tell us about language evolution, the focus has thus far been on properties that can be imputed to protolanguage. The extent to which pragmatics figures in the use of pidgins can be taken to correlate with the restricted nature of their linguistic resources. If protolanguage was similarly restricted, then these factors would have to be assigned a significant role (Botha 2006b). The next pertinent question is whether the evolution from simpler to more complex systems in the remote past could have analogues in processes that are observable in or inferable from modern language.

On the basis of evidence from grammaticalization, whereby lexical items acquire specialized grammatical meanings in a unidirectional progression, Heine and Kuteva (2002a, 2007, this volume) wish to show how language systems could have become increasingly complex once humans had achieved a state of language readiness. 'Early language'—at the point at which mutability becomes an inherent characteristic—can be thought of as an essentially lexical stage that saw the emergence of nouns and verbs but must have lacked function words and grammatical morphemes; the structure hypothesized resembles that of incipient pidgins (cf. also Hurford 2003a; Tallerman 2007). Once a noun–verb distinction is in place, 'many other design features can collect around it' (Jackendoff 2002: 259), and 'grammaticalization now becomes the driving force of grammatical evolution' (Heine and Kuteva 2007: 303). Botha's (2009b) criticism of Heine and Kuteva's position concentrates on an ill-defined notion of 'early language' and associated conflation of language evolution and language change, the latter of which is non-phylogenetic.

One factor that differentiates modern pidgins from the situation of ancestral forms of communication is that the former have been developed largely through interactions between adults who are in possession of a fully evolved *faculté de langage* and have proficiency in one or more modern languages (McDaniel 2005; Heine and Kuteva 2007; Mufwene 2008). According to a widely held view, pidginization involves severe reduction (loss of referential and non-referential power) and simplification (regularization) of full languages (Heine and Kuteva 2002a, 2007; Jackendoff 2002; Mufwene 2008). In this respect, directionality in pidgin formation (from complex to less complex systems) would seem exactly the opposite of how language evolution must have proceeded (Botha 2006b; Heine and Kuteva 2007). Moreover, linguistic objects (i.e. beyond lexis) can be drawn directly or adapted from the languages in contact. Mufwene (2008: 283) goes so far as to assert that most, if not all grammatical features of pidgins have been selected from the relevant superstrate and/or substrate languages. If pidgins 'inherit' a portion of their structural features from pre-existing languages, then their significance for our present purpose is diminished (cf. Comrie 2000; Heine and Kuteva 2002a, 2007).

The 'constructive' model of Baker (2000) sets aside the proposition that each pidgin represents a 'degraded' version of a pre-existing language. One language in the mix typically provides the bulk of lexis in the emerging MIC, but speakers are not attempting to acquire that language in any meaningful sense. The process is one of communal language construction rather than partial L2-acquisition and/or L1-restructuring. Baker's model and its implications for evolutionary linguistics are examined in detail in Roberge (2009). What follows is a précis of the main points.

Jargons, which are often indiscriminately lumped together with pidgins (in the restrictive sense discussed earlier), are aggregates of individual solutions to the problem of interethnic communication. They are characterized by a high degree of variability, transfer from languages known to the speakers, feature stripping, and a lack of linguistic norms (although at a minimal level they do share properties with the pre-Basic and Basic Variety, described in Benazzo 2009). The transition from jargon to stable pidgin coincides with the formation of a language community and the emergence of socially accepted norms, which occurs when none of the languages in a heterogeneous milieu serves as a target language (Mühlhäusler 1997). Directionality during the stabilization of pidgins is internal; that is, the target is the linguistic system that speakers are actually constructing (Thomason and Kaufman 1988; Baker 1997; Mühlhäusler 1997).

Moreover—critically—when a highly diverse population participates in the construction of a MIC, L1-transfer should not be of great significance beyond the jargon phase. In such an ecology, innovative solutions to the problem of interethnic communication are preferred; areal and linguistic-typological heterogeneity inhibits the selection of patterns that are characteristic of one group (cf. Mühlhäusler 1997). Of central interest to the study of language evolution are the competition and selection of features during the emergence of communal norms (cf. Mufwene 2008), and the creation of structures and grammatical categories *de novo*, that is, without reference to linguistic objects in the contact languages. Consider, for example, the Cape Dutch Pidgin datum *baasje loop haal vuur* (literally 'little-boss go fetch fire'—a slave is speaking to his owner's son; the meaning is roughly 'Young master, go get me a light (for my pipe)'). The juxtaposition of andative *loop* 'go, walk, run' with the lexical verb *haal* represents a bridge from the unregulated concatenation of words to a wholly innovated syntactic structure, specifically, V+V incorporation (found in vernacular Afrikaans *Hy loop koop toe 'n nuwe kar* 'He then went off and bought a new car' beside Standard *Hy loop toe 'n nuwe kar koop*, with V2/OV order). It is this complexification of grammar through innovation that is claimed to have had analogues in language evolution.

The ecologies in which early language emerged and in which modern pidgins have formed are generally assumed to differ in important ways (Botha 2006b; Heine and Kuteva 2007; Mufwene 2008). Pidgin use is confined to a small number of communicative domains. There is no reason to suppose that early human language was so confined. Here, one should recall that the interlingual function is at the core of what characterizes a pidgin. All pidgins and creoles are—or were, formerly—MICs. The pressures driving the stabilization and structural elaboration of pidgins can be related to expanding domains of communication and the need for predictability and automaticity.

The elaboration of modern human language out of protolanguage can only have coincided with the increasing complexity of early human society (Givón 1998: 96; Johansson 2005: 239). Since Saussure (1916[1976: 263]), proposals that languages ultimately share a common origin in one place and time and in a single group have faced at best a mixed reception. Indeed, there can have been no single moment at which the language faculty itself crystallized (see Hurford and Dediu 2009). More probable is that human language commenced with the appearance of more or less discrete communication systems within small bands of people; see Nichols, this volume. Characteristic of human culture is its cumulative nature and growth in complexity and diversity with time, indeed at such a rate that our ancestors 'could not communicate about their world without constantly evolving better ways of communicating' (Odling-Smee and Laland 2009: 120). Diversity in material culture creates the opportunity for trade; 'with trade comes negotiation, and further selection for effective communication' (ibid). With higher frequencies of contact between bands came an increased need for individuals to exchange information in group-external settings and the establishment of cross-group communication net-works. Increasingly complex grammars took shape as communicative require-ments become more demanding.

This brings us to the commensurability of the cognitive capacities of the agents of grammar construction. Givón believes that *Homo sapiens* built its communica-tion system on a pre-existing 'neuro-cognitive platform' that included semantic memory (words), event representation (word concatenation), and event-episodic representation (clause concatenation) (2009: 336). The adaptive impetus to go beyond this platform was rooted in the demands of communication. The windows approach postulates that modern pidgin speakers return to the pregrammatical mode of speaking and can (under the right conditions) create new, language-independent rules in order to meet their expanding communicative needs. The developmental processes they utilize (e.g. the Merge operation, extrapolation of functional categories out of lexical meaning) are presumed to recapitulate those of our hominin ancestors. But at present, it is unclear to what extent the possession of full language is a factor in modern constructions of a grammatical mode of speaking. Kihm (2002) and Benazzo (2009) believe that comparison with other processes that illustrate the creation of language anew is indicated, specifically the spontaneous invention of signed languages. Nevertheless, a properly constructed pidgin window on language evolution holds great heuristic promise.

..................................................

# CHAPTER 57

# WHAT MODERN-DAY GESTURE CAN TELL US ABOUT LANGUAGE EVOLUTION

..................................................

## SUSAN GOLDIN-MEADOW

### 57.1 INTRODUCTION

..................................................................................

Humans are equipotential with respect to language-learning—if exposed to language in the manual modality, children will learn a sign language as quickly and effortlessly as they learn a spoken language. Why then has the oral modality become the modality of choice for languages around the globe? The oral modality might have triumphed over the manual modality simply because it is so good at encoding messages in the segmented and combinatorial form that human languages have come to assume. But this is not the case—the manual modality is just as good as the oral modality at segmented and combinatorial encoding, as evidenced by sign languages of the deaf. There is thus little to choose between sign and speech on these grounds. However, language serves another important function—it conveys information imagistically. The oral modality is not well suited to this function, but the manual modality excels at it. Indeed, the manual modality has taken over this role (in the form of spontaneous gestures that accompany speech) in all cultures. It is possible, then, that the oral modality assumes the segmented and combinatorial format not because of its strengths, but to compensate for its weaknesses (Goldin-Meadow and McNeill 1999).

This argument rests on a crucial assumption—that imagistic information is an important aspect of human communication and that it is well served by representation in the manual modality. The present chapter examines the gestures that hearing speakers produce when they talk to provide evidence for this assumption and focuses on two roles of gesture: when the manual modality works along with speech to fulfil the functions of language, (1) its imagistic encoding fills in gaps left by speech and thus plays an important communicative role for the listener, and (2) its imagistic encoding helps speakers think and thus plays an important cognitive role for the speaker. The chapter then explores the changes that take place in the manual modality when it is called upon to fulfil the functions of language on its own, that is, when it works alone without speech in both established and newly-emerging sign languages. The chapter ends with a brief discussion of the advantages of a language system that contains both an imagistic and a segmented format, and the implications of the phenomenon for linguistic evolution.

## 57.2 WHEN THE MANUAL MODALITY SHARES THE FUNCTIONS OF LANGUAGE WITH THE ORAL MODALITY

### 57.2.1 The properties of gesture accompanying speech

McNeill (1992) has argued that the gestures that accompany speech form a single integrated system with that speech, with each modality best suited to expressing its own set of meanings. Speech reflects a linear-segmented, hierarchical linguistic structure, utilizing a grammatical pattern that embodies the language's standards of form and drawing on an agreed-upon lexicon of words. In contrast, gesture reflects a global-synthetic image. It is idiosyncratic and constructed at the moment of speaking—it does not belong to a conventional code. Consider, for example, a speaker who is describing the east coast of the United States and produces a gesture tracing the shape of the coastline. The gesture conveys nuances of the coastline that are difficult, if not impossible, to capture in speech. Gesture thus allows speakers to convey thoughts that may not easily fit into the categorical system that their conventional language offers (Goldin-Meadow 2003a).

McNeill (1992: 41) lists the fundamental properties of the gestures that accompany speech as follows:

(i) Gestures are global in meaning. The meanings of the parts of a gesture are determined by the whole (and not *vice versa,* as is the case in speech). Indeed, the parts of a gesture cannot really be considered isolable units, as they are dependent for their meaning on the whole. In contrast to the bottom-up structure of sentences, there is consequently a top-down structure *within a gesture.*

(ii) Gestures are non-combinatoric. Gestures do not combine to form larger, hierarchically structured gestures. Most gestures are one to a clause and, even when there are successive gestures within a clause, each corresponds to an idea unit in and of itself. There is, as a result, no hierarchical structure *across gestures* (though there may be other kinds of non-hierarchical structure; see McNeill (1992)).

(iii) Gestures are context-sensitive. They are free to incorporate only the salient and relevant aspects of the context. Each gesture is created at the moment of speaking and highlights what is relevant. Because of the sensitivity of gestures to the context of the moment, there is variability in the forms gesture takes *within a speaker.*

(iv) Gestures do not have standards of form. Different speakers display the same meanings in idiosyncratic ways. There is consequently variability in the forms gesture takes *across speakers.* Even when there is cross-speaker similarity, this is not because of standards but because of similarity of meaning—similar meanings engender similar gestures.

It is often easy to analyse a given gesture into parts, but these parts have a different status from the parts of sentences—they are individually constructed with meanings that are determined by the context and that percolate from the top down. For example, in describing an individual running, a speaker moved his hand forward while wiggling his index and middle fingers (McNeill 1992). The parts of this gesture gain meaning because of the meaning of the whole; the wiggling fingers mean 'running' only because we know that the gesture, as a whole, depicts someone running and not because this speaker uses wiggling fingers to mean running in any other context. Indeed, in other gestures produced by this same speaker, wiggling fingers may well have a very different meaning (such as indecision between two alternatives). To argue that the wiggling fingers gesture is composed of separately meaningful parts, one would have to show that each of the three components that comprise the gesture—the V handshape, the wiggling motion, and the forward motion—is used for a stable meaning across the speaker's gestural repertoire. There is no evidence for stability of this sort in co-speech gestures (McNeill 1992; Goldin-Meadow et al. 1995).

Thus, the gestures that accompany speech are not composed of parts but instead have parts that derive from wholes. Moreover, they are wholes that represent by way of imagery. Because the gesture as a whole must be a good (that is, relatively transparent) representation of its referent, the addition of semantic information to a spontaneous gesture never decreases its iconicity.

## 57.2.2 The imagistic information encoded in the manual modality plays a role in communication

The imagistic base of gesture allows it to capture and reveal information that speakers may have difficulty expressing in speech. As a result, gesture offers listeners insight into information that cannot be gotten by listening. Gesture thus has the potential to play a unique role in communication.

Take as an example a child describing why she thinks that the water in a tall, thin container is a different amount from the water in a short, fat container. She says, 'it's different because this one's tall and that one's short', while holding a flat palm first at the height of the water in the tall container and then at the height of the water in the short container. The child focuses on the height dimension of the containers in both speech and gesture. Now consider a child who also focuses on height in his speech, but does so while producing first a narrow C-shaped gesture indicating the width of the tall container and then a larger C-shaped gesture indicating the width of the short container. This child focuses on the height of the containers in speech, but their width in gesture.

In order to fully understand that the amount of water in the two containers is the same, the child needs to understand that height and width compensate for one another—that the taller height of the first container is offset by its narrower width, and that the shorter height of the second container is offset by its larger width. The second child has noticed both dimensions and, although he says that the amount of water in the two containers is different, he is well on his way toward grasping the concept of conservation of quantity. When both children are given instruction in the concept, the second child, the one whose gestures convey information *not* found in speech, is more likely to benefit from the instruction than the first, whose gestures convey the same information in gesture and speech (Church and Goldin-Meadow 1986).

If gesture can reveal unspoken thoughts, those thoughts are then 'out there' and can be part of the conversation—assuming, of course, that gesture can be read by ordinary listeners in ordinary circumstances. And it can. Everyone can read gesture, young or old, in an experiment or in real-life communication. In fact, the information we take from speech is affected by the gestures that accompany speech (Goldin-Meadow and Sandhofer 1999). For example, children and adults are *more* likely to glean the message conveyed in speech when it is accompanied by gesture conveying the same information than when it is accompanied by no gesture at all. Conversely, listeners are *less* likely to glean the message in speech when it is accompanied by gesture conveying a different message than when it is accompanied by no gesture.

These facts raise the possibility that, by playing a role in communication, gesture can lead to cognitive change in the gesturer. If children reveal their readiness for instruction simply by moving their hands, and if listeners are attentive to those movements and change their responses accordingly, gesture can provide an indirect way for children (and all learners) to tell their teachers what they need next. A teacher would be able to recognize that the two children described earlier in the conservation of quantity example differ in how well they understand conservation only if the teacher paid attention to the children's gestures as well as their speech. Teachers do, in fact, attend to the gestures that their pupils produce. Moreover, they alter the instruction they give their pupils (both their speech and their gestures) as a function of the children's gestures (Goldin-Meadow and Singer 2003). Gesture can thus change the course of learning by influencing the kind of input the learner receives.

Interestingly, speakers are often not aware that they are moving their hands when they speak, and listeners rarely know whether the information they glean from a conversation comes from the speaker's hands or mouth. Nonetheless, gestures that seem to be invisible have a noticeable impact on communication.

## 57.2.3 The imagistic information encoded in the manual modality plays a role in thinking

Gesture thus has an impact on listeners. But it can also have an effect on the speakers themselves. We have all had the experience of finding ourselves gesturing when no one is watching. We may feel sheepish about it but that does not stop us. Why do we gesture when we speak? Perhaps because gesturing helps us think. Indeed, there is evidence that gesturing can make it easier to retrieve words (Krauss et al. 2000), to package ideas into words (Kita 2000), to tie words to the real world (Glenberg and Robertson 1999), and to remember an unrelated list of words (Goldin-Meadow et al. 2001). By freeing resources that can be used for other tasks, gesturing has the potential to contribute to cognitive growth.

Gesture can also play a role in cognitive growth by providing an imagistic route through which ideas can be made active or brought into the learner's repertoire. For example, telling children to gesture while they explain their solutions to a maths problem brings out new, and correct, ideas in gesture about how to solve the problem. Interestingly, at the same time that they are producing these correct ideas in gesture, the children continue to solve the problems incorrectly and to produce incorrect problem-solving strategies in speech. However, if the children are then given instruction in how to solve the problems, they are more likely to profit from the instruction than children who were told not to gesture (Broaders et al. 2007). Gesturing thus brings out implicit ideas, which, in turn, can lead to learning.

Even more striking, we can introduce new ideas into children's cognitive repertoires by telling them how to move their hands. For example, if we make children sweep their left hand under the left side of the mathematical equation $3+6+4=\_\_+4$ and their right hand under the right side of the equation during instruction, they learn how to solve problems of this type. Moreover, they are more likely to succeed on the problems than children told to say, 'The way to solve the problem is to make one side of the problem equal to the other side' (Cook et al. 2007).

How does gesturing promote new ideas? The children may be extracting meaning from the hand movements they are told to produce. If so, they should be sensitive to the particular movements they produce and learn accordingly. Alternatively, all that may matter is that the children are moving their hands. If so, they should learn regardless of which movements they produce. In fact, children who were told to produce movements instantiating a correct rendition of the grouping strategy during instruction (such as a V-hand placed under the 3 and 6 in the $3+6+4=\_\_+4$ problem, followed by a point at the blank) solved more problems correctly after instruction than children told to produce movements instantiating a partially correct strategy (such as a V-hand placed under the 6 and 4, followed by a point at the blank), and the latter group, in turn, solved more problems correctly than children told not to gesture at all (Goldin-Meadow et al. 2009). Importantly, this effect was mediated by whether children added the grouping strategy to their post-instruction spoken repertoires. Because the grouping strategy was never expressed in speech during instruction by either child or teacher, nor was it expressed in gesture by the teacher, the information that children incorporated into their post-instruction speech must have come from their own gestures. We may be able to lay foundations for new knowledge simply by telling learners how to move their hands.

Moreover, the manual modality may be a particularly good venue for innovation because ideas expressed in this modality may be less likely to be challenged (or even noticed) than ideas expressed in the more explicit and recognized oral modality. Because gesture is less codified and less monitored than speech, it may be more welcoming of fresh ideas than speech.

## 57.3 WHEN THE MANUAL MODALITY TAKES OVER ALL OF THE FUNCTIONS OF LANGUAGE

We have seen that the manual modality conveys information imagistically, and that this information has an important role to play in both communication and thinking. The manual modality assumes an imagistic form when it is used in conjunction with a segmented and combinatorial system (i.e. speech). But what happens when the manual modality must fulfil all of the functions of language on its own? It turns out that, under these circumstances, the manual modality changes its form and itself becomes segmented and combinatorial. We see this phenomenon in conventional sign languages passed down from one generation to the next, but it is also found, and is particularly striking, in emerging sign languages.

## 57.3.1 Conventional sign languages

Sign languages of the deaf are autonomous languages, independent of the spoken languages of hearing cultures. Despite the fact that they are processed by the hand and the eye and not the mouth and the ear, sign languages have the essential properties of segmentation and combination that characterize all spoken language systems (Klima and Bellugi 1979; Sandler and Lillo-Martin 2006). Sign languages are structured at the sentence level (syntactic structure), at the sign level (morphological structure), and at the level of sub-sign, and have meaningless elements akin to phonemes ('phonological' structure). Just like words in spoken languages (but unlike the gestures that accompany speech), signs combine to create larger wholes (sentences) that are typically characterized by a basic order, for example, SVO (Subject–Verb–Object) in American Sign Language (ASL); SOV in Sign Language of the Netherlands. Moreover, the signs that comprise the sentences are themselves composed of meaningful components (morphemes).

Although the signs in a language like ASL often look iconic, this iconicity does not appear to play an important role in the way signers process sign, nor in the way children acquire sign. For example, young children are just as likely to learn a sign whose form does not resemble its referent as a sign whose form is an iconic depiction of the referent. Moreover, many signs and grammatical devices do not have an iconic relation to the meanings they represent. For example, the sign for 'slow' in ASL is made by moving one hand across the back of the other hand. When the sign is modified to be 'very slow', it is made more rapidly since this is the particular modification of movement associated with an intensification meaning in ASL (Klima and Bellugi 1979). Thus, modifying the meaning of a sign can reduce its iconicity in a conventional sign language simply because the meaning of the sign as a whole is made up of the meanings of the components that comprise it.

In contrast, as described earlier, the gestures that accompany speech are not composed of parts but are instead non-compositional wholes. Since the gesture as a whole must be a good representation of its referent, the addition of semantic information to a spontaneous gesture always increases its iconicity—if something is thought of as very slow, the gesture for it is also very slow (McNeill 1992). The gesture *as a whole* represents 'very slow', and although one could, in principle, break up the gesture into two parts (such as 'slow', a movement across the back of the hand, and 'very', an exaggerated and slowed movement), there is no evidence that these particular forms have independent and consistent meaning across a range of gestures—as they would have to if they were part of a combinatorial system in a conventional sign language (we later consider whether signers gesture).

## 57.3.2 Emerging sign languages

Not only is segmentation and combination characteristic of communication in the manual modality when that communication has been conventionalized within a community over generations, but it is also a salient feature of emerging manual communication systems. We consider three different systems, all of which display the properties of segmentation and combination: (1) the gestures invented by a deaf child who has not been exposed to a conventional sign language to communicate with hearing individuals—a system of homesigns developed over a period of years by a deaf child; (2) the gestures that arise when homesigners are brought together for the first time and that change over time as new learners enter the community—newly developing sign languages developed over decades by a community; (3) the gestures that hearing individuals create in an experimental situation when asked to communicate using their hands and not their mouths—signs developed on-the-spot by hearing adults.

### 57.3.2.1 *Signs invented by a homesigner*

Deaf children exposed from birth to a conventional sign language such as ASL acquire that language in stages comparable to those followed by hearing children acquiring a spoken language. However, 90% of deaf children are not born to deaf parents who can provide early exposure to conventional sign language. Rather, they are born to hearing parents who, not surprisingly, speak to their children. Unfortunately, it is extremely uncommon for deaf children with severe to profound hearing losses to acquire spontaneously the spoken language of their hearing parents and, even with intensive instruction, their speech is very likely to be markedly delayed. In addition, unless hearing parents send their deaf children to a school in which sign language is used, the children are not likely to be exposed to a conventional sign system.

Despite their lack of a usable model of conventional language, deaf children of hearing parents manage to communicate and do so by means of a self-created system of homesigns. These systems are characterized by a variety of language-like properties, including segmentation and combination (Goldin-Meadow 2003b, 2005). Rather than communicate the way a mime artist would, enacting an event as veridically as possible, the child conveys messages using segmented gestures combined into a consistently structured string. For example, rather than going over to the cookie jar and pretending to remove the cookie and eat it, the child points toward the cookie and then jabs her hand several times toward her mouth, effectively conveying 'cookie-eat'. The gesture strings generated by each of the deaf children can be described in terms of very simple patterns. These patterns predict which semantic elements are likely to be gestured and where in the gesture string those elements are likely to be produced. For example, deaf children inventing homesigns in different countries (China, United States) tend to leave gestures for the agent (S) out of their gesture sentences, as do many languages (even English has a form that permits agent omission, the truncated passive: *the ball was hit*, as opposed to *the ball was hit by the boy*). The deaf children typically produce a gesture for the object (O) and a gesture for the action (V) and, importantly, they produce these gestures in a consistent order, placing the O gesture before the V gesture; in other words, they follow an OV order (Goldin-Meadow and Mylander 1998). The gesture systems thus have sentence-like structure.

In addition to structure at the sentence level, each deaf child's homesign system also has structure at the word level (Goldin-Meadow et al. 1995, 2007). Each gesture is composed of a handshape and a motion component, and the meaning of the gesture as a whole is determined by the meanings of each of these parts. For example, a child moves his hand shaped like an O in a short motion arcing downward to request the experimenter to lay a penny down flat. The O-handshape represents a 'round object' (the penny) in this gesture and in the child's entire corpus of gestures, and the short-arc motion represents 'put down', again across the entire gesture corpus. When produced together within a single gesture, the component parts combine to create the meaning of the whole, 'put down a round object'.

Importantly, the structure found at the sentence and word levels in each of the deaf children's gesture systems cannot be traced back to the spontaneous gestures that their hearing parents produced while talking to them. The children see the global and unsegmented gestures that their parents produce. But when gesturing themselves, they generate gestures that are discrete, segmented forms joined together into structured strings. The children thus transform the unsegmented gestures they see into a segmented and combinatorial system of their own.

### 57.3.2.2 *Signs invented by a community of homesigners*

Nicaraguan Sign Language offers a unique opportunity to watch a sign language become increasingly complex over generations of creators. The initial step in the creation process took place when deaf children in Managua were brought together for the first time in an educational setting. The deaf children had been born to hearing parents and each was likely to have invented his or her own homesign system. When brought together, they needed to develop a common sign language. Not surprisingly given its homesign roots, the system generated by this first cohort of signers was characterized by segmentation and combination (Kegl et al. 1999). But Nicaraguan Sign Language did not stop there. Every year, new students entered the school and learned to sign among their peers. The second cohort of signers had as its input the sign system developed by the first cohort and, over the course of two decades, changed the system so that it became more language-like (Senghas and Coppola 2001).

The second cohort of signers, in a sense, stands on the shoulders of the first. It does not need to introduce segmentation and combination into the system—those properties are already present in their input. They can therefore take the transformation process one step further. But it may be the Nicaraguan homesigners (and homesigners all over the globe) who take the first, and perhaps the most transformative, step—they change hearing speakers' gestures, which are global and synthetic, into a segmented and combinatorial system. Subsequent learners are then able to build on these properties, creating a system that looks more and more like the natural languages of the world.

The situation in Nicaragua is not unique. As another example, a community, now in its seventh generation and containing 3500 members, was founded 200 years ago in Israel by the Al-Sayyid Bedouins. Within the last three generations, 150 deaf individuals were born into this community, all descended from two of the founders' five sons. Al-Sayyid Bedouin Sign Language (ABSL) was thus born (Sandler et al. 2005). With three generations of signers, there is an opportunity not only to glimpse a language in its infant stages but also to watch how it has grown. For example, highly regular sign order evolved to mark grammatical relations in ABSL within the first generation; the particular order used is SOV. However, the language appears to have developed very little, if any, complex morphology (Aronoff et al. 2004, although it is worth noting that not all spoken languages have rich morphological structure either).

ABSL is not yet a mature language and thus is still undergoing change. As a result, signers from each of the three generations are likely to differ, and to differ systematically, in the system of signs they use. By observing signers from each generation, we can therefore make good guesses as to when a particular linguistic property first entered the language. Moreover, because the individual families in the community are tightly knit, with strong bonds within families but not across them, we can chart changes in the language in relation to the social network of the community. We can determine when properties remained within a single family and when they did not, and thus follow the trajectory that particular linguistic properties took as they spread (or failed to spread) throughout the community. This small and self-contained community consequently offers a unique perspective on some classic questions in historical linguistics.

Like Nicaraguan Sign Language, ABSL has arisen with no influence from any established language, either signed or spoken. However, ABSL differs from Nicaraguan Sign Language in that it is developing in a socially stable community with children learning the system from their parents. The differences and similarities between the two systems can thus provide useful information about the trajectories that languages follow as they grow from a homesign system into a fully formed conventional sign language.

## 57.3.2.3  *Signs invented by a hearing adult*

The findings reviewed thus far suggest that segmentation and combination are fundamental to human language. Note that these properties are not forced upon language by the modality in which it is expressed. Segmentation and combination are found in human language whether it is produced in the oral or manual modality. Moreover, segmentation and combination are not inevitable in the manual modality—they are not found when the manual modality is used along with speech, that is, when hearing people produce co-speech gestures.

What then determines when segmentation and combination will arise in the manual modality? One possibility is that segmentation and combination crop up in the manual modality only when it takes on the primary burden of communication. To test this hypothesis, we can examine hearing adults' gestures when those gestures are produced with speech (sharing the communicative burden) and when they are produced instead of speech (shouldering the entire communicative burden). The gestures adults produce without speech ought to display segmentation and combination and thus be distinct from the gestures the adults produce with speech.

This prediction was confirmed (Goldin-Meadow et al. 1996). When they produced gesture without speech, the adults frequently combined those gestures into strings and the strings were consistently ordered, with gestures for certain semantic elements occurring in particular positions in the string; that is, there was structure across the gestures at the sentence level. In addition, the verb-like action gestures that the adults produced could be divided into handshape and motion parts, with the handshape of the action frequently conveying information about the objects in its semantic frame; that is, there was structure within the gesture at the word level (although the adults did not develop a system of contrasts within their gestures, a characteristic of deaf homesigners' systems; Goldin-Meadow et al. 1995, 2007). Thus, the adults produced gestures characterized by segmentation and combination and did so with essentially no time for reflection on what might be fundamental to language-like communication.

The appearance of segmentation and combination in adults' gestures produced without speech is particularly striking given that these properties were *not* found in the gestures that these same adults produced *with* speech—their co-speech gestures were rarely combined into strings, and handshape was rarely used to convey object information within a gesture (Goldin-Meadow et al. 1996). In other words, the adults did not use their gestures as building blocks for larger sentence or word units. Rather, they used their gestures to imagistically depict the scenes they described, as speakers typically do when they spontaneously gesture along with their talk.

Interestingly, when hearing speakers of a variety of languages (Chinese, Turkish, and Spanish, as well as English) are asked to describe a series of events using only their hands, they not only produce strings of segmented gestures characterized by consistent order, but those strings all display the same gesture order—even though the speakers use the predominant orders of their respective languages (and thus use different orders) when describing the same scenes in speech (Goldin-Meadow et al. 2008). The gesture order that all speakers-turned-signers use is SOV—precisely the order that we see in the early stages of other emerging sign systems (ABSL and the homesigns developed by individual deaf children). This order may reflect a natural ordering that humans exploit when creating a communication system over short and long time spans.

## 57.4 THE ADVANTAGES OF A COMMUNICATION SYSTEM WITH BOTH A SEGMENTED AND AN IMAGISTIC REPRESENTATIONAL FORMAT

Modern-day human communication systems are based on a segmented and combinatorial mode of representation (typically conveyed in the oral modality) that gives the system its generative capacity. But they also have an imagistic mode of representation (in the manual modality) that exists alongside, and that gives the system the ability to be responsive to the communicative needs of the moment. The gestures that speakers produce in the manual modality can express information that they are often not able to express within the codified spoken system. This information is processed by the listener (not necessarily consciously) and becomes part of the conversation. Moreover, once information has been expressed in the manual modality, it can catalyse change in the speaker and eventually find its way into the oral modality. Thus, there is an imagistic side to human communication that plays an important role in both communication and thinking.

If we grant that there are advantages to a communication system with both a segmented/combinatorial format and an imagistic format, we can then understand why language is the province of the oral modality. Whereas the oral modality and the manual modality can assume the segmented and combinatorial format equally well, the manual modality is particularly well suited to the imagistic format. It therefore takes over this function, leaving segmentation and combination, the hallmarks of the linguistic code, to the oral modality.

This speculation raises an interesting question about sign language. In sign, the manual modality assumes the segmented and combinatorial format essential to human language. Can the manual modality at the same time be used for imagistic expression? In other words, do signers gesture? They may (Emmorey 1999), perhaps with their mouths (for instance, one Israeli signer puffed out her cheek when signing about carrying a valise; her mouth gesture, and only her mouth gesture, made it clear that the valise was full; Sandler 2003). But the oral modality can also be used in limited ways for imagistic expression (for instance, the speed at which an object moves can be captured in the speed of the speech describing it; Shintel et al. 2006). Although it is possible to have both functions served by the same modality, it may be more efficient to separate the imagistic and segmented/combinatorial forms of representation by modality.

Does the fact that there is both an imagistic and a segmented side to modern-day communication bear on the question of linguistic evolution? It is possible, as Donald argues (1991, this volume), that the mimetic function preceded and, over evolutionary time, led to the current day analytic structures that characterize language. But it is equally possible that the two functions were present in our communicative efforts from the beginning, and that the oral and manual modalities have always worked together to fulfil our communicative needs, evolving together to produce the single system that characterizes our modern-day language.

# CHAPTER 58

# MONOGENESIS OR POLYGENESIS: A SINGLE ANCESTRAL LANGUAGE FOR ALL HUMANITY?

## JOHANNA NICHOLS

## 58.1 INTRODUCTION

Comparative-historical linguistics cannot tell us whether all the world's languages descend from a single ancestor, as its resolution seems to fade out not far beyond the roughly 6000–7000 years representing the age of the oldest reconstructable families. Typology and linguistic geography can have greater temporal scope, and though they cannot identify or reconstruct protolanguages they do have something to say on the matter of monogenesis.

The term *language* is used here to mean modern human language as we know it; *pre-language* refers to whatever was immediately prior and ancestral to language (with no claims about its structure). *Proto-World* will be used of a hypothetical monogenetic ancestor language, with no claim as to its reality. *Pre-modern humans* is a very broad term covering all ancestral and archaic types up to the development of modern humans some 180–200 kya (thousand years ago), but in fact referring here primarily to the immediate ancestors and near-contemporaries of the first modern humans (when it is necessary to make this explicit I use *late pre-modern humans*). For simplicity I deal only with spoken language, though the same arguments apply if gesture is included.

## 58.2 THE TRANSITION TO LANGUAGE

Beginning sometime after our divergence from chimpanzees, a suite of physiological, neurological, developmental, and behavioural changes was set into motion that eventually resulted in language, with phonological and grammatical complexity, a brain wired for language, a vocal tract uniquely adapted to speech, and acquisition of language by young children with little or no instruction. Late pre-modern humans had a largely modern anatomy, including braincase, jaw, and hyoid bone anatomy that were the apparent product of selection for the ability to function in speech production (MacLarnon, this volume). Early modern humans, beginning close to 100 kya, leave cultural remains indicating symbolic capacity whenever demographic circumstances are favourable, and this suggests that the cognitive capacity for abstract thinking, symbolic behaviour, and complex knowledge was present in modern humans from the very beginning, but the possibility of the actual behaviour being innovated and transmitted must have depended on regional population size (Powell et al. 2009). These things are consistent with an assumption that late pre-modern humans had at least pre-language and early modern humans had full language capacity and therefore language. For simplicity, in what follows I will operate with the assumption that the transition from anatomically pre-modern to modern coincided with the transition from pre-language to language; this of course schematizes what must have been a gradual matter both physiologically and linguistically. The argument that follows amounts to showing that on the schematic view language could not have had a single ancestor, and a fortiori it could not have had one in less schematic reality; even pre-language could not be said to have had a single ancestor.

Though the grammatical structure of pre-language is unknowable, its general functional aspects can safely be assumed. As a transmitted phenomenon, like language it was learned by children who had an innate capacity to learn it. It had words with forms and meanings. The acoustic capacities of male, female, and child vocal tracts were different, individual voices and speech differed, yet different sexes and age groups communicated with each other and could say and understand the same words. If pre-language had these properties, then it was a population phenomenon with variation and change, and therefore it could develop dialects, isoglosses, distinct mutually unintelligible pre-languages, and phylogenetic families. These things imply a geography: dialects, pre-languages, and families had ranges that were the result of spreads and migrations; there was diffusion, and innovative and archaic forms; bilinguals, multilinguals, and monolinguals; second language learning, areality and contact phenomena (Pakendorf, this volume).

Language-family diversity must have been high throughout the range of pre-modern humans. In historical times and reconstructable prehistory, language-family diversity is high by default unless depressed by political-economic organization (diversity is reduced by states and empires, because state and trade languages replace local ones) or availability of resources (diversity is low in deserts, in continental interiors, and at high latitudes, where resources are thin and each social unit needs a large range); see Austerlitz (1980); Nichols (1992, 1997); Nettle (1999). The pre-modern human range excluded high latitudes and probably deserts, and certainly included no states or empires. Therefore it probably exhibited high genealogical and typological diversity of pre-languages, at least as high as that achieved by historical hunter-gatherer cultures in rich ecologies at lower latitudes, as in northern Australia and parts of South America.

Note that this view of pre-modern linguistic geography and diversity assumes no more than that pre-modern humans had some form of transmitted oral communication. It is the transmission, rather than the exact structure of the communicative system and its possibilities for representing content, that necessarily implies diachronic differentiation and the development of dialects and genealogical lineages in the communicative systems.

It is important to distinguish the evolution of language capacity from the evolution of actual transmitted languages (i.e. particular codes). Language capacity includes an appropriate vocal tract, articulatory dexterity, appropriate hearing, what might be called acoustic dexterity (ability to segment and decode speech at its spoken rate), ability to acquire language in childhood, and cooperative communication (this term from Tomasello 2008). It must have evolved as a set of phenomena that had selective value especially as a set and especially after its bearers had reached critical mass in the population. That point or interval when critical mass was reached can be called the transition to full language capacity. The first steps toward language capacity as we now know it began to occur several million years ago (chimpanzees have some of the fundamental communicative capacities, gestural rather than spoken: Tomasello 2008) and its symptoms are visible in the evolving cranium and vocal tract, so it can be assumed that vocal communication was in use at the time of the transition interval.

## 58.3 THE INITIAL LINGUISTIC POPULATION

Many linguists discussing the origin of language assume there was a single origin of language and therefore a single ancestral language, a Proto-World, whether or not reconstructable from modern data. In fact the single origin and the single language are two very different things, but in what follows I will treat the single-origin–single-language assumption as the null hypothesis and show that several different considerations undermine it. Consistent with the null hypothesis, we will need to make the assumed proto-conditions approximate as closely as possible the single Pleistocene tribe with its distinct single language. That means assuming the smallest plausible population sizes and territorial ranges at the time of the transition from pre-modern to modern humans.

At about 100 kya, a small plausible range for modern humans is approximately the southern half to two-thirds of the Rift Valley in Africa and nearby coastal areas. This area is comparable in size to New Guinea or northern Australia, areas which harbour large numbers of languages and language families. Northern Australia is the best comparandum, as its people were hunter-gatherers with a Stone Age technology at European contact. Some dozen language families (some of them small and at least one an isolate) and some 100 languages inhabited this range at contact and just before (Evans 2003; Bowern and Koch 2004). Given the linear shape of the Rift Valley, groups at the far reaches of the range would have had no contact with each other. Thus considerable typological diversity is likely to have existed, as it does in northern Australia.

Though the matter is still disputed, at least some evidence points to the possibility of a population bottleneck in the early prehistory of modern humans, with the entire population reduced to as few as 10,000 breeding females or a total population of about 30,000 individuals (Harpending et al. 1993, 1998; Hawks et al. 2000; Manica et al. 2007).[1] Even if there was no bottleneck, the early human population was always small. For the null hypothesis, then, assume that language arose in a population whose size was 30,000 individuals. This is smaller than the pre-colonial aboriginal population of northern Australia, but nonetheless large enough to comprise 50 or more ethnolinguistic tribes of around 500 people each, an estimate of the modal tribal size for Australia at contact and for Pleistocene tribes in general (Birdsell 1953, 1957). Thus even the smallest plausible population was large enough to harbour considerable diversity of languages and language families.

Given what is known about all traditional human societies, the late pre-modern and early modern human population must have been structured into family-like

---

[1] But Premo and Hublin (2009) show that the genetic profile indicating a bottleneck can also be achieved if there are occasional genetic sweeps within local populations. This means that there may never have been any drastic reduction of the human population.

and/or band-like groups and possibly larger groups speaking the same pre-language. Mates probably moved into the group from nearby groups. The family or band was the locus of (pre-)language transmission and transmission of cultural knowledge. As noted above, the cognitive capacity for symbolic behaviour and complex knowledge is likely to have been present in modern humans from the very beginning, but its manifestation in actual transmitted behaviour must have depended on population size (Powell et al. 2009).

To summarize so far, either the small range or the bottlenecked population, or both simultaneously, would still predict considerable diversity of language families and language types under historically attested and reconstructable conditions. If a population bottleneck occurred after the dispersal from the original range was in process, the surviving tribes and languages would have been geographically, typologically, and genealogically more distant from each other than if it occurred at the outset.

Pre-modern humans spread across the Old World tropics and subtropics and occupied that large range for hundreds of thousands of years, and the genealogical and structural diversity of pre-languages developing during that long time must have become extraordinary by about 60 kya, when modern humans spread out of Africa to displace pre-modern humans throughout the range of the latter, and then expanded beyond that range.

Now consider what the transition to full language capacity meant, viewed as a process going on in late pre-modern societies in one part of the pre-modern range represented by southern Africa. Consider first a scenario where language capacity evolves gradually, and assume that the final transition to language is set up when some fine-tuning of articulation, perception, memory, cooperative communicative capacity, or the like arises as a genetic mutation and gradually spreads through a set of bands linked by kinship. As individuals born with full language capacity approach critical mass in the population, more and more language-ready infants go through acquisition, the first ones with pre-language-speaking parents and peers and then more and more of them with parents and peers who have full language capacity. The grammar they impose on what they hear may differ from what their parents have; a more language-like grammar has emerged out of the normal acquisition process. Young adults, some with full language capacity and some without, marry into nearby bands and may become L2 learners of other pre-languages, and perhaps those with full language capacity impose a language-like grammar on the pre-language they hear. When the number of individuals with full language capacity reaches critical mass their capacities begin to guide language learning and language change. No new language has arisen. The genealogical affinity and wordstock of the language they speak is unaffected by this evolutionary change. The same thing is happening in adjacent speech communities. Eventually an entire swath of pre-languages is structurally transformed, though their genealogical lineages and wordstocks are inherited from pre-languages. The transition to language takes place gradually over a whole population and affects a number of different languages from different linguistic families.

The rise of language in this sense was a slow process; over 100,000 years passed between the appearance of the first archaic modern humans and the spread of modern humans out of Africa. By 60 kya, modern humans (and their languages) had reached the limits of the pre-modern range, and the centre of world expansion for people and languages shifted to Southeast Asia. Most of the vast structural and genealogical diversity of pre-language went extinct in this spread. The spread of late pre-modern humans at the expense of their earlier predecessors must have involved a similar process of preservation of a number of varieties and lineages and extinction of others, and probably likewise for previous spreads. If it were possible to go back in time and observe the whole prehistory of language and pre-language, we would come to a point where the communication system could no longer be considered language or even pre-language before all lines converged in a single ancestor—if they ever did. The single-ancestor scenario is possible only if the population of the entire species was too small to support more than one language (which would probably mean fewer than 500 individuals, an improbably small viable species population).

Alternatively, a single-ancestor origin is possible if, at some very early stage in the evolution of language, the communicative system was not even pre-language but a set of innate calls that were not learned but instinctive; in this case the entire species uses the same set of calls. At some point a mutation occurs that disconnects the hard-wiring and requires the mutant individuals to learn the calls. In animals without the requisite learning capacity such a mutation would be deleterious to the group, but as soon as the pre-human line developed the relevant learning capacity it made no difference whether the signals were instinctive or learned. If the learners increase in a population and reach critical mass, the set of calls becomes a (very early) pre-language and begins to develop dialects and eventually mutually unin-telligible pre-languages. If the spread of learners across the population occurs rapidly enough that no deep dialect division separates the innovative learned varieties from the peripheral instinctive ones by the time the peripheral ones also make the transition, then we have a single-ancestor development of pre-language. But this pre-language is so primitive as to consist, initially, of only a set of discrete symbols with whatever simple combinatorics may have governed an innate set of calls. This was a communicative system but it is not a language by linguistic criteria.

This section is grounded in the basics of linguistic geography and diversity analysis, together with some knowledge about palaeodemography and learning, but it took the form of a thought experiment because nothing can be known about the structure, words, etc. of late pre-language and early language. The following sections show why these things are unknowable.

## 58.4 SELECTED TYPOLOGICAL FEATURES

This section surveys retention rates in three structural properties that might at first glance seem to be candidates for fossils inherited from a Proto-World. All of them seem to be more prone to be inherited intact than to be innovated, and for none of them are there known causes that favour their rise. All diffuse to some extent but not readily. All characterize only a minority of languages. Thus, given current typological knowledge, inheritance from an ancestor seems to be the most parsimonious explanation for the presence of one or another of them in a language or a language family. Nonetheless, a cross-linguistic survey shows that none of them could be a detectable survival from a Proto-World grammar. Table 58.1 shows some retention rates over 5000-year increments (that being a rounded average age of the older families surveyed) and the surviving percentages that would be expected after various time spans. A property would have to be inherited with well over 90% fidelity per descent line per 5000 years in order to have higher than rare frequency in today's languages. Though such transmission fidelity levels are occasionally found in language families, they are exceptional. They cannot be assumed for all or most languages and for the entire expanse of time since language developed.

**Table 58.1. Expected retentions at various rates with 5000-year increments (rounded).**
Entries are the percents of daughter languages expected to retain the property. To use the table, determine or assume a rate of retention for some language property (e.g. verb-final word order, prefixal person agreement, one cognate word); the table returns the percent of daughter languages in the family expected to retain that property after various numbers of years.

| | Retention rates | | | | | | |
|---|---|---|---|---|---|---|---|
| | 50% | 60% | 70% | 80% | 90% | 95% | 99% |
| Retention after: | | | | | | | |
| 10,000 years | 25% | 36% | 49% | 64% | 8% | 90% | 98% |
| 20,000 years | 6% | 13% | 24% | 41% | 66% | 81% | 96% |
| 40,000 years | 1% | 2% | 6% | 17% | 43% | 66% | 92% |
| 60,000 years | 0 | 0 | 1% | 7% | 28% | 54% | 89% |
| 80,000 years | 0 | 0 | 0 | 3% | 19% | 44% | 85% |
| 100,000 years | 0 | 0 | 0 | 1% | 12% | 36% | 82% |
| 150,000 years | 0 | 0 | 0 | 0 | 4% | 21% | 74% |

## 58.4.1 Morphological ergativity

Ergativity is the identical coding of subject of intransitive verb and object of transitive verb, with subject of transitive verb differently marked. Languages with ergative case paradigms of nouns include Basque, Georgian, and Chukchi. About 21% of the world's languages have ergative noun morphology, another 5% split ergative/accusative, 24% accusative, 47% neutral, and 4% other.[2] Morphological ergativity seems to be a good example of a property more easily lost than gained (Nichols 1994). Still, though a few families have very high retention rates

Table 58.2. Survival rates of morphological ergativity in nouns in families that have it (and where it is old or original).

(Worldwide frequency in all families and isolates is 12%.) Only the major or productive noun inflection pattern is considered. Erg = number of sampled daughter languages with ergative noun inflection. Families were sampled at approximately one language per highest branch; * = sampled more densely.

|  |  | N | Erg | % Erg |
|---|---|---|---|---|
| Nakh-Daghestanian* | Eurasia | 10 | 10 | 1.00 |
| Kartvelian | Eurasia | 4 | 3 | 0.75 |
| W. Caucasian | Eurasia | 4 | 3 | 0.75 |
| Chukchi-Kamchatkan | Eurasia | 2 | 2 | 1.00 |
| Sino-Tibetan | Eurasia | 7 | 5 | 0.71 |
| Pama-Nyungan* | Pacific | 10 | 8 | 0.80 |
| Tangkic | Pacific | 3 | 1 | 0.33 |
| Madang | Pacific | 4 | 1 | 0.25 |
| S. Bougainville | Pacific | 2 | 1 | 0.50 |
| Austronesian* | Pacific | 13 | 4 | 0.31 |
| Eskimo-Aleut | Americas | 3 | 2 | 0.67 |
| Mixe-Zoque | Americas | 2 | 1 | 0.50 |
| Macro-Ge | Americas | 3 | 1 | 0.33 |
| Pano-Tacanan | Americas | 3 | 3 | 1.00 |
| TOTAL |  | 70 | 45 |  |
| World mean |  |  |  | 0.64 |

[2] These and other typological frequencies cited here come from sampling the Autotyp database (Bickel and Nichols 2002). Counted are the most frequent alignments per language. Nearly every language has some minor patterns in addition to a most frequent one. Ergativity is not limited to noun morphology, but this is the most frequent locus.

(Table 58.2), the worldwide average is too low for any appreciable number of the families with ergativity to have retained it from the time of earliest language.

If there was a Proto-World and it was ergative, the frequencies of alignments in today's languages does not enable us to reconstruct that ergativity to Proto-World. Ergativity is not evenly distributed worldwide, and is almost entirely lacking in Africa. The modern human emigration from Africa began probably between 85 and 55 kya and reached the Indian Ocean coast by ca. 60 kya (Forster and Matsumura 2005, with further references). Could it be that ergativity was absent in language as it first developed in Africa, and arose once in the emigrant population that provided most of the rest of the world's languages? Even with this later starting date, the survival rate for ergativity (Table 58.2) would predict a near-zero modern frequency, much lower than is actually attested.[3]

Macaulay et al. (2005) estimate that the population that emigrated from Africa comprised several hundred females. Assuming this means a total population of at most a few thousand, it could have supported only a few languages. A chance change in alignment in even just one of them would have had a drastic effect on the subsequent frequencies of alignments. Maslova (2000) shows mathematically that, if the initial population is small, the statistically catastrophic effects of early random changes make it impossible to reconstruct initial frequencies of types after many millennia; but if the initial population is large, frequencies will settle toward equilibrium, also making it impossible to reconstruct initial frequencies. Bickel (2008) uses simulation to reach the same conclusion: an initial skewing of typological variables (such as a dominance of ergativity) is not detectable after anything like 100,000 or 60,000 years, at probabilities of change at all similar to what is observed cross-linguistically in large samples.

Thus, the survey of survival rates given here, Maslova's analysis, and Bickel's simulation all show that we cannot know the frequencies of different alignments in the earliest language population. In the case of ergativity, the near-zero frequency of ergative alignment in the African sample is the equilibrium that would be expected worldwide if today's frequencies result primarily from inheritance. Therefore, though in some places ergativity indicates areal connections that seem to go back to earlier than the oldest levels reachable by standard comparative method, such connections cannot be traced back as far as the origin of language or the migration out of Africa. The same reasoning applies to all other structural properties.

---

[3] Furthermore, the calculated survival rate is for language families that do have some ergativity, while a worldwide survival rate could also be calculated as the frequency of ergativity in all families (noun ergativity 12%) or the percent of stocks surveyed that attest some ergativity (18%).

## 58.4.2  Inclusive/exclusive pronouns

Inclusive/exclusive pronouns distinguish, in the first person non-singular forms ('we', 'us'), one that refers to speaker and hearer (inclusive) from one that refers to speaker and other(s) but not hearer (exclusive). Inclusive/exclusive systems are unknown in western Europe and fairly rare in Eurasia and Africa generally, but frequent in the Pacific and the Americas (Bickel and Nichols 2005); they are found, for instance, in Fula, Tibetan, Tagalog, Warlpiri and other Australian languages, Lakhota, and Quechuan languages. For inclusive/exclusive oppositions the retention rate in families is

**Table 58.3. Retention rates for inclusive/exclusive in families that have it at all.**
(Worldwide frequency in all families and isolates is 40%.) Conventions as on Table 58.2.

| Stock | Area | N | Incl | % incl. |
|---|---|---|---|---|
| Chadic | Africa | 3 | 1 | 0.33 |
| Cushitic | Africa | 3 | 1 | 0.33 |
| East Sudanic | Africa | 4 | 1 | 0.25 |
| Kartvelian | Eurasia | 3 | 1 | 0.33 |
| Tungusic | Eurasia | 3 | 2 | 0.67 |
| Nakh-Daghestanian* | Eurasia | 36 | 20 | 0.56 |
| Sino-Tibetan | Eurasia | 12 | 5 | 0.42 |
| Austroasiatic | Eurasia | 5 | 4 | 0.80 |
| Pama-Nyungan* | Pacific | 14 | 8 | 0.57 |
| Nyulnyul | Pacific | 3 | 3 | 1.00 |
| Austronesian* | Pacific | 32 | 31 | 0.97 |
| Border (N.G.) | Pacific | 4 | 3 | 0.75 |
| West Papuan | Pacific | 3 | 3 | 1.00 |
| Wakashan | Americas | 2 | 1 | 0.50 |
| Algic | Americas | 4 | 2 | 0.50 |
| Uto-Aztecan | Americas | 5 | 1 | 0.20 |
| Otomanguean | Americas | 3 | 3 | 1.00 |
| Mixe-Zoque | Americas | 3 | 3 | 1.00 |
| Cariban | Americas | 4 | 3 | 0.75 |
| Guaycurú | Americas | 2 | 1 | 0.50 |
| Pano-Tacanan | Americas | 2 | 1 | 0.50 |
| Chibchan | Americas | 3 | 2 | 0.67 |
| Macro-Ge | Americas | 4 | 3 | 0.75 |
| TOTAL | | 157 | 103 | |
| World mean | | | | 0.62 |

rather similar to that for ergativity (Nichols (1992, 1995) finds the opposition quite stable; Wichmann and Holmann (2009) find it not particularly stable). Therefore neither the total frequency of inclusive/exclusive opposition worldwide nor the frequency skewings between the Old World, New World, and Pacific can reflect original or very early frequencies or skewings. Inclusive/exclusive oppositions are known to diffuse in contact situations (Jacobsen 1980), though they diffuse less readily than, say, phonological properties. (See Table 58.3.)

## 58.4.3 Grammatical gender

Gender is the grammatical and usually covert classification of nouns, where a noun's gender is revealed in the forms of words that agree with nouns, such as verbs and/or adjectives. Most western European languages have gender (e.g. German, Spanish, Greek), though English does not. In all large-scale surveys, gender proves to be one of the most stably inherited properties (see Nichols 1995; Matasović 2004, 2007; Wichmann and Holman 2009). Gender per se is not known to be diffusion-prone (loss of gender, however, is often attributed to contact: e.g. Matasović (2004) for Indo-European), though worldwide, gender does seem to form large-scale clusters (Nichols 1992). Though highly stable, its modern frequencies and skewings cannot reflect just inheritance and loss from an original situation. (See Table 58.4.)

Thus, though for all three structural features it is presently easier to explain retention and loss than innovative new cases, this cannot be taken to mean that their

Table 58.4. Survival rates for gender in language families that have any. Worldwide frequency in all families and isolates is 30%.

| Stock | Continent | N | Yes | % |
| --- | --- | --- | --- | --- |
| Atlantic | Africa | 2 | 2 | 1.00 |
| Benue-Congo | Africa | 2 | 1 | 0.50 |
| Cushitic | Africa | 3 | 2 | 0.67 |
| Chadic | Africa | 3 | 1 | 0.33 |
| Semitic | Africa | 3 | 3 | 1.00 |
| Indo-European | Eurasia | 12 | 9 | 0.75 |
| Nakh-Daghestanian | Eurasia | 33 | 29 | 0.88 |
| Gunwingguan | Pacific | 2 | 2 | 1.00 |
| Sepik | Pacific | 2 | 1 | 0.50 |
| Algic | Americas | 3 | 2 | 0.67 |
| TOTAL | | 65 | 52 | |
| World mean | | | | 0.73 |

presence in modern languages reflects the structural type of the earliest linguistic population. There is probably no grammatical phenomenon whose modern frequencies (in the world or in large areas) reflect skewed frequencies of the earliest modern linguistic population. Even for the most stable features, only up to about 20,000 years do expected survival rates differ appreciably from zero. Modern frequencies evidently result from relatively recent innovations and diffusions.

## 58.5 SINGULARITIES, ESPECIALLY AFRICAN SINGULARITIES

A singularity is a linguistic phenomenon well-attested only in one area or family on earth. Singularities show that highly unusual grammatical properties are hard to innovate, hence easier to acquire by diffusion or inheritance than by innovation.

The clearest example of a singularity is clicks, which are robustly attested in all three of the endemic language families of southern Africa and also well-installed in some of the intrusive Bantu languages. They are also found as outliers in two language isolates (Sandawe, Hadza) of the southern Horn of Africa and one Cushitic language there (Dahalo), and the usual interpretation is that these survive from a once larger click-using area that has now been mostly overrun in the Bantu expansion of some 3000 years ago (Güldemann and Vossen 2000; Tishkoff et al. 2005; Güldemann 2010; Güldemann and Elderkin 2010). Clicks are the anchor point of a consonantism and syllable structure that are distinctive but use the standard points of articulation and are well integrated with morphologies of a variety of common language types, so there is no obvious reason why they could not have developed more than once. Could it be, then, that pre-Bantu southern African languages all descend from an ancient ancestor that happened to use clicks, while the other languages of the world descend from ancestors that happened not to use clicks? Only if the retention fidelity for clicks is on the order of the 99+% needed to guarantee very long-term survival. This is implausible, but since the ages of the click-using language families are unknown and the families and languages are few, a retention rate cannot be determined.

It has also been suggested that clicks are an archaism surviving only in Africa from very early language (A. Knight et al. 2003). Though the monogenetic origin which this suggests may not reflect the authors' current thinking, it is worth addressing linguistically. The fact that clicks are unique to Africa does not make them an archaism; genetically, what marks Africa as the origin point of humanity is the diversity of genetic lineages there, not the presence of any one rare lineage. Probably the strongest argument against interpreting clicks as a Proto-World survival is indeed the geographical localization of clicks. An ancestor language spoken at the dawn of language can be expected to have descendants in more than one part of the linguistic world. In linguistic geographical terms, an archaism should recur at the periphery of a spread, not occur (as clicks do) once near the centre of dispersal. Rather, the present-day distribution of clicks is neatly areal, and it calls for an areal explanation: Africa has the greatest variety of airstream mechanisms of any large language area, and clicks, an extremely complex type of consonant, could have arisen only in this typological context.

Tracing clicks to an early or ultimate ancestor language makes an implicit assumption that rare phenomena must be ancient (this is relatively explicit in Tishkoff et al. 2007)—that is, structural diversity has decreased over time. In fact though, as clicks show, unusual types simply have preconditions which take time to develop.

# 58.6 PROTO-WORLD VOCABULARY

A line of inquiry best represented in several chapters of Ruhlen (1994) traces resemblant words found here and there in the world's languages back to a Proto-World. Bengtson and Ruhlen (1994) propose 27 global etymologies drawn from the cognate sets and putative cognate sets in published work on 30 families (e.g. Indo-European, Uralic), macrofamilies (e.g. Afroasiatic, Niger-Congo), pseudofamilies (e.g. Amerind, Indo-Pacific), and isolates (e.g. Basque, Burushaski). Some of the sets are from peer-reviewed work on proven families and are demonstrated cognates displaying regular sound correspondences (the Indo-European words are of this type); some are not. Formal and semantic ranges are considerable. Not all of the 30 groups have representatives in each of the 27 etymologies (no etymology has all groups), and not every branch of every family (or every putative branch of every macrogroup) is represented in every set. For instance, the set for no. 9 KUAN 'dog' (pp. 302–303) lists forms from 17 of the 30 groups. The glosses given in these forms range over 'hyena', 'dog', 'wolf', 'bitch', 'wild dog', 'wolverine', 'fox', 'coyote', and 'lynx', with 'dog' most common. The initial sounds in the forms range over velars, uvulars, and occasional others (palatal, zero) in different manners of articulation. Not all forms have a labial element and not all have a nasal later element. (The following set no. 10 KU(N) 'who' (pp. 303–305) has the same first two segments K and U, but the putative cognates reported, where they come from the same families as those for 'dog', do not always have the same initial sounds, showing that what was sought was not corresponding sounds but just similar sounds.) Thus it seems that the set was assembled by searching the sources for words referring to any canid or other predator and beginning with any velar or uvular (and possibly other sounds) and also containing a labial and/or a nasal element. The wordlists surveyed for each group entry ranged from a few hundred or more proposed cognate sets to several thousand words (in dictionaries of individual language). The 30 groups surveyed include the pseudofamilies Amerind (which in reality comprises over 100 unrelated language families of the Americas), Indo-Pacific (in reality over 50 unrelated families of New Guinea), Australian (some 20 families), Nilo-Saharan (about 10–12 families), and Caucasian (two families), and for all of these only a minority of the families actually have putative cognates in the set for 'dog' (e.g. Amerind, 17 languages from 15 families); Caucasian, one branch of one family); this means that the actual range of the search is not 30 groups but the 300+ demonstrated language families on earth (for the figure of 300+ see Hammarström (2007: 23) and Nichols and Bickel (2009); Campbell (2010) gives a total number but no listing of families), and the success rate is actually about 36 out of 300+. With this amount of freedom in searches, such a success rate falls easily within the range of chance.

The formal and semantic ranges in these sets and the partial representation across subgroups are comparable to what one sees in established cognate sets in proven families. However, what Bengtson and Ruhlen are doing is not describing word histories in an established family but presenting evidence of relatedness. Now, describing word histories and establishing relatedness of languages are very different undertakings with different standards of adequacy. In tracing word histories one works with established regular sound correspondences and proven or provable cognate relationships, so that the formal differences in the daughter languages are fully accounted for. In demonstrating relatedness one needs to show that the number of resemblant forms exceeds what is expected by chance for a given formal and semantic range and for a given number of words or protoforms that one sorts through in seeking resemblants. The burden of proof is on the proponent of relatedness, who needs to show what the thresholds are for chance and significance. This burden is not addressed by Bengtson and Ruhlen or in any other work on putative Proto-World cognates, while there have been several demonstrations that the resemblances are within the range of chance (Nichols 1996, 2010a, b; Campbell and Poser 2008 review other literature; these sources deal with both Proto-World and mega-macrofamily claims).

Thus, while it is theoretically possible that a few words from the earliest languages might survive here and there in today's languages, given their likely phonological and semantic differences and small numbers they cannot be detectably different from chance.[4] In any event, as shown above, there is no reason to think that all languages share a single ancestor.

---

[4] Glottochronology, a method of estimating ages of language families based on survival rates of cognates in a fixed wordlist in binary tests of pairs of sister languages (Swadesh 1955 and various recent historical linguistics handbooks) assumes an 86% retention rate per millennium. This amounts to 45% per 5000 years—low stability compared to Table 58.1. This is for retention of known cognates, in the same sense, from a fixed wordlist, and from a fixed language list, while the Proto-World efforts do not prove cognacy in advance and place no limits on wordlist, sense, or choice of languages.

## 58.7 Conclusions

To summarize, principles of linguistic geography and palaeodemography indicate that language originated gradually over a diverse population of pre-languages and pre-language families. There was no single ancestral language. If some remote ancestor to pre-language did actually comprise a single communicative community, that communicative system cannot have been language and its signals were not words. These conclusions are reached not by reconstruction and not by calculation of typological frequencies but by inference from the study of linguistic geography, linguistic diversity, and language acquisition. Another point emerging from these considerations is that, in the 100,000 or 200,000 years since the origin of language, languages have barely scratched the surface of possible structural and genealogical diversity; the pre-languages that went extinct in the spread of modern humans and their languages had been diversifying for close to a million years and must have been incomparably more diverse.

CHAPTER 59

# PREHISTORIC POPULATION CONTACT AND LANGUAGE CHANGE

## BRIGITTE PAKENDORF

## 59.1 INTRODUCTION

Molecular anthropology is the branch of biological anthropology that uses molecular genetic methods to study the origin, relationships, history, and migration patterns of human populations. The combination of such different fields as genetics (molecular anthropology) and linguistics may appear rather incongruous; however, joint investigations can elucidate some of the factors involved in prehistoric language contact, since molecular anthropology can provide insights into prehistoric events, which in turn can help inform historical linguistic analyses. This will be outlined below.

Language change is a ubiquitous process, although it is rarely noticed at an individual level, and we lack historical documentation over extensive periods of time for most areas of the world. Nevertheless, sound changes are attested in the histories of many language families, as are changes at the lexical level; words become obsolete and are replaced by others for various reasons, for instance when they become associated with taboo meanings or are replaced by erstwhile metaphors (cf. Hock 1991). Similarly, grammatical structures change over time; for example, in the process called grammaticalization (Bybee, this volume; Heine and Kuteva, this volume), separate words in frequently used constructions become shorter and fuse into one word, changing their meaning over time as they do so and resulting in a new construction with a new meaning.

However, although languages change all the time for different internally-conditioned reasons, language change can also be triggered or accelerated through contact. In this event, the knowledge that people have of a second language influences the way they use their primary language; this in turn leads to copies of words or structures from the second language entering and changing their primary language. Conversely, the patterns of a person's primary language can influence the patterns of a language learnt later in life, leading, for example, to foreign accents or to the diverse variants of former colonial languages.

Several factors might have an impact in situations of language contact. Was there extensive intermarriage between the two groups? Did the groups keep socially apart, reserving interactions for a tightly defined sphere, such as the market place? Did one group formerly speak a different language and shift to their current language? These are important questions in the field of language contact research, since it is assumed that distinct factors involved in different contact situations will affect the linguistic outcome of that contact. Since multilingualism has been widespread throughout the history of modern humans (Nichols, this volume), language contact can be assumed to have played an important role in shaping the patterns of modern linguistic variation. Research into the factors that influence the outcome of language contact is therefore important to further our understanding of language evolution.

Difficulties arise in the assessment of situations of population and language contact when the contact took place in prehistoric times, so that little is known about the contact situation, and all we have to work with is the linguistic outcome of the contact. Given that the vast majority of human languages were spoken in prehistoric contexts, without standard languages, nation states, or orthographies, and therefore without any written documents available to illustrate the changes they have undergone, these difficulties beset a large proportion of possible contact situations. Careful analyses can tell us what kinds of change a language has undergone under contact influence, but without knowing anything about the actual contact situation, it is difficult, if not impossible, to come to definitive conclusions as to what conditioned the linguistic results of the contact. It is precisely in such cases that molecular anthropology can be of help, as will be outlined below.

## 59.2 LANGUAGE CHANGE THROUGH
## CONTACT INFLUENCE

A brief note on terminology may be useful at the outset: since the word 'borrowing' is used in the literature with numerous distinct meanings (Pakendorf 2007), I prefer to avoid it; instead, I use the term 'copying' to cover all instances of transfer of items from one language to another.

In the past 20 years, research on language contact has burgeoned (for extensive introductions see Thomason 2001, Winford 2003 and Matras 2009), triggered to a large extent by the seminal monograph by Thomason and Kaufman (1988). It has become clear that anything can be copied from one language to another, both actual forms of words or morphemes as well as structural patterns. Although words from the cultural lexicon (e.g. words for 'computer', 'car', or 'television') are copied most frequently, since they are introduced into a language at the same time as the object they denote is introduced into the society, basic lexical items (e.g. words for 'sister', 'face', or 'to boil') and morphemes can also be copied. Structural patterns can be copied as well, such as word order patterns or the usage patterns of case markers. Some of the most striking examples of structural copies that languages can introduce are known from the Indian village of Kupwar, where Kannada, Marathi, and Urdu are spoken (Gumperz and Wilson 1971); from Northwest New Britain (Thurston 1987), where the Non-Austronesian language Anêm is spoken in contact with several Austronesian languages; and from Karkar Island off the coast of Papua New Guinea (Ross 1996), which is inhabited by speakers of the Austronesian language Takia and the Non-Austronesian language Waskia. In all of these cases, although the languages in contact have retained separate lexicons, the syntactic patterns have aligned to such a degree that '[i]t is possible to translate one sentence into the other by simple morph for morph substitution' (Gumperz and Wilson 1971: 155).

The factors leading to the transfer of different kinds of copies are quite diverse, ranging from 'cultural contact' in which speakers of the recipient language do not necessarily know the model language (e.g. the copying of English words into Japanese, cf. Ross 2003) to long-term bilingualism (for example, in the above-mentioned cases of Kupwar, Karkar Island, and New Britain, as well as in Arnhem Land (Heath 1978) and Amazonia (Aikhenvald 2002)) or to language shift (Thomason and Kaufman 1988; Ross 2003). The impact of linguistically mixed households has not yet been systematically investigated; however, Ross (2003) suggests that the regular introduction of spouses from one linguistic group to another might lead to both phonological and structural change in the language of the receiving group.

Thus, contact between populations speaking different languages is expected to lead to noticeable changes in the languages concerned. However, notwithstanding the large amounts of data amassed over recent years, as yet no consensus has been reached on what kinds of linguistic change result from which kind of contact, nor are the actual processes involved in contact-induced change clear. Various factors have been proposed as playing a role, such as the structural similarity/dissimilarity between the languages in contact (L. Johanson 2002), the attitudes of speakers towards their own and the contact language as well as towards copies introduced from one to the other (Gumperz and Wilson 1971; Heath 1978), or the sociopolitical status of the languages in contact (e.g. L. Johanson 2002; Sakel 2007); however, none of these is unanimously accepted.

It is difficult to study the factors involved in the different linguistic outcomes of language contact solely with linguistic methods, as the nature of the contact situation is often not known. For example, it is often unclear whether specific changes were introduced through long-term bilingualism, or instead through shift from one language to another. It is here that molecular anthropological investigations can be of use, as will be outlined below.

## 59.3 MOLECULAR ANTHROPOLOGY AND ITS USES IN LANGUAGE CONTACT RESEARCH

Two parts of the human genome are studied most widely in molecular anthropology, due to their very specific mode of inheritance: mitochondrial DNA (mtDNA) and the Y-chromosome (Cann, this volume). (For a more detailed overview of molecular anthropology for non-geneticists see Appendix 1 in Pakendorf (2007); for reviews of the use of mtDNA and the Y-chromosome in molecular anthropological studies see Pakendorf and Stoneking (2005), and Jobling and Tyler-Smith (2003), respectively; for an in-depth introduction to molecular anthropology see Jobling et al. (2004).)

MtDNA is a small circular molecule that exists in large copy numbers in special little organelles in the cell called mitochondria. Its special advantage in molecular anthropological studies lies in the fact that it is inherited solely in the maternal line—although both men and women carry mtDNA, the small number of molecules of the father's mtDNA that enter the egg get eliminated within days after fertilization. The Y-chromosome, on the other hand, is one of two sex chromosomes found in the human genome, with the X-chromosome being its counterpart; women carry two X-chromosomes, while men carry one X-chromosome and one Y-chromosome. From this it follows that the Y-chromosome is male-specific, being inherited solely in the paternal line, from fathers to sons. Thus, mtDNA analyses highlight female-specific evolutionary processes, while Y-chromosomal analyses furnish insights into male-specific events.

Molecular anthropological analyses can provide indications of prehistoric admixture events, sex-biased migration patterns, decreases or increases of population size, and settlement practices (matri- versus patrilocality). These results allow insights into prehistoric sociocultural practices that may have had an effect on language change in contact situations. Of particular importance with respect to the study of language contact is the detection of prehistoric language shift, in other words when a population has given up its language in favour of a different one. No agreement has yet been reached amongst linguists on what changes occur in languages that were the target of a shift, since such a shift is frequently not historically documented. However, language shift can result in a mismatch between the genetic and linguistic affiliation of a group (that is, a group is genetically more similar to its geographic neighbours than to its linguistic relatives), which can be detected with genetic methods. Thus, linguistic investigations of languages which can be shown genetically to have been the target of a language shift can provide evidence for what linguistic changes, if any, such a shift produces.

A good example of the genetic detection of prehistoric language shift is the case of Azerbaijanian from the south Caucasus, which is closely related to Turkish. Analyses of mtDNA and Y-chromosomal variation in Azerbaijanis have demonstrated that this group is genetically more closely related to their geographic neighbours from the Caucasus than to their linguistic relatives (Nasidze and Stoneking 2001; Nasidze et al. 2003). From historical sources it is known that a Turkic-speaking group, the Seljuks, invaded what is now Azerbaijan in the 11th century, establishing their rule over the indigenous populations. The genetic results indicate that this immigrating Turkic-speaking group was numerically quite small, but that it managed to impose its language on the resident population without contributing much to the local gene pool. Interestingly, linguistic traces of this pre-Turkic substrate can be found in the phonology and structure of Azerbaijanian (Stilo 1994: 88–91), thus confirming the idea of a prehistoric language shift.

The detection of sex-biased gene flow, such as the introduction of foreign spouses into a group, is facilitated through the comparison of the mtDNA and Y-chromosomal affiliation of a group. For example, research has shown that Polynesian mtDNAs (i.e. the maternal lineages) are of predominantly Asian origin (with 94% of mtDNA lineages being traced back to Asia), while their Y-chromosomes (i.e. the paternal lineages) have a major component (66%) of Melanesian origin, indicating that a large number of Melanesian men were incorporated into the pre-Polynesian societies before these societies migrated to Polynesia. This might be an indication that the ancient Austronesian groups were matrilocal, that is, husbands moved in with their wives' families (Kayser et al. 2006). The linguistic effects of such sex-biased gene flow have yet to be investigated.

## 59.4 COMBINING LINGUISTIC AND GENETIC ANALYSES TO INVESTIGATE PREHISTORIC CONTACT: A CASE STUDY

I illustrate the application of combined molecular anthropological and linguistic investigations of a prehistoric contact event with a case study from Siberia which deals with the prehistoric contact undergone by the Sakha (Yakuts) (for details see Pakendorf 2007). The Sakha are Turkic-speaking cattle and horse pastoralists who immigrated to the middle reaches of the Lena river in north-eastern Siberia from a more southerly point of origin. This migration, assumed to have taken place in the 13th or 14th century CE (Gogolev 1993), brought the ancestors of the Sakha into contact with Tungusic-speaking hunters and reindeer herders, mainly Evenks. Starting in the late 17th century, the Sakha expanded territorially under pressure of Russian colonization, and settled in large areas of north-eastern Siberia, where they are nowadays the numerically and linguistically dominant indigenous group (Forsyth 1992). During this expansion they further encroached upon the territory of other indigenous peoples, namely the Tungusic-speaking Evenks and Evens as well as Yukaghirs, who speak a language which might possibly be distantly related to the Uralic language family.

A number of ethnographers have mentioned the intermarriage of the Sakha people with indigenous north Siberian groups as well as the linguistic assimilation of the latter in the course of Sakha prehistory (e.g. Seroševskij [1896] 1993; Dolgix 1960; Tugolukov 1985). This would imply that differences between the Sakha language and its Turkic relatives are due to the shift of these indigenous groups from their native languages to Sakha. However, combined molecular anthropological (Pakendorf et al. 2006) and linguistic investigations of the possible contact undergone by the Sakha lead to somewhat unexpected results.

The Y-chromosomal analyses provide convincing evidence that no admixture with Evenks took place in the paternal line. This implies that no shift of entire groups of Evenki-speakers (i.e. of both women and men) to the Sakha language and identity occurred, contrary to previous proposals. Based on mtDNA analyses, no conclusive evidence for admixture in the maternal line could be detected; however, some intermarriage of the immigrating Sakha with Evenk women cannot be excluded, either. These somewhat inconclusive results regarding potential admixture in the maternal line are due to the fact that the Sakha, Evenks, and Evens, as well as South Siberian Turkic groups all share certain mtDNA lineages. This indicates that these groups intermarried amongst each other, probably at a time when both the ancestors of the Sakha and the ancestors of the Evenks and Evens were still settled in southern Siberia in the vicinity of Turkic groups. However, since it can be assumed that the ancestors of the Sakha who migrated to north-eastern

Siberia carried at least some of these shared lineages with them, later intermarriage with Evenk women carrying the same lineages would not be detectable with the methods used. Therefore, more finely-grained analyses of the entire mtDNA molecule are necessary to resolve the issue of whether the Sakha ancestors intermarried with the neighbouring Evenks or not.

Turning to the linguistic investigations, we find that interestingly, although the number of loanwords from Evenki is quite small, the Sakha language can be shown to have undergone structural changes under Evenki influence. For example, Sakha lost the genitive case, which in other Turkic languages marks the possessor in possessive noun phrases, since Evenki, like other Tungusic languages, does not mark the possessor. Furthermore, although the Turkic languages lost the separate case to mark coordinate subjects (called comitative case) and nowadays use the same marker to express instruments and coordinate subjects (very similar to English 'with'), in Sakha two separate case suffixes were retained. Although such a distinction is cross-linguistically widespread, and so might have been retained in Sakha for language-internal reasons, the similarity in form between the Evenki comitative case suffix and a variant of the Sakha suffix points towards Evenki influence. Other features of Sakha that are arguably due to contact influence from Evenki include the following: the development of a case suffix to mark indefinite direct objects in the imperative mood (that is, a different case suffix is used on 'horse' in sentences such as 'Catch me a horse!' from that used in a sentence like 'Catch me that horse!'); the development of a future imperative mood (i.e. there is a separate verb form in Sakha to express commands that are to be fulfilled at a later point in time rather than immediately); as well as certain pragmatic uses of the possessive suffixes.

It is notable that nearly all of these contact-induced changes are of a purely structural nature, without the copying of any forms. These kinds of changes are indicative of bilingualism in Evenki by the ancestors of the Sakha, since in order to copy structural patterns from one language to the other, speakers of Sakha had to be closely acquainted with both languages. There is thus an interesting mismatch between the genetic results (no evidence of language shift of entire groups of Evenks to Sakha, though possibly some intermarriage in the maternal line) and the linguistic data, which indicate more than just a casual knowledge of Evenki by the ancestors of the Sakha. From a modern-day perspective it is somewhat hard to imagine that the Sakha might at some time have been bilingual in Evenki, since nowadays they are the linguistically dominant group in north-eastern Siberia. However, the Y-chromosomal analyses demonstrate that the ancestors of the Sakha underwent a severe reduction in their genetic diversity (a so-called founder event) in the paternal line during their history, which indicates that only a small group of Sakha migrated to the north. In the initial period after their migration to the Lena river this small group of immigrants would have been quite vulnerable in the new environment and harsher climate, and therefore dependent on the indigenous Evenki-speaking population (Pakendorf 2007; cf. Güldemann 2006, on a similar dependency of immigrating pastoralist Khoe-speakers on their hunter-gatherer neighbours in southern Africa). During this period of dependency it is probable that they used their neighbours' language for intergroup communication (cf. Khanina, ms.).

## 59.5 CONCLUSIONS

As has been demonstrated through this brief case study, the combination of in-depth molecular anthropological analyses and linguistic investigations can open up new insights into the factors at work in prehistoric population and language contact. This is a highly important area of investigation, since multilingualism has been the norm throughout human history (Nichols, this volume), and therefore language contact will have been an important source of change in the evolution of human languages. However, there are several parameters that might play a role, and one case study alone is not enough to develop predictions for language contact phenomena in general. An important role in contact between human populations is played by social factors, such as the kind of interaction that takes place between groups speaking different languages, or the attitudes towards language mixing. Therefore, it is highly desirable to add sociolinguistic investigations to the multidisciplinary approach to language contact studies, in order to obtain a comprehensive view of the parameters at work. Furthermore, since the social factors are expected to be different depending on differing environmental factors (for example, contact in the scarcely populated expanses of Siberia was probably very unlike that in densely populated areas of Africa), it is desirable to undertake multidisciplinary investigations of potential contact situations in various regions of the world. Only when data from several such studies have been gathered and analysed will we be able to make inductions about one of the great forces that have shaped human languages.

## ACKNOWLEDGEMENTS

I thank Mark Stoneking and Dejan Matić for helpful comments on a draft version of the manuscript.

..................................................

# CHAPTER 60

# WHY FORMAL MODELS ARE USEFUL FOR EVOLUTIONARY LINGUISTS

..................................................

## KENNY SMITH

A large proportion of the community actively involved in publishing research on the origins and evolution of language use formal (i.e. mathematical or computational) models. This chapter briefly outlines what formal models can contribute, addresses some common criticisms of formal models, and outlines future directions.[1]

## 60.1 COMPLEXITY, PREDICTION, AND THE ROLE OF FORMAL MODELS

### 60.1.1 The complexity problem

Language is a complex phenomenon which is an outcome of several processes (social learning, cultural, and biological evolution) which are themselves complex

---

[1] This article is not intended to be a review of the modelling literature, and as such, illustrative examples are drawn almost exclusively from the work of the language evolution group in Edinburgh, most notably Simon Kirby.

(Kirby, this volume). In order to understand the evolution of language, we therefore need to understand these processes and their interaction: we need to build theories of how they work, and test those theories. Do they account for the data they claim to account for? Do they make accurate predictions beyond the data which was used to build them? To do this, we need a mechanism for working out the predictions of a theory. One way of doing this is to work through the consequences of a theory verbally. However, verbal reasoning depends on our intuitions being reliable, and the reliability of our intuitions breaks down as the complexity of the system we are reasoning about increases—particularly problematic for evolutionary linguists, given the nature of the system we are interested in. Formal models offer a solution to this problem, and consequently are widely used in fields devoted to understanding systems of this nature (on learning, see Elman et al. 1996; on cultural evolution, see Boyd and Richerson 1985; on evolutionary biology, see Futuyma 1997).

A formal model is any description of a system that is sufficiently precise that predictions about the behaviour of that system can be more or less mechanically produced from that description. Two types of formal model are commonly used: mathematical and computational models. Both allow the components of a system and the way in which they interact to be specified. The resulting model can then be used to explore how the system behaves. Predictions can be mechanically derived from the detailed specification of the model, for example, by running a number of simulations using a computational model or by finding numerical or analytic solutions to a mathematical model—we don't have to trust the reliability of our intuitions to generate predictions from the formal specification of our theory. This is useful in circumstances where those intuitions are unreliable, and for this reason Di Paolo et al. (2000) suggest that formal models can be thought of as tools for running 'opaque thought experiments', where the opacity lies between the set of assumptions and their consequences.

Formal models are therefore simply a tool to allow the consequences of a given set of assumptions to be explored (see below for more on assumptions), which in turn allows the modeller to test whether (1) a theory of a system matches the real-world data that the theory is intended to account for, or (2) the theory does not, but can be made to match the real-world data by the addition of some remedial assumptions, or (3) the theory can never in fact account for the real-world data, and must be rejected. However, as pointed out by Di Paolo et al. (2000), formal models introduce an opacity of their own: automatically-derived predictions from a model may themselves require some reflection or exploration to understand. The more complex the system being modelled, the less reliable a verbal model will be and the more necessary a formal model, but (typically) the greater the effort required to understand the behaviour of the model in its own right. We'll return to this issue of model complexity and opacity in the third section. The point here is simply that, if the predictions of the model are to be any real use, it's often necessary to construct a verbal explanation of how those predictions relate to the initial assumptions embodied in the model. As such, formal models often feel like scaffolds which are needed to build new verbal models: we start with a theory whose predictions are unclear, produce a formal model of that system, interpret its results, then produce a verbal description of the process which stands alongside of (and perhaps is independent from) the formal model.

## 60.1.2 An example

One of the best-known formal models in evolutionary linguistics is Kirby's (2000) model of the cultural evolution of recursive compositionality. This model explores the theory (expressed verbally by, for example, Wray 1998) that cultural transmission can produce a structured language from an initially unstructured, holistic protolanguage, through a historical process of cumulative fractionation. Kirby's computational model shows that, under certain assumptions (including assumptions about how learners build grammars from data, and about the kind of data that learners can expect to see), a recursively compositional language can indeed evolve from a non-compositional predecessor through purely cultural processes. Furthermore, the model reveals that a parameter not central to pre-existing verbal arguments (e.g. Wray's) turns out to be crucial. The learning bottleneck (the extent to which learners are forced to generalize beyond their training data, producing utterances to convey meanings which they themselves never encountered while learning) drives the evolution of structure: pressure for generalization introduced by the learning bottleneck favours generalizable languages, and the language of the population therefore evolves over time to become increasingly generalizable. Since compositional languages are highly generalizable, compositional languages emerge from this process (Kirby's manipulation of the learning bottleneck parameter in the original paper is somewhat minimal, but subsequent papers taking a similar approach test the impact of the learning bottleneck more fully: e.g. Kirby and Hurford 2002; K. Smith et al. 2003a).

Kirby explains this result in terms of competition among linguistic replicators with varying degrees of generality, and makes an explicit link between the learning bottleneck (which introduces a pressure for generalization) and an advantage to linguistic replicators of greater generality. This insight, more than the specifics of his model, led to a series of follow-up studies which identify other features impacting on the relative advantages of compositionality (for instance, frequency of occurrence: see Kirby 2001; meaning space structure: Brighton 2002; distribution of meanings in meaning space: K. Smith et al. 2003a).

Implementing a verbal theory often requires a far more rigorous definition of the components of that theory—one of the advantages (and challenges) of formal modelling is that it forces a high level of explicitness. The implementational decisions made when building a model add additional assumptions to the original theory, and the results produced by that model can sometimes depend on these additional assumptions. To return to our example: Kirby (2000), in implementing a particular learning model, assumes that learners ignore data which would lead to ambiguity (i.e. two or more distinct meanings being expressed using a single utterance). Brighton et al. (2005) show that this bias against ambiguity plays an important role: in the absence of such a bias, maximally ambiguous, unstructured grammars evolve, rather than compositionally structured grammars (see Kirby et al. 2008 for an experimental demonstration of the same result, and Steels and Kaplan 2002 for a related result on lexical ambiguity). Again, this outcome can be explained with reference to Kirby's insight regarding selection for generalizability—ambiguity (everything is expressed using the same signal) constitutes a highly viable generalization ('no matter what you want to say, just say X'), and consequently prospers for precisely the same reasons as compositionality. This model therefore reveals two key assumptions which must be in place for Wray's original theory to stand up: the learning bottleneck, and some mechanism (perhaps arising from the biases of learners or functional considerations) for blocking ambiguity.

## 60.2 BUILDING IN RESULTS, AND JUSTIFYING ASSUMPTIONS

To summarize so far: formal models make excellent tools for testing the predictions of theories about the interaction of (multiple) complex systems, which are otherwise difficult to analyse. Using such models can confirm, refine, or contradict our verbal predictions, and potentially sharpen our understanding of the phenomenon we are interested in, for example, by foregrounding the importance of assumptions which were previously more or less hidden (in our example, the learning bottleneck), or by identifying the need for such assumptions in the first place (such as the assumption about how learners handle ambiguity described above).

If the consequences of those assumptions do not match with the real-world data that the model is intended to account for, then we know that one or more of the assumptions is wrong. Conversely, if the assumptions necessary to yield a particular set of consequences can be shown to be incorrect (for instance, if we have to make assumptions about the processes of learning which we know to conflict with the developmental literature) then the model can be used to show that a particular theory must be abandoned or further refined. Explicitly or implicitly, modellers must seek to justify the assumptions of their models against the kind of criticism levelled at formal models by Bickerton:

Somewhere among them [i.e. published formal models, KS] one can find almost all the initial conditions that one could imagine, save for those that most likely obtained when language began in reality. Powerful and potentially interesting though this approach is, its failure to incorporate more realistic conditions (perhaps because these would be more difficult to simulate) sharply reduces any contribution it might make towards unravelling language evolution. So far, it is a classic case of looking for your car-keys where the street-lamps are (Bickerton 2007: 522).

The way to avoid this sort of criticism is to start from theories that are well grounded in the empirical literature, and aim to explain a well-understood phenomenon at an appropriate level of abstraction: the reasonableness of a set of assumptions is of course an empirical matter, and the main contribution of formal models is to show what follows from a given set of assumptions. Importantly, the consequences of a particular set of assumptions may itself be a means to rejecting those assumptions, if the formal model reveals predictions implicit in those assumptions which contradict the real-world behaviour of interest.

One common reaction to formal models which produce a surprising or interesting result is 'well, of course it produces that result, you've built it in to your model'. Of course, this accusation is entirely true: building results into models is *the entire point of formal modelling*. In a formal model, the outcomes of the model are inherent in the assumptions built into that model: if a particular result is produced by that model then it must be due to those assumptions. The interesting question is *what* has to be built in to yield a particular result. Models allow us to vary parameters of interest to see how they influence the result in question, as in the example above, where factors like the severity of the transmission bottleneck, the structure of the semantic space, and the ambiguity biases of learners can be manipulated and be shown to impact on the evolution of linguistic structure. The emergence of structure in these models is 'built in' in the interesting sense that it follows mechanically from the right sets of assumptions.

## 60.3 SIMPLE VERSUS COMPLEX

A simple model includes only the minimal set of assumptions required to test the relevant aspects of the theory and, as far as possible, abstracts away from everything else. For example, a recent tendency in part of the formal modelling literature has seen the replacement of relatively complex models with much simpler, much more abstract models. For example, Kirby et al. (2007) present an extremely simple model (where languages are simply treated as associations between a small number of atomic, unstructured meanings and signals) which allows the same points to be made about the relationship between linguistic regularity, the learning bottleneck, frequency, and learner bias as earlier, more complex models (as exemplified, for instance, by Kirby (2000), where language is treated as a mapping between complex meanings and complex signals, underpinned by a grammar specifying that mapping), but with a much simpler, cleaner model of learning and far fewer assumptions. Related models (e.g. Griffiths and Kalish 2007) allow analytic results to be derived, in this case, describing the relationship between the biases of language learners and the outcomes of cultural evolution in populations of such learners: rather than necessitating running a number of simulations or performing a number of numerical calculations, these simple models are more amenable to mathematical analyses that allow us to prove what outcomes will *necessarily* hold under a certain set of assumptions, rather than results that seem generally to occur in a certain (usually small) number of simulation runs.

Some non-modellers are troubled by the abstraction of formal models in general (for all formal models abstract away from detail, even complex ones) and simple models in particular. Similarly, some modellers feel that the logical next step is to move in the direction of increasing complexity, in order to produce more *realistic* models that can be more easily related to real-world data. However, complex models suffer from shortcomings of their own. Firstly, a model as complex as the original phenomenon is pointless, because it presents an opacity problem (how are the outcomes of the model related to the assumptions of the model?) as challenging as our original problem of understanding the real-world phenomenon. Simple models are also more amenable to analytic treatments, which allow us to move away from interpretation of simulation or numerical results and start making more definitive assertions about (abstract) states of affairs that must necessarily hold under given sets of assumptions. However, perhaps the most persuasive argument for simplicity appeals to *insight*. In his excellent book on modelling in ecology and evolutionary biology, Karl Sigmund (1995) argues strongly that the measure of a successful formal model should not necessarily be the predictions it yields but the insight it affords:

Predictions are not the pinnacle of science. They are useful, especially for falsifying theories. However, predicting can't be a model's *only* purpose. This is not meant as an attempt to falsify Popperianism (I wouldn't know how to begin). But surely the *insights* offered by a model are at least as important as its *predictions*: they help in understanding things by playing with them (Sigmund 1995: 4).

Simpler models afford better insights—they highlight the key factors, naked of additional unnecessary assumptions, and therefore allow us a better feel for whatever system we are playing with. To take an example: a number of models (including all of those cited here) make the abstraction that learners are exposed to utterance-meaning pairs during learning, rather than utterances and situations in the world from which meaning can be derived: this abstraction is dubbed the 'assumption of explicit meaning transfer' in A. Smith (2003). This simplification is clearly a distortion of reality: we of course know that meanings aren't explicitly transmitted from individual to individual during language learning. But the insight that models making this assumption afford (namely that languages adapt, and that structure can be an adaptation for generalization) is worth the sacrifice in realism (see Chater and Christiansen, this volume).

## 60.4 Moving beyond models

Recent years have seen modellers become interested in testing the assumptions and predictions of their models on real human beings, in laboratory experiments. There are two ways in which this can be achieved. One approach is to test the predictions of models directly in laboratory populations. For example, we can test the predictions of a formal model of cultural evolution using an experimental version of the parlour game Chinese Whispers (for a recent overview of this 'diffusion chain' methodology see K. Smith et al. 2008; see also Kirby, this volume). Kirby et al. (2008) use such a methodology to test the formal modelling prediction that languages should adapt to become learnable, and do so by becoming generalizable. In this experiment, the solutions to the generalization problem closely resemble those which we see in the formal models, including systematic ambiguity (when ambiguity is permitted) or compositional structure (when ambiguity is blocked).

A second line of development, suggested in K. Smith (2008), is to begin to test the *assumptions* of the formal models directly, rather than their predictions. To return to our earlier example: Kirby (2000) necessarily makes a number of assumptions about the nature of the learning process, and in particular the ways in which learners attempt to generalize over linguistic data items. While some justification can be sought from the developmental literature, it should also be possible to test these assumptions in the lab. Do learners really learn like this? Can we show it in the lab, perhaps through use of tailored artificial language learning experiments? Ultimately, the relationship between formal model and experiment should be reciprocal. If we find through experimentation that human learners diverge from the assumptions made in formal models, we can feed this information back in to the models to see how a better set of assumptions impacts on the predictions of those models. For example, if experiments suggest that learners learn in a radically different way to that envisaged by Kirby, will we still see the cultural evolution of linguistic structure, or does something else happen? Does this revised model require further remedial assumptions, which can in turn be tested?

## 60.5 CONCLUSIONS

Formal models provide a means of testing our theories, by allowing us to mechanically work through the outcomes of the set of assumptions embodied in a particular theory. This is a useful tool, particularly (as is the case in evolutionary linguistics) when dealing with multiple complex systems (learning, culture, evolution) which interact to yield a behaviour (language) which is itself complex. Perhaps more importantly, formal models are an excellent way of gaining insight into these processes: by abstracting the system down to its bare bones and then playing with it, formal models help us to sharpen our intuitions about how the complex systems shaping language might work.

# CHAPTER 61

# LANGUAGE IS AN ADAPTIVE SYSTEM: THE ROLE OF CULTURAL EVOLUTION IN THE ORIGINS OF STRUCTURE

## SIMON KIRBY

## 61.1 INTRODUCTION: A MULTIPLICITY OF MECHANISMS

Understanding the origins of human language is one of the most, if not the most, challenging topics of modern scientific enquiry (Christiansen and Kirby 2003). One of the reasons for this is that the underlying processes that ultimately give rise to language are uniquely complex and entangled. In order to understand why the language we speak has the structure it does, we need to consider how each of us came to have internalized the knowledge of that structure. In other words, we need to understand how, during development, we were exposed to instances of language use and used that experience to become competent users of that language. However, this only really scratches the surface. Even if we were to completely understand the process of language acquisition, this simply pushes the explanatory challenge back, leaving open the question of why the language we are exposed to during acquisition came to have the particular properties it does. Furthermore, if we believe that the mechanisms of language acquisition form part of the explanation of language structure, we can ask how those mechanisms came to be the way they are too.

One way of thinking about these explanatory challenges is in terms of the dynamical systems that give rise to language. Here I will outline three, although there may be other ways of dividing things up:

- *Individual learning.* This is the process that takes instances of language use as input and 'reverse engineers' some kind of system (i.e. a grammar) that is capable of producing similar usage.
- *Socio/cultural transmission.* The language we speak is, in one sense, the result of all the utterances ever spoken within earshot of anyone who we have ever heard speak, and all the utterances ever spoken to the speakers of those utterances, and so on back through time. Languages are thus the product of a breathtakingly rich pattern of cultural inheritance as information about the structure of a language flows through social networks and over historical time.
- *Biological evolution.* Our species is unique in having a learned system of communication which employs a structured (and therefore extensible) mapping between meanings and signals. This uniqueness is ultimately explained by our unique biology. In particular, our ability to learn language is underpinned by a biological endowment that arose through a process of biological evolution. In other words, we have inherited our ability to acquire language from a long line of language-acquiring ancestors.

These three dynamical systems—all uncontroversially implicated in some way with the structure of the languages we speak—operate at different timescales: the *ontogenetic* timescale of the individual; the timescale of the history of a language, or more broadly languages in general (what Hurford 1990b calls the *glossogenetic* timescale); and the timescale of the evolution of the species, which might be referred to as the *phylogenetic* timescale. These timescales may appear to be quite separate. Indeed they are typically tackled by distinct subdisciplines in linguistics: language acquisition; historical/sociolinguistics; and language evolution respectively. However, there is a commonality that it is worth pointing out between the processes that operate in each. Learning, cultural transmission, and biological evolution are all complex adaptive systems. In other words, they are processes involving a number of interacting parts which give rise to emergent properties that show the appearance of design. Biological evolution is the classic example of a complex adaptive system: organisms exhibit the appearance of being

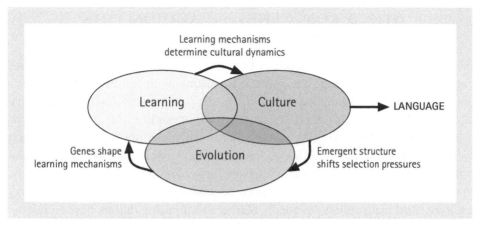

**Figure 61.1. The three complex adaptive systems that give rise to language and their interactions.**

designed for survival in their niche, despite the absence of any intelligent designer, by virtue of the way in which genetic information is passed on. Similarly, learning can be seen as a complex adaptive system that gives rise to brains which are better adapted to a particular task. It is perhaps less self-evident that cultural transmission is adaptive, but I argue in this chapter that this is the case, especially for language.

In addition to their common status as complex adaptive systems, there is another reason why we should be wary of compartmentalizing the study of learning, cultural transmission, and biological evolution in linguistics. It turns out that there are significant interactions between these three, as shown in Figure 61.1.

Firstly, the way in which we acquire language is determined, at least in part, by our particular cognitive make-up, which is ultimately influenced by our genes. (Note that this is not the same as saying that we have a domain-specific language faculty, although it is of course consistent with that view.) Secondly, it is the way in which we learn language that drives the cultural evolution of language. Finally, the universal properties of language arising from this cultural process have the potential to alter the selection pressures driving biological evolution.

These interactions underline the need for a broad understanding of what we mean by evolutionary linguistics. To gain a truly explanatory account of why human language is the way it is (arguably the goal for linguistics as a whole) we need to understand language as an evolutionary system that operates on multiple interdependent timescales. Evolutionary linguistics, therefore, should not be taken to mean simply that subarea of linguistics dealing with biological evolution, but rather the approach to linguistics that treats language as a complex adaptive system.

In the following sections, I will examine these interactions in turn, and argue that, taken together, they suggest rather different conclusions of the role of biology in the explanation of linguistic structure than is often assumed.

## 61.2 FROM GENES TO ACQUISITION

There are clear anatomical differences between humans and our nearest relatives that are relevant to language. However, it is reasonable to assume that part of the biological difference that makes us able to acquire language resides in our cognitive machinery. In other words, there is something about our brains that predisposes us to learn language that no other species shares. This assumption underpins what might be considered the 'orthodox' evolutionary psychology position on the evolution of language set out most clearly by Pinker and Bloom (1990). Put simply, they suggest that the approach to language acquisition based on work by Chomsky (e.g. 1965) and many others, is broadly correct in supposing that we have an innate, species-specific, and domain-specific faculty for language. This faculty, they argue, has two important features: it is complex, and it is adaptive.

There are many fascinating issues and debates that spring from these two claims (for example, much of the debate between Hauser et al. (2002) on the one hand, and Pinker and Jackendoff (2005) on the other revolves around how complex the domain-specific aspects of the language faculty really are). However, if Pinker and Bloom (1990) are right about the language faculty, what does it tell us? If the language faculty is innate and drives our process of language acquisition, then we have a causal link between our genes and language. Furthermore, if the faculty is complex and adaptive, then Pinker and Bloom (1990) argue that the only explanation for the structure of the language faculty is a Darwinian one. In other words, we also have a causal link between the structure of language and our genes.

One interesting corollary of this position is that our capacity for language is not only innate, but also domain-specific, at least in one reading of what domain-specificity is. It is a truism to state that our genetic endowment affects our ability to learn language (how could it be any other way?), but to state that we have genes that are in some sense specifically for learning language, we need to show that they arose through selection *for* that function. This is essentially the Pinker and Bloom (1990) position. However, as we shall see, it is not the only coherent one.

## 61.3 FROM LEARNING TO CULTURAL EVOLUTION

A simplification underlying the picture sketched above is that there is some simple relationship between any innate capacity for language that we have and the languages that we actually speak. To put this more precisely, we can think of the language faculty in terms of the set of languages that it allows us to acquire. In some models of language acquisition, such as Principles and Parameters (Chomsky 1981), this is made formally explicit: the language faculty constrains the search space for learning by ruling out some logically possible language types. If evolution is to respond to the particulars of the language faculty, then different constraints or biases imposed by our genes must make their presence felt in the types of language that are actually spoken. In other words, the pattern of cross-linguistic variation must directly reflect the nature of the language faculty; language universals should mirror Universal Grammar. But is this assumption valid? Can we be confident that the distribution of language types spoken by a population of individuals will necessarily directly reflect the state of their cognitive machinery? To approach this question, we need to understand exactly how properties of an individual's learning mechanism can shape language universals. In other words, we need to solve a 'problem of linkage' (Kirby 1999) between explanans (our biology) and explanandum (language structure).

The solution to the problem of linkage turns out to lie in socio/cultural transmission, the final dynamical system we listed in the introduction. Language does not spring directly from our language faculty. Rather, it is inherited and constantly shaped by our membership of a speech community. It is only by taking this point seriously that we can begin to understand how individual properties (e.g. features of an individual's learning mechanism) end up making their influence felt at the population level in the actual structure of language.

It is crucial for a truly explanatory linguistics to take seriously the potential disconnect between individual-level and population-level explanation, but interestingly the evolutionary orthodoxy sketched out by Pinker and Bloom (1990) in some sense fails to do this. Although biological evolution is an adaptive system that is all about populations, the assumption that there is a straightforward link between the properties of the language acquisition device and the universal properties of language may arise from the notion of an ideal speaker-listener in a homogeneous speech community (Chomsky 1965), a foundational idealization of much of generative grammar. Whilst this idealization has its place, and much progress on understanding the structure of language has flowed from it, we need to move beyond it when considering language as an adaptive system. In other words, it has no place in an evolutionary approach to linguistics. Accordingly, we should expand our picture of the causal connections in the evolution of language to include cultural transmission.

## 61.4 Methodology

An obvious question at this stage is how exactly we are to go about uncovering the role that cultural transmission plays in our explanation of linguistic structure. One approach, following on from foundational work by Hurford (1989), is to build working models of populations made up of individuals that interact and acquire language from each other, with the hope of uncovering the general relationship between learning biases/constraints and emergent language universals. The idea is that our intuitive understanding of interacting dynamical systems is poor, but models allow us to study the basic mechanisms in an idealized setting. Ultimately, the aim is to take the understanding gained this way and apply it later to the real systems.

There have been three broad approaches to this kind of modelling (although there is substantial overlap between these):

- *Computational/robotic.* This approach has been extensively explored since the late 1980s (e.g. Hurford 1989). Models of language learning 'agents' interact in simulated populations. The literature in this area is vast, but there are several accessible introductory reviews (see Kirby 2002; Steels 2003; Jäger et al. 2009; Cangelosi, this volume) as well as an edited collection of works (Cangelosi and Parisi 2002) and a practical introduction to the field in preparation (Kirby et al., in preparation).
- *Mathematical.* Although less common, there are a number of papers that use mathematical techniques rather than multiagent computational simulation (e.g. Niyogi 2006; Griffiths and Kalish, 2007; Kirby et al. 2007).
- *Experimental.* More recently, there has been the growth of a new approach to modelling cultural transmission and its influence on language using real human participants in a laboratory setting (e.g. Kirby et al. 2008; Reali and Griffiths 2009).

    There are a number of ways these models could be configured, but the Iterated Learning Model (ILM) provides a framework which characterizes many of them. The guiding principles for the ILM are as follows:

- Individuals are explicitly modelled. In other words, population-level behaviour must be *emergent* from the interactions of individuals.
- Individuals *learn* by observing instances of behaviour.
- Individuals also *produce* behaviour as a result of learning that then goes on to be input to other individuals' learning.

Within this broad framework, there are many ways in which specific models can vary. For example, a key design question for modellers is to consider how learning works. Guiding questions might be: how domain-specific will the model of learning be? How constrained will it be? Will the learning model be the same for all individuals in the population, or will it vary? Another important axis of variation concerns what is being learned. For example, individuals might have a task of simply discovering a mapping between meanings and signals, or they might be embedded in a more ecologically relevant context where they must solve some communicative problem. Finally, there are important variables relating to the structure of the population, such as size; spatial structure; social networks; population turnover (i. e. birth and death); and the mix of horizontal versus vertical transmission.

Rather than try and exemplify all these possible variants in the literature, I will go into three examples in more detail after considering what have been the central lessons learned so far from this modelling work.

## 61.5 THE MAIN RESULT

Despite the wide range of models, it is increasingly clear that, as noted in the introduction, socio/cultural transmission is an adaptive system. Specifically, what we see again and again in models of iterated learning is that language can exhibit the appearance of design. Normally we think of there being only two possible sources of design in nature: biological evolution by natural selection, or intelligent design by intentional agents. The iterated learning models suggest a third alternative. Cultural evolution can deliver design-like solutions.

But what does this mean for language? In what way is language adapting through iterated learning? The simple answer is that language is adapting in such a way as to ensure its own survival through the transmission process. As Deacon (1997) and Christiansen and Chater (2008; Chater and Christiansen, this volume) have pointed-ed out, there is a clear imperative on a culturally transmitted language: to be transmitted with fidelity from one individual to the next (and the next, and so on) a language must be learnable despite any constraints placed on that transmission. For example, languages have to be learned by children from a subset. This poverty of the stimulus acts as an informational bottleneck on the transmission of language. If a language (or more accurately some feature or variant in a language) is suboptimal from the perspective of transmission, say if it is difficult to learn accurately, then inevitably its long-term survival through repeated cycles of learning and production such as those seen in the iterated learning model will be in doubt.

What modelling allows us to do is vary the nature of this bottleneck on transmission from one individual to the next and observe the resulting adaptations by the culturally transmitted language. For example, a number of modellers have been interested in testing the hypothesis that structure in the mapping between signals and meanings in language is a response to the cultural transmission bottleneck. It is clear that languages are strikingly non-random, in that they have a partially predictable relationship between meanings and signals. In other words, if we know some meaning-signal pairs in a human language, we can often reliably predict other such pairs. This is an enormously important feature of language—it is what enables us to talk about things that we have never heard talked about before and reliably be understood. In this respect, it is arguably more important than recursion as a core property of human language. This compositionality in the encoding of meanings in utterances is also uniquely human, or very nearly so[1] (see Smith and Kirby 2011 for discussion).

# 61.6 A COMPUTATIONAL MODEL

Many computational implementations of the iterated learning model have looked precisely at how this compositionality emerges (see Brighton et al. 2005 for review). In order to do this, they obviously need to demonstrate a transition from a signalling system that is entirely non-compositional to one that is. What would a signalling system that is non-compositional look like? Simply put, the relationship between meanings and signals would be completely arbitrary—with no systematic internal structure to the mapping. In other words, in this initial state, signals are related to meanings holistically. This can be created either by starting the simulations with a 'language'[2] whose signals are entirely randomly generated with no regard to the meanings they correspond to. Alternatively, some simulations start with no language at all, and agents are allowed to 'invent' strings at random whenever they are required to.

These simulations show that features of linguistic structure, such as compositionality, emerge naturally from the process of iterated learning. For example, in Brighton's (2002) model, simulated agents try and learn a language pairing strings of letters with simple idealized meanings consisting of a number of features, each of which can take one of a finite set of values. For example, an 'utterance' in this

---

[1] Arguably, there are some other cases of compositionality in animal communication. For example, the dance of the honeybee carries different aspects of meaning with different aspects of the signal (von Frisch 1974). However, in this case, there is no open-ended recombination of signal components.

[2] Two objections may arise from the use of the term 'language' to refer to the model signal systems in these, and similar, simulations. Firstly, in the initial state, by virtue of being non-compositional they lack the very feature that we are arguing is definitional of human language. An alternative would be to refer to the signalling systems as 'protolanguage' until that point in the simulation where compositionality emerges. Indeed, this would have close parallels with at least one account of protolanguage as a non-compositional system (Wray 1998). This is problematic, not least because 'protolanguage' has different meanings for different authors, and the transition observed in simulations turns out to be gradual. Secondly, it could be argued that the final system in these simulations, albeit compositional, lacks any number of other features of human language that we might be interested in. Of course, this misses the point that any successful model must focus in on the object of study, in this case the transition from non-compositional to compositional meaning-signal mappings, by appropriate abstraction and idealization. We are choosing to focus here on compositionality, since it has been studied extensively using models. It is by no means the only feature of language that has been explored this way, of course.

language might be the string 'gkptb' paired with the three-featured meaning [3,2,4]. It doesn't matter what these features or values actually correspond to, because this model is not grounded in the real world (although some models are, such as Steels 2003). Nor is it important what the symbols in the string correspond to (syllables, perhaps). For Brighton's models, all that is important is that both strings and meanings are potentially decomposable into subparts. I say 'potentially' here, because it is crucial for these models of the emergence of compositionality not to assume initially a particular decomposition. In Brighton's model, the agents' learning algorithm instead starts with the assumption that the language they are exposed to is in fact completely non-compositional. The learners simply store all the string-meaning pairs unanalysed essentially as a list. Obviously, if this was all that happened, then it would not be a particularly interesting model of learning. There would not, for example, be any possibility of learners generalizing to unseen meanings. Accordingly, the model looks for any generalizations that are supported by the data. It does this by using a machine learning technique known as minimum description length learning. The learner tries to build a finite state model[3] of the language that is as concise as possible while at the same time predicting the data well.

Given a random (holistic) language, in which there is no systematic relationship between meanings and signals, then very little compression is possible of the maximal grammar (i.e. one which simply lists each meaning-string pair). Accordingly, only minimal generalization is possible. However, what is striking about Brighton's model, and indeed all other simulations of the iterated learning process, is that this state of affairs is not maintained. In each generation of the simulation, an agent is called on to produce strings for a random selection of meanings, which they do as best they can with the grammar they have acquired. The resulting meaning-string pairs are then input to the next generation's learner and the process repeats. What happens depends on the size of the bottleneck on transmission, in other words, the size of the set of randomly chosen meanings that each agent is given to produce for the next learner's input. With a wide bottleneck where all possible meanings are likely to be observed by every learner, nothing much happens: the language remains a holistic, unstructured system. However, if the bottleneck is tightened then a dramatically different result is observed. Over a number of generations, the size of the grammars is reduced and the resulting languages are highly structured and compositional (see Figure 61.2 for a series of grammars from a typical simulation run).

These languages late in the simulation are relatively stable—that is, they are learnable by each generation despite the existence of the transmission bottleneck. The result of iterated learning, therefore, is an adaptation of the language being

---

[3] Minimum description length learning can be applied to formalisms that are not finite state. However, a finite state model of this simple language is sufficient to explore the topic of interest to Brighton, namely compositionality, and proves to be significantly more computationally tractable.

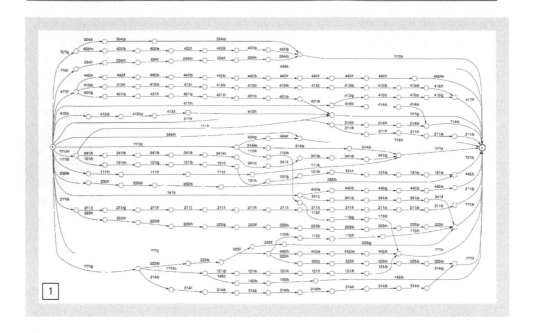

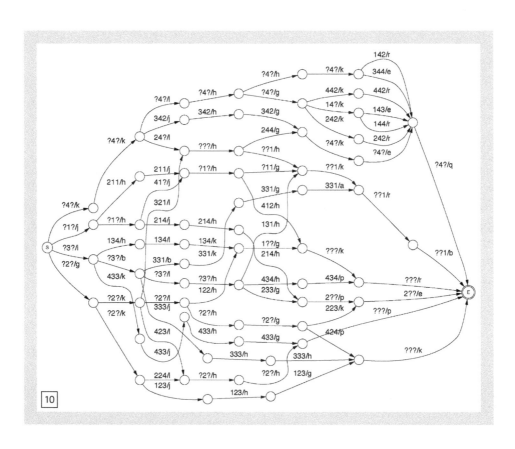

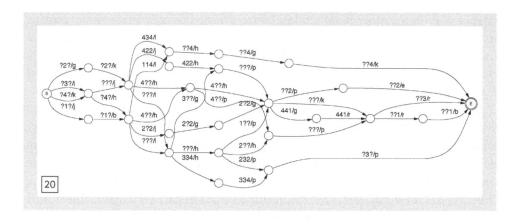

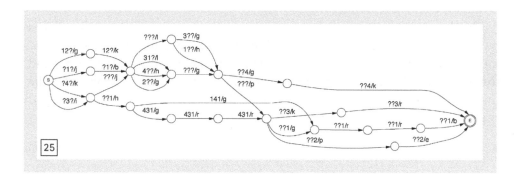

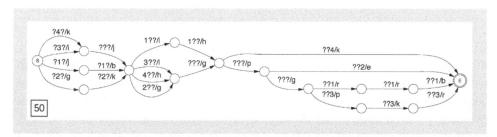

**Figure 61.2. Example grammars from a run of Brighton's simulation, with generation numbers shown.**

Note that the grammars become smaller and simpler. At the same time they become more learnable, more compositional, and more general. To see more details of these grammars, please refer to Brighton et al. (2005) from which these figures are adapted.

transmitted to the pressures placed on that transmission by the bottleneck. Languages that are difficult to fit through the bottleneck (i.e. to learn) will result in noisy transmission because of the failure of reliable generalization and the introduction of randomness. Any generalizable feature of language that arises by chance will on the other hand tend to be transmitted reliably precisely because of its generalizability. It is more able to pass through a narrow bottleneck. The inevitable result is a gradual but snowballing accretion of increasingly generalizable structure in the language. As Hurford (2000) puts it in the title of his article, 'social transmission favours linguistic generalization'.

Brighton's results and others like them show us that languages adapt to be learnable in the presence of a transmission bottleneck. But what can we expect languages that have adapted in this way to look like? In the simulations I have described, the answer is that they become compositionally structured, with the meanings of the whole signal being made up of the combination of meanings of the subparts of that signal. However, this result depends in part on a reasonable model of learning. For example, if Brighton had used a representation of languages that did not allow strings to be decomposed into substrings, then obviously no such evolution could have occurred.

This leaves the reasonable question: what is the relationship between what is built into the learner in a computational model and the results that we see in that model? The results show we cannot simply equate the structure of the learner and the structure of languages that emerge (because the models have demonstrated the importance of the bottleneck in determining the result), but we have not escaped the fact that there is some relationship between the two.

## 61.7 A MATHEMATICAL MODEL

Kirby et al. (2007), building on work by Griffiths and Kalish (2007), used a mathematical model of learning placed within the iterated learning framework to try and answer precisely how the nature of the learner impacts on the structure of language. In order to give a more general answer to this problem than is provided by the typical computational simulation, a Bayesian model of learning is used, which allows us to provide a very transparent representation of what is innate, and what comes from the data in learning.

The Bayesian approach treats learning as a process of hypothesis selection given some a priori bias over possible hypotheses—a measure of our beliefs about hypotheses in advance of any data heard. If we assume that the learner wants to pick the most likely hypothesis $h$ for a given set of data heard $d$, then we need some way of working out the probability of each hypothesis given that data set, $P(h|d)$. How can we get at this probability for a particular hypothesis? It is reasonable to assume that a learner has ready access to a related value: the probability of the data the learner heard given a hypothesis, $P(d|h)$. This is because we can assume the learner has some model of language that relates hypothesis (i.e. grammars) to data (i.e. utterances). After all, this is what it means to be a speaker: we know what utterances a grammar produces. Naively, we might think that these two probabilities will be the same, that $P(h|d)=P(d|h)$. This is akin to saying that the best hypothesis is the one that best fits the data. However, this ignores the fact that some hypotheses might be more likely a priori than others. In other words, learning may have a prior bias.

Bayes' rule solves the problem for us by allowing us to determine the probability, $P(h|d)$, of some hypothesis $h$ given some data $d$ in terms of the probability of that data given the hypothesis, $P(d|h)$, and the prior probability of the hypothesis, $P(h)$[4]:

$$P(h|d) \propto P(d|h)P(h)$$

The last term, the prior, is whatever the learner brings to the task of language learning that is independent of the data. In other words, $P(h)$, is a model of innateness, if we take innateness in its broadest sense (i.e. something that may or may not be language-specific). So, Bayes' rule gives us a model of learning that makes explicit the separation of the contribution of data and the contribution of prior bias from the learner herself. This model of learning can be placed within the iterated learning framework to understand how prior bias affects the cultural evolution process. Kirby et al. (2007) detail how, mathematically, a prediction can be made of what languages should look like as a result of cultural evolution given any prior bias. Formally, they show how to calculate the *stationary distribution* over languages resulting from iterated learning. This distribution is the expected frequency of each language in the limit of cultural evolution. In other words, it is a complete description of the language universals that can be predicted, assuming cultural evolution has run for sufficient time. They show how, under a range of reasonable assumptions, this stationary distribution depends on the particular prior bias, the frequency distribution over meanings, and the number of utterances a learner hears.

Put simply, then, this general model of iterated Bayesian learning allows us to calculate exactly what language universals will emerge given any particular model of innateness and details of the bottleneck on cultural transmission.

The headline result from Kirby et al. (2007) is that, although the nature of the prior bias is important in determining the shape of language universals, the strength of that prior bias does not determine how strongly constraining those universals are. In fact, the bias can be arbitrarily weak or strong and have the same effect. Instead, as was predicted by the computational models of cultural evolution, the crucial factor is the bottleneck. The less data a learner hears, the more the

---

[4] To calculate the actual probability, we would also need to normalize by dividing by the probability of the data summed over all hypotheses. However, since this is constant for any given set of data, we can ignore this value if we are simply looking for the best hypothesis.

languages that emerge reflect the prior preferences of the learner. So, for example, if a learner has even the tiniest preference for regular, predictable languages, then the languages that emerge from cultural evolution will exhibit regularity and structure wherever data is sparse but not necessarily where data is abundant. In the realm of morphology, for instance, this would be reflected in the distribution of regular versus irregular paradigms. This is precisely what we see in human languages, where irregularity is seen to correlate with frequency (Bybee 2006a). Note, however, that the iterated Bayesian learning model is entirely general and can be applied to any situation where we need to understand how individual psychology shapes the behaviour of populations through cultural transmission (see Kalish et al. 2007, for examples of it being applied to fields outside of language).

## 61.8 AN EXPERIMENTAL MODEL

A recent emerging trend is the use of experimental techniques with human participants to build close analogues to the computational and mathematical models of iterated learning in the laboratory. The strength of this approach is firstly that we can test the generality of our conclusions from models in a situation where the prior bias is provided by real human biology. Secondly, we can see whether results like the emergence of compositionality from a holistic protolanguage (Wray 1998) can really occur in a feasible timescale.

So how can we observe the cultural evolution of language in the lab? Kirby et al. (2008) present the first of a series of experiments inspired by work on the emergence of communicative conventions in language game studies (e.g. Galantucci 2005). Whereas the earlier experimental studies demonstrate clearly that novel coordinated communication systems can emerge among participants who are intentionally trying to construct such a system, Kirby et al. (2008) endeavour to show that simply the process of cultural transmission alone was enough to 'design' a structured linguistic system. In their experiment, participants are exposed to an artificial language made up of written strings of syllables paired with simple geometric pictures (i.e. meanings). They are then tested on their ability to recall the strings they had seen given a set of pictures. What the participants are not told is that some of the pictures they are tested on were ones that they did not see in training.

So far, this is a pretty standard artificial language learning study. What makes this a cultural evolution experiment is that the data produced during testing by one participant forms the language that the next participant in the experiment is trained on. In this way, the experimenter has control only over the initial language fed into the 'chain' of participants, and then observes how that language evolves culturally as it is passed from one to the next.

A key feature of the design of these human iterated learning experiments is how the language output by one participant is transformed into the data given to the next. For example, by only showing a subset of the language, a transmission bottleneck can be implemented. In addition, Kirby et al. (2008) experiment with other ways in which the data can be 'filtered'. In one condition, for example, any ambiguity that emerges in the languages the participants produce is filtered out by removing items so that there is never more than one picture that is assigned the same string (see the original paper for more details).

In every run of the experiment, the languages became increasingly learnable as they were transmitted from participant to participant, but in the case of filtering for ambiguity the results were particularly intriguing. The input to the start of the experiment was a randomly constructed holistic language, but gradually over the generations this evolved towards a compositionally structured one in which subparts of the signal corresponded to subparts of the meaning. In every case, as the language became easier and easier for participants to learn, so too did it become more and more structured. Just as in the computational models, compositionality had emerged from holism.

It is important to note that the participants were not aware of the contribution they were making to the emerging structure. Participants believed they were simply learning as best they could the language that was presented to them. In this case, as in the computational and mathematical models, it is language that is adapting to the pressures placed on it by the nature of the cultural transmission bottleneck, rather than individuals intentionally constructing a structured language.

## 61.9 CONCLUSION: FROM CULTURAL EVOLUTION TO BIOLOGICAL FITNESS?

What all these models of cultural evolution demonstrate is that the relationship between genes and language structure is indirect. The mathematical models show that we cannot infer strong innate constraints even in the case where we see strongly constraining universals of language structure. Equally, all the models of iterated learning show that we cannot infer that a biological process of natural selection of language-related genes is in play where we observe adaptive structure in human language. Rather, the very fact that language is culturally transmitted can itself explain the emergence of adaptations. So where does this leave biological evolution? If we assume that language is in some way relevant to fitness, then it seems likely that the structure of language that emerges from the process of cultural evolution will affect the fitness landscape of the learners acquiring that language. Of course, any changes in biology of language-learning individuals may affect their prior biases and hence in turn alter the trajectory of cultural evolution and eventually the structure of language.

Understanding this co-evolutionary dynamic is a topic of intense current research. For example, there are vigorous debates about the relevance of the 'Baldwin effect' and genetic assimilation whereby features of the environment that were at one stage learned may become innately canalized (see, for instance, Briscoe 2000; Chater et al. 2009; Anderson, this volume). An emerging line of enquiry concerns the role of 'masking' and 'unmasking' in the evolution of language, where traits are masked from the view of natural selection by the effect of cultural transmission and other very different traits are unmasked and brought under selection as a side effect (see Smith and Kirby 2008; Deacon 2009, 2010).

One thing, however, is abundantly clear. There is *something* biologically special about humans that gives us this unique behaviour called language. To discover what this is, we need to be clear about all the adaptive systems that underpin the emergence of language. Ultimately, it may be the existence of these systems themselves that provides the requisite uniqueness. Although there are other species that can culturally transmit a structured signalling system (for instance, songbirds), only humans have the capacity to transmit culturally complex signals mapped onto complex meanings. In all the models of iterated learning of language, be they computational, mathematical, or experimental, this ability has had to be built in or assumed. Without it, the emergence of linguistic structure appears impossible. Once it is in place—as the growing number of models looking at everything from phonemic coding (Zuidema and de Boer 2009), through compositionality (Kirby 2001), to recursive syntax (Batali 2002), attest—the emergence of language appears almost inevitable.

# CHAPTER 62

# ROBOTICS AND EMBODIED AGENT MODELLING OF THE EVOLUTION OF LANGUAGE

## ANGELO CANGELOSI

### 62.1 GROUNDING LANGUAGE IN PERCEPTION AND ACTION: THE EMBODIED AGENTS AND ROBOTICS APPROACH

Computational approaches to the modelling of the evolution of communication and language have significantly contributed to an increased research interest in language origins (Cangelosi and Parisi 2002). Models based on experiments with robots and embodied multiagent systems (Steels 2003; Mirolli and Nolfi 2009; Cangelosi 2010) help us understand the evolutionary and developmental dynamics linking language with other sensorimotor, affective, and cognitive capabilities, in the context of social and cultural learning. The modelling approach is consistent with embodied cognition theories and the symbol grounding approach to language (Harnad 1990; Cangelosi 2010). For example, some language origin theories focus specifically on the link between language and action, as in the mirror neuron hypothesis (Arbib, this volume) and the link between language evolution and hand manipulation skills (Corballis 2002, this volume).

This chapter provides a brief overview of major seminal work on the modelling of language evolution through experiments with robots and embodied agents. 'Robots' in this sense are simulated and/or physical artefacts that can interact with the world through sensors (e.g. microphone for sounds, camera for images, touch sensors) and actuators (e.g. wheels for spatial exploration, and arms and hands for manipulation of objects). Robot language experiments typically involve tasks in which the robots must communicate about objects and entities in the environment (Steels 1999), about their physical interaction with objects (Marocco et al. 2003; Cangelosi et al. 2010), and about their body posture (Steels and Spranger 2009). 'Embodied agents' are multiagent systems in which a population of simulated agents live in a shared environment, can receive visual, auditory, and tactile information about the world, and can act on it. These experiments typically involve communication about spatial navigation and foraging tasks (Cangelosi 2001). However, the differences between the two approaches should not be considered crucial, given the imprecise distinction between experiments with (simulated) robots and the use of embodied agents with rich sensorimotor properties, and also because robotic studies are often at least partially based on simulation experiments.

The next section outlines embodied models of the evolution of signalling behaviour and coordination, after which I look at models of the evolution of lexicons and referential capability. The final main section details models of the evolution of syntax. For more comprehensive analysis, see Cangelosi and Parisi (2002), Steels (2003), Lyon et al. (2007), Mirolli and Nolfi (2009), and Vogt and de Boer (2010).

## 62.2 MODELLING THE EVOLUTION OF SIGNALLING BEHAVIOUR AND COORDINATION

An early application of robot models in language origins research used wheeled mobile robots to investigate the emergence of social coordination and prelinguistic and signalling communication. Quinn (2001) studied how two robots can coordinate their behaviour without using any additional communication channel (e.g. sound), simply relying on adaptive behavioural strategies. Two mobile robots are placed in an arena and are evolved for a capacity to move together, following each other within a limited distance. Although no explicit roles are allocated to the two robots, the agents evolve a strategy where one agent takes on the role of leader, and the other, follower. This is achieved through a dynamic coordination of their behaviour: the robots first align to face each other; then, if an agent perceives the presence of the other robot whilst it is still rotating to align, it adopts the leader role. Overall, this robotic model successfully demonstrates the emergence of a functional, but non-communicative, behaviour strategy which evolves in the early stages of the simulation.

Robotics models subsequently simulated the dynamics of (prelinguistic) communication through the addition of signalling capability (continuous sound or light). Marocco and Nolfi (2007) use an evolutionary robotics approach for a model of communication in a group of robots. The environment has four robots that move within a rectangular arena with two target (homing) areas. The agents have to perform a collective navigation task. In order for their evolutionary fitness to increase, only two robots at a time can be in each of the target areas. In addition to exploring the arena, the robots produce a continuous sound (one channel only) by varying its pitch. At the end of the evolutionary experiments, the robots have developed a non-trivial communication system that exploits the difference in the sound communication modalities. This model also shows that the co-adaptation of the robots' individual and communicative behaviours permits the evolution of more complex and effective individuals.

In a more recent study, Mitri et al. (2009) investigate the evolution of information suppression in communicating robots with conflicting interests. A population of robots are evolved for their foraging skills. Robots compete for limited food resources and can also emit a signal (blue light). During evolution, after just a few generations the robots evolve the behaviour of emitting a high intensity of light when they are near the food, thus helping the other robots to find food more rapidly. In subsequent stages of evolution, the robots learn to conceal this information, as they are competing for food. However, the robots are never able to completely cease to produce the signal. The explanation is that they have reached a stable evolutionary equilibrium with considerable variation in communicative behaviour, resulting from random mutation.

Finally, other embodied agent models have looked at the emergence of a shared repertoire of phonetic systems preceding semantic communication (see de Boer, Chapter 63).

## 62.3 MODELLING THE EVOLUTION OF SHARED LEXICONS AND REFERENTIAL CAPABILITIES

Robotic and embodied agent models have made a significant contribution to the understanding of genetic and cultural evolution dynamics in language origins, where both the semantic system and the lexicon interact and co-adapt during linguistic evolution. Robotics models have mostly focused on the emergence of shared lexicons through cultural evolution. Simulated embodied agent models, on the other hand, have mostly investigated the genetic evolution of shared languages.

One of the first models of the emergence of a shared lexicon in a group of robots was developed by Steels and Vogt (1997). Two mobile robots are placed in a structured environment and start to interact with each other without any shared lexicon or representation of their environment (i.e. meaning). They play language games in which each speaker generates new meanings and negotiates words for these meanings with the hearer. The agents take turns to be speakers and hearers. This study investigates the minimal conditions under which verbal communication may evolve, and the results show that a shared lexicon can emerge, even though there are strong limits on the size and stability of this lexicon.

The 'Talking Heads' model of the emergence of communication in robotic agents is one of the best-known works (Steels 1999, 2003). Here, two robot heads look at a whiteboard containing a variety of coloured shapes. Each individual robot can autonomously create a categorical representation of the objects. In addition, these perceptual categories become associated with words that the agents use to communicate with each other in numerous language games. Crucially, the association of a specific perceptual category with a word is mediated by social interaction with other agents. This therefore leads to the cultural evolution of a shared set of words. Numerous experiments using this set-up have analysed the dynamics of the evolution of the lexicon, including the emergence of synonyms and other language game dynamics (Baronchelli et al. 2008).

This modelling approach has been extended to human–robot communication systems, such as training the AIBO pet dog to name objects (Steels and Kaplan 2002). More recently, Steels and Spranger (2009) have extended it by using humanoid robots.

Simulation models of embodied agents have been employed to model the genetic evolution of shared lexicons. As evolutionary studies require large populations of agents and also the simulation of the process of selection and reproduction from one generation to the next, the simulated multiagent approach provides a more suitable methodology (Cangelosi and Parisi 2002).

Cangelosi and Parisi (1998) report on an early model of the evolutionary emergence of shared lexicons. Simulated embodied agents live in a two-dimensional grid world, performing foraging tasks and learning to differentiate between 'edible mushrooms' (that when eaten increase the chances of survival and reproduction) and 'toadstools' (which cause a decrease in fitness). Agents can perceive the location and visual properties of food, and autonomously learn to categorize foods into the edible and inedible categories, as a condition for selective reproduction. An artificial neural network controls the agents' perceptual and motor system, as well as their linguistic behaviour. As agents are allowed to communicate with each other about their food, this causes the gradual evolution of a shared lexicon. This foraging model was also extended to specifically investigate the 'Symbolic Theft Hypothesis' of language origins (Cangelosi and Harnad 2000).

## 62.4 MODELLING THE EVOLUTION OF SYNTAX

The embodied modelling approach has also been employed specifically to look at the evolutionary emergence of syntax, with particular focus on compositionality. An early application of cognitive linguistic approaches to the robotic modelling of language origins is the Fluid Construction Grammar framework, proposed by Steels (2004). In an experiment with the AIBO robot, Steels demonstrates the suitability of Fluid Construction Grammar for experiments in syntactic evolution. Two robots play language games and are equipped with a complex sensory-motor system which can detect objects and can also build an analogue world model of the objects' location and trajectories. The experiments demonstrate that additional syntactic constraints (e.g. word order, agreement, semantic and syntactic subcategorization) help the hearer in its language comprehension tasks. These constraints provide cues that the agent uses to significantly reduce the searching of parse hypotheses not intended by the speaker.

Embodied multiagent systems have also been used for modelling the cultural evolution of syntax. Vogt (2005) developed a simulation model of the Talking Heads scenario to investigate the evolution of compositionality within the iterated learning model protocol (Kirby and Hurford 2002). Simulation robotic experiments demonstrate that the transmission bottleneck serves as a pressure mechanism for the emergence of compositionality (see Kirby, this volume), and that the emerging languages reflect the compositional structure of the objects in the world.

With embodied multiagent models it has also been possible to investigate the interaction between phylogenetic and ontogenetic (cultural) evolution phenomena in the origins of language and compositionality. Cangelosi (2001) employs a foraging task where the agents must learn the hierarchical relationships between perceptual categories of food and the actions to perform on each category. The agents can use two-word utterances to describe their behaviour. In particular, each child agent uses its own parents' two-word description to learn what to do with the food, but also to learn to imitate its parents' language. Simulation results show a systematic advantage for the evolution of compositional lexicons, where one word indicates the main action to perform on food ('avoid'/'approach') and the second describes the three different types of food upon which the main action is performed. This preference for compositional lexicons is explained by the formation of structured semantic representations in the agents' neural network.

An extension of the above model looked specifically at the Baldwin effect phenomenon, and the role of cultural variation and learning costs in the evolution of language (Munroe and Cangelosi 2003). In this model, the cost of learning is varied so that when an agent eats a 'poisonous mushroom', this results in fitness loss (in the high learning cost condition) or has no effect (no learning cost condition). As for cultural variation, in one condition, agents must learn their parents' two-word utterance precisely (no cultural variation), whilst in the other case they are allowed to change part of the lexicon through added noise in the learning (high cultural variation). Simulation results show that when there is a high cost associated with language learning, the agents gradually assimilate in their genome some explicit features (e.g. words) of the specific language they are exposed to. When the structure of the language is allowed to vary using a process of cultural transmission, Baldwinian processes cause the assimilation of a predisposition to learn quickly whichever lexicons the environment provides, rather than any structural properties associated with a specific lexicon.

## 62.5 CONCLUSION AND FUTURE DIRECTIONS

The studies outlined above show that a robotic and embodied approach to the modelling of the evolution of language can successfully tackle various aspects of language origins, from prelinguistic social coordination and signalling behaviour, to the emergence of compositional lexicons. Moreover, implementing both linguistic and cognitive/sensorimotor properties within the same cognitive model allows researchers to test theories of language evolution that hypothesize a direct link between the emergence of linguistic knowledge and other internal representations and cognitive phenomena.

This embodied approach is nicely complemented by other methodologies employed in the computational modelling of language evolution. For example, analytic models based on mathematical techniques can be used to investigate the language game dynamics originally studied in the Talking Heads robot model (Baronchelli et al. 2008). Other non-embodied multiagent approaches focus on syntactic phenomena, with fixed semantic configurations (e.g. Kirby and Hurford 2002). Moreover, laboratory investigations into the emergence of communication allow computational hypotheses to be closely compared and tested (Galantucci and Garrod 2010).

Finally, an important advantage of computational and robotics approaches to language evolution is their interdisciplinary nature. This enables a direct dialogue with empirical disciplines interested in language and cognition, such as cognitive neuroscience, psychology, cognitive linguistics, primatology, and anthropology (Cangelosi and Parisi 2002; Steels 2006). Constraining robotics models with empirical data also improves the ability of both robotics and computer models to generate predictions, based on descriptive theories, which can be further validated or falsified by new empirical and modelling studies (Galantucci and Garrod 2010; Vogt and de Boer 2010).

# CHAPTER 63

# SELF-ORGANIZATION AND LANGUAGE EVOLUTION

## BART DE BOER

## 63.1 INTRODUCTION

Language can be considered from two perspectives. It can be considered as behaviour and knowledge of an individual, and it can also be considered as a system of conventions in a language community. In fact, these two perspectives can be said to define two levels at which language can be observed. One is the individual level, where detailed individual behaviour is studied. The other is the population level, where individual behaviour is averaged and abstracted, and more general trends and processes are studied. Examples of subfields of linguistics at the two levels will be given below. Of course, both levels are intertwined and interdependent. Individuals' behaviour is determined by conventions in the group, but at the same time, group conventions are created and maintained through individual behaviour. Such interaction between the levels can lead to a phenomenon called self-organization. In this chapter I focus on these two levels: although self-organization at the neural level is important in, for example, development of sensory capacities, and plausibly in learning of speech, it falls into the domain of neurology, rather than linguistics.

Self-organization in its contemporary meaning is the spontaneous emergence of order in a system. Generally this involves repeated interaction between elements on a microscopic scale that results in organization on a macroscopic scale. The macroscopic scale can then be described with far fewer parameters than would be necessary to describe the behaviour on the microscopic scale. In language the individual level corresponds to the microscopic scale, while the population level corresponds to the macroscopic scale.

The term self-organization appears to have been coined (with a slightly different meaning) by W. Ross Ashby (1947) in the context of cybernetics and the nervous system. Ashby intended the term self-organization to refer to the possibility for a system to control its own behaviour. However, in his mathematical formulation the notion of two interacting levels is already present. The notion of self-organization as the spontaneous emergence of order stems more from physics and chemistry, for example, the work of Prigogine (Nicolis and Prigogine 1977).

A classical example from biology is the honeycomb. Through interaction between individual bees, and only through such interaction, a regular structure of hexagonal cells is formed that is much larger than the bees themselves. There is no need for a central controlling force, or for precise behavioural programmes in the individual bees. Flocking of birds, schooling of fish, and trail formation by ants (or university students on campus lawns) are other basic examples of self-organization. A system in which self-organization can occur must consist of a (large) number of interacting elements. In language these elements could be speakers in a population, different sounds or words in the language itself, or (if one looks at the neural level) neurons interacting in the brain.

Emergence of order means that the system evolves towards a macroscopic state that can be described with fewer parameters (or in terms of information theory, with fewer bits of information) than the possible states at the microscopic level. This means that the behaviour of the individuals must become coupled: an individual's behaviour is no longer independent of the behaviour of the other members of the population. In the example of language in a population of speakers, this means that the language of individuals cannot be arbitrarily different from that of the rest of the population.

A final requirement on self-organization is that the emergence of order must be spontaneous. This excludes systems controlled by an outside force, or a system that is structured beforehand in a way that imposes order on the elements of the system. The solar system illustrates a system controlled by an outside force: the motion of the planets is orderly, but only because of solar gravitation, acting as a global force. An example of a structured system is any hierarchical system: behaviour of elements on a lower level is directly controlled by elements at higher levels. Self-organization must really be the result of the interaction between the elements of the system. No small subclass of elements in the system should have complete control over other elements of the system.

The above implies that there must be feedback between the individual (microscopic) level and the population (macroscopic) level. Individuals must be able to sense the population behaviour somehow, and adapt their behaviour accordingly. In order to allow one macroscopic state to dominate the population, this must be a self-amplifying effect: once a certain state begins to dominate, more and more individuals will conform to it. This is called positive feedback. In language, the interaction between the two levels can be illustrated by the emergence of new words for new objects. At first, several words will be coined by different individual speakers. However, since for successful communication shared words are necessary, individuals adopt words that are also used by other speakers. This process starts a positive feedback loop: more frequent words will be more successful in spreading. Eventually all speakers may come to perceive that there is one 'correct' word at the population level, and they will adopt this word. The above-mentioned processes are quite basic, and therefore natural examples of self-organization abound in physical, chemical, biological, and neurological systems. It is even likely that self-organization occurs in social and economic systems, but in these contexts, the term self-organization is often applied in an imprecise way and therefore uncontroversial examples are more difficult to identify.

## 63.2 SELF-ORGANIZATION AND EVOLUTION

Self-organization can help simplify biological and genetic accounts of evolution. If complex structures can be explained as the result of self-organization, this means that such structures need not be genetically coded. Only the much simpler behaviours that lead to self-organization need to be coded. This tends to simplify the account of how complex structures evolved. In the case of linguistic structures, explanations based on self-organization usually depend on general cognitive mechanisms already present to some degree in other animals, as well as on functional constraints due to imperfect articulation, perception, and processing. Such mechanisms and constraints entail more continuity with evolutionary ancestors than language-specific adaptations. Language-specific adaptations are illustrated by the Principles and Parameters model (e.g. Baker 2001), or the capacity for recursion as proposed by Hauser et al. (2002). Such adaptations would require more complex and therefore vulnerable genetic coding, and this makes it more problematic to explain how language evolved relatively rapidly. Self-organization, in providing an alternative to biological evolution for complexity to emerge, helps to reduce the amount of adaptation that needs to be explained by genetic, biological evolution.

The interaction between self-organization and biological evolution is fundamental to understanding the evolution of language. Biological evolution determines the dynamics and the boundary conditions of the self-organizing process. Self-organization causes the language to converge on a limited number of states, the properties of which then determine the fitness of the language-using agents. Biological evolution then selects for adaptations that help cope with the properties of the states resulting from self-organization. For example, Zuidema and de Boer (2009) have shown that systems of utterances under pressure from acoustic distinctiveness tend to self-organize towards having combinatorial structure, even though the agents that use these utterances are not aware of this structure. However, once combinatorial structure is present, biological adaptations for using this combinatorial structure increase fitness. This solves part of the riddle of how ape-like vocalizations might have evolved into human speech. Ape vocalizations are holistic in the sense that utterances generally consist of single articulatory gestures (possibly repeated multiple times); apes make no use of internally-structured signals. Human speech makes extensive and productive use of internally-structured utterances, and is therefore combinatorial. The riddle is that if all agents in the population use a holistic system, then how could an evolutionary adaptation for using combinatorial structure ever increase fitness? Self-organization here provides a means for a system of signals with combinatorial properties to be present in a population of language users before the language users are aware of this structure.

The example above illustrates a general point about language evolution: fitness of adaptations for language is in general frequency-dependent, meaning that a single agent with the adaptation does not have increased fitness, but that multiple agents with the adaptation do. However, self-organization can move a population of agents towards states where a single individual with a mutation for language does have increased fitness. Self-organization thus helps solve the apparent paradox of how innovative adaptations for language can have increased fitness, even if only one agent in the population has this adaptation.

## 63.3 INVESTIGATING SELF-ORGANIZATION IN LANGUAGE

Although the idea of self-organization is reasonably intuitive, it nevertheless requires interaction between large numbers of individuals as well as feedback between the population and individuals. Especially in the case of human behaviour, this can become complex. This complexity is most likely why self-organization in language has only relatively recently been studied in linguistics. Although the individual and collective levels of language clearly influence each other, modern linguists generally choose to study them separately. Subfields like historical and descriptive linguistics study language at the collective level (although descriptions of dialects are often based on single informants, they are nevertheless taken to be representative of a whole language population). Subfields like the study of speech errors, of language acquisition, or of psycholinguistics on the other hand are based on individual behaviour. Both Saussure (1916/1976) and Chomsky (1965), in defining theoretical frameworks for studying language, abstracted away from the interaction between individual and collective levels. They either defined idealizations of the collective language (Saussure's *langue*) or assumed that in the ideal case individual knowledge and collective language are the same (Chomsky's *competence*). Such idealizations are generally in order when producing descriptive grammars of a given dialect at a given time, but are inadequate when the processes of language change and language emergence are under investigation. Sociolinguistics and the studies of language birth, change, and death, as well as the study of the evolution of linguistic abilities are therefore the prime fields within modern linguistics which investigate the interaction between individual and collective behaviour. It is therefore not surprising that these are also the fields where the idea of self-organization is most influential.

Probably the first linguistics paper to use the term self-organization explicitly was Lindblom et al. (1984) on the emergence of syllable systems. Since then, much work has been produced that links self-organization, language, and language evolution. Most of this work in some way makes use of computer models, which have no difficulties dealing with the repeated complex interactions inherent to self-organizing systems. (Overviews can be found in Cangelosi and Parisi 2002; Kirby 2002, this volume; de Boer 2005b; Kirby et al. 2008; K. Smith, this volume.)

Two perspectives on self-organization in language will be discussed here. The first is the perspective of an individual's linguistic knowledge: linguistic items such as words or speech sounds can be considered as the microscopic level and the complete linguistic system can be considered as the macroscopic level. The second perspective is that of language in a population of speakers, where individual language users constitute the microscopic level, and the whole language community constitutes the macroscopic level.

Studies explaining the structure of systems of speech sounds as the result of self-organization (Liljencrants and Lindblom 1972; Lindblom et al. 1984; Schwartz et al. 1997; Redford et al. 2001; Ke et al. 2003) illustrate the perspective of self-organization at the level of an individual's knowledge. In this context, the micro-level consists of the individual speech sounds, and the macro-level is the sound system as a whole. Speech sounds have both perceptual and articulatory properties and these properties have continuous values. This means that some speech sounds are close together in either articulatory or acoustic space, while others are further apart. At the level of the whole sound system, this results in certain systems of speech sounds being more suitable for communication than others, either because they are easier to produce or because they are easier to distinguish, while most likely some systems are also easier to learn than others. This puts pressure on the individual sounds to be as distinct as possible, while at the same time being easy to pronounce and to learn. This is a form of feedback (through use) from the macro-level (the whole system of speech sounds) to the micro-level (the individual speech sounds). This view abstracts away from how the feedback is implemented (this is investigated by the population view of self-organization explained below) and sees sound systems as the self-organized outcome of interactions within sets of speech sounds.

Using this perspective, acoustic distinctiveness turns out to be sufficient to explain the structure of small to medium vowel systems (Liljencrants and Lind-blom 1972; Schwartz et al. 1997). Ke et al. (2003) have shown that systems of tones can also be explained as the result of maximizing acoustic distinctiveness. For systems that include consonants, and for larger vowel systems, other factors also play a role. Articulatory ease can partly explain the structure of syllable systems (Lindblom et al. 1984; Redford et al. 2001). Syllable systems turn out to be a compromise between acoustic distinctiveness on the one hand, and articulatory ease on the other. However, learnability might also be important. Systems that reuse the same features are preferred over others, a factor investigated and modelled by Schwartz et al. (2007).

Because of the complexity of interactions between different elements of a system of speech sounds, a lot of calculation is involved in determining what the outcome of self-organization would be. This is especially true if multiple conflicting factors (such as articulatory ease and acoustic distinctiveness) are modelled. Most of this work was therefore undertaken using computer simulations.

The models of self-organization at the level of the sound system address the question why sound systems are the way they are, but abstract away from the question of how linguistic systems came to be the way they are. This is addressed by agent-based models of (cultural) language evolution. Such models (Hurford 1987; Steels 1995, 1998; Batali 1998; Kirby 2002) take the perspective of self-organization at the level of the population. These models directly investigate the link between individual behaviour and emergence and change of language at the level of the population. In an agent-based model, individual behaviour is modelled directly; the agents are generally small computer programs that model some aspect (language use, language learning) of an individual's behaviour. The model contains many such agents, and all these agents interact repeatedly. Two main paradigms are found in the literature. One is the iterated learning model, advocated by Hurford and Kirby (see Kirby, this volume; Smith, this volume) while the other is the language game model, advocated by Steels.

Iterated learning focuses on transmission from generation to generation. In a typical iterated learning model, each generation consists of one agent, while only two generations exist simultaneously (the parent and child generation). At each point in time the parent agent produces language, while the child agent learns. After a while the parent agent 'dies', the child agent grows up and becomes adult, and a new child agent is born. This process is iterated. In this way, iterated learning models can focus precisely on which aspects of language structure can be explained by transmission from one generation to the next.

In the language game model, on the other hand, transmission and emergence of language within one large population of agents is typically modelled. All agents simultaneously produce, perceive, and learn language, and even invent new language when the need arises. In this way the emergence and spread of language in an existing population of speakers can be investigated, including such phenomena as linguistic innovations, the effects of population structure, or the emergence of linguistic diversity.

Aspects of both paradigms can be combined to form a continuum of possible models. One could, for example, increase population size in the iterated learning paradigm, or model agent birth and death in the language game model. In this way a complete spectrum of possible sociolinguistic situations can be modelled using agent-based models.

A typical example of iterated learning is Kirby and colleagues' (e.g. Kirby 1999) work on the emergence of compositional syntax (Kirby, this volume). In this model, a parent agent produces a set of sentences about a very simple world, involving an agent, an action, and possibly a patient. The child agent learns the language on the basis of these sentences using a learning mechanism that detects regular correspondences between the intended meaning and the utterance used. Initially, agents just use random utterances to describe situations in the world. It turns out that compositional syntactic structure emerges after a number of generations. This happens only when the number of utterances observed is smaller than the number needed to describe all situations in the world (but large enough, of course, so that all objects and actions occur in the examples). In this situation, accidental regularities in the initially random utterances are amplified, as fewer examples are needed to learn a regular language than a random language.

A typical example of a language game is the naming game, as described by Steels (1995). In the simplest version, a population of agents starts out without any linguistic knowledge at all, but they are faced with the task of establishing names for each agent in the population. Agents engage in interactions with one other agent at a time, in which they try to identify a third agent by name. If an agent has no name for the third agent, it creates a random word. If it has one or more candidate names, it selects one at random, with a probability proportional to the previous success of the name. If the agents agree on the identification, the success score of the name is increased, otherwise it is decreased. In this model, a population of agents rapidly converge on a unique set of names. Initially, different names will be coined for the same agent, but through positive feedback, names used more often become more successful, and end up being used even more often. In this way it is shown that lexicons can emerge rapidly without central control.

When investigating the emergence of sound systems with agent-based models, it is possible to combine the two forms of self-organization. This was done first at the Institut de Communication Parlée (Glotin 1995; Berrah and Laboissière 1999) and is worked out in more detail by de Boer (2000). Oudeyer (2005) has combined all three levels of self-organization by including self-organizing neural maps in his models. In de Boer's (2000) model, a population of agents develops a shared system of vowels that must be as large and as successful as possible. The setting is that of the language game: a large (but fixed) population starts out with empty vowel systems, and each agent develops a set of vowels through interaction with the other agents. Initially, vowels are generated randomly, but once signals are established, agents learn from each other. Successful vowels are kept, and unsuccessful ones are removed. Evaluation of vowels is done through imitation: one agent chooses a vowel from its repertoire and produces it (with noise). The second agent hears this vowel and finds the vowel in its repertoire that is closest to it. This amounts to categorical perception. Finally, the second agent produces the vowel it thinks it heard, and the first agent finds its closest vowel. If this is the same as the one it initially selected, the game is successful, otherwise it is a failure. This imitation game puts pressure on signals to be as distinct as possible, without the need of semantics (which would be necessary in a more realistic system). Through repeated interactions, vowel systems emerge that are very much like the ones found in human languages. Because of the randomness inherent in the imitation game, different vowel systems emerge for different runs. However, the frequency with which different vowel systems of a given number of vowels emerge is comparable to the frequency with which these systems are found in human languages.

The emergence of a range of different vowel systems (something which occurs in all these population-based models) indicates that it is not only optimal systems that emerge. This is perhaps what one would expect if the only factor at play was self-organization within an individual—the type of self-organization described in the previous section. However, the fact that agents need to conform to what already exists in a population tends to stabilize less-than-optimal vowel systems. Stability is, of course, relative; historical processes will have a higher probability of ending up with more optimal vowel systems (and therefore these will be more frequent) but there is always a small probability that a population will self-organize towards a suboptimal system.

Finally, a few papers have investigated models with self-organization from a mathematical perspective. For example, De Vylder and Tuyls (2006) have investigated convergence of naming games, while Kirby et al. (2007) have investigated properties of the states that iterated learning converges to. Other work, such as Wang and Minett (2005), investigates the actual trajectories with which language changes. Such mathematical analysis provides more fundamental insight than computer simulations alone. However, systems necessarily have to be simplified in order to do the mathematical analysis, but it is hard to determine which simplifications still result in interesting and realistic behaviour without doing computer simulations. Therefore the combination of exploratory computer simulation and mathematical analysis is probably the best way to make progress in investigating the role of self-organization in language and its evolution.

# CHAPTER 64

........................................................................

# STATISTICAL LEARNING AND LANGUAGE ACQUISITION

........................................................................

## KATHARINE GRAF ESTES

## 64.1 INTRODUCTION

........................................................................

Infants exhibit remarkable abilities to discover structure in their vastly complex linguistic environments (see Jusczyk 1997). This precocity has motivated the search for mechanisms underlying language acquisition. Discovering the foundations of acquisition may also elucidate forces that have shaped the organization of human languages. One promising language acquisition mechanism is statistical learning, the process of detecting structure in the environment by tracking patterns in the input. Developments in computational modelling and analyses of child-directed speech corpora have revealed that the speech stream contains a wealth of distributional cues to linguistic structure (e.g. Elman et al. 1996; Mintz et al. 2002; see also de Boer, Chapter 33). Experimental evidence indicates that infants, as well as children and adults, possess powerful statistical learning mechanisms capable of rapidly tracking regularities in sounds, words, and grammars (Gómez 2007). From this account, language learners do not require innate universal grammar knowledge to acquire linguistic structure, but rather rely on distributional information present in the input and on mechanisms that exploit the information. This chapter focuses on the role of statistical learning in infants' lexical and syntactic acquisition. I address how the study of statistical learning contributes to the understanding of language development and the interaction between human learning mechanisms and human languages.

## 64.2 STATISTICAL LEARNING AND LEXICAL ACQUISITION

Infants' statistical learning abilities were first investigated to understand the mechanisms used to segment words from fluent speech, an important first step in acquiring new words. Segmentation is not a trivial task because speech contains no obvious and fully reliable word boundary indicators. To examine infants' detection of statistical word segmentation cues, Saffran et al. (1996) presented 8-month-olds with an artificial language that contained no pauses or stressed syllables, forming a continuous speech sequence (e.g. *golabupadotitupirogolabu...*). The only available segmentation cue was transitional probability information, a cue present in natural speech. Syllables that are part of the same word occur together more predictably (i.e. with higher probability) than syllables that cross word boundaries, because a huge range of words can follow any given word. Learners may find word boundaries by detecting low probability syllable sequences. After two minutes of artificial language exposure, listening time measures showed that infants distinguished high transitional probability 'words' (i.e. highly predictable sequences from the language such as *golabu*, which contained perfect transitional probability between syllables) from novel sequences (e.g. *tilado*) and from familiar low probability sequences that spanned words (e.g. *bupado* from *golabu#padoti*). Thus, infants can rapidly track statistical cues that help them access individual words. Statistical learning is not restricted to syllables, but could be used to segment words based on other probabilistic cues as well, such as stress and phonotactic patterns (it is also not limited to speech; cf. Kirkham et al. 2002).

Going beyond word detection, there is evidence that infants can apply statistical learning to a key task in lexical development: linking the sounds of words with their meanings. Graf Estes et al. (2007) found that 17-month-olds readily learned new object labels that they had previously segmented from an artificial language (i.e. high probability syllable sequences). They failed to learn labels consisting of novel sequences or familiar, low probability sequences. These findings suggest that statistical learning may help infants discover segmented units which are then ready to be mapped to meanings. Furthermore, they demonstrate a way that statistical segmentation supports learning of another level of linguistic structure, lexical acquisition.

## 64.3 STATISTICAL LEARNING AND SYNTACTIC ACQUISITION

Studies of the connection between statistical learning and lexical acquisition examined regularities in adjacent elements. However, if statistical learning is a significant component of syntactic development, it must be capable of additional levels of analysis. Chomsky (1957), among others, argued that statistical patterns have limited utility for acquiring syntax because sentences are not simple strings of associated words, but are linked in phrases as part of hierarchical structures. Furthermore, countless statistical patterns can be calculated between linguistic units at multiple levels of analysis (phonetic features, segments, syllables, words, and phrases) and most correlations are uninformative (e.g. between every fifth word).

Recent investigations demonstrate that human learners are not limited to simple adjacent probabilities, but seem to track the types of patterns necessary to exploit distributional cues to syntactic structures. Gómez and Gerken (1999) tested 1-year-olds' ability to learn a simple finite-state grammar (see also Saffran and Wilson 2003). After listening to a set of sentences in an artificial language, infants discriminated novel sentences with grammatical versus ungrammatical word orders. Simple memorization cannot explain their performance; infants generalized beyond the training set to discriminate grammatical from ungrammatical sentences containing new vocabulary items. Because no learner is exhaustively exposed to all allowable sentences in a language, this ability to abstract beyond the details of the input is essential for the acquisition of natural language syntax.

Gómez (2002) examined infants' learning of another fundamental aspect of syntax, non-adjacent dependencies (see Tallerman, Chapter 48). Many naturally-occurring grammatical patterns involve dependencies spanning intervening words and phrases (e.g. verb agreement: *the cats in the bed are sleeping*). Gómez presented 18-month-olds with three-word sequences (e.g. *vot kicey jic*) in which the first and third elements reliably co-occurred. Infants learned the regularities connecting non-adjacent elements when they could take advantage of variability in the identity of the intervening element (*vot kicey jic, vot wadim jic*, etc.). Variation in the middle element highlighted the consistency of the first and third elements, promoting learning. Another feature of non-adjacent dependencies is that they can provide learners with word category information. In child-directed speech analyses,

Mintz (2003) found that statistical regularities in highly consistent non-adjacent dependencies, termed frequent frames (e.g. *you ___ it, the ___and*), led to accurate categorization of the intervening words. Words that occurred in the same frame tended to come from the same category (e.g. verbs, nouns). The findings from Gómez and Mintz indicate that infants are capable of learning non-adjacent dependencies, and that speech input conveys valuable distributional information through such dependencies. More broadly, these investigations strengthen the argument that distributional learning can meet many challenges of natural language acquisition.

One objection to statistical approaches to language acquisition is that learners must be computationally overwhelmed. However, there is evidence for constraints on learners' computations. For example, Newport and Aslin (2004) reported that adults in word segmentation tasks failed to learn non-adjacent patterns over syllables (e.g. syllables 1 and 3, *badite, bakute*), but successfully learned patterns over vowels (e.g. *tedoki, bepogi*) and consonants (*dokibae, dakube*). The key distinction is that regularities across phonetic segments occur in the words of natural languages, such as Hebrew and Arabic, whereas regularities over syllables are not common. Infants also display learning biases linked to natural language structures (e.g. Saffran and Thiessen 2003). Saffran and colleagues (2008) examined 12-month-olds' learning of an artificial language that incorporated an important feature of natural languages, phrases marked by predictive dependencies. Words from one category required the presence of words from another category, and together they formed phrases. For example, in English, articles like *a* or *the* require a subsequent noun (sometimes with intervening words), but nouns can occur without articles. A dependency in the artificial language was that in A-phrases, D-words (a category of nonsense words) always followed A-words, but A-words also occurred without D-words. Another group of 12-month-olds heard a language that lacked predictive dependencies; no word category predicted the occurrence of another (e.g. A-words occurred with and without D-words, and vice versa), although there were rules governing word combinations (e.g. A-words preceded D-words, which preceded C-words). The lack of dependencies is unlikely in natural languages. Infants successfully learned the language containing predictive dependencies; they discriminated grammatical from ungrammatical sentences. Infants failed to learn the language lacking predictive dependencies (see Saffran 2002 for similar findings with adults). Demonstrations of learning biases suggest that statistical learning is selective in ways that relate to the organization of natural languages. Humans readily learn regularities that commonly occur across human languages, but have greater difficulty learning regularities that do not.

Studies of statistical learning of syntax indicate that these powerful learning capacities include important constraints that help to address the problem of the potentially overburdened distributional learner; learners may be biased to perform certain computations. Intriguingly, the constraints or biases also appear to act on non-linguistic input (e.g. computer alert sounds, visual nonsense shapes; Saffran 2002). Thus, the constraints that are highly suited to discovering linguistic structure may not be specific to language, but general characteristics of human learning. Statistical learning accounts of language acquisition present an alternative to the traditional innate universal grammar explanation for syntactic acquisition and for the striking similarities in organization across the world's languages. The parallels between the distributional regularities that humans readily learn and the structures that languages exhibit support the hypothesis that constraints on human learning mechanisms have shaped the design of human languages (e.g. Newport and Aslin 2000; Christiansen and Dale 2004; Chater and Christiansen, this volume). Human languages may have evolved to take advantage of how humans learn.

In summary, although much remains to be investigated, the findings to date indicate that very early in life, learners possess statistical learning abilities that may help them access some of the structure in the immense complexity of their native languages. Tracking distributional regularities in speech may facilitate lexical acquisition by promoting word segmentation and readying sounds to link to meanings. Statistical learning may also contribute to syntactic acquisition, as infants can detect regularities beyond simple adjacent transitional probabilities. Importantly, statistical learning is not without limits; constraints appear to focus learning in essential ways. The ongoing study of statistical learning promises to reveal a great deal about how infants learn their native languages and connections between human learning mechanisms and what humans learn.

# CHAPTER 65

# A SOLUTION TO THE LOGICAL PROBLEM OF LANGUAGE EVOLUTION: LANGUAGE AS AN ADAPTATION TO THE HUMAN BRAIN

NICK CHATER AND MORTEN H. CHRISTIANSEN

## 65.1 INTRODUCTION

Chomsky's proposal (e.g. 1965, 1980) that human language is underpinned by a genetically specified universal grammar (UG) is astonishingly bold. Generative grammar is seen not primarily as concerned with finding the most elegant account of the linguistic patterns observed in the world's languages, but rather as a part of biology: it is viewed as specifying the structure of a 'language organ' whose development unfolds under genetic control. Thus, according to this perspective, language acquisition should not, strictly speaking, be viewed as a process of learning at all; it should be viewed as a process of growth, analogous to the growth of the arm or the liver. But the proposal that generative grammar aims to characterize UG (interpreted as an abstract specification of a biological organ) comes at a price: the putative language organ, like any other biological structure, must have explicable origins in the framework of natural selection.

The evolution of UG, though, appears deeply puzzling, as we shall argue below. Indeed, we present positive reasons to doubt that an evolutionary account of the origin of UG, as classically conceived, is viable. These arguments thereby cast doubt on the viability of the concept of UG, as an abstract specification of biological structure.

If UG is abandoned, what alternative theoretical synthesis is possible? How can the apparent 'fit' between languages and language learners be explained? How might universal, but often apparently arbitrary, patterns across the world's languages arise? In short, what theoretical options are available, if the concept of UG is abandoned?

In this chapter, we sketch a framework in which we hope a new synthesis can be constructed—this viewpoint is developed in more detail in Christiansen and Chater (2008). We suggest that this framework provides an alternative way of integrating insights from biology, the cognitive and brain sciences, and linguistics, and that it provides, in particular, an evolutionarily plausible account of the biological basis for language acquisition. This synthesis, as we shall see, inverts the explanatory structure underlying the postulation of UG. Instead of seeing the brain as a genetically specified system for language, which must have somehow arisen over the course of biological evolution, we view the key to language evolution to consist in evolutionary processes over language itself. Specifically, language should be viewed as an evolving system, in which the features of languages have been shaped by the process of acquisition and transmission across successive generations of language users. In particular, aspects of language that are easy to learn and process, or are communicatively effective, tend to be retained and amplified; aspects of language which are difficult to learn or process, or which hinder communication, will, if they arise at all, rapidly be stamped out. According to this perspective, the 'fit' between the structure of language and the brains of language users comes about not, primarily, because the brain has somehow evolved a genetically specified UG capturing the universal principles of language, but instead because language itself is shaped by the brain.

The remainder of this chapter outlines this viewpoint in four main sections. We begin by framing what we call the *logical problem of language evolution* that arises from a conventional UG perspective. We next consider how language might, instead, be viewed as a cultural product, shaped by successive generations of speakers. We argue that biological and cognitive constraints cannot be left out—they are likely to be crucial in explaining the cultural evolution of language. We first sketch some of these constraints. The core of our account is that language evolves to fit the brain; but can the brain also adapt to deal with language? We then describe circumstances under which such co-evolution can or cannot occur, suggesting that the brain may have adapted to stable, 'functional' aspects of languages, even though it could not have internalized the types of arbitrary linguistic constraints captured by a putative UG. Finally, we briefly sketch some future directions for research.

## 65.2 THE LOGICAL PROBLEM
### OF LANGUAGE EVOLUTION

How might a language organ have evolved? How might the principles of UG, specifying, by assumption, highly complex and arbitrary constraints on the structure of language, become genetically encoded? As with any other putative biological structure, an evolutionary story can take one of two routes. One route is to assume that specialized brain mechanisms specific to language have evolved over long periods of natural selection (e.g. Pinker and Bloom 1990). The other route rejects the idea that UG has arisen through adaptation and proposes that UG has emerged through some non-adaptationist route (e.g. Lightfoot 2000, this volume), just as it has suggested that many biological structures are not the product of adaptation. Yet both routes run into fundamental difficulties; see also Bickerton, this volume.

### 65.2.1 Problems for the adaptationist account

The idea of linguistically-driven biological adaptation as the origin of a genetically specified UG faces a fundamental problem. UG is intended to characterize a set of universal grammatical principles (for instance, governing phrase structure, case marking, and agreement) that hold across all languages. It is a central assumption, as we have noted, that these principles are arbitrary in the sense that they are not determined by functional considerations, such as constraints on learning, memory, cognitive abilities, or communicative effectiveness (see, for instance, Chomsky 1980). Indeed, the highly abstract principles of UG have even been suggested to hinder communication (Chomsky 2005). This arbitrariness implies that any combination of arbitrary principles will be equally adaptive—as long as speakers adopt the *same* arbitrary principles. Pinker and Bloom (1990) draw an analogy with intercomputer communication: it does not matter what specific settings (principles) are adopted as long as everyone adopts the same set of settings. Yet the claim that a particular 'protocol' can become genetically embedded through adaptation faces three fundamental difficulties, relating to the dispersion of human populations, language change, and the question of what is genetically encoded.

The first problem stems from the fact that, according to a broad range of different scenarios concerning language evolution and human migration (e.g. Hawks et al. 2000), divergent populations of language users would have arisen; see Nichols, this volume. Each of these different groups would have adapted to its own linguistic environment, rather than developing a universal language faculty. Indeed, salvaging the evolution of UG would require a very specific scenario of gradual adaptation over a long period within a single, highly localized, population, prior to the dispersion and dominance of that population (at which point language divergence would begin); and an abrupt cessation of biological adaptation to language henceforth. The wide geographical spread of human populations throughout the last several hundred thousand years, during which it is typically assumed that language arose, seems to count against this viewpoint (Hawks et al. 2000). Second, the adaptationist account of UG faces the problem that even within a single population, linguistic conventions change much more rapidly than genes change, thus creating a 'moving target' for natural selection. Computational simulations have shown that under conditions of relatively slow linguistic change, arbitrary principles cannot become genetically fixed—even when the genetic make-up of the learners is allowed to affect the direction of linguistic change (Chater et al. 2009). Third, natural selection produces adaptations designed to fit the environment in which selection occurs; see Számadó and Szathmáry, this volume. It is thus puzzling that an adaptation for UG would have resulted in the genetic underpinnings of a system capturing the highly abstract features of all possible human languages, rather than fixing the superficial, and specific, properties of the first language-like communication systems developed by early hominins. After all, hominins would have been positively selected for ability to learn and process the *specific* communication system they actually employed, not for the hypothetical ability to learn any of a large space of languages which have never been encountered.

It remains possible, though, that the origin of language did have a substantial impact on human genetic evolution. The above arguments only preclude biological adaptations for arbitrary features of language, whereas there might be features that are universally stable across linguistic environments (such as the means of producing speech (Lieberman 1984); or the need for enhanced memory capacity, or complex pragmatic inferences (Levinson 2000; Givón and Malle 2002)) which might lead to biological adaptation, as we discuss below. However, these language features are likely to be functional, to facilitate language learning and use—and thus would typically not be considered part of UG.

## 65.2.2 Problems for the non-adaptationist account

The non-adaptationist account fares no better. The putative language organ, embodying the genetically specified UG, must capture an enormously complex and subtle set of constraints. In the Government and Binding framework (Chomsky 1981), for example, UG is presumed to contain binding principles, theta theory, and so on, in an intricately interlocking system. The non-adaptationist account boils down to the idea that some process of *chance variation* maps existing biological structures on to UG. Yet the probability of randomly building a fully functioning, and completely novel, biological function by chance is infinitesimally small (Christiansen and Chater 2008). To be sure, modern genetics shows how small genetic changes can lead, via a cascade of genetic ramifications, to dramatic phylogenetic consequences (e.g. additional pairs of legs instead of antennae; Carroll 2005). But such mechanisms go no way towards explaining how a completely new and functioning system can arise *de novo* (Finlay 2007).

## 65.2.3 Is minimalism a solution?

The formulation of the meta-theory concerning the biological basis of UG formed the basis of 'mid-period' Chomskyan generative grammar. It might be suggested that recent developments in syntax, and in particular, the Minimalist Program (Chomsky 1995) may cast these theoretical issues in a different light. For example, Hauser et al. (2002) suggest that the content of UG (or what they term the 'narrow faculty of language') may be extremely modest, consisting purely of the principle of recursion (see also Chomsky 2005; Boeckx, this volume; Bickerton, this volume). This appears to signal an almost complete retreat from the original UG perspective. One rationale for UG was to explain how language acquisition is possible, given that the linguistic input to the child is noisy and incomplete, and the regularities of natural language are both arbitrary and highly complex (in other words, UG was presumed to resolve the 'poverty of the stimulus' argument; see Chomsky 1980; Pullum and Scholz 2002; Chater and Vitányi 2007). If UG consists only of recursion, this solution collapses. Moreover, linguistics can no longer be viewed as a part of biology, capturing innate knowledge of language, if the language-specific element of this knowledge consists only of recursion. Current writings on minimalism by no means suggest wholehearted acceptance of the consequences of this retreat (Boeckx 2006).

In any case, the supposed simplicity of the mechanisms of the Minimalist Program is achieved by sleight of hand. A single Merge operation composes structures together; but this is more than balanced by a spectacular increase in the complexity of the lexicon. Moreover, sentence structure becomes surprisingly intricate—Boeckx (2006) notes approvingly that one 'discovery' of the minimalist account is that typical declarative sentences may consist of around 50 phrases, embedded inside one another (for discussion, see Chater and Christiansen 2007). Thus, it is by no means clear that minimalism plays any role in simplifying accounts either of language evolution or, indeed, language acquisition.

## 65.3 LANGUAGE AS SHAPED BY CULTURAL TRANSMISSION

If we do away with the assumption that language requires a dedicated, genetically specified UG, then it is natural to view language as a cultural product—that is, a collective construction, across individuals and across generations of language users. From this standpoint, language has the same status as other cultural products, such as styles of dress, art, music, social structure, moral codes, or patterns of religious beliefs. Language may, of course, be particularly central to culture—indeed, language is presumably the primary vehicle through which much other cultural information is transmitted, and hence may have formed a crucial catalytic role in the development of other aspects of human culture and society. Nonetheless, language should, from this perspective, be viewed as a creation of a human mind that is not specifically hard-wired for language, rather than as directly emerging from a genetically-specified UG. This is, in short, to return to a pre-Chomskyan conception of language (e.g. Bloomfield 1933).

From this standpoint, the evolution of language is not, at least primarily, the story of how human biology has become shaped to support language. Instead, language itself is viewed as an evolving system, transmitted from generation to generation of language-users by processes of cultural transmission. On this view, it is natural to see language evolution as language-change writ large: thus, the study of diachronic linguistics (i.e. the study of processes of change in current, or at least recent, languages) becomes a potentially crucial window on the processes that may have led to the emergence of language (Bybee, this volume; Heine and Kuteva, this volume). Moreover, the study of the creation of new linguistic systems, over one or two generations of learners, as in Nicaraguan Sign Language (Senghas et al. 2004), and in the transition from pidgins to creoles (Hymes 1971), can be viewed as exhibiting the processes of cultural invention and transmission that underpin language evolution.

Accordingly, it seems natural to see content words, referring to objects, properties, and actions, which can be communicatively useful, even in the absence of a fully structured grammatical system, as the starting points for language (Bickerton, this volume). Such items might initially be strung together somewhat arbitrarily; over time (both within individuals and across generations) particular patterns may then come to have conventionalized significance. For example, an item of particular importance might be signalled, pragmatically, by being, for instance, clause-initial; this, or some other, pattern may gradually become a language-internal cue, and, eventually, a conventionalized syntactic property signalling default subject position (Levinson 2000; Jackendoff 2002).

Similarly, content words, which initially have a narrow linguistic function, may come to be used more and more widely to signal general syntactic properties, a process known as grammaticalization (Hopper and Traugott 2003; Bybee, this volume; Heine and Kuteva, this volume). Thus, the English number *one* may be the origin of the determiner *a(n)*. Similarly, the Latin *cantare habeo* ('I have (something) to sing') mutated into *chanterai, cantaré, cantarò* ('I will sing' in French, Spanish, Italian). The suffix corresponds phonologically to 'I have' in each language (respectively, *ai, he, ho*—the 'have' element has collapsed into inflectional morphology; Fleischman 1982), but comes to have a purely grammatical function—signalling future tense. Over time, such morphological forms may be eroded or modified, typically to make them easier or quicker to say, often yielding an increasingly irregular morphological system. Indeed, morphological structure can sometimes become so eroded that a new content word is co-opted to signal the grammatical distinction, and the cycle begins again (Fleischman 1982).

Some theorists see the view that language emerges through cultural processes as indicating that language is relatively unconstrained by biological factors (e.g. Bybee 2009). We argue, by contrast, that processes of cultural transmission alone do not place sufficient constraints on the patterns of viable languages to explain the specific patterns of natural language and the specific patterns of linguistic change that give rise to them. Rather, we suggest that biological and cognitive constraints should be seen as helping to determine *which* types of linguistic structure tend to be learned, processed, and hence transmitted from person to person, and from generation to generation. Thus, we see the processes of cultural transmission that have shaped the creation of natural languages as grounded in prior human neural and cognitive capacities.

## 65.4 THE NEURAL AND COGNITIVE
### BASIS OF LANGUAGE

If language is a collective cultural creation, then its properties may be expected to reflect the neural and cognitive machinery of language users. In other cultural domains, this is a familiar observation. Musical patterns appear to be rooted, in part at least, in machinery of the human auditory and motor systems (Sloboda 1985); art is partially shaped by the properties of human visual perception

(Gombrich 1960); tools, such as scissors or spades, are built around the constraints of the human body; aspects of religious belief may connect, among other things, with the human propensity for folk-psychological explanation (Boyer 1994). But the general observation that language may be adapted, over generations of cultural transmission, to the human brain gains bite only if specific aspects of language, particularly those typically identified as emerging from UG, can be seen as arising from particular aspects of human learning and processing capacities. To this end, Christiansen and Chater (2008) identify four overlapping sets of factors: thought, pragmatics, perceptuo-motor factors, and cognition, which we now briefly review in turn.

## 65.4.1  Constraints from thought

Language allows us to communicate our thoughts—and hence the nature of those thoughts must surely strongly influence the structure of language. Thus, the meaning of content words is, presumably, closely constrained, at least in concrete domains, by the objects and categories delivered by the perceptual and attentional system. Quine (1960) observed that, for a translator of a newly encountered language, hearing a cry of 'gavagai!' while a rabbit races by might, in principle, lead to an infinity of hypotheses concerning its meaning, from 'Lo, food'; 'Let's go hunting'; 'Lo, a momentary rabbit-stage'; 'Lo, a detached rabbit-part'. Developmental psychologists have established that a range of powerful perceptual and attentional constraints allow children to consider only a tiny fraction of possible meanings (e.g. Bloom 2000). With regard to grammar, the representational complexity of thought presumably determines that no finite inventory of messages could provide a practicable linguistic system, and instead requires that language has a compositional structure, using a finite set of lexical and grammatical resources to encode an unlimited set of possible messages (e.g. Brighton et al. 2005). More broadly, while there is continuing controversy concerning the Whorfian hypothesis that language influences thought, there can be little doubt that thought profoundly influences language.

## 65.4.2  Pragmatic constraints

The communicative function of language is likely to shape language structure not only in relation to the thoughts that are transmitted, but regarding the processes of pragmatic interpretation that people use to understand each others' behaviour (whether linguistic or otherwise). For example, one pragmatic principle is that people typically aim to convey as much information as possible in their utterances. So, for example, *John admires himself* is specific in that *himself* can refer only to

John. In *John admires him*, *him* is much less specific—it must refer to a (contextually obvious) male. But pragmatic constraints would indicate that, were this person John, then *himself* would have been used (because this would have been more specific); hence, if *him* is used, it should not refer to John. This pattern may, through repetition, then become 'fossilized' in the syntax of the language: new generations of learners may never observe *him* to be used to refer 'reflexively', and hence may assume that this pattern is not grammatically acceptable (rather than acceptable, but pragmatically awkward). Thus, to adapt a phrase of Givón (1979b), today's syntax may be, in part at least, yesterday's pragmatics. Levinson (2000) has developed this line of argument to provide an account of a wide range of related phenomena, traditionally described by purely abstract, and apparently entirely arbitrary, syntactic principles (the 'binding constraints', Chomsky 1981).

## 65.4.3  Cognitive mechanisms of learning and processing

A further source of constraints derives from the nature of cognitive architecture, including learning, processing, and memory. In particular, language processing involves generating and decoding regularities from highly complex sequential input, indicating a connection between general-purpose cognitive mechanisms for learning and processing sequential material, and the structure of natural language. For this reason, sequential learning tasks have become an important experimental paradigm for studying language acquisition and processing (in areas including 'artificial language learning' or 'statistical learning': see Gómez and Gerken 2000; Graf Estes, this volume); and computational models of sequence learning have been used to explain patterns of language structure. For example, Christiansen and Devlin (1997) aimed to explain statistical consistency in the head-order of the world's languages using a connectionist network, the simple recurrent network (SRN; Elman 1990). They trained SRNs to predict the next lexical category in a sentence on corpora generated by 32 different grammars, differing in head-order consistency (i.e. inconsistent grammars would mix head-first and head-last phrases). Although lacking built-in linguistic biases, the SRNs' performance was nonetheless sensitive to the amount of head-order consistency found in the grammar: the more inconsistent the grammar, the harder it was to learn. Christiansen and Devlin further analysed frequency data on the world's natural languages concerning head-order, and found that languages incorporating patterns that the networks found hard to learn tended to be less frequent.

If language has adapted to pre-existing cognitive machinery, then this raises the possibility that human sequential learning abilities may be one of the key pre-adaptations that allowed human language processing to 'take-off'. Conway and Christiansen (2001) reviewed sequential learning in non-human primates and argued that non-human primates cannot match human performance regarding hierarchical sequential structure. This may be part of the explanation for the uniqueness of human language. Finally, note that people with acquired agrammatic aphasia, typically viewed as a language-specific impairment, also show impairment of sequential learning abilities in a non-linguistic artificial sequence learning task (Christiansen et al. 2008).

## 65.4.4  Perceptuo-motor factors

The perceptual and motor basis of language is also a powerful influence on language structure. For example, the serial character of vocal output forces a sequential construction of messages. Moreover, a perceptual system with a strictly limited capacity for storing sensory input, where new sensory information typically overwrites old, demands a linguistic code which can be interpreted incrementally (in contrast to standard codes used in communication engineering, where information is stored in large blocks). The noisiness and variability (across contexts and speakers) of linguistic production, and of the acoustic environment, may, moreover, force a 'digital' communication system, in which lexical items are encoded as sequences of a small number of basic units, phonemes, to support error-correction; these discrete units in turn appear closely related to the vocal apparatus and to 'natural' perceptual boundaries (Kuhl 1987). Thus, the boundaries between phonemes are not chosen arbitrarily, but are easy to produce and perceive distinctly, given perceptual and motor equipment which pre-dates the development of language. Some theorists have argued for deeper impacts. Thus, MacNeilage (1998; this volume) argues that syllable structure may be parasitic on the jaw movements used in eating; and for some cognitive linguists, the machinery of the perceptuo-motor system crucially underpins language content and structure via embodied image schemas (e.g. Hampe 2006). The depth of the influence of perceptual and motor factors on more abstract aspects of language is controversial, but such influence may be substantial.

## 65.4.5  The importance of multiple constraints and reconsidering the problem of language acquisition

We have sketched a few of the constraints that may have shaped language. In reality, we suggest that many aspects of language may be shaped by the interaction of a wide range of constraints. Thus, for example, the tendency for linguistic constraints to be local, rather than long-distance, might be shaped by restrictions on memory, the communicative pressure for incremental interpretation, and preferences for nested hierarchical structural relationships. Similarly, processes of morphological erosion (Carstairs-McCarthy, Chapter 47; Heine and Kuteva,

Chapter 54) might be affected by ease of articulation, communicative pressure for rapid communication, aspects of perceptual discrimination, and pressures of learnability.

The more numerous and more complex these constraints, the more challenging it will be for theorists to unpick them. Yet, perhaps paradoxically, postulating a greater number of constraints simplifies the problem of language acquisition. This is because constraints on language structure will be *shared* across people. And given that the same biases regarding pragmatics, perception, motor control, thought, or learning will be shared across the population, this drastically prunes the number of options that the language learner need consider (Chater and Christiansen 2010).

Crucially, a learner embodying these biases will typically make the *right* guesses, given a relatively small amount of linguistic input—precisely because the learner embodies the *same* constraints that have driven previous generations of language users to settle on particular linguistic structures.

Indeed, while there are positive results concerning the learnability of languages from corpora of linguistic input alone, with no language-specific bias (e.g. Chater and Vitányi 2007), we suggest that rapid and robust language learning is likely to be guided by powerful biases within the learner. Rather than conceiving of these biases as arising from a dedicated, genetically specified UG, the present viewpoint is that natural languages have themselves been constrained, through processes of cultural transmission and evolution, to lie within a small region of the space of logically possible communication systems—those which best fit the multiple constraints that shape the evolution of language. From this perspective, though, it seems unlikely that the world's languages will fit within a single parametrized framework (e.g. Baker 2001), and more likely that languages will provide a diverse, and somewhat unruly, set of solutions to a hugely complex problem of multiple constraint satisfaction, as appears consistent with research on language typology (Comrie 1989; Evans and Levinson 2009). Thus, language universals are therefore best construed, on our account, as probabilistic tendencies, akin to Wittgenstein's (1953) notion of 'family resemblances', rather than rigid properties that hold across all languages.

# 65.5 Problems of gene–language co-evolution

We argued above that genes for arbitrary features of language, as postulated in UG, could not have co-evolved with natural language itself—and, more broadly, that UG, as standardly construed, is implausible on evolutionary grounds. In essence, the problem is that, prior to the existence of putative language genes, such arbitrary features of language will be highly variable over time. Such linguistic change is likely to be very much faster than genetic change, so that the linguistic environment provides a 'moving target', to which putative language genes would be unable to adapt. Moreover, the diffusion of human populations would be expected to lead to a wide diversity of languages (and, indeed, human languages diverge very rapidly—New Guinea contains perhaps one-quarter of the world's languages, exhibiting an extraordinary diversity of phonology and syntax, despite being settled only within the last 50,000 years; Diamond 1991). Gene–language co-evolution can, of course, only adapt to the current linguistic environment. Hence, any such co-evolution would generate different selective pressures on 'language genes', as we noted above. Yet modern human populations do not seem to be selectively adapted to learn their own language groups—instead, every human appears, to a first approximation, equally ready to learn any of the world's languages (although see Dediu and Ladd 2007).

It is important to stress, however, that our arguments have been directed only against a genetic basis for putatively arbitrary aspects of language; they do not necessarily apply to *functional* aspects. Functional aspects of language, perhaps including vocabulary size, the emphasis on local linguistic processes, the layered digital codes of phonological and syntactic structure, and compositional semantics (Brighton et al. 2005) may be stable aspects of the linguistic environment, precisely because of their functional role in subserving effective communication. Thus, while (prior to the emergence of putative UG) arbitrary linguistic conventions may be expected to change rapidly, functionally important constraints may be stable—hence providing stable aspects of the linguistic environment against which biological natural selection can take place. Thus, it is possible that language has co-evolved with genes associated with, for example, particular perceptuo-motor processing machinery, specialization of the articulatory apparatus, large long-term memory, general sequential processing abilities, and so on.

Finally, note that our arguments concerning the co-evolution of language and language genes are instances of a broader line of argument. For example, evolutionary biologists interested in the evolution of a species in the context of a fast-changing environment (here, the linguistic environment) typically argue that 'generalist' behavioural strategies typically dominate—because specific adaptations to today's environment are typically poorly matched with the challenge encountered tomorrow (Thompson 1994). Moreover, the considerations arguing against the co-evolution of arbitrary linguistic structure and language genes apply equally to other, putatively arbitrary, cultural 'universals', such as a putative universal 'moral grammar' (Hauser 2006).

## 65.6 FUTURE DIRECTIONS

If language has been shaped by pre-existing human neural and cognitive abilities, rather than guided by a genetically specific UG encoding arbitrary linguistic principles, the implications for the study of language are far-reaching. Indeed, Christiansen and Chater (2008) argue that this perspective may help create a new synthesis for the interdisciplinary study of language.

Most immediately, from this viewpoint, the study of language evolution is directly connected with diachronic linguistics, the study of language change (McMahon 1994), instead of being viewed as fundamentally different (i.e. one being concerned with the evolution of the genetically specified UG; the other being concerned with language change within the bounds set by UG). Thus, as we have argued, processes of language change, such as grammaticalization, may illustrate broader processes of language evolution, in microcosm; and processes of language transmission may be studied using formal and computational methods (e.g. Brighton et al. 2005). Moreover, language typology (Comrie 1989) can also be reconnected with the study of the neural and cognitive foundations of language— basic cognitive, perceptual, learning, and communicative principles may help explain patterns in the bewildering variety observed across the world's languages (see also Evans and Levinson 2009 for a similar point). Further, this variety is likely to prove a powerful tool for constraining such principles, particularly those initially created in the context of English, or at best a small number of European languages.

The present viewpoint, as noted above, casts the problem of language acquisition in a fresh light—as being tractable precisely because of the multiple constraints that are shared by language users and new language learners. Thus, understanding the constraints on language structure may potentially connect directly with empirical and theoretical work on language acquisition. One recent development which fits this pattern is the emergence of Construction Grammar in linguistics (e.g. Goldberg 2006; Bybee, this volume), and the parallel development of usage-based accounts of language acquisition, which stress the construction-specific character of early language acquisition, and the fact that more abstract linguistic generalizations (e.g. over entire syntactic categories, rather than specific lexical items) emerge late in acquisition (Tomasello 2003a).

To sum up, viewing language as shaped by the brain explains the fit between language and language users by viewing language as adapted to prior biological and cognitive biases, rather than postulating the existence of a language-specific UG. We hope that this standpoint may help synthesize an integrated study of language, incorporating descriptive and theoretical linguistics, and providing a new connection between linguistics and the brain and cognitive sciences.

# ACKNOWLEDGMENTS

NC was supported by a Major Research Fellowship from the Leverhulme Trust and by ESRC Grant Number RES-000-22-2768; MHC was supported by a Charles A. Ryskamp Fellowship from the American Council of Learned Societies and by the Santa Fe Institute.

# REFERENCES

ABLER, W. (1989). On the particulate principle of self-diversifying systems. *Journal of Social and Biological Structures* 12: 1–13.

ABOITIZ, F., GARCIA, R., BOSMAN, C., and BRUNETTI, E. (2006). Cortical memory mechanisms and language origins. *Brain and Language* 98: 40–56.

ADAMS, A.-M. and GATHERCOLE, S. E. (2000). Limitations in working memory: Implications for language development. *International Journal of Language and Communication Disorders* 35: 95–116.

AIELLO, L. C. (1996). Terrestriality, bipedalism and the origin of language. *Proceedings of the British Academy* 88: 269–289.

AIELLO, L. C. (1998). The foundation of human language. In Jablonski and Aiello (eds.), 21–34.

AIELLO, L. C. and DEAN, M. C. (1990). *An introduction to human evolutionary anatomy.* London: Academic Press.

AIELLO, L. C. and DUNBAR, R. I. M. (1993). Neocortex size, group size and the evolution of language. *Current Anthropology* 34: 184–193.

AIELLO, L. C. and WHEELER, P. (1995). The expensive-tissue hypothesis: The brain and the digestive system in human and primate evolution. *Current Anthropology* 36: 199–221.

AIELLO, L. C., BATES, N., and JOFFE, T. (2001). In defense of the extensive tissue hypothesis. In Falk and Gibson (eds.), 57–78.

AIKHENVALD, A. Y. (2002). *Language contact in Amazonia.* Oxford and New York: Oxford University Press.

AITCHISON, J. (1996). *The seeds of speech: Language origin and evolution.* Cambridge: Cambridge University Press.

ALEMSEGED, Z., SPOOR, F., KIMBEL, W. H., BOBE, R., GERAADS, D., REED, D., and WYNN, J. G. (2006). A juvenile early hominin skeleton from Dikika, Ethiopia. *Nature* 443: 296–301.

ALEXANDER, R. D. (1989). Evolution of the human psyche. In Mellars and Stringer (eds.), 455–513.

ALEXEEV, V. (1986). *The origin of the human race.* Moscow: Progress Publishers.

ALLEY, T. R. (1980). Infantile coloration as an elicitor of caretaking behavior in old-world primates. *Primates* 21: 416–429.

ALON, U. (2007). *An introduction to systems biology.* New York: Chapman and Hall/CRC.

ALPERSON-AFIL, N., RICHTER, D., and GOREN-INBAR, N. (2007). Phantom hearths and the use of fire at Gesher Benot Ya'aqov, Israel. *PaleoAnthropology* 2007: 1–15.

AMBROSE, S. H. (2001). Paleolithic technology and human evolution. *Science* 291: 1748–1753.

AMBROSE, S. H. (2008). Coevolution of composite tool technology, working memory and language: Implications for the evolution of modern human behavior. Paper presented at the Wenner-Gren Foundation Symposium 139: Working Memory and the Evolution of Modern Thinking, Cascais, Portugal.

AMUNTS, K., SCHLAUG, G., JÄNCKE, L., STEINMETZ, H., SCHLEICHER, A., DABRINGHAUS, A., and ZILLES, K. (1997). Motor cortex and hand motor skills: Structural compliance in the human brain. *Human Brain Mapping* 5: 206–215.

AMUNTS, K., SCHLEICHER, A., BURGEL, U., MOHLBERG, H., UYLINGS, H. B., and ZILLES, K. (1999). Broca's region revisited: Cytoarchitecture and intersubject variability. *Journal of Comparative Neurology* 412: 319–341.

ANDERSON, J. R. (1993). *Rules of the mind.* Hillsdale, NJ: Erlbaum.

ANDERSON, S. R. (2004). *Doctor Dolittle's delusion: Animals and the uniqueness of human language.* New Haven, CT and London: Yale University Press.

ANDERSON, S. R. (2008). The logical structure of linguistic theory. *Language* 84: 795–814.

ANDERSON, S. R. and LIGHTFOOT, D. W. (2002). *The language organ: Linguistics as cognitive physiology.* Cambridge: Cambridge University Press.

ANDREW, R. J. (2002). The earliest origins and subsequent evolution of lateralization. In L. J. Rogers and R. J. Andrew (eds.), *Comparative vertebrate lateralization.* Cambridge: Cambridge University Press, 70–93.

APICELLA, C. L., FEINBERG, D. R., and MARLOWE, F. W. (2007). Voice pitch predicts reproductive success in male hunter-gatherers. *Biology Letters* 3: 682–684.

ARAMBOURG, C. and COPPENS, Y. (1968). Decouverte d'un australopithecien nouveau dans les Gisements de L'Omo (Ethiopie). *South African Journal of Science* 64: 58–59.

ARBIB, M. A. (2002). The mirror system, imitation, and the evolution of language. In Dautenhahn and Nehaniv (eds.), 229–280.

ARBIB, M. A. (2003). The evolving mirror system: A neural basis for language readiness. In Christiansen and Kirby (eds.), 182–200.

ARBIB, M. A. (2005a). From monkey-like action recognition to human language: an evolutionary framework for neurolinguistics. *Behavioral and Brain Sciences* 28: 105–167.

ARBIB, M. A. (2005b). Interweaving protosign and protospeech: Further developments beyond the mirror. *Interaction Studies* 6: 145–171.

ARBIB, M. A. (ed.) (2006). *Action to language via the mirror neuron system.* Cambridge: Cambridge University Press.

ARBIB, M. A. (2008). From grasp to language: Embodied concepts and the challenge of abstraction. *Journal of Physiology Paris* 102: 4–20.

ARBIB, M. A. (2009). Invention and community in the emergence of language: A perspective from new sign languages. In S. M. Platek and T. K. Shackelford (eds.), *Foundations in evolutionary cognitive neuroscience: Introduction to the discipline.* Cambridge: Cambridge University Press, 117–152.

ARBIB, M. A. (2012). *How the brain got language: The mirror system hypothesis.* Oxford: Oxford University Press.

ARBIB, M. A., LIEBAL, K., and PIKA, S. (2008). Primate vocalization, gesture, and the evolution of human language. *Current Anthropology* 49: 1053–1076.

ARENSBURG, B., TILLIER, A. M., VANDERMEERSCH, B., DUDAY, H., SCHEPARTZ, L. A., and RAK, Y. (1989). A Middle Palaeolithic human hyoid bone. *Nature* 338: 758–760.

ARENSBURG, B., SCHEPARTZ, L. A., TILLIER, A. M., VANDERMEERSCH, B., and RAK, Y. (1990). A reappraisal of the anatomical basis for speech in Middle Palaeolithic hominids. *American Journal of Physical Anthropology* 83: 137–146.

ARIEW, A. (1999). Innateness is canalization: In defense of a developmental account of innateness. In V. G. Hardcastle (ed.), *Where biology meets psychology.* Cambridge, MA: MIT Press, 117–138.

ARISTOTLE (1984). *The complete works of Aristotle.* Edited by Jonathan Barnes. Princeton, NJ: Princeton University Press. (Citations from *On interpretation, On soul, Prior analytics.*)

ARMSTRONG, D. F. and WILCOX, S. E. (2007). *The gestural origin of language.* Oxford: Oxford University Press.

ARNOLD, K. and ZUBERBÜHLER, K. (2006a). Language evolution: Semantic combinations in primate calls. *Nature* 441: 303.

ARNOLD, K. and ZUBERBÜHLER, K. (2006b). The alarm-calling system of adult male putty-nosed monkeys, *Cercopithecus nictitans martini. Animal Behaviour* 72: 643–653.

ARNOLD, K. and ZUBERBÜHLER, K. (2008). Meaningful call combinations in a non-human primate. *Current Biology* 18: R202–R203.

ARNOLD, K., POHLNER, Y., and ZUBERBÜHLER, K. (2008). A forest monkey's alarm call series to predator models. *Behavioral Ecology and Sociobiology* 62: 549–559.

ARONOFF, M., MEIR, I., PADDEN, C., and SANDLER, W. (2004). Morphological universals and the sign language type. In G. Booij and J. van Marle (eds.), *Yearbook of morphology 2004.* Dordrecht and Boston, MA: Kluwer Academic Publishers, 19–39.

ARONOV, D., ANDALMAN, A. S., and FEE, M. S. (2008). A specialized forebrain circuit for vocal babbling in the juvenile songbird. *Science* 320: 630–634.

ASFAW, B., WHITE, T., LOVEJOY, O., LATIMER, B., SIMPSON, S., and SUWA, G. (1999). *Australopithecus garhi*: A new species of early hominid from Ethiopia. *Science* 284: 629–635.

ASHBY, W. R. (1947). Principles of the self-organizing dynamic system. *Journal of General Psychology* 37: 125–128.

AU, W. W. L. (1993). *The sonar of dolphins.* New York: Springer.

AUSTERLITZ, R. (1980). Language-family density in North America and Eurasia. *Ural-Altaische Jahrbücher* 51: 1–10.

AUSTIN, J. L. (1962). *How to do things with words.* Cambridge, MA: Harvard University Press.

AUSTIN, P. and BRESNAN, J. (1996). Non-configurationality in Australian Aboriginal languages. *Natural Language and Linguistic Theory* 14: 215–268.

AVISE, J. C. (2005). *Molecular markers, natural history and evolution* (2nd revised edn.). Sunderland, MA: Sinauer Associates Inc.

BADDELEY, A. D. (2000). The episodic buffer: A new component of working memory? *Trends in Cognitive Sciences* 4: 417–423.

BADDELEY, A. D. (2001). Is working memory still working? *American Psychologist* 11: 851–864.

BADDELEY, A. D. and HITCH, G. J. (1974). Working memory. In G. A. Bower (ed.), *Recent advances in learning and motivation.* New York: Academic Press, 47–90.

BADDELEY, A. D. and LOGIE, R. H. (1999). Working memory: The multiple-component model. In A. Miyake and P. Shah (eds.), *Models of working memory: Mechanisms of active maintenance and executive control.* New York: Cambridge University Press, 28–61.

BADDELEY, A. D., GATHERCOLE, S., and PAPAGNO, C. (1998). The phonological loop as a language learning device. *Psychological Review* 105: 158–173.

BAE, C. J. (2010). The late Middle Pleistocene hominin fossil record of Eastern Asia: Synthesis and review. *Yearbook of Physical Anthropology* 53: 75–93.

BAILEY, D. H. and GEARY, D. C. (2009). Hominid brain structure: Testing climatic, ecological and social competition models. *Human Nature* 20: 67–79.

BAILEY, P., VON BONIN, G., and McCULLOCH, W. S. (1950). *The isocortex of the chimpanzee.* Urbana-Champaign, IL: University of Illinois Press.

BAKER, M. C. (2001). *The atoms of language: The mind's hidden rules of grammar.* New York: Basic Books.

BAKER, P. (1990). Off target? *Journal of Pidgin and Creole Languages* 5: 107–119.

BAKER, P. (1997). Directionality in pidginization and creolization. In A. K. Spears and D. Winford (eds.), *The structure and status of pidgins and creoles.* Amsterdam: John Benjamins, 91–109.

BAKER, P. (2000). Theories of creolization and the degree and nature of restructuring. In I. Neumann-Holzschuh and E. W. Schneider (eds.), *Degrees of restructuring in creole languages.* Amsterdam: John Benjamins, 41–63.

BAKKER, P. (1987). *Autonomous languages: Signed and spoken languages created by children in the light of Bickerton's bioprogram hypothesis.* Publikaties van het Instituut voor Algemene Taalwetenschap 53. Amsterdam: University of Amsterdam.

BAKKER, P. (2006). Twins' languages as windows on language genesis. Paper presented at the Netherlands Institute for Advanced Study, Wassenaar, 13 June 2006.

BALABAN, M. and WAXMAN, S. (1992). Words may facilitate categorization in 9-month-old infants. *Journal of Experimental Child Psychology* 64: 3–26.

BALDWIN, D. A. (1991). Infants' contribution to the achievement of joint reference. *Child Development* 62: 875–890.

BALDWIN, D. A. (1995). Understanding the link between joint attention and language. In C. Moore and P. J. Dunham (eds.), *Joint attention.* Hillsdale, NJ: Lawrence Erlbaum, 131–158.

BALDWIN, J. M. (1902). *Development and evolution.* New York: Macmillan.

BALL, P. (1999). *The self-made tapestry.* New York: Oxford University Press.

BALLENTIJN, M. R. and TEN CATE, C. (1999). Variation in the number of elements in the perch-coo vocalization of the collared dove (*Streptopelia decaocto*) and what it may tell about the sender. *Behaviour* 136: 847–864.

BALTER, M. (2005). Are human brains still evolving? Brain genes show signs of selection. *Science* 309: 1662–1663.

BARHAM, L. (2002). Systematic pigment use in the Middle Pleistocene of South-Central Africa. *Current Anthropology* 43: 181–190.

BARONCHELLI, A., LORETO, V., and STEELS, L. (2008). In-depth analysis of the naming game dynamics: The homogeneous mixing case. *International Journal of Modern Physics C* 19: 785–812.

BARON-COHEN, S. (1995). *Mindblindness: An essay on autism and theory of mind.* Cambridge, MA: MIT Press.

BATALI, J. (1998). Computational simulations of the emergence of grammar. In Hurford et al. (eds.), 405–426.

BATALI, J. (2002). The negotiation and acquisition of recursive grammars as a result of competition among exemplars. In Briscoe (ed.), 111–172.

BATES, E., THAL, D., and MARCHMAN, V. (1991). Symbols and syntax: A Darwinian approach to language development. In Krasnegor et al. (eds.), 29–65.

BATESON, P. (2002). The corpse of a wearisome debate. *Science* 297: 2212–2213.

BATESON, P. (2004). The origins of human differences. *Daedalus* 133: 36–46.

BAZIN, E., GLÉMIER, S., and GALTIER, N. (2006). Population size does not influence mitochondrial genetic diversity in animals. *Science* 312: 570–572.

BEARZI, M. and STANFORD, C. (2010). A bigger, better brain. *American Scientist* 98: 402–409.

BECKERS, G. J. L., NELSON, B., and SUTHERS, R. A. (2004). Vocal-tract filtering by lingual articulation in a parrot. *Current Biology* 14: 1592–1597.

BEDNARIK, R. (2008). The mythical moderns. *Journal of World Prehistory* 21: 85–102.

BEECHER, M. D. and CAMPBELL, S. E. (2005). The role of unshared songs in singing interactions between neighbouring song sparrows. *Animal Behaviour* 70: 1297–1304.

BEECHER M. D., CAMPBELL, S. E., BURT, J. M., HILL, C. E., and NORDBY, J. C. (2000). Song-type matching between neighbouring song sparrows. *Animal Behaviour* 59: 21–27.

BEHAR, D. M., VILLEMS, R., SOODYALL, H., BLUE-SMITH, J., PEREIRA, L., METSPALU, E., SCOZZARI, R., MAKKAN, H., TZUR, S., COMAS, D., BERTRANPETIT, J., QUINTANA-MURCI, L., TYLER-SMITH, C., SPENCER WELLS, R., ROSSET, S., and THE GENOGRAPHIC CONSORTIUM. (2008). The dawn of human matrilineal diversity. *American Journal of Human Genetics* 82: 1130–1140.

BENAZZO, S. (2009). The emergence of temporality: From restricted linguistic systems to early human language. In Botha and de Swart (eds.), 21–57.

BENGTSON, J. and RUHLEN, M. (1994). Global etymologies. In M. Ruhlen, *On the origin of languages: Studies in linguistic taxonomy*. Stanford, CA: Stanford University Press, 277–329.

BENNETT, E. I., DIAMOND, M. C., KRECH, D., and ROSENZWIEG, M. R. (1964). Chemical and anatomical plasticity of the brain. *Science* 146: 610–619.

BENTON, M. J. and DONOGHUE, P. C. (2007). Palaeontological evidence to date the tree of life. *Molecular Biology and Evolution* 25: 26–53.

BERGER, L. R., DE RUITER, D. J., CHURCHILL, S. E., SCHMID, P., CARLSON, K. J., DIRKS, P. H. G. M., and KIBII, J. M. (2010). *Australopithecus sediba*: A new species of *Homo*-like australopith from South Africa. *Science* 328: 195–204.

BERGMAN, T. J., BEEHNER, J. C., CHENEY, D. L., and SEYFARTH, R. M. (2003). Hierarchical classification by rank and kinship in baboons. *Science* 302: 1234–1236.

BERK, L. (1999). Children's private speech: An overview of theory and the status of research. In P. Lloyd and C. Fernyhough (eds.), *Lev Vygotsky: Critical assessments. Vol II, Thought and language*. Florence, KY: Taylor & Francis/Routledge, 33–70.

BERKO, J. (1958). The child's learning of English morphology. *Word* 14: 150–177.

BERRAH, A.-R. and LABOISSIÈRE, R. (1999). Species: An evolutionary model for the emergence of phonetic structures in an artificial society of speech agents. In D. Floreano, J.-D. Nicoud, and F. Mondada (eds.), *Advances in artificial life: Lecture notes in artificial intelligence* Vol. 1674. Berlin: Springer Verlag, 674–678.

BERSAGLIERI, T., SABETI, P. C., PATTERSON, N., VANDERPLOEG, T., SCHAFFNER, S. F., DRAKE, J. A., RHODES, M., REICH, D. E., and HIRSCHHORN, J. N. (2004). Genetic signatures of strong recent positive selection at the Lactase gene. *American Journal of Human Genetics* 74: 1111–1120.

BIBEN, M. and SYMMES, D. (1986). Play vocalizations of squirrel monkeys (*Saimiri sciureus*). *Folia Primatologica* 46: 173–182.

BICKEL, B. (2008). A general method for the statistical evaluation of typological universals. Ms, University of Leipzig. www.uni-leipzig.de/~bickel (accessed February 15, 2010).

BICKEL, B. and NICHOLS, J. (2002). The AUTOTYP research program. http://www.uni-leipzig.de/~autotyp/

BICKEL, B. and NICHOLS, J. (2005). Inclusive/exclusive as person vs. number categories worldwide. In E. Filimonova (ed.), *Clusivity*. Amsterdam: John Benjamins, 47–70.

BICKERTON, D. (1981). *Roots of language*. Ann Arbor, MI: Karoma.

BICKERTON, D. (1984). The language bioprogram hypothesis. *Behavioral and Brain Sciences* 7: 173–221.

BICKERTON, D. (1988). Seselwa serialization and its significance. *Journal of Pidgin and Creole Languages* 4: 155–183.

BICKERTON, D. (1990). *Language and species*. Chicago, IL: University of Chicago Press.

BICKERTON, D. (1995). *Language and human behavior.* Seattle, WA: University of Washington Press/London: UCL Press.

BICKERTON, D. (1998). Catastrophic evolution: The case for a single step from protolanguage to full human language. In Hurford et al. (eds.), 341–358.

BICKERTON, D. (2000). How protolanguage became language. In Knight et al. (eds.), 264–284.

BICKERTON, D. (2003). Symbol and structure: A comprehensive framework for language evolution. In Christiansen and Kirby (eds.), 77–93.

BICKERTON, D. (2007). Language evolution: A brief guide for linguists. *Lingua* 117: 510–526.

BICKERTON, D. (2008). *Bastard tongues.* New York: Farrar, Straus and Giroux.

BICKERTON, D. (2009a). *Adam's tongue: How humans made language, how language made humans.* New York: Hill and Wang/Farrar, Straus and Giroux.

BICKERTON, D. (2009b). Recursion: Core of complexity or artifact of analysis? In T. Givón and M. Shibatani (eds.), *Syntactic complexity: Diachrony, acquisition, neuro-cognition, evolution.* Amsterdam: John Benjamins, 531–544.

BICKERTON, D. (2009c). Syntax for non-syntacticians: A brief primer. In Bickerton and Szathmáry (eds.), 3–13.

BICKERTON, D. (2010). On two incompatible theories of language evolution. In Larson et al. (eds.), 199–210.

BICKERTON, D. and ODO, C. (1976). *General phonology and pidgin syntax.* Final Report on NSF Grant No. 39748. University of Hawaii.

BICKERTON, D. and SZATHMÁRY, E. (eds.) (2009). *Biological foundations and origins of syntax.* Strüngmann Forum Reports, Vol. 3. Cambridge, MA: MIT Press.

BIRD, C. D. and EMERY, N. J. (2009). Insightful problem solving and creative tool modification by captive nontool-using rooks. *Proceedings of the National Academy of Sciences of the USA* 106: 10370–10375.

BIRDSELL, J. B. (1953). Some environmental and cultural factors influencing the structuring of Australian Aboriginal populations. *American Naturalist* 87: 171–207.

BIRDSELL, J. B. (1957). Some population problems involving Pleistocene man. *Cold Spring Harbor Symposia on Quantitative Biology* 22: 47–69.

BISANG, W. (2004). Grammaticalization without co-evolution of form and meaning: The case of tense-aspect-modality in East and Mainland Southeast Asia. In Bisang et al. (eds.), 109–138.

BISANG, W. (2009). On the evolution of complexity – sometimes less is more in East and mainland Southeast Asia. In Sampson et al. (eds.), 19–33.

BISANG, W., HIMMELMANN, N., and WIEMER, B. (eds.) (2004). *What makes grammaticalization? A look from its fringes and its components.* Berlin/New York: Mouton de Gruyter.

BLACKING, J. (1973). *How musical is man?* Seattle, WA: University of Washington Press.

BLAKEMORE, S. and CHOUDHURY, S. (2006). Development of the adolescent brain: Implications for executive function and social cognition. *Journal of Child Psychology and Psychiatry* 47: 296–312.

BLEED, P. (1986). The optimal design of hunting weapons: Maintainability or reliability? *American Antiquity* 51: 737–747.

BLEVINS, J. (1995). The syllable in phonological theory. In J. Goldsmith (ed.), *Handbook of phonological theory.* Oxford: Blackwell, 206–244.

BLEVINS, J. (2004). *Evolutionary phonology: The emergence of sound patterns.* Cambridge: Cambridge University Press.

BLONDIN-MASSÉ, A., CHICOISNE, G., GARGOURI, Y., HARNAD, S., PICARD, O., and MARCOTTE, O. (2008). How is meaning grounded in dictionary definitions? In *Proceedings of the 3rd Textgraphs Workshop on Graph-Based Algorithms for Natural Language Processing*, 17–24.

BLOOM, P. (2000). *How children learn the meaning of words.* Cambridge, MA: MIT Press.

BLOOMFIELD, L. (1933). *Language.* New York: Henry Holt and Co.

BOECKX, C. (2006). *Linguistic minimalism: Origins, concepts, methods, and aims.* Oxford: Oxford University Press.

BOECKX, C. (2008). Did we really solve Plato's Problem (abstractly)? In Y. Otsu (ed.), *Proceedings of the 9th Tokyo Conference on Psycholinguistics.* Tokyo: Hituzi Syobo, 1–25.

BOECKX, C. (2009). Linguistic minimalism. In B. Heine and H. Narrog (eds.), *Oxford handbook of grammatical analysis.* Oxford: Oxford University Press, 537–562.

BOECKX, C. (2011). Some reflections on Darwin's problem in the context of Cartesian Biolinguistics. In A.-M. di Sciullo and C. Boeckx (eds.), *The biolinguistic enterprise: New perspectives on the evolution and nature of the human language faculty.* Oxford: Oxford University Press, 42–64.

BOECKX, C. and GROHMANN, K. K. (2007). The *Biolinguistics* manifesto. *Biolinguistics* 1: 1–8.

BOEHM, C. (2001). *Hierarchy in the forest: The evolution of egalitarian behavior.* Cambridge, MA: Harvard University Press.

BOESCH, C. and BOESCH, H. (1989). Hunting behavior of wild chimpanzees in the Taï National Park. *American Journal of Physical Anthropology* 78: 547–573.

BOESCH, C. and BOESCH-ACHERMANN, H. (2000). *The chimpanzees of the Taï forest: Behavioral ecology and evolution.* Oxford and New York: Oxford University Press.

BOLHUIS, J. J. and GAHR, M. (2006). Neural mechanisms of birdsong memory. *Nature Reviews Neuroscience* 7: 347–357.

BOOGERT, N. J., GIRALDEAU, L-A., and LEFEBVRE, L. (2008). Song complexity correlates with learning ability in zebra finch males. *Animal Behaviour* 76: 1735–1741.

BOOTH, A. E. and WAXMAN, S. R. (2002). Object names and object functions serve as cues to categories in infancy. *Developmental Psychology* 38: 948–957.

BORAN, J. R. and HEIMLICH, S. (1999). Social learning in cetaceans: Hunting, hearing and hierarchies. In Box and Gibson (eds.), 282–307.

BORDEN, G. J., HARRIS, K. S., and RAPHAEL, L. J. (2003). *Speech science primer: Physiology, acoustics, and perception of speech.* Philadelphia, PA: Lippincott Williams and Wilkins.

BORDES, F. (1968). *The Old Stone Age.* New York: World University Library.

BORG, E. (2007). If mirror neurons are the answer, what was the question? *Journal of Consciousness Studies* 14: 5–19.

BOTHA, R. (2003). *Unravelling the evolution of language.* Amsterdam: Elsevier.

BOTHA, R. (2006a). On the windows approach to language evolution. *Language and Communication* 26: 129–43.

BOTHA, R. (2006b). Pidgin languages as a putative window on language evolution. *Language and Communication* 26: 1–14.

BOTHA R. (2008). Prehistoric shell beads as a window on language evolution. *Language and Communication* 28: 197–212.

BOTHA, R. (2009a). On musilanguage/'Hmmmmm' as an evolutionary precursor to language. *Language and Communication* 29: 61–76.

BOTHA, R. (2009b). Theoretical underpinnings of inferences about language evolution: The syntax used at Blombos Cave. In Botha and Knight (eds.), (2009a), 93–111.

BOTHA R. (2009c). What are windows on language evolution? In Botha and de Swart (eds.), 1–25.

BOTHA R., and DE SWART, H. (eds.) (2009). *Language evolution: The view from restricted linguistic systems.* Utrecht: LOT.

BOTHA R. and KNIGHT, C. (eds.) (2009a). *The cradle of language.* Oxford: Oxford University Press.

BOTHA, R. and KNIGHT, C. (eds.) (2009b). *The prehistory of language.* Oxford: Oxford University Press.

BOUGHMAN, J. W. (1998). Vocal learning by greater spear-nosed bats. *Proceedings of the Royal Society of London B* 265: 227–233.

BOWERN, C. and KOCH, H. (2004). *Australian languages: Classification and the comparative method.* Amsterdam/Philadelphia, PA: John Benjamins.

BOWIE, J. (2008). Proto-discourse and the emergence of compositionality. *Interaction Studies* 9: 18–33.

BOX, H. O. and GIBSON, K. R. (eds.) (1999). *Mammalian social learning: Comparative and ecological perspectives.* Cambridge: Cambridge University Press.

BOYD, R. and RICHERSON, P. J. (1985). *Culture and the evolutionary process.* Chicago, IL: University of Chicago Press.

BOYD, R. and SILK, J. B. (2003). *How humans evolved.* New York: W. W. Norton.

BOYER, P. (1994). *The naturalness of religious ideas: A cognitive theory of religion.* Berkeley, CA: University of California Press.

BOYLAND, J. T. (1996). Morphosyntactic change in progress: A psycholinguistic approach. Unpublished PhD thesis. Berkeley, CA: University of California.

BRAIN, C. K. and SILLEN, A. (1988). Evidence from the Swartkrans cave for the earliest use of fire. *Nature* 336: 464–466.

BRAINE, M. D. (1994). Is nativism sufficient? *Journal of Child Language* 21: 9–31.

BRAMBLE, D. M. and LIEBERMAN, D. E. (2004). Endurance running in the evolution of *Homo. Nature* 432: 345–352.

BRANTINGHAM, P. J., KUHN, S. L., and KERRY, K.W. (eds.) (2004). *The early Upper Paleolithic beyond Western Europe.* Berkeley, CA: University of California Press.

BRIGHTON, H. (2002). Compositional syntax from cultural transmission. *Artificial Life* 8: 25–54.

BRIGHTON, H., KIRBY, S., and SMITH, K. (2005a). Cultural selection for learnability: Three principles underlying the view that language adapts to be learnable. In Tallerman (ed.), 291–333.

BRIGHTON, H., SMITH, K., and KIRBY, S. (2005b). Language as an evolutionary system. *Physics of Life Reviews* 2: 177–226.

BRISCOE, T. (2000). Grammatical acquisition: Inductive bias and coevolution of language and the language acquisition device. *Language* 76: 245–296.

BRISCOE, T. (ed.) (2002). *Linguistic evolution through language acquisition: Formal and computational models.* Cambridge: Cambridge University Press.

BRISCOE, T. (2009). What can formal or computational models tell us about how (much) language shaped the brain? In Bickerton and Szathmáry (eds.), 369–382.

BROADERS, S., COOK, S. W., MITCHELL, Z., and GOLDIN-MEADOW, S. (2007). Making children gesture brings out implicit knowledge and leads to learning. *Journal of Experimental Psychology: General* 136: 539–550.

BROCA, P. (1861). Remarques sur le siège de la faculté du langage articulé; suivies d'une observation d'aphémie. *Bulletin de la Société Anatomique* 6: 330–357.

BROOM, R. (1938). The Pleistocene anthropoid apes of South Africa. *Nature* 142: 377–379.

BROWMAN, C. P. and GOLDSTEIN, L. (1992). Articulatory phonology: An overview. *Phonetica* 49: 155–180.

BROWN, J. C. (1966). *Loglan: A logical language.* Gainesville, FL: The Loglan Institute.

BROWN, K. S., MAREAN, C. W., HERRIES, A. I. R., JACOBS, Z., TRIBOLO, C., BRAUN, D., ROBERTS, D. L., MEYER, M. C., and BERNATCHEZ, J. (2009). Fire as an engineering tool of early modern humans. *Science* 325: 859–862.

BROWN, S. (2000). The 'musilanguage' model of human evolution. In Wallin et al. (eds.), 271–300.

BRUNET, M., BEAUVILAIN, A., COPPENS, Y., HEINTZ, E., MOUTAYE, A. H. E., and PILBEAM, D. (1996). *Australopithecus bahrelghazali,* une nouvelle espèce d'Hominide ancien de la région de Koro Toro (Tchad). *Comptes rendus de l'Académie des sciences* 322: 907–913.

BRUNET, M., GUY, F., PILBEAM, D., MACKAYE, H. T., LIKIUS, A., AHOUNTA, D., BEAUVILAIN, A., BLONDEL, C., BOCHERENS, H., BOISSERIE, J.-R., DE BONIS, L., COPPENS, Y., DEJAX, J., DENYS, C., DURINGER, P., EISENMANN, V., GONGDIBE, F., FRONTY, P., GERAADS, D., LEHMANN, T., LIHOREAU, F., LOUCHART, A., MAHAMAT, A., MERCERON, G., MOUCHELIN, G., OTERO, O., CAMPOMANES, P. P., DE LEON, M. P., RAGE, J.-C., SAPANET, M., SCHUSTER, M., SUDRE, J., TASSY, P., VALENTIN, X., VIGNAUD, P., VIRIOT, L., ZAZZO, A., and ZOLLIKOFER, C. (2002). A new hominid from the Upper Miocene of Chad, Central Africa. *Nature* 418: 145–151.

BUGNYAR, T. and KOTRSCHAL, K. (2002). Observational learning and the raiding of food caches in ravens, *Corvus corax:* Is it tactical deception? *Animal Behaviour* 64: 185–195.

BURLING, R. (1993). Primate calls, human language, and nonverbal communication. *Current Anthropology* 34: 25–53.

BURLING, R. (2002). The slow growth of language in children. In Wray (ed.), 297–310.

BURLING, R. (2005). *The talking ape: How language evolved.* Oxford: Oxford University Press.

BURT, J. M., BARD, S. C., CAMPBELL, S. E., and BEECHER, M. D. (2002). Alternative forms of song matching in song sparrows. *Animal Behaviour* 63: 1143–1151.

BUSS, D. M. (2003). *The evolution of desire: Strategies of human mating.* Revised edition. New York: Basic Books.

BUSTAMANTE, C. D., FLEDEL-ALON, A., WILLIAMSON, S., NIELSEN, R., HUBISZ, M. T., GLANOWSKI, S., TANENBAUM, D. M., WHITE, T. J., SNINSKY, J. J., HERNANDEZ, R. D., CIVELLO, D., ADAMS, M. D., CARGILL, M., and CLARK, A. G. (2005). Natural selection on protein-coding genes in the human genome. *Nature* 437: 1153–1157.

BUXHOEVEDEN, D. P. and CASANOVA, M. (2000). Comparative lateralisation patterns in the language area of human, chimpanzee, and rhesus monkey brains. *Laterality* 4: 315–330.

BUXHOEVEDEN, D. P., SWITALA, A. E., LITAKER, M., ROY, E., and CASANOVA, M. F. (2001a). Lateralization of minicolumns in human planum temporale is absent in non-human primate cortex. *Brain, Behavior and Evolution* 57: 349–358.

BUXHOEVEDEN, D. P., SWITALA, A. E., LITAKER, M., ROY, E., and CASANOVA, M. F. (2001b). Morphological differences between minicolumns in human and nonhuman primate cortex. *American Journal of Physical Anthropology* 115: 361–371.

BYBEE, J. L. (1998). A functionalist approach to grammar and its evolution. *Evolution of Communication* 2: 249–278.

BYBEE, J. L. (2006a). *Frequency of use and the organization of language.* Oxford: Oxford University Press.

BYBEE, J. L. (2006b). From usage to grammar: The mind's response to repetition. *Language* 82: 711–733.

BYBEE, J. L. (2009). Language universals and usage-based theory. In M. H. Christiansen, C. Collins, and S. Edelman (eds.), *Language universals*. Oxford: Oxford University Press, 17–39.

BYBEE, J. L. (2010). *Language, usage and cognition*. Cambridge: Cambridge University Press.

BYBEE, J. L. and MCCLELLAND, J. (2005). Alternatives to the combinatorial paradigm of linguistic theory based on domain general principles of human cognition. *The Linguistic Review* 22: 381–410.

BYBEE, J. L., PERKINS, R., and PAGLIUCA, W. (1994). *The evolution of grammar: Tense, aspect and modality in the languages of the world*. Chicago, IL: University of Chicago Press.

BYRNE, R. W. (1995). *The thinking ape: Evolutionary origins of intelligence*. Oxford: Oxford University Press.

BYRNE, R. W. and BATES, L. A. (2010). Primate social cognition: Uniquely primate, uniquely social, or just unique? *Neuron* 65: 815–830.

BYRNE, R. W. and BYRNE, J. M. E. (1991). Hand preferences in the skilled gathering tasks of mountain gorillas (*Gorilla g. beringei*). *Cortex* 27: 521–46.

BYRNE, R. W. and BYRNE, J. M. E. (1993). Complex leaf-gathering skills of mountain gorillas (*Gorilla g. beringei*): Variability and standardization. *American Journal of Primatology* 31: 241–261.

BYRNE, R. W. and CORP, N. (2004). Neocortex size predicts deception rate in primates. *Proceedings of the Royal Society of London B* 271: 1693–1699.

BYRNE, R. W. and RUSSON, A. (1998). Learning by imitation: A hierarchical approach. *Behavioral and Brain Sciences* 21: 667–721.

BYRNE, R. W. and WHITEN, A. (1988). *Machiavellian intelligence: Social expertise and the evolution of intellect in monkeys, apes and humans*. Oxford: Clarendon Press.

BYRNE, R. W. and WHITEN, A. (1992). Cognitive evolution in primates: Evidence from tactical deception. *Man NS* 27: 609–627.

BYRNE, R. W., BATES, L.A., and MOSS, C. J. (2009). Elephant cognition in primate perspective. *Comparative cognition and behavior reviews* 4: 65–79.

CAIN, D. P. and WADA, J. A. (1979). An anatomical asymmetry in the baboon brain. *Brain, Behavior and Evolution* 16: 222–226.

CALL, J. and TOMASELLO, M. (eds.) (2007). *The gestural communication of apes and monkeys*. Mahwah, NJ: Lawrence Erlbaum/London: Taylor and Francis.

CALL, J. and TOMASELLO, M. (2008). Does the chimpanzee have a theory of mind? 30 years later. *Trends in Cognitive Science* 12: 187–192.

CALVIN, W. H. (1985). A stone's throw and its launch window: Timing, precision and its implications for language and hominid brains. *Journal of Theoretical Biology* 104: 121–135.

CALVIN, W. H. (1993). The unitary hypothesis: A common neural circuitry for novel manipulations, language, plan-ahead and throwing? In Gibson and Ingold (eds.), 230–250.

CALVIN, W. H. and BICKERTON, D. (2000). *Lingua ex machina: Reconciling Darwin and Chomsky with the human brain*. Cambridge, MA: MIT Press.

CAMPBELL, E. J. M. (1968). The respiratory muscles. *Annals of the New York Academy of Sciences* 155: 135–40.

CAMPBELL, L. (2010). Language isolates and their history: What's weird anyway? Paper presented at 36th Annual Meeting, Berkeley Linguistics Society.

CAMPBELL, L. and POSER, W. J. (2008). *Language classification: History and method.* Cambridge: Cambridge University Press.

CAMPS, M. and URIAGEREKA, J. (2006). The Gordian knot of linguistic fossils. In J. Rossello and J. Martin (eds.), *The biolinguistic turn.* Barcelona: Publicacions Universitat de Barcelona, 34–65.

CANGELOSI, A. (2001). Evolution of communication and language using signals, symbols and words. *IEEE Transactions on Evolutionary Computation* 5: 93–101.

CANGELOSI, A. (2010). Grounding language in action and perception: From cognitive agents to humanoid robots. *Physics of Life Reviews* 7: 139–151.

CANGELOSI, A. and HARNAD, S. (2000). The adaptive advantage of symbolic theft over sensorimotor toil: Grounding language in perceptual categories. *Evolution of Communication* 4: 117–142.

CANGELOSI, A. and PARISI, D. (1998). The emergence of a 'language' in an evolving population of neural networks. *Connection Science* 10: 83–97.

CANGELOSI, A. and PARISI, D. (eds.) (2002). *Simulating the evolution of language.* Berlin: Springer Verlag.

CANGELOSI, A., SMITH, A. D. M., and SMITH, K. (eds.) (2006). *Proceedings of the 6th International Conference on the Evolution of Language (EVOLANG6).* Singapore: World Scientific.

CANN, R. L., STONEKING, M., and WILSON, A. C. (1987). Mitochondrial DNA and human evolution. *Nature* 325: 31–36.

CANTALUPO, C. and HOPKINS, W. D. (2001). Asymmetric Broca's area in Great Apes. *Nature* 414: 505.

CAPASSO, L., MICHETTI, E., and D'ANASTASIO, R. (2008). A *Homo erectus* hyoid bone: Possible implications for the origin of the human capability for speech. *Collegium Antropologicum* 4: 1007–1011.

CARLSON, S. M. and MOSES, L. J. (2001). Individual differences in inhibitory control and children's theory of mind. *Child Development* 72: 1032–1053.

CARLSON, S. M., MOSES, L. J., and CLAXTON, L. J. (2004). Individual differences in executive functioning and theory of mind: An investigation of inhibitory control and planning ability. *Journal of Experimental Child Psychology* 87: 299–319.

CARROLL, S. B. (2003). Genetics and the making of *Homo sapiens. Nature* 422: 849–857.

CARROLL, S. B. (2005). *Endless forms most beautiful: The new science of evo devo and the making of the animal kingdom.* New York: W. W. Norton.

CARROLL, S. B. and BOYD, C. (1992). Host race radiation in the soapberry bug: Natural history with the history. *Evolution* 46: 1052–1069.

CARROLL, S. B., DINGLE, H., and KLASSEN, S. P. (1997). Genetic differentiation of fitness-associated traits among rapidly evolving populations of the soapberry bug. *Evolution* 51: 1182–1188.

CARROLL, S. B., LOYE, J. E., DINGLE, H., MATHIESON, M., FAMULA, T. R., and ZALUCKI, M. P. (2005). And the beak shall inherit – evolution in response to invasion. *Ecology Letters* 8: 944–951.

CARROLL, S. B., HENDRY, A. P., REZNICK, D. N., and FOX, C. W. (2007). Evolution on ecological time-scales. *Functional Ecology* 21: 387–393.

CARRUTHERS, P. (2006). *The architecture of the mind: Massive modularity and the flexibility of thought.* Oxford: Oxford University Press.

CARSTAIRS-McCARTHY, A. (1999). *The origins of complex language: An inquiry into the evolutionary beginnings of sentence, syllables and truth.* Oxford: Oxford University Press.

CARSTAIRS-McCARTHY, A. (2005). The evolutionary origin of morphology. In Tallerman (ed.), 166–184.

CARSTAIRS-McCARTHY, A. (2010). *The evolution of morphology.* Oxford: Oxford University Press.

CARTMILL, E. A. and BYRNE, R. W. (2007). Orangutans modify their gestural signaling according to their audience's comprehension. *Current Biology* 17: 1345–1348.

CASE, R. (1985). *Intellectual development: Birth to adulthood (Developmental psychology series).* New York: Academic Press.

CATANI, M. and FFYTCHE, D. H. (2005). The rises and falls of disconnection syndromes. *Brain* 128: 2224–2239.

CATCHPOLE, C. K. (2000). Sexual selection and the evolution of song and brain structure in *Acrocephalus* warblers. In P. J. B. Slater, J. S. Rosenblatt, C. T. Snowdon, and T. J. Roper (eds.), *Advances in the study of behavior 29.* San Diego, CA: Academic Press, 45–97.

CATCHPOLE, C. K. and SLATER, P. J. B. (1995/2008), *Bird song: Biological themes and variations.* Cambridge: Cambridge University Press.

CAVALLI-SFORZA, L. L. and FELDMAN, M. W. (2003). The application of molecular approaches to the study of human evolution. *Nature Genetics* 33 (Suppl): 266–275.

CHAMBERLAIN, A. T. and WOOD, B. A. (1985). A reappraisal of variation in hominid mandibular corpus dimensions. *American Journal of Physical Anthropology* 66: 399–405.

CHANGEUX, J. P. and Chavallion, J. (eds.) (1995). *Origins of the human brain.* Oxford: Clarendon Press.

CHASE, P. G. (1999). Symbolism as reference and symbolism as culture. In Dunbar et al. (eds.), 34–49.

CHATER, N. and CHRISTIANSEN, M. H. (2007). Two views of simplicity in linguistic theory: Which connects better with cognitive science? *Trends in Cognitive Sciences* 8: 324–326.

CHATER, N. and CHRISTIANSEN, M. H. (2010). Language acquisition meets language evolution. *Cognitive Science* 34: 1131–1157.

CHATER, N. and VITÁNYI, P. (2007). 'Ideal learning' of natural language: Positive results about learning from positive evidence. *Journal of Mathematical Psychology* 51: 135–163.

CHATER, N., REALI, F., and Christiansen, M. H. (2009). Restrictions on biological adaptation in language evolution. *Proceedings of the National Academy of Sciences of the USA* 106: 1015–1020.

CHENEY, D. L. and SEYFARTH, R. M. (1990). *How monkeys see the world: Inside the mind of another species.* Chicago, IL: University of Chicago Press.

CHENEY, D. L. and SEYFARTH, R. M. (1998). Why monkeys don't have language. In G. Petersen (ed.), *The Tanner lectures on human values, Vol. 19.* Salt Lake City, UT: University of Utah Press, 175–219.

CHENEY, D. L. and SEYFARTH, R. M. (2005). Constraints and preadaptations in the earliest stages of language evolution. *The Linguistic Review* 22: 135–159.

CHENEY, D. L. and SEYFARTH, R. M. (2007). *Baboon metaphysics: The evolution of a social mind.* Chicago, IL: University of Chicago Press.

CHENG, L. L. S. (1997). *On the typology of wh-questions.* New York: Garland.

CHICOISNE, G., BLONDIN-MASSÉ, A., PICARD, O., and HARNAD, S. (2008). Grounding abstract word definitions in prior concrete experience. Paper presented at the Sixth

Annual Conference on the Mental Lexicon, University of Alberta, Banff Alberta, 7–10 October 2008. http://eprints.ecs.soton.ac.uk/16618/

CHOMSKY, N. (1957). *Syntactic structures.* The Hague: Mouton.

CHOMSKY, N. (1959). Review of 'Verbal behavior' by B. F. Skinner. *Language* 35: 26–58.

CHOMSKY, N. (1965). *Aspects of the theory of syntax.* Cambridge, MA: MIT Press.

CHOMSKY, N. (1966). *Cartesian linguistics.* New York: Harper and Row.

CHOMSKY, N. (1975). *Reflections on language.* New York: Pantheon.

CHOMSKY, N. (1980). *Rules and representations.* New York: Columbia University Press.

CHOMSKY, N. (1981). *Lectures on government and binding.* Dordrecht: Foris.

CHOMSKY, N. (1986). *Knowledge of language.* New York: Praeger.

CHOMSKY, N. (1995). *The Minimalist Program.* Cambridge, MA: MIT Press.

CHOMSKY, N. (1999). Reluctant icon: Noam Chomsky interviewed by Tim Halle. http://www.chomsky.info/interviews/1999----.htm. Accessed 1 July 2008.

CHOMSKY, N. (2000a). *On nature and language.* New York and Cambridge: Cambridge University Press.

CHOMSKY, N. (2000b). *The architecture of language.* Oxford: Oxford University Press.

CHOMSKY, N. (2001). Derivation by phase. In M. Kenstowicz (ed.), *Ken Hale. A life in language.* Cambridge, MA: MIT Press, 1–52.

CHOMSKY, N. (2005). Three factors in language design. *Linguistic Inquiry* 36: 1–22.

CHOMSKY, N. (2007). Approaching UG from below. In U. Sauerland and H. M. Gärtner (eds.), *Interfaces + recursion = language?* Berlin: Mouton de Gruyter, 1–29.

CHOMSKY, N. (2008). On phases. In R. Freidin, C. Otero, and M.-L. Zubizarreta (eds.), *Foundational issues in linguistic theory.* Cambridge, MA: MIT Press, 133–166.

CHOMSKY, N. (2010). Some simple evo devo theses: How true might they be for language? In Larson et al. (eds.), 45–62.

CHOU, H. H., HAYAKAWA, T., DIAZ, S., KRINGS, M., INDRIATI, E., LEAKEY, M., PÄÄBO, S., SATTA, Y., TAKAHATA, N., and VARKI, A. (2002). Inactivation of CMP-N-acetylneuraminic acid hydroxylase occurred prior to brain expansion during human evolution. *Proceedings of the National Academy of Sciences of the USA* 99: 11736–11741.

CHRISTIANSEN, M. H. and CHATER, N. (2008). Language as shaped by the brain. *Behavioral and Brain Sciences* 31: 489–509.

CHRISTIANSEN, M. H. and DALE, R. (2004). The role of learning and development in the evolution of language: A connectionist perspective. In Oller and Griebel (eds.), 90–109.

CHRISTIANSEN, M. H. and DEVLIN, J. T. (1997). Recursive inconsistencies are hard to learn: A connectionist perspective on universal word order correlations. In M. G. Shafto and P. Langley (eds.), *Proceedings of the 19th Annual Conference of the Cognitive Science Society.* Mahwah, NJ: Lawrence Erlbaum, 113–118.

CHRISTIANSEN, M. H. and KIRBY, S. (2003). Language evolution: The hardest problem in science? In Christiansen and Kirby (eds.), 1–15.

CHRISTIANSEN, M. H. and Kirby, S. (eds.) (2003). *Language evolution.* Oxford: Oxford University Press.

CHRISTIANSEN, M. H., KELLY, L., SHILLCOCK, R., and GREENFIELD, K. (2008). Impaired artificial grammar learning in agrammatism. Submitted manuscript.

CHURCH, R. B. and GOLDIN-MEADOW, S. (1986). The mismatch between gesture and speech as an index of transitional knowledge. *Cognition* 23: 43–71.

CHURCHILL, S. E., FRANCISCO, R. G., McKEAN-PERAZA, H. A., DANIEL, J. A., and WAREN B. R. (2009). Shanidar 3 Neandertal rib puncture wound and Paleolithic weaponry. *Journal of Human Evolution* 57: 163–178.

CLAPHAM, P. J., LEIMKUHLER, E., GRAY, B. K., and MATTILA, D. K. (1995). Do humpback whales exhibit lateralized behaviour? *Animal Behaviour* 50: 73–82.

CLARK, A. (2008). *Supersizing the mind: Embodiment, action, and cognitive extension.* Oxford: Oxford University Press.

CLARK, C. W. (1995). Application of US Navy underwater hydrophone arrays for scientific research on whales. *Reports of the International Whaling Commission* 45: 210–212.

CLARK, E. V. (1993). *The lexicon in acquisition.* Cambridge: Cambridge University Press.

CLARKE, E., REICHARD, U., and ZUBERBÜHLER, K. (2006). The syntax and meaning of wild gibbon songs. *PLoS ONE* 1: e73.

CLAY, Z. and ZUBERBÜHLER, K. (2009). Food-associated calling sequences in bonobos. *Animal Behaviour* 77: 1387–1396.

CLAY, Z. and ZUBERBÜHLER, K. (2011). Bonobos extract meaning from call sequences. *PLoS ONE* 6: e18786.

CLAYTON, N. S. and DICKINSON, A. (1998). Episodic-like memory during cache recovery by scrub jays. *Nature* 395: 272–274.

CLAYTON, N. S., GRIFFITHS, D., EMERY, N., and DICKINSON, A. (2001). Elements of episodic-like memory in animals. *Philosophical Transactions of the Royal Society of London B* 356: 1483–1491.

CLAYTON, N. S., BUSSEY, T. J., EMERY, N. J., and DICKINSON, A. (2003). Prometheus to Proust: The case for behavioural criteria for mental 'time travel'. *Trends in Cognitive Sciences* 7: 436–437.

CLUTTON-BROCK, T. H. (2006). Cooperative breeding in mammals. In P. M. Kappeler and C. P. Van Schaik (eds.), *Cooperation in primates and humans.* Berlin: Springer Verlag, 173–190.

COCHRAN, G. and HARPENDING, H. (2009). *The 10,000 year explosion: How civilization accelerated human evolution.* New York: Basic Books.

COHEN, H. and LEFEBVRE, C. (eds.) (2005). *Handbook of categorization in cognitive science.* Amsterdam: Elsevier.

COMRIE, B. (1989). *Language universals and linguistic typology: Syntax and morphology* (2nd edn.). Oxford: Blackwell.

COMRIE, B. (1992). Before complexity. In Hawkins and Gell-Mann (eds.), 193–211.

COMRIE, B. (2000). From potential to realization: An episode in the origin of language. *Linguistics* 38: 989–1004.

COMRIE, B. (2003). Reconstruction, typology and reality. In Hickey (ed.), 243–257.

CONNOR, R. C. and SMOLKER, R. A. (1996). 'Pop' goes the dolphin: A vocalization male bottlenose dolphins produce during consortships. *Behaviour* 133: 643–662.

CONVERSE, L. J., CARLSON, A. A., ZIEGLER, T. E., and SNOWDON, C. T. (1995). Communication of ovulatory state to mates by female pygmy marmosets, *Cebuella pygmaea. Animal Behaviour* 49: 615–621.

CONWAY, C. M. and CHRISTIANSEN, M. H. (2001). Sequential learning in non-human primates. *Trends in Cognitive Sciences* 5: 539–546.

COOK, M. L. H., SAYIGH, L. S., BLUM, J. E., and WELLS, R. S. (2004). Signature-whistle production in undisturbed free-ranging bottlenose dolphins (*Tursiops truncatus*). *Proceedings of the Royal Society of London B* 271: 1043–1049.

COOK, R., BROWN, M., and RILEY, D. (1983). Flexible memory processing by rats: Use of prospective and retrospective information. *Journal of Experimental Psychology: Animal Behavior Processes* 11: 453–469.

COOK, S. W., MITCHELL, Z., and GOLDIN-MEADOW, S. (2007). Gesturing makes learning last. *Cognition* 106: 1047–1058.

COOLIDGE, F. L. and WYNN, T. (2001). Executive functions of the frontal lobes and the evolutionary ascendancy of *Homo sapiens. Cambridge Archaeological Journal* 11: 255–260.

COOLIDGE, F. L. and WYNN, T. (2005). Working memory, its executive functions, and the emergence of modern thinking. *Cambridge Archaeological Journal* 15: 5–26.

COOLIDGE, F. L. and WYNN, T. (2009a). Recursion, phonological storage capacity, and the evolution of modern speech. In Botha and Knight (eds.) (2009b), 244–254.

COOLIDGE, F. L. and WYNN, T. (2009b). *The rise of* Homo sapiens*: The evolution of modern thinking.* Chichester: John Wiley and Sons.

COOPER, D. L. (2006). Broca's Arrow: Evolution, prediction and language in the brain. *The Anatomical Record (Part B: New Anatomy)* 289B: 9–24.

COOPER, M. D. and ALDER, M. N. (2006). The evolution of adaptive immune systems. *Cell* 124: 815–822.

CORBALLIS, M. C. (1993). *The lopsided ape: Evolution of the generative mind.* Oxford: Oxford University Press.

CORBALLIS, M. C. (2002). *From hand to mouth: The origins of language.* Princeton, NJ: Princeton University Press.

CORBALLIS, M. C. (2003). From mouth to hand: Gesture, speech, and the evolution of right-handedness. *Behavioral and Brain Sciences* 26: 199–260.

CORBALLIS, M. C. (2004). The origins of modernity: Was autonomous speech the critical factor? *Psychological Review* 111: 543–552.

CORBALLIS, M. C. (2009). Mental time travel and the shaping of language. *Experimental Brain Research* 192: 553–560.

CORBALLIS, M. C. and LEA, S. E. G. (eds.) (1999). *The descent of mind: Psychological perspectives on hominid evolution.* Oxford: Oxford University Press.

COUDÉ, G., FERRARI, P. F., RODA, F., and MARANESI, M., VERONI, V., MONTI, F., RIZZOLATTI, G., and FOGASSI, L. (2007). Neuronal responses during vocalization in the ventral premotor cortex of macaque monkeys. Society for Neuroscience Annual Meeting (San Diego California), Abstract 636.3.

CRAIN, S. (1991). Language acquisition in absence of experience. *Behavioral and Brain Sciences* 14: 597–650.

CROCKFORD, C. and BOESCH, C. (2003). Context-specific calls in wild chimpanzees, *Pan troglodytes verus*: Analysis of barks. *Animal Behaviour* 66: 115–125.

CROCKFORD, C. and BOESCH, C. (2005). Call combinations in wild chimpanzees. *Behaviour* 142: 397–421.

CROCKFORD, C., HERBINGER, I., VIGILANT, L., and BOESCH, C. (2004). Wild chimpanzees produce group-specific calls: A case for vocal learning? *Ethology* 110: 221–243.

CROFT, W. A. (1991). The evolution of negation. *Journal of Linguistics* 27: 1–27.

CROFT, W. A. (2000). *Explaining language change.* Harlow: Longman Linguistic Library.

CROFT, W. A. (2001). *Radical construction grammar: Syntactic theory in typological perspective.* Oxford: Oxford University Press.

CROW, T. J. (2004). Directional asymmetry is the key to the origin of modern *Homo sapiens* (the Broca-Annett axiom): A reply to Rogers' review of 'The speciation of modern *Homo sapiens*'. *Laterality: Asymmetries of Body, Brain and Cognition* 9: 233–242.

CULICOVER, P. W. and JACKENDOFF, R. (2005). *Simpler syntax*. Oxford: Oxford University Press.

CURRAT, M., EXCOFFIER, L., MADDISON, W, OTTO, S. P., RAY, N., WHITLOCK, M. C., and YEAMAN, S. (2006). Comment on 'Ongoing Adaptive Evolution of *ASPM*, a Brain Size Determinant in *Homo sapiens*' and '*Microcephalin*, a Gene Regulating Brain Size, Continues to Evolve Adaptively in Humans'. *Science* 313: 172.

CURTISS, S. (1977). *Genie: A psycholinguistic study of a modern-day 'wild child'*. New York: Academic Press.

DAHL, Ö. (2004). *The growth and maintenance of linguistic complexity*. Amsterdam/Philadelphia: John Benjamins.

DAMASIO, H. and DAMASIO, A. R. (1989). *Lesion analysis in neuropsychology*. New York: Oxford University Press.

DART, R. A. (1925). *Australopithecus africanus*: The man-ape of South Africa. *Nature* 115: 195–199.

DARWIN, C. (1871). *The descent of man and selection in relation to sex*. London: John Murray.

DARWIN, C. (1872). *The expression of the emotions in man and animals*. London: John Murray.

DAUTENHAHN, K. and NEHANIV, C. L. (eds.) (2002). *Imitation in animals and artifacts: Complex adaptive systems*. Cambridge, MA: MIT Press.

DAVIDSON, I. (2003). The archaeological evidence of language origins: State of art. In Christiansen and Kirby (eds.), 140–157.

DAVIDSON, R. J., SHACKMAN, A. J., and MAXWELL, J. S. (2004). Asymmetries in face and brain related to emotion. *Trends in Cognitive Sciences* 8: 389–391.

DAVIES, A. G. and OATES, J. F. (1994). *Colobine monkeys: Their ecology, behaviour and evolution*. Cambridge: Cambridge University Press.

DAWKINS, R. (1986). *The blind watchmaker*. New York: W. W. Norton.

DAWKINS, R. (1995). *River out of Eden: A Darwinian view of life*. New York: Basic Books.

DAWKINS, R. (1996). *Climbing mount improbable*. New York: W. W. Norton.

DEACON, T. W. (1997). *The symbolic species: The coevolution of language and the brain*. New York: W. W. Norton and Company/London: Penguin Press.

DEACON, T. W. (2003). Universal Grammar and semiotic constraints. In Christiansen and Kirby (eds.), 111–140.

DEACON, T. W. (2009). Relaxed selection and the role of epigenesis in the evolution of language. In M. S. Blumberg, J. H. Freeman, and S. R. Robinson (eds.), *Oxford handbook of developmental behavioral neuroscience*. New York: Oxford University Press, 730–752.

DEACON, T. W. (2010). A role for relaxed selection in the evolution of the language capacity. *Proceedings of the National Academy of Sciences of the USA* 107: 9000–9006.

DE BOER, B. (2000). Self organization in vowel systems. *Journal of Phonetics* 28: 441–465.

DE BOER, B. (2001). *The origins of vowel systems*. Oxford: Oxford University Press.

DE BOER, B. (2003). Conditions for stable vowel systems in a population. In W. Banzhaf, T. Christaller, P. Dittrich, J. T. Kim, and J. Ziegler (eds.), *Advances in artificial life: Lecture notes in computer science 2801*. Berlin: Springer, 415–424.

DE BOER, B. (2005a). Infant directed speech and the evolution of language. In Tallerman (ed.), 100–121.

DE BOER, B. (2005b). Self-organisation in language. In C. Hemelrijk (ed.), *Self-organisation and evolution of social systems.* Cambridge: Cambridge University Press, 123–139.

DE BOER, B. and KUHL, P. K. (2003). Investigating the role of infant-directed speech with a computer model. *Acoustics Research Letters Online* 4: 129–134.

DE CASTRO, J. and NICOLAS, M. (1997). Palaeodemography of the Atapuerca-SH Middle Pleistocene hominid sample. *Journal of Human Evolution* 33: 333–355.

DEDIU, D. and LADD, D. R. (2007). Linguistic tone is related to the population frequency of the adaptive haplogroups of two brain size genes: *ASPM* and *Microcephalin. Proceedings of the National Academy of Sciences of the USA* 104: 10944–10949.

DEGUSTA, D., GILBERT, W. H., and TURNER, S. P. (1999). Hypoglossal canal size and hominid speech. *Proceedings of the National Academy of Sciences of the USA* 96: 1800–1804.

DEHAENE, S. (1997). *The number sense.* Oxford: Oxford University Press.

DEHAENE, S., PEGADO, F., BRAGA, L. W., VENTURA, P., NUNES FILHO, G., JOBERT, A., DEHAENE-LAMBERTZ, G., KOLINSKY, R., MORAIS, J., and COHEN, L. (2010). How learning to read changes the cortical networks for vision and language. *Science* 330: 1359–1364.

DE LA TORRE, S. and SNOWDON, C. T. (2009). Dialects in pygmy marmosets? Population variation in call structure. *American Journal of Primatology* 71: 333–342.

DE LA TORRE, I., MORA, R., DOMINGUEZ-RODRIGO, M., DE LUQUE, L., and ALCALA, L. (2003). The Oldowan industry of Peninj and its bearing on the reconstruction of the technological skill of Lower Pleistocene hominids. *Journal of Human Evolution* 44: 203–224.

DELGADO, R. A. (2006). Sexual selection in the loud calls of male primates: Signal content and function. *International Journal of Primatology* 27: 5–25.

DENNELL, R. and ROEBROEKS, W. (2005). An Asian perspective on early human dispersal from Africa. *Nature* 438: 1099–1104.

DENNETT, D. (1995). *Darwin's dangerous idea: Evolution and the meaning of life.* New York: Simon and Schuster.

DENT, M. L., PIERCE, A., BRITTAN-POWELL, E. F., and DOOLING, R. J. (1997). Perception of synthetic /ba/-/wa/ speech continuum by budgerigars (*Melopsittacus undulates*). *Journal of the Acoustical Society of America* 102: 1891–1897.

D'ERRICO, F. (2005). The invisible frontier: A multiple species model for the origin of behavioral modernity. *Evolutionary Anthropology* 12: 188–202.

D'ERRICO, F. and VANHAEREN, M. (2009). Earliest personal ornaments and their significance for the origin of language debate. In Botha and Knight (eds.) (2009a), 16–40.

D'ERRICO F., HENSHILWOOD, C., LAWSON, G., VANHAEREN, M., TILLIER, A.-M., SORESSI, M., BRESSON, F., MAUREILLE, B., NOWELL, A., LAKARA, J., BACKWELL, L., and JULIEN, M. (2003). Archaeological evidence for the emergence of language, symbolism, and music – An alternative multidisciplinary perspective. *Journal of World Prehistory* 17: 1–70.

D'ERRICO, F., HENSHILWOOD, C., VANHAEREN, M., and VAN NIEKERK, K. (2005). *Nassarius kraussianus* shell beads from Blombos Cave: Evidence for symbolic behaviour in the Middle Stone Age. *Journal of Human Evolution* 48: 3–24.

D'ERRICO, F., VANHAEREN, M., BARTON, N., BOUZOUGGAR, A., MIENIS, H., RICHTER, D., HUBLIN, J-J., McPHERRON, S., and LOZOUET, P. (2009). Additional evidence on the use of personal ornaments in the Middle Paleolithic of North Africa. *Proceedings of the National Academy of Sciences of the USA* 106: 16051–16056.

DE SMET, H. J., BAILLIEUS, H., DE DEYN, P. P., MARIEN, P., and PAQUIER, P. (2007). The cerebellum and language: The story so far. *Folia Phoniatrica et Logopaedica* 7: 165–170.

DE SOUSA, A. and WOOD, B. (2007). The hominin fossil record and the emergence of the modern human central nervous system. In J. H. Kaas (ed.), *Evolution of nervous systems: A comprehensive reference. Vol. 4: The evolution of primate nervous systems.* Oxford: Elsevier, 291–336.

DESSALLES, J.-L. (1998). Altruism, status and the origin of relevance. In Hurford et al. (eds.), 130–147.

DE VYLDER, B. and TUYLS, K. (2006). How to reach linguistic consensus: A proof of convergence for the naming game. *Journal of Theoretical Biology* 242: 818–831.

DE WAAL, F. B. M. (1982). *Chimpanzee politics: Power and sex among apes.* London: Jonathan Cape/New York: Harper and Row.

DE WAAL, F. B. M. (1988). The communicative repertoire of captive bonobos (*Pan paniscus*) compared to that of chimpanzees. *Behaviour* 106: 183–251.

DE WAAL, F. B. M. (2003). Darwin's legacy and the study of primate visual communication. In P. Ekman, J. J. Campos, R. J. Davidson, and F. B. M. de Waal (eds.), *Emotions inside out: 130 years after Darwin's 'The expression of the emotions in man and animals'.* New York: New York Academy of Sciences, 7–31.

DE WAAL, F. B. M. and VAN HOOFF, J. A. R. A. M. (1981). Side-directed communication and agonistic interactions in chimpanzees. *Behaviour* 77: 164–198.

DIAMOND, J. (1991/2004). *The third chimpanzee: The evolution and future of the human animal.* New York: Harper Collins.

DILLER, K. and CANN, R. L. (2009). Evidence against a genetic-based revolution in language 50,000 years ago. In Botha and Knight (eds.) (2009a), 135–149.

DI PAOLO, E. A., NOBLE, J., and BULLOCK, S. (2000). Simulation models as opaque thought experiments. In M. A. Bedau, J. S. McCaskill, N. H. Packard, and S. Rasmussen (eds.), *Artificial Life VII: Proceedings of the Seventh International Conference on Artificial Life.* Cambridge, MA: MIT Press, 497–506.

DOBZHANSKY, T. (1937). *Genetics and 'The origin of species'.* New York: Columbia University Press.

DOBZHANSKY, T. (1973). Nothing makes sense in biology except in the light of evolution. *The American Biology Teacher* 35: 125–129.

DOLGIX, B. O. (1960). *Rodovoy i plemennoy sostav narodov Sibiri v XVII veke.* [The tribal composition of the peoples of Siberia in the 17th century]. Moscow: Izdatel'stvo Akademii Nauk SSSR.

DOMINGUEZ-RODRIGO, M., SERRALLONGA, J., JUAN-TRESSERRAS, J., ALCALA, L., and LUQUE, L. (2001). Woodworking activities by early humans: A plant residue analysis on Acheulean stone tools from Peninj (Tanzania). *Journal of Human Evolution* 40: 289–299.

DONALD M. (1991). *Origins of the modern mind: Three stages in the evolution of culture and cognition.* Cambridge, MA: Harvard University Press.

DONALD, M. (1993). Précis of 'Origins of the modern mind' with multiple reviews and author's response. *Behavioral and Brain Sciences* 16: 737–791.

DONALD, M. (1998). Mimesis and the executive suite: Missing links in language evolution. In Hurford et al. (eds.), 44–67.

DONALD, M. (1999). Preconditions for the evolution of protolanguages. In Corballis and Lea (eds.), 138–154.

DONALD, M. (2009). Sixteen years after the fact: Revisiting a theory of human cognitive evolution. In G. Hatfield and H. Pittman (eds.), *The co-evolution of mind, brain and culture*. Philadelphia, PA: University of Pennsylvania Museum of Archaeology and Anthropology.

DORUS, S., VALLENDER, E. J., EVANS, P. D., MAHOWALD, M., WYCKOFF, G. J., MALCOM, C. M., and LAHN, B. T. (2004). Accelerated evolution of nervous system genes in the origin of *Homo sapiens*. *Cell* 119: 1027–1040.

DOUPE, A. J. and KUHL, P. K. (1999). Birdsong and human speech: Common themes and mechanisms. *Annual Review of Neuroscience* 22: 567–631.

DREA, C. M. and CARTER, A. (2009). Cooperative problem solving in a social carnivore. *Animal Behaviour* 78: 967–977.

DUCHIN, L. E. (1990). The evolution of articulate speech: Comparative anatomy of the oral cavity in *Pan* and *Homo*. *Journal of Human Evolution* 19: 687–697.

DUNBAR, R. I. M. (1991). Functional significance of social grooming in primates. *Folia Primatologica* 57: 121–131.

DUNBAR, R. I. M. (1992). Neocortex size as a constraint on group size in primates. *Journal of Human Evolution* 22: 469–493.

DUNBAR, R. I. M. (1993). Coevolution of neocortex size, group size and language in humans. *Behavioral and Brain Sciences* 16: 681–735.

DUNBAR, R. I. M. (1996). *Grooming, gossip and the evolution of language*. London: Faber and Faber/Cambridge MA: Harvard University Press.

DUNBAR, R. I. M. (2003). The social brain: Mind, language, and society in evolutionary perspective. *Annual Review of Anthropology* 32: 163–181.

DUNBAR, R. I. M. (2008). Mind the gap: Or why humans aren't just great apes. *Proceedings of the British Academy* 154: 403–423.

DUNBAR, R. I. M. (2009). Why only humans have language. In Botha and Knight (eds.) (2009b), 12–35.

DUNBAR, R. I. M. and DUNBAR, P. (1975). *Social dynamics of gelada baboons*. Basel: Karger.

DUNBAR, R. I. M. and SHULTZ, S. (2007a). Evolution in the social brain. *Science* 317: 1344–1347.

DUNBAR, R. I. M. and SHULTZ, S. (2007b). Understanding primate brain evolution. *Philosophical Transactions of the Royal Society of London B* 362: 649–658.

DUNBAR, R. I. M., DUNCAN, N., and NETTLE, D. (1995). Size and structure of freely forming conversational groups. *Human Nature* 6: 67–78.

DUNBAR, R. I. M., DUNCAN, N., and MARRIOT, A. (1997). Human conversational behaviour. *Human Nature* 8: 231–246.

DUNBAR, R. I. M., KNIGHT, C., and POWER, C. (eds.) (1999). *The evolution of culture: An interdisciplinary view*. Edinburgh: Edinburgh University Press.

DUNBAR, R. I. M., KORSTJENS, A. H., and LEHMANN, J. (2009). Time as an ecological constraint. *Biological Reviews* 84: 413–429.

DURIE, M. and ROSS, M. (eds.) (1996). *The comparative method reviewed: Regularity and irregularity in language change*. New York and Oxford: Oxford University Press.

EDELMAN, G. (1987). *Neural Darwinism: The theory of neuronal group selection*. New York: Basic Books.

EGNOR, S. E. R. and HAUSER, M. D. (2004). A paradox in the evolution of primate vocal learning. *Trends in Neurosciences* 27: 649–654.

EKMAN, P. (ed.) (1972a). *Emotion in the human face: Guide-lines for research and an integration of findings*. New York: Pergamon Press.

EKMAN, P. (1972b). Universals and cultural differences in facial expressions of emotion. In J. Cole (ed.), *Nebraska Symposium on motivation 1971*. Lincoln, NE: University of Nebraska Press, 207–283.

EKMAN, P. and FRIESEN, W. V. (1969). The repertoire of non-verbal behavior: Categories, origins, usage, and coding. *Semiotica* 1: 49–98.

EKMAN, P. and FRIESEN, W. V. (1971). Constants across cultures in the face and emotion. *Journal of Personality and Social Psychology* 17: 124–129.

ELLIS, N. C. (1996). Sequencing in SLA: Phonological memory, chunking and points of order. *Studies in Second Language Acquisition* 18: 91–126.

ELLIS, N. C. and LARSEN-FREEMAN, D. (eds.) (2009). *Language learning Volume 59: Supplement 1.*

ELMAN, J. L. (1990). Finding structure in time. *Cognitive Science* 14: 179–211.

ELMAN, J. L., BATES, E., JOHNSON, M. H., KARMILOFF-SMITH, A., PARISI, D., and PLUNKETT, K. (1996). *Rethinking innateness: A connectionist perspective on development.* Cambridge, MA: MIT Press.

ELOWSON, A. M. and SNOWDON, C. T. (1994). Pygmy marmosets, *Cebuella pygmaea*, modify vocal structure in response to changed social environment. *Animal Behaviour* 47: 1267–1277.

ELOWSON, A. M., SNOWDON, C. T., and LAZARO-PEREA, C. (1998a). 'Babbling' and social context in infant monkeys: Parallels to human infants. *Trends in Cognitive Sciences* 2: 31–37.

ELOWSON, A. M., SNOWDON, C. T., and LAZARO-PEREA, C. (1998b). Infant 'babbling' in a nonhuman primate: Complex vocal sequences with repeated call types. *Behaviour* 135: 643–664.

EMERY, N. J. and CLAYTON, N. S. (2001). Effects of experience and social context on prospective caching strategies by scrub jays. *Nature* 414: 443–446.

EMERY, N. J. and CLAYTON, N. S. (2004). The mentality of crows: Convergent evolution of intelligence in corvids and apes. *Science* 306: 1903–1907.

EMMOREY, K. (1999). Do signers gesture? In L. S. Messing and R. Campbell (eds.), *Gesture, speech, and sign.* Oxford: Oxford University Press, 133–159.

EMMOREY, K. (2002). *Language, cognition, and brain: Insights from sign language research.* Hillsdale, NJ: Lawrence Erlbaum.

ENARD, W., PRZEWORSKI, M., FISHER, S. E., LAI, C., WIEBE, V., KITANO, T., MONACO, A., and PÄÄBO, S. (2002). Molecular evolution of FOXP2: A gene involved in speech and language. *Nature* 418: 869–872.

ENDICOTT, P., HO, S., and STRINGER, C. B. (2010). Using genetic evidence to evaluate four palaeoanthropological hypotheses for the timing of Neanderthal and modern human origins. *Journal of Human Evolution* 59: 87–95.

ENFIELD, N. J. and LEVINSON, S. C. (eds.) (2006). *Roots of human sociality: Culture, cognition and interaction.* Oxford: Berg.

ENGH, A. E., HOFFMEIER, R., CHENEY, D. L., and SEYFARTH, R. M. (2006). Who, me? Can baboons infer the target of a vocalization? *Animal Behaviour.* 71: 381–387.

ENGLE, R. W. and KANE, M. J. (2004). Executive attention, working memory capacity, and a two-factor theory of cognitive control. In B. Ross (ed.), *The psychology of learning and motivation, Vol. 44.* New York, NY: Elsevier, 145–199.

ERDAL, D. and WHITEN, A. (1994). On human egalitarianism: An evolutionary product of Machiavellian status escalation? *Current Anthropology* 35: 175–183.

ERIKSSON, P. S., PERFILIEVA, E., BJÖRK-ERIKSSON, T., ALBORN, A., NORDBORG, C., PETERSON, D. A., and GAGE, F. H. (1998). Neurogenesis in the adult human hippocampus. *Nature Medicine* 4: 1313–1317.

ERMAN, B. and WARREN, B. (2000). The idiom principle and the open choice principle. *Text* 20: 29–62.

ERREN, T. C., CULLEN, P., and ERREN, M. (2008). Neanderthal, chimp and human genomes: Hypotheses wanted for research into brain evolution. *Medical Hypotheses* 70: 4–7.

ESWARAN, V., HARPENDING, H., and ROGERS, A. R. (2005). Genomics refutes an exclusively African origin of humans. *Journal of Human Evolution* 49: 1–18.

ETTLINGER, G. F. (1988). Hand preference, ability and hemispheric specialization. How far are these factors related in the monkey? *Cortex* 24: 389–398.

EVANS, C. S., EVANS, L., and MARLER, P. (1993). On the meaning of alarm calls: Functional reference in an avian vocal system. *Animal Behaviour* 46: 23–38.

EVANS, N. (ed.) (2003). *The Non-Pama-Nyungan languages of Northern Australia: Comparative studies of the continent's most linguistically complex region.* Canberra: Research School of Pacific Studies, Australian National University.

EVANS, N. and LEVINSON, S. C. (2009). The myth of language universals: Language diversity and its importance for cognitive science. *Behavioral and Brain Sciences* 32: 429–492.

EVANS, P. D., ANDERSON, J. R., VALLENDER, E. J., CHOI, S. S., and LAHN, B. T. (2004a). Reconstructing the evolutionary history of *microcephalin*, a gene controlling human brain size. *Human Molecular Genetics*, 13: 1139–1145.

EVANS, P. D., ANDERSON, J. R., VALLENDER, E. J., GILBERT, S. L., MALCOM, C. M., DORUS, S., and LAHN, B. T. (2004b). Adaptive evolution of *ASPM*, a major determinant of cerebral cortical size in humans. *Human Molecular Genetics* 13: 489–494.

EVANS, P. D., GILBERT, S. L., MEKEL-BOBROV, N., VALLENDER, E. J., ANDERSON, J. R., VAEZ-AZIZI, L. M., TISHKOFF, S. A., HUDSON, R. R., and LAHN, B. T. (2005). Microcephalin, a gene regulating brain size, continues to evolve adaptively in humans. *Science* 309: 1717–1720.

EVERETT, D. L. (2005). Cultural constraints on grammar and cognition in Pirahã: Another look at the design features of human language. *Current Anthropology* 46: 621–646.

EVERETT, D. L. (2009). Pirahã culture and grammar: a response to some criticisms. *Language* 85: 405–442.

FAGOT, J. and VAUCLAIR, J. (1993). Manual and hemispheric specialization in the manipulation of a joystick by baboons *(Papio papio). Behavioral Neuroscience* 107: 210–214.

FALK, D. (1980). A re-analysis of the South African Australopithecine natural endocasts. *American Journal of Physical Anthropology* 53: 525–539.

FALK, D. (1983). The Taung endocast: A reply to Holloway. *American Journal of Physical Anthropology* 60: 479–480.

FALK, D. (2004). Prelinguistic evolution in early Hominins: Whence motherese? *Behavioral and Brain Sciences* 27: 491–503.

FALK, D. (2009). *Finding our tongues: Mothers, infants and the origins of language.* New York: Basic Books.

FALK, D. and GIBSON, K. R. (eds.) (2001). *External anatomy of the primate cerebral cortex.* Cambridge: Cambridge University Press.

FALK, D., CHEVERUD, J., VANNIER, M. W., and CONROY, G. C. (1986). Advanced computer-graphics technology reveals cortical asymmetry in endocasts of rhesus monkeys. *Folia Primatologica* 46: 98–103.

FALK, D., HILDEBOLT, C., CHEVERUD, J., VANNIER, M., HELMKAMP, R. C., and KONIGSBERG, L. (1990). Cortical asymmetries in the frontal lobe of rhesus monkeys (*Macaca mulatta*). *Brain Research* 512: 40–45.

FANT, G. (1960). *Acoustic theory of sound production*. The Hague: Mouton.

FARRAR, M. J. (1990). Discourse and the acquisition of grammatical morphemes. *Journal of Child Language* 17: 607–624.

FARRIES, M. A. (2004). The avian song system in comparative perspective. *Annals of the New York Academy of Sciences* 1016: 61–76.

FEENDERS, G., LIEDVOGEL, M., RIVAS, J., ZAPKA, M., HORITA, H., HARA, E., WADA, K., MOURITSEN, H., and JARVIS, E. D. (2008). Molecular mapping of movement-associated areas in the avian brain: A motor theory for vocal learning. *PLoS ONE* 3: e1768.

FERGUSON, C. A. (1964). Baby talk in six languages. *American Anthropologist* 66: 103–114.

FERGUSON, C. A. and FARWELL, C. B. (1975). Words and sounds in early language acquisition. *Language* 51: 419–430.

FERNALD, A. (1985). Four-month-old infants prefer to listen to motherese. *Infant Behavior and Development* 8: 181–195.

FERNALD, A. (1992). Meaningful melodies in mothers' speech. In H. Papoušek, U. Jürgens, and M. Papoušek (eds.), *Nonverbal vocal communication: Comparative and developmental perspectives*. Cambridge: Cambridge University Press, 262–282.

FERNALD, A. (1994). Human maternal vocalizations to infants as biologically relevant signals: An evolutionary perspective. In P. Bloom (ed.), *Language acquisition: Core readings*. Cambridge, MA: MIT Press, 51–94.

FERNALD, A., TAESCHNER, T., DUNN, J., PAPOUSEK, M., DE BOYSSON-BARDIES, B., and FUKUI, I. (1989). A cross-language study of prosodic modifications in mothers' and fathers' speech to preverbal infants. *Journal of Child Language* 16: 477–501.

FERNALD, R. D. (2003). How does behavior change the brain? Multiple methods to answer old questions. *Integrative and Comparative Biology* 43: 771–779.

FERNANDEZ-CARRIBA, S., LOECHES, A., MORCILLO, A., and HOPKINS, W. D. (2002). Asymmetry in facial expression of emotions by chimpanzees. *Neuropsychologia* 40: 1523–1533.

FERRARI, P. F., GALLESE, P., RIZZOLATTI, G., and FOGASSI, L. (2003). Mirror neurons responding to the observation of ingestive and communicative mouth movements in the monkey ventral premotor cortex. *European Journal of Neuroscience* 17: 1703–1714.

FILLMORE, C. J., KAY, P., and O'CONNOR, M. C. (1988). Regularity and idiomaticity in grammatical constructions. *Language* 64: 501–538.

FINLAY, B. L. (2007). Endless minds most beautiful. *Developmental Science* 10: 30–34.

FINLAY, B. L., and DARLINGTON, R. B. (1995). Linked regularities in the development and evolution of mammalian brains. *Science* 268: 1578–1584.

FINLAYSON, C. (2004). *Neanderthals and modern humans: An ecological and evolutionary perspective*. New York and Cambridge: Cambridge University Press.

FISHER, C. and GLEITMAN, L. R. (2002). Language acquisition. In H. F. Pashler and C. R. Gallistel (eds.), *Stevens' handbook of experimental psychology, Vol. 3: Learning and motivation*. New York: Wiley, 445–496.

FISHER, R. A. (1930). *The genetical theory of natural selection*. Oxford: Clarendon Press.

FISMAN, R., IYENGAR, S. S., KAMENICA, E., and SIMONSON, I. (2006). Gender differences in mate selection: Evidence from a speed dating experiment. *Quarterly Journal of Economics* 121: 673–697.

FITCH, W. T. (2000a). The evolution of speech: A comparative review. *Trends in Cognitive Sciences* 4: 258–267.

FITCH, W. T. (2000b). The phonetic potential of nonhuman vocal tracts: Comparative cineradiographic observations of vocalizing animals. *Phonetics* 57: 205–218.

FITCH, W. T. (2002). Comparative vocal production and the evolution of speech: Reinterpreting the descent of the larynx. In Wray (ed.), 21–45.

FITCH, W. T. (2004). Kin selection and 'mother tongues': A neglected component in language evolution. In Oller and Griebel (eds.), 275–296.

FITCH, W. T. (2005). The evolution of language: A comparative review. *Biology and Philosophy* 20: 193–230.

FITCH, W. T. (2007). The evolution of language: A comparative perspective. In G. Gaskell (ed.), *Oxford handbook of psycholinguistics*. Oxford: Oxford University Press, 787–804.

FITCH, W. T. (2010a). *The evolution of language*. Cambridge: Cambridge University Press.

FITCH, W. T. (2010b). Three meanings of 'recursion': Key distinctions for biolinguistics. In Larson et al. (eds.), 73–90.

FITCH, W. T. and HAUSER, M. D. (2004). Computational constraints on syntactic processing in a nonhuman primate. *Science* 303: 377–380.

FITCH, W. T. and REBY, D. (2001). The descended larynx is not uniquely human. *Proceedings of the Royal Society of London B* 268: 1669–1675.

FITCH, W. T., HAUSER, M. D., and CHOMSKY, N. (2005). The evolution of the language faculty: Clarifications and implications. *Cognition* 97: 179–210.

FLAVELL, J. H. (1992). Perspectives on perspective taking. In H. Beilin and P. Pufall (eds.), *Piaget's theory: Prospects and possibilities*. Hillsdale, NJ: Lawrence Erlbaum, 107–139.

FLEISCHMAN, S. (1982). *The future in thought and language: Diachronic evidence from Romance*. Cambridge: Cambridge University Press.

FOCQUAERT, F., BRAECKMAN, J., and PLATEK, S. (2008). An evolutionary cognitive neuroscience perspective on human self-awareness and theory of mind. *Philosophical Psychology* 21: 47–68.

FODOR, J. A. (1983). *The modularity of mind: An essay on faculty psychology*. Cambridge, MA: MIT Press.

FODOR, J. A. and PIATTELLI-PALMARINI, M. (2010). *What Darwin got wrong*. New York: Farrar, Straus and Giroux.

FORD, J. K. B. (1991). Vocal traditions among resident killer whales (*Orcinus orca*) in coastal waters of British Columbia. *Canadian Journal of Zoology* 69: 1454–1483.

FORGACS, G. and NEWMAN, S. (2005). *Biological physics of the developing embryo*. Cambridge: Cambridge University Press.

FORSTER, P. and MATSUMURA, S. (2005). Did early humans go north or south? *Science* 308: 965–966.

FORSTER, S. and CORDS, M. (2005). Socialization of infant blue monkeys (*Cercopithecus mitis stuhlmanni*): Allomaternal interactions and sex differences. *Behaviour* 142: 869–896.

FORSYTH, J. (1992). *A history of the peoples of Siberia, Russia's North Asian colony 1581–1990*. Cambridge: Cambridge University Press.

FOUNDAS, A. L., LEONARD, C., and HEILMAN, K. (1995). Morphological cerebral asymmetries and handedness: The pars triangularis and planum temporale. *Archives of Neurology* 52: 501–508.

FOUNDAS, A. L., EURE, K. F., LUEVANO, L. F., and WEINBERGER, D. R. (1998). MRI asymmetries of Broca's area: The pars triangularis and pars opercularis. *Brain and Language* 64: 282–296.

FOUTS, R. S. (1975). Capacities for language in the great apes. In R. H. Tuttle (ed.), *Socio-ecology and psychology of primates*. The Hague/Paris: Mouton, 371–390.

FOUTS, R. S. and MILLS, S. T. (1997). *Next of kin: My conversations with chimpanzees*. New York: William Morrow.

FOUTS, R. S. and RIGBY, R. L. (1977). Man-chimpanzee communication. In Sebeok (ed.), 1034–1054.

FRANKEL, A. S., CLARK, C. W., HERMAN, L. M., and GABRIELE, C. M. (1995). Spatial distribution, habitat utilization, and social interactions of humpback whales, *Megaptera novaeangliae*, off Hawai'i, determined using acoustic and visual techniques. *Canadian Journal of Zoology* 73: 1134–1146.

FRANKS, B. K., and RIGBY, K. (2005). Deception and mate selection: Some implications for relevance and the evolution of language. In Tallerman (ed.), 208–229.

FRAYER, D. W. and NICOLAY, C. (2000). Fossil evidence on the origin of speech sounds. In N. L. Wallin, B. Merker, and S. Brown (eds.), *The origin of music*. Cambridge, MA: MIT Press, 217–234.

FREEBERG, T. M. (2006). Social complexity can drive vocal complexity. *Psychological Science* 17: 557–561.

FRIPP, D., OWEN, C., QUINTANA-RIZZO, E., SHAPIRO, A., BUCKSTAFF, K., JANKOWSKI, K., WELLS, R. S., and TYACK, P. L. (2005). Bottlenose dolphin (*Tursiops truncatus*) calves appear to model their signature whistles on the signature whistles of community members. *Animal Cognition* 8: 17–26.

FRISHBERG, N. (1975). Arbitrariness and iconicity in American Sign Language. *Language* 51: 696–719.

FROMKIN, V. (ed.) (1978). *Tone: A linguistic survey*. New York: Academic Press.

FUSTER, J. M. (1997). *The prefrontal cortex: Anatomy, physiology, and neuropsychology of the frontal lobe* (3rd edn.). Philadelphia, PA: Lippincott-Raven.

FUTUYMA, D. J. (1997). *Evolutionary biology*. Sunderland, MA: Sinauer Associates.

GALANTUCCI, B. (2005). An experimental study of the emergence of human communication systems. *Cognitive Science* 29: 737–767.

GALANTUCCI, B. and GARROD, S. (2010). Experimental semiotics: A new approach for studying the emergence and the evolution of human communication. *Interaction Studies* 11: 1–13.

GALANTUCCI, B., FOWLER, C. A., and TURVEY, M. T. (2006). The motor theory of speech perception reviewed. *Psychonomic Bulletin and Review* 13: 361–377.

GANNON, P. J., HOLLOWAY, R. L., BROADFIELD, D. C., and BRAUN, A. R. (1998). Asymmetry of chimpanzee planum temporale: Humanlike pattern of Wernicke's brain language area homolog. *Science* 279: 220–222.

GANNON, P. J., KHECK, N. M., BRAUN, A. R., and HOLLOWAY, R. L. (2005). Planum parietale of chimpanzees and orangutans: A comparative resonance of human-like planum temporale asymmetry. *The Anatomical Record* 287: 1128–1141.

GANNON, P. J., KHECK, N. M., and HOF, P. R. (2008). Leftward interhemispheric asymmetry of macaque monkey temporal lobe language area homolog is evident at the cytoarchitectural, but not gross anatomic level. *Brain Research* 1199: 62–73.

GARDNER, R. A. and GARDNER, B. T. (1969). Teaching sign language to a chimpanzee. *Science* 165: 664–672.

GARDNER, R. A., GARDNER, B. T., and VAN CANTFORT, T. E. (eds.) (1989). *Teaching sign language to chimpanzees*. Albany, NY: State University of New York Press.

GARSTANG, W. (1922). The theory of recapitulation: A critical re-statement of the biogenetic law. *Journal of the Linnaean Society (Zoology)* 35: 81–101.

GATHERCOLE, S. E., PICKERING, S. J., AMBRIDGE, B., and WEARING, H. (2004). A structural analysis of working memory from 4 to 15 years of age. *Developmental Psychology* 40: 177–190.

GAZDA, S. K., CONNOR, R. C., EDGAR, R. K., and COX, F. (2005). A division of labour with role specialization in group-hunting bottlenose dolphins (*Tursiops truncatus*) off Cedar Key, Florida. *Proceedings of the Royal Society of London B* 272: 135–140.

GEISSMANN, T. (2000). Gibbon songs and human music from an evolutionary perspective. In Wallin et al. (eds.), 103–124.

GENTILUCCI, M. and CORBALLIS, M. C. (2006). From manual gesture to speech: A gradual transition. *Neuroscience and Biobehavioral Reviews* 30: 949–960.

GENTNER, T. Q., FENN, K. J., MARGOLIASH, D., and NUSBAUM, H. C. (2006). Recursive syntactic pattern learning by songbirds. *Nature* 440: 1204–1207.

GESCHWIND, N. (1965). Disconnexion syndromes in animal and man. *Brain* 88: 585–644.

GESCHWIND, N. and GALABURDA, A. M. (1985). Cerebral lateralization: Biological mechanisms, associations and pathology: I. A hypothesis and a program for research. *Archives of Neurology* 42: 428–459.

GESCHWIND, N. and LEVITSKY, W. (1968). Human brain: Left-right asymmetries in temporal speech region. *Science* 161: 186–187.

GHAZANFAR, A. and HAUSER, M. D. (2001). The auditory behavior of primates: A neuroethological perspective. *Current Opinion in Neurobiology* 11: 712–720.

GHAZANFAR, A., MAIER, J. X., HOFFMAN, K. L., and LOGOTHETIS, N. (2005). Multisensory integration of dynamic faces and voices in rhesus monkey auditory cortex. *Journal of Neuroscience* 25: 5004–5012.

GIBBONS, A. (2006). *The first human*. New York: Doubleday.

GIBSON, K. R. (1990). Neurological perspectives on comparative animal and human intelligence: New approaches to the instinct versus learning controversy. In Parker and Gibson (eds.), 97–128.

GIBSON, K. R. (1991). Myelination and behavioral development: A comparative perspective on questions of neoteny, altriciality, and intelligence. In Gibson and Petersen (eds.), 29–64.

GIBSON, K. R. (1993). Tool use, language and social behavior in relationship to information processing capacities. In Gibson and Ingold (eds.), 251–269.

GIBSON, K. R. (1996a). The ontogeny and evolution of the brain, cognition and language. In Lock and Peters (eds.), 409–433.

GIBSON, K. R. (1996b). The biocultural brain: Seasonal migrations and the emergence of the Upper Paleolithic. In P. A. Mellars and K. R. Gibson (eds.), *Modelling the early human mind*. McDonald Institute Monographs. Cambridge: McDonald Institute for Archaeological Research, 33–48.

GIBSON, K. R. (2002). Evolution of human intelligence: The roles of brain size and mental construction. *Brain, Behavior and Evolution* 59: 10–20.

GIBSON, K. R. (2005). Epigenesis, brain plasticity, and behavioral versatility: Alternatives to standard evolution psychology models. In S. McKinnon and S. Silverman (eds.),

*Complexities: Anthropological challenges to reductive accounts of bio-social life.* Chicago, IL: University of Chicago Press, 23–42.

GIBSON, K. R. and INGOLD, T. (eds.) (1993). *Tools, language and cognition in human evolution.* Cambridge: Cambridge University Press.

GIBSON, K. R. and JESSEE, S. (1999). Language evolution and expansions of multiple neural processing areas. In B. King (ed.), *The evolution of language: Assessing the evidence from the non-human primates.* Santa Fe, NM: School for American Research, 189–228.

GIBSON, K. R. and PETERSEN, A. C. (eds.) (1991). *Brain maturation and cognitive development: Comparative and cross-cultural perspectives.* Hawthorne, NY: Aldine de Gruyter.

GIL, D. (1994). The structure of Riau Indonesian. *Nordic Journal of Linguistics* 17: 179–200.

GIL, D. (2000). Syntactic categories, cross-linguistic variation and universal grammar. In P. M. Vogel and B. Comrie (eds.), *Approaches to the typology of word classes.* Berlin: Mouton de Gruyter, 173–216.

GIL, D. (2005). Isolating-Monocategorial-Associational language. In Cohen and Lefebvre (eds.), 347–379.

GIL, D. (2008). How much grammar does it take to sail a boat? (Or, what can material artefacts tell us about the evolution of language?). In A. D. M. Smith et al. (eds.), 123–130.

GILBERT, W. H. (2008). Hominid systematics. In W. H. Gilbert and B. Asfaw (eds.), *Homo erectus. Pleistocene evidence from the Middle Awash, Ethiopia.* Berkeley, CA: University of California Press, 349–371.

GIL-DA-COSTA, R., BRAUN, A., LOPES, M., HAUSER, M. D., CARSON, R., HERSCOVITCH, P., and MARTIN, A. (2004). Toward an evolutionary perspective on conceptual representation: Species-specific calls activate visual and affective processing systems in the macaque. *Proceedings of the National Academy of Sciences of the USA* 101: 17516–17521.

GIL-DA-COSTA, R., MARTIN, A., LOPES, M. A., MUNOZ, M., FRITZ, J. B., and BRAUN, A. R. (2006). Species-specific calls activate homologs of Broca's and Wernicke's areas in the macaque. *Nature Neuroscience* 9: 1064–1070.

GILISSEN, E. (1992). The neocortical sulci of the capuchin monkey (*Cebus*): Evidence for asymmetry in the sylvian sulcus and comparison with other primates. *Comptes Rendus de l'Academie de Sciences Paris, Series III* 314: 165–170.

GILISSEN, E. (2001). Structural symmetries and asymmetries in human and chimpanzee brains. In Falk and Gibson (eds.), 187–215.

GIRET, N., MIKLÓSI, A., KREUTZER, M., and BOVET, D. (2009). Use of experimenter-given cues by African Gray parrots (*Psittacus erithacus*). *Animal Cognition* 12: 1–10.

GISINER, R. C. and SCHUSTERMAN, R. J. (1992). Combinatorial relationships learned by a language-trained sea lion. In J. Thomas, R. A. Kastelein, and A. Y. Supin. (eds.), *Marine mammal sensory systems.* New York: Plenum Press, 643–662.

GIVÓN, T. (1971). Historical syntax and synchronic morphology: An archaeologist's field trip. In D. Adams, M. A. Campbell, V. Cohen, J. Lovins, E. Maxwell, C. Nygren, and J. Reighard (eds.), *Papers from the Seventh Regional Meeting of the Chicago Linguistic Society.* University of Chicago, Chicago, IL, 394–415.

GIVÓN, T. (1979a). *Discourse and syntax.* New York: Academic Press.

GIVÓN, T. (1979b). *On understanding grammar.* New York: Academic Press.

GIVÓN, T. (1998). On the co-evolution of language, mind and brain. *Evolution of Communication* 2: 45–116.

GIVÓN, T. (2003). *Bio-linguistics.* Amsterdam: John Benjamins.

GIVÓN, T. (2009). *The genesis of syntactic complexity.* Amsterdam: John Benjamins.

Givón, T. and Malle, B. F. (eds.) (2002). *The evolution of language out of pre-language.* Amsterdam: John Benjamins.

Glass, L. and Mackey, M. C. (1988). *From clocks to chaos.* Princeton, NJ: Princeton University Press.

Glenberg, A. M. and Robertson, D. A. (1999). Indexical understanding of instructions. *Discourse Processes* 28: 1–26.

Glotin, H. (1995). *La vie artificielle d'une société de robots parlants: Émergence et changement du code phonétique.* Grenoble: DEA sciences cognitives-Institut National Polytechnique de Grenoble.

Gogolev, A. I. (1993). *Jakuty. Problemy ètnogeneza i formirovanija kul'tury.* [The Yakuts. Problems of their ethnogenesis and the formation of their culture] Yakutsk: Izdatel'stvo JaGU.

Goldberg, A. E. (1995). *Constructions: A construction grammar approach to argument structure.* Chicago, IL: University of Chicago Press.

Goldberg, A. E. (2006). *Constructions at work. The nature of generalization in language.* Oxford: Oxford University Press.

Goldberg, A. E. (2008). Universal Grammar? Or prerequisites for natural language? *Behavioral and Brain Sciences* 31: 522–523.

Goldin-Meadow, S. (2003a). *Hearing gesture: How our hands help us think.* Cambridge, MA: Harvard University Press.

Goldin-Meadow, S. (2003b). *The resilience of language: What gesture creation in deaf children can tell us about how all children learn language.* New York: Psychology Press.

Goldin-Meadow, S. (2005). What language creation in the manual modality tells us about the foundations of language. *The Linguistic Review* 22: 199–225.

Goldin-Meadow, S., Cook, S. W., and Mitchell, Z. A. (2009). Gesturing gives children new ideas about math. *Psychological Science* 20: 267–272.

Goldin-Meadow, S. and McNeill, D. (1999). The role of gesture and mimetic representation in making language the province of speech. In Corballis and Lea (eds.), 155–172.

Goldin-Meadow, S. and Mylander, C. (1998). Spontaneous sign systems created by deaf children in two cultures. *Nature* 91: 279–281.

Goldin-Meadow, S. and Sandhofer, C. (1999). Gestures convey substantive information about a child's thoughts to ordinary listeners. *Developmental Science* 2: 67–74.

Goldin-Meadow, S. and Singer, M. A. (2003). From children's hands to adults' ears: Gesture's role in teaching and learning. *Developmental Psychology* 39: 509–520.

Goldin-Meadow, S., Mylander, C., and Butcher, C. (1995). The resilience of combinatorial structure at the word level: Morphology in self-styled gesture systems. *Cognition* 56: 195–262.

Goldin-Meadow, S., McNeill, D., and Singleton, J. (1996). Silence is liberating: Removing the handcuffs on grammatical expression in the manual modality. *Psychological Review* 103: 34–55.

Goldin-Meadow, S., Nusbaum, H., Kelly, S. D., and Wagner, S. (2001). Explaining math: Gesturing lightens the load. *Psychological Science* 12: 516–522.

Goldin-Meadow, S., Mylander, C., and Franklin, A. (2007). How children make language out of gesture: Morphological structure in gesture systems developed by American and Chinese deaf children. *Cognitive Psychology* 55: 87–135.

GOLDIN-MEADOW, S., SO, W. C., ÖZYÜREK, A., and MYLANDER, C. (2008). The natural order of events: How speakers of different languages represent events nonverbally. *Proceedings of the National Academy of Sciences of the USA* 105: 9163–9168.

GOLDSTEIN, L. (2003). Emergence of discrete gestures. In M. J. Solé, D. Recasens, and J. Romero (eds.), *Proceedings of the 15th International Congress of Phonetic Sciences.* Barcelona: Universitat Autònoma de Barcelona, 85–86.

GOLDSTEIN, L. and FOWLER, C. A. (2003). Articulatory phonology: A phonology for public language use. In N. O. Schiller and A. S. Meyers (eds.), *Phonetics and phonology in language comprehension and production.* New York: Mouton de Gruyter, 159–207.

GOLDSTEIN, L., BYRD, D., and SALTZMAN, E. (2006). The role of vocal tract gestural action units in understanding the evolution of phonology. In Arbib (ed.), 215–249.

GOLDSTEIN, M. H., KING, A. P., and WEST, M. J. (2003). Social interaction shapes babbling: Testing parallels between birdsong and speech. *Proceedings of the National Academy of Sciences of the USA* 100: 8030–8035.

GOLDSTONE, R. L. (1994). Influences of categorization on perceptual discrimination. *Journal of Experimental Psychology: General* 123: 178–200.

GOLDSTONE, R. L. (1998). Perceptual learning. *Annual Review of Psychology* 49: 585–612.

GOMBRICH, E. H. (1960). *Art and illusion: A study in the psychology of pictorial representation.* Princeton, NJ: Princeton University Press.

GÓMEZ, J. C. (2005). Requesting gestures in captive monkeys and apes: Conditioned responses or referential behaviours? *Gesture* 5: 91–105.

GÓMEZ, R. L. (2002). Variability and detection of invariant structure. *Psychological Science* 13: 431–436.

GÓMEZ, R. L. (2007). Statistical learning in infant language development. In M. G. Gaskell (ed.), *The Oxford handbook of psycholinguistics.* Oxford: Oxford University Press, 601–616.

GÓMEZ, R. L. and GERKEN, L. (1999). Artificial grammar learning by 1-year-olds leads to specific and abstract knowledge. *Cognition* 70: 109–135.

GÓMEZ, R. L. and GERKEN, L. A. (2000). Infant artificial language learning and language acquisition. *Trends in Cognitive Sciences* 4: 178–186.

GOOD, C. D., JOHNSTRUDE, I., ASHBURNER, J., HENSON, R. N. A., FRISTON, K. J., and FRACKOWIAK, R. S. J. (2001). Cerebral asymmetry and the effects of sex and handedness on brain structure: A voxel-based morphometric analysis of 465 normal human brains. *NeuroImage* 14: 685–700.

GOODALL, J. (1968). The behaviour of free-living chimpanzees in the Gombe Stream Reserve. *Animal Behaviour Monographs* 1: 161–311.

GOODALL, J. (1986). *The chimpanzees of Gombe: Patterns of behavior.* Cambridge, MA: Belknap Press of Harvard University Press.

GOODALL, J. (1989). Gombe: Highlights and current research. In P. G. Heltne and L. A. Marquardt (eds.), *Understanding chimpanzees.* Cambridge, MA: Harvard University Press, 2–21.

GOODMAN, M. (1996). Epilogue: A personal account of the origins of a new paradigm. *Molecular Phylogenetics and Evolution* 5: 269–285.

GOPNIK, M. and CRAGO, M. B. (1991). Familial aggregation of a developmental language disorder. *Cognition* 39: 1–50.

GORDON, R. G. (2005). *Ethnologue: Languages of the world. 15th Edition.* Dallas, TX: Summer Institute of Linguistics.

GOTTLIEB, G. (1992). *Individual development and evolution.* New York: Oxford University Press.

GOULD, J. L. and MARLER, P. (1987). Learning by instinct. *Scientific American* 256: 74–85.

GOULD, S. J. (1977). *Ontogeny and phylogeny.* Cambridge, MA: Belknap Press of Harvard University Press.

GOULD, S. J. (1991). Exaptation: A crucial tool for evolutionary psychology. *Journal of Social Issues* 47: 43–65.

GOULD, S. J. (1994). *Eight little piggies.* New York: W. W. Norton.

GOULD, S. J. (1997). *Evolution: The pleasures of pluralism.* New York Review of Books, June 26.

GOULD, S. J. (2002). *The structure of evolutionary theory.* Cambridge, MA: Belknap Press of Harvard University Press.

GOULD, S. J. and ELDREDGE, N. (1977). Punctuated equilibria: The 'tempo' and 'mode' of evolution reconsidered. *Paleobiology* 3: 115–151.

GOULD, S. J. and LEWONTIN, R. (1999). The spandrels of San Marco and the Panglossian paradigm: A critique of the adaptationist program. *Proceedings of the Royal Society of London B* 205: 581–598.

GOULD, S. J. and VRBA, E. S. (1982). Exaptation: A missing term in the science of form. *Paleobiology* 8: 4–15.

GRAF ESTES, K., EVANS, J. L., ALIBALI, M. W., and SAFFRAN, J. R. (2007). Can infants map meaning to newly segmented words? Statistical segmentation and word learning. *Psychological Science* 18: 254–260.

GRAFTON, S. T., ARBIB, M. A., FADIGA, L., and RIZZOLATTI, G. (1996). Localization of grasp representations in humans by positron emission tomography: 2. Observation compared with imagination. *Experimental Brain Research* 112: 103–111.

GRANT, B. R. and GRANT, P. R. (1996). Cultural inheritance of song and its role in the evolution of Darwin's finches. *Evolution* 50: 2471–2487.

GRANT, P. R. and GRANT, B. R. (2002). Unpredictable evolution in a 30-year study of Darwin's finches. *Science* 296: 707–711.

GRANT, P. R. and GRANT, B. R. (2006). Evolution of character displacement in Darwin's finches. *Science* 313: 224–226.

GRAVES, P. (1994). Flakes and ladders: What the archaeological record cannot tell us about the origins of language. *World Archaeology* 26: 158–171.

GREEN, R. E., KRAUSE, J., BRIGGS, A. W., MARICIC, T., STENZEL, U., KIRCHER, M., PATTERSON, N., LI, H., ZHAI, W., FRITZ, M. H.-Y., HANSEN, N. F., DURAND, E. Y., MALASPINAS, A.-S., JENSEN, J. D., MARQUES-BONET, T., ALKAN, C., PRÜFER, K., MEYER, M., BURBANO, H. A., GOOD, J. M., SCHULTZ, R., AXIMU-PETRI, A., BUTTHOF, A., HÖBER, B., HÖFFNER, B., SIEGEMUND, M., WEIHMANN, A., NUSBAUM, C., LANDER, E. S., RUSS, C., NOVOD, N., AFFOURTIT, J., EGHOLM, M., VERNA, C., RUDAN, P., BRAJKOVIC, D., KUCAN, Z., GUŠIC, I., DORONICHEV, V. B., GOLOVANOVA, L. V., LALUEZA-FOX, C., DE LA RASILLA, M., FORTEA, J., ROSAS, A., SCHMITZ, R. W., JOHNSON, P. L. F., EICHLER, E. E., FALUSH, D., BIRNEY, E., MULLIKIN, J. C., SLATKIN, M., NIELSEN, R., KELSO, J., LACHMANN, M., REICH, D., and PÄÄBO, S. (2010). A draft sequence of the Neanderthal genome. *Science* 328: 710–722.

GREENBERG, J. H. (1966). Synchronic and diachronic universals on phonology. *Language* 42: 508–517.

GREENBERG, J. H. (1969). Some methods of dynamic comparison in linguistics. In J. Puhvel (ed.), *Substance and structure of language.* Berkeley/Los Angeles, CA: University of California Press, 147–203.

GREENBERG, J. II. (1978). How does a language acquire gender markers? In J. H. Greenberg, C. A. Ferguson, and E. Moravcsik (eds.), *Universals of human language. Volume 3: Word structure*. Stanford, CA: Stanford University Press, 47–82.

GREENBERG, J. H. (1992). Preliminaries to a systematic comparison between biological and linguistic evolution. In Hawkins and Gell-Mann (eds.), 139–158.

GREENBERG, J. H. (2000). *Indo-European and its closest relatives*. Stanford, CA: Stanford University Press.

GREENFIELD, P. M. (1991). Language, tools and brain: The ontogeny and phylogeny of hierarchically organized sequential behaviour. *Behavioral and Brain Sciences* 14: 531–595 (with continuing commentary and a new response (1998), 21: 154–163).

GREENFIELD, P. M. and SAVAGE-RUMBAUGH, E. S. (1990). Grammatical combination in *Pan paniscus*: Processes of learning and invention in the development and evolution of language. In Parker and Gibson (eds.), 540–578.

GREENFIELD, P. M. and SAVAGE-RUMBAUGH, E. S. (1991). Imitation, grammatical development, and the invention of protogrammar by an ape. In Krasnegor et al. (eds.), 235–258.

GREENFIELD, P. M. and SAVAGE-RUMBAUGH, E. S. (1993). Comparing communicative competence in child and chimp: The pragmatics. *Journal of Child Language* 20: 1–26.

GRICE, H. P. (1957). Meaning. *Philosophical Review* 66: 377–388.

GRIFFITHS, P. E. (2002). What is innateness? *The Monist* 85: 70–85.

GRIFFITHS, T. L. and KALISH, M. L. (2007). Language evolution by iterated learning with Bayesian agents. *Cognitive Science* 31: 441–480.

GRINE, F. E. and FLEAGLE, J. G. (2009). The first humans: a summary perspective on the origin and early evolution of the Genus *Homo*. In Grine et al. (eds.), 197–207.

GRINE, F. E., FLEAGLE, J. G., and LEAKEY, R. E. (eds.) (2009). *The first humans: Origin and early evolution of the genus* Homo. New York: Springer.

GROMAN, J. D. and PELLMYR, O. (2000). Rapid evolution and specialization following host colonization in yucca moth. *Journal of Evolutionary Biology* 13: 223–236.

GROVES, C. P. (1989). *A theory of primate and human evolution*. Oxford: Oxford University Press.

GUILFORD, T. and DAWKINS, M. S. (1991). Receiver psychology and the evolution of animal signals. *Animal Behaviour* 42: 1–14.

GÜLDEMANN, T. (2006). Structural isoglosses between Khoekhoe and Tuu: The Cape as a linguistic area. In Y. Matras, A. McMahon, and N. Vincent (eds.), *Linguistic areas: convergence in historical and typological perspective*. Houndmills: Palgrave Macmillan, 99–134.

GÜLDEMANN, T. (2008). The Macro-Sudan belt: Toward identifying a linguistic area in northern sub-Saharan Africa. In B. Heine and D. Nurse (eds.), *Africa as a Linguistic Area*. Cambridge: Cambridge University Press, 151–185.

GÜLDEMANN, T. (2010). 'Sprachraum' and geography: Linguistic macro-areas in Africa. In A. Lameli, R. Kehrein, and S. Rabanus (eds.), *The handbook of language mapping*. Berlin: Mouton de Gruyter, 561–585.

GÜLDEMANN, T. and ELDERKIN, E. D. (2010). On external genealogical relationships of the Khoe family. In M. Brenzinger and C. König (eds.), *Khoisan languages and linguistics: Proceedings of the 1st International Symposium January 4–8, 2003*. Riezlern/Kleinwalsertal: Rüdiger Köppe Verlag.

GÜLDEMANN, T. and VOSSEN, R. (2000). Khoisan. In B. Heine and D. Nurse (eds.), *African languages: An introduction*. Cambridge: Cambridge University Press, 99–122.

GUMPERZ, J. J. and WILSON, R. (1971). Convergence and creolization: A case from the Indo-Aryan/Dravidian border in India. In D. Hymes (ed.), *Pidginization and Creolization of Languages. Proceedings of a Conference held at the University of the West Indies, Mona, Jamaica, April 1968*. Cambridge: Cambridge University Press, 151–167.

GUTIÉRREZ, G., SÁNCHEZ, D., and MARÍN, A. (2002). A reanalysis of the ancient mitochondrial DNA sequences recovered from Neandertal bones. *Molecular Biology and Evolution* 19: 1359–1366.

HAILE-SELASSIE, Y., SUWA, G., and WHITE, T. D. (2004). Late Miocene teeth from Middle Awash, Ethiopia, and early hominid dental evolution. *Science* 303: 1503–1505.

HAILMAN, J. P. (1969). How an instinct is learned. *Scientific American* 221: 98–106.

HAIMAN, J. (1994). Ritualization and the development of language. In W. Pagliuca (ed.), *Perspectives on grammaticalization*. Amsterdam: John Benjamins Publishing Company, 3–28.

HAIMOFF, E. H. (1983). Occurrence of anti-resonance in the song of the siamang (*Hylobates syndactylus*). *American Journal of Primatology* 5: 249–256.

HAMES, R. B. (1988). The allocation of parental care among the Ye'kwana. In L. Betzig, M. Borgerhoff-Mulder, and P. Turke (eds.), *Human reproductive behaviour: A Darwinian perspective*. Cambridge: Cambridge University Press, 237–251.

HAMILTON A. F. and GRAFTON, S. T. (2006). Goal representation in human anterior intraparietal sulcus. *Journal of Neuroscience* 26: 1133–1137.

HAMILTON, C. R. and VERMEIRE, B. A. (1988). Complementary hemispheric specialization in monkeys. *Science* 242: 1691–1694.

HAMILTON, W. D. (1964). The genetical evolution of social behavior. *Journal of Theoretical Biology* 7: 1–52.

HAMMARSTRÖM, H. (2007). *Handbook of descriptive language knowledge: A full-scale reference guide for typologists*. Munich: Lincom Europa.

HAMMERSCHMIDT, K. and FISCHER, J. (2008). Constraints in primate vocal production. In Oller and Griebel (2008b) (eds.), 93–119.

HAMPE, B. (ed.) (2006). *From perception to meaning: Image schemas in cognitive linguistics*. Berlin: Mouton de Gruyter.

HANDFORD, P. (1988). Trill rate dialects in the rufous-collared sparrow, *Zonotrichia capensis*, in northwestern Argentina. *Canadian Journal of Zoology* 66: 2658–2670.

HARDUS, M. E., LAMEIRA, A. R., VAN SCHAIK, C. P., and WICH, S. A. (2009a) Tool use in wild orang-utans modifies sound production: a functionally deceptive innovation? *Proceedings of the Royal Society of London B* 276: 3689–3694.

HARDUS, M. E., LAMEIRA, A. R., SINGLETON, I., MORROGH-BERNARD, H., KNOTT, C.D., ANCRENAZ, M., UTAMI ATMOKO, S. S., and WICH, S. A. (2009b). A description of the orangutan's vocal and sound repertoire, with a focus on geographical variation. In S. A. Wich, S. S. Utami Atmoko, T. Mitra Setia, and C. P. van Schaik (eds.), *Orangutans: Geographical variation in behavioral ecology and conservation*. Oxford: Oxford University Press, 49–64.

HARE, B. and TOMASELLO, M. (1999). Domestic dogs (*Canis familiaris*) use human and conspecific social cues to locate hidden food. *Journal of Comparative Psychology* 113: 173–177.

HARE, B. and TOMASELLO, M. (2005). Human-like social skills in dogs? *Trends in Cognitive Sciences* 9: 439–444.

HARE, B., CALL, J., AGNETTA, B., and TOMASELLO, M. (2000). Chimpanzees know what conspecifics do and do not see. *Animal Behavior* 59: 771–785.

HARE, B., CALL, J., and TOMASELLO, M. (2001). Do chimpanzees know what conspecifics know? *Animal Behaviour* 61: 139–151.

HARLEY, H. E., PUTMAN, E. A., and ROITBLAT, H. L. (2003). Bottlenose dolphins perceive object features through echolocation. *Nature* 424: 667–669.

HARLOW, J. M. (1868). Recovery from the passage of an iron bar through the head. *Publications of the Massachusetts Medical Society* 2: 327–347.

HARNAD, S. (1990). The symbol grounding problem. *Physica D* 42: 335–346.

HARNAD, S. (2000). From sensorimotor praxis and pantomine to symbolic representations. *The evolution of language. Proceedings of 3rd International Conference (EVOLANG 3) Paris*, 118–125.

HARNAD, S. (2005). To cognize is to categorize: Cognition is categorization. In Cohen and Lefebvre (eds.), 19–43.

HARNAD, S. (2007). From knowing how to knowing that: Acquiring categories by word of mouth. Kaziemierz Naturalized Epistemology Workshop (KNEW), Kaziemierz, Poland, 2 September 2007.

HARNAD, S. STEKLIS, H. D., and LANCASTER. J. B. (eds.) (1976). *Origins and evolution of language and speech. Annals of the New York Academy of Sciences* 280.

HARPENDING, H. C., SHERRY, S. T., ROGERS, A. R., and STONEKING, M. (1993). The genetic structure of ancient human populations. *Current Anthropology* 34: 483–496.

HARPENDING, H. C., BATZER, M. A., GURVEN, M., JORDE, L. B., ROGERS, A. R., and SHERRY, S. T. (1998). Genetic traces of ancient demography. *Proceedings of the National Academy of Sciences USA* 95: 1961–1967.

HARRISON, R. M. and NYSTROM, P. (2008). Handedness in captive bonobos (*Pan paniscus*). *Folia Primatologica* 79: 253–268.

HART, D. and SUSSMAN, R. (2005). *Man the hunted: Primates, predators and human evolution*. Boulder, CO: Westview Press.

HASLER, A. D. (1960). Guideposts of migrating fishes. *Science* 132: 785–792.

HASPELMATH, M. (1999). Why is grammaticalization irreversible? *Linguistics* 37: 1043–1068.

HASSELQUIST, D., BENSCH, S., and VON SCHANTZ, T. (1996). Correlation between male song repertoire, extra-pair paternity and offspring survival in the great reed warbler. *Nature* 381: 229–232.

HAST, M. H., FISCHER, J. M., WETZEL, A. B., and THOMPSON, V. E. (1974). Cortical motor representation of the laryngeal muscles in *Macaca mulatta*. *Brain Research* 73: 229–240.

HAUSER, M. D. (1993). Right hemisphere dominance for the production of facial expression in monkeys. *Science* 261: 475–477.

HAUSER, M. D. (1996). *The evolution of communication*. Cambridge, MA: MIT Press.

HAUSER, M. D. (2000). *Wild minds: What animals really think*. New York: Henry Holt.

HAUSER, M. D. (2006). *Moral minds*. New York: Ecco Press.

HAUSER, M. D. (2009a). Origin of the mind. *Scientific American* September 2009: 44–51.

HAUSER, M. D. (2009b). The possibility of impossible cultures. *Nature* 460: 190–196.

HAUSER, M. D. (2010). On obfuscation, obscurantism and opacity: Evolving conceptions of the faculty of language. In Larson et al. (eds.), 91–99.

HAUSER, M. D. and AKRE, K. (2001). Asymmetries in the timing of facial and vocal expressions by rhesus monkeys: Implications for hemispheric specialization. *Animal Behaviour* 61: 391–400.

HAUSER, M. D. and CAREY, S. (1998). Building a cognitive creature from a set of primitives: Evolutionary and developmental insights. In D. D. Cummins and C. Allen (eds.), *The evolution of the mind*. Oxford: Oxford University Press, 51–106.

HAUSER, M. D., CHOMSKY, N., and FITCH, W. T. (2002). The faculty of language: What is it, who has it, and how did it evolve? *Science* 298: 1569–1579.

HAUSER, M. D., BARNER, D., and O'DONNELL, T. (2007). Evolutionary linguistics: A new look at an old landscape. *Language Learning and Development* 3: 101–132.

HAWKES, K. (1990). Showing off: Tests of an hypothesis about men's foraging goals. *Ethology and Sociobiology* 12: 29–54.

HAWKES, K., O'CONNELL, J. F., BLURTON JONES, N. G., ALVAREZ, H., and CHARNOV, E. L. (1998). Grandmothering, menopause, and the evolution of human life histories. *Proceedings of the National Academy of Sciences of the USA* 95: 1336–1339.

HAWKINS, J. A. (1994). *A performance theory of order and constituency*. Cambridge: Cambridge University Press.

HAWKINS, J. A. (2004). *Efficiency and complexity in grammars*. Oxford: Oxford University Press.

HAWKINS, J. A. and GELL-MANN, M. (eds.) (1992). *The evolution of human language. Proceedings of the Workshop on the Evolution of Human Languages, August 1989, Santa Fe, New Mexico*. Santa Fe, NM: Addison-Wesley Publishing Company.

HAWKS, J., HUNLEY, K., LEE, S.-H., and WOLPOFF, M. (2000). Population bottlenecks and Pleistocene human evolution. *Molecular Biology and Evolution* 17: 2–22.

HAWKS, J., WANG, E. T., COCHRAN, G. M., HARPENDING, H. C., and MOYZIS, R. K. (2007). Recent acceleration of human adaptive evolution. *Proceedings of the National Academy of Sciences of the USA* 52: 20753–20758.

HAYES, C. (1952). *The ape in our house*. London: Gollancz.

HAYES, K. J. and NISSEN, C. H. (1971). Higher mental functions of a home-raised chimpanzee. In A. M. Schrier and F. Stollnitz (eds.), *Behavior of nonhuman primates: Modern research trends*. New York: Academic Press, 59–115.

HAZY, T., FRANK, M., and O'REILLY, R. (2006). Banishing the homunculus: Making working memory work. *Neuroscience* 139: 105–118.

HEATH, J. (1978). *Linguistic diffusion in Arnhem Land*. Canberra: Australian Institute of Aboriginal Studies.

HEBB, D. O. (1949). *The organization of behavior*. New York: Wiley.

HEFFNER, H. E. and HEFFNER, R. S. (1984). Temporal lobe lesions and perception of species-specific vocalizations by macaques. *Science* 226: 75–76.

HEILBRONNER, P. L. and HOLLOWAY, R. L. (1988). Anatomical brain asymmetries in New World and Old World monkeys: Stages of temporal lobe development in primate evolution. *American Journal of Physical Anthropology* 76: 39–48.

HEIM, J. L. (1989). La nouvelle reconstitution du crane Néandertalien de La Chapelle-Aux-Saints: méthode et résultats. *Bulletins et Mémoires de la Société d'Anthropologie de Paris* 1: 95–118.

HEINE, B. (1993). *Auxiliaries: Cognitive forces and grammaticalization*. New York and Oxford: Oxford University Press.

HEINE, B. and KUTEVA, T. (2002a). On the evolution of grammatical forms. In Wray (ed.), 376–397.

HEINE, B. and KUTEVA, T. (2002b). *World lexicon of grammaticalization*. Cambridge: Cambridge University Press.

HEINE, B. and KUTEVA, T. (2007). *The genesis of grammar: A reconstruction.* Oxford: Oxford University Press.

HEINE, B. and REH, M. (1984). *Grammaticalization and reanalysis in African languages.* Hamburg: Buske.

HEINE, B., CLAUDI, U., and HÜNNEMEYER, F. (1991). *Grammaticalization: A conceptual framework.* Chicago, IL: University of Chicago Press.

HENRY, P. I., MORELLI, G. A., and TRONICK, E. Z. (2005). Child caretakers among Efe foragers of the Ituri Forest. In Hewlett and Lamb (eds.), 191–213.

HENSHILWOOD, C. S. and DUBREUIL, B. (2009). Reading the artefacts: Gleaning language skills from the Middle Stone Age in Southern Africa. In Botha and Knight (eds.) (2009a), 41–61.

HENSHILWOOD C. S. and MAREAN, C. W. (2003). The origin of modern human behaviour: Critique of the models and their test implications. *Current Anthropology* 44: 627–651.

HENSHILWOOD, C. S., D'ERRICO, F., YATES, R., JACOBS, Z., TRIBOLO, C., DULLER, N. M., SEALY, J. C., VALLADAS, H., WATTS, I., and WINTLE, A. G. (2002). Emergence of modern human behaviour: Middle Stone Age engravings from South Africa. *Science* 295: 1278–1280.

HENSHILWOOD, C. S., D'ERRICO, F., VANHAEREN, M., VAN NIEKERK, K., and JACOBS, Z. (2004). Middle Stone Age shell beads from South Africa. *Science* 304: 404.

HERBINGER, I., PAPWORTH, S., BOESCH, C., and ZUBERBÜHLER, K. (2009). Vocal, gestural and locomotor responses of wild chimpanzees to familiar and unfamiliar intruders: A playback study. *Animal Behaviour* 78: 1389–1396.

HERMAN, L. M. (1980). Cognitive characteristics of dolphins. In L. M. Herman (ed.), *Cetacean behavior: Mechanisms and functions.* New York: John Wiley and Sons, 363–429.

HERMAN, L. M. (1987). Receptive competencies of language-trained animals. In J. S. Rosenblatt, C. Beer, M.-C. Busnel, and P. J. B. Slater (eds.), *Advances in the study of behavior 17.* Orlando, FL: Academic Press, 1–60.

HERMAN, L. M. (2002). Vocal, social, and self-imitation by bottlenosed dolphins. In Dautenhahn and Nehaniv (eds.), 63–108.

HERMAN, L. M. and FORESTELL, P. H. (1985). Reporting presence or absence of named objects by a language-trained dolphin. *Neuroscience and Biobehavioral Reviews* 9: 667–681.

HERMAN, L. M. and GORDON, J. A. (1974). Auditory delayed matching in the bottlenose dolphin. *Journal of the Experimental Analysis of Behavior* 21: 19–26.

HERMAN, L. M., RICHARDS, D. G., and WOLZ, J. P. (1984). Comprehension of sentences by bottlenosed dolphins. *Cognition* 16: 129–219.

HERMAN, L. M., KUCZAJ, S. A. II., and HOLDER, M. D. (1993). Responses to anomalous gestural sequences by a language-trained dolphin: Evidence for processing of semantic relations and syntactic information. *Journal of Experimental Psychology: General* 122: 184–194.

HERMAN, L. M., ABICHANDANI, S. L., ELHAJI, A. N., HERMAN, E. Y. K., SANCHEZ, J. L., and PACK, A. A. (1999). Dolphins (*Tursiops truncatus*) comprehend the referential character of the human pointing gesture. *Journal of Comparative Psychology* 111: 347–364.

HERREL, A., HUYGHE, K., VANHOOYDONCK, B., BACKELJAU, T., BREUGELMANS, K., GRBAC, I., VAN DAMME, R., and IRSCHICK, D. J. (2008). Rapid large-scale evolutionary divergence in morphology and performance associated with exploitation of a different dietary resource. *Proceedings of the National Academy of Sciences of the USA* 105: 4792–4795.

HERRMANN, E., CALL, J., HERNANDEZ-LLOREDA, M. V., HARE, B., and TOMASELLO, M. (2007). Humans have evolved specialized skills of social cognition: The cultural intelligence hypothesis. *Science* 317: 1360–1366.

HERSHKOVITZ, P. (1977). *Living New World monkeys.* Chicago, IL: University of Chicago Press.

HESS, E. (2008). *Nim Chimpsky: The chimp who would be human.* New York: Bantam.

HEWES, G. (1973). Primate communication and the gestural origin of language. *Current Anthropology* 14: 5–25.

HEWITT, G. P., MacLARNON, A. M., and JONES, K. E. (2002). The functions of laryngeal air sacs in primates: A new hypothesis. *Folia Primatologica* 73: 70–94.

HEWLETT, B. S. and LAMB, M. E. (2005). *Hunter-gatherer childhoods.* New Brunswick, NJ: Aldine Transaction Publishers.

HEYES, C. M. and GALEF, B. G. (eds.) (1996). *Social learning in animals: The roots of culture.* San Diego, CA: Academic Press.

HICKEY, R. (ed.) (2003). *Motives for language change.* Cambridge: Cambridge University Press.

HILL, J. A. C. (1983). A computational model of language acquisition in the two-year-old. *Cognition and Brain Theory* 6: 287–317.

HILL, K. C. (ed.) (1979). *The genesis of language.* Ann Arbor, MI: Karoma Publishers.

HILLIARD, A. T. and WHITE, S. A. (2009). Possible precursors of syntactic components in other species. In Bickerton and Szathmáry (eds.), 161–183.

HILLIX, W. A. and RUMBAUGH, D. M. (2003). *Animal bodies, human minds: Ape, dolphin, and parrot language skills.* New York: Springer.

HINDE, R. A. (1966). *Animal behavior: A synthesis of ethology and comparative psychology.* New York: McGraw Hill.

HOCK, H. H. (1991). *Principles of historical linguistics.* Berlin/New York: Mouton de Gruyter.

HOCKETT, C. F. (1958). In search of Jove's brow. *American Speech* 53: 243–313.

HOCKETT, C. F. (1960). Logical considerations in the study of animal communication. In W. E. Lanyon and W. N. Tavolga (eds.), *Animal sounds and animal communication.* Washington, DC: American Institute of Biological Sciences, 392–430.

HOELZEL, A. R. (1991). Killer whale predation on marine mammals at Punta Norte, Argentina; Food sharing, provisioning and foraging strategy. *Behavioral Ecology and Sociobiology* 29: 197–204.

HOIT, J. D., SHEA, S. A., and BANZETT, R. B. (1994). Speech production during mechanical ventilation in tracheostomized individuals. *Journal of Speech and Hearing Research* 37: 53–63.

HOLDEN, C. (2006). Random samples: *Polly Pachyderm. Science* 314: 29.

HOLEKAMP, K. E., SAKAI, S. T., and LUNDRIGAN, B. L. (2007). Social intelligence in the spotted hyena (*Crocuta crocuta*). *Philosophical Transactions of the Royal Society B* 362: 523–538.

HOLLOWAY, R. L. (1968). The evolution of the primate brain: Some aspects of quantitative relations. *Brain research* 7: 121–172.

HOLLOWAY, R. L. (1969). Culture: A human domain. *Current Anthropology* 10: 395–412.

HOLLOWAY, R. L. (1975). *Role of social behavior in the evolution of the brain.* 43rd James Arthur lecture. New York: American Museum of Natural History.

HOLLOWAY, R. L. (1978). Problems of brain endocast interpretation and African hominid evolution. In C. Jolly (ed.), *Early hominids of Africa.* New York: St. Martin's Press, 379–401.

HOLLOWAY, R. L. (1981). Culture, symbols and human brain evolution: A synthesis. *Dialectical Anthropology* 5: 287–303.

HOLLOWAY, R. L. (1983). Human paleontological evidence relevant to language behavior. *Human Neurobiology* 2: 105–114.

HOLLOWAY, R. L. (1995). Toward a synthetic theory of human brain evolution. In Changeux and Chavallion (eds.), 42–60.

HOLLOWAY, R. L. (1996). Evolution of the human brain. In Lock and Peters (eds.), 74–116.

HOLLOWAY, R. L. (2009). Brain fossils: Endocasts. In L. R. Squire (ed.), *Encyclopedia of Neuroscience, Vol 2*. Oxford: Academic Press, 353–361.

HOLLOWAY, R. L. and DE LACOSTE-LAREYMONDIE, M. C. (1982). Brain endocast asymmetry in pongids and hominids: Some preliminary findings on the paleontology of cerebral dominance. *American Journal of Physical Anthropology* 58: 101–110.

HOLVECK, M-J., VIERA DE CASTRO, A. C., LACHLAN, R. F., TEN CATE, C., and RIEBEL, K. (2008). Accuracy of song syntax learning and singing consistency signal early condition in zebra finches. *Behavioral Ecology* 19: 1267–1281.

HOOK-COSTIGAN, M. A. and ROGERS, L. J. (1998). Lateralized use of the mouth in production of vocalizations by marmosets. *Neuropsychologia* 36: 1265–1273.

HOPKINS, W. D. (1995). Hand preferences for a coordinated bimanual task in 110 chimpanzees (*Pan troglodytes*): Cross-sectional analysis. *Journal of Comparative Psychology* 109: 291–297.

HOPKINS, W. D. (2006). Comparative and familial analysis of handedness in great apes. *Psychological Bulletin* 132: 538–559.

HOPKINS, W. D. (ed.) (2007). *Evolution of hemispheric specialization in primates*. Oxford: Elsevier.

HOPKINS, W. D. and CANTALUPO, C. (2004). Handedness in chimpanzees is associated with asymmetries in the primary motor cortex but not with homologous language areas. *Behavioral Neuroscience* 118: 1176–1183.

HOPKINS, W. D. and DE WAAL, F. B. M. (1995). Behavioral laterality in captive bonobos (*Pan paniscus*): Replication and extension. *International Journal of Primatology* 16: 261–276.

HOPKINS, W. D. and MARINO L. (2000). Asymmetries in cerebral width in nonhuman primate brains as revealed by magnetic resonance imaging (MRI). *Neuropsychologia* 38: 493–499.

HOPKINS, W. D. and NIR, T. (2010). Planum temporale surface area and grey matter asymmetries in chimpanzees (*Pan troglodytes*): The effect of handedness and comparison with findings in humans. *Behavioural Brain Research* 208: 436–443.

HOPKINS, W. D., MARINO, L., RILLING, J. K., and MACGREGOR, L. A. (1998). Planum temporale asymmetries in Great Apes as revealed by magnetic resonance imaging. *Neuroreport* 9: 2913–2918.

HOPKINS, W. D., PILCHER, D. L., and MACGREGOR, L. A. (2000). Sylvian fissure length asymmetries in primates revisited: A comparative MRI study. *Brain, Behavior and Evolution* 56: 293–299.

HOPKINS, W. D., RUSSELL, J. L., FREEMAN, H., BUEHLER, N., REYNOLDS, E., and SCHAPIRO, S. (2005). The distribution and development of handedness for manual gestures in captive chimpanzees (*Pan troglodytes*). *Psychological Science* 16: 487.

HOPKINS, W. D., RUSSELL, J. L., and CANTALUPO, C. (2007a). Neuroanatomical correlates of handedness for tool use in chimpanzees (*Pan troglodytes*): Implication for theories on the evolution of language. *Psychological Science* 18: 971–977.

HOPKINS, W. D., TAGLIALATELA, J. P., and LEAVENS, D. A. (2007b). Chimpanzees differentially produce novel vocalizations to capture the attention of a human. *Animal Behaviour* 73: 281–286.

HOPPER, P. J. (1998). Emergent grammar. In M. Tomasello (ed.), *The new psychology of language*. Mahwah, NJ: Lawrence Erlbaum, 155–175.

HOPPER, P. J. and TRAUGOTT, E. C. (2003). *Grammaticalization*. Second edition. Cambridge: Cambridge University Press.

HOSTETTER, A. B., CANTERO, M., and HOPKINS, W. D. (2001). Differential use of vocal and gestural communication by chimpanzees (*Pan troglodytes*) in response to the attentional status of a human (*Homo sapiens*). *Journal of Comparative Psychology* 115: 337–343.

HOWELL, F. C. (1951). The place of Neanderthal Man in human evolution. *American Journal of Physical Anthropology* 9: 379–416.

HRDY, S. B. (1976). Care and exploitation of nonhuman primate infants by conspecifics other than the mother. In J. S. Rosenblatt (ed.), *Advances in the study of behavior 6*. New York: Academic Press, 101–158.

HRDY, S. B. (1999). *Mother nature: Maternal instincts and how they shape the human species*. New York: Random House.

HRDY, S. B. (2009). *Mothers and others: The evolutionary origins of mutual understanding*. Cambridge, MA: Belknap Press of Harvard University Press.

HUBLIN, J.-J. (1998). Climatic changes, paleogeography, and the evolution of the Neandertals. In T. Akazawa, K. Aoki, and O. Bar-Yosef (eds.), *Neandertals and modern humans in Western Asia*. New York: Plenum Press, 295–310.

HUGHES, C. and ENSOR, R. (2007). Executive function and theory of mind: Predictive relations from ages 2- to 4-years. *Developmental Psychology* 43: 1447–1459.

HUGHES, C. and ENSOR, R. (2008). Does executive function matter for preschoolers' problem behaviors? *Journal of Abnormal Child Psychology* 36: 1–14.

HUNT, G. R. and GRAY, R. D. (2004). Direct observations of pandanus-tool manufacture and use by a New Caledonian crow (*Corvus moneduloides*). *Animal Cognition* 7: 114–120.

HURFORD, J. R. (1987). *Language and number*. Oxford: Blackwell.

HURFORD, J. R. (1989). Biological evolution of the Saussurean sign as a component of the language acquisition device. *Lingua* 77: 187–222.

HURFORD, J. R. (1990a). Beyond the roadblock in linguistic evolution studies. *Behavioral and Brain Sciences* 13: 736–737.

HURFORD, J. R. (1990b). Nativist and functional explanations in language acquisition. In I. M. Roca (ed.), *Logical issues in language acquisition*. Dordrecht: Foris, 85–136.

HURFORD, J. R. (2000). Social transmission favours linguistic generalization. In Knight et al. (eds.), 324–352.

HURFORD, J. R. (2002). The roles of expression and representation in language evolution. In Wray (ed.), 311–334.

HURFORD, J. R. (2003a). The language mosaic and its evolution. In Christiansen and Kirby (eds.), 38–57.

HURFORD, J. R. (2003b). The neural basis of predicate-argument structure. *Behavioral and Brain Sciences* 26: 261–283.

HURFORD, J. R. (2007). *The origins of meaning: Language in the light of evolution*. Oxford: Oxford University Press.

HURFORD, J. R. (2011). *The origins of grammar: Language in the light of evolution*. Oxford: Oxford University Press.

HURFORD, J. R. and DEDIU, D. (2009). Diversity in languages, genes, and the language faculty. In Botha and Knight (eds.) (2009a), 167–188.

HURFORD, J. R., STUDDERT-KENNEDY, M., and KNIGHT, C. (eds.) (1998). *Approaches to the evolution of language: Social and cognitive bases.* Cambridge: Cambridge University Press.

HURST, J. A., BARAITSER, M., AUGER, E., GRAHAM, F., and NOREL, S. V. (1990). An extended family with a dominantly inherited speech disorder. *Developmental Medicine and Child Neurology* 32: 352–355.

HYMES, D. (1971). *Pidginization and creolization of languages.* Cambridge: Cambridge University Press.

INTERNATIONAL HUMAN GENOME SEQUENCING CONSORTIUM (2004). Finishing the euchromatic sequence of the human genome. *Nature* 431: 931–945.

IRIE-SUGIMOTO, N., KOBAYASHI, T., SATO, T., and HASEGAWA, T. (2008). Evidence of means–end behavior in Asian elephants (*Elephas maximus*). *Animal Cognition* 11: 359–365.

IZARD, C. E. (1971). *The face of emotion.* New York: Appleton-Century-Crofts.

IZARD, C. E. (1980). Cross-cultural perspectives on emotions and emotion communication. In H. C. Triandis and W. Lonner (eds.), *Handbook of cross-cultural psychology: Vol. 3 Basic Processes.* Boston, MA: Allyn and Bacon, 185–222.

JABLONSKI, N. G. and AIELLO, L. C. (eds.) (1998). *The origin and diversification of language.* San Francisco, CA: California Academy of Sciences.

JACKENDOFF, R. (1999). Possible stages in the evolution of the language capacity. *Trends in Cognitive Sciences* 3: 272–279.

JACKENDOFF, R. (2002). *Foundations of language: Brain, meaning, grammar, evolution.* Oxford: Oxford University Press.

JACKENDOFF, R. (2010). Your theory of language evolution depends on your theory of language. In Larson et al (eds.), 63–72.

JACKENDOFF, R. and PINKER, S. (2005). The nature of the language faculty and its implications for evolution of language (Reply to Fitch, Hauser, and Chomsky). *Cognition* 97: 211–225.

JACKSON, A. P., EASTWOOD, H., BELL, S. M., ADU, J., TOOMES, C., CARR, I. M., ROBERTS, E., HAMPSHIRE, D. J., CROW, Y. J., MIGHELL, A. J., KARBANI, G., JAFRI, H., RASHID, Y., MUELLER, R. F., MARKHAM, A. F., and WOODS, C. G. (2002). Identification of microcephalin, a protein implicated in determining the size of the human brain. *American Journal of Human Genetics* 71: 136–42.

JACOBS, Z., ROBERTS, R. G., GALBRAITH, R. F., DEACON, H. J., GRÜN, R., MACKAY, A., MITCHELL, P., VOGELSANG, R., and WADLEY, L. (2008). Ages for the Middle Stone Age of Southern Africa: Implications for human behavior and dispersal. *Science* 322: 733–735.

JACOBSEN, W. H., Jr. (1980). Inclusive/exclusive: A diffused pronominal category in native western North America. In J. Kreiman and A. E. Ojeda (eds.), *Papers from the parasession on pronouns and anaphora.* Chicago, IL: Chicago Linguistics Society, 204–227.

JÄGER, H., BARONCHELLI, A., BRISCOE, E., CHRISTIANSEN, M. H., GRIFFITHS, T., JÄGER, G., KIRBY, S., KOMAROVA, N., RICHERSON, P. J., STEELS, L., and TRIESCH, J. (2009). What can mathematical, computational and robotic models tell us about the origins of syntax? In Bickerton and Szathmáry (eds.), 385–410.

JAKOBSON, R. (1967). About the relation between visual and auditory signs. In W. Wathen-Dunn (ed.), *Models for the perception of speech and visual form.* Cambridge, MA: MIT Press, 1–7.

Janda, R. D. (2001). Beyond 'pathways' and 'unidirectionality': On the discontinuity of language transmission and the counterability of grammaticalization. In L. Campbell (ed.), *Grammaticalization: A critical assessment* (Special issue of *Language Sciences*), 265–340.

Janik, V. M. (1999). Origins and implications of vocal learning in bottlenose dolphins. In Box and Gibson (eds.), 308–326.

Janik, V. M. (2000a). Food-related bray calls in wild bottlenose dolphins (*Tursiops truncatus*). *Proceedings of the Royal Society of London B* 267: 923–927.

Janik, V. M. (2000b). Source levels and the estimated active space of bottlenose dolphin (*Tursiops truncatus*) whistles in the Moray Firth, Scotland. *Journal of Comparative Physiology A* 186: 673–680.

Janik, V. M. (2000c). Whistle matching in wild bottlenose dolphins (*Tursiops truncatus*). *Science* 289: 1355–1357.

Janik, V. M. (2005). Acoustic communication networks in marine mammals. In P. K. McGregor (ed.), *Animal communication networks*. Cambridge: Cambridge University Press, 390–415.

Janik, V. M. and Slater, P. J. B. (1997). Vocal learning in mammals. In P. J. B. Slater, C. T. Snowdon, J. S. Rosenblatt, and M. Milinkski (eds.), *Advances in the study of behavior* 26. San Diego, CA: Academic Press, 59–99.

Janik, V. M., Sayigh, L. S., and Wells, R. S. (2006). Signature whistle contour shape conveys identity information to bottlenose dolphins. *Proceedings of the National Academy of Sciences of the USA* 103: 8293–8297.

Jarvis, E. D. (2004). Learned birdsong and the neurobiology of human language. *Annals of the New York Academy of Sciences*, 1016: 749–777.

Jarvis, E. D., Güntürkün, O., Bruce, L., Csillag, A., Karten, H. J., Kuenzel, W., Medina, L., Paxinos, G., Perkel, D. J., Shimizu, T., Striedter, G. F., Wild, M., Ball, G. F., Dugas-Ford, J., Durand, S., Hough, G., Husband, S., Kubikova, L., Lee, D. W., Mello, C. V., Powers, A., Siang, C., Smulders, T. V., Wada, K., White, S. A., Yamamoto, K., Yu, J., Reiner, A., and Butler, A. B. (2005). Avian brains and a new understanding of vertebrate evolution. *Nature Reviews Neuroscience* 6: 151–159.

Jenkins, L. (2000). *Biolinguistics: Exploring the biology of language*. Cambridge: Cambridge University Press.

Jerison, H. J. (1973). *Evolution of the brain and intelligence*. New York: Academic Press.

Jerison, H. J. (1982). Allometry, brain size, cortical surface, and convolutedness. In E. Armstrong and D. Falk (eds.), *Primate brain evolution: Methods and concepts*. New York: Plenum Press, 77–84.

Jespersen, O. (1895/1983). *Progress in language*. Amsterdam: John Benjamins Publishing Company.

Jobling, M. A. and Tyler-Smith, C. (2003). The human Y chromosome: An evolutionary marker comes of age. *Nature Reviews Genetics* 4: 598–612.

Jobling, M. A., Hurles, M. E., and Tyler-Smith, C. (2004). *Human evolutionary genetics*. New York: Garland Science.

Johanson, D. C., White, T. D., and Coppens, Y. (1978). A new species of the genus *Australopithecus* (Primates: Hominidae) from the Pliocene of East Africa. *Kirtlandia* 28: 1–14.

Johanson, L. (2002). Contact-induced change in a code-copying framework. In M. C. Jones and E. Esch (eds.), *Language change: The interplay of internal, external and extra-linguistic factors*. Berlin/New York: Mouton de Gruyter, 285–313.

JOHANSSON, S. (2005). *Origins of language: Constraints on hypotheses.* Amsterdam: John Benjamins.

JOHANSSON, S. (2008). Seeking compositionality in holistic protolanguage without substructure – do counterexamples overwhelm the fractionation process? In A. D. M. Smith et al. (eds.), 171–178.

JOHNSON-PYNN, J., FRAGASZY, D. M., HIRSH, E. M., BRAKKE, K. E., and GREENFIELD, P. M. (1999). Strategies used to combine seriated cups by chimpanzees (*Pan troglodytes*), bonobos (*Pan paniscus*), and capuchins (*Cebus apella*). *Journal of Comparative Psychology* 113: 37–48.

*Journal of Human Evolution* 37(3–4) (1999). Special issue devoted to the Pleistocene site of Gran Dolina, Sierra de Atapuerca, Spain, 309–700.

JUNGERS, W. L., POKEMPNER, A. A., KAY, R. F., and CARTMILL, M. (2003). Hypoglossal canal size in living hominoids and the evolution of human speech. *Human Biology* 75: 473–484.

JÜRGENS, U. (1998). Neuronal control of mammalian vocalization, with special reference to the squirrel monkey. *Naturwissenschaften* 85: 376–388.

JÜRGENS, U. (2002). Neural pathways underlying vocal control. *Neuroscience and Biobehavioural Reviews* 26: 235–258.

JÜRGENS, U. and SCHRIEVER, S. (1991). Respiratory muscle activity during vocalization in the squirrel monkey. *Folia Primatologia* 56: 121–132.

JUSCZYK, P. W. (1997). *The discovery of spoken language.* Cambridge, MA: MIT Press.

JUST, M. A. and CARPENTER, P. A. (1992). A capacity theory of comprehension: Individual differences in working memory. *Psychological Review* 99: 122–149.

KAKO, E. (1999a). Elements of syntax in the systems of three language-trained animals. *Animal Learning and Behavior* 27: 1–14.

KAKO, E. (1999b). Response to Pepperberg; Herman and Uyeyama; and Shanker, Savage-Rumbaugh, and Taylor. *Animal Learning and Behavior* 27: 26–27.

KALISH, M. L., GRIFFITHS, T. L., and LEWANDOWSKY, S. (2007). Iterated learning: Intergenerational knowledge transmission reveals inductive biases. *Psychonomic Bulletin and Review* 14: 288–294.

KAMINSKI, J., CALL, J., and FISCHER, J. (2004). Word learning in a domestic dog: Evidence for fast mapping. *Science* 304: 1682–1683.

KANE, M. J. and ENGLE, R. W. (2002). The role of prefrontal cortex in working-memory capacity, executive attention, and general fluid intelligence: An individual-differences perspective. *Psychonomic Bulletin and Review* 9: 637–671.

KAPLAN, H. S., HILL, K., LANCASTER, J. B., and HURTADO, A. M. (2000). A theory of human life history evolution: Brains, learning and longevity. *Evolutionary Anthropology* 9: 156–185.

KARMILOFF, K. and KARMILOFF-SMITH, A. (2001). *Pathways to language: From fetus to adolescent.* Boston, MA: Harvard University Press.

KATZ, J. J. (1976). The effability hypothesis. In Harnad et al. (eds.), 445–455.

KATZ, P. A. (1963). Effects of labels on children's perception and discrimination learning. *Journal of Experimental Psychology* 66: 423–428.

KAUFFMAN, S. A. (1993). *The origins of order.* Oxford: Oxford University Press.

KAWAI, M. (1965). Newly-acquired pre-cultural behavior of the natural troop of Japanese monkeys on Koshima islet. *Primates* 6: 1–30.

KAY, R. F., ROSS, C., and WILLIAMS, B. A. (1997). Anthropoid origins. *Science* 275: 797–804.

KAY, R. F., CARTMILL, M., and BALOW, M. (1998). The hypoglossal canal and the origin of human vocal behavior. *Proceedings of the National Academy of Sciences of the USA* 95: 5417–5419.

KAYSER, M., BRAUER, S., CORDAUX, R., CASTO, A., LAO, O., ZHIVOTOVSKY, L. A., MOYSE-FAURIE, C., RUTLEDGE, R. B., SCHIEFENHOEVEL, W., GIL, D., LIN, A. A., UNDERHILL, P. A., OEFNER, P. J., TRENT, R. J., and STONEKING, M. (2006). Melanesian and Asian origins of Polynesians: mtDNA and Y chromosome gradients across the Pacific. *Molecular Biology and Evolution* 23: 2234–2244.

KE, J., MINETT, J. W., AU, C.-P., and WANG, W. S.-Y. (2002). Self-organization and selection in the emergence of vocabulary. *Complexity* 7: 41–54.

KE, J., OGURA, M., and WANG, W. S.-Y. (2003). Optimization models of sound systems using genetic algorithms. *Computational Linguistics* 29: 1–18.

KEGL, J., SENGHAS, A., and COPPOLA, M. (1999). Creation through contact: Sign language emergence and sign language change in Nicaragua. In M. DeGraff (ed.), *Language creation and language change: Creolization, diachrony, and development*. Cambridge, MA: MIT Press, 179–237.

KELEMEN, G. (1969). Anatomy of the larynx and the anatomical basis of vocal performance. In G. H. Bourne (ed.), *The chimpanzee*. Basel: Karger, 165–186.

KELLER, G. B. and HAHNLOSER, R. H. R. (2009). Neural processing of auditory feedback during vocal practice in a songbird. *Nature* 457: 187–190.

KELLER, R. (1994). *On language change: The invisible hand in language*. London: Routledge.

KELLER, S. S., HIGHLEY, J. R., GARCIA-FINANA, M., SLUMING, V., REZAIE, R., and ROBERTS, N. (2007). Sulcal variability, stereological measurement and asymmetry of Broca's area on MR images. *Journal of Anatomy* 211: 534–555.

KELLER, S. S., CROW, T. J., FOUNDAS, A. L., AMUNTS, K., and ROBERTS, N. (2009a). Broca's area: Nomenclature, anatomy, typology and asymmetry. *Brain and Language* 109: 29–48.

KELLER, S. S., ROBERTS, N., and HOPKINS, W. D. (2009b). A comparative Magnetic Resonance Imaging study of the anatomy, variability and asymmetry of Broca's area in the human and chimpanzee brain. *Journal of Neuroscience* 29: 14607–14616.

KELLOGG, W. N. and KELLOGG, L. A. (1933). *The ape and the child: A comparative study of the environmental influence upon early behaviour*. New York and London: Hafner Publishing Company.

KEMPE, V. and BROOKS, P. (2001). The role of diminutives in the acquisition of Russian gender: Can elements of child-directed speech aid in learning morphology? *Language Learning* 51: 221–256.

KENDON, A. (1995). Gestures as illocutionary and discourse structure markers in Southern Italian conversation. *Journal of Pragmatics* 23: 247–279.

KHANINA, O. (No date). *A case-study in historical sociolinguistics: Reconstructing the pattern of multilingualism of Enets (1850-1950)*. Ms.

KIER, W. M. and SMITH, K. K. (1985). Tongues, tentacles and trunks: The biomechanics of movement in muscular-hydrostats. *Zoological Journal of the Linnean Society* 83: 307–324.

KIHM, A. (2002). Langues créoles et origine du langage: État de la question. *Langages* 146: 59–69.

KILIAN, A., VON FERSEN, L., and GÜNTÜRKÜN, O. (2000). Lateralization of visuospatial processing in the bottlenose dolphin (*Tursiops truncatus*). *Behavioural Brain Research* 116: 211–215.

KILIAN, A., VON FERSEN, L., and GÜNTÜRKÜN, O. (2005). Left hemispheric advantage for numerical abilities in the bottlenose dolphin. *Behavioural Processes* 68: 179–184.

KIMBEL, W. H. (2009). The origin of *Homo*. In Grine et al. (eds.), 31–37.

KIMBEL, W. H., WALTER, R. C., JOHANSON, D. C., REED, K. E., ARONSON, J. L., ASSEFA, Z., MAREAN, C. W., ECK, G. G., BOBE, R., HOVERS, E., RAK, Y., VONDRA, C., YEMANE, T., YORK, D., CHEN, Y., EVENSEN, N. M., and SMITH, P. E. (1996). Late Pliocene *Homo* and Oldowan tools for the Hadar formation (Kada Hadar member) Ethiopia. *Journal of Human Evolution* 31: 549–561.

KIMBEL, W. H., JOHANSON, D. C., and RAK, Y. (1997). Systematic assessment of a maxilla of *Homo* from Hadar, Ethiopia. *American Journal of Physical Anthropology* 103: 235–262.

KINDERMAN, P., DUNBAR, R. I. M., and BENTALL, R. P. (1998). Theory-of-mind deficits and causal attributions. *British Journal of Psychology* 89: 191–204.

KINSELLA, A. (2009). *Language evolution and syntactic theory*. Cambridge: Cambridge University Press.

KIRBY, S. (1999). *Function, selection and innateness: The emergence of language universals*. Oxford: Oxford University Press.

KIRBY, S. (2000). Syntax without natural selection: How compositionality emerges from vocabulary in a population of learners. In Knight et al. (eds.), 303–323.

KIRBY, S. (2001). Spontaneous evolution of linguistic structure: An iterated learning model of the emergence of regularity and irregularity. *IEEE Transactions on Evolutionary Computation* 5: 102–110.

KIRBY, S. (2002). Natural language from artificial life. *Artificial Life* 8: 185–215.

KIRBY, S. and HURFORD, J. R. (2002). The emergence of linguistic structure: An overview of the iterated learning model. In Cangelosi and Parisi (eds.), 121–148.

KIRBY, S., SMITH, K., and BRIGHTON, H. (2004). From UG to universals: Linguistic adaptation through iterated learning. *Studies in Language* 28: 587–607.

KIRBY, S., DOWMAN, M., and GRIFFITHS, T. L. (2007). Innateness and culture in the evolution of language. *Proceedings of the National Academy of Sciences of the USA* 104: 5241–5245.

KIRBY, S., CORNISH, H., and SMITH, K. (2008). Cumulative cultural evolution in the laboratory: An experimental approach to the origins of structure in human language. *Proceedings of the National Academy of Sciences of the USA* 105: 10681–10686.

KIRBY, S., CHRISTIANSEN, M. H., and CHATER, N. (2009). Syntax as an adaptation to the learner. In Bickerton and Szathmáry (eds.), 325–343.

KIRBY, S., SMITH, A., and SMITH, K. (In preparation). *Evolving language: Exploring the evolution of communication through working models*.

KIRIAZIS, J. and SLOBODCHIKOFF, C. N. (2006). Perceptual specificity in the alarm calls of Gunnison's prairie dogs. *Behavioural Processes* 73: 29–35.

KIRKHAM, N. Z., SLEMMER, J. A., and JOHNSON, S. P. (2002). Visual statistical learning in infancy: Evidence for a domain general learning mechanism. *Cognition* 83: B35–B42.

KIRSCHNER, M. W. and GERHART, J. (2005). *The plausibility of life: Resolving Darwin's dilemma*. New Haven, CT: Yale University Press.

KITA, S. (2000). How representational gestures help speaking. In McNeill (ed.), 162–185.

KLEIN, R. G. (1989). *The human career: Human biological and cultural origins*. Chicago, IL: University of Chicago Press.

KLEIN, R. G. (1992). The archaeology of modern human origins. *Evolutionary Anthropology* 1: 5–14.

KLEIN, R. G. (1998). Why anatomically modern people did not disperse from Africa 100,000 years ago. In T. Akazawa, K. Aoki, and O. Bar-Yosef (eds.), *Neanderthals and modern humans in Western Asia*. New York: Plenum, 509–522.

KLEIN, R. G. (2003). Whither the Neanderthals? *Science* 299: 1525–1527.

KLEIN, R. G. and EDGAR, B. (2002). *The dawn of human culture*. New York: John Wiley and Sons.

KLEIN, W. and PERDUE, C. (1992). *Utterance structure: Developing grammars*. Amsterdam: John Benjamins.

KLEIN, W. and PERDUE, C. (1997). The Basic Variety (or: Couldn't natural languages be much simpler?). *Second Language Research* 13: 301–347.

KLIMA, E. and BELLUGI, U. (1979). *The signs of language*. Cambridge, MA: Harvard University Press.

KNECHT, S., DRAGER, B., DEPPE, M., BOBE, L., LOHMANN, H., FLOEL, A., RINGELSTEIN, E. B., and HENNINGSEN, H. (2000). Handedness and hemispheric language dominance in healthy humans. *Brain* 123: 2512–2518.

KNIGHT, A., UNDERHILL, P. A., MORTENSEN, H. M., ZHIVOTOVSKY, L. A., LI, A. A., HENN, B. M., LOUIS, D., RUHLEN, M., and MOUNTAIN, J. L. (2003). African Y chromosome and mtDNA divergence provides insight into the history of click languages. *Current Biology* 13: 464–473.

KNIGHT, C. (2008). Early human kinship was matrilineal. In N. J. Allen, H. Callan, R. I. M. Dunbar, and W. James (eds.), *Early human kinship*. Oxford: Blackwell, 61–82.

KNIGHT, C. (2009). Language, ochre and the rule of law. In Botha and Knight (eds.) (2009a), 281–303.

KNIGHT, C., STUDDERT-KENNEDY, M., and HURFORD, J. R. (eds.) (2000). *The evolutionary emergence of language: Social function and the origins of linguistic form*. Cambridge: Cambridge University Press.

KNÖRNSCHILD, M., BEHR, O., and VON HELVERSEN, O. (2006). Babbling behavior in the sac-winged bat (*Saccopteryx bilineata*). *Naturwissenschaften* 93: 451–454.

KOHLER, E., KEYSERS, C., UMILTÀ, C. A., FOGASSI, L., GALLESE, V., and RIZZOLATTI, G. (2002). Hearing sounds, understanding actions: Action representation in mirror neurons. *Science* 297: 846–848.

KOOPS, K., McGREW, W. C., and MATSUZAWA, T. (2010). Do chimpanzees (*Pan troglodytes*) use cleavers and anvils to fracture *Treculia africana* fruits? Preliminary data on a new form of percussive technology. *Primates* 51: 175–178.

KRASNEGOR, N. A., RUMBAUGH, D. M., SCHIEFELBUSCH, R. L., and STUDDERT-KENNEDY, M. (eds.) (1991). *Biological and behavioral determinants of language development*. Hillsdale, NJ: Lawrence Erlbaum.

KRAUSE, J., LALUEZA-FOX, C., ORLANDO, L., ENARD, W., GREEN, R. E., BURBANO, H. A., HUBLIN, J.-J., HANNI, C., FORTEA, J., de la RASILLA, M., BERTRANPETIT, J., ROSAS, A., and PÄÄBO, S. (2007). The derived FOXP2 variant of modern humans was shared with Neandertals. *Current Biology* 17: 1908–1912.

KRAUSS, R. M., CHEN, Y., and GOTTESMAN, R. F. (2000). Lexical gestures and lexical access: A process model. In McNeill (ed.), 261–283.

KREBS, J. R. and DAWKINS, R. (1984). Animal signals: Mind-reading and manipulation. In J. R. Krebs and N. B. Davies (eds.), *Behavioural ecology: An evolutionary approach*. Oxford: Blackwell Scientific Publications, 380–402.

KRIEG, W. J. S. (1954). *Connections of the frontal lobe of the monkey*. Springfield, IL: Charles C. Thomas.

KROODSMA, D. E. (2005). *The singing life of birds*. New York: Houghton Mifflin.

KROODSMA, D. E., HOULIHAN, P. W., FALLON, P. A., and WELLS, J. A. (1997). Song development in grey catbirds. *Animal Behaviour* 54: 457–464.

KUCZAJ, S. A. II and WALKER, R. T. (2006). How do dolphins solve problems? In E. A. Wasserman and T. R. Zentall (eds.), *Comparative cognition: Experimental explorations of animal intelligence*. Oxford: Oxford University Press, 580–601.

KUHL, P. K. (1981). Discrimination of speech by nonhuman animals: Basic auditory sensitivities conducive to the perception of speech-sound categories. *Journal of the Acoustical Society of America* 70: 340–349.

KUHL, P. K. (1987). The special mechanisms debate in speech research: Categorization tests on animals and infants. In S. Harnad (ed.) *Categorical perception: The groundwork of cognition*. Cambridge: Cambridge University Press, 355–386.

KUHL, P. K., ANDRUSKI, J. E., CHISTOVICH, I. A., CHISTOVICH, L. A., KOZHEVIKOVA, E. V., RYSINKA, V. L., STOLYAROVA, E. I., SUNDBERG, U., and LACERDA, F. (1997). Cross-language analysis of phonetic units in language addressed to infants. *Science* 277: 684–686.

KUHL, P. K., TSAO, F. M., and LIU, H. M. (2003). Foreign-language experience in infancy: Effects of short-term exposure and social interaction on phonetic learning. *Proceedings of the National Academy of Sciences of the USA* 100: 9096–9101.

KUHN, S. L. and STINER, M. C. (2006). What's a mother to do: The division of labor among Neandertals and modern humans in Eurasia. *Current Anthropology* 47: 953–980.

KUHN S. L. and STINER M. C. (2007). Body ornamentation as information technology: Towards an understanding of the significance of early beads. In Mellars et al. (eds.), 45–54.

KUMAR, S., FILIPSKI, A., SWARNA, V., WALKER, A., and HEDGES, S. B. (2005). Placing confidence limits on the molecular age of the human–chimpanzee divergence. *Proceedings of the National Academy of Sciences of the USA* 102: 18842–18847.

KUTEVA, T. (2001). *Auxiliation: An enquiry into the nature of auxiliation*. Oxford: Oxford University Press.

KUTEVA, T. (2010). Are there languages without grammar? E-publication proceedings: SICOL-2010.

KUYPERS, H. G. J. M. (1958). Corticobulbar connexions to the pons and lower brain-stem in man: An anatomical study. *Brain* 10: 371–375.

LACHLAN, R. F. and SLATER, P. J. B. (1999). The maintenance of vocal learning by gene-culture interaction: The cultural trap hypothesis. *Proceedings of the Royal Society of London B* 266: 701–706.

LADD, D. R., DEDIU, D., and KINSELLA, A. R. (2008). Language and genes: Reflections on biolinguistics and the nature-nurture question. *Biolinguistics* 2: 114–126.

LADEFOGED, P. (1982). *A course in phonetics*. San Diego, CA: Harcourt Brace Jovanovich.

LADEFOGED, P. (2006). *Features and parameters for different purposes*. http://www.linguistics.ucla.edu/people/ladefoge/PLfeaturesParameters.pdf

LADEFOGED, P. and MADDIESON, I. (1996). *The sounds of the world's languages*. Malden, MA: Blackwell.

LAI, C. S., FISHER, S. E., HURST, J. A., VARGHA-KHADEM, F., and MONACO, A. P. (2001). A forkhead-domain gene is mutated in a severe speech and language disorder. *Nature* 413: 519–523.

LAI, C. S., GERELLI, D., MONACO, A. P., FISHER, S. E., and COPP, A. J. (2003). *FOXP2* expression during brain development coincides with adult sites of pathology in a severe speech and language disorder. *Brain* 126: 2455–2462.

LAITMAN, J. T., HEIMBUCH, R. C., and CRELIN, E. S. (1979). The basicranium of fossil hominids as an indicator of their upper respiratory systems. *American Journal of Physical Anthropology* 51: 15–34.

LALAND, K. N. and BROWN, G. R. (2002). *Sense and nonsense*. Oxford: Oxford University Press.

LALAND, K. N., ODLING-SMEE, J., and FELDMAN, M. W. (2001). Cultural niche construction and human evolution. *Journal of Evolutionary Biology* 14: 22–33.

LANCASTER, J. B. and KAPLAN, H. S. (2007). Chimpanzee and human intelligence: Life history, diet and the mind. In S. W. Gangestad and J. A. Simpson (eds.), *The evolution of mind: Fundamental questions and controversies*. New York: Guilford Press, 111–118.

LANCASTER J. B. and LANCASTER, C. S. (1983). Parental investment: The hominid adaptation. In D. Ortner (ed.), *How humans adapt: A biocultural odyssey*. Washington, DC: Smithsonian Institution Press, 33–66.

LANGACKER, R. (1987). *Foundations of cognitive grammar, Vol. 1. Theoretical prerequisites*. Stanford, CA: Stanford University Press.

LAPORTE, M. N. C. and ZUBERBÜHLER, K. (2010). Vocal greeting behaviour in wild chimpanzee females. *Animal Behaviour* 80: 467–473.

LARSON, R. K., DÉPREZ, V., and YAMAKIDO, H. (eds.) (2010). *The evolution of human language: Biolinguistic perspectives*. Cambridge: Cambridge University Press.

LEAKEY, L. S. B. (1959). A new fossil skull from Olduvai. *Nature* 184: 491–493.

LEAKEY, L. S. B., TOBIAS, P. V., and NAPIER, J. R. (1964). A new species of the genus *Homo* from Olduvai Gorge. *Nature* 202: 7–9.

LEAKEY, M. G., FEIBEL, C. S., McDOUGALL, I., and WALKER, A. (1995). New four-million-year-old hominid species from Kanapoi and Allia Bay, Kenya. *Nature* 376: 565–571.

LEAKEY, M. G., SPOOR, F., BROWN, F. H., GATHOGO, P. N., KIARIE, C., LEAKEY, L. N., and McDOUGALL, I. (2001). New hominin genus from eastern Africa shows diverse middle Pliocene lineages. *Nature* 410: 433–440.

LEAVENS, D. A., HOSTETTER, A. B., WESLEY, M. J., and HOPKINS, W. D. (2004). Tactical use of unimodal and bimodal communication by chimpanzees, *Pan troglodytes*. *Animal Behaviour* 67: 467–476.

LEAVENS, D. A., HOPKINS, W. D., and BARD, K. A., (2005). Understanding the point of chimpanzee pointing: Epigenesis and ecological validity. *Current Directions in Psychological Science* 14: 185–189.

LEE, C. E. (1999). Rapid and repeated invasions of fresh water by the copepod *Eurytemora affinis*. *Evolution* 53: 1423–1434.

LEGER, D. W. (2005). First documentation of combinatorial song syntax in a suboscine passerine species. *The Condor* 107: 765–774.

LEHMANN, C. (1982/1995). *Thoughts on grammaticalization*. Munich: Lincom Europa.

LEHMANN, J., KORSTJENS, A. H., and DUNBAR, R. I. M. (2007). Group size, grooming and social cohesion in primates. *Animal Behaviour* 74: 1617–1629.

LEHRMAN, D. S. (1953). A critique of Konrad Lorenz's theory of instinctive behavior. *Quarterly Review of Biology* 28: 337–363.

LEITÃO, A., TEN CATE, C., and RIEBEL, K. (2006). Within-song complexity in a songbird is meaningful to both male and female receivers. *Animal Behaviour* 71: 1289–1296.

LEMASSON, A. and HAUSBERGER, M. (2004). Patterns of vocal sharing and social dynamics in a captive group of Campbell's monkeys (*Cercopithecus campbelli campbelli*). *Journal of Comparative Psychology* 118: 347–359.

LEMASSON, A., GAUTIER, J. P. and HAUSBERGER, M. (2003). Vocal similarities and social bonds in Campbell's monkey (*Cercopithecus campbelli*). *Comptes Rendus Biologies* 326: 1185–1193.

LEMASSON, A., HAUSBERGER, M., and ZUBERBÜHLER, K. (2005). Socially meaningful vocal plasticity in adult Campbell's monkeys (*Cercopithecus campbelli*). *Journal of Comparative Psychology* 119: 220–229.

LEMAY, M. (1977). Asymmetries of the skull and handedness. *Journal of Neurological Sciences* 32: 243–253.

LEMAY, M. (1985). Asymmetries of the brains and skulls of nonhuman primates. In S. D. Glick (ed.), *Cerebral lateralization in nonhuman species*. New York: Academic Press, 223–245.

LEMAY, M. and GESCHWIND, N. (1975). Hemispheric differences in the brains of great apes. *Brain, Behavior and Evolution* 11: 48–52.

LENNEBERG, E. H. (1967). *Biological foundations of language*. New York: Riley.

LEVINSON, S. C. (2000). *Presumptive meanings: The theory of generalized conversational implicature*. Cambridge, MA: MIT Press.

LEWONTIN, R. C. (1974). The analysis of variance and the analysis of causes. *American Journal of Human Genetics* 26: 400–411.

LEWONTIN, R. C. (1998). The evolution of cognition: Questions we will never answer. In D. Scarborough, S. Sternberg, and D. N. Osherson (eds.), *An invitation to cognitive science*. Cambridge, MA: MIT Press, 107–132.

LEWONTIN, R. C. (2000). *The triple helix: Gene, organism, and environment*. Cambridge, MA: Harvard University Press.

LIBERMAN, A. M. and MATTINGLY, I. G. (1989). A specialization for speech perception. *Science* 243: 489–494.

LIBERMAN, A. M., COOPER F. S., SHANKWEILER, D. P., and STUDDERT-KENNEDY, M. (1967). Perception of the speech code. *Psychological Review* 74: 431–461.

LIBERT, A. (2000). *A priori artificial languages*. Munich: Lincom Europa.

LICKLITER, R. (2008). The growth of developmental thought: Implications for a new evolutionary psychology. *New Ideas in Psychology* 26: 353–367.

LIEBAL, K., CALL, J., and TOMASELLO, M. (2004). Use of gesture sequences in chimpanzees. *American Journal of Primatology* 64: 377–396.

LIEBAL, K., PIKA, S., and TOMASELLO, M. (2006). Gestural communication in orang-utans. *Gesture* 6: 1–38.

LIEBER, R. (1992). *Deconstructing morphology: Word formation in syntactic theory*. Chicago, IL: University of Chicago Press.

LIEBERMAN, D. E. (2008). Speculations about the selective basis for modern human craniofacial form. *Evolutionary Anthropology* 17: 55–68.

LIEBERMAN, D. E. and McCARTHY, R. C. (1999). The ontogeny of cranial base angulation in humans and chimpanzees and its implications for reconstructing pharyngeal dimensions. *Journal of Human Evolution* 36: 487–517.

LIEBERMAN, D. E., McCARTHY, R. C., HIIEMAE, K. M., and PALMER, J. B. (2001). Ontogeny of postnatal hyoid and larynx descent in humans. *Archives of Oral Biology* 46: 117–128.

LIEBERMAN, D. E., McBRATNEY, B. M., and KROVITZ, G. (2002). The evolution and development of cranial form in *Homo sapiens*. *Proceedings of the National Academy of Sciences of the USA* 99: 1134–1139.

LIEBERMAN, E., MICHEL, J., JACKSON, J., TANG, T., and NOWAK, M. (2007). Quantifying the evolutionary dynamics of language. *Nature* 449: 713–716.

Lieberman, P. (1980). On the development of vowel production in young children. In G. H. Yeni-Komshian, J. F. Kavanagh, and C. A. Ferguson (eds.), *Child phonology, perception and production. Volume 1: Production.* New York: Academic Press, 113–142.

Lieberman, P. (1984). *The biology and evolution of language.* Cambridge, MA: Harvard University Press.

Lieberman, P. (1991). *Uniquely human: The evolution of speech, thought, and selfless behavior.* Cambridge, MA: Harvard University Press.

Lieberman, P. (2000). *Human language and our reptilian brain.* Cambridge, MA: Harvard University Press.

Lieberman, P. (2002). On the nature and evolution of the neural bases of human language. *Yearbook of Physical Anthropology* 45: 36–62.

Lieberman, P. (2006). *Toward an evolutionary biology of language.* Cambridge, MA and London: Harvard University Press.

Lieberman, P. (2007). The evolution of speech: Its anatomical and neural bases. *Current Anthropology* 48: 39–66.

Lieberman, P. and Crelin, E. S. (1971). On the speech of Neanderthal man. *Linguistic Inquiry* 2: 203–222.

Lieberman, P., Crelin, E. S., and Klatt, D. H. (1972). Phonetic ability and the related anatomy of the newborn and adult human, Neanderthal man, and the chimpanzee. *American Anthropologist* 74: 287–307.

Lieberman, P., Laitman, J. T., Reidenberg, J. S., and Gannon, P. J. (1992). The anatomy, physiology, acoustics and perception of speech: Essential elements in analysis of the evolution of human speech. *Journal of Human Evolution* 23: 447–467.

Lightfoot, D. W. (1979). *Principles of diachronic syntax.* Cambridge: Cambridge University Press.

Lightfoot, D. W. (1991). Subjacency and sex. *Language and Communication* 11: 67–69.

Lightfoot, D. W. (1999). *The development of language: Acquisition, change and evolution.* Oxford: Blackwell.

Lightfoot, D. W. (2000). The spandrels of the linguistic genotype. In Knight et al. (eds.), 231–247.

Lightfoot, D. W. (2006). *How new languages emerge.* Cambridge: Cambridge University Press.

Liljencrants, J. and Lindblom, B. (1972). Numerical simulations of vowel quality systems. *Language* 48: 839–862.

Lin, J.-W. (2005). Time in a language without tense: The case of Chinese. *Journal of Semantics* 23: 1–53.

Lindblom, B. (1986). Phonetic universals in vowel systems. In J. J. Ohala and J. J. Jaeger (eds.), *Experimental phonology.* Orlando, FL: Academic Press, 13–44.

Lindblom, B. (1998). Systemic constraints and adaptive change in the formation of sound structure. In Hurford et al. (eds.), 242–264.

Lindblom, B. (2011). Evolution of phonology. In P. C. Hogan (ed.), *The Cambridge encyclopedia of the language sciences.* Cambridge: Cambridge University Press.

Lindblom, B. and Maddieson, I. (1988). Phonetic universals in consonant systems. In L. M. Hyman and C. N. Li (eds.), *Language, speech and mind.* London: Routledge, 62–78.

Lindblom, B., MacNeilage, P. F., and Studdert-Kennedy, M. (1984). Self-organizing processes and the explanation of language universals. In M. Butterworth, B. Comrie, and

Ö. Dahl (eds.), *Explanations for language universals*. Berlin: Walter de Gruyter and Co., 181–203.

LINDBLOM, B., DIEHL, R., PARK, S.-H., and SALVI, G. (2011). Sound systems are shaped by their users: The recombination of phonetic substance. In G. N. Clements and R. Ridouane (eds.), *Where do phonological contrasts come from? Cognitive, physical and developmental bases of phonological features*. Amsterdam: John Benjamins, 65–98.

LIU, H.-M., KUHL, P. K., and TSAO, F.-M. (2003). An association between mothers' speech clarity and infants' speech discrimination skills. *Developmental Science* 6: F1–F10.

LIU, S. T. and PHILLIPS, K. A. (2009). Sylvian fissure asymmetries in capuchin monkeys (*Cebus apella*). *Laterality* 14: 217–227.

LIU, W., JIN, C., ZHANG, Y., CAI, Y., XING, S., WU, X., CHENG, H., EDWARDS, R. L., PAN, W., QIN, D., AN, Z., TRINKAUS, E., and WU, X. (2010). Human remains from Zhirendong, South China, and modern human emergence in East Asia. *Proceedings of the National Academy of Sciences of the USA* 107: 19201–19206.

LOCK, A. and PETERS, C. R. (eds.) (1996). *Handbook of human symbolic evolution*. New York: Clarendon Press.

LOCKE, J. L. (1983). *Phonological acquisition and change*. New York: Academic Press.

LOCKE, J. L. (1993). *The child's path to spoken language*. Cambridge, MA: Harvard University Press.

LOCKE, J. L. (1998). Social sound-making as a precursor to spoken language. In Hurford et al. (eds.), 190–201.

LOCKE, J. L. (2001a). First communion: The emergence of vocal relationships. *Social Development* 10: 294–308.

LOCKE, J. L. (2001b). Vocal development in the human infant: functions and phonetics. In N. Hewlett, L. Kelly, and F. Windsor (eds.), *Themes in clinical linguistics and phonetics*. Mahwah, NJ: Lawrence Erlbaum, 243–256.

LOCKE, J. L. (2001c). Rank and relationships in the evolution of spoken language. *Journal of the Royal Anthropological Institute* 7: 37–50.

LOCKE, J. L. (2004). How do infants come to control the organs of speech? In B. Maassen, R. D. Kent, H. F. M. Peters, P. H. H. M. van Lieshout, and W. Hulstijn (eds.), *Speech motor control in normal and disordered speech*. Oxford: Oxford University Press, 175–190.

LOCKE, J. L. (2006). Parental selection of vocal behavior: Crying, cooing, babbling and the evolution of language. *Human Nature* 17: 155–168.

LOCKE, J. L. (2008a). Cost and complexity: Selection for speech and language. *Journal of Theoretical Biology* 25: 640–652.

LOCKE, J. L. (2008b). The trait of human language: Lessons from the canal boat children of England. *Biology and Philosophy* 23: 347–361.

LOCKE, J. L. (2009). Evolutionary developmental linguistics: Naturalization of the faculty of language. *Language Sciences* 31: 33–59.

LOCKE, J. L. (2010). The development of linguistic systems: Insights from evolution. In J. Guendouzi, F. Loncke, and M. J. Williams (eds.), *Handbook of psycholinguistic and cognitive processes: Perspectives in communication disorders*. London: Psychology Press, 3–29.

LOCKE, J. L. and BOGIN, B. (2006). Language and life history: A new perspective on the evolution and development of linguistic communication. *Behavioral and Brain Sciences* 29: 259–325.

LOMBARD, M. and PHILLIPSON, L. (2010). Indications of bow and stone-tipped arrow use 64000 years ago in KwaZulu-Natal, South Africa. *Antiquity* 84: 635–648.

LORENZ, K. (1965). *Evolution and modification of behavior.* Chicago, IL: University of Chicago Press.

LORENZO, G. and LONGA, V. M. (2003). Homo loquens: *Biologia y evolucion del lenguaje.* Lugo: Tris Tram.

LOSIN, E. R., FREEMAN, H., RUSSELL, J. L., MEGUERDITCHIAN, A., and HOPKINS, W. D. (2008). Left hemisphere specialization for oro-facial movements of learned vocal signals by captive chimpanzees. *Plos ONE* 3: 1–7.

LOSOS, J. B., WARHEIT, K. I., and SCHOENER, T. W. (1997). Adaptive differentiation following experimental island colonizations in *Anolis* lizards. *Nature* 387: 70–73.

LOU, H., LUBER, B., CRUPAIN, M., KEENAN, J. P., NOWAK, M., and KJAER, T. (2004). Who am I? On the nature of subjectivity. *Proceedings of the National Academy of Sciences of the USA* 101: 6827–6832.

LUPYAN, G. (2006). Labels facilitate learning of novel categories. In Cangelosi et al. (eds.), 190–197.

LURIA, A. R. (1966). *Higher cortical functions in man.* New York: Basic Books.

LURIA, A. R., TSVETKOVA, L. S., and FUTER, D. S. (1965). *Journal of Neurological Science* 2: 288–292.

LYON, B. E., EADIE, J. M., and HAMILTON, L. D. (1994). Parental choice selects for ornamental plumage in American coot chicks. *Nature* 37: 240–243.

LYON C., NEHANIV C. L., and CANGELOSI A. (eds.) (2007). *Emergence of communication and language.* London: Springer.

MACAULAY, V., HILL, C., ACHILLI, A., RENGO, C., CLARKE, D., MEEHAN, W., BLACKBURN, J., SEMINO, O., SCOZZARI, R., CRUCIANI, F., TAHA, A., SHAARI, N. K., RAJA, J. M., ISMAIL, P., ZAINUDDIN, Z., GOODWIN, W., BULBECK, D., BANDELT, H. J., OPPENHEIMER, S., TORRONI, A., and RICHARDS, M. (2005). Single, rapid coastal settlement of Asia revealed by analysis of complete mitochondrial genomes. *Science* 308: 1034–1036.

MCBREARTY, S. (2007). Down with the revolution. In Mellars et al. (eds.), 133–151.

MCBREARTY, S. and BROOKS, A. S. (2000). The revolution that wasn't: A new interpretation of the origin of modern human behavior. *Journal of Human Evolution* 39: 453–563.

MCCOMB, K. and SEMPLE, S. (2005). Coevolution of vocal communication and sociality in primates. *Biology Letters* 1: 381–385.

MCCOMB, K., MOSS, C., SAYIALEL, S., and BAKER, L. (2000). Unusually extensive networks of vocal recognition in African elephants. *Animal Behaviour* 69: 1103.

MCCUNE, L. (1999). Children's transition to language. In B. King (ed.), *The origins of language: What non-human primates can tell us.* Santa Fe, NM: School for American Research, 269–306.

MCCUNE, L., VIHMAN, M. M., ROUG-HELLICHIUS, L., DELERY, D. B., and GOGATE, L. (1996). Grunt communication in human infants (*Homo sapiens*). *Journal of Comparative Psychology* 110: 27–37.

MCDANIEL, D. (2005). The potential role of production in the evolution of syntax. In Tallerman (ed.), 153–165.

MCDOUGALL, I., BROWN, F. H., and FLEAGLE, J. G. (2005). Stratigraphic placement and age of modern humans from Kibish, Ethiopia. *Nature* 433: 733–736.

MCGREW, W. C. (2010). Evolution: Chimpanzee technology. *Science* 328: 579–580.

MCGREW, W. C. and TUTIN, C. E. G. (1978). Evidence for a social custom in wild chimpanzees? *Man* 13: 234–251.

MCGURK, H. and MACDONALD, J. (1976). Hearing lips and seeing voices. *Nature* 264: 746–748.

MACKEN, M. A. (1979). Developmental reorganization of phonology: A hierarchy of basic units of acquisition. *Lingua* 49: 11–49.

MacLARNON, A. M. (1993). The vertebral canal. In A. Walker and R. Leakey (eds.), *The* Nariokotome Homo erectus *skeleton*. Cambridge, MA: Harvard University Press, 359–390.

MacLARNON, A. M. (1995). The distribution of spinal cord tissues and locomotor adaptation in primates. *Journal of Human Evolution* 29: 463–482.

MacLARNON, A. M. and HEWITT, G. P. (1999). The evolution of human speech: The role of enhanced breathing control. *American Journal of Physical Anthropology* 109: 341–363.

MacLARNON, A. M. and HEWITT, G. P. (2004). Increased breathing control: Another factor in the evolution of human language. *Evolutionary Anthropology* 13: 181–197.

MACLAURIN, J. (2002). The resurrection of innateness. *The Monist* 85: 105–130.

McMAHON, A. (1994). *Understanding language change*. Cambridge: Cambridge University Press.

MacNEILAGE, P. F. (1998). The frame/content theory of evolution of speech production. *Behavioral and Brain Sciences* 21: 499–511.

MacNEILAGE, P. F. (2008). *The origin of speech*. Oxford: Oxford University Press.

MacNEILAGE, P. F. and DAVIS, B. L. (2000). On the origin of the internal structure of word forms. *Science* 288: 527–531.

MacNEILAGE, P. F. and DAVIS, B. L. (2005). The frame/content theory of evolution of speech: Comparison with a gestural origins theory. *Interaction Studies* 6: 173–199.

MacNEILAGE, P. F., DAVIS, B. L., KINNEY, A., and MATYEAR, C. L. (1999). Origin of serial output complexity in speech. *Psychological Science* 10: 459–460.

MacNEILAGE, P. F., DAVIS, B. L., KINNEY, A., and MATYEAR, C. L. (2000). The motor core of speech: A comparison of serial organization patterns in infants and languages. *Child Development* 71: 153–163.

MacNEILAGE, P. F., ROGERS, L. J., and VALLORTIGARA, G. (2009). Origins of the left and right brain. *Scientific American* 300: 60–67.

McNEILL, D. (1992). *Hand and mind*. Chicago, IL: University of Chicago Press.

McNEILL, D. (ed.) (2000). *Language and gesture*. Cambridge: Cambridge University Press.

McNEILL, D., DUNCAN, S. D., COLE, J., GALLAGHER, S., and BERTENTHAL, B. (2008). Growth points from the very beginning. *Interaction Studies* 9: 117–132.

McPHERRON, A., ALEMSEGED, A., MAREAN, C., WYNN, J., REED, D., GERAADS, D., BOBE, R., and BÉARAT, H. A. (2010). Evidence for stone-tool-assisted consumption of animal tissues before 3.39 million years ago at Dikika, Ethiopia. *Nature* 466: 857–860.

McSHANE, J. (1979). The development of naming. *Linguistics* 17: 879–905.

McSHANE, J. (1980). *Learning to talk*. Cambridge: Cambridge University Press.

MacWHINNEY, B. (1999). *The emergence of language*. Mahwah, NJ: Lawrence Erlbaum.

McWHORTER, J. (2005). *Defining creole*. Oxford: Oxford University Press.

MAESS, B., KOELSCH, S., GUNTER, T. C., and FRIEDERICI, A. D. (2001). Musical syntax is processed in Broca's area: An MEG study. *Nature Neuroscience* 4: 540–545.

MAGUIRE, E. A., GADIAN, D. J., JOHNSRUDE, I. S., GOOD, C. D., ASHBURNER, J., FRACKOWIAK, R. S. J., and FRITH, C. D. (2000). Navigation-related structural change in the hippocampi of taxi drivers. *Proceedings of the National Academy of Sciences of the USA* 97: 4398–4403.

MAMELI, M. and BATESON, P. (2006). Innateness and the sciences. *Biology and Philosophy* 21: 155–188.

MANICA, A., AMOS, W., BALLOUX, F., and HANIHARA, T. (2007). The effect of ancient population bottlenecks on human phenotypic variation. *Nature* 448: 346–348.

MARANTZ, A. (1983). Before Babel: The misguided quest for the origins of language. *The Sciences* 23: 16–20.

MARATSOS, M. (1998). The acquisition of grammar. In D. Kuhn and R. S. Siegler (eds.), *Handbook of child psychology. Volume 2. Cognition, perception, and language*. New York: John Wiley and Sons, 421–466.

MARCUS, G., VIJAYAN, S., BANDI RAO, S., and VISHTON, P. M. (1999). Rule leaning by seven-month-old infants. *Science* 283: 77–80.

MARKMAN, E. M. (1989). *Categorization and naming in children: Problems of induction*. Cambridge, MA: MIT Press.

MAREAN, C. W. (2010a). Pinnacle Point cave 13B (Western Cape Province, South Africa) in context: the Cape floral kingdom, shellfish, and modern human origins. *Journal of Human Evolution* 59: 425–443.

MAREAN, C. W. (2010b). When the sea saved humanity. *Scientific American* 303: 54–61.

MAREAN, C. W., BAR-MATTHEWS, M., BERNATCHEZ, J., FISHER, E., GOLDBERG, P., HERRIES, A. I. R., JACOBS, Z., JERARDINO, A., KARKANAS, P., MINICHILLO, T., NILSSEN, P. J., THOMPSON, E., WATTS, I., WILLIAMS, H. W. (2007). Early human use of marine resources and pigment in South Africa during the Middle Pleistocene. *Nature* 449: 905–908.

MARLER, P. (1970). Birdsong and speech development: Could there be parallels? *American Scientist* 58: 669–673.

MARLER, P. (1977). The structure of animal communication sounds. In T. H. Bullock (ed.), *Recognition of complex acoustic signals*. Berlin: Dahlem Konferenzen, 17–35.

MARLER, P. (1991). The instinct to learn. In S. Carey and R. Gelman (eds.), *The epigenesis of mind*. Hillsdale, NJ: Lawrence Erlbaum Associates, 37–66.

MARLER, P. (1999). On innateness: Are sparrow songs 'learned' or 'innate'? In M. D. Hauser and M. Konishi (eds.), *The design of animal communication*. Cambridge, MA: MIT Press, 293–318.

MARLER, P. and TENAZA, R. (1977). Signaling behavior of apes with special reference to vocalizations. In Sebeok (ed.), 965–1033.

MARLOWE, F. W. (2006). Central place provisioning: The Hadza as an example. In G. Hohmann, M. M. Robbins, and C. Boesch (eds.), *Feeding ecology in apes and other primates: Ecological, physical and behavioral aspects*. Cambridge: Cambridge University Press, 359–377.

MARLOWE, F. W. (2010). *The Hadza: Hunter-gatherers of Tanzania*. Berkeley, CA: University of California Press.

MAROCCO, D. and NOLFI, S. (2007). Emergence of communication in embodied agents evolved for the ability to solve a collective navigation problem. *Connection Science* 19: 53–74.

MARSHALL, A., WRANGHAM, R., and CLARK ARCADI, A. (1999). Does learning affect the structure of vocalizations in chimpanzees? *Animal Behaviour* 58: 825–830.

MARSHALL, L. (1976). *The Kung of Nyae Nyae*. Cambridge, MA: Harvard University Press.

MARTIN, A. R. and REEVES, R. R. (2002). Diversity and zoogeography. In A. R. Hoelzel (ed.), *Marine mammal biology: An evolutionary approach*. Oxford: Blackwell Science, 1–37.

MARTÍNEZ, I., ARSUAGA, J. L., QUAM, R., CARRETERO, J. M., GRACIA, A., and RODRÍGUEZ, L. (2008). Human hyoid bones from the middle Pleistocene site of the Sima de los Huesos (Sierra de Atapuerca, Spain). *Journal of Human Evolution* 54: 118–124.

MASATAKA, N. (1992). Motherese in a signed language. *Infant Behavior and Development* 15: 453–460.

MASLOVA, E. (2000). A dynamic approach to the verification of distributional universals. *Linguistic Typology* 4: 307–333.

MATASOVIĆ, R. (2004). *Gender in Indo-European.* Heidelberg: Winter.

MATASOVIĆ, R. (2007). The diachronic stability of gender revisited. Paper presented at the Association for Linguistic Typology 8th Biennial Meeting.

MATRAS, Y. (2009). *Language contact.* Cambridge: Cambridge University Press.

MAYR, E. (1982). *The growth of biological thought.* Cambridge, MA: Belknap Press of the Harvard University Press.

MEDAWAR, P. B. (1967). A biological retrospect. In P. B. Medawar (ed.), *The art of the soluble.* London: Methuen, 97–110.

MEDIN, D. L. and ATRAN, S. (2004). The native mind: Biological categorization, reasoning and decision making in development across cultures. *Psychological Review* 111: 960–983.

MEGUERDITCHIAN, A. and VAUCLAIR, J. (2006). Baboons communicate with their right hand. *Behavioural Brain Research* 171: 170–174.

MEGUERDITCHIAN, A. and VAUCLAIR, J. (2008). Vocal and gestural communication in nonhuman primates and the question of the origin of language. In L. Roska-Hardy and E. M. Neumann-Held (eds.), *Learning from animals?* London: Psychology Press, 61–85.

MEGUERDITCHIAN, A., VAUCLAIR, J., and HOPKINS, W. D. (2010). Captive chimpanzees use their right hand to communicate with each other: Implications for the origins of hemispheric specialization for language. *Cortex* 46: 40–48.

MEKEL-BOBROV, N. and LAHN, B. T. (2007). Response to comments by Timpson et al. and Yu et al. *Science* 317: 1036.

MEKEL-BOBROV, N., GILBERT, S. L., EVANS, P. D., VALLENDER, E. J., ANDERSON, J. R., HUDSON, R. R., TISHKOFF, S. A., and LAHN, B. T. (2005). Ongoing adaptive evolution of *ASPM*, a brain size determinant in *Homo sapiens. Science* 309: 1720–1722.

MEKEL-BOBROV, N., EVANS, P. D., GILBERT, S. L., VALLENDER, E. J., HUDSON, R. R., and LAHN, B. T. (2006). Response to comment on 'Ongoing adaptive evolution of ASPM, a brain size determinant in *Homo sapiens*' and 'Microcephalin, a gene regulating brain size, continues to evolve adaptively in humans' *Science* 313: 172.

MELIS, A. P., HARE, B., and TOMASELLO, M. (2006). Chimpanzees recruit the best collaborators. *Science* 311: 1297–1300.

MELLARS, P. A. (1989a). Major issues in the emergence of modern humans. *Current Anthropology* 30: 349–385.

MELLARS, P. A. (1989b). Technological changes at the Middle-Upper Palaeolithic transition: Economic, social and cognitive perspectives. In Mellars and Stringer (eds.), 338–365.

MELLARS, P. A. (1996). *The Neanderthal legacy: An archaeological perspective from western Europe.* Princeton, NJ: Princeton University Press.

MELLARS, P. A. (1998a). Neanderthals, modern humans and the archaeological evidence for language. In Jablonski and Aiello (eds.), 98–115.

MELLARS, P. A. (1998b). Modern humans, language and the symbolic explosion. *Cambridge Archaeological Journal* 8: 88–90.

MELLARS, P. A. (2010). Neanderthal symbolism and ornament manufacture: The bursting of a bubble? *Proceedings of the National Academy of Sciences of the USA* 107: 20147–20148.

MELLARS, P. A. and STRINGER, C. B. (eds.) (1989). *The human revolution: Behavioral and biological perspectives on the origin of modern humans.* Princeton, NJ: Princeton University Press.

MELLARS, P. A., Boyle, K., BAR-YOSEF, O., and STRINGER, C. (eds.) (2007). *Rethinking the human revolution.* Cambridge: McDonald Institute Monographs.

MELTZOFF, A. N. (1996). The human infant as imitative generalist: A 20-year progress report on infant imitation with implications for comparative psychology. In Heyes and Galef (eds.), 347–370.

MELTZOFF, A. N., and MOORE, K. M. (1997). Explaining facial imitation: A theoretical model. *Early Development and Parenting* 6: 179–192.

MENN, L. (1983). Development of articulatory, phonetic and phonological capabilities. In B. Butterworth (ed.), *Language production Volume II.* London: Academic Press, 3–50.

MENZEL, C. (2005). Progress in the study of chimpanzee recall and episodic memory. In Terrace and Metcalfe (eds.), 188–224.

MENZEL, E. W. (1972). Spontaneous invention of ladders in a group of young chimpanzees. *Folia Primatologica* 17: 87–106.

MENZEL, E. W. (1978). Implications of chimpanzee language training experiments for primate field research – and vice versa. In D. J. Chivers and J. Herbert (eds.), *Recent advances in primatology. 1: Behaviour.* London: Academic Press, 883–895.

MENZEL, R., GREGGERS, U., SMITH, A., BERGER, S., BRANDT, R., BRUNKE, S., BUNDROCK, G., HÜLSE, S., PLÜMPE, T., SCHAUPP, F., SCHÜTTLER, E., STACH, S., STINDT, J., STOLLHOFF, N., and WATZL, S. (2005). Honey bees navigate according to a map-like spatial memory. *Proceedings of the National Academy of Sciences of the USA* 102: 3040–3045.

*Merriam-Webster's Collegiate Dictionary* (2000). Tenth edition. Springfield, MA: Merriam-Webster.

MESOUDI, A., WHITEN, A., and DUNBAR, R. I. M. (2006). A bias for social information in human cultural transmission. *British Journal of Psychology* 97: 405–423.

MIELKE, J. (2008). *The emergence of distinctive features.* Oxford: Oxford University Press.

MIESTAMO, M., SINNEMÄKI, K., and KARLSSON, F. (eds.) (2008). *Language complexity: Typology, contact, change.* Amsterdam/Philadelphia, PA: John Benjamins.

MILES, H. L. (1990). The cognitive foundations for reference in a signing orangutan. In Parker and Gibson (eds.), 511–539.

MILES, H. L. (1999). Symbolic communication with and by great apes. In Parker et al. (eds.), 197–210.

MILLARD, A. R. (2008). Critique of the chronometric evidence for hominid fossils: I. Africa and the Near East 500–50ka. *Journal of Human Evolution* 54: 848–874.

MILLER, G. F. (2000). *The mating mind: How sexual choice shaped the evolution of human nature.* London: William Heinemann.

MILLER, L. K. (1989). *Musical savants: Exceptional skill in the mentally retarded.* Hillsdale, NJ: Lawrence Erlbaum.

MINTZ, T. H. (2003). Frequent frames as a cue for grammatical categories in child directed speech. *Cognition* 90: 91–117.

MINTZ, T. H., NEWPORT, E. L., and BEVER, T. G. (2002). The distributional structure of grammatical categories in speech to young children. *Cognitive Science* 26: 393–424.

MIROLLI M. and NOLFI, S. (eds.) (2010). *Evolution of communication and language in embodied agents.* Berlin: Springer Verlag.

MITANI, J. C. (1996). Comparative studies of African ape vocal behavior. In W. C. McGrew, L. F. Marchant, and T. Nishida (eds.), *Great ape societies.* Cambridge: Cambridge University Press, 241–254.

MITANI, J. C. and WATTS, D. P. (1997). The evolution of non-maternal caretaking among anthropoid primates: Do helpers help? *Behavioral Ecology and Sociobiology* 40: 213–220.

MITANI, J. C., HUNLEY, K. L., and MURDOCH, M. E. (1999). Geographic variation in the calls of wild chimpanzees: A reassessment. *American Journal of Primatology* 47: 133–151.

MITANI, J. C., WATTS, D. P., and AMSLER, S. J. (2010). Lethal intergroup aggression leads to territorial expansion in wild chimpanzees. *Current Biology* 20: R507–R508.

MITHEN, S. (1996). *The prehistory of the mind: A search for the origins of art, science and religion.* London: Thames and Hudson.

MITHEN, S. (1999a). Imitation and cultural change: A view from the Stone Age, with specific reference to the manufacture of hand axes. In Box and Gibson (eds.), 389–400.

MITHEN, S. (1999b). Symbolism and the supernatural. In Dunbar et al. (eds.), 147–169.

MITHEN, S. (2005). *The singing Neanderthals: The origins of music, language, mind and body.* London: Weidenfeld and Nicholson.

MITHEN, S. (2009). Holistic communication and the co-evolution of language and music: Resurrecting an old idea. In Botha and Knight (eds.) (2009b), 58–76.

MITRI, S., FLOREANO, D., and KELLER, L. (2009). The evolution of information suppression in communicating robots with conflicting interests. *Proceedings of the National Academy of Sciences of the USA* 106: 15786–15790.

MIVART, ST. G. J. (1871). *On the genesis of species.* London: Macmillan.

MIYAKE, A. and SHAH, P. (eds.) (1999). *Models of working memory: Mechanisms of active maintenance and executive control.* Cambridge: Cambridge University Press.

MOGGI-CECCHI, J. and COLLARD, M. (2002). A fossil stapes from Sterkfontein, South Africa, and the hearing capabilities of early hominids. *Journal of Human Evolution* 42: 259–265.

MONNOT, M. (1999). Function of infant-directed speech. *Human Nature* 10: 415–443.

MORA, R. and DE LA TORRE, I. (2005). Percussion tools in Olduvai Beds I and II (Tanzania): Implications for early human activities. *Journal of Anthropological Archaeology* 24: 179–192.

MORLEY, I. (2002). Evolution of the physiological and neurological capacities for music. *Cambridge Archaeological Journal* 16: 97–112.

MUELLER, G. and S. NEWMAN (eds.) (2003). *Origination of organismal form.* Cambridge, MA: MIT Press.

MUFWENE, S. S. (2008). What do creoles and pidgins tell us about the evolution of language? In B. Laks (ed.), *Origin and evolution of languages: Approaches, models, paradigms.* London: Equinox, 272–297.

MÜHLHÄUSLER, P. (1997). *Pidgin and creole linguistics* (2nd edn.). London: University of Westminster Press.

MUI, R., HASELGROVE, M., PEARCE, J. M., and HEYES, C. M. (2008). Automatic imitation in budgerigars. *Proceedings of the Royal Society of London B* 275: 2547–2553.

MUNROE, S. and CANGELOSI, A. (2002). Learning and the evolution of language: The role of cultural variation and learning cost in the Baldwin effect. *Artificial Life* 8: 311–339.

NAIGLES, L. and HOFF-GINSBERG, E. (1998). Why are some verbs learned before other verbs? Effects on input frequency and structure on children's early verb use. *Journal of Child Language* 25: 95–120.

NASIDZE, I. and STONEKING, M. (2001). Mitochondrial DNA variation and language replacements in the Caucasus. *Proceedings of the Royal Society of London B* 268: 1197–1206.

NASIDZE, I., SARKISIAN, T., KERIMOV, A., and STONEKING, M. (2003). Testing hypotheses of language replacement in the Caucasus: Evidence from the Y-chromosome. *Human Genetics* 112: 255–261.

NEGUS, V. E. (1929). *The mechanism of the larynx.* London: Heinemann.

NEGUS, V. E. (1949). *The comparative anatomy and physiology of the larynx.* New York: Hafner.

NETTLE, D. (1999). *Linguistic diversity.* Oxford: Oxford University Press.

NETTLE, D. and DUNBAR, R. I. M. (1997). Social markers and the evolution of reciprocal exchange. *Current Anthropology* 38: 93–99.

NEVILLE, H. J. (1991). Neurobiology of cognitive and language processing: Effects of early experience. In Gibson and Petersen (eds.), 355–380.

NEVINS, A., PESETSKY, D., and RODRIGUES, C. (2009a). Evidence and argumentation: A reply to Everett (2009). *Language* 85: 671–681.

NEVINS, A., PESETSKY, D., and RODRIGUES, C. (2009b). Pirahã exceptionality: A reassessment. *Language* 85: 355–404.

NEWMEYER, F. J. (1991). Functional explanation in linguistics and the origin of language. *Language and Communication* 11: 3–28.

NEWMEYER, F. J. (1998). *Language form and language function.* Cambridge, MA: MIT Press.

NEWMEYER, F. J. (2004). *Cognitive and functional factors in the evolution of grammar.* http://www.interdisciplines.org/coevolution/papers/3.

NEWMEYER, F. J. (2005). *Possible and probable languages: A generative perspective on linguistic typology.* Oxford: Oxford University Press.

NEWPORT, E. L. and ASLIN, R. N. (2000). Innately constrained learning: Blending old and new approaches to language acquisition. In S. C. Howell, S. A. Fish, and T. Keith-Lucas (eds.), *Proceedings of the 24th Annual Boston University Conference on Language Development.* Somerville, MA: Cascadilla Press.

NEWPORT, E. L. and ASLIN, R. N. (2004). Learning at a distance I. Statistical learning of non-adjacent dependencies. *Cognitive Psychology* 48: 127–162.

NEWPORT, E. L., HAUSER, M. D., SPAEPEN, G., and ASLIN, R. N. (2004). Learning at a distance II. Statistical learning of non-adjacent dependencies in a non-human primate. *Cognitive Psychology* 49: 85–117.

NICOLIS, G. and PRIGOGINE, I. (1977). *Self-organization in non-equilibrium systems.* New York: John Wiley.

NICHOLS, J. (1992). *Linguistic diversity in space and time.* Chicago, IL: University of Chicago Press.

NICHOLS, J. (1994). Ergativity and linguistic geography. *Australian Journal of Linguistics* 13: 39–89.

NICHOLS, J. (1995). Diachronically stable structural features. In H. Andersen (ed.), *Historical linguistics 1993: Papers from the Eleventh International Conference on Historical Linguistics.* Amsterdam: John Benjamins, 337–356.

NICHOLS, J. (1996). The comparative method as heuristic. In Durie and Ross (eds.), 39–71.

NICHOLS, J. (1997). Modeling ancient population structures and movement in linguistics. *Annual Review of Anthropology* 26: 359–384.

NICHOLS, J. (2010a). Proof of Dene-Yeniseian relatedness. In J. Kari and B. A. Potter (eds.), *The Dene-Yeniseian connection.* Fairbanks, AK: Alaska Native Language Center, 266–278.

NICHOLS, J. (2010b). Macrofamilies, macroareas, and contact. In R. Hickey (ed.), *The handbook of language contact.* Oxford: Wiley-Blackwell, 361–378.

NICHOLS, J. and BICKEL, B. (2009). *The Autotyp genealogical and geographical classification.* http://www.uni-leipzig.de/~autotyp/

NIELSEN, R., BUSTAMANTE, C., CLARK, A. G., GLANOWSKI, S., SACKTON, T. B., HUBISZ, M. J., FLEDEL-ALON, A., TANENBAUM, D. M., CIVELLO, D., WHITE, T. J., SNINSKY, J. J., ADAMS, M. D., and CARGILL, M. (2005). A scan for positively selected genes in the genomes of humans and chimpanzees. *PLoS Biology* 3: e170.

NISHIDA, T. (1980). The leaf-clipping display: A newly discovered expressive gesture in wild chimpanzees. *Journal of Human Evolution* 9: 117–128.

NISHIMURA, T., MIKAMI, A., SUZUKI, J., and MATSUZAWA, T. (2006). Descent of the hyoid in chimpanzees: Evolution of face flattening and speech. *Journal of Human Evolution* 51: 244–254.

NISHITANI, N., SCHURMANN, M., AMUNTS, K., and HARI, R. (2005). Broca's region: From action to language. *Physiology* 20: 60–67.

NIYOGI, P. (2006). *The computational nature of language learning and evolution.* Cambridge, MA: MIT Press.

NOAD, M. J., CATO, D. H., BRYDEN, M. M., JENNER, M. N., and JENNER, K. C. S. (2001). Cultural revolution in whale song. *Nature* 408: 537.

NOLTE, J. (2008). *The human brain: An introduction to its functional anatomy* (8th edn.). St. Louis, MO: Mosby.

NOONAN, J. P. (2010). Neanderthal genomes and the evolution of modern humans. *Genome Research* 20: 457–553.

NOWICKI, S., SEARCY, W. A., and PETERS, S. (2002). Brain development, song learning and mate choice in birds: A review and experimental test of the 'nutritional stress hypothesis'. *Journal of Comparative Physiology A* 188: 1003–1014.

NUDO, R. J. and MASTERTON, R. B. (1990). Descending pathways to the spinal cord, IV: Some factors related to the amount of cortex devoted to the corticospinal tract. *Journal of Comparative Neurology* 296: 584–597.

OCHS, E. (1983). Cultural dimensions of language acquisition. In E. Ochs and B. B. Schieffelin (eds.), *Acquiring conversational competence.* London: Routledge and Kegan Paul, 185–191.

OCHS, E. (1992). Indexing gender. In A. Duranti and C. Goodwin (eds.), *Rethinking context: Language as an interactive phenomenon.* Cambridge: Cambridge University Press, 325–358.

OCHS, E. and SCHIEFFELIN, B. B. (1984). Language acquisition and socialization: Three developmental stories and their implications. In R. A. Shweder and R. A. LeVine (eds.), *Culture theory: Essays on mind, self, and emotion.* Cambridge: Cambridge University Press, 277–320.

O'CONNELL, J. F., HAWKES, K., and BLURTON JONES, N. G. (1999). Grandmothering and the evolution of *Homo erectus. Journal of Human Evolution* 36: 461–485.

ODLING-SMEE, F. J. and LALAND, K. N. (2009). Cultural niche construction: Evolution's cradle of language. In R. Botha and C. Knight (eds.) (2009b), 99–121.

ODLING-SMEE, F. J., LALAND, K. N., and FELDMAN, M. W. (2003). *Niche construction: The neglected process in evolution.* Princeton, NJ: Princeton University Press.

O'DONNELL, T., HAUSER, M. D., and FITCH, T. (2005). Using mathematical models of language experimentally. *Trends in Cognitive Sciences* 9: 284–289.

OKANOYA, K. (2002). Sexual display as a syntactical vehicle: The evolution of syntax in birdsong and human language through sexual selection. In Wray (ed.), 46–63.

OLLER, D. K. (2000). *The emergence of the speech capacity.* Mahwah, NJ: Lawrence Erlbaum.

OLLER, D. K. and GRIEBEL, U. (eds.) (2004). *The evolution of communication systems: A comparative approach.* Cambridge, MA: MIT Press.

OLLER, D. K. and GRIEBEL, U. (2008a). Contextual flexibility in infant vocal development and the earliest steps in the evolution of language. In Oller and Griebel (2008b) (eds.), 141–168.

OLLER, D. K. and GRIEBEL, U. (eds.) (2008b). *Evolution of communicative flexibility: Complexity, creativity, and adaptability in human and animal communication.* Cambridge, MA: MIT Press.

OLLER, D. K., EILERS, R. E., BULL, D. H., and CARNEY, A. E. (1985). Prespeech vocalizations of a deaf infant. *Journal of Speech and Hearing Research* 28: 47–63.

O'SULLIVAN, C. and YEAGER, C. P. (1989). Communicative competence and linguistic competence: The effects of social setting on chimpanzees' conversational skill. In Gardner et al. (eds.), 269–279.

OTERO, C. (1990).The emergence of homo loquens and the laws of physics. *Behavioral and Brain Sciences* 13: 747–750.

OTT, D. (2009). The evolution of I-language: Lexicalization as the key evolutionary novelty. *Biolinguistics* 3: 255–269.

OUATTARA, K., ZUBERBÜHLER, K., N'GORAN, E. K., GOBERT, J.-E., and LEMASSON, A. (2009). The alarm call system of female Campbell's monkeys. *Animal Behaviour* 78: 35–44.

OUDEYER, P.-Y. (2005). The self-organization of speech sounds. *Journal of Theoretical Biology* 233: 435–449.

OUDEYER, P.-Y. (2006). *Self-organization in the evolution of speech.* Oxford: Oxford University Press.

OWREN, M. J. and GOLDSTEIN, M. H. (2008). Scaffolds for babbling: Innateness and learning in the emergence of contextually flexible vocal production in human infants. In Oller and Griebel (2008b) (eds.), 169–192.

OWREN, M. J., DIETER, J. A., SEYFARTH, R. M., and CHENEY, D. L. (1993). Vocalizations of rhesus and Japanese macaques cross-fostered between species show evidence of only limited modification. *Developmental Psychobiology* 26: 389–406.

OWREN, M. J., SEYFARTH, R. M., and CHENEY, D. L. (1997). The acoustic features of vowel-like grunt calls in chacma baboons (*Papio cynocephalus ursinus*): Implications for production processes and functions. *Journal of the Acoustical Society of America* 101: 2951–2963.

OYAMA, S. (1985). *The ontogeny of information.* Cambridge: Cambridge University Press.

PACK, A. A. and HERMAN, L. M. (1995). Sensory integration in the bottlenosed dolphin: Immediate recognition of complex shapes across the senses of echolocation and vision. *Journal of the Acoustical Society of America* 98: 722–733.

PAGEL, M., ATKINSON, Q. D., and MEADE, A. (2007). Frequency of word-use predicts rates of lexical evolution throughout Indo-European history. *Nature* 449: 717–720.

PAKENDORF, B. (2007). *Contact in the prehistory of the Sakha (Yakuts): Linguistic and genetic perspectives.* Utrecht: LOT.

PAKENDORF, B. and STONEKING, M. (2005). Mitochondrial DNA and human evolution. *Annual Review of Genomics and Human Genetics* 6: 165–183.

PAKENDORF, B., NOVGORODOV, I. N., OSAKOVSKIJ, V. L., DANILOVA, A. P., PROTOD'JAKONOV, A. P., and STONEKING, M. (2006). Investigating the effects of prehistoric migrations in Siberia: Genetic variation and the origins of Yakuts. *Human Genetics* 120: 334–353.

PAPOUSEK, M., PAPOUSEK, H., and SYMMES, D. (1991). The meanings of melodies in motherese in tone and stress languages. *Infant Behavior and Development* 14: 415–440.

PAPWORTH, S., BÖSE, A.-S., BARKER, J., and ZUBERBÜHLER, K. (2008). Male blue monkeys alarm call in response to danger experienced by others. *Biology Letters* 4: 472–475.

PARKER, A. R. (2005). Evolving the narrow language faculty: Was recursion the pivotal step? Unpublished ms., Language Evolution and Computation Research Unit, University of Edinburgh.

PARKER, S. T. and GIBSON, K. R. (1977). Object manipulation, tool use and sensorimotor intelligence as feeding adaptations in Cebus monkeys and great apes. *Journal of Human Evolution* 6: 623–641.

PARKER, S. T. and GIBSON, K. R. (1979). A model of the evolution of language and intelligence in early hominids. *Behavioral and Brain Sciences* 2: 367–407.

PARKER, S. T. and GIBSON, K. R. (eds.) (1990). *'Language' and intelligence in monkeys and apes: Comparative developmental perspectives.* Cambridge: Cambridge University Press.

PARKER, S. T., MITCHELL, R. W., and MILES, H. L. (eds.) (1999). *The mentalities of gorillas and orangutans: Comparative perspectives.* Cambridge: Cambridge University Press.

PARSONS, L. (2003). Exploring the functional neuroanatomy of music performance, perception and comprehension. In Peretz and Zatorre (eds.), 247–268.

PASSINGHAM, R. E. (1975). Changes in size and organization of the brain of man and his ancestors. *Brain, Behavior and Evolution* 11: 73–90.

PATEL, A. D. (2003). Language, music, syntax and the brain. *Nature Neuroscience* 6: 674–681.

PATEL, A. D. (2007). *Music, language, and the brain.* New York: Oxford University Press.

PATTERSON, D. K. and PEPPERBERG, I. M. (1994). A comparative study of human and parrot phonation: Acoustic and articulatory correlates of vowels. *Journal of the Acoustical Society of America* 96: 634–648.

PATTERSON, D. K. and PEPPERBERG, I. M. (1998). Acoustic and articulatory correlates of stop consonants in a parrot and a human subject. *Journal of the Acoustical Society of America* 103: 2197–2215.

PATTERSON, F. G. (1978). The gestures of a gorilla: Language acquisition in another pongid. *Brain and Language* 5: 72–97.

PATTERSON, F. G. and LINDEN, E. (1981). *The education of Koko.* New York: Holt, Rinehart and Winston.

PATTERSON, N., RICHTER, D. J., GNERRE, S., LANDER, E. S., and REICH, D. (2006). Genetic evidence for complex speciation of humans and chimpanzees. *Nature* 441: 1103–1108.

PAVARD, S., SIBERT, A., and HEYER, E. (2007). The effect of maternal care on child survival: A demographic, genetic, and evolutionary perspective. *Evolution* 61: 1153–1161.

PAWLEY, A., and SYDER, F. H. (1983). Two puzzles for linguistic theory: Nativelike selection and nativelike fluency. In J. C. Richards and R. W. Schmidt (eds.), *Language and communication.* London: Longman, 191–226.

PAYNE, K. (2000). The progressively changing songs of humpback whales: A window on the creative process in a wild animal. In Wallin et al. (eds.), 135–150.

PAYNE, K. and PAYNE, R. (1985). Large scale changes over 19 years in songs of humpback whales in Bermuda. *Zeitschrift für Tierpsychologie* 68: 89–114.

PAYNE, K., TYACK, P., and PAYNE, R. (1983). Progressive changes in the songs of humpback whales (*Megaptera novaeangliae*): A detailed analysis of two seasons in Hawaii. In R. Payne (ed.), *Communication and behavior of whales.* Boulder, CO: Westview Press, 9–57.

PEIRCE, C. S. (1931). *Collected papers of Charles Sanders Peirce. Vol. II Elements of logic.* C. Hartshorn and P. Weiss (eds.) Cambridge, MA: Harvard University Press.

PENN, D. C., HOLYOAK, K., and POVINELLI, D. (2008). Darwin's mistake: Explaining the discontinuity between human and nonhuman minds. *Behavioral and Brain Sciences* 31: 109–178.

PENNINGTON, B. F. (2002). *The development of psychopathology.* New York: Guilford Press.

PEPPERBERG, I. M. (2000). *The Alex studies: Cognitive and communicative abilities of Grey parrots.* Cambridge, MA: Harvard University Press.

PEPPERBERG, I. M. (2005). An avian perspective on language evolution: Implications of simultaneous development of vocal and phsyical object combinations by a Grey parrot (*Psittacus erithacus*). In Tallerman (ed.), 239–261.

PEPPERBERG, I. M. (2007a). Emergence of linguistic communication: Studies on Grey parrots. In Lyon et al. (eds.), 355–386.

PEPPERBERG, I. M. (2007b). Grey parrots do not always 'parrot': Roles of imitation and phonological awareness in the creation of new labels from existing vocalizations. *Language Sciences* 29: 1–13.

PEPPERBERG, I. M. (2010). Vocal learning in Grey parrots: A brief review of perception, production, and cross-species comparisons. *Brain and Language* 115: 81–91.

PEPPERBERG, I. M. (2013). Evolution of vocal communication: an avian model. In J. J. Bolhuis and M. Everaert (eds.), Birdsong, speech, and language: *Exploring the evolution of mind and brain.* Cambridge, MA: MIT Press, 261–274.

PEPPERBERG, I. M. and GORDON, J. D. (2005). Numerical comprehension by a Grey parrot (*Psittacus erithacus*), including a zero-like concept. *Journal of Comparative Psychology* 119: 197–209.

PEPPERBERG, I. M. and SCHINKE-LLANO, L. (1991). Language acquisition and use in a bilingual environment: A framework for studying birdsong in zones of sympatry. *Ethology* 89: 1–28.

PEPPERBERG, I. M. and SHIVE, H. (2001). Simultaneous development of vocal and physical object combinations by a Grey parrot (*Psittacus erithacus*): Bottle caps, lids, and labels. *Journal of Comparative Psychology* 115: 376–384.

PERETZ, I. and ZATORRE, R. J. (eds.) (2003). *The cognitive neuroscience of music.* Oxford: Oxford University Press.

PERETZ, I., AYOTTE, J., ZATORRE, R. J., MEHLER, J., AHAD, P., PENHUNE, B., and JUTRAS, B. (2002). Congenital amusia: A disorder of fine-grained pitch discrimination. *Neuron* 33: 185–191.

PERKEL, D. J. (2004). Origin of the anterior forebrain pathway. *Annals of the New York Academy of Sciences* 1016: 736–748.

PERNER, J., LANG, B., and KLOO, D. (2002). Theory of mind and self-control: More than a common problem of inhibition. *Child Development* 73: 752–767.

PETRIDES, M., CADORET, G., and MACKEY, S. (2005). Orofacial somatomotor responses in the macaque monkey homologue of Broca's area. *Nature* 435: 1235–1238.

PHELPS, E. A. (2004). Human emotion and memory: Interactions of the amygdala and hippocampal complex. *Current Opinion in Neurobiology* 14: 198–202.

PIATTELLI-PALMARINI, M. (1974). Transcript of the 'Debate on Biolinguistics' meeting held at Endicott House, Dedham, Mass., May 20–21, 1974. Ms.

PIATTELLI-PALMARINI, M. (1989). Evolution, selection, and cognition: From 'learning' to parameter setting in biology and in the study of language. *Cognition* 31: 1–44.

PIATTELLI-PALMARINI, M. (1990). An ideological battle over modals and quantifiers. *Behavioral and Brain Sciences* 13: 752–754.

PIATTELLI-PALMARINI, M. (2006). The return of the laws of form. Life on the Edge (*La Vita in Bilico*). C. P. Manzù. Roma (Italy), Centro Pio Manzu'. Volume 2 (Workshop 1): 45–57.

PIATTELLI-PALMARINI, M. (2010). What is language, that it may have evolved, and what is evolution, that it may apply to language? In Larson et al. (eds.), 148–162.

PIATTELLI-PALMARINI, M. and URIAGEREKA, J. (2011). A geneticist's dream, a linguist's nightmare: The case of FOXP2. In A.-M. Di Sciullo and C. Boeckx (eds.), *The biolinguistic enterprise*. Oxford: Oxford University Press, 100–125.

PIERREHUMBERT, J. (2001). Exemplar dynamics: Word frequency, lenition and contrast. In J. Bybee and P. Hopper (eds.), *Frequency and the emergence of linguistic structure*. Amsterdam/Philadelphia: John Benjamins, 137–157.

PIETRANDREA, P. (2002). Iconicity and arbitrariness in Italian Sign Language. *Sign Language Studies* 2: 296–321.

PIETROSKI, P. (2008). Minimalist meaning, internalist interpretation. *Biolinguistics* 2: 317–341.

PIGLIUCCI, M. (2007). Do we need an extended evolutionary synthesis? *Evolution* 61: 2743–2749.

PIKA, S. and MITANI, J. C. (2009). The directed scratch: Evidence for a referential gesture in chimpanzees? In Botha and Knight (eds.) (2009b), 166–180.

PIKA, S. and ZUBERBÜHLER, K. (2008). Social games between bonobos and humans: Evidence for shared intentionality? *American Journal of Primatology* 70: 207–210.

PIKA, S., LIEBAL, K., and TOMASELLO, M. (2003). Gestural communication in young gorillas (*Gorilla gorilla*): Gestural repertoire, learning, and use. *American Journal of Primatology* 60: 95–111.

PIKA, S., LIEBAL, K., CALL, J., and TOMASELLO, M. (2005a). The gestural communication of apes. *Gesture* 5: 41–56.

PIKA, S., LIEBAL, K., and TOMASELLO, M. (2005b). Gestural communication in subadult bonobos (*Pan paniscus*): Repertoire and use. *American Journal of Primatology* 65: 39–61.

PINKER, S. (1997). *How the mind works*. New York: W.W. Norton.

PINKER, S. (2003). Language as an adaptation to the cognitive niche. In Christiansen and Kirby (eds.), 16–37.

PINKER, S. (2004). Why nature and nurture won't go away. *Daedalus* 133: 5–17.

PINKER, S. and BLOOM, P. (1990). Natural language and natural selection. *Behavioral and Brain Sciences* 13: 707–784.

PINKER, S. and JACKENDOFF, R. (2005). The faculty of language: What's special about it? *Cognition* 95: 201–236.

PINKER, S., NOWAK, M. A., and LEE, J. J. (2007). The logic of indirect speech. *Proceedings of the National Academy of Sciences of the USA* 105: 833–838.

PIPITONE, R. N. and GALLUP, G. G. (2008). Women's voice attractiveness varies across the menstrual cycle. *Evolution and Human Behavior* 29: 268–274.

PLOOG, D. (2002). Is the neural basis of vocalisation different in non-human primates and *Homo sapiens*? In T. J. Crow (ed.), *The speciation of modern* Homo sapiens. Oxford: Oxford University Press, 121–135.

PODOS, J., HUBER, S. K., and TAFT, B. (2004). Bird song: The interface of evolution and mechanism. *Annual Review of Ecology, Evolution and Systematics* 35: 55–87.

POIRER, F. E. (1970). The Nilgiri langur (*Presbytis johnii*) of South India. In L. A. Rosenblum (ed.), *Primate behaviour: Developments in field and laboratory*. New York: Academic Press, 251–383.

POLLICK, A. S. (2006). Gestures and multimodal signalling in bonobos and chimpanzees. *Dissertation Abstracts International: Section B: The Sciences and Engineering* 67: 1744.

POLLICK, A. S. and DE WAAL, F. B. M. (2007). Ape gestures and language evolution. *Proceedings of the National Academy of Sciences of the USA* 104: 8184–8189.

POLLICK, A. S., JENESON, A., and DE WAAL, F. B. M. (2008). Gestures and multimodal signalling in bonobos. In T. Furuichi and J. Thompson (eds.), *The bonobos: Behavior, ecology, and conservation.* New York: Springer, 75–94.

POOLE, J. H., TYACK, T. L., STOEGER-HORWATH, A. S., and WATWOOD, S. (2005). Animal behaviour: Elephants are capable of vocal learning. *Nature* 434: 455–456.

POPPE, N. N. (1960). *Buriat grammar.* Bloomington, IN: Indiana University.

POREMBA, A., MALLOY, M., SAUNDERS, R., CARSON, R., HERSKOVITCH, P., and MISHKIN, M. (2004). Species-specific calls evoke asymmetric activity in the monkey's temporal poles. *Nature* 427: 448–451.

POULIN-DUBOIS, D., GRAHAM, S., and SIPPOLA, L. (1995). Early lexical development: The contribution of parent labeling and infants' categorization abilities. *Journal of Child Language* 22: 325–343.

POWELL, A., SHENNAN, S., and THOMAS, M. G. (2009). Late Pleistocene demography and the appearance of modern human behavior. *Science* 324: 1298–1301.

POWELL, G. V. N. and BJORK, R. D. (2004). Habitat linkages and the conservation of tropical biodiversity as indicated by seasonal migrations of three-wattled bellbirds. *Conservation Biology* 18: 500–509.

POWER, C. and AIELLO, L. C. (1997). Female proto-symbolic strategies. In L. D. Hager (ed.), *Women in human evolution.* New York and London: Routledge, 153–171.

PRATHER, J. F., PETERS, S., NOWICKI, S., and MOONEY, R. (2008). Precise auditory-vocal mirroring in neurons for learned vocal communication. *Nature* 451: 305–310.

PREMACK, D. (1977). *Intelligence in ape and man.* Mahwah, NJ: Lawrence Erlbaum.

PREMACK, D. (1985). 'Gavagai!' or the future history of the animal language controversy. *Cognition* 19: 207–296.

PREMACK, D. and WOODRUFF, G. (1978). Does the chimpanzee have a theory of mind? *Behavioral and Brain Sciences* 1: 515–526.

PREMO, L. S. and HUBLIN, J.-J. (2009). Culture, population structure, and low genetic diversity in Pleistocene hominins. *Proceedings of the National Academy of Sciences of the USA* 106: 33–37.

PREUSS, T. M. (2007). Evolutionary specializations of primate brain systems. In M. J. Ravosa and M. Dagasto (eds.), *Primate origins: Adaptations and evolution.* New York: Springer, 625–675.

PRINCE, A. and SMOLENSKY, P. (1997). Optimality: From neural networks to universal grammar. *Science* 275: 1604–1610.

PROGOVAC, L. and LOCKE, J. L. (2009). Exocentric compounds, ritual insult, and the evolution of syntax. *Biolinguistics* 3: 337–354.

PROOPS, L., McCOMB, K., and REBY, D. (2008). Cross-modal individual recognition in domestic horses (*Equus caballus*). *Proceedings of the National Academy of Sciences of the USA* 106: 947–951.

PRUETZ, J. D. and BERTOLANI, P. (2007). Savanna chimpanzees, *Pan troglodytes verus*, hunt with tools. *Current Biology* 17: 412–417.

PULLUM, G. K. and SCHOLZ, B. C. (2002). Empirical assessment of stimulus poverty arguments. *The Linguistic Review* 19: 9–50.

QUARTZ, S. R. and SEJNOWSKI, T. J. (1997). The neural basis of cognitive development: A constructivist manifesto. *Behavioral and Brain Sciences* 20: 537–596.

QUINE, W. V. O. (1960). *Word and object*. Cambridge, MA: MIT Press.

QUINN, M. (2001). Evolving communication without dedicated communication channels. In J. Kelemen and P. Sosík (eds.), *Proceedings of ECAL01*. London: Springer, 357–366.

RADFORD, A. N. and DU PLESSIS, M. A. (2008). Dual function of allopreening in the cooperatively breeding green woodhoopoe, *Pheoniculus purpureus. Behavioral Ecology and Sociobiology* 61: 221–230.

RALLS, K., FIORELLI, P., and GISH, S. (1985). Vocalizations and vocal mimicry in captive harbor seals, *Phoca vitulina. Canadian Journal of Zoology* 63: 1050–1056.

RANKIN, S., OSWALD, J., BARLOW, J., and LAMMERS, M. (2007). Patterned burst-pulse vocalizations of the northern right whale dolphin, *Lissodelphis borealis. Journal of the Acoustical Society of America* 121: 1213–1218.

RAYMOND, M. and PONTIER, D. (2004). Is there geographical variation in human handedness? *Laterality* 9: 35–51.

REALI, F. and GRIFFITHS, T. L. (2009). The evolution of frequency distributions: Relating regularization to inductive biases through iterated learning. *Cognition* 111: 317–328.

REDFORD, M. A., CHEN, C. C., and MIIKKULAINEN, R. (2001). Constrained emergence of universals and variation in syllable systems. *Language and Speech* 44: 27–56.

REDICAN, W. K. and MITCHELL, G. (1974). Play between adult male and infant Rhesus monkeys. *American Zoologist* 14: 295–302.

REICH, D., GREEN, R. E., KIRCHER, M., KRAUSE, J., PATTERSON, N., DUR, E. Y., VIOLA, B., BRIGGS, A. W., STENZEL, U., JOHNSON, P. L. F., MARICIC, T., GOOD, J. M., MARQUES-BONET, T., ALKAN, C., FU, Q., MALLICK, S., LI, H., MEYER, M., EICHLER, E. E., STONEKING, M., RICHARDS, M., TALAMO, S., SHUNKOV, M. V., DEREVIANKO, A. P., HUBLIN, J.-J., KELSO, J., SLATKIN, M., and PÄÄBO, S. (2010). Genetic history of an archaic hominin group from Denisova Cave in Siberia. *Nature* 468: 1053–1060.

REISS, D. and McCOWAN, B. (1993). Spontaneous vocal mimicry and production by bottlenose dolphins (*Tursiops truncatus*): Evidence for vocal learning. *Journal of Comparative Psychology* 107: 301–312.

REISS, D. and MARINO, L. (2001). Mirror self-recognition in the bottlenose dolphin: A case of cognitive convergence. *Proceedings of the National Academy of Sciences of the USA* 98: 5937–5942.

RENDELL, L. E. and WHITEHEAD, H. (2003). Acoustic clans in sperm whales (*Physeter macrocephalus*). *Proceedings of the Royal Society of London B* 270: 225–231.

REULAND, E. (2008). Imagination, planning, and working memory: The emergence of language. Paper presented at the Wenner-Gren Foundation Symposium 139: Working Memory and the Evolution of Modern Thinking, Cascais, Portugal.

REZNICK, D. N. and GHALAMBOR, C. K. (2005). Selection in nature: Experimental manipulations of natural populations. *Integrative and Comparative Biology* 45: 456–462.

REZNICK, D. N., BRYGA, H., and ENDLER, J. A. (1990). Experimentally induced life-history evolution in a natural population. *Nature* 346: 357–359.

RICHARDS, D. G., WOLZ, J. P., and HERMAN, L. M. (1984). Vocal mimicry of computer-generated sounds and vocal labeling of objects by a bottlenosed dolphin, *Tursiops truncatus. Journal of Comparative Psychology* 98: 10–28.

RICHMAN, B. (1987). Rhythm and melody in gelada vocal exchanges. *Primates* 28: 199–223.

RIDLEY, M. (1993). *Evolution*. Cambridge, MA: Blackwell Scientific.

RIEDE, T. and ZUBERBÜHLER, K. (2003a). Pulse register phonation in Diana monkey alarm calls. *Journal of the Acoustical Society of America* 113: 2919–2926.

Riede, T. and Zuberbühler, K. (2003b). The relationship between acoustic structure and semantic information in Diana monkey alarm vocalization. *Journal of the Acoustical Society of America* 114: 1132–1142.

Riede, T., Bronson, E., Hatzikirou, H., and Zuberbühler, K. (2005). Vocal production mechanisms in a non-human primate: Morphological data and a model. *Journal of Human Evolution* 48: 85–96.

Riede, T., Bronson, E., Hatzikirou, H., and Zuberbühler, K. (2006). Multiple discontinuities in nonhuman vocal tracts: A response to Lieberman (2006). *Journal of Human Evolution* 50: 222–225.

Riel-Salvatore, J. (2010). A niche construction perspective on the Middle-Upper Paleolithic transition in Italy. *Journal of Archaeological Method and Theory* 17: 323–355.

Rightmire, G. P. (1990). *The evolution of* Homo erectus. Cambridge: Cambridge University Press.

Rightmire, G. P. and Lordkipanidze, D. (2009). Comparisons of Early Pleistocene skulls from East Africa and the Georgian Caucasus: Evidence bearing on the origin and systematic of Genus *Homo*. In Grine et al. (eds.) 39–48.

Rizzi, L. (2009). Some elements of syntactic computations. In Bickerton and Szathmáry (eds.), 63–87.

Rizzolatti, G. and Arbib, M. A. (1998). Language within our grasp. *Trends in Neurosciences* 21: 188–194.

Rizzolatti, G. and Sinigaglia, C. (2008). *Mirrors in the brain.* Oxford: Oxford University Press.

Rizzolatti, G., Fadiga, L., Gallese, V., and Fogassi, L. (1996a). Premotor cortex and the recognition of motor actions. *Cognitive Brain Research* 3: 131–141.

Rizzolatti, G., Fadiga, L., Matelli, M., Bettinardi, V., Paulesu, E., Perani, D., and Fazio, F. (1996b). Localization of grasp representations in humans by PET: 1. Observation versus execution. *Experimental Brain Research* 111: 246–252.

Roberge, P. T. (2009). The creation of pidgins as a possible window on language evolution. In Botha and de Swart (eds.), 101–137.

Robinson, J. T. (1960). The affinities of the new Olduvai australopithecine. *Nature* 186: 456–458.

Roche, H., Blumenschine, R. J., and Shea, J. J. (2009). Origins and adaptations of early *Homo*: What archaeology tells us. In Grine et al. (eds.), 135–147.

Rogers, A. R., Wooding, S., Chad, C. D., Batzer, M. A., and Jorde, L. B. (2007). Ancestral alleles and population origins: Inferences depend on mutation rate. *Molecular Biology and Evolution* 24: 990–997.

Rogers, L. J. and Andrew, R. J. (2002). *Comparative vertebrate lateralization.* Cambridge: Cambridge University Press.

Rosenberg, J. and Tunney, R. J. (2008). Human vocabulary use as display. *Evolutionary Psychology* 6: 538–549.

Ross, C. and MacLarnon, A. (2000). The evolution of non-maternal care in anthropoid primates: A test of the hypotheses. *Folia Primatologica* 71: 93–113.

Ross, C. and Regan, G. (2000). Allocare, predation risk, social structure and natal coat colour in anthropoid primates. *Folia Primatologica* 71: 67–76.

Ross, M. (1996). Contact-induced change and the comparative method: Cases from Papua New Guinea. In Durie and Ross (eds.), 180–217.

Ross, M. (2003). Diagnosing prehistoric language contact. In Hickey (ed.), 174–198.

Rougier, II., Milota, Ş., Rodrigo, R. R., Gherase, M., Sarcina, L., Moldovan, O., Zilhão, J., Constantin, S., Franciscus, R. G., Zollikofer, C. P. E., Ponce de León, M., and Trinkaus, E. (2007). Peştera cu Oase 2 and the cranial morphology of early modern Europeans. *Proceedings of the National Academy of Sciences of the USA* 104: 1165–1170.

Rousset, I. (2003). From lexical to syllabic organization: Favored and disfavored co-occurrences. *Proceedings of the 15th International Congress of Phonetics*. Barcelona: Autonomous University of Barcelona, 2705–2708.

Rumbaugh, D. M. (ed.) (1977). *Language learning by a chimpanzee. The Lana project.* New York: Academic Press.

Russon, A. E. and Galdikas, B. M. F. (1993). Imitation in free-ranging rehabilitant orangutans (*Pongo pygmaeus*). *Journal of Comparative Psychology* 107: 147–161.

Russon, A. E. and Galdikas, B. M. F. (1995). Constraints on great apes' imitation: Model and action selectivity in rehabilitant orangutan (*Pongo pygmaeus*) imitation. *Journal of Comparative Psychology* 109: 5–17.

Sabeti, P. C., Reich, D. E., Higgins, J. M., Levine, H. Z. P., Richter, D. J., Schaffner, S. F., Gabriel, S. B., Platko, J. V., Patterson, N. J., McDonald, G. J., Ackerman, H. C., Campbell, S. J., Altshuler, D., Cooper, R., Kwiatkowski, D., Ward, R., and Lander, E. S. (2002). Detecting recent positive selection in the human genome from haplotype structure. *Nature* 419: 832–837.

Sabeti, P. C., Schaffner, S. F., Fry, B., Lohmueller, J., Varilly, P., Shamovsky, O., Palma, A., Mikkelsen, T. S., Altshuler, D., and Lander, E. S. (2006). Positive natural selection in the human lineage. *Science* 312: 1614–1620.

Sadato, N., Pascual-Leone, A., Grafman, J., Deiber, M. P., Ibañez, V., and Hallett, M. (1998). Neural networks for Braille reading by the blind. *Brain* 121: 1213–1229.

Saffran, J. R. (2002). Constraints on statistical language learning. *Journal of Memory and Language* 47: 172–196.

Saffran, J. R. and Thiessen, E. D. (2003). Pattern induction by infant language learners. *Developmental Psychology* 39: 484–494.

Saffran, J. R. and Wilson, D. P. (2003). From syllables to syntax: Multilevel statistical learning by 12-month-old infants. *Infancy* 4: 273–284.

Saffran, J. R., Aslin, R. N., and Newport, E. L. (1996). Statistical learning by 8-month-old infants. *Science* 274: 1926–1928.

Saffran, J. R., Hauser, M. D., Seibel, R., Kapfhamer, J., Tsao, F., and Cushman, F. (2008). Grammatical pattern learning by human infants and cotton-top tamarin monkeys. *Cognition* 107: 479–500.

Saino, N., Ninni, P., Calza, S., Martinelli, R., De Berardi, F., and Moller, A. P. (2000). Better red than dead: Carotenoid-based mouth coloration reveals infection in barn swallow nestlings. *Proceedings of the Royal Society of London B* 26: 57–61.

St-Louis, B., Corbeil, M., Achim, A., and Harnad, S. (2008). Acquiring the mental lexicon through sensorimotor category learning. Sixth Annual Conference on the Mental Lexicon, University of Alberta, Banff Alberta, 7–10 October 2008. http://eprints.ecs.soton.ac.uk/16620/

Sakai, M., Hishii, T., Takeda, S., and Kohshima, S. (2006). Laterality of flipper rubbing behaviour in wild bottlenose dolphins (*Tursiops aduncus*): Caused by asymmetry of eye use? *Behavioral Brain Research* 170: 204–210.

SAKEL, J. (2007). Type of loan: Matter and pattern. In Y. Matras and J. Sakel (eds.), *Grammatical borrowing in cross-linguistic perspective*. Berlin and New York: Mouton de Gruyter, 15–29.

SALTZMAN, E. L. and MUNHALL, K. G. (1989). A dynamical approach to gestural patterning in speech production. *Ecological Psychology* 1: 333–382.

SAMPSON, G., GIL, D., and TRUDGILL, P. (eds.) (2009). *Language complexity as an evolving variable*. Oxford: Oxford University Press.

SAMUELS, B. (2009a). The structure of phonological theory. Unpublished PhD thesis, Harvard University.

SAMUELS, B. (2009b). The third factor in phonology. *Biolinguistics* 3: 355–382.

SAMUELS, R. (2004). Innateness in cognitive science. *Trends in Cognitive Sciences* 8: 136–141.

SANDLER, W. (2003). On the complementarity of signed and spoken language. In Y. Levy and J. Schaeffer (eds.), *Language competence across populations: On the definition of SLI*. Mahwah, NJ: Lawrence Erlbaum, 383–409.

SANDLER, W. and LILLO-MARTIN, D. (2006). *Sign language and linguistic universals*. Cambridge: Cambridge University Press.

SANDLER, W., MEIR, I., PADDEN, C., and ARONOFF, M. (2005). The emergence of grammar: Systematic structure in a new language. *Proceedings of the National Academy of Sciences of the USA* 102: 2661–2665.

SANKOFF, G. (1979). The genesis of a language. In Hill (ed.), 23–47.

SANTONJA, M. and VILLA, P. (1990). The Lower Paleolithic of Spain and Portugal. *Journal of World Prehistory* 4: 45–94.

SAPIR, E. (1921). *Language: An introduction to the study of speech*. New York: Harcourt Brace.

SARICH, V. M. (1984). Pygmy chimpanzee systematics: A molecular perspective. In R. L. Sussman (ed.), *The Pygmy chimpanzee: Evolutionary biology and behavior*. New York: Plenum Press, 43–48.

SARICH V. M. and WILSON, A. C. (1967). Immunological time scale for hominoid evolution. *Science* 158: 1200–1203.

SAUSSURE, F. DE (1916/1976). *Cours de linguistique générale* (edited by C. Bally, A. Sechehaye, and A. Riedlinger; critical edn. by T. de Mauro). Paris: Payot.

SAUSSURE, F. DE (1983). *Course in General Linguistics* (edited by C. Bally and A. Sechehaye. Translated by Roy Harris). La Salle, IL: Open Court.

SAVAGE-RUMBAUGH, E. S. (1986). *Ape language: From conditioned response to symbol*. New York: Columbia University Press.

SAVAGE-RUMBAUGH, E. S. (1991). Language learning in the bonobo: How and why they learn. In Krasnegor et al. (eds.), 209–233.

SAVAGE-RUMBAUGH, E. S. and FIELDS, W. (2006). Rules and tools: Beyond anthropomorphism. In N. Toth and K. Schick (eds.), *The Oldowan: Case studies into the earliest Stone Age*. Gosport, IN: Stone Age Institute Press, 223–242.

SAVAGE-RUMBAUGH, E. S. and LEWIN, R. (1994). *Kanzi: The ape at the brink of the human mind*. New York: John Wiley and Sons.

SAVAGE-RUMBAUGH, E. S., RUMBAUGH, D. M., and BOYSEN, S. (1978). Linguistically mediated tool use and exchange by chimpanzees (*Pan troglodytes*). *Behavioral and Brain Sciences* 1: 539–554.

SAVAGE-RUMBAUGH, E. S., MURPHY, J., SEVCIK, R. A., BRAKKE, K. E., WILLIAMS, S. L., and RUMBAUGH, D. M. (1993). *Language comprehension in ape and child. Monographs of the Society for Research in Child Development* 58.

SAVAGE-RUMBAUGH, E. S., SHANKAR, S. G., and TAYLOR, T. (1998). *Apes, language, and the human mind.* New York and Oxford: Oxford University Press.

SAYIGH, L. S., ESCH, H. C., WELLS, R. S., and JANIK, V. M. (2007). Facts about signature whistles of bottlenose dolphins (*Tursiops truncatus*). *Animal Behaviour* 74: 1631–1642.

SCELZA, B. A. (2009). The grandmaternal niche: Critical caretaking among Martu Aborigines. *American Journal of Human Biology* 21: 448–454.

SCHEIBEL, A. B., PAUL, L. A., FRIED, I., FORSYTHE, A. B., TOMIYASU, U., WECHSLER, W., KAO, A., and SLOTNICK, J. (1985). Dendritic organization of the anterior speech area. *Experimental Neurology* 87: 109–117.

SCHEL, A. M., TRANQUILLI, S., and ZUBERBÜHLER, K. (2009). The alarm call system of two species of black-and-white colobus monkeys (*Colobus polykomos* and *Colobus guereza*). *Journal of Comparative Psychology* 123: 136–150.

SCHENKER, N. M., BUXHOEVEDEN, D. P., BLACKMON, W. L., AMUNTS, K., ZILLES, K., and SEMENDEFERI, K. (2008). A comparative quantitative analysis of cytoarchitecture and minicolumnar organization in Broca's area in humans and great apes. *Journal of Comparative Neurology* 510: 117–128.

SCHENKER, N. M., HOPKINS, W. D., SPOCTER, M. A., GARRISON, A., STIMPSON, C. D., ERWIN, J. M., HOF, P. R., and SHERWOOD, C. C. (2009). Broca's area homologue in chimpanzees (*Pan troglodytes*): Probabilistic mapping, asymmetry and comparison to humans. *Cerebral Cortex* 20: 730–742.

SCHERER, S. (2008). *A short guide to the human genome.* Cold Spring Harbor, NY: Cold Spring Harbor Press.

SCHICK, K. and TOTH, N. (1993). *Making silent stones speak: Human evolution and the dawn of technology.* New York: Simon and Schuster.

SCHICK, K., TOTH, N., GARUFI, G., SAVAGE-RUMBAUGH, E. S., RUMBAUGH, D., and SEVCIK, R. (1999). Continuing investigations into the stone tool-making capabilities of a bonobo (*Pan paniscus*). *Journal of Archaeological Science* 26: 821–832.

SCHIEFFELIN, B. B. (1985). The acquisition of Kaluli. In D. I. Slobin (ed.), *The crosslinguistic study of language acquisition Vol. 1.* Hillsdale, NJ: Lawrence Erlbaum, 525–593.

SCHIEFFELIN, B. B. (1990). *The give and take of everyday life: Language socialization of Kaluli children.* Cambridge: Cambridge University Press.

SCHÖN YBARRA, M. A. (1995). A comparative approach to the non-human primate vocal tract: Implications for sound production. In E. Zimmermann, J. D. Newman, and U. Jürgens (eds.), *Current topics in primate vocal communication.* New York: Plenum, 185–198.

SCHULTZ, A. H. (1969). *The life of primates.* New York: Universe Books.

SCHUSTERMAN, R. J. (2008). Vocal learning in mammals with special emphasis on pinnipeds. In Oller and Griebel (2008b) (eds.), 41–70.

SCHUSTERMAN, R. J. and GISINER, R. C. (1988). Artificial language comprehension in dolphins and sea lions: The essential cognitive skills. *Psychological Record* 38: 311–348.

SCHUSTERMAN, R. J. and GISINER, R. C. (1997). Pinnipeds, porpoises, and parsimony: Animal language research viewed from a bottom-up perspective. In R. W. Mitchell, N. S. Thompson, and H. L. Miles (eds.), *Anthropomorphism, anecdotes, and animals.* New York: State University of New York Press, 370–382.

SCHWARTZ, B. L., MEISSNER, C. A., HOFFMAN, M. L., EVANS, S., and FRAZIER, L. D. (2004). Event memory and misinformation effects in a gorilla (*Gorilla gorilla gorilla*). *Animal Cognition* 7: 93–100.

SCHWARTZ, B. L., HOFFMAN, M. L., and EVANS, S. (2005). Episodic-like memory in a gorilla: A review and new findings. *Learning and Motivation* 36: 226–244.

SCHWARTZ, J.-L., BOË, L.-J., VALLÉE, N., and ABRY, C. (1997). The Dispersion-Focalization Theory of vowel systems. *Journal of Phonetics* 25: 255–286.

SCHWARTZ, J.-L., BOË, L.-J., and ABRY, C. (2007). Linking the dispersion-focalization theory (DFT) and the Maximum Utilization of the Available Distinctive Features (MUAF) principle in a Perception-For-Action-Control Theory (PACT). In M. J. Solé, P. S. Beddor, and M. Ohala (eds.), *Experimental approaches to phonology.* Oxford: Oxford University Press, 104–124.

SCOTT-PHILLIPS, T. C. (2006). Why talk? Speaking as selfish behaviour. In Cangelosi et al. (eds.), 299–306.

SCOTT-PHILLIPS, T. C., KIRBY, S., and RITCHIE, G. R. S. (2007). Signalling signalhood: An exploratory study into the emergence of communicative intentions. In A. Benz, C. Ebert, and R. van Rooij (eds.), *Proceedings of the ESSLLI 2007 workshop on Language, Games and Evolution.* Bielefeld: Universität Bielefeld, 77–84.

SCOTT-PHILLIPS, T. C., KIRBY, S., and RITCHIE, G. R. S. (2008). Signalling signalhood and the emergence of communication. In A. D. M. Smith et al. (eds.), 497–498.

SEBEOK, T. A. (ed.) (1977). *How animals communicate.* Bloomington, IN: Indiana University Press.

SEED, A. M., CLAYTON, N. S., and EMERY, N. J. (2008). Cooperative problem solving in rooks (*Corrus frugilegus*). *Proceedings of the Royal Society B: Biological Sciences* 275 : 1421–1429.

SELKIRK, E. O. (1982). *The syntax of words.* Cambridge, MA: MIT Press.

SEMAW, S., RENNE, P., HARRIS, J., FEIBEL, C. S., BERNOR, R., FESSEHA, N., and MOWBRAY, K. (1997). 2.5-million-year-old stone tools from Gona, Ethiopia. *Nature* 385: 333–336.

SENGHAS, A. and COPPOLA, M. (2001). Children creating language: How Nicaraguan Sign Language acquired a spatial grammar. *Psychological Science* 12: 323–328.

SENGHAS, A., KITA, S., and ÖZYÜREK, A. (2004). Children creating core properties of language: Evidence from an emerging sign language in Nicaragua. *Science* 305: 1779–1782.

SENUT, B., PICKFORD, M., GOMMERY, D., MEIN, P., CHEBOI, K., and COPPENS, Y. (2001). First hominid from the Miocene (Lukeino Formation, Kenya). *Comptes Rendus de l'Academie des Sciences* 332: 137–144.

SEROŠEVSKIJ, V. L. ([1896] 1993). *Jakuty.* [The Yakuts]. Moscow: Rossijskaja političeskaja enciklopedija (ROSSPEN).

SEYFARTH, R. M. (2005). Continuities in vocal communication argue against a gestural origin of language. *Behavioral and Brain Sciences* 28: 144–145.

SEYFARTH, R. M. and CHENEY, D. L. (1997). Some general features of vocal development in non-human primates. In Snowdon and Hausberger (eds.), 249–273.

SEYFARTH, R. M. and CHENEY, D. L. (2010). Production, usage, and comprehension in animal vocalizations. *Brain and Language* 115: 92–100.

SEYFARTH, R. M., CHENEY, D. L., and MARLER, P. (1980). Vervet monkey alarm calls: Semantic communication in a free ranging primate. *Animal Behaviour* 28: 1070–1094.

SEYFARTH, R. M., CHENEY, D. L., and BERGMAN, T. J. (2005). Primate social cognition and the origins of language. *Trends in Cognitive Sciences* 9: 264–266.

SHAFER, D. D. (1993). Patterns of hand preference in gorillas and children. In J. P. Ward and W. D. Hopkins (eds.), *Primate laterality: Current behavioral evidence of primate asymmetries.* New York: Springer, 267–284.

SHAFER, D. D. (1997). Hand preference behaviors shared by two groups of captive bonobos. *Primates* 38: 303–313.

SHAPIRO, G. I. and GALDIKAS, B. M. F. (1999). Early sign performance in a free-ranging, adult orangutan. In Parker et al. (eds.), 265–282.

SHAPLESKE, J., ROSSELL, S. L., WOODRUFF, P. W., and DAVID, A. S. (1999). The planum temporale: A systematic, quantitative review of its structural, functional and clinical significance. *Brain Research Reviews* 29: 26–49.

SHEA, J. J., FLEAGLE, J. G., and ASSEFA, Z. (2007). Context and chronology of early *Homo sapiens* fossils from the Omo Kibish. In Mellars et al. (eds.), 153–162.

SHEN, G., GAO, X., GAO, B., and GRANGER, D. E. (2009). Age of Zhoukoudian *Homo erectus* determined with $^{26}Al/^{10}Be$ burial dating. *Nature* 458: 198–200.

SHERWOOD, C. S., BROADFIELD, D. C., HOLLOWAY, R. L., GANNON, P. J., and HOF, P. R. (2003). Variability of Broca's area homologue in great apes: Implication for language evolution. *The Anatomical Record* 217A: 276–285.

SHINTEL, H., NUSBAUM, H. C., and OKRENT, A. (2006). Analog acoustic expression in speech communication. *Journal of Memory and Language* 55: 167–177.

SIGMUND, K. (1995). *Games of life: Explorations in ecology, evolution and behaviour.* London: Penguin.

SILK, J. B., ALTMANN, J., and ALBERTS, S. C. (2006a). Social relationships among adult female baboons (*Papio cynocephalus*). I: Variation in the strength of social bonds. *Behavioral Ecology and Sociobiology* 61: 183–195.

SILK, J. B., ALTMANN, J., and ALBERTS, S. C. (2006b) Social relationships among adult female baboons (*Papio cynocephalus*). II: Variation in the quality and stability of social bonds. *Behavioral Ecology and Sociobiology* 61: 197–204.

SILVERI, M. C. and MISCIAGNA, S. (2000). Language, memory, and the cerebellum. *Journal of Neurolinguistics* 13: 129–143.

SIMONS, E. and PILBEAM, D. (1972). Hominoid paleoprimatology. In R. Tuttle (ed.), *The functional and evolutionary biology of primates.* Chicago, IL: Aldine-Atherton, 22–62.

SIMONYAN, K. and JÜRGENS, U. (2002). Cortico-cortical projections of the motorcortical larynx area in the rhesus monkey. *Brain Research* 949: 23–31.

SIMONYI, S. (1907). *Die ungarische Sprache: Geschichte und Charakteristik.* Strasbourg: Trübner.

SINGH, M. (2005). Essential fatty acids, DHA, and human brain. *Indian Journal of Pediatrics*, 72: 239–242.

SKINNER, B. F. (1957). *Verbal behavior.* New York: Appleton-Century-Crofts.

SLATER, P. J. B. (2000). Bird song repertoires, their organization and use. In Wallin et al. (eds.), 49–63.

SLOBIN, D. I. (2002). Language evolution, acquisition and diachrony: Probing the parallels. In Givón and Malle (eds.), 375–392.

SLOBODA, J. A. (1985). *The musical mind: The cognitive psychology of music.* Oxford: Oxford University Press.

SLOBODCHIKOFF, C. N., PASEKA, A., and VERDOIN, J. L. (2009a). Prairie dog alarm calls encode labels about predator colors. *Animal Cognition* 12: 435–439.

SLOBODCHIKOFF, C. N., PERLA, B., and VERDOIN, J. L. (2009b). *Prairie dogs: Communication and community in an animal society.* Cambridge, MA: Harvard University Press.

SLOCOMBE, K. E. and ZUBERBÜHLER, K. (2005a). Functionally referential communication in a chimpanzee. *Current Biology* 15: 1779–1784.

SLOCOMBE, K. E. and ZUBERBÜHLER, K. (2005b). Agonistic screams in wild chimpanzees (*Pan troglodytes schweinfurthii*) vary as a function of social role. *Journal of Comparative Psychology* 119: 67–77

SLOCOMBE, K. E. and ZUBERBÜHLER, K. (2006). Food-associated calls in chimpanzees: Responses to food types or food preferences? *Animal Behaviour* 72: 989–999.

SLOCOMBE, K. E. and ZUBERBÜHLER, K. (2007). Chimpanzees modify recruitment screams as a function of audience composition. *Proceedings of the National Academy of Sciences of the USA* 104: 17228–17233.

SLOCOMBE, K. E., TOWNSEND, S. W., and ZUBERBÜHLER, K. (2009). Wild chimpanzees (*Pan troglodytes schweinfurthii*) distinguish between different scream types: Evidence from a playback study. *Animal Cognition* 12: 441–449.

SLOCOMBE. K. E., KALLER, T., CALL, J., and ZUBERBÜHLER, K. (2010a) Chimpanzees extract social information from agonistic screams. *PLoS ONE* 5: e 11473.

SLOCOMBE, K. E., KALLER, T., TURMAN, L., TOWNSEND, S. W., PAPWORTH, S., and ZUBERBÜHLER, K. (2010b). Production of food-associated calls in wild male chimpanzees is dependent on the composition of the audience. *Behavioral Ecology and Sociobiology* 64: 1959–1966.

SLOCOMBE, K. E, WALLER, B., and LIEBAL, K. (2011). The language void: The need for multimodality in primate communication research. *Animal Behaviour* 81: 919–924.

SLOCOMBE, K. E., KALLER, T., CALL, J., and ZUBERBÜHLER, K. (In prep). Chimpanzee responses to calls elicited by foods of different types and values: a playback study.

SMITH, A. D. M. (2003). Intelligent meaning creation in a clumpy world helps communication. *Artificial Life* 9: 175–190.

SMITH, A. D. M. (2008). Protolanguage reconstructed. *Interaction Studies* 9: 100–116.

SMITH, A. D. M., SMITH, K., and FERRER I CANCHO, R. (eds.) (2008). *The evolution of language: Proceedings of the 7th International Conference (EVOLANG7)*. Singapore: World Scientific.

SMITH, B. L. and OLLER, D. K. (1981). A comparative study of the development of stop consonant production in normal and Down's syndrome children. *Journal of Speech and Hearing Disorders* 48: 114–118.

SMITH, C. (1997). *The parameter of aspect*. Dordrecht: Kluwer.

SMITH, J. D., SCHULL, J., STROTE, J., MCGEE, K., EGNOR, R., and ERB, L. (1995). The uncertain response in the bottlenose dolphin (*Tursiops truncatus*). *Journal of Experimental Psychology: General* 124: 391–408.

SMITH, J. D., SHIELDS, W. E., and WASHBURN, D. A. (1997). The uncertain response in humans and animals. *Cognition* 62: 75–97.

SMITH, J. N., GOLDIZEN, A. W., DUNLOP, R. A., and NOAD, M. J. (2008). Songs of male humpback whales, *Megaptera novaeangliae*, are involved in intersexual interactions. *Animal Behaviour* 76: 467–477.

SMITH, K. (2008). Is a holistic protolanguage a plausible precursor to language? A test case for a modern evolutionary linguistics. *Interaction Studies* 9: 1–17.

SMITH, K. and KIRBY, S. (2008). Cultural evolution: Implications for understanding the human language faculty and its evolution. *Philosophical Transactions of the Royal Society B* 363: 3591–3603.

SMITH, K. and KIRBY, S. (2011). Compositionality and linguistic evolution. In M. Werning, W. Hinzen, and E. Machery (eds.), *Oxford handbook of compositionality*. Oxford: Oxford University Press.

SMITH, K., BRIGHTON, H., and KIRBY, S. (2003a). Complex systems in language evolution: The cultural emergence of compositional structure. *Advances in Complex Systems* 6: 537–558.

SMITH, K., KIRBY, S., and BRIGHTON, H. (2003b). Iterated learning: A framework for the emergence of language. *Artificial Life* 9: 371–386.

SMITH, K., KALISH, M. L., GRIFFITHS, T. L., and LEWANDOWSKY, S. (2008). Introduction. Cultural transmission and the evolution of human behaviour. *Philosophical Transactions of the Royal Society of London* 363: 3469–3476.

SMITH, R. J. (2005). Species recognition in paleoanthropology: Implications of small sample sizes. In D. E. Lieberman, R. J. Smith, and J. Kelley (eds.), *Interpreting the past: Essays on human, primate, and mammal evolution in honor of David Pilbeam*. Boston, MA: Brill Academic Publishers, 207–219.

SMITH, W. J. and SMITH, A. M. (1996). Information about behaviour provided by Louisiana waterthrush, *Seurus motacilla* (Parulinae), songs. *Animal Behaviour* 51: 785–799.

SNOW, B. K. (1977). Territorial behaviour and courtship of the male three-wattled bellbird. *Auk* 94: 623–645.

SNOW, D. W. (1982). *The Cotingas*. Ithaca, NY: Cornell University Press.

SNOWDON, C. T. (1997). Affiliative processes and vocal development. *Annals of the New York Academy of Sciences* 807: 340–351.

SNOWDON, C. T. and ELOWSON, A. M. (2001). 'Babbling' in pygmy marmosets: Development after infancy. *Behaviour* 138: 1235–1248.

SNOWDON, C. T. and HAUSBERGER, M. (eds.) (1997). *Social influences on vocal development*. Cambridge: Cambridge University Press.

SNOWDON, C. T. and HODUN, A. (1981). Acoustic adaptations in pygmy marmoset contact calls: Locational cues vary with distances between conspecifics. *Behavioral Ecology and Sociobiology* 9: 295–300.

SOBER, E. (1998). Innate knowledge. In E. Craig (ed.), *Routledge encyclopedia of philosophy*. London: Routledge, 794–797.

SOLOMON, N. G. and FRENCH, J. A. (1997). *Cooperative breeding in mammals*. Cambridge: Cambridge University Press.

SPELKE, E. S. (2003). What makes us smart? Core knowledge and natural language. In D. Gentner and S. Goldin-Meadow (eds.), *Language in mind: Advances in the investigation of language and thought*. Cambridge, MA: MIT Press, 277–312.

SPITERI, E., KONOPKA, G., COPPOLA, G., BOMAR, J., OLDHAM, M., OU, J., VERNES, S. C., FISHER, S. E., REN, B., and GESCHWIND, D. H. (2007). Identification of the transcriptional targets of *FOXP2*, a gene linked to speech and language, in developing human brain. *American Journal of Human Genetics* 81: 1144–1157.

SPONHEIMER, M. and LEE-THORP, J. A. (1999). Isotopic evidence for the diet of an early hominid, *Australopithecus africanus*. *Science* 283: 368–370.

SRINIVASAN, M. V., ZHANG, S., ALTWEIN, M., and TAUTZ, J. (2000). Honeybee navigation: Nature and calibration of the 'odometer'. *Science* 287: 851–853.

STEELS, L. (1995). A self-organizing spatial vocabulary. *Artificial Life* 2: 319–332.

STEELS, L. (1998). Synthesising the origins of language and meaning using co-evolution, self-organisation and level formation. In Hurford et al. (eds.), 384–404.

STEELS, L. (1999). *The talking heads experiment Volume 1. Words and meaning*. Laboratorium, Antwerp.

STEELS, L. (2003). Evolving grounded communication for robots. *Trends in Cognitive Science* 7: 308–312.

STEELS, L. (2004). Constructivist development of grounded construction grammars. In D. Scott, W. Daelemans, and M. Walker (eds.), *Proceedings of the 42nd Annual Meeting of the Association for Computational Linguistics*, Barcelona, 9–19.

STEELS, L. (2006). How to do experiments in artificial language evolution and why. In Cangelosi et al. (eds.), 323–332.

STEELS, L. and KAPLAN, F. (2000). AIBO's first words, the social learning of language and meaning. *Evolution of Communication* 4: 3–32.

STEELS, L. and KAPLAN, F. (2002). Bootstrapping grounded word semantics. In Briscoe (ed.), 53–73.

STEELS, L. and SPRANGER, M. (2009). How experience of the body shapes language about space. *IJCAI'09: Proceedings of the 21st International Joint Conference on Artificial Intelligence*. San Francisco, CA: Morgan Kaufmann, 14–19.

STEELS, L. and VOGT, P. (1997). Grounding adaptive language games in robotic agents. In P. Harvey and P. Husbands (eds.), *Proceedings of the 4th European Conference on Artificial Life*. Cambridge, MA: MIT Press, 474–482.

STEIPER, M. E. and YOUNG, N. M. (2006). Primate molecular divergence dates. *Molecular Phylogenetics and Evolution* 41: 384–394.

STEIPER, M. E., YOUNG, N. M., and SUKARNA, T. Y. (2004). Genomic data support the hominoid slowdown and an Early Oligocene estimate for the hominoid-cercopithecoid divergence. *Proceedings of the National Academy of Sciences of the USA* 101: 17021–17026.

STEKLIS, H. D. and HARNAD, S. (1976). From hand to mouth: Some critical stages in the evolution of language. In Harnad et al. (eds.), 445–455.

STEPHAN, C. and ZUBERBÜHLER, K. (2008). Predation increases acoustic complexity in primate alarm calls. *Biology Letters* 4: 641–644.

STEVENS, K. N. (1972). The quantal nature of speech: Evidence from articulatory-acoustic data. In P. B. Denes and E. E. David Jr. (eds.), *Human communication: A unified view*. New York: McGraw-Hill, 51–66.

STICH, S. P. (1975). The idea of innateness. In S. P. Stich (ed.), *Innate ideas*. Berkeley, CA: University of California Press, 1–22.

STILO, D. L. (1994). Phonological systems in contact in Iran and Transcaucasia. In M. Marashi (ed.), *Persian studies in North America: Studies in honor of Mohammad Ali Jazayery*. Bethesda, MD: Iranbooks, 75–94.

STRIEDTER, G. F. (2005). *Principles of brain evolution*. Sunderland, MA: Sinaur Associates.

STRINGER, C. and MCKIE, R. (1996). *African exodus*. London: Pimlico.

STROMSWOLD, K. (2001). The heritability of language: A review and metanalysis of twin, adoption and linkage studies. *Language* 77: 647–723.

STROMSWOLD, K. (2010). Genetics and the evolution of language: What genetic studies reveal about the evolution of language. In Larson et al. (eds.), 176–190.

STRUHSAKER, T. (1967). Auditory communication among vervet monkeys (*Cercopithecus aethiops*). In A. Altmann (ed.), *Social communication among primates*. Chicago, IL: Chicago University Press, 281–324.

STUDDERT-KENNEDY, M. (1998). The particulate origins of language generativity: From syllable to gesture. In Hurford et al. (eds.), 202–221.

STUDDERT-KENNEDY, M. (2002). Mirror neurons, vocal imitation and the evolution of particulate speech. In M. I. Stamenov and V. Gallese (eds.), *Mirror neurons and the evolution of brain and language*. Amsterdam: John Benjamins, 207–227.

STUDDERT-KENNEDY, M. (2005). How did language go discrete? In Tallerman (ed.), 48–67.

STUDDERT-KENNEDY, M. and GOLDSTEIN, L. (2003). Launching language: The gestural origin of discrete infinity. In Christiansen and Kirby (eds.), 235–254.

STUDDERT-KENNEDY, M. and GOODELL, E. W. (1995). Gestures, features and segments in early child speech. In B. de Gelder and J. Morais (eds.), *Speech and reading: A comparative approach*. Hove: Lawrence Erlbaum/Taylor & Francis, 65–88.

STUDDERT-KENNEDY, M. and LANE, H. (1980). Clues from the difference between signed and spoken languages. In U. Bellugi and M. Studdert-Kennedy (eds.), *Signed and spoken language: Biological constraints on linguistic form*. Berlin: Verlag Chemie, 29–40.

SUDDENDORF, T. and BUSBY, J. (2003a). Like it or not? The mental time travel debate: Reply to Clayton et al. *Trends in Cognitive Sciences* 7: 437–438.

SUDDENDORF, T. and BUSBY, J. (2003b). Mental time travel in animals? *Trends in Cognitive Sciences* 7: 391–396.

SUDDENDORF, T. and CORBALLIS, M. C. (1997). Mental time travel and the evolution of the human mind. *Genetic, Social, and General Psychology Monographs* 123: 133–167.

SWADESH, M. (1955). Toward greater accuracy in lexicostatistic dating. *International Journal of American Linguistics* 21: 121–137.

SZÁMADÓ, S. and SZATHMÁRY, E. (2006). Competing selective scenarios for the emergence of natural language. *Trends in Ecology and Evolution* 21: 555–561.

SZÁMADÓ, S., HURFORD, J., BISHOP, D., DEACON, T., D'ERRICO, F., FISCHER, J., OKANOYA, K., SZATHMÁRY, E., and WHITE, S. (2009). What are the possible biological and genetic foundations for syntactic phenomena? In Bickerton and Szathmáry (eds.), 207–236.

SZATHMÁRY, E. and SZÁMADÓ, S. (2008). Being human: Language: A social history of words. *Nature* 456: 40–41.

TAGLIALATELA, J. P., SAVAGE-RUMBAUGH, E. S., and BAKER, L. A. (2003). Vocal production by a language-competent *Pan paniscus*. *International Journal of Primatology* 24: 1–17.

TAGLIALATELA, J. P., CANTALUPO, C., and HOPKINS, W. D. (2006). Gesture handedness predicts asymmetry in the chimpanzee inferior frontal gyrus. *NeuroReport* 17: 923–927.

TAGLIALATELA, J. P., DADDA, M., and HOPKINS, W. D. (2007). Sex differences in asymmetry of the planum parietale in chimpanzees *(Pan troglodytes)*. *Behavioural Brain Research* 184: 185–191.

TAGLIALATELA, J. P., RUSSELL, J. L., SCHAEFFER, J. A., and HOPKINS, W. D. (2008). Communicative signaling activates 'Broca's' homologue in chimpanzees. *Current Biology* 18: 343–348.

TAGLIALATELA, J. P., RUSSELL, J. L., SCHAEFFER, J. A. and HOPKINS, W. D. (2009). Visualizing vocal perception in the chimpanzee brain. *Cerebral Cortex* 19: 1151–1157.

TAKAI, M., ANAYA, F., SHIGEHARA, N., and SETOGUCHI, T. (2000). New fossil materials of the earliest New World monkey, *Branisella boliviana*, and the problems of platyrrhine origins. *American Journal of Physical Anthropology* 111: 263–281.

TAKEMOTO, H. (2008). Morphological analyses and 3D modelling of the tongue musculature of the chimpanzee (*Pan troglodytes*). *American Journal of Primatology* 70: 966–975.

TALLERMAN, M. (ed.) (2005). *Language origins: Perspectives on evolution*. Oxford: Oxford University Press.

TALLERMAN, M. (2007). Did our ancestors speak a holistic protolanguage? *Lingua* 117: 579–604.

TALLERMAN, M. (2008a). Holophrastic protolanguage: Planning, processing, storage, and retrieval. *Interaction Studies* 9: 84–99.

TALLERMAN, M. (2008b). Kin selection and linguistic complexity. In A. D. M. Smith et al. (eds.), 307–314.

TALLERMAN, M. (2009). The origins of the lexicon: How a word store evolved. In Botha and Knight (eds.) (2009a), 181–200.

TALLERMAN, M. (2011). Kin selection, pedagogy, and linguistic complexity: Whence proto-language? In R. Botha and M. Everaert (eds.), *The evolutionary emergence of human language*. Oxford: Oxford University Press.

TALMY, L. (2007). Recombinance in the evolution of language. In J. E. Cihlar, D. Kaiser, I. Kimbara, and A. Franklin (eds.), *Proceedings of the 39th Annual Meeting of the Chicago Linguistic Society: The Panels, Vol. 39*. Chicago, IL: Chicago Linguistic Society, 26–60.

TANNER, J. E. and BYRNE, R. W. (1996). Representation of action through iconic gesture in a captive lowland gorilla. *Current Anthropology* 37: 162–173.

TANNER, N. and ZIHLMAN, A. (1978). Women in evolution Part I. Innovation and selection in human origins. *Signs: Journal of Women in Culture and Society* 1: 558–608.

TATTERSALL, I. (1998a). *Becoming human: Evolution and human uniqueness*. New York: Harcourt Brace.

TATTERSALL, I. (1998b). *The origin of the human capacity*. New York: The American Museum of Natural History.

TATTERSALL, I. (1999). *The last Neandertal*. Boulder, CO: Westview Press.

TATTERSALL, I. (2010). A putative role for language in the origin of human consciousness. In Larson et al. (ed.), 193–198.

TAYLER, C. K. and SAAYMAN, G. S. (1973). Imitative behaviour by Indian Ocean bottlenose dolphins (*Tursiops aduncus*) in captivity. *Behaviour* 44: 286–297.

TEAFORD, M. F. and UNGAR, P. S. (2000). Diet and the evolution of the earliest human ancestors. *Proceedings of the National Academy of Sciences of the USA* 97: 13506–13511.

TEMPLETON, A. R. (2007). Genetics and recent human evolution. *Evolution* 61: 1507–1519.

TERRACE, H. S. (1979). *Nim*. New York: Knopf.

TERRACE, H. S. (2005). Metacognition and the evolution of language. In Terrace and Metcalfe (eds.), 84–115.

TERRACE, H. S. and METCALFE, J. (eds.) (2005). *The missing link in cognition: Origins of self-reflective consciousness*. Oxford: Oxford University Press.

TERRACE, H. S., PETITTO, L. A., SANDERS, R. J., and BEVER, T. G. (1979). Can an ape create a sentence? *Science* 206: 891–902.

TEYSSANDIER, N. (2008). Revolution or evolution: The emergence of the Upper Paleolithic in Europe. *World Archaeology* 40: 493–519.

THIEME, H. (1997). Lower Palaeolithic hunting spears from Germany. *Nature* 385: 807–810.

THOMAS, D. A. (1995). *Music and the origins of language. Theories from the French enlightenment*. Cambridge: Cambridge University Press.

THOMASON, S. G. (2001). *Language contact: An introduction*. Edinburgh: Edinburgh University Press.

THOMASON, S. G. and KAUFMAN, T. (1988). *Language contact, creolization, and genetic linguistics*. Berkeley, CA: University of California Press.

THOMPSON, D. W. (1961). *On growth and form* (Abridged edn., ed. J. T. Bonner). Cambridge: Cambridge University Press.

THOMPSON, J. N. (1994). *The coevolutionary process*. Chicago, IL: University of Chicago Press.

THOMPSON, P., KUTTAB-BOULOS, H., WITONSKY, D., YANG, L., ROE, B. A., and DI RIENZO, A. (2001). Genetic influences on brain structure. *Nature Neuroscience* 4: 1253–1258.

THOMPSON, R. K. R. and HERMAN, L. M. (1977). Memory for lists of sounds by the bottlenosed dolphin: Convergence of memory processes with humans? *Science* 195: 501–503.

THORPE, W. H. (1963). *Learning and instinct in animals.* Cambridge, MA: Harvard University Press.

THURSTON, W. R. (1987). *Processes of change in the languages of North-Western New Britain.* Canberra: Department of Linguistics, Research School of Pacific Studies, The Australian National University.

TIMPSON, N., HERON, J., SMITH, G. D., and ENARD, W. (2007). Comment on papers by Evans et al. and Mekel-Bobrov et al. on evidence for positive selection of MCPH1 and ASPM. *Science* 317: 1036.

TINBERGEN, N. (1952). Derived activities: Their causation, biological significance, origin and emancipation during evolution. *Quarterly Review of Biology* 27: 1–32.

TINBERGEN, N. (1963). On aims and methods of ethology. *Zeitschrift für Tierpsychologie* 20: 410–433.

TISHKOFF, S. A., VARKONYI, R., CAHINHINAN, N., ABBES, S., ARGYROPOULOS, G., DESTRO-BISOL, G., DROUSIOTOU, A., DANGERBELD, B., LEFRANC, G., LOISELET, J., PIRO, A., STONEKING, M., TAGARELLI, A., TAGARELLI, G., TOUMA, E. H., WILLIAMS, S. M., and CLARK, A. G. (2001). Haplotype diversity and linkage disequilibrium at human G6PD: Recent origin of allels that confer malaria resistance. *Science* 293: 455–462.

TISHKOFF, S. A., GONDER, M. K., HENN, B. M., MORTENSEN, H., KNIGHT, A., GIGNOUX, C., FENANDOPULLE, N., LEMA, G., NYAMBO, T. B., RAMAKRISHNAN, U., REED, F. A., and MOUNTAIN, J. L. (2005). History of click-speaking populations of Africa inferred from mtDNA and Y chromosome genetic variation. *Molecular Biology and Evolution* 24: 2180–2195.

TISHKOFF, S. A., REED, F. A., FRIEDLAENDER, F., EHRET, R. C., RANCIARO, A., FROMENT, A., HIRBO, J. B., AWOMOYI, A. A., BODO, J. M., DOUMBO, O., IBRAHIM, M., JUMA, A. T., KOTZE, M. J., LEMA, G., MOORE J. H., MORTENSEN, H., NYAMBO, T. B., OMAR, S. A., POWELL, K., PRETORIUS, G. S., SMITH, M. W., THERA, M. A., WAMBEBE, C., WEBER, J. L., and WILLIAMS, S. M. (2009). The genetic structure and history of Africans and African Americans. *Science* 324: 1035–1044.

TOBIAS, P. V. (1995). The brain of the first hominids. In Changeux and Chavallion (eds.), 61–83.

TOBIAS, P. V. (2001). The promise and the peril in hominin brain evolution. In Falk and Gibson (eds.), 241–256.

TODT, D. and HULTSCH, H. (1998). How songbirds deal with large amounts of serial information. *Cybernetics* 79: 487–500.

TOMAIUOLO, F., MACDONALD, J. D., CARAMANOS, Z., POSNER, G., CHIAVARAS, M., EVANS, A. C., and PETRIDES, M. (1999). Morphology, morphometry and probability mapping of the pars opercularis of the inferior frontal gyrus: An *in vivo* MRI analysis. *European Journal of Neuroscience* 11: 3033–3046.

TOMASELLO, M. (1996). Do apes ape? In Heyes and Galef (eds.), 319–346.

TOMASELLO, M. (1999). *The cultural origins of human cognition.* Cambridge, MA: Harvard University Press.

TOMASELLO, M. (2003a). *Constructing a language: A usage-based theory of language acquisition.* Cambridge, MA: Harvard University Press.

TOMASELLO, M. (2003b). On the different origins of symbols and grammar. In Christiansen and Kirby (eds.), 94–110.

Tomasello, M. (2005). Beyond formalities: The case of language acquisition. *The Linguistic Review* 22: 183–197.

Tomasello, M. (2006). Why don't apes point? In Enfield and Levinson (eds.), 506–524.

Tomasello, M. (2007). If they're so good at grammar, why don't they talk? *Language, Learning, and Development* 3: 133–156.

Tomasello, M. (2008). *Origins of human communication.* Cambridge, MA: MIT Press.

Tomasello, M. (2009a). Universal grammar is dead. *Behavioral and Brain Sciences* 32: 470–471.

Tomasello, M. (2009b). *Why we cooperate.* Cambridge, MA: MIT Press.

Tomasello, M. and Call, J. (1997). *Primate cognition.* New York: Oxford University Press.

Tomasello, M. and Camaioni, L. (1997). A comparison of the gestural communication of apes and human infants. *Human Development* 40: 7–24.

Tomasello, M. and Carpenter, M. (2007). Shared intentionality. *Developmental Science* 10: 121–125.

Tomasello, M., Carpenter, M., Call, J., Behne, T., and Moll, H. (2005). Understanding and sharing intentions: The origins of cultural cognition. *Behavioral and Brain Sciences* 28: 675–691.

Tooby, J. and Cosmides, L. (1990). The past explains the present: Emotional adaptations and the structure of ancestral environments. *Ethology and Sociobiology* 11: 375–424.

Tooby, J. and DeVore, I. (1987). The reconstruction of hominid behavioral evolution through strategic modeling. In W. Kinzey (ed.), *The evolution of human behavior: Primate models.* Albany: State University of New York Press, 183–238.

Toth, N. and Schick, K. (2009). The Oldowan: The tool making of early hominins and chimpanzees compared. *Annual Review of Anthropology* 38: 289–305.

Toth, N., Schick, K., Savage-Rumbaugh, E. S., Sevcik, R., and Rumbaugh, D. (1993). Pan the tool-maker: Investigations into the stone tool-making and tool-using capabilities of a bonobo (*Pan paniscus*). *Journal of Archaeological Science* 20: 81–91.

Townsend, S. W., Slocombe, K. E., Emery-Thompson, M., and Zuberbühler, K. (2007). Female-led infanticide in wild chimpanzees. *Current Biology* 17: R355–R356.

Townsend, S. W., Deschner, T. and Zuberbühler, K. (2008). Female chimpanzees use copulation calls flexibly to prevent social competition. *PLoS ONE* 3: e2431.

Traugott, E. C., and Dasher, R. B. (2002). *Regularity in semantic change.* Cambridge: Cambridge University Press.

Trehub, S. E. (2003). Musical predispositions in infancy: An update. In Peretz and Zatorre (eds.), 3–20.

Trivers, R. L. (1974). Parent-offspring conflict. *American Zoologist* 14: 249–264.

Tsao, F.-M., Liu, H.-M., and Kuhl, P. K. (2004). Speech perception in infancy predicts language development in the second year of life: A longitudinal study. *Child Development* 75: 1067–1084.

Tschauner, H. (1996). Middle-range theory, behavioral archaeology, and post-empiricist philosophy of science in archaeology. *Journal of Archaeological Method and Theory* 3: 3–30.

Tschudin, A. J. P. C. (2006). Belief attribution tasks with dolphins: What social minds can reveal about animal rationality. In S. Hurley and M. Nudds (eds.), *Rational animals?* Oxford: Oxford University Press, 413–436.

Tugolukov, V. A. (1985). *Tungusy (èvenki i èveny) Srednej i Zapadnoj Sibiri. (The Tungus (Evenks and Evens) of Central and Western Siberia).* Moscow: Izdatel'stvo 'Nauka'.

Tulving, E. (1999). Episodic vs semantic memory. In R. A. Wilson and F. C. Keil (eds.), *The MIT encyclopedia of the cognitive sciences.* Cambridge, MA: MIT Press, 278–280.

Tulving, E. (2005). Episodic memory and autonoesis: Uniquely human? In Terrace and Metcalfe (eds.), 3–56.

Turner, A. (1984). Human migration into high latitudes as part of a large-mammal community. In Foley, R. (ed.), *Hominid evolution and community ecology: prehistoric human adaptation in the Pleistocene*. New York: Academic Press, 193–217.

Tyack, P. L. (1986). Population biology, social behaviour, and communication in whales and dolphins. *Trends in Ecology and Evolution* 1: 144–150.

Tyack, P. L. and Clark, C. W. (2000). Communication and acoustic behavior of dolphins and whales. In W. W. L. Au, A. N. Popper, and R. R. Fay (eds.), *Hearing by whales and dolphins*. New York: Springer Verlag, 156–224.

Tyack, P. L. and Sayigh, L. S. (1997). Vocal learning in cetaceans. In Snowdon and Hausberger (eds.), 208–233.

Ungar, P. S. and Scott, R. S. (2009). Dental evidence for diets of early *Homo*. In Grine et al. (eds.), 121–134.

Uriagereka, J. (1998). *Rhyme and reason: An introduction to Minimalist syntax*. Cambridge, MA: MIT Press.

Uylings, H., Jacobsen, A., Zilles, K., and Amunts, K. (2006). Left-right asymmetry in volume and number of neurons in adult Broca's area. *Cortex* 42: 652–658.

Vallabha, G. K., McClelland, J. L., Pons, F., Werker, J. F., and Amano, S. (2007). Unsupervised learning of vowel categories from infant-directed speech. *Proceedings of the National Academy of Sciences of the USA* 104: 13273–13278.

Vallender, E. J. and Lahn, B. T. (2004). Positive selection on the human genome. *Human Molecular Genetics* 13: R245–R254.

Vallender, E. J., Mekel-Bobrov, N., and Lahn, B. T. (2008). Genetic basis of human brain evolution. *Trends in Neurosciences* 31: 637–644.

Vallet, E. and Kreutzer, M. (1995). Female canaries are sexually responsive to special song phrases. *Animal Behaviour* 49: 1603–1610.

Vandermeersch, B. (1993). Appendix. Was the Sainte-Césaire discovery a burial? In F. Lévêque, A. M. Backer, and M. Guilbaud (eds.), *Context of a late Neandertal*. Madison, WI: Prehistory Press, 129–131.

Vanhaeren, M. (2005). The evolutionary significance of beadmaking and use. In F. d'Errico and L. Backwell (eds.), *From tools to symbols, from early hominids to modern humans: Proceedings of the International Round Table, Johannesburg, South Africa, 16-18 March 2003*. Johannesburg: Wits University Press, 525–553.

Vanhaeren, M. and d'Errico, F. (2006). Aurignacian ethno-linguistic geography of Europe revealed by personal ornaments. *Journal of Archaelogical Science* 33: 1105–1128.

van Hooff, J. A. R. A. M. (1967). Facial displays of the catarrhine monkeys and apes. In D. Morris (ed.), *Primate ethology*. London: Weidenfield and Nicholson, 7–68.

van Hooff, J. A. R. A. M. (1973). A structural analysis of the social behavior of a semi-captive group of chimpanzees. In M. von Cranach and I. Vine (eds.), *Social communication and movement*. New York: Academic Press, 75–162.

Van Schaik, C. P. and Deaner, R. O. (2003). Life history and cognitive evolution in primates. In F. B. M. de Waal and P. L. Tyack (eds.), *Animal social complexity: Intelligence, culture, and individualized societies*. Cambridge, MA: Harvard University Press, 5–25.

Van Valen, L. (1966). On discussing human races. *Perspectives on Biology and Medicine* 9: 377–383.

VERNES, S. C., SPITERI, E., NICOD, J., GROSZER, M., TAYLOR, J. M., DAVIES, K. E., GESCHWIND, D. H., and FISHER, S. E. (2007). High-throughput analysis of promoter occupancy reveals direct neural targets of FOXP2, a gene mutated in speech and language disorders. *American Journal of Human Genetics* 81: 1232–1250.

VERNES, S. C., NEWBURY, D. F., ABRAHAMS, B. S., WINCHESTER, L., NICOD, J., GROSZER, M., ALARCÓN, M., OLIVER, P. L., DAVIES, K. E., GESCHWIND, D. H., MONACO, A. P., and FISHER, S. E. (2008). A functional genetic link between distinct developmental language disorders. *New England Journal of Medicine* 359: 2337–2345.

VESTERGAARD, M., OBEL, C., HENRIKSEN, T. B., SØRENSEN, H. T., SKAJAA, E., and ØSTERGAARD, J. (1999). Duration of breastfeeding and developmental milestones during the latter half of infancy. *Acta Paediatrica* 88: 1327–1332.

VIHMAN, M. M. and VELLEMAN S. L. (1989). Phonological reorganization: A case study. *Language and Speech* 32: 149–170.

VISALBERGHI, E. and FRAGASZY, D. M. (1990). Do monkeys ape? In Parker and Gibson (eds.), 247–273.

VOGT, K. C. (1867). *Mémoire sur les microcéphales ou hommes-singes*. Geneva and Basel: Georg.

VOGT, P. (2005). The emergence of compositional structures in perceptually grounded language games. *Artificial Intelligence* 167: 206–242.

VOGT, P. and DE BOER, B. (2010). Language evolution: Computer models for empirical data. *Adaptive Behavior* 18: 5–11.

VOIGHT, B. F., KUDARAVALLI, S., and PRITCHARD, J. K. (2006). A map of recent positive selection in the human genome. *PLoS Biology* 4: e72.

VON BONIN, G. and BAILEY, P. (1947). The neocortex of *Macaca mulatta*. Urbana, IL: University of Illinois Press.

VON FRISCH, K. (1974). Decoding the language of the bee. *Science* 185: 663–668.

VON HUMBOLDT, W. 1826 [2005]. Über den grammatischen Bau der chinesischen Sprache. In W. von Humboldt, 1826 [2005]. *Grundzüge des sprachlichen Typus*. Berlin. 241–257.

VORPERIAN, H. K., KENT, R. D., LINDSTROM, M. J., KALINA, C. M., GENTRY, L. R., and YANDELL, B. S. (2005). Development of vocal tract length during early childhood: A magnetic resonance imaging study. *Journal of the Acoustical Society of America* 117: 338–350.

VUKOVIC, J., FEINBERG, D. R., JONES, B. C., DEBRUINE, L. M., WELLING, L. L. M., LITTLE, A. C., and SMITH, F. G. (2008). Self-rated attractiveness predicts individual differences in women's preferences for masculine men's voices. *Personality and Individual Differences* 45: 451–456.

WADDINGTON, C. H. (1942). The canalization of development and the inheritance of acquired characters. *Nature* 150: 563–565.

WADDINGTON, C. H. (1953). Genetic assimilation of an acquired character. *Evolution* 7: 118–126.

WADLEY, L. (2001). What is cultural modernity? A general view and a South African perspective from Rose Cottage Cave. *Cambridge Archaeological Journal* 11: 201–221.

WADLEY, L. (2010). Were snares and traps used in the Middle Stone Age and does it matter? A review and a case study from Sibudu, South Africa. *Journal of Human Evolution* 58: 179–192.

WAGNER, A. (1999). Causality in complex systems. *Biology and Philosophy* 14: 83–101.

WAKEFIELD, J. L. and WILKINS, W. K. (2007). Conceptual space. In S. Karimi, V. Samiian, and W. K. Wilkins (eds.), *Phrasal and clausal architecture: Syntactic derivation and interpretation*. Amsterdam: John Benjamins, 365–395.

WALKER, A. and LEAKEY, R. E. (eds.) (1993). *The Nariokotome* Homo erectus *skeleton.* Cambridge, MA: Harvard University Press.

WALLACE, D. C. (2007). Why do we still have maternally inherited mitochondrial DNA? Insights from evolutionary medicine. *Annual Review of Biochemistry* 76: 781–821.

WALLIN, N. L., MERKER, B., and BROWN, S. (eds.) (2000). *The origins of music.* Cambridge, MA: MIT Press.

WANG, W. S.-Y. and MINETT, J. W. (2005). The invasion of language: Emergence, change and death. *Trends in Ecology and Evolution* 20: 263–269.

WANKER, R., SUGAMA, Y., and PRINAGE, S. (2005). Vocal labelling of family members in spectacled parrotlets, *Forpus conspicillatus. Animal Behaviour* 70: 111–118.

WARNEKEN, F., CHEN, F., and TOMASELLO, M. (2006). Co-operative activities in young children and chimpanzees. *Child Development* 77: 640–663.

WARREN, J. M. (1980). Handedness and laterality in humans and other animals. *Physiological Psychology* 8: 351–359.

WASHBURN, S. L. (1960). Tools and human evolution. *Scientific American* 203: 63–75.

WATERSON, N. (1971). Child phonology: A prosodic view. *Journal of Linguistics* 7: 179–211.

WATKINS, K. E., PAUS, T., LERCH, J. P., ZIJDENBOS, A., COLLINS, D. L., NEELIN, P., TAYLOR, J., WORSLEY, K. J., and EVANS, A. C. (2001). Structural asymmetries in the human brain: A voxel-based statistical analysis of 142 MRI scans. *Cerebral Cortex* 11: 868–877.

WATKINS, K. E., DRONKERS, N. F., and VARGHA-KHADEM, F. (2002a). Behavioural analysis of an inherited speech and language disorder: Comparison with acquired aphasia. *Brain* 125: 452–464.

WATKINS, K. E., VARGHA-KHADEM, F., ASHBURNER, J., PASSINGHAM, R. E., CONNELLY, A., FRISTON, K. J., FRACKOWIAK, R. S., MISHKIN, M., and GADIAN, D. G. (2002b). MRI analysis of an inherited speech and language disorder: Structural brain abnormalities. *Brain* 125: 465–478.

WATSON, J. S., GERGELY, G., CSANYI, V., TOPAL, J., GACSI, J. M., and SARKOZI, Z. (2001). Distinguishing logic from association in the solution of an invisible displacement task by children (*Homo sapiens*) and dogs (*Canis familiaris*): Using negation of disjunction. *Journal of Comparative Psychology* 115: 219–226.

WATWOOD, S. L., TYACK, P. L., and WELLS, R. S. (2004). Whistle sharing in paired male bottlenose dolphins, *Tursiops truncatus. Behavioral Ecology and Sociobiology* 55: 531–543.

WEBER, B. H. and DEPEW, D. J. (eds.) (2003). *Evolution and learning: The Baldwin effect reconsidered.* Cambridge, MA: MIT Press.

WEIR, A. A. S., CHAPPELL, J., and KACELNIK, A. (2002). Shaping of hooks in New Caledonian Crows. *Science* 297: 981.

WEISSENGRUBER, G. E., FORSTENPOINTNER, G., PETERS, G., KÜBLER-HEISS, A., and FITCH, W. T. (2002). Hyoid apparatus and pharynx in the lion (*Panthera leo*), jaguar (*Panthera onca*), cheetah (*Acinonyx jubatus*) and domestic cat (*Felis silvestris f. catus*). *Journal of Anatomy* 201: 195–209.

WELLS, R., BONESS, D. J., and RATHBUN, G. B. (1999). Behavior. In J. E. Reynolds and S. A. Rommel (eds.), *Biology of marine mammals.* Washington, DC: Smithsonian Institution Press, 324–422.

WERNICKE, C. (1874). *Der aphasische Symptomenkomplex.* Breslau: Cohn, Weigert.

WEST, G. B., BROWN, J. H., and ENQUIST, B. J. (1997). A general model for the origin of the allometric scaling laws in biology. *Science* 276: 122–126.

WEST-EBERHARD, M. J. (1989). Phenotypic plasticity and the origins of diversity. *Annual Review of Ecology and Systematics* 20: 249–278.

WEST-EBERHARD, M. J. (2003). *Developmental plasticity and evolution.* Oxford: Oxford University Press.

WHEELER, B. C. (2009). Monkeys crying wolf? Tufted capuchin monkeys use anti-predator calls to usurp resources from conspecifics. *Proceedings of the Royal Society of London B* 276: 3013–3018.

WHITE, T. D., SUWA, G., and ASFAW, B. (1994). *Australopithecus ramidus*, a new species of early hominid from Aramis, Ethiopia. *Nature* 371: 306–312.

WHITE, T. D., SUWA, G., and ASFAW, B. (1995). *Australopithecus ramidus*, a new species of early hominid from Aramis, Ethiopia – a corrigendum. *Nature* 375: 88.

WHITE, T. D., ASFAW, B., DEGUSTA, D., GILBERT, H., RICHARDS, G. D., SUWA, G., and HOWELL, F. C. (2003). Pleistocene *Homo sapiens* from Middle Awash, Ethiopia. *Nature* 423: 742–747.

WHITE, T. D., ASFAW, B., BEYENE, Y., HAILE-SELASSIE, Y., LOVEJOY, C. O., SUWA, G., WOLDEGABRIEL, G., (2009). *Ardipithecus ramidus* and the paleobiology of early hominids. *Science* 326: 75–86.

WHITEN, A. (1999). The evolution of deep social mind in humans. In Corballis and Lea (eds.), 173–193.

WICH, S. A. and DE VRIES, H. (2006). Male monkeys remember which group members have given alarm calls. *Proceedings of the Royal Society of London B* 273: 735–740.

WICH, S. A., SWARTZ, K. B., HARDUS, M. E., LAMEIRA, A. R., STROMBERG, E., and SHUMAKER, R. W. (2009). A case of spontaneous acquisition of a human sound by an orangutan. *Primates* 50: 56–64.

WICHMANN, S. and HOLMAN, E. W. (2009). *Assessing temporal stability for linguistic typological features.* Munich: Lincom Europa.

WIEMER, B. (2002). *Grammatikalisierungstheorie. Derivation und Konstruktionen: Am Beispiel des klassifizierenden Aspektes, des Passivs und des Subjektimpersonal im slavisch-baltischen Areal.* Unpublished Habilitationsschrift, University of Konstanz.

WIEMER, B. (2004). The evolution of passives as grammatical constructions in Northern Slavic and Baltic languages. In Bisang et al. (eds.), 271–331.

WIESENDANGER, M. (1999). Manual dexterity and the making of tools: An introduction from an evolutionary perspective. *Experimental Brain Research* 128: 1–5.

WILD, M. (1997). Neural pathways for control of birdsong production. *Journal of Neurobiology* 33: 653–670.

WILKINS, W. K. (2005). Anatomy matters. *The Linguistic Review* 22: 271–288.

WILKINS, W. K. (2009). Mosaic neurobiology and anatomical plausibility. In Botha and Knight (eds.) (2009b), 266–350.

WILKINS, W. K. and WAKEFIELD, J. L. (1995a). Brain evolution and neurolinguistic preconditions. *Behavioral and Brain Sciences* 18: 161–182.

WILKINS, W. K. and WAKEFIELD, J. L. (1995b). Issues and non-issues in the origins of language. *Behavioral and Brain Sciences* 18: 205–226.

WILLIAMS, H. and NOTTEBOHM, F. (1985). Auditory responses in avian vocal motor neurons: A motor theory for song perception in birds. *Science* 229: 279–282.

WILLIAMSON, S. H., HUBISZ, M. J., CLARK, A. G., PAYSEUR, B. A., BUSTAMANTE, C. D., and NIELSEN, R. (2007). Localizing recent adaptive evolution in the human genome. *PLoS Genetics* 3: e90.

WILSON, D. S. and SOBER, E. (1994). Reintroducing group selection to the human behavioral sciences. *Behavioral and Brain Sciences* 17: 585–654.

WIMSATT, W. C. (1986). Developmental constraints, generative entrenchment and the innate/acquired distinction. In W. Bechtel (ed.), *Integrating scientific disciplines*. Dordrecht: Nijhoff, 185–208.

WINFORD, D. (2003). *An introduction to contact linguistics*. Malden: Blackwell Publishing.

WINKWORTH, A. L., DAVIS, P. J., ADAMS, R. D., and ELLIS, E. (1995). Breathing patterns during spontaneous speech. *Journal of Speech and Hearing Research* 38: 124–144.

WITTGENSTEIN, L. (1953). *Philosophical investigations*. London: Blackwell.

WITTIG, R. (2010). The function and cognitive underpinnings of post-conflict affiliation in wild chimpanzees. In E. Lonsdorf, S. Ross, and T. Matsuzawa (eds.), *The mind of the chimpanzee: Ecological and experimental perspectives*. Chicago, IL: University of Chicago Press, 208–219.

WITTIG, R., CROCKFORD, C., WIKBERG, E., SEYFARTH, R. M., and CHENEY, D. L. (2007). Kin-mediated reconciliation substitutes for direct reconciliation in baboons. *Proceedings of the Royal Society of London B* 274: 1109–1115.

WOBBER, V. and HARE, B. (2009). Testing the social dog hypothesis: Are dogs also more skilled than chimpanzees in non-communicative social tasks? *Behavioural Processes* 81: 423–428.

WOHLSCHLÄGER, A., GATTIS, M., and BEKKERING, H. (2003). Action generation and action perception in imitation: An instance of the ideomotor principle. *Philosophical Transactions of the Royal Society of London* 358: 501–515.

WOLFF, P. (1969). The natural history of crying and other vocalizations in early infancy. In B. M. Foss (ed.), *Determinants of infant behavior IV*. London: Methuen, 81–109.

WOLPOFF, M. H. (1989). Multiregional evolution: The fossil alternative to Eden. In Mellars and Stringer (eds.), 62–108.

WOLPOFF, M. H. (1996). *Human evolution*. New York: McGraw Hill.

WOLPOFF, M. H. and CASPARI, R. (1997). *Race and human evolution*. New York: Simon and Schuster.

WOLPOFF, M. H., MANNHEIM, B., MANN, A., HAWKS, J., CASPARI, R., ROSENBERG, K. R., FRAYER, D. W., GILL, G. W., and CLARK, G. (2004). Why not the Neandertals? *World Archaeology* 36: 527–546.

WONG, K. (2010). Fossils in our family. *Scientific American* 302: 12–14.

WOOD, B. A. (1992). Origin and evolution of the genus *Homo*. *Nature* 355: 783–790.

WOOD, B. A. and COLLARD, M. (1999). The human genus. *Science* 284: 65–71.

WORDEN, R. (1998). The evolution of language from social intelligence. In Hurford et al. (eds.), 148–168.

WRANGHAM, R. (2009). *Catching fire: How cooking made us human*. New York: Basic books.

WRANGHAM, R., CHENEY, D., SEYFARTH, R., and SARMIENTO, E. (2009). Shallow-water habitats as sources of fallback foods for hominins. *American Journal of Physical Anthropology* 140: 630–642.

WRAY, A. (1998). Protolanguage as a holistic system for social interaction. *Language and Communication* 18: 47–67.

WRAY, A. (2000). Holistic utterances in protolanguage: The link from primates to humans. In Knight et al. (eds.), 285–302.

WRAY, A. (2002a). Dual processing in protolanguage: Performance without competence. In Wray (ed.), 113–137.

Wray, A. (2002b). *Formulaic language and the lexicon.* Cambridge: Cambridge University Press.

Wray, A. (ed.) (2002). *The transition to language.* Oxford: Oxford University Press.

Wright, R. (1994). *The moral animal: Why we are the way we are: The new science of evolutionary psychology.* New York: Random House.

Wright, T. F. and Wilkinson, G. S. (2001). Population genetic structure and vocal dialects in an Amazon parrot. *Proceedings of the Royal Society of London B* 268: 609–616.

Wu X. (1981). A well-preserved cranium of an archaic type of early *Homo sapiens* from Dali, China. *Scientia Sinica* 24: 530–539.

Würsig, B. and Clark, C. W. (1993). Behavior. In J. J. Burns, J. J. Montague, and C. J. Cowles (eds.), *The bowhead whale.* Lawrence, KS: Society of Marine Mammalogy, 157–199.

Wynn, T. (1993). Layers of tool behavior. In Gibson and Ingold (eds.), 407–428.

Wynn, T. (2002). Archaeology and cognitive evolution. *Behavioral and Brain Sciences* 25: 389–438.

Wynn, T. and Coolidge, F. L. (2007). Did a small but significant enhancement in working memory capacity power the evolution of modern thinking? In Mellars et al. (eds.), 79–90.

Wynn, T. and Coolidge, F. L. (eds.) (2010). *Working memory: Beyond language and symbolism.* Chicago, IL: University of Chicago Press.

Wynne, C. D. L. (2001). *Animal cognition: The mental lives of animals.* Basingstoke: Palgrave.

Xiao, R. and McEnery, T. (2004). *Aspect in Mandarin Chinese. A corpus-based study.* Amsterdam: John Benjamins.

Xitco, M. J. and Roitblat, H. L. (1996). Object recognition through eavesdropping: Passive echolocation in bottlenose dolphins. *Animal Learning and Behavior* 24: 355–365.

Xitco, M. J., Gory, J. D., and Kuczaj, S. A. II. (2001). Spontaneous pointing by bottlenose dolphins (*Tursiops truncatus*). *Animal Cognition* 4: 115–123.

Xu, F. (2002). The role of language in acquiring object kind concepts in infancy. *Cognition* 85: 223–250.

Yamauchi, H. (2004). *Baldwinian accounts of language evolution.* Unpublished doctoral thesis, University of Edinburgh.

Yang, Y. (2007). *Tense and aspect in Chinese Pidgin English.* Unpublished MA thesis, University of Düsseldorf.

Yellen, J., Brooks, A. S., Cornelissen, E., Mehlman, M., and Stewart, K. (1995). A Middle Stone Age worked bone industry from Katanda, Upper Simliki Valley, Zaire. *Science* 268: 553–556.

Yeni-Komshian, G. and Benson, D. (1976). Anatomical study of cerebral asymmetry in the temporal lobe of humans, chimpanzees and monkeys. *Science* 192: 387–389.

Yu, F., Hill, R. S., Schaffner, S. F., Sabeti, P. C., Wang, E. T., Mignault, A. A., Ferland, R. J., Moyzis, R. K., Walsh, C. A., and Reich, D. (2007). Comment on 'Ongoing adaptive evolution of *ASPM*, a brain size determinant in *Homo sapiens*'. *Science* 316: 370.

Zahavi, A. and Zahavi, A. (1997). *The handicap principle.* New York and Oxford: Oxford University Press.

Zeskind, P. S., Sale, J., Maio, M. L., Huntington, L., and Weiseman, J. R. (1985). Adult perceptions of pain and hunger cries: A synchrony of arousal. *Child Development* 56: 549–554.

Zilhão, J. (2006). Neandertals and modern humans mixed, and it matters. *Evolutionary Anthropology* 15: 183–195.

ZILHÃO, J., D'ERRICO, F., BORDES, J.-G., LENOBLE, A., TEXIER, J.-P., and RIGAUD, J.-P. (2006). Analysis of Aurignacian interstratification at the Châtelperronian-type site and implications for the behavioral modernity of Neandertals. *Proceedings of the National Academy of Sciences of the USA* 103: 12643–12648.

ZIPURSKY, S. L. (2010). Driving self-recognition. *The Scientist* 24: 40.

ZITO, K. and SVOBODA, K. (2002). Activity-dependent synaptogenesis in the adult mammalian cortex. *Neuron* 35: 1015–1017.

ZUBERBÜHLER, K. (2000a). Interspecific semantic communication in two forest monkeys. *Proceedings of the Royal Society of London B* 267: 713–718.

ZUBERBÜHLER, K. (2000b). Causal cognition in a non-human primate: Field playback experiments with Diana monkeys. *Cognition* 76: 195–207.

ZUBERBÜHLER, K. (2002). A syntactic rule in forest monkey communication. *Animal Behaviour* 63: 293–299.

ZUBERBÜHLER, K. (2008). Audience effects. *Current Biology* 18: R189–R190.

ZUBEBÜHLER, K. and JENNY, D. (2002). Leopard predation and primate evolution. *Journal of Human Evolution* 43: 873–886.

ZUBERBÜHLER, K., NOË, R. and SEYFARTH, R. M. (1997). Diana monkey long-distance calls: Messages for conspecifics and predators. *Animal Behaviour* 53: 589–604.

ZUBERBÜHLER, K., CHENEY, D. L., and SEYFARTH, R. M. (1999a). Conceptual semantics in a nonhuman primate. *Journal of Comparative Psychology* 113: 33–42.

ZUBERBÜHLER, K., JENNY, D. and BSHARY, R. (1999b). The predator deterrence function of primate alarm calls. *Ethology* 105: 477–490.

ZUIDEMA, W. and DE BOER, B. (2009). The evolution of combinatorial phonology. *Journal of Phonetics* 3: 125–144.

ZWICKY, A. (1969). Review of Brown (1966). *Language* 45: 444–457.

# AUTHOR INDEX

# Subject Index